BRITISH WRITERS

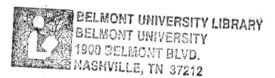

BRITISH WRITERS

JAY PARINI
Editor

SUPPLEMENT IX

Charles Scribner's Sons
an imprint of the Gale Group
New York • Detroit • San Francisco • London • Boston • Woodbridge, CT

British Writers Supplement IX

Jay Parini, Editor in Chief

© 2004 by Charles Scribner's Sons. Charles Scribner's Sons is an imprint of The Gale Group, Inc., a division of Thomson Learning, Inc.

Charles Scribner's Sons™ and Thomson Learning™ are trademarks used herein under license.

For more information, contact
Charles Scribner's Sons
An imprint of The Gale Group
300 Park Avenue South, 9th Floor
New York, NY 10010
Or you can visit our Internet site at
http://www.gale.com

For permission to use material from this product, submit your request via Web at http://www.gale-edit.com/permissions, or you may download our Permissions Request form and submit your request by fax or mail to:

Permissions Department
The Gale Group, Inc.
27500 Drake Rd.
Farmington Hills, MI 48331-3535
Permissions Hotline:
248 699-8006 or 800 877-4253, ext. 8006
Fax: 248 699-8074 or 800 762-4058

LIBRARY OF CONGRESS CATALOGING-IN-PUBLICATION DATA

British Writers Supplement IX / Jay Parini, editor.
 p. cm.
Includes bibliographical references and index.
 ISBN 0-684-31237-9 (hardcover : alk. paper)
 1. English literature–20th century–Bio-bibliography. 2. English literature–20th century–History and criticism. 3. Commonwealth literature (English)–History and criticism. 4. Commonwealth literature (English)–Bio-bibliography. 5. Authors, Commonwealth–20th century–Biography. 6. Authors, English–20th century–Biography. I. Parini, Jay. II. Title.
 PR85 .B688 Suppl. 9
 820.9'0091–dc22   2003014871

Printed in the United States of America
10 9 8 7 6 5 4 3 2 1

Acknowledgments

Acknowledgment is gratefully made to those publishers and individuals who permitted the use of the following materials in copyright:

CAROLINE BLACKWOOD Blackwood, Caroline. From *For All That I Found There*. Duckworth, 1973. Copyright © 1973 by Caroline Blackwood. All rights reserved. Reproduced by permission of Sheil Land Associates Ltd. —Blackwood, Caroline. From *Good Night Sweet Ladies*. Heinemann, 1983. Copyright © 1978, 1983 by Caroline Blackwood. All rights reserved. Reproduced by permission of Sheil Land Associates Ltd. Lowell, Robert. From "For Sheridan" in *Day By Day*. Farrar, Straus and Giroux, 1977. Copyright © 1975, 1976, 1977 by Robert Lowell. All rights reserved. Reproduced by permission of Farrar, Straus and Giroux. LLC and Faber and Faber. *Encounter*, v. 12, June, 1959 for "Portrait of the Beatnik: Letter from California" by Caroline Blackwood; v. 16, April, 1961 for "The Mystique of Ingmar Bergman" by Caroline Blackwood. Reproduced by permission of Sheil Land Associates Ltd.

CHRISTOPHER CAUDWELL Caudwell, Christopher. From *Poems*. John Lame the Bodley Head, 1939. Reproduced by permission.

BRUCE CHATWIN *Granta*, v. 21, Spring, 1987 for "An Interview with Bruce Chatwin" by M. Ignatieff. Reproduced by permission of A.P. Watt Ltd on behalf of Michael Ignatieff.

EDWIN MORGAN Morgan, Edwin. From *Collected Poems*. Carcanet, 1996. Copyright © 1990 by Edwin Morgan. All rights reserved. Reproduced by permission of Carcanet Press Limited. Morgan, Edwin. From *From Glasgow to Saturn*. Carcanet, 1973. Copyright © 1973 by Edwin Morgan. All rights reserved. Reproduced by permission of Carcanet Press Limited. Morgan, Edwin. From *The New Divan*. Carcanet, 1977. Copyright © 1977 by Edwin Morgan. All rights reserved. Reproduced by permission of Carcanet Press Limited. Morgan, Edwin. From *The Second Life*. Carcanet, 1968. Copyright © 1968 by Edwin Morgan and Edinburgh University Press. All rights reserved. Reproduced by permission of Carcanet Press Limited.

MARY RENAULT Carlston, Erin G. From *RePresenting Bisexualities: Subjects and Cultures of Fluid Desire*. Edited by Donald E. Hall and Maria Pramaggiore. New York University Press, 1996. Copyright ©

1996 by New York University. All rights reserved. Reproduced by permission.

RUTH RENDELL Parr, Susan Resneck. From *Dictionary of Literary Biography, Volume 87: British Mystery and Thriller Writers Since 1940*. Edited by Bernard Benstock and Thomas F. Staley. Gale Research, Inc., 1989. Copyright © Gale Research Inc. All rights reserved. Reproduced by permission of The Gale Group.

IAIN CHRICHTON SMITH Smith, Iain Crichton. From *A Life*. Carcanet, 1986. Copyright © 1986 by Iain Crichton Smith. All rights reserved. Reproduced by permission of Carcanet Press Limited. Smith, Iain Crichton. From *From Bourgeois Land*. Victor Gollancz Ltd., 1969. Copyright © 1969 by Iain Crichton Smith. All rights reserved. Reproduced by permission. Smith, Iain Crichton. From *In the Middle*. Victor Gollancz Ltd., 1977. Copyright © 1977 by Iain Crichton Smith. Reproduced by permission. All rights reserved. Reproduced by permission. Smith, Iain Crichton. From *Love Poems and Elegies*. Victor Gollancz Ltd., 1972. Copyright © 1971, 1972 by Iain Crichton Smith. All rights reserved. Reproduced by permission. Smith, Iain Crichton. From *The Exiles*. Carcanet, 1984. Copyright © 1984 by Iain Crichton Smith. All rights reserved. Reproduced by permission of Carcanet Press Limited. Smith, Iain Crichton. From *The Law and the Grace*. Eyre & Spottiswoode, 1965. Copyright © 1965 by Iain Crichton Smith. All rights reserved. Reproduced by permission. Smith, Iain Crichton. From *Thistles and Roses*. Eyre & Spottiswoode, 1961. Copyright © 1961 by Iain Crichton Smith. All rights reserved. Reproduced by permission. Smith, Lain Crichton. From *Ends and Beginnings*. Carcanet, 1994. Copyright © 1994 by Lain Crichton Smith. All rights reserved. Reproduced by permission of Carcanet Press Limited.

EMMA TENNANT *New Statesman and Society*, v. 6, November 26, 1993. © 1993 Statesman & Nation Publishing Company Limited. Reproduced by permission.

CHARLES WALTER STANSBY WILLIAMS Williams, Charles. From *Poetry at Present*. Clarendon Press, 1930. Reproduced by permission of Oxford

ACKNOWLEDGMENTS

University Press. Williams, Charles. From *Taliessin Through Logres*. Oxford University Press, 1938. Reproduced by permission of the author. Williams, Charles. From *The Region of the Summer Stars*. Oxford University Press, 1948. Reproduced by permission of the author.

Editorial and Production Staff

Project Editor
PAMELA PARKINSON

Copyeditors
SHANE DAVIS
MELISSA DOBSON
LINDA SANDERS

Proofreader
CAROL HOLMES

Indexer
REBECCA VALENTINE

Permission Researcher
JULE VAN PELT

Composition Specialist
GARY LEACH

Buyer
STACY MELSON

Publisher
FRANK MENCHACA

Contents

Subjects in Supplement IX

Introduction

"Writing is not literature unless it gives to the reader a pleasure which arises not only from the things said, but from the way in which they are said," observed Stopford Brooke, a Victorian essayist. To this day, one of the major functions of the critic is simply to notice the way things are said—how the language of a given text works to embody meaning. The essays in Supplement IX of *British Writers* are focused with considerable intensity on the language of eighteen of our most interesting (and often neglected) writers, mostly contemporary, although some are from the past. In each case they are written to increase the reader's pleasure in the work of each writer and to make the shape of that career, its evolution and influence, comprehensible.

This series brings together a wide range of articles on British writers, most of them modern or contemporary, although a couple of them consider neglected, but interesting, writers from the literary past. As in previous volumes, the subjects have all been chosen for their significant contribution to the traditions of literature, and each has influenced intellectual life in Britain in some way. Readers will find these eighteen essays lively and intelligent, designed to interest readers unfamiliar with their work and to assist those who know the work quite well by providing close readings of individual texts and a sense of the biographical, cultural, and critical context of that work.

British Writers was originally an off-shoot of a series of monographs that appeared between 1959 and 1972, the *Minnesota Pamphlets on American Writers*. These pamphlets were incisively written and informative, treating ninety-seven American writers in a format and style that attracted a devoted following of readers. The series proved invaluable to a generation of students and teachers, who could depend on these reliable and interesting critiques of major figures. The idea of reprinting these essays occurred to Charles Scribner, Jr., an innovative publisher during the middle decades of the twentieth century. The series appeared in four volumes entitled *American Writers: A Collection of Literary Biographies* (1974). *British Writers* began with a series of essays originally published by the British Council, and regular supplements have followed. The goal of the supplements has been consistent with the original idea of the series: to provide clear, informative essays aimed at the general reader. These essays often rise to a high level of craft and critical vision, but they are meant to introduce a writer of some importance in the history of British or Anglophone literature, and to provide a sense of the scope and nature of the career under review.

The authors of these critical articles are mostly teachers, scholars, and writers. Most have published books and articles in their field, and several are well-known writers of poetry or fiction as well as critics. As anyone glancing through this volume will see, they have been held to the highest standards of clear writing and sound scholarship. Jargon and theoretical musings have been discouraged, except when strictly relevant. Each of the essays concludes with a select bibliography of works by the author under discussion and secondary works that might be useful to those who wish to pursue the subject further.

Supplement IX focuses on a wide range of authors who have had little sustained attention from critics, although most are well known. For example Caroline Blackwood, Bruce Chatwin, Alasdair Gray, Patrick McCabe, Brian Moore, Mary Renault, and Emma Tennant have all been written about in the review pages of newspapers and magazines, often at considerable length, and their books have acquired a substantial following, but their work has yet to attract significant scholarship. That will certainly follow, but the essays included in this volume constitute a beginning of sorts, an attempt to map out the particular universe of each writer.

Two unusual writers from the distant past considered in this supplement are John Trevisa, a

INTRODUCTION

medieval writer and translator, and Anne Finch, a seventeenth century poet whose work has only been rediscovered by critics in recent years. Other writers, such as Denton Welch and Charles Williams, have attracted a cult following but not yet been considered in this series as major writers. Both deserve this quality of attention. The poets discussed in this volume are Norman Cameron, Edwin Morgan, and Iain Chrichton Smith. These are well-known figures in the literary world, major voices, and it is time they were added to the series. Among other writers discussed in this volume are Christopher Caudwell (the Marxist poet, critic, historian, and culture critic), and two popular mystery writers, Ruth Rendell and Reginal Hill, both of whom, in very different ways, have attracted strong interest from readers.

As ever, our purpose in these presenting these critical and biographical essays is to bring readers back to the texts discussed, to help them in their reading. These are especially strong and stimulating essays, and they should enable students and general readers to enter into the world of these writers freshly, encouraging them on their intellectual journeys. They should help readers to appreciate the way things are said by these authors, thus enhancing their pleasure in the texts.

—*JAY PARINI*

Chronology

CHRONOLOGY

CHRONOLOGY

1566   William Painter's *Palace of Pleasure*, a miscellany of prose stories, the source of many dramatists' plots

1567   Darnley murdered at Kirk o'Field
Mary Queen of Scots marries the earl of Bothwell

1569   Rebellion of the English northern earls suppressed

1570   Roger Ascham's *The Schoolmaster*

1571   Defeat of the Turkish fleet at Lepanto

ca. 1572   Ben Jonson born

1572   St. Bartholomew's Day massacre
John Donne born

1574   The earl of Leicester's theater company formed

1576   The Theater, the first permanent theater building in London, opened
The first Blackfriars Theater opened with performances by the Children of St. Paul's
John Marston born

1576–1578   Martin Frobisher's voyages to Labrador and the northwest

1577–1580   Sir Francis Drake sails around the world

1577   Holinshed's *Chronicles of England, Scotlande, and Irelande*

1579   John Lyly's *Euphues: The Anatomy of Wit*
Thomas North's translation of *Plutarch's Lives*

1581   The Levant Company founded
Seneca's *Ten Tragedies* translated

1582   Richard Hakluyt's *Divers Voyages Touching the Discoverie of America*

1584–1585   Sir John Davis' first voyage to Greenland

1585   First English settlement in America, the "Lost Colony" comprising 108 men under Ralph Lane, founded at Roanoke Island, off the coast of North Carolina

1586   Kyd's *Spanish Tragedy*
Marlowe's *Tamburlaine*
William Camden's *Britannia*
The Babington conspiracy against Queen Elizabeth
Death of Sir Philip Sidney

1587   Mary Queen of Scots executed

    Birth of Virginia Dare, first English child born in America, at Roanoke Island

1588   Defeat of the Spanish Armada
Marlowe's *Dr. Faustus*

1590   Spenser's *The Faerie Queen*, Cantos 1–3

1592   Outbreak of plague in London; the theaters closed
Henry King born

1593   Death of Christopher Marlowe

1594   The Lord Chamberlain's Men, the company to which Shakespeare belonged, founded
The Swan Theater opened
Death of Thomas Kyd

1595   Ralegh's expedition to Guiana
Sidney's *Apology for Poetry*

1596   The earl of Essex's expedition captures Cadiz
The second Blackfriars Theater opened

ca. 1597   Death of George Peele

1597   Bacon's first collection of *Essays*

1598   Jonson's *Every Man in His Humor*

1598–1600   Richard Hakluyt's *Principal Navigations, Voyages, Traffics, and Discoveries of the English Nation*

1599   The Globe Theater opened
Death of Edmund Spenser

1600   Death of Richard Hooker

1601   Rebellion and execution of the earl of Essex

1602   The East India Company founded
The Bodleian Library reopened at Oxford

1603–1625   Reign of James I

1603   John Florio's translation of Montaigne's *Essays*
Cervantes' *Don Quixote* (Part 1)
The Gunpowder Plot
Thomas Browne born

1604   Shakespeare's *Othello*

ca. 1605   Shakespears's *King Lear*
Tourneur's *The Revenger's Tragedy*

1605   Bacon's *Advancement of Learning*

1606   Shakespeare's *Macbeth*
Jonson's *Volpone*
Death of John Lyly
Edmund Waller born

1607   The first permanent English colony established at Jamestown, Virginia

CHRONOLOGY

1608   John Milton born

1609   Kepler's *Astronomia nova*
John Suckling born

1610   Galileo's *Sidereus nuncius*

1611   The Authorized Version of the Bible
Shakespeare's *The Tempest*

1612   Death of Prince Henry, King James's eldest son
Webster's *The White Devil*
Bacon's second collection of *Essays*

ca. 1613   Richard Crashaw born

1613   The Globe Theatre destroyed by fire
Webster's *The Duchess of Malfi*

1614   Ralegh's *History of the World*

1616   George Chapman's translation of Homer's *Odyssey*
Deaths of William Shakespeare, Francis Beaumont, and Miguel Cervantes

ca. 1618   Richard Lovelace born

1618   The Thirty Years' War begins
Sir Walter Ralegh executed
Abraham Cowley born

1619   The General Assembly, the first legislative assembly on American soil, meets in Virginia
Slavery introduced at Jamestown

1620   The Pilgrims land in Massachusetts
John Evelyn born

1621   Francis Bacon impeached and fined
Robert Burton's *Anatomy of Melancholy*
Andrew Marvell born

1622   Middleton's *The Changeling*
Henry Vaughan born

1623   The First Folio of Shakespeare's plays
Visit of Prince Charles and the duke of Buckingham to Spain; failure of attempts to negotiate a Spanish marriage

1624   War against Spain

1625–1649   Reign of Charles I

1625   Death of John Fletcher
Bacon's last collection of *Essays*

1626   Bacon's *New Atlantis*, appended to *Sylva sylvarum*
Dutch found New Amsterdam
Death of Cyril Tourneur
Death of Francis Bacon

1627   Ford's *'Tis Pity She's a Whore*
Cardinal Richelieu establishes the Company of New France with monopoly over trade and land in Canada
Buckingham's expedition to the Isle of Ré to relieve La Rochelle
Death of Thomas Middleton

1627–1628   Revolt and siege of La Rochelle, the principal Huguenot city of France

1628   Buckingham assassinated
Surrender of La Rochelle
William Harvey's treatise on the circulation of the blood (*De motu cordis et sanguinis*)
John Bunyan born

1629   Ford's *The Broken Heart*
King Charles dismisses his third Parliament, imprisons nine members, and proceeds to rule for eleven years without Parliament
The Massachusetts Bay Company formed

1629–1630   Peace treaties with France and Spain

1631   John Dryden born
Death of John Donne

1633   William Laud appointed archbishop of Canterbury
Death of George Herbert
Samuel Pepys born

1634   Deaths of George Chapman and John Marston

1635   The Académie Française founded
George Etherege born

1636   Pierre Corneille's *Le Cid*
Harvard College founded

ca. 1637   Thomas Traherne born

1637   Milton's "Lycidas"
Descartes's *Discours de la méthode*
King Charles's levy of ship money challenged in the courts by John Hampden
The introduction of the new English Book of Common Prayer strongly opposed in Scotland
Death of Ben Jonson

ca. 1638   Death of John Webster

1638   The Scots draw up a National Covenant to defend their religion

ca. 1639   Death of John Ford

xvi

CHRONOLOGY

1639   Parliament reassembled to raise taxes
        Death of Thomas Carew
        Charles Sedley born
1639–1640   The two Bishops' Wars with Scotland
1640   The Long Parliament assembled
        The king's advisers, Archbishop Laud and the earl of Strafford, impeached
        Aphra Behn born
1641   Strafford executed
        Acts passed abolishing extraparliamentary taxation, the king's extraordinary courts, and his power to order a dissolution without parliamentary consent
        The Grand Remonstrance censuring royal policy passed by eleven votes
        William Wycherley born
1642   Parliament submits the nineteen Propositions, which King Charles rejects as annihilating the royal power
        The Civil War begins
        The theaters close
        Royalist victory at Edgehill; King Charles established at Oxford
        Death of Sir John Suckling
1643   Parliament concludes the Solemn League and Covenant with the Scots
        Louis XIV becomes king of France
        Charles Sackville, earl of Dorset, born
1644   Parliamentary victory at Marston Moor
        The New Model army raised
        Milton's *Areopagitica*
1645   Parliamentary victory under Fairfax and Cromwell at Naseby
        Fairfax captures Bristol
        Archbishop Laud executed
1646   Fairfax besieges King Charles at Oxford
        King Charles takes refuge in Scotland; end of the First Civil War
        King Charles attempts negotiations with the Scots
        Parliament's proposals sent to the king and rejected

1647   Conflict between Parliament and the army
        A general council of the army established that discusses representational government within the army
        The Agreement of the People drawn up by the Levelers; its proposals include manhood suffrage
        King Charles concludes an agreement with the Scots
        George Fox begins to preach
        John Wilmot, earl of Rochester, born
1648   Cromwell dismisses the general council of the army
        The Second Civil War begins
        Fairfax defeats the Kentish royalists at Maidstone
        Cromwell defeats the Scots at Preston
        The Thirty Years' War ended by the treaty of Westphalia
        Parliament purged by the army
1649–1660   Commonwealth
1649   King Charles I tried and executed
        The monarchy and the House of Lords abolished
        The Commonwealth proclaimed
        Cromwell invades Ireland and defeats the royalist Catholic forces
        Death of Richard Crashaw
1650   Cromwell defeats the Scots at Dunbar
1651   Charles II crowned king of the Scots, at Scone
        Charles II invades England, is defeated at Worcester, escapes to France
        Thomas Hobbes's *Leviathan*
1652   War with Holland
1653   The Rump Parliament dissolved by the army
        A new Parliament and council of state nominated; Cromwell becomes Lord Protector
        Walton's *The Compleat Angler*
1654   Peace concluded with Holland
        War against Spain
1655   Parliament attempts to reduce the army and is dissolved
        Rule of the major-generals

xvii

CHRONOLOGY

1656   Sir William Davenant produces *The Siege of Rhodes*, one of the first English operas

1657   Second Parliament of the Protectorate
Cromwell is offered and declines the throne
Death of Richard Lovelace

1658   Death of Oliver Cromwell
Richard Cromwell succeeds as Protector

1659   Conflict between Parliament and the army

1660   General Monck negotiates with Charles II
Charles II offers the conciliatory Declaration of Breda and accepts Parliament's invitation to return
Will's Coffee House established
Sir William Davenant and Thomas Killigrew licensed to set up two companies of players, the Duke of York's and the King's Servants, including actors and actresses
Pepys's *Diary* begun

1660–1685   Reign of Charles II

1661   Parliament passes the Act of Uniformity, enjoining the use of the Book of Common Prayer; many Puritan and dissenting clergy leave their livings
Anne Finch born

1662   Peace Treaty with Spain
King Charles II marries Catherine of Braganza
The Royal Society incorporated (founded in 1660)

1664   War against Holland
New Amsterdam captured and becomes New York
John Vanbrugh born

1665   The Great Plague
Newton discovers the binomial theorem and invents the integral and differential calculus, at Cambridge

1666   The Great Fire of London
Bunyan's *Grace Abounding*
London Gazette founded

1667   The Dutch fleet sails up the Medway and burns English ships

The war with Holland ended by the Treaty of Breda
Milton's *Paradise Lost*
Thomas Sprat's *History of the Royal Society*
Death of Abraham Cowley

1668   Sir Christopher Wren begins to rebuild St. Paul's Cathedral
Triple Alliance formed with Holland and Sweden against France
Dryden's *Essay of Dramatick Poesy*

1670   Alliance formed with France through the secret Treaty of Dover
Pascal's *Pensées*
The Hudson's Bay Company founded
William Congreve born

1671   Milton's *Samson Agonistes* and *Paradise Regained*

1672   War against Holland
Wycherley's *The Country Wife*
King Charles issues the Declaration of Indulgence, suspending penal laws against Nonconformists and Catholics

1673   Parliament passes the Test Act, making acceptance of the doctrines of the Church of England a condition for holding public office

1674   War with Holland ended by the Treaty of Westminster
Deaths of John Milton, Robert Herrick, and Thomas Traherne

1676   Etherege's *The Man of Mode*

1677   Baruch Spinoza's *Ethics*
Jean Racine's *Phèdre*
King Charles's niece, Mary, marries her cousin William of Orange

1678   Fabrication of the so-called popish plot by Titus Oates
Bunyan's *Pilgrim's Progress*
Dryden's *All for Love*
Death of Andrew Marvell
George Farquhar born

1679   Parliament passes the Habeas Corpus Act
Rochester's *A Satire Against Mankind*

1680   Death of John Wilmot, earl of Rochester

1681   Dryden's *Absalom and Achitophel* (Part 1)

CHRONOLOGY

1682   Dryden's *Absalom and Achitophel* (Part 2)
Thomas Otway's *Venice Preserv'd*
Philadelphia founded
Death of Sir Thomas Browne

1683   The Ashmolean Museum, the world's first public museum, opens at Oxford
Death of Izaak Walton

1685–1688   Reign of James II

1685   Rebellion and execution of James Scott, duke of Monmouth
John Gay born

1686   The first book of Newton's *Principia—De motu corporum*, containing his theory of gravitation—presented to the Royal Society

1687   James II issues the Declaration of Indulgence
Dryden's *The Hind and the Panther*
Death of Edmund Waller

1688   James II reissues the Declaration of Indulgence, renewing freedom of worship and suspending the provisions of the Test Act
Acquittal of the seven bishops imprisoned for protesting against the Declaration
William of Orange lands at Torbay, Devon
James II takes refuge in France
Death of John Bunyan
Alexander Pope born

1689–1702   Reign of William III

1689   Parliament formulates the Declaration of Rights
William and Mary accept the Declaration and the crown
The Grand Alliance concluded between the Holy Roman Empire, England, Holland, and Spain
War declared against France
King William's War, 1689–1697 (the first of the French and Indian wars)
Samuel Richardson born

1690   James II lands in Ireland with French support, but is defeated at the battle of the Boyne
John Locke's *Essay Concerning Human Understanding*

1692   Salem witchcraft trials

     Death of Sir George Etherege

1694   George Fox's *Journal*
Voltaire (François Marie Arouet) born
Death of Mary II

1695   Congreve's *Love for Love*
Death of Henry Vaughan

1697   War with France ended by the Treaty of Ryswick
Vanbrugh's *The Relapse*

1698   Jeremy Collier's *A Short View of the Immorality and Profaneness of the English Stage*

1699   Fénelon's *Les Aventures de Télémaque*

1700   Congreve's *The Way of the World*
Defoe's *The True-Born Englishman*
Death of John Dryden
James Thomson born

1701   War of the Spanish Succession, 1701–1714 (Queen Anne's War in America, 1702–1713)
Death of Sir Charles Sedley

1702–1714   Reign of Queen Anne

1702   Clarendon's *History of the Rebellion* (1702–1704)
Defoe's *The Shortest Way with the Dissenters*

1703   Defoe is arrested, fined, and pilloried for writing *The Shortest Way*
Death of Samuel Pepys

1704   John Churchill, duke of Marlborough, and Prince Eugene of Savoy defeat the French at Blenheim
Capture of Gibraltar
Swift's *A Tale of a Tub* and *The Battle of the Books*
The Review founded (1704–1713)

1706   Farquhar's *The Recruiting Officer*
Deaths of John Evelyn and Charles Sackville, earl of Dorset

1707   Farquhar's *The Beaux' Stratagem*
Act of Union joining England and Scotland
Death of George Farquhar
Henry Fielding born

1709   The *Tatler* founded (1709–1711)
Nicholas Rowe's edition of Shakespeare
Samuel Johnson born
Marlborough defeats the French at Malplaquet

CHRONOLOGY

Charles XII of Sweden defeated at Poltava

1710 South Sea Company founded
First copyright act

1711 Swift's *The Conduct of the Allies*
The *Spectator* founded (1711–1712; 1714)
Marlborough dismissed
David Hume born

1712 Pope's *The Rape of the Lock* (Cantos 1–2)
Jean Jacques Rousseau born

1713 War with France ended by the Treaty of Utrecht
The *Guardian* founded
Swift becomes dean of St. Patrick's, Dublin
Addison's *Cato*
Laurence Sterne born

1714–1727 Reign of George I
1714 Pope's expended version of *The Rape of the Lock* (Cantos 1–5)

1715 The Jacobite rebellion in Scotland
Pope's translation of Homer's *Iliad* (1715–1720)
Death of Louis XIV

1716 Death of William Wycherley
Thomas Gray born

1717 Pope's *Eloisa to Abelard*
David Garrick born
Horace Walpole born

1718 Quadruple Alliance (Britain, France, the Netherlands, the German Empire) in war against Spain

1719 Defoe's *Robinson Crusoe*
Death of Joseph Addison

1720 Inoculation against smallpox introduced in Boston
War against Spain
The South Sea Bubble
Gilbert White born
Defoe's *Captain Singleton* and *Memoirs of a Cavalier*

1721 Tobias Smollett born
William Collins born

1722 Defoe's *Moll Flanders*, *Journal of the Plague Year*, and *Colonel Jack*

1724 Defoe's *Roxana*
Swift's *The Drapier's Letters*

1725 Pope's translation of Homer's *Odyssey* (1725–1726)

1726 Swift's *Gulliver's Travels*

Voltaire in England (1726–1729)
Death of Sir John Vanbrugh

1727–1760 Reign of George II
1728 Gay's *The Beggar's Opera*
Pope's *The Dunciad* (Books 1–2)
Oliver Goldsmith born

1729 Swift's *A Modest Proposal*
Edmund Burke born
Deaths of William Congreve and Sir Richard Steele

1731 Navigation improved by introduction of the quadrant
Pope's *Moral Essays* (1731–1735)
Death of Daniel Defoe
William Cowper born

1732 Death of John Gay

1733 Pope's *Essay on Man* (1733–1734)
Lewis Theobald's edition of Shakespeare

1734 Voltaire's *Lettres philosophiques*

1736 James Macpherson born

1737 Edward Gibbon born

1738 Johnson's *London*

1740 War of the Austrian Succession, 1740–1748 (King George's War in America, 1744–1748)
George Anson begins his circumnavigation of the world (1740–1744)
Frederick the Great becomes king of Prussia (1740–1786)
Richardson's *Pamela* (1740–1741)
James Boswell born

1742 Fielding's *Joseph Andrews*
Edward Young's *Night Thoughts* (1742–1745)
Pope's *The New Dunciad* (Book 4)

1744 Johnson's *Life of Mr. Richard Savage*
Death of Alexander Pope

1745 Second Jacobite rebellion, led by Charles Edward, the Young Pretender
Death of Jonathan Swift

1746 The Young Pretender defeated at Culloden
Collins' *Odes on Several Descriptive and Allegorical Subjects*

1747 Richardson's *Clarissa Harlowe* (1747–1748)
Franklin's experiments with electricity announced

CHRONOLOGY

Voltaire's *Essai sur les moeurs*

1748 War of the Austrian Succession ended by the Peace of Aix-la-Chapelle

Smollett's *Adventures of Roderick Random*

David Hume's *Enquiry Concerning Human Understanding*

Montesquieu's *L'Esprit des lois*

1749 Fielding's *Tom Jones*

Johnson's *The Vanity of Human Wishes*

Bolingbroke's *Idea of a Patriot King*

1750 The *Rambler* founded (1750–1752)

1751 Gray's *Elegy Written in a Country Churchyard*

Fielding's *Amelia*

Smollett's *Adventures of Peregrine Pickle*

Denis Diderot and Jean le Rond d'Alembert begin to publish the *Encyclopédie* (1751–1765)

Richard Brinsley Sheridan born

1752 Frances Burney and Thomas Chatterton born

1753 Richardson's *History of Sir Charles Grandison* (1753–1754)

Smollett's *The Adventures of Ferdinand Count Fathom*

1754 Hume's *History of England* (1754–1762)

Death of Henry Fielding

George Crabbe born

1755 Lisbon destroyed by earthquake

Fielding's *Journal of a Voyage to Lisbon* published posthumously

Johnson's *Dictionary of the English Language*

1756 The Seven Years' War against France, 1756–1763 (the French and Indian War in America, 1755–1760)

William Pitt the elder becomes prime minister

Johnson's proposal for an edition of Shakespeare

1757 Robert Clive wins the battle of Plassey, in India

Gray's "The Progress of Poesy" and "The Bard"

Burke's *Philosophical Enquiry into the Origin of Our Ideas of the Sublime and Beautiful*

Hume's *Natural History of Religion*

William Blake born

1758 The *Idler* founded (1758–1760)

1759 Capture of Quebec by General James Wolfe

Johnson's *History of Rasselas, Prince of Abyssinia*

Voltaire's *Candide*

The British Museum opens

Sterne's *The Life and Opinions of Tristram Shandy* (1759–1767)

Death of William Collins

Mary Wollstonecraft born

Robert Burns born

1760–1820 Reign of George III

1760 James Macpherson's *Fragments of Ancient Poetry Collected in the Highlands of Scotland*

William Beckford born

1761 Jean-Jacques Rousseau's *Julie, ou la nouvelle Héloïse*

Death of Samuel Richardson

1762 Rousseau's *Du Contrat social* and *Émile*

Catherine the Great becomes czarina of Russia (1762–1796)

1763 The Seven Years' War ended by the Peace of Paris

Smart's *A Song to David*

1764 James Hargreaves invents the spinning jenny

1765 Parliament passes the Stamp Act to tax the American colonies

Johnson's edition of Shakespeare

Walpole's *The Castle of Otranto*

Thomas Percy's *Reliques of Ancient English Poetry*

Blackstone's *Commentaries on the Laws of England* (1765–1769)

1766 The Stamp Act repealed

Swift's *Journal to Stella* first published in a collection of his letters

Goldsmith's *The Vicar of Wakefield*

Smollett's *Travels Through France and Italy*

Lessing's *Laokoon*

Rousseau in England (1766–1767)

1768 Sterne's *A Sentimental Journey Through France and Italy*

CHRONOLOGY

The Royal Academy founded by George III
First edition of the *Encyclopaedia Britannica*
Maria Edgeworth born
Death of Laurence Sterne

1769 David Garrick organizes the Shakespeare Jubilee at Stratford-upon-Avon
Sir Joshua Reynolds' *Discourses* (1769–1790)
Richard Arkwright invents the spinning water frame

1770 Boston Massacre
Burke's *Thoughts on the Cause of the Present Discontents*
Oliver Goldsmith's *The Deserted Village*
Death of Thomas Chatterton
William Wordsworth born

1771 Arkwright's first spinning mill founded
Deaths of Thomas Gray and Tobias Smollett
Walter Scott born

1772 Samuel Taylor Coleridge born

1773 Boston Tea Party
Goldsmith's *She Stoops to Conquer*
Johann Wolfgang von Goethe's *Götz von Berlichingen*

1774 The first Continental Congress meets in Philadelphia
Goethe's *Sorrows of Young Werther*
Death of Oliver Goldsmith
Robert Southey born

1775 Burke's speech on American taxation
American War of Independence begins with the battles of Lexington and Concord
Samuel Johnson's *Journey to the Western Islands of Scotland*
Richard Brinsley Sheridan's *The Rivals* and *The Duenna*
Beaumarchais's *Le Barbier de Séville*
James Watt and Matthew Boulton begin building steam engines in England
Births of Jane Austen, Charles Lamb, Walter Savage Landor, and Matthew Lewis

1776 American Declaration of Independence
Edward Gibbon's *Decline and Fall of the Roman Empire* (1776–1788)
Adam Smith's *Inquiry into the Nature & Causes of the Wealth of Nations*
Thomas Paine's *Common Sense*
Death of David Hume

1777 Maurice Morgann's *Essay on the Dramatic Character of Sir John Falstaff*
Sheridan's *The School for Scandal* first performed (published 1780)
General Burgoyne surrenders at Saratoga

1778 The American colonies allied with France
Britain and France at war
Captain James Cook discovers Hawaii
Death of William Pitt, first earl of Chatham
Deaths of Jean Jacques Rousseau and Voltaire
William Hazlitt born

1779 Johnson's *Prefaces to the Works of the English Poets* (1779–1781); reissued in 1781 as *The Lives of the Most Eminent English Poets*
Sheridan's *The Critic*
Samuel Crompton invents the spinning mule
Death of David Garrick

1780 The Gordon Riots in London
Charles Robert Maturin born

1781 Charles Cornwallis surrenders at Yorktown
Immanuel Kant's *Critique of Pure Reason*
Friedrich von Schiller's *Die Räuber*

1782 William Cowper's "The Journey of John Gilpin" published in the *Public Advertiser*
Choderlos de Laclos's *Les Liaisons dangereuses*
Rousseau's *Confessions* published posthumously

1783 American War of Independence ended by the Definitive Treaty of Peace, signed at Paris
William Blake's *Poetical Sketches*

CHRONOLOGY

George Crabbe's *The Village*

William Pitt the younger becomes prime minister

Henri Beyle (Stendhal) born

1784 Beaumarchais's *Le Mariage de Figaro* first performed (published 1785)

Death of Samuel Johnson

1785 Warren Hastings returns to England from India

James Boswell's *The Journey of a Tour of the Hebrides, with Samuel Johnson, LL.D.*

Cowper's *The Task*

Edmund Cartwright invents the power loom

Thomas De Quincey born

Thomas Love Peacock born

1786 William Beckford's *Vathek* published in English (originally written in French in 1782)

Robert Burns's *Poems Chiefly in the Scottish Dialect*

Wolfgang Amadeus Mozart's *The Marriage of Figaro*

Death of Frederick the Great

1787 The Committee for the Abolition of the Slave Trade founded in England

The Constitutional Convention meets at Philadelphia; the Constitution is signed

1788 The trial of Hastings begins on charges of corruption of the government in India

The Estates-General of France summoned

U.S. Constitution is ratified

George Washington elected president of the United States

Giovanni Casanova's *Histoire de ma fuite* (first manuscript of his memoirs)

The *Daily Universal Register* becomes the *Times* (London)

George Gordon, Lord Byron born

1789 The Estates-General meets at Versailles

The National Assembly (Assemblée Nationale) convened

The fall of the Bastille marks the beginning of the French Revolution

The National Assembly draws up the Declaration of Rights of Man and of the Citizen

First U.S. Congress meets in New York

Blake's *Songs of Innocence*

Jeremy Bentham's *Introduction to the Principles of Morals and Legislation* introduces the theory of utilitarianism

Gilbert White's *Natural History of Selborne*

1790 Congress sets permanent capital city site on the Potomac River

First U.S. Census

Burke's *Reflections on the Revolution in France*

Blake's *The Marriage of Heaven and Hell*

Edmund Malone's edition of Shakespeare

Wollstonecraft's *A Vindication of the Rights of Man*

Death of Benjamin Franklin

1791 French royal family's flight from Paris and capture at Varennes; imprisonment in the Tuileries

Bill of Rights is ratified

Paine's *The Rights of Man* (1791–1792)

Boswell's *The Life of Johnson*

Burns's *Tam o'Shanter*

The *Observer* founded

1792 The Prussians invade France and are repulsed at Valmy September massacres

The National Convention declares royalty abolished in France

Washington reelected president of the United States

New York Stock Exchange opens

Mary Wollstonecraft's *Vindication of the Rights of Woman*

William Bligh's voyage to the South Sea in H.M.S. *Bounty*

Percy Bysshe Shelley born

1793 Trial and execution of Louis XVI and Marie-Antoinette

France declares war against England

CHRONOLOGY

The Committee of Public Safety (Comité de Salut Public) established
Eli Whitney devises the cotton gin
William Godwin's *An Enquiry Concerning Political Justice*
Blake's *Visions of the Daughters of Albion and America*
Wordsworth's *An Evening Walk* and *Descriptive Sketches*

1794 Execution of Georges Danton and Maximilien de Robespierre
Paine's *The Age of Reason* (1794–1796)
Blake's *Songs of Experience*
Ann Radcliffe's *The Mysteries of Udolpho*
Death of Edward Gibbon

1795 The government of the Directory established (1795–1799)
Hastings acquitted
Landor's *Poems*
Death of James Boswell
John Keats born
Thomas Carlyle born

1796 Napoleon Bonaparte takes command in Italy
Matthew Lewis' *The Monk*
John Adams elected president of the United States
Death of Robert Burns

1797 The peace of Campo Formio: extinction of the Venetian Republic
XYZ Affair
Mutinies in the Royal Navy at Spithead and the Nore
Blake's *Vala, Or the Four Zoas* (first version)
Mary Shelley born
Deaths of Edmund Burke, Mary Wollstonecraft, and Horace Walpole

1798 Napoleon invades Egypt
Horatio Nelson wins the battle of the Nile
Wordsworth's and Coleridge's *Lyrical Ballads*
Landor's *Gebir*
Thomas Malthus' *Essay on the Principle of Population*

1799 Napoleon becomes first consul
Pitt introduces first income tax in Great Britain

Sheridan's *Pizarro*
Honoré de Balzac born
Thomas Hood born
Alexander Pushkin born

1800 Thomas Jefferson elected president of the United States
Alessandro Volta produces electricity from a cell
Library of Congress established
Death of William Cowper
Thomas Babington Macaulay born

1801 First census taken in England

1802 The Treaty of Amiens marks the end of the French Revolutionary War
The *Edinburgh Review* founded

1803 England's war with France renewed
The Louisiana Purchase
Robert Fulton propels a boat by steam power on the Seine

1804 Napoleon crowned emperor of the French
Jefferson reelected president of the United States
Blake's *Milton* (1804–1808) and *Jerusalem*
The Code Napoleon promulgated in France
Beethoven's *Eroica* Symphony
Schiller's *Wilhelm Tell*
Benjamin Disraeli born

1805 Napoleon plans the invasion of England
Battle of Trafalgar
Battle of Austerlitz
Beethoven's *Fidelio* first produced
Scott's *Lay of the Last Minstrel*

1806 Scott's *Marmion*
Death of William Pitt
Death of Charles James Fox
Elizabeth Barrett born

1807 France invades Portugal
Aaron Burr tried for treason and acquitted
Byron's *Hours of Idleness*
Charles and Mary Lamb's *Tales from Shakespeare*
Thomas Moore's *Irish Melodies*
Wordsworth's *Ode on the Intimations of Immortality*

1808 National uprising in Spain against the French invasion

CHRONOLOGY

The Peninsular War begins
James Madison elected president of the United States
Covent Garden theater burned down
Goethe's *Faust* (Part 1)
Beethoven's Fifth Symphony completed
Lamb's *Specimens of English Dramatic Poets*

1809 Drury Lane theater burned down and rebuilt
The *Quarterly Review* founded
Byron's *English Bards and Scotch Reviewers*
Byron sails for the Mediterranean
Goya's *Los Desastres de la guerra* (1809–1814)
Alfred Tennyson born
Edward Fitzgerald born

1810 Crabbe's *The Borough*
Scott's *The Lady of the Lake*
Elizabeth Gaskell born

1811–1820 Regency of George IV

1811 Luddite Riots begin
Coleridge's *Lectures on Shakespeare* (1811–1814)
Jane Austen's *Sense and Sensibility*
Shelley's *The Necessity of Atheism*
John Constable's *Dedham Vale*
William Makepeace Thackeray born

1812 Napoleon invades Russia; captures and retreats from Moscow
United States declares war against England
Henry Bell's steamship *Comet* is launched on the Clyde river
Madison reelected president of the United States
Byron's *Childe Harold* (Cantos 1–2)
The Brothers Grimm's *Fairy Tales* (1812–1815)
Hegel's *Science of Logic*
Robert Browning born
Charles Dickens born

1813 Wellington wins the battle of Vitoria and enters France
Jane Austen's *Pride and Prejudice*
Byron's *The Giaour* and *The Bride of Abydos*
Shelley's *Queen Mab*
Southey's *Life of Nelson*

1814 Napoleon abdicates and is exiled to Elba; Bourbon restoration with Louis XVIII
Treaty of Ghent ends the war between Britain and the United States
Jane Austen's *Mansfield Park*
Byron's *The Corsair* and *Lara*
Scott's *Waverley*
Wordsworth's *The Excursion*

1815 Napoleon returns to France (the Hundred Days); is defeated at Waterloo and exiled to St. Helena
U.S.S. *Fulton*, the first steam warship, built
Scott's *Guy Mannering*
Schlegel's *Lectures on Dramatic Art and Literature* translated
Wordsworth's *The White Doe of Rylstone*
Anthony Trollope born

1816 Byron leaves England permanently
The Elgin Marbles exhibited in the British Museum
James Monroe elected president of the United States
Jane Austen's *Emma*
Byron's *Childe Harold* (Canto 3)
Coleridge's *Christabel, Kubla Khan: A Vision, The Pains of Sleep*
Benjamin Constant's *Adolphe*
Goethe's *Italienische Reise*
Peacock's *Headlong Hall*
Scott's *The Antiquary*
Shelley's *Alastor*
Rossini's *Il Barbiere di Siviglia*
Death of Richard Brinsley Sheridan
Charlotte Brontë born

1817 *Blackwood's Edinburgh* magazine founded
Jane Austen's *Northanger Abbey* and *Persuasion*
Byron's *Manfred*
Coleridge's *Biographia Literaria*
Hazlitt's *The Characters of Shakespeare's Plays* and *The Round Table*
Keats's *Poems*
Peacock's *Melincourt*
David Ricardo's *Principles of Political Economy and Taxation*
Death of Jane Austen
Death of Mme de Staël
Branwell Brontë born

CHRONOLOGY

Henry David Thoreau born

1818 Byron's *Childe Harold* (Canto 4), and *Beppo*
Hazlitt's *Lectures on the English Poets*
Keats's *Endymion*
Peacock's *Nightmare Abbey*
Scott's *Rob Roy* and *The Heart of Mid-Lothian*
Mary Shelley's *Frankenstein*
Percy Shelley's *The Revolt of Islam*
Emily Brontë born
Karl Marx born
Ivan Sergeyevich Turgenev born

1819 The *Savannah* becomes the first steamship to cross the Atlantic (in 26 days)
Peterloo massacre in Manchester
Byron's *Don Juan* (1819–1824) and *Mazeppa*
Crabbe's *Tales of the Hall*
Géricault's *Raft of the Medusa*
Hazlitt's *Lectures on the English Comic Writers*
Arthur Schopenhauer's *Die Welt als Wille und Vorstellung (The World as Will and Idea)*
Scott's *The Bride of Lammermoor* and *A Legend of Montrose*
Shelley's *The Cenci*, "The Masque of Anarchy," and "Ode to the West Wind"
Wordsworth's *Peter Bell*
Queen Victoria born
George Eliot born

1820–1830 Reign of George IV
1820 Trial of Queen Caroline
Cato Street Conspiracy suppressed; Arthur Thistlewood hanged
Monroe reelected president of the United States
Missouri Compromise
The *London* magazine founded
Keats's *Lamia, Isabella, The Eve of St. Agnes, and Other Poems*
Hazlitt's *Lectures Chiefly on the Dramatic Literature of the Age of Elizabeth*
Charles Maturin's *Melmoth the Wanderer*
Scott's *Ivanhoe* and *The Monastery*
Shelley's *Prometheus Unbound*

Anne Brontë born

1821 Greek War of Independence begins
Liberia founded as a colony for freed slaves
Byron's *Cain, Marino Faliero, The Two Foscari*, and *Sardanapalus*
Hazlitt's *Table Talk* (1821–1822)
Scott's *Kenilworth*
Shelley's *Adonais* and *Epipsychidion*
Death of John Keats
Death of Napoleon
Charles Baudelaire born
Feodor Dostoyevsky born
Gustave Flaubert born

1822 The Massacres of Chios (Greeks rebel against Turkish rule)
Byron's *The Vision of Judgment*
De Quincey's *Confessions of an English Opium-Eater*
Peacock's *Maid Marian*
Scott's *Peveril of the Peak*
Shelley's *Hellas*
Death of Percy Bysshe Shelley
Matthew Arnold born

1823 Monroe Doctrine proclaimed
Byron's *The Age of Bronze* and *The Island*
Lamb's *Essays of Elia*
Scott's *Quentin Durward*

1824 The National Gallery opened in London
John Quincy Adams elected president of the United States
The *Westminster Review* founded
Beethoven's Ninth Symphony first performed
William (Wilkie) Collins born
James Hogg's *The Private Memoirs and Confessions of a Justified Sinner*
Landor's *Imaginary Conversations* (1824–1829)
Scott's *Redgauntlet*
Death of George Gordon, Lord Byron

1825 Inauguration of steam-powered passenger and freight service on the Stockton and Darlington railway
Bolivia and Brazil become independent Alessandro Manzoni's *I Promessi Sposi* (1825–1826)

CHRONOLOGY

1826 André-Marie Ampère's *Mémoire sur la théorie mathématique des phénomènes électrodynamiques*
James Fenimore Cooper's *The Last of the Mohicans*
Disraeli's *Vivian Grey* (1826–1827)
Scott's *Woodstock*

1827 The battle of Navarino ensures the independence of Greece
Josef Ressel obtains patent for the screw propeller for steamships
Heinrich Heine's *Buch der Lieder*
Death of William Blake

1828 Andrew Jackson elected president of the United States
Henrik Ibsen born
George Meredith born
Dante Gabriel Rossetti born
Leo Tolstoy born

1829 The Catholic Emancipation Act
Robert Peel establishes the metropolitan police force
Greek independence recognized by Turkey
Balzac begins *La Comédie humaine* (1829–1848)
Peacock's *The Misfortunes of Elphin*
J. M. W. Turner's *Ulysses Deriding Polyphemus*

1830–1837 Reign of William IV

1830 Charles X of France abdicates and is succeeded by Louis-Philippe
The Liverpool-Manchester railway opened
Tennyson's *Poems, Chiefly Lyrical*
Death of William Hazlitt
Christina Rossetti born

1831 Michael Faraday discovers electromagnetic induction
Charles Darwin's voyage on H.M.S. *Beagle* begins (1831–1836)
The Barbizon school of artists' first exhibition
Nat Turner slave revolt crushed in Virginia
Peacock's *Crotchet Castle*
Stendhal's *Le Rouge et le noir*
Edward Trelawny's *The Adventures of a Younger Son*

1832 The first Reform Bill
Samuel Morse invents the telegraph
Jackson reelected president of the United States
Disraeli's *Contarini Fleming*
Goethe's *Faust* (Part 2)
Tennyson's *Poems, Chiefly Lyrical*, including "The Lotus-Eaters" and "The Lady of Shalott"
Death of Johann Wolfgang von Goethe
Death of Sir Walter Scott
Lewis Carroll born

1833 Robert Browning's *Pauline*
John Keble launches the Oxford Movement
American Anti-Slavery Society founded
Lamb's *Last Essays of Elia*
Carlyle's *Sartor Resartus* (1833–1834)
Pushkin's *Eugene Onegin*
Mendelssohn's *Italian Symphony* first performed

1834 Abolition of slavery in the British Empire
Louis Braille's alphabet for the blind
Balzac's *Le Père Goriot*
Nikolai Gogol's *Dead Souls* (Part 1, 1834–1842)
Death of Samuel Taylor Coleridge
Death of Charles Lamb
William Morris born

1835 Hans Christian Andersen's *Fairy Tales* (1st ser.)
Robert Browning's *Paracelsus*
Births of Samuel Butler and Mary Elizabeth Braddon
Alexis de Tocqueville's *De la Democratie en Amerique* (1835–1840)

1836 Martin Van Buren elected president of the United States
Dickens' *Sketches by Boz* (1836–1837)
Landor's *Pericles and Aspasia*

1837–1901 Reign of Queen Victoria

1837 Carlyle's *The French Revolution*
Dickens' *Oliver Twist* (1837–1838) and *Pickwick Papers*
Disraeli's *Venetia* and *Henrietta Temple*

1838 Chartist movement in England

CHRONOLOGY

National Gallery in London opened
Elizabeth Barrett Browning's *The Seraphim and Other Poems*
Dickens' *Nicholas Nickleby* (1838–1839)

1839   Louis Daguerre perfects process for producing an image on a silver-coated copper plate Faraday's *Experimental Researches in Electricity* (1839–1855)
First Chartist riots
Opium War between Great Britain and China
Carlyle's *Chartism*

1840   Canadian Act of Union
Queen Victoria marries Prince Albert
Charles Barry begins construction of the Houses of Parliament (1840–1852)
William Henry Harrison elected president of the United States
Robert Browning's *Sordello*
Thomas Hardy born

1841   New Zealand proclaimed a British colony
James Clark Ross discovers the Antarctic continent
Punch founded
John Tyler succeeds to the presidency after the death of Harrison
Carlyle's *Heroes and Hero-Worship*
Dickens' *The Old Curiosity Shop*

1842   Chartist riots
Income tax revived in Great Britain
The Mines Act, forbidding work underground by women or by children under the age of ten
Charles Edward Mudie's Lending Library founded in London
Dickens visits America
Robert Browning's *Dramatic Lyrics*
Macaulay's *Lays of Ancient Rome*
Tennyson's *Poems*, including "Morte d'Arthur," "St. Simeon Stylites," and "Ulysses"
Wordsworth's *Poems*

1843   Marc Isambard Brunel's Thames tunnel opened
The Economist founded
Carlyle's *Past and Present*
Dickens' *A Christmas Carol*

John Stuart Mill's *Logic*
Macaulay's *Critical and Historical Essays*
John Ruskin's *Modern Painters* (1843–1860)

1844   Rochdale Society of Equitable Pioneers, one of the first consumers' cooperatives, founded by twenty-eight Lancashire weavers
James K. Polk elected president of the United States
Elizabeth Barrett Browning's *Poems*, including "The Cry of the Children"
Dickens' *Martin Chuzzlewit*
Disraeli's *Coningsby*
Turner's *Rain, Steam and Speed*
Gerard Manley Hopkins born

1845   The great potato famine in Ireland begins (1845–1849)
Disraeli's *Sybil*

1846   Repeal of the Corn Laws
The *Daily News* founded (edited by Dickens the first three weeks)
Standard-gauge railway introduced in Britain
The Brontës' pseudonymous *Poems by Currer, Ellis and Action Bell*
Lear's *Book of Nonsense*

1847   The Ten Hours Factory Act
James Simpson uses chloroform as an anesthetic
Anne Brontë's *Agnes Grey*
Charlotte Brontë's *Jane Eyre*
Emily Brontë's *Wuthering Heights*
Bram Stoker born
Tennyson's *The Princess*

1848   The year of revolutions in France, Germany, Italy, Hungary, Poland
Marx and Engels issue *The Communist Manifesto*
The Chartist Petition
The Pre-Raphaelite Brotherhood founded
Zachary Taylor elected president of the United States
Anne Brontë's *The Tenant of Wildfell Hall*
Dickens' *Dombey and Son*
Elizabeth Gaskell's *Mary Barton*
Macaulay's *History of England* (1848–1861)

CHRONOLOGY

Mill's *Principles of Political Economy*
Thackeray's *Vanity Fair*
Death of Emily Brontë

1849 Bedford College for women founded
Arnold's *The Strayed Reveller*
Charlotte Brontë's *Shirley*
Ruskin's *The Seven Lamps of Architecture*
Death of Anne Brontë

1850 The Public Libraries Act
First submarine telegraph cable laid between Dover and Calais
Millard Fillmore succeeds to the presidency after the death of Taylor
Elizabeth Barrett Browning's *Sonnets from the Portuguese*
Carlyle's *Latter-Day Pamphlets*
Dickens' *Household Words* (1850–1859) and *David Copperfield*
Charles Kingsley's *Alton Locke*
The Pre-Raphaelites publish the *Germ*
Tennyson's *In Memoriam*
Thackeray's *The History of Pendennis*
Wordsworth's *The Prelude* is published posthumously

1851 The Great Exhibition opens at the Crystal Palace in Hyde Park
Louis Napoleon seizes power in France
Gold strike in Victoria incites Australian gold rush
Elizabeth Gaskell's *Cranford* (1851–1853)
Meredith's *Poems*
Ruskin's *The Stones of Venice* (1851–1853)

1852 The Second Empire proclaimed with Napoleon III as emperor
David Livingstone begins to explore the Zambezi (1852–1856)
Franklin Pierce elected president of the United States
Arnold's *Empedocles on Etna*
Thackeray's *The History of Henry Esmond, Esq.*

1853 Crimean War (1853–1856)

Arnold's *Poems*, including "The Scholar Gypsy" and "Sohrab and Rustum"
Charlotte Brontë's *Villette*
Elizabeth Gaskell's *Crawford and Ruth*

1854 Frederick D. Maurice's Working Men's College founded in London with more than 130 pupils
Battle of Balaklava
Dickens' *Hard Times*
James George Frazer born
Theodor Mommsen's *History of Rome* (1854–1856)
Tennyson's "The Charge of the Light Brigade"
Florence Nightingale in the Crimea (1854–1856)
Oscar Wilde born

1855 David Livingstone discovers the Victoria Falls
Robert Browning's *Men and Women*
Elizabeth Gaskell's *North and South*
Olive Schreiner born
Tennyson's *Maud*
Thackeray's *The Newcomes*
Trollope's *The Warden*
Death of Charlotte Brontë

1856 The Treaty of Paris ends the Crimean War
Henry Bessemer's steel process invented
James Buchanan elected president of the United States
H. Rider Haggard born

1857 The Indian Mutiny begins; crushed in 1858
The Matrimonial Causes Act
Charlotte Brontë's *The Professor*
Elizabeth Barrett Browning's *Aurora Leigh*
Dickens' *Little Dorritt*
Elizabeth Gaskell's *The Life of Charlotte Brontë*
Thomas Hughes's *Tom Brown's School Days*
Trollope's *Barchester Towers*

1858 Carlyle's *History of Frederick the Great* (1858–1865)
George Eliot's *Scenes of Clerical Life*

CHRONOLOGY

Morris' *The Defense of Guinevere*
Trollope's *Dr. Thorne*

1859 Charles Darwin's *The Origin of Species*
Dickens' *A Tale of Two Cities*
Arthur Conan Doyle born
George Eliot's *Adam Bede*
Fitzgerald's *The Rubaiyat of Omar Khayyám*
Meredith's *The Ordeal of Richard Feverel*
Mill's *On Liberty*
Samuel Smiles's *Self-Help*
Tennyson's *Idylls of the King*

1860 Abraham Lincoln elected president of the United States
The *Cornhill* magazine founded with Thackeray as editor
James M. Barrie born
William Wilkie Collins' *The Woman in White*
George Eliot's *The Mill on the Floss*

1861 American Civil War begins
Louis Pasteur presents the germ theory of disease
Arnold's *Lectures on Translating Homer*
Dickens' *Great Expectations*
George Eliot's *Silas Marner*
Meredith's *Evan Harrington*
Francis Turner Palgrave's *The Golden Treasury*
Trollope's *Framley Parsonage*
Peacock's *Gryll Grange*
Death of Prince Albert

1862 George Eliot's *Romola*
Meredith's *Modern Love*
Christina Rossetti's *Goblin Market*
Ruskin's *Unto This Last*
Trollope's *Orley Farm*

1863 Thomas Huxley's *Man's Place in Nature*

1864 The Geneva Red Cross Convention signed by twelve nations
Lincoln reelected president of the United States
Robert Browning's *Dramatis Personae*
John Henry Newman's *Apologia pro vita sua*
Tennyson's *Enoch Arden*

Trollope's *The Small House at Allington*

1865 Assassination of Lincoln; Andrew Johnson succeeds to the presidency
Arnold's *Essays in Criticism* (1st ser.)
Carroll's *Alice's Adventures in Wonderland*
Dickens' *Our Mutual Friend*
Meredith's *Rhoda Fleming*
A. C. Swinburne's *Atalanta in Calydon*

1866 First successful transatlantic telegraph cable laid
George Eliot's *Felix Holt, the Radical*
Elizabeth Gaskell's *Wives and Daughters*
Beatrix Potter born
Swinburne's *Poems and Ballads*

1867 The second Reform Bill
Arnold's *New Poems*
Bagehot's *The English Constitution*
Carlyle's *Shooting Niagara*
Marx's *Das Kapital* (vol. 1)
Trollope's *The Last Chronicle of Barset*
George William Russell (AE) born

1868 Gladstone becomes prime minister (1868–1874)
Johnson impeached by House of Representatives; acquitted by Senate
Ulysses S. Grant elected president of the United States
Robert Browning's *The Ring and the Book* (1868–1869)
Collins' *The Moonstone*

1869 The Suez Canal opened
Girton College, Cambridge, founded
Arnold's *Culture and Anarchy*
Mill's *The Subjection of Women*
Trollope's *Phineas Finn*

1870 The Elementary Education Act establishes schools under the aegis of local boards
Dickens' *Edwin Drood*
Disraeli's *Lothair*
Morris' *The Earthly Paradise*
Dante Gabriel Rossetti's *Poems*
Saki [Hector Hugh Munro] born

CHRONOLOGY

1871 Trade unions legalized
Newnham College, Cambridge, founded for women students
Carroll's *Through the Looking Glass*
Darwin's *The Descent of Man*
Meredith's *The Adventures of Harry Richmond*
Swinburne's *Songs Before Sunrise*

1872 Max Beerbohm born
Samuel Butler's *Erewhon*
George Eliot's *Middlemarch*
Grant reelected president of the United States
Hardy's *Under the Greenwood Tree*

1873 Arnold's *Literature and Dogma*
Mill's *Autobiography*
Pater's *Studies in the History of the Renaissance*
Trollope's *The Eustace Diamonds*

1874 Disraeli becomes prime minister
Hardy's *Far from the Madding Crowd*
James Thomson's *The City of Dreadful Night*

1875 Britain buys Suez Canal shares
Trollope's *The Way We Live Now*
T. F. Powys born

1876 F. H. Bradley's *Ethical Studies*
George Eliot's *Daniel Deronda*
Henry James's *Roderick Hudson*
Meredith's *Beauchamp's Career*
Morris' *Sigurd the Volsung*
Trollope's *The Prime Minister*

1877 Rutherford B. Hayes elected president of the United States after Electoral Commission awards him disputed votes
Henry James's *The American*

1878 Electric street lighting introduced in London
Hardy's *The Return of the Native*
Swinburne's *Poems and Ballads* (2d ser.)
Births of A. E. Coppard and Edward Thomas

1879 Somerville College and Lady Margaret Hall opened at Oxford for women
The London telephone exchange built
Gladstone's Midlothian campaign (1879–1880)
Browning's *Dramatic Idyls*
Meredith's *The Egoist*

1880 Gladstone's second term as prime minister (1880–1885)
James A. Garfield elected president of the United States
Browning's *Dramatic Idyls Second Series*
Disraeli's *Endymion*
Radclyffe Hall born
Hardy's *The Trumpet-Major*
Lytton Strachey born

1881 Garfield assassinated; Chester A. Arthur succeeds to the presidency
Henry James's *The Portrait of a Lady* and *Washington Square*
D. G. Rossetti's *Ballads and Sonnets*
P. G. Wodehouse born

1882 Triple Alliance formed between German empire, Austrian empire, and Italy
Leslie Stephen begins to edit the *Dictionary of National Biography*
Married Women's Property Act passed in Britain
Britain occupies Egypt and the Sudan

1883 Uprising of the Mahdi: Britain evacuates the Sudan
Royal College of Music opens
T. H. Green's *Ethics*
T. E. Hulme born
Stevenson's *Treasure Island*

1884 The Mahdi captures Omdurman: General Gordon appointed to command the garrison of Khartoum
Grover Cleveland elected president of the United States
The *Oxford English Dictionary* begins publishing
The Fabian Society founded
Hiram Maxim's recoil-operated machine gun invented

1885 The Mahdi captures Khartoum: General Gordon killed
Haggard's *King Solomon's Mines*
Marx's *Das Kapital* (vol. 2)
Meredith's *Diana of the Crossways*
Pater's *Marius the Epicurean*

CHRONOLOGY

1886   The Canadian Pacific Railway completed
        Gold discovered in the Transvaal
        Births of Frances Cornford, Ronald Firbank, and **Charles Stansby Walter Williams**
        Henry James's *The Bostonians* and *The Princess Casamassima*
        Stevenson's *The Strange Case of Dr. Jekyll and Mr. Hyde*

1887   Queen Victoria's Golden Jubilee
        Rupert Brooke born
        Haggard's *Allan Quatermain* and *She*
        Hardy's *The Woodlanders*
        Edwin Muir born

1888   Benjamin Harrison elected president of the United States
        Henry James's *The Aspern Papers*
        Kipling's *Plain Tales from the Hills*
        T. E. Lawrence born

1889   Yeats's *The Wanderings of Oisin*
        Death of Robert Browning

1890   Morris founds the Kelmscott Press
        Agatha Christie born
        Frazer's *The Golden Bough* (1st ed.)
        Henry James's *The Tragic Muse*
        Morris' *News From Nowhere*
        Jean Rhys born

1891   Gissing's *New Grub Street*
        Hardy's *Tess of the d'Urbervilles*
        Wilde's *The Picture of Dorian Gray*

1892   Grover Cleveland elected president of the United States
        Conan Doyle's *The Adventures of Sherlock Holmes*
        Shaw's *Widower's Houses*
        J. R. R. Tolkien born
        Rebecca West born
        Wilde's *Lady Windermere's Fan*

1893   Wilde's *A Woman of No Importance* and *Salomé*

1894   Kipling's *The Jungle Book*
        Moore's *Esther Waters*
        Marx's *Das Kapital* (vol. 3)
        Audrey Beardsley's *The Yellow Book* begins to appear quarterly
        Shaw's *Arms and the Man*

1895   Trial and imprisonment of Oscar Wilde

William Ramsay announces discovery of helium
        The National Trust founded
        Conrad's *Almayer's Folly*
        Hardy's *Jude the Obscure*
        Wells's *The Time Machine*
        Wilde's *The Importance of Being Earnest*
        Yeats's *Poems*

1896   William McKinley elected president of the United States
        Failure of the Jameson Raid on the Transvaal
        Housman's *A Shropshire Lad*

1897   Queen Victoria's Diamond Jubilee
        Conrad's *The Nigger of the Narcissus*
        Havelock Ellis' *Studies in the Psychology of Sex* begins publication
        Henry James's *The Spoils of Poynton* and *What Maisie Knew*
        Kipling's *Captains Courageous*
        Shaw's *Candida*
        Stoker's *Dracula*
        Wells's *The Invisible Man*

1898   Kitchener defeats the Mahdist forces at Omdurman: the Sudan reoccupied
        Hardy's *Wessex Poems*
        Henry James's *The Turn of the Screw*
        C. S. Lewis born
        Shaw's *Caesar and Cleopatra* and *You Never Can Tell*
        Alec Waugh born
        Wells's *The War of the Worlds*
        Wilde's *The Ballad of Reading Gaol*

1899   The Boer War begins
        Elizabeth Bowen born
        Noël Coward born
        Elgar's *Enigma Variations*
        Kipling's *Stalky and Co.*

1900   McKinley reelected president of the United States
        British Labour party founded
        Boxer Rebellion in China
        Reginald A. Fessenden transmits speech by wireless
        First Zeppelin trial flight
        Max Planck presents his first paper on the quantum theory
        Conrad's *Lord Jim*

CHRONOLOGY

Elgar's *The Dream of Gerontius*
Sigmund Freud's *The Interpretation of Dreams*
V. S. Pritchett born
William Butler Yeats's *The Shadowy Waters*

1901–1910 Reign of King Edward VII
1901 William McKinley assassinated; Theodore Roosevelt succeeds to the presidency
First transatlantic wireless telegraph signal transmitted
Chekhov's *Three Sisters*
Freud's *Psychopathology of Everyday Life*
Rudyard Kipling's *Kim*
Thomas Mann's *Buddenbrooks*
Potter's *The Tale of Peter Rabbit*
Shaw's *Captain Brassbound's Conversion*
August Strindberg's *The Dance of Death*

1902 Barrie's *The Admirable Crichton*
Arnold Bennett's *Anna of the Five Towns*
Cézanne's *Le Lac D'Annecy*
Conrad's *Heart of Darkness*
Henry James's *The Wings of the Dove*
William James's *The Varieties of Religious Experience*
Kipling's *Just So Stories*
Maugham's *Mrs. Cradock*
Stevie Smith born
Times Literary Supplement begins publishing

1903 At its London congress the Russian Social Democratic Party divides into Mensheviks, led by Plekhanov, and Bolsheviks, led by Lenin
The treaty of Panama places the Canal Zone in U.S. hands for a nominal rent
Motor cars regulated in Britain to a 20-mile-per-hour limit
The Wright brothers make a successful flight in the United States
Burlington magazine founded
Samuel Butler's *The Way of All Flesh* published posthumously
Cyril Connolly born

George Gissing's *The Private Papers of Henry Ryecroft*
Thomas Hardy's *The Dynasts*
Henry James's *The Ambassadors*
Alan Paton born
Shaw's *Man and Superman*
Synge's *Riders to the Sea* produced in Dublin
Yeats's *In the Seven Woods* and *On Baile's Strand*

1904 Roosevelt elected president of the United States
Russo-Japanese war (1904–1905)
Construction of the Panama Canal begins
The ultraviolet lamp invented
The engineering firm of Rolls Royce founded
Barrie's *Peter Pan* first performed
Cecil Day Lewis born
Chekhov's *The Cherry Orchard*
Conrad's *Nostromo*
Henry James's *The Golden Bowl*
Kipling's *Traffics and Discoveries*
Georges Rouault's *Head of a Tragic Clown*
G. M. Trevelyan's *England Under the Stuarts*
Puccini's *Madame Butterfly*
First Shaw-Granville Barker season at the Royal Court Theatre
The Abbey Theatre founded in Dublin

1905 Russian sailors on the battleship Potemkin mutiny
After riots and a general strike the czar concedes demands by the Duma for legislative powers, a wider franchise, and civil liberties
Albert Einstein publishes his first theory of relativity
The Austin Motor Company founded
Bennett's *Tales of the Five Towns*
Claude Debussy's *La Mer*
E. M. Forster's *Where Angels Fear to Tread*
Richard Strauss's *Salome*
H. G. Wells's *Kipps*
Oscar Wilde's *De Profundis*
Births of **Norman Cameron**, Henry Green, and **Mary Renault**

CHRONOLOGY

1906   Liberals win a landslide victory in the British general election
The Trades Disputes Act legitimizes peaceful picketing in Britain
Captain Dreyfus rehabilitated in France
J. J. Thomson begins research on gamma rays
The U.S. Pure Food and Drug Act passed
Churchill's *Lord Randolph Churchill*
William Empson born
Galsworthy's *The Man of Property*
Kipling's *Puck of Pook's Hill*
Shaw's *The Doctor's Dilemma*
Yeats's *Poems 1899–1905*

1907   Exhibition of cubist paintings in Paris
Henry Adams' *The Education of Henry Adams*
Henri Bergson's *Creative Evolution*
Conrad's *The Secret Agent*
Births of Barbara Comyns, Daphne du Maurier, and Christopher Fry
Forster's *The Longest Journey*
André Gide's *La Porte étroite*
Shaw's *John Bull's Other Island* and *Major Barbara*
Synge's *The Playboy of the Western World*
Trevelyan's *Garibaldi's Defence of the Roman Republic*
Christopher Caudwell (Christopher St. John Sprigg) born

1908   Herbert Asquith becomes prime minister
David Lloyd George becomes chancellor of the exchequer
William Howard Taft elected president of the United States
The Young Turks seize power in Istanbul
Henry Ford's Model T car produced
Bennett's *The Old Wives' Tale*
Pierre Bonnard's *Nude Against the Light*
Georges Braque's *House at L'Estaque*
Chesterton's *The Man Who Was Thursday*

Jacob Epstein's *Figures* erected in London
Forster's *A Room with a View*
Anatole France's *L'Ile des Pingouins*
Henri Matisse's *Bonheur de Vivre*
Elgar's First Symphony
Ford Madox Ford founds the *English Review*

1909   The Young Turks depose Sultan Abdul Hamid
The Anglo-Persian Oil Company formed
Louis Bleriot crosses the English Channel from France by monoplane
Admiral Robert Peary reaches the North Pole
Freud lectures at Clark University (Worcester, Mass.) on psychoanalysis
Serge Diaghilev's Ballets Russes opens in Paris
Galsworthy's *Strife*
Hardy's *Time's Laughingstocks*
Malcolm Lowry born
Claude Monet's *Water Lilies*
Stephen Spender born
Trevelyan's *Garibaldi and the Thousand*
Wells's *Tono-Bungay* first published (book form, 1909)

1910–1936   Reign of King George V

1910   The Liberals win the British general election
Marie Curie's *Treatise on Radiography*
Arthur Evans excavates Knossos
Edouard Manet and the first post-impressionist exhibition in London
Filippo Marinetti publishes "Manifesto of the Futurist Painters"
Norman Angell's *The Great Illusion*
Bennett's *Clayhanger*
Forster's *Howards End*
Galsworthy's *Justice* and *The Silver Box*
Kipling's *Rewards and Fairies*
Norman MacCaig born
Rimsky-Korsakov's *Le Coq d'or*
Stravinsky's *The Firebird*
Vaughan Williams' *A Sea Symphony*
Wells's *The History of Mr. Polly*

CHRONOLOGY

Wells's *The New Machiavelli* first published (in book form, 1911)

1911 Lloyd George introduces National Health Insurance Bill

Suffragette riots in Whitehall

Roald Amundsen reaches the South Pole

Bennett's *The Card*

Chagall's *Self Portrait with Seven Fingers*

Conrad's *Under Western Eyes*

D. H. Lawrence's *The White Peacock*

Katherine Mansfield's *In a German Pension*

Edward Marsh edits *Georgian Poetry*

Moore's *Hail and Farewell* (1911–1914)

Flann O'Brien born

Strauss's *Der Rosenkavalier*

Stravinsky's *Petrouchka*

Trevelyan's *Garibaldi and the Making of Italy*

Wells's *The New Machiavelli*

Mahler's *Das Lied von der Erde*

1912 Woodrow Wilson elected president of the United States

SS *Titanic* sinks on its maiden voyage

Five million Americans go to the movies daily; London has four hundred movie theaters

Second post-impressionist exhibition in London

Bennett's and Edward Knoblock's *Milestones*

Constantin Brancusi's *Maiastra*

Wassily Kandinsky's *Black Lines*

D. H. Lawrence's *The Trespasser*

1913 Second Balkan War begins

Henry Ford pioneers factory assembly technique through conveyor belts

Epstein's *Tomb of Oscar Wilde*

New York Armory Show introduces modern art to the world

Alain Fournier's *Le Grand Meaulnes*

Freud's *Totem and Tabu*

D. H. Lawrence's *Sons and Lovers*

Mann's *Death in Venice*

Proust's *Du Côté de chez Swann* (first volume of *À la recherche du temps perdu*, 1913–1922)

Barbara Pym born

Ravel's *Daphnis and Chloé*

1914 The Panama Canal opens (formal dedication on 12 July 1920)

Irish Home Rule Bill passed in the House of Commons

Archduke Franz Ferdinand assassinated at Sarajevo

World War I begins

Battles of the Marne, Masurian Lakes, and Falkland Islands

Joyce's *Dubliners*

Norman Nicholson born

Shaw's *Pygmalion* and *Androcles and the Lion*

Yeats's *Responsibilities*

Wyndham Lewis publishes *Blast* magazine and *The Vorticist Manifesto*

1915 The Dardanelles campaign begins

Britain and Germany begin naval and submarine blockades

The *Lusitania* is sunk

Hugo Junkers manufactures the first fighter aircraft

First Zeppelin raid in London

Brooke's *1914: Five Sonnets*

Norman Douglas' *Old Calabria*

D. W. Griffith's *The Birth of a Nation*

Gustav Holst's *The Planets*

D. H. Lawrence's *The Rainbow*

Wyndham Lewis's *The Crowd*

Maugham's *Of Human Bondage*

Pablo Picasso's *Harlequin*

Sibelius' Fifth Symphony

Denton Welch born

1916 Evacuation of Gallipoli and the Dardanelles

Battles of the Somme, Jutland, and Verdun

Britain introduces conscription

The Easter Rebellion in Dublin

Asquith resigns and David Lloyd George becomes prime minister

The Sykes-Picot agreement on the partition of Turkey

First military tanks used

CHRONOLOGY

Wilson reelected president president of the United States
Henri Barbusse's *Le Feu*
Griffith's *Intolerance*
Joyce's *Portrait of the Artist as a Young Man*
Jung's *Psychology of the Unconscious*
Moore's *The Brook Kerith*
Edith Sitwell edits *Wheels* (1916–1921)
Wells's *Mr. Britling Sees It Through*

1917 United States enters World War I
Czar Nicholas II abdicates
The Balfour Declaration on a Jewish national home in Palestine
The Bolshevik Revolution
Georges Clemenceau elected prime minister of France
Lenin appointed chief commissar; Trotsky appointed minister of foreign affairs
Conrad's *The Shadow-Line*
Douglas' *South Wind*
Eliot's *Prufrock and Other Observations*
Modigliani's *Nude with Necklace*
Sassoon's *The Old Huntsman*
Prokofiev's *Classical Symphony*
Yeats's *The Wild Swans at Coole*

1918 Wilson puts forward Fourteen Points for World Peace
Central Powers and Russia sign the Treaty of Brest-Litovsk
Execution of Czar Nicholas II and his family
Kaiser Wilhelm II abdicates
The Armistice signed
Women granted the vote at age thirty in Britain
Rupert Brooke's *Collected Poems*
Gerard Manley Hopkins' *Poems*
Joyce's *Exiles*
Lewis's *Tarr*
Sassoon's *Counter-Attack*
Oswald Spengler's *The Decline of the West*
Strachey's *Eminent Victorians*
Béla Bartók's *Bluebeard's Castle*
Charlie Chaplin's *Shoulder Arms*

1919 The Versailles Peace Treaty signed

J. W. Alcock and A. W. Brown make first transatlantic flight
Ross Smith flies from London to Australia
National Socialist party founded in Germany
Benito Mussolini founds the Fascist party in Italy
Sinn Fein Congress adopts declaration of independence in Dublin
Eamon De Valera elected president of Sinn Fein party
Communist Third International founded
Lady Astor elected first woman Member of Parliament
Prohibition in the United States
John Maynard Keynes's *The Economic Consequences of the Peace*
Eliot's *Poems*
Maugham's *The Moon and Sixpence*
Shaw's *Heartbreak House*
The Bauhaus school of design, building, and crafts founded by Walter Gropius
Amedeo Modigliani's *Self-Portrait*

1920 The League of Nations established
Warren G. Harding elected president of the United States
Senate votes against joining the League and rejects the Treaty of Versailles
The Nineteenth Amendment gives women the right to vote
White Russian forces of Denikin and Kolchak defeated by the Bolsheviks
Karel Čapek's *R.U.R.*
Galsworthy's *In Chancery* and *The Skin Game*
Sinclair Lewis' *Main Street*
Katherine Mansfield's *Bliss*
Matisse's *Odalisques* (1920–1925)
Ezra Pound's *Hugh Selwyn Mauberly*
Paul Valéry's *Le Cimetière Marin*
Yeats's *Michael Robartes and the Dancer*
Edwin Morgan born

1921 Britain signs peace with Ireland

CHRONOLOGY

First medium-wave radio broadcast in the United States

The British Broadcasting Corporation founded

Braque's *Still Life with Guitar*

Chaplin's *The Kid*

Aldous Huxley's *Crome Yellow*

Paul Klee's *The Fish*

D. H. Lawrence's *Women in Love*

John McTaggart's *The Nature of Existence* (vol. 1)

Moore's *Héloïse and Abélard*

Eugene O'Neill's *The Emperor Jones*

Luigi Pirandello's *Six Characters in Search of an Author*

Shaw's *Back to Methuselah*

Strachey's *Queen Victoria*

Births of George Mackay Brown and **Brian Moore**

1922 Lloyd George's Coalition government succeeded by Bonar Law's Conservative government

Benito Mussolini marches on Rome and forms a government

William Cosgrave elected president of the Irish Free State

The BBC begins broadcasting in London

Lord Carnarvon and Howard Carter discover Tutankhamen's tomb

The PEN club founded in London

The *Criterion* founded with T. S. Eliot as editor

Kingsley Amis born

Eliot's *The Waste Land*

A. E. Housman's *Last Poems*

Joyce's *Ulysses*

D. H. Lawrence's *Aaron's Rod* and *England, My England*

Sinclair Lewis's *Babbitt*

O'Neill's *Anna Christie*

Pirandello's *Henry IV*

Edith Sitwell's *Façade*

Virginia Woolf's *Jacob's Room*

Yeats's *The Trembling of the Veil*

Donald Davie born

1923 The Union of Soviet Socialist Republics established

French and Belgian troops occupy the Ruhr in consequence of Germany's failure to pay reparations

Mustafa Kemal (Ataturk) proclaims Turkey a republic and is elected president

Warren G. Harding dies; Calvin Coolidge becomes president

Stanley Baldwin succeeds Bonar Law as prime minister

Adolf Hitler's attempted coup in Munich fails

Time magazine begins publishing

E. N. da C. Andrade's *The Structure of the Atom*

Brendan Behan born

Bennett's *Riceyman Steps*

Churchill's *The World Crisis* (1923–1927)

J. E. Flecker's *Hassan* produced

Nadine Gordimer born

Paul Klee's *Magic Theatre*

Lawrence's *Kangaroo*

Rainer Maria Rilke's *Duino Elegies* and *Sonnets to Orpheus*

Sibelius' *Sixth Symphony*

Picasso's *Seated Woman*

William Walton's *Façade*

1924 Ramsay MacDonald forms first Labour government, loses general election, and is succeeded by Stanley Baldwin

Calvin Coolidge elected president of the United States

Noël Coward's *The Vortex*

Forster's *A Passage to India*

Mann's *The Magic Mountain*

Shaw's *St. Joan*

1925 Reza Khan becomes shah of Iran

First surrealist exhibition held in Paris

Alban Berg's *Wozzeck*

Chaplin's *The Gold Rush*

John Dos Passos' *Manhattan Transfer*

Theodore Dreiser's *An American Tragedy*

Sergei Eisenstein's *Battleship Potemkin*

F. Scott Fitzgerald's *The Great Gatsby*

André Gide's *Les Faux Monnayeurs*

Hardy's *Human Shows and Far Phantasies*

CHRONOLOGY

Huxley's *Those Barren Leaves*
Kafka's *The Trial*
O'Casey's *Juno and the Paycock*
Virginia Woolf's *Mrs. Dalloway*
and *The Common Reader*
Brancusi's *Bird in Space*
Shostakovich's *First Symphony*
Sibelius' *Tapiola*

1926   Ford's *A Man Could Stand Up*
Gide's *Si le grain ne meurt*
Hemingway's *The Sun also Rises*
Kafka's *The Castle*
D. H. Lawrence's *The Plumed Serpent*
T. E. Lawrence's *Seven Pillars of Wisdom* privately circulated
Maugham's *The Casuarina Tree*
O'Casey's *The Plough and the Stars*
Puccini's *Turandot*

1927   General Chiang Kai-shek becomes prime minister in China
Trotsky expelled by the Communist party as a deviationist; Stalin becomes leader of the party and dictator of the Soviet Union
Charles Lindbergh flies from New York to Paris
J. W. Dunne's *An Experiment with Time*
Freud's *Autobiography* translated into English
Albert Giacometti's *Observing Head*
Ernest Hemingway's *Men Without Women*
Fritz Lang's *Metropolis*
Wyndham Lewis' *Time and Western Man*
F. W. Murnau's *Sunrise*
Proust's *Le Temps retrouvé* posthumously published
Stravinsky's *Oedipus Rex*
Virginia Woolf's *To the Lighthouse*

1928   The Kellogg-Briand Pact, outlawing war and providing for peaceful settlement of disputes, signed in Paris by sixty-two nations, including the Soviet Union
Herbert Hoover elected president of the United States
Women's suffrage granted at age twenty-one in Britain
Alexander Fleming discovers penicillin
Bertolt Brecht and Kurt Weill's *The Three-Penny Opera*
Eisenstein's *October*
Huxley's *Point Counter Point*
Christopher Isherwood's *All the Conspirators*
D. H. Lawrence's *Lady Chatterley's Lover*
Wyndham Lewis' *The Childermass*
Matisse's *Seated Odalisque*
Munch's *Girl on a Sofa*
Shaw's *Intelligent Woman's Guide to Socialism*
Virginia Woolf's *Orlando*
Yeats's *The Tower*
Iain Chrichton Smith born

1929   The Labour party wins British general election
Trotsky expelled from the Soviet Union
Museum of Modern Art opens in New York
Collapse of U.S. stock exchange begins world economic crisis
Robert Bridges's *The Testament of Beauty*
William Faulkner's *The Sound and the Fury*
Robert Graves's *Goodbye to All That*
Hemingway's *A Farewell to Arms*
Ernst Junger's *The Storm of Steel*
Hugo von Hoffmansthal's *Poems*
Henry Moore's *Reclining Figure*
J. B. Priestley's *The Good Companions*
Erich Maria Remarque's *All Quiet on the Western Front*
Shaw's *The Applecart*
R. C. Sheriff's *Journey's End*
Edith Sitwell's *Gold Coast Customs*
Thomas Wolfe's *Look Homeward, Angel*
Virginia Woolf's *A Room of One's Own*
Yeats's *The Winding Stair*
Second surrealist manifesto; Salvador Dali joins the surrealists
Epstein's *Night and Day*

CHRONOLOGY

Mondrian's *Composition with Yellow Blue*

1930 Allied occupation of the Rhineland ends

Mohandas Gandhi opens civil disobedience campaign in India

The *Daily Worker*, journal of the British Communist party, begins publishing

J. W. Reppe makes artificial fabrics from an acetylene base

John Arden born

Auden's *Poems*

Coward's *Private Lives*

Eliot's *Ash Wednesday*

Wyndham Lewis's *The Apes of God*

Maugham's *Cakes and Ale*

Ezra Pound's *XXX Cantos*

Evelyn Waugh's *Vile Bodies*

Ruth Rendell born

1931 The failure of the Credit Anstalt in Austria starts a financial collapse in Central Europe

Britain abandons the gold standard; the pound falls by twenty-five percent

Mutiny in the Royal Navy at Invergordon over pay cuts

Ramsay MacDonald resigns, splits the Cabinet, and is expelled by the Labour party; in the general election the National Government wins by a majority of five hundred seats

The Statute of Westminster defines dominion status

Ninette de Valois founds the Vic-Wells

Ballet (eventually the Royal Ballet)

Coward's *Cavalcade*

Dali's The *Persistence of Memory*

John le Carré born

O'Neill's *Mourning Becomes Electra*

Anthony Powell's *Afternoon Men*

Antoine de Saint-Exupéry's *Vol de nuit*

Walton's *Belshazzar's Feast*

Virginia Woolf's *The Waves*

Caroline Blackwood born

1932 Franklin D. Roosevelt elected president of the United States

Paul von Hindenburg elected president of Germany; Franz von Papen elected chancellor

Sir Oswald Mosley founds British Union of Fascists

The BBC takes over development of television from J. L. Baird's company

Basic English of 850 words designed as a prospective international language

The Folger Library opens in Washington, D.C.

The Shakespeare Memorial Theatre opens in Stratford-upon-Avon

Faulkner's *Light in August*

Huxley's *Brave New World*

F. R. Leavis' *New Bearings in English Poetry*

Boris Pasternak's *Second Birth*

Ravel's *Concerto for Left Hand*

Peter Redgrove born

Rouault's *Christ Mocked by Soldiers*

Waugh's *Black Mischief*

Yeats's *Words for Music Perhaps*

1933 Roosevelt inaugurates the New Deal

Hitler becomes chancellor of Germany

The Reichstag set on fire

Hitler suspends civil liberties and freedom of the press; German trade unions suppressed

George Balanchine and Lincoln Kirstein found the School of American Ballet

Beryl Bainbridge born

Lowry's *Ultramarine*

André Malraux's *La Condition humaine*

Orwell's *Down and Out in Paris and London*

Gertrude Stein's *The Autobiography of Alice B. Toklas*

Anne Stevenson born

1934 The League Disarmament Conference ends in failure

The Soviet Union admitted to the League

Hitler becomes Führer

CHRONOLOGY

Civil war in Austria; Engelbert Dollfuss assassinated in attempted Nazi coup
Frédéric Joliot and Irene Joliot-Curie discover artificial (induced) radioactivity
Einstein's *My Philosophy*
Fitzgerald's *Tender Is the Night*
Graves's *I, Claudius* and *Claudius the God*
Toynbee's *A Study of History* begins publication (1934–1954)
Waugh's *A Handful of Dust*
Births of Alan Bennett, Christopher Wallace-Crabbe, and **Alasdair Gray**

1935 Grigori Zinoviev and other Soviet leaders convicted of treason
Stanley Baldwin becomes prime minister in National Government; National Government wins general election in Britain
Italy invades Abyssinia
Germany repudiates disarmament clauses of Treaty of Versailles
Germany reintroduces compulsory military service and outlaws the Jews
Robert Watson-Watt builds first practical radar equipment
Karl Jaspers' *Suffering and Existence*
André Brink born
Ivy Compton-Burnett's *A House and Its Head*
Eliot's *Murder in the Cathedral*
Barbara Hepworth's *Three Forms*
George Gershwin's *Porgy and Bess*
Greene's *England Made Me*
Isherwood's *Mr. Norris Changes Trains*
Malraux's *Le Temps du mépris*
Yeats's *Dramatis Personae*
Klee's *Child Consecrated to Suffering*
Benedict Nicholson's *White Relief*

1936 Edward VII accedes to the throne in January; abdicates in December
1936–1952 Reign of George VI
1936 German troops occupy the Rhineland

Ninety-nine percent of German electorate vote for Nazi candidates
The Popular Front wins general election in France; Léon Blum becomes prime minister
Roosevelt reelected president of the United States
The Popular Front wins general election in Spain
Spanish Civil War begins
Italian troops occupy Addis Ababa; Abyssinia annexed by Italy
BBC begins television service from Alexandra Palace
Auden's *Look, Stranger!*
Auden and Isherwood's *The Ascent of F-6*
A. J. Ayer's *Language, Truth and Logic*
Chaplin's *Modern Times*
Greene's *A Gun for Sale*
Huxley's *Eyeless in Gaza*
Keynes's *General Theory of Employment*
F. R. Leavis' *Revaluation*
Mondrian's *Composition in Red and Blue*
Dylan Thomas' *Twenty-five Poems*
Wells's *The Shape of Things to Come* filmed
Reginald Hill born

1937 Trial of Karl Radek and other Soviet leaders
Neville Chamberlain succeeds Stanley Baldwin as prime minister
China and Japan at war
Frank Whittle designs jet engine
Picasso's *Guernica*
Shostakovich's Fifth Symphony
Magritte's *La Reproduction interdite*
Hemingway's *To Have and Have Not*
Malraux's *L'Espoir*
Orwell's *The Road to Wigan Pier*
Priestley's *Time and the Conways*
Virginia Woolf's *The Years*
Emma Tennant born
Death of Christopher Caudwell (Christopher St. John Sprigg)

1938 Trial of Nikolai Bukharin and other Soviet political leaders

CHRONOLOGY

Austria occupied by German troops and declared part of the Reich

Hitler states his determination to annex Sudetenland from Czechoslovakia

Britain, France, Germany, and Italy sign the Munich agreement

German troops occupy Sudetenland

Edward Hulton founds *Picture Post*

Cyril Connolly's *Enemies of Promise*

du Maurier's *Rebecca*

Faulkner's *The Unvanquished*

Graham Greene's *Brighton Rock*

Hindemith's *Mathis der Maler*

Jean Renoir's *La Grande Illusion*

Jean-Paul Sartre's *La Nausée*

Yeats's *New Poems*

Anthony Asquith's *Pygmalion* and Walt Disney's *Snow White*

Ngũgĩ wa Thiong'o born

1939 German troops occupy Bohemia and Moravia; Czechoslovakia incorporated into Third Reich

Madrid surrenders to General Franco; the Spanish Civil War ends

Italy invades Albania

Spain joins Germany, Italy, and Japan in anti-Comintern Pact

Britain and France pledge support to Poland, Romania, and Greece

The Soviet Union proposes defensive alliance with Britain; British military mission visits Moscow

The Soviet Union and Germany sign nonaggression treaty, secretly providing for partition of Poland between them

Germany invades Poland; Britain, France, and Germany at war

The Soviet Union invades Finland

New York World's Fair opens

Eliot's *The Family Reunion*

Births of Seamus Heaney and Michael Longley

Isherwood's *Good-bye to Berlin*

Joyce's *Finnegans Wake* (1922–1939)

MacNeice's *Autumn Journal*

Powell's *What's Become of Waring?*

1940 Churchill becomes prime minister

Italy declares war on France, Britain, and Greece

General de Gaulle founds Free French Movement

The Battle of Britain and the bombing of London

Roosevelt reelected president of the United States for third term

Betjeman's *Old Lights for New Chancels*

Angela Carter born

Chaplin's *The Great Dictator*

Bruce Chatwin born

J. M. Coetzee born

Disney's *Fantasia*

Greene's *The Power and the Glory*

Hemingway's *For Whom the Bell Tolls*

C. P. Snow's *Strangers and Brothers* (retitled *George Passant* in 1970, when entire sequence of ten novels, published 1940–1970, was entitled *Strangers and Brothers*)

1941 German forces occupy Yugoslavia, Greece, and Crete, and invade the Soviet Union

Lend-Lease agreement between the United States and Britain

President Roosevelt and Winston Churchill sign the Atlantic Charter

Japanese forces attack Pearl Harbor; United States declares war on Japan, Germany, Italy; Britain on Japan

Auden's *New Year Letter*

James Burnham's *The Managerial Revolution*

F. Scott Fitzgerald's *The Last Tycoon*

Huxley's *Grey Eminence*

Derek Mahon born

Shostakovich's *Seventh Symphony*

Tippett's *A Child of Our Time*

Orson Welles's *Citizen Kane*

Virginia Woolf's *Between the Acts*

1942 Japanese forces capture Singapore, Hong Kong, Bataan, Manila

German forces capture Tobruk

U.S. fleet defeats the Japanese in the Coral Sea, captures Guadalcanal

CHRONOLOGY

Battle of El Alamein
Allied forces land in French North Africa
Atom first split at University of Chicago
William Beveridge's *Social Insurance and Allied Services*
Albert Camus's *L'Étranger*
Joyce Cary's *To Be a Pilgrim*
Edith Sitwell's *Street Songs*
Waugh's *Put Out More Flags*

1943　German forces surrender at Stalingrad
German and Italian forces surrender in North Africa
Italy surrenders to Allies and declares war on Germany
Cairo conference between Roosevelt, Churchill, Chiang Kai-shek
Teheran conference between Roosevelt, Churchill, Stalin
Eliot's *Four Quartets*
Henry Moore's *Madonna and Child*
Sartre's *Les Mouches*
Vaughan Williams' *Fifth Symphony*

1944　Allied forces land in Normandy and southern France
Allied forces enter Rome
Attempted assassination of Hitler fails
Liberation of Paris
U.S. forces land in Philippines
German offensive in the Ardennes halted
Roosevelt reelected president of the United States for fourth term
Education Act passed in Britain
Pay-as-You-Earn income tax introduced
Beveridge's *Full Employment in a Free Society*
Cary's *The Horse's Mouth*
Huxley's *Time Must Have a Stop*
Maugham's *The Razor's Edge*
Sartre's *Huis Clos*
Edith Sitwell's *Green Song and Other Poems*
Graham Sutherland's *Christ on the Cross*
Trevelyan's *English Social History*
W. G. Sebald born

1945　British and Indian forces open offensive in Burma
Yalta conference between Roosevelt, Churchill, Stalin
Mussolini executed by Italian partisans
Roosevelt dies; Harry S. Truman becomes president
Hitler commits suicide; German forces surrender
The Potsdam Peace Conference
The United Nations Charter ratified in San Francisco
The Labour Party wins British General Election
Atomic bombs dropped on Hiroshima and Nagasaki
Surrender of Japanese forces ends World War II
Trial of Nazi war criminals opens at Nuremberg
All-India Congress demands British withdrawal from India
De Gaulle elected president of French Provisional Government; resigns the next year
Betjeman's *New Bats in Old Belfries*
Britten's *Peter Grimes*
Orwell's *Animal Farm*
Russell's *History of Western Philosophy*
Sartre's *The Age of Reason*
Edith Sitwell's *The Song of the Cold*
Waugh's *Brideshead Revisited*
Births of Wendy Cope and Peter Reading

1946　Bills to nationalize railways, coal mines, and the Bank of England passed in Britain
Nuremberg Trials concluded
United Nations General Assembly meets in New York as its permanent headquarters
The Arab Council inaugurated in Britain
Frederick Ashton's *Symphonic Variations*
Britten's *The Rape of Lucretia*
David Lean's *Great Expectations*
O'Neill's *The Iceman Cometh*

CHRONOLOGY

Roberto Rosselini's *Paisà*
Dylan Thomas' *Deaths and Entrances*

1947   President Truman announces program of aid to Greece and Turkey and outlines the "Truman Doctrine"
Independence of India proclaimed; partition between India and Pakistan, and communal strife between Hindus and Moslems follows
General Marshall calls for a European recovery program
First supersonic air flight
Britain's first atomic pile at Harwell comes into operation
Edinburgh festival established
Discovery of the Dead Sea Scrolls in Palestine
Princess Elizabeth marries Philip Mountbatten, duke of Edinburgh
Auden's *Age of Anxiety*
Camus's *La Peste*
Chaplin's *Monsieur Verdoux*
Lowry's *Under the Volcano*
Priestley's *An Inspector Calls*
Edith Sitwell's *The Shadow of Cain*
Waugh's *Scott-King's Modern Europe*
Dermot Healy born

1948   Gandhi assassinated
Czech Communist Party seizes power
Pan-European movement (1948–1958) begins with the formation of the permanent Organization for European Economic Cooperation (OEEC)
Berlin airlift begins as the Soviet Union halts road and rail traffic to the city
British mandate in Palestine ends; Israeli provisional government formed
Yugoslavia expelled from Soviet bloc
Columbia Records introduces the long-playing record
Truman elected of the United States for second term
Greene's *The Heart of the Matter*
Huxley's *Ape and Essence*
Leavis' *The Great Tradition*

Pound's *Cantos*
Priestley's *The Linden Tree*
Waugh's *The Loved One*
Death of Denton Welch

1949   North Atlantic Treaty Organization established with headquarters in Brussels
Berlin blockade lifted
German Federal Republic recognized; capital established at Bonn
Konrad Adenauer becomes German chancellor
Mao Tse-tung becomes chairman of the People's Republic of China following Communist victory over the Nationalists
Peter Ackroyd born
Simone de Beauvoir's *The Second Sex*
Cary's *A Fearful Joy*
Arthur Miller's *Death of a Salesman*
Orwell's *Nineteen Eighty-four*

1950   Korean War breaks out
Nobel Prize for literature awarded to Bertrand Russell
R. H. S. Crossman's *The God That Failed*
T. S. Eliot's *The Cocktail Party*
Fry's *Venus Observed*
Doris Lessing's *The Grass Is Singing*
C. S. Lewis' *The Chronicles of Narnia* (1950–1956)
Wyndham Lewis' *Rude Assignment*
George Orwell's *Shooting an Elephant*
Carol Reed's *The Third Man*
Dylan Thomas' *Twenty-six Poems*
A. N. Wilson born

1951   Guy Burgess and Donald Maclean defect from Britain to the Soviet Union
The Conservative party under Winston Churchill wins British general election
The Festival of Britain celebrates both the centenary of the Crystal Palace Exhibition and British postwar recovery
Electric power is produced by atomic energy at Arcon, Idaho

CHRONOLOGY

W. H. Auden's *Nones*
Samuel Beckett's *Molloy* and *Malone Dies*
Benjamin Britten's *Billy Budd*
Greene's *The End of the Affair*
Akira Kurosawa's *Rashomon*
Wyndham Lewis' *Rotting Hill*
Anthony Powell's *A Question of Upbringing* (first volume of *A Dance to the Music of Time*, 1951–1975)
J. D. Salinger's *The Catcher in the Rye*
C. P. Snow's *The Masters*
Igor Stravinsky's *The Rake's Progress*

1952– Reign of Elizabeth II
At Eniwetok Atoll the United States detonates the first hydrogen bomb
The European Coal and Steel Community comes into being
Radiocarbon dating introduced to archaeology
Michael Ventris deciphers Linear B script
Dwight D. Eisenhower elected president of the United States
Beckett's *Waiting for Godot*
Charles Chaplin's *Limelight*
Ernest Hemingway's *The Old Man and the Sea*
Arthur Koestler's *Arrow in the Blue*
F. R. Leavis' *The Common Pursuit*
Lessing's *Martha Quest* (first volume of *The Children of Violence*, 1952–1965)
C. S. Lewis' *Mere Christianity*
Thomas' *Collected Poems*
Evelyn Waugh's *Men at Arms* (first volume of *Sword of Honour*, 1952–1961)
Angus Wilson's *Hemlock and After*

1953 Constitution for a European political community drafted
Julius and Ethel Rosenberg executed for passing U.S. secrets to the Soviet Union
Cease-fire declared in Korea
Edmund Hillary and his Sherpa guide, Tenzing Norkay, scale Mt. Everest

Nobel Prize for literature awarded to Winston Churchill
General Mohammed Naguib proclaims Egypt a republic
Beckett's *Watt*
Joyce Cary's *Except the Lord*
Robert Graves's *Poems 1953*
Death of Norman Cameron

1954 First atomic submarine, *Nautilus,* is launched by the United States
Dien Bien Phu captured by the Vietminh
Geneva Conference ends French dominion over Indochina
U.S. Supreme Court declares racial segregation in schools unconstitutional
Nasser becomes president of Egypt
Nobel Prize for literature awarded to Ernest Hemingway
Kingsley Amis' *Lucky Jim*
John Betjeman's *A Few Late Chrysanthemums*
William Golding's *Lord of the Flies*
Christopher Isherwood's *The World in the Evening*
Koestler's *The Invisible Writing*
Iris Murdoch's *Under the Net*
C. P. Snow's *The New Men*
Thomas' *Under Milk Wood* published posthumously

1955 Warsaw Pact signed
West Germany enters NATO as Allied occupation ends
The Conservative party under Anthony Eden wins British general election
Cary's *Not Honour More*
Greene's *The Quiet American*
Philip Larkin's *The Less Deceived*
F. R. Leavis' *D. H. Lawrence, Novelist*
Vladimir Nabokov's *Lolita*
Patrick White's *The Tree of Man*
Patrick McCabe born

1956 Nasser's nationalization of the Suez Canal leads to Israeli, British, and French armed intervention
Uprising in Hungary suppressed by Soviet troops

CHRONOLOGY

Khrushchev denounces Stalin at Twentieth Communist Party Congress

Eisenhower reelected president of the United States

Anthony Burgess' *Time for a Tiger*

Golding's *Pincher Martin*

Murdoch's *Flight from the Enchanter*

John Osborne's *Look Back in Anger*

Snow's *Homecomings*

Edmund Wilson's *Anglo-Saxon Attitudes*

1957   The Soviet Union launches the first artificial earth satellite, *Sputnik I*

Eden succeeded by Harold Macmillan

Suez Canal reopened

Eisenhower Doctrine formulated

Parliament receives the Wolfenden Report on Homosexuality and Prostitution

Nobel Prize for literature awarded to Albert Camus

Beckett's *Endgame* and *All That Fall*

Lawrence Durrell's *Justine* (first volume of *The Alexandria Quartet*, 1957–1960)

Ted Hughes's *The Hawk in the Rain*

Murdoch's *The Sandcastle*

V. S. Naipaul's *The Mystic Masseur*

Eugene O'Neill's *Long Day's Journey into Night*

Osborne's *The Entertainer*

Muriel Spark's *The Comforters*

White's *Voss*

1958   European Economic Community established

Khrushchev succeeds Bulganin as Soviet premier

Charles de Gaulle becomes head of France's newly constituted Fifth Republic

The United Arab Republic formed by Egypt and Syria

The United States sends troops into Lebanon

First U.S. satellite, *Explorer 1*, launched

Nobel Prize for literature awarded to Boris Pasternak

Beckett's *Krapp's Last Tape*

John Kenneth Galbraith's *The Affluent Society*

Greene's *Our Man in Havana*

Murdoch's *The Bell*

Pasternak's *Dr. Zhivago*

Snow's *The Conscience of the Rich*

1959   Fidel Castro assumes power in Cuba

St. Lawrence Seaway opens

The European Free Trade Association founded

Alaska and Hawaii become the forty-ninth and fiftieth states

The Conservative party under Harold Macmillan wins British general election

Brendan Behan's *The Hostage*

Golding's *Free Fall*

Graves's *Collected Poems*

Koestler's *The Sleepwalkers*

Harold Pinter's *The Birthday Party*

Snow's *The Two Cultures and the Scientific Revolution*

Spark's *Memento Mori*

1960   South Africa bans the African National Congress and Pan-African Congress

The Congo achieves independence

John F. Kennedy elected president of the United States

The U.S. bathyscaphe *Trieste* descends to 35,800 feet

Publication of the unexpurgated *Lady Chatterley's Lover* permitted by court

Auden's *Hommage to Clio*

Betjeman's *Summoned by Bells*

Pinter's *The Caretaker*

Snow's *The Affair*

David Storey's *This Sporting Life*

1961   South Africa leaves the British Commonwealth

Sierra Leone and Tanganyika achieve independence

The Berlin Wall erected

The New English Bible published

Beckett's *How It Is*

Greene's *A Burnt-Out Case*

Koestler's *The Lotus and the Robot*

Murdoch's *A Severed Head*

Naipaul's *A House for Mr Biswas*

CHRONOLOGY

Osborne's *Luther*
Spark's *The Prime of Miss Jean Brodie*
White's *Riders in the Chariot*

1962 John Glenn becomes first U.S. astronaut to orbit earth
The United States launches the spacecraft *Mariner* to explore Venus
Algeria achieves independence
Cuban missile crisis ends in withdrawal of Soviet missiles from Cuba
Adolf Eichmann executed in Israel for Nazi war crimes
Second Vatican Council convened by Pope John XXIII
Nobel Prize for literature awarded to John Steinbeck
Edward Albee's *Who's Afraid of Virginia Woolf?*
Beckett's *Happy Days*
Anthony Burgess' *A Clockwork Orange* and *The Wanting Seed*
Aldous Huxley's *Island*
Isherwood's *Down There on a Visit*
Lessing's *The Golden Notebook*
Nabokov's *Pale Fire*
Aleksandr Solzhenitsyn's *One Day in the Life of Ivan Denisovich*

1963 Britain, the United States, and the Soviet Union sign a test-ban treaty
Birth of Simon Armitage
Britain refused entry to the European Economic Community
The Soviet Union puts into orbit the first woman astronaut, Valentina Tereshkova
Paul VI becomes pope
President Kennedy assassinated; Lyndon B. Johnson assumes office
Nobel Prize for literature awarded to George Seferis
Britten's *War Requiem*
John Fowles's *The Collector*
Murdoch's *The Unicorn*
Spark's *The Girls of Slender Means*
Storey's *Radcliffe*
John Updike's *The Centaur*

1964 Tonkin Gulf incident leads to retaliatory strikes by U.S. aircraft against North Vietnam
Greece and Turkey contend for control of Cyprus
Britain grants licenses to drill for oil in the North Sea
The Shakespeare Quatercentenary celebrated
Lyndon Johnson elected president of the United States
The Labour party under Harold Wilson wins British general election
Nobel Prize for literature awarded to Jean-Paul Sartre
Saul Bellow's *Herzog*
Burgess' *Nothing Like the Sun*
Golding's *The Spire*
Isherwood's *A Single Man*
Stanley Kubrick's *Dr. Strangelove*
Larkin's *The Whitsun Weddings*
Naipaul's *An Area of Darkness*
Peter Shaffer's *The Royal Hunt of the Sun*
Snow's *Corridors of Power*

1965 The first U.S. combat forces land in Vietnam
The U.S. spacecraft Mariner transmits photographs of Mars
British Petroleum Company finds oil in the North Sea
War breaks out between India and Pakistan
Rhodesia declares its independence
Ontario power failure blacks out the Canadian and U.S. east coasts
Nobel Prize for literature awarded to Mikhail Sholokhov
Robert Lowell's *For the Union Dead*
Norman Mailer's *An American Dream*
Osborne's *Inadmissible Evidence*
Pinter's *The Homecoming*
Spark's *The Mandelbaum Gate*

1966 The Labour party under Harold Wilson wins British general election
The Archbishop of Canterbury visits Pope Paul VI
Florence, Italy, severely damaged by floods
Paris exhibition celebrates Picasso's eighty-fifth birthday

CHRONOLOGY

Fowles's *The Magus*
Greene's *The Comedians*
Osborne's *A Patriot for Me*
Paul Scott's *The Jewel in the Crown*
(first volume of *The Raj Quartet*,
1966–1975)
White's *The Solid Mandala*

1967 Thurgood Marshall becomes first black U.S. Supreme Court justice
Six-Day War pits Israel against Egypt and Syria
Biafra's secession from Nigeria leads to civil war
Francis Chichester completes solo circumnavigation of the globe
Dr. Christiaan Barnard performs first heart transplant operation, in South Africa
China explodes its first hydrogen bomb
Golding's *The Pyramid*
Hughes's *Wodwo*
Isherwood's *A Meeting by the River*
Naipaul's *The Mimic Men*
Tom Stoppard's *Rosencrantz and Guildenstern Are Dead*
Orson Welles's *Chimes at Midnight*
Angus Wilson's *No Laughing Matter*

1968 Violent student protests erupt in France and West Germany
Warsaw Pact troops occupy Czechoslovakia
Violence in Northern Ireland causes Britain to send in troops
Tet offensive by Communist forces launched against South Vietnam's cities
Theater censorship ended in Britain
Robert Kennedy and Martin Luther King Jr. assassinated
Richard M. Nixon elected president of the United States
Booker Prize for fiction established
Durrell's *Tunc*
Graves's *Poems 1965–1968*
Osborne's *The Hotel in Amsterdam*
Snow's *The Sleep of Reason*
Solzhenitsyn's *The First Circle* and *Cancer Ward*
Spark's *The Public Image*

1969 Humans set foot on the moon for the first time when astronauts descend to its surface in a landing vehicle from the U.S. spacecraft *Apollo 11*
The Soviet unmanned spacecraft *Venus V* lands on Venus
Capital punishment abolished in Britain
Colonel Muammar Qaddafi seizes power in Libya
Solzhenitsyn expelled from the Soviet Union
Nobel Prize for literature awarded to Samuel Beckett
Carter's *The Magic Toyshop*
Fowles's *The French Lieutenant's Woman*
Storey's *The Contractor*

1970 Civil war in Nigeria ends with Biafra's surrender
U.S. planes bomb Cambodia
The Conservative party under Edward Heath wins British general election
Nobel Prize for literature awarded to Aleksandr Solzhenitsyn
Durrell's *Nunquam*
Hughes's *Crow*
F. R. Leavis and Q. D. Leavis' *Dickens the Novelist*
Snow's *Last Things*
Spark's *The Driver's Seat*

1971 Communist China given Nationalist China's UN seat
Decimal currency introduced to Britain
Indira Gandhi becomes India's prime minister
Nobel Prize for literature awarded to Heinrich Böll
Bond's *The Pope's Wedding*
Naipaul's *In a Free State*
Pinter's *Old Times*
Spark's *Not to Disturb*
Birth of Sarah Kane

1972 The civil strife of "Bloody Sunday" causes Northern Ireland to come under the direct rule of Westminster
Nixon becomes the first U.S. president to visit Moscow and Beijing

CHRONOLOGY

The Watergate break-in precipitates scandal in the United States
Eleven Israeli athletes killed by terrorists at Munich Olympics
Nixon reelected president of the United States
Bond's *Lear*
Snow's *The Malcontents*
Stoppard's *Jumpers*

1973 Britain, Ireland, and Denmark enter European Economic Community
Egypt and Syria attack Israel in the Yom Kippur War
Energy crisis in Britain reduces production to a three-day week
Nobel Prize for literature awarded to Patrick White
Bond's *The Sea*
Greene's *The Honorary Consul*
Lessing's *The Summer Before the Dark*
Murdoch's *The Black Prince*
Shaffer's *Equus*
White's *The Eye of the Storm*

1974 Miners strike in Britain
Greece's military junta overthrown
Emperor Haile Selassie of Ethiopia deposed
President Makarios of Cyprus replaced by military coup
Nixon resigns as U.S. president and is succeeded by Gerald R. Ford
Betjeman's *A Nip in the Air*
Bond's *Bingo*
Durrell's *Monsieur* (first volume of *The Avignon Quintet*, 1974–1985)
Larkin's *The High Windows*
Solzhenitsyn's *The Gulag Archipelago*
Spark's *The Abbess of Crewe*

1975 The U.S. *Apollo* and Soviet *Soyuz* spacecrafts rendezvous in space
The Helsinki Accords on human rights signed
U.S. forces leave Vietnam
King Juan Carlos succeeds Franco as Spain's head of state
Nobel Prize for literature awarded to Eugenio Montale

1976 New U.S. copyright law goes into effect

Israeli commandos free hostages from hijacked plane at Entebbe, Uganda
British and French SST Concordes make first regularly scheduled commercial flights
The United States celebrates its bicentennial
Jimmy Carter elected president of the United States
Byron and Shelley manuscripts discovered in Barclay's Bank, Pall Mall
Hughes's *Seasons' Songs*
Koestler's *The Thirteenth Tribe*
Scott's *Staying On*
Spark's *The Take-over*
White's *A Fringe of Leaves*

1977 Silver jubilee of Queen Elizabeth II celebrated
Egyptian president Anwar el-Sadat visits Israel
"Gang of Four" expelled from Chinese Communist party
First woman ordained in the U.S. Episcopal church
After twenty-nine years in power, Israel's Labour party is defeated by the Likud party
Fowles's *Daniel Martin*
Hughes's *Gaudete*

1978 Treaty between Israel and Egypt negotiated at Camp David
Pope John Paul I dies a month after his coronation and is succeeded by Karol Cardinal Wojtyla, who takes the name John Paul II
Former Italian premier Aldo Moro murdered by left-wing terrorists
Nobel Prize for literature awarded to Isaac Bashevis Singer
Greene's *The Human Factor*
Hughes's *Cave Birds*
Murdoch's *The Sea, The Sea*

1979 The United States and China establish diplomatic relations
Ayatollah Khomeini takes power in Iran and his supporters hold U.S. embassy staff hostage in Teheran
Rhodesia becomes Zimbabwe
Earl Mountbatten assassinated

CHRONOLOGY

The Soviet Union invades Afghanistan

The Conservative party under Margaret Thatcher wins British general election

Nobel Prize for literature awarded to Odysseus Elytis

Golding's *Darkness Visible*

Hughes's *Moortown*

Lessing's *Shikasta* (first volume of *Canopus in Argos, Archives*)

Naipaul's *A Bend in the River*

Spark's *Territorial Rights*

White's *The Twyborn Affair*

1980   Iran-Iraq war begins

Strikes in Gdansk give rise to the Solidarity movement

Mt. St. Helen's erupts in Washington State

British steelworkers strike for the first time since 1926

More than fifty nations boycott Moscow Olympics

Ronald Reagan elected president of the United States

Burgess's *Earthly Powers*

Golding's *Rites of Passage*

Shaffer's *Amadeus*

Storey's *A Prodigal Child*

Angus Wilson's *Setting the World on Fire*

1981   Greece admitted to the European Economic Community

Iran hostage crisis ends with release of U.S. embassy staff

Twelve Labour MPs and nine peers found British Social Democratic party

Socialist party under François Mitterand wins French general election

Rupert Murdoch buys *The Times* of London

Turkish gunman wounds Pope John Paul II in assassination attempt

U.S. gunman wounds President Reagan in assassination attempt

President Sadat of Egypt assassinated

Nobel Prize for literature awarded to Elias Canetti

Spark's *Loitering with Intent*

1982   Britain drives Argentina's invasion force out of the Falkland Islands

U.S. space shuttle makes first successful trip

Yuri Andropov becomes general secretary of the Central Committee of the Soviet Communist party

Israel invades Lebanon

First artificial heart implanted at Salt Lake City hospital

Bellow's *The Dean's December*

Greene's *Monsignor Quixote*

1983   South Korean airliner with 269 aboard shot down after straying into Soviet airspace

U.S. forces invade Grenada following left-wing coup

Widespread protests erupt over placement of nuclear missiles in Europe

The £1 coin comes into circulation in Britain

Australia wins the America's Cup

Nobel Prize for literature awarded to William Golding

Hughes's *River*

Murdoch's *The Philosopher's Pupil*

1984   Konstantin Chernenko becomes general secretary of the Central Committee of the Soviet Communist party

Prime Minister Indira Gandhi of India assassinated by Sikh bodyguards

Reagan reelected president of the United States

Toxic gas leak at Bhopal, India, plant kills 2,000

British miners go on strike

Irish Republican Army attempts to kill Prime Minister Thatcher with bomb detonated at a Brighton hotel

World Court holds against U.S. mining of Nicaraguan harbors

Golding's *The Paper Men*

Lessing's *The Diary of Jane Somers*

Spark's *The Only Problem*

1985   United States deploys cruise missiles in Europe

CHRONOLOGY

Mikhail Gorbachev becomes general secretary of the Soviet Communist party following death of Konstantin Chernenko

Riots break out in Handsworth district (Birmingham) and Brixton

Republic of Ireland gains consultative role in Northern Ireland

State of emergency is declared in South Africa

Nobel Prize for literature awarded to Claude Simon

A. N. Wilson's *Gentlemen in England*

Lessing's *The Good Terrorist*

Murdoch's *The Good Apprentice*

Fowles's *A Maggot*

1986   U.S. space shuttle *Challenger* explodes

United States attacks Libya

Atomic power plant at Chernobyl destroyed in accident

Corazon Aquino becomes president of the Philippines

Giotto spacecraft encounters Comet Halley

Nobel Prize for literature awarded to Wole Soyinka

Final volume of *Oxford English Dictionary* supplement published

Amis's *The Old Devils*

Ishiguro's *An Artist of the Floating World*

A. N. Wilson's *Love Unknown*

Powell's *The Fisher King*

1987   Gorbachev begins reform of Communist party of the Soviet Union

Stock market collapses

Iran-contra affair reveals that Reagan administration used money from arms sales to Iran to fund Nicaraguan rebels

Palestinian uprising begins in Israeli-occupied territories

Nobel Prize for literature awarded to Joseph Brodsky

Golding's *Close Quarters*

Burgess's *Little Wilson and Big God*

Drabble's *The Radiant Way*

1988   Soviet Union begins withdrawing troops from Afghanistan

Iranian airliner shot down by U.S. Navy over Persian Gulf

War between Iran and Iraq ends

George Bush elected president of the United States

Pan American flight 103 destroyed over Lockerbie, Scotland

Nobel Prize for literature awarded to Naguib Mafouz

Greene's *The Captain and the Enemy*

Amis's *Difficulties with Girls*

Rushdie's *Satanic Verses*

1989   Ayatollah Khomeini pronounces death sentence on Salman Rushdie; Great Britain and Iran sever diplomatic relations

F. W. de Klerk becomes president of South Africa

Chinese government crushes student demonstration in Tiananmen Square

Communist regimes are weakened or abolished in Poland, Czechoslovakia, Hungary, East Germany, and Romania

Lithuania nullifies its inclusion in Soviet Union

Nobel Prize for literature awarded to José Cela

Second edition of *Oxford English Dictionary* published

Drabble's *A Natural Curiosity*

Murdoch's *The Message to the Planet*

Amis's *London Fields*

Ishiguro's *The Remains of the Day*

Death of Bruce Chatwin

1990   Communist monopoly ends in Bulgaria

Riots break out against community charge in England

First women ordained priests in Church of England

Civil war breaks out in Yugoslavia; Croatia and Slovenia declare independence

Bush and Gorbachev sign START agreement to reduce nuclear-weapons arsenals

President Jean-Baptiste Aristide overthrown by military in Haiti

CHRONOLOGY

Boris Yeltsin elected president of Russia

Dissolution of the Soviet Union

Nobel Prize for literature awarded to Nadine Gordimer

1992 U.N. Conference on Environment and Development (the "Earth Summit") meets in Rio de Janeiro

Prince and Princess of Wales separate

War in Bosnia-Herzegovina intensifies

Bill Clinton elected president of the United States in three-way race with Bush and independent candidate H. Ross Perot

Nobel Prize for literature awarded to Derek Walcott

1993 Czechoslovakia divides into the Czech Republic and Slovakia; playwright Vaclav Havel elected president of the Czech Republic

Britain ratifies Treaty on European Union (the "Maastricht Treaty")

U.S. troops provide humanitarian aid amid famine in Somalia

United States, Canada, and Mexico sign North American Free Trade Agreement

Nobel Prize for literature awarded to Toni Morrison

1994 Nelson Mandela elected president in South Africa's first post-apartheid election

Jean-Baptiste Aristide restored to presidency of Haiti

Clinton health care reforms rejected by Congress

Civil war in Rwanda

Republicans win control of both houses of Congress for first time in forty years

Prime Minister Albert Reynolds of Ireland meets with Gerry Adams, president of Sinn Fein

Nobel Prize for literature awarded to Kenzaburo Õe

Amis's *You Can't Do Both*

Naipaul's *A Way in the World*

1995 Britain and Irish Republican Army engage in diplomatic talks

Barings Bank forced into bankruptcy as a result of a maverick bond trader's losses

United States restores full diplomatic relations with Vietnam

NATO initiates air strikes in Bosnia

Death of Stephen Spender

Israeli Prime Minister Yitzhak Rabin assassinated

Nobel Prize for literature awarded to Seamus Heaney

1996 IRA breaks cease-fire; Sein Fein representatives barred from Northern Ireland peace talks

Prince and Princess of Wales divorce

Cease-fire agreement in Chechnia; Russian forces begin to withdraw

Boris Yeltsin reelected president of Russia

Bill Clinton reelected president of the United States

Nobel Prize for literature awarded to Wislawa Szymborska

Death of Caroline Blackwood

1996 British government destroys around 100,000 cows suspected of infection with Creutzfeldt-Jakob, or "mad cow" disease

1997 Diana, Princess of Wales, dies in an automobile accident

Unveiling of first fully-cloned adult animal, a sheep named Dolly

Booker McConnell Prize for fiction awarded to Arundhati Roy

1998 United States renews bombing of Bagdad, Iraq

Independent legislature and Parliaments return to Scotland and Wales

Booker McConnell Prize for fiction awarded to Ian McEwan

Nobel Prize for literature awarded to Jose Saramago

1999 King Hussein of Jordan dies

United Nations responds militarily to Serbian President Slobodan Milosevic's escalation of crisis in Kosovo

Booker McConnell Prize for fiction awarded to J. M. Coetzee

Nobel Prize for literature awarded to Günter Grass

CHRONOLOGY

Deaths of Ted Hughes, **Brian Moore**, and **Iain Chrichton Smith**

2000   Penelope Fitzgerald dies

J. K. Rowling's *Harry Potter and the Goblet of Fire* sells more than 300,000 copies in its first day

Oil blockades by fuel haulers protesting high oil taxes bring much of Britain to a standstill

Slobodan Milosevic loses Serbian general election to Vojislav Kostunica

Death of Scotland's First Minister, Donald Dewar

Nobel Prize for literature awarded to Gao Xingjian

Booker McConnell Prize for fiction awarded to Margaret Atwood

George W. Bush, son of former president George Bush, becomes president of the United States after Supreme Court halts recount of closest election in history

Death of former Canadian Prime Minister Pierre Elliot Trudeau

Human Genome Project researchers announce that they have a complete map of the genetic code of a human chromosome

Vladimir Putin succeeds Boris Yeltsin as president of Russia

British Prime Minister Tony Blair's son Leo is born, making him the first child born to a sitting prime minister in 152 years

2001   In Britain, the House of Lords passes legislation that legalizes the creation of cloned human embryos

British Prime Minister Tony Blair wins second term

Margaret Atwood's *The Blind Assassin* wins Booker McConnell Prize for fiction

Kazuo Ishiguro's *When We Were Orphans*

Trezza Azzopardi's *The Hiding Place*

Terrorists attack World Trade Center and Pentagon with hijacked airplanes, resulting in the collapse of the World Trade Center towers and the deaths of thousands. Passengers of a third hijacked plane thwart hijackers, resulting in a crash landing in Pennsylvania. The attacks are thought to be organized by Osama bin Laden, the leader of an international terrorist network known as al Qaeda

Ian McEwan's *An Atonement*

Salman Rushdie's *Fury*

Peter Carey's *True History of the Kelly Gang*

Deaths of Eudora Welty and W. G. Sebald

2002   Former U.S. President Jimmy Carter awarded the Nobel Peace Prize

Europe experiences its worst floods in 100 years as floodwaters force thousands of people out of their homes

Wall Street Journal reporter Daniel Pearl kidnapped and killed in Karachi, Pakistan while researching a story about Pakistani militants and suspected shoe bomber Richard Reid. British-born Islamic militant Ahmad Omar Saeed Sheikh sentenced to death for the crime. Three accomplices receive life sentences.

Slobodan Milosevic goes on trial at the U.N. war crimes tribunal in The Hague on charges of masterminding ethnic cleansing in the former Yugoslavia.

Yann Martel's *Life of Pi* wins Booker McConnell Prize for fiction

Nobel Prize for literature awarded to Imre Kertész

List of Contributors

JAMES P. AUSTIN. Graduate student in the M.F.A. program in fiction at the University of California at Irvine. He holds a B.A. in English from Wittenberg University (Ohio) and an M.A. in English from Iowa State University. He is presently at work on his first short story collection. **Patrick McCabe**

CHARLES ROBERT BAKER. Poet, short-story writer and essayist. Baker has made many Contributions to the *American Writers*, *British Writers*, and *American Writers Classics* series. His latest published fiction is a Christmas story, "The Harp." Mr. Baker lives in Dallas, Texas and is curator of "Mark Twain: Father of Modern American Literature" at Bridwell Library, Southern Methodist University. **Charles Walter Stansby Williams**

JANE BEAL. Faculty Fellow in the English Department at University of California Davis. Beal received her Ph.D in English Literature from the University of California, Davis. She is revising her dissertation, *John Trevisa and the English Polychronicon: Authority and Vernacular Translation in Late-Medieval England,* into a book. Her published articles have appeared in *Studies in Philology, Fourteenth-Century England,* and the *Oxford Encyclopedia of American Literature.* In addition to teaching and writing poetry, Jane enjoys playing flute, studying Chinese, and traveling in the U.S., Europe, and West Africa. **John Trevisa**

REBECCA BERG. Freelance writer and editor. Her publications include the short stories "A History of Song," which appeared in the *Five Fingers Review*, and "The Shriek of a Heron," which appeared in the *Talus Review*. Recently, she has completed work on a novel. She earned her Ph.D. in English from Cornell University. **Ruth Rendell**

DAVID BREITHAUPT. Writer. His fiction and poetry have appeared in numerous magazines, including volume 2 of Andrei Codrescu's *Thus Spake the Corpse (Best of the Exquisite Corpse)*. Contributed an essay on James Purdy for Scribner's American Writers series. He has also edited an anthology of poet Charles Plymell called *Hand on the Doorknob* (Water Row Press, 2000). Breithaupt has also worked as an archivist for poet and writer Allen Ginsberg. He lives in Gambier, Ohio with his family while working a variety of odd jobs to supplement his income from freelance writing. He has traveled widely but never left the planet. **Denton Welch**

GERRY CAMBRIDGE. Poet and Editor. Edits the Scottish-American poetry magazine, *The Dark Horse*. His own books of verse include *The Shell House* (Scottish Cultural Press, 1995), *'Nothing But Heather!': Scottish Nature in Poems, Photographs and Prose* (Luath Press, 1999), illustrated with his own natural history photographs, and *The Praise of Swans* (Shoestring Press, 2000). Cambridge was the 1997–1999 Brownsbank Fellow, based at Hugh MacDiarmid's former home, Brownsbank Cottage, near Biggar in Scotland. His latest collection is *Madame Fi Fi's Farewell and Other Poems* (Luath Press, 2002). **Iain Chrichton Smith**

RICHARD DAVENPORT-HINES. Formerly on the staff on the London School of Economics and a freelance author since 1986. He is a trustee of the London Library, a fellow of the Royal Historical Society, a research associate of the *Oxford Dictionary of National Biography*, and a

CONTRIBUTORS

past winner of the Wolfson Prize for History and Biography. His biography of W.H. Auden was first published in 1996, and re-issued in 2003. Other recent books include Gothic: *Four Hundred Years of Excess, Horror, Evil and Rain (1999) and the Pursuit of Oblivion: A Global History of Narcotics (2002)*. **Caroline Blackwood**

JENNIFER E. DUNN. D.Phil. candidate at Oxford University. She is writing a dissertation on Emma Tennant and other Anglo-American women writers, with a focus on their use of supernatural tropes. Her research interests include the gothic and neogothic novel, postmodernism, feminist theory, and women's writing. She teaches at Oxford and is a contributor to the *Oxonian Review of Books*. **Emma Tennant**

NIKOLAI ENDRES. Professor. Received his Ph.D. in Comparative Literature from the University of North Carolina at Chapel Hill. As assistant professor at Western Kentucky University, he teaches Great Books, British literature, classics, and gay and lesbian studies. He has published on André Gide, Oscar Wilde, Mary Renault, Gore Vidal, and Petronius. He has two book projects in mind: Platonic love in the *Symposium and Phaedrus*, Petronius' *Satyricon*, Oscar Wilde's *The Picture of Dorian Gray*, E. M. Forster's *Maurice*, Thomas Mann's *Death in Venice*, André Gide's *Corydon*, Gore Vidal's *The City and the Pillar*, Mary Renault's *The Charioteer*, and Marguerite Yourcenar's *Memoirs of Hadrian*; and a study of Petronius's *Nachleben* in modern literature. The university just awarded him a Junior Faculty Fellowship to facilitate his research. MARY RENAULT

AMANDA FIELDS. M.F.A. student in Nonfiction at the University of Minnesota, Minneapolis. She received her B.A. in English from Millikin University and her M.A. in English from Iowa State University. She is currently working on a manuscript about farming and family life in Illinois and teaching creative writing and literature at the University of Minnesota. **Dermot Healey**

CHRIS JONES. Lecturer in English at the University of St. Andrews in Scotland, Jones won the 2001 *Review of English Studies Essay Prize* for work on Auden and his use of Old English poetry (published in the May 2002 issue). He has forthcoming articles with the journals *TEXT* and *Paideuma* and is currently writing a book on Old English as used by nineteenth- and twentieth-century poets. **Edwin Morgan**

TOM JONES. Lecturer in English at the University of St Andrews. Jones has a B.A. and Ph.D. from the University of Cambridge. He has written on Pope's reading in and relation to Greek philosophers, and is currently writing a book on philosophies of language and Pope's poetry with a particular focus on the British Empiricists.**Anne Finch**

GAVIN MILLER. Writer. He received his Ph.D. in English Literature from the University of Edinburgh in 2000. Since then he has worked on *A Dictionary of the Older Scottish Tongue* for the Department of English Literature, University of Dundee, and as a faculty assistant to the Department of English Literature, University of Glasgow. His research interests include contemporary British and American literature, the history of ideas in Scotland, and the philosophy of psychiatry. He is currently working on a book on the work of the psychiatrist, R. D. Laing. **Alasdair Gray**

JOHN LENNARD. Professor and writer. Lennard teaches for the University of Notre Dame and the British-American Drama Academy in London, at Cambridge University, and on-line for Fairleigh Dickinson. He is the author of two best-selling textbooks, *The Poetry Handbook* and (with Mary Luckhurst) *The Drama Handbook*, both published by Oxford University Press, and of monographs on punctuation history and Anglo-India. **Reginald Hill**

HELENA NELSON. Writer and Lecturer. Born in Cheshire, England in 1953, Nelson holds a B.A. from the University of York and an M.A. in Eighteenth-Century literature from the University of Manchester. She has written romantic fiction and is a full-time lecturer in English and Com-

CONTRIBUTORS

munication Studies at Glenrothes College in Scotland. Nelson is the main writer and editor of the further education resource *Core.com 2002*. Her poetry collections include: *Mr and Mrs Philpott on Holiday at Auchterawe, Kettillonia 2001 and Starlight on Water*, Rialto Press, 2003. **Norman Cameron**

ROBERT SULLIVAN. Writer. Sullivan has taught at Brown University, the University of Illinois, and was a Fulbright Professor at the University of Zagreb from 1997 to 2000. He is the author of *A Matter of Faith, Christopher Caudwell*, and numerous articles on modern and contemporary literature. Research projects include participation in the *Modernist Journalist Project*. **Christopher Caudwell and Brian Moore**

THOMAS WRIGHT. Writer. Editor of *Table Talk*, the first English language anthology of Oscar Wilde's spoken stories, and reviewer for a number of English publications such as the *Daily Telegraph*, the *Independent on Sunday*, and the *Times Literary Supplement*. Wright has written articles on Peter Ackroyd for *British Writers Supplement VI* and Oscar Wilde for *British Writers Retrospective Supplement II*. **Bruce Chatwin**

BRITISH WRITERS

CAROLINE BLACKWOOD

(1931–1996)

Richard Davenport-Hines

LADY CAROLINE MAUREEN Hamilton-Temple-Blackwood was born on 16 July 1931, at 4, Hans Crescent, Knightsbridge, her parents' large town house in London. She was the eldest of three children of Basil Sheridan Hamilton-Temple-Blackwood, fourth marquess of Dufferin and Ava (1909–1945), an aristocrat from Northern Ireland, and his wife, Maureen Constance Guinness (1907–1998).

Her great-grandfather, the first marquess of Dufferin and Ava, was not only British ambassador to Russia, Turkey, Italy, and France during the late nineteenth century but also governor general and commander in chief of Canada in the 1870s and viceroy of India during the 1880s. As a reward for his part in the annexation of Burma, he was promoted to the rank of marquess in 1888. He also had many literary connections. His mother had been a poet and was granddaughter of the playwright Richard Brinsley Sheridan. Her sister Caroline Norton was a successful Victorian novelist whose notoriously unhappy marriage provided the foundation for the plot in George Meredith's *Diana of the Crossways* (1885). Another cousin was Sheridan Le Fanu, author of *Uncle Silas* (1864) and of the gothic stories *In a Glass Darkly* (1872). The historian and biographer Sir Harold Nicolson was also a cousin.

The first marquess of Dufferin and Ava was a man of outstanding charm, subtlety, and intelligence. When young he proved his literary powers with his compelling *Narrative of a Journey from Oxford to Skibbereen During the Year of the Irish Famine* (1847). His beguiling account of a cruise toward the North Pole, *Letters from High Latitudes* (1857), has often been reprinted. Later the marquess had too many official duties to allow for literary composition, but he sought out the company of poets; his speeches,

government reports, and dispatches show his pleasure in the sensual use of the English language.

All his life the marquess was short of money, and in his final years his financial resources were depleted after he became involved in a fraudulently managed mining company. His ancestral home, Clandeboye, in County Down, fell into decay and neglect; all his sons were relatively impoverished. This situation was solved when Caroline's father, the first marquess's only grandson in the male line, married Maureen Guinness in July 1930. It was an ardent love match on both sides, but with the advantage for the Dufferins that the bride was an heiress, whose money revived their fortunes. A fortnight after the marriage the groom's father was killed in an air crash, so that Basil Ava was married and inherited his marquessate almost simultaneously at the age of twenty-one.

Caroline Blackwood's parents strongly marked her character and conduct. Her father was a gifted but vulnerable man who had been damaged by the effects of his mother's mental illness: she believed that she was a fairy queen and jabbered with elation about her powers. Less amusingly, she was convinced that Basil and his sister Veronica were demon changelings who had been substituted for her real children by bad fairies. Her occasional affectionate embraces of her children therefore felt like unpleasant assaults. Basil Ava was emotionally scarred by these troubles. He won a prize scholarship to Oxford University, where he was a pupil of the famous economist Sir Roy Harrod—"in some respects the most brilliant one I ever had," Harrod judged (Kay Halle, comp., *Randolph Churchill: The Young Unpretender,* 1971, pp. 30–31). Ava edited the prestigious student magazine *Cherwell* as well as the *Oxford University Review.* The poet John

Betjeman fell in love with him: his elegy "In Memory of Basil, Marquess of Dufferin and Ava" testifies to his enduring affection for his "humorous, reckless, loyal, / my kind, heavy-lidded companion." Edward James, later an important English surrealist, was also in love with Ava at Oxford. "He was a shy boy, most attractive with very black hair and an Irish face, and brilliant . . . [but] terribly nervous," James wrote in *Swans Reflecting Elephants* (1982). He recalled an occasion in Oxford when "Ava was leaning against the mantelpiece and knocked over the fire irons in the grate. They fell down with a terrible clatter, and it took Ava a minute and a half to recover his wits" (p. 64). At Oxford, Ava learned to soothe his nerves and insecurity with alcohol: he would start drinking port in mid-morning.

As the marquess of Dufferin and Ava he held junior posts in the Conservative government of the late 1930s, but he declined a government position when Churchill became prime minister in 1940 because he wanted to fight in the war. After a strenuous effort, he managed to control his drinking before leaving for combat in Asia. In 1945, in the closing months of World War II, he was killed in action in Burma. His dark beauty and striking voice as much as his acute, almost palpable anxiety and his susceptibility to alcohol became characteristics too of his eldest child, Caroline. John Betjeman, who had loved Ava's "guttersnipe looks, his big, brown, sensual eyes, sensual lips, dirtiness generally" met Caroline once when she was a young woman "and was so moved by her resemblance to Ava, and so attracted to her, that he decided he could never meet her again" (Lees-Milne, p. 101). Caroline's character, like her father's, was a startling amalgam of sophistication and innocence; they were both powerfully intelligent, sensual, eloquent, sharing a capacity for devastating repartee and a tendency to grubbiness.

Caroline's mother had a different influence. Maureen Guinness was two years older than Basil Ava and during the 1920s had been one of the "Bright Young Things" celebrated in the early novels of Evelyn Waugh. She and her two sisters, the Guinness girls, were gossip column celebrities of the period. Maureen was a great joker, who defied pomposity and lived with resolute gaiety. On one occasion she planted a shopwindow dummy in the bed of an admiral; on another she told King George V that he was "bogus." She had many enduring friendships of great warmth and loyalty, but some detractors too. The photographer and diarist Sir Cecil Beaton described her in 1935 as "the biggest bitch in London" (Philip Hoare, "Maureen, Marchioness of Dufferin and Ava," *Independent*, 23 May 1998).

During the 1930s Maureen Dufferin pioneered platform shoes (her famous "pinnacles") in London society, and in 1948 she was the first woman in England to carry a transparent plastic handbag. Her appearance and whimsicality inspired the character of Maudie, countess of Littlehampton, heroine of the cartoons drawn by Sir Osbert Lancaster and enjoyed every morning by readers of the *Daily Express* in the 1950s and 1960s. She was grief-stricken by her husband's death and subsequently discovered that he had mortgaged the house to cover secret gambling debts. She remarried twice, first to a young antiques dealer, and then to a judge. After her father's death, she inherited a large shareholding in the Guinness family's brewery business, of which she became a director in 1949 (passing the directorship to her son Sheridan in 1979). She was financially generous to each of her children.

At the age of two and a half, in 1934, Caroline was photographed for the London newspapers sitting in her pram reading a Beatrix Potter book. Another society column carried her photograph in 1938 exercising one of her mother's Pekingese dogs in Hyde Park. But she found her childhood irretrievably unhappy and bore grudges against her mother for most of her life. With the outbreak of war in 1939, the three Dufferin children were sent for safety to live at Clandeboye. Caroline gave a somewhat fanciful account of the damp, discomfort, and decay at Clandeboye in her descriptions of Dunmartin Hall in her autobiographical novel *Great Granny Webster* (1977). In her version it resembled Mervyn Peake's grim Castle of Gormenghast peopled with absurd characters from Monty Python.

CAROLINE BLACKWOOD

The three children were put in the charge of a series of misfit nannies. The first died, the second left to marry, the third was committed to a mental asylum, and the fourth was an unbalanced brute called Miss Alley. This large, terrifying, greedy woman ate the children's wartime food rations, punished them when they took fruit from the garden, and deliberately starved them. Caroline's brother Sheridan developed rickets. Miss Alley resented the privileges of her charges and treated them with calculated sadism. As Sheridan Dufferin recalled (in "Growing Up at Clandeboye," Ulster Architectural Heritage Society, *Clandeboye,* 1985):

> Like most children at this period we were produced every day for an hour or so at tea, all spruced up and polished, when my mother would read stories or games would be played involving the other guests. Back we would then go to nanny's kingdom and an early lesson in the harsh reality of life. As a child I was extremely frightened of the dark and sought to allay my terror by humming myself to sleep. The noise irritated my nanny . . . and I remember being snatched out of the bed at one o'clock in the morning and held out of the window at arm's length with the threat that if I didn't shut up she would drop me. . . . I got my revenge later by peeing on that particular nanny's hatbox with the hat in it.

> (p. 5)

As girls Caroline and her sister Perdita loved to caress and ride horses. Yet, as she recounted in *For All That I Found There* (1973), the happiness of this pleasure would be suddenly spoiled. Every morning a toothless, bandy-legged old jockey named McAfee would take the two girls out riding on plump little barrel-bellied ponies. "You're alright," he'd call if they fell off when jumping walls. Perdita's collarbone was never set after she broke it in a fall because McAfee told her not to fuss or tell anyone. McAfee, who had a rasping Ulster accent, liked little girls. Finally he made an assignation with Caroline to meet in a lonely wood. He emerged from some laurel bushes, wearing his best shiny bowler hat, rolling his eyes, whispering. There were white pills that he wanted her to take, and when she panicked and bicycled off, he was aghast. "Caroline, Caroline, what I have done?" he kept repeating. As she peddled away, he called, "please, please, never breathe a word!" (p. 124). This sinister encounter began her lethal complicity with men.

Blackwood was scantily educated. Because of wartime gas rationing, she attended the nearest private school to Clandeboye, Rockport, a boarding school for boys. It is the basis for Stoneyport School in her story about childhood bullying, "Piggy," in *For All That I Found There.* Subsequently she attended other schools, including a "finishing school" for young ladies at Lausanne in Switzerland, where she was supposed to learn decorum.

A BOHEMIAN IN LONDON AND PARIS

During puberty Blackwood was plump, ungainly, and lacking in confidence; her stockings were always falling down. Thirteen-year-old Renata in her first novel, *The Stepdaughter* (1976), is Blackwood's partial self-portrait in early adolescence. By the age of eighteen, however, perhaps to her astonishment, she had matured into a captivating beauty. She had huge, avid blue eyes, wonderful blond hair, and a luscious figure. Perhaps as a young, intelligent but nervous and unsure woman she was sometimes a victim of her beauty.

She came out as a debutante in 1949 at a ball held at Londonderry House, a great house on Park Lane, London, owned by the marquess of Londonderry, whose Irish seat, Mount Stewart, was near Clandeboye. Afterward she took a secretarial job with *Picture Post*, a London magazine covering political and other news stories with profuse, high-quality photographs, published by the Hulton Press. The magazine had leftist tendencies. After the left-wing journalist Claud Cockburn gave her small reporting assignments, Blackwood gained some reputation as a radical, although in fact she was apolitical. Her political responses were conditioned by her scorn for stupidity. Political ideas seemed to her people's pretext for foolish behavior.

As she became more estranged from her mother, Blackwood took as her social mentor a waspish, highly strung, and highly sexed woman called Ann Rothermere, wife of the newspaper magnate Lord Rothermere. It was perhaps Ann Rothermere's influence that obtained Blackwood's job at *Picture Post*. Lady Rothermere was at this time the acknowledged lover and subsequently the wife of Ian Fleming, creator of James Bond. In 1951 she gave a ball at Warwick House, the Rothermeres' superb home in London, where Caroline Blackwood met another of Ann Rothermere's protégés, the painter Lucian Freud (b. 1922). He was a grandson of the founder of psychoanalysis, Sigmund Freud, had come to England as a refugee from Hitler, and had a pronounced taste for titled women both as models and as lovers. Like Caroline's father, Lucian Freud was ferociously intelligent and fiercely handsome. Freud and Blackwood became involved, to the distress of Maureen Dufferin and to the distaste of some of their set. On one occasion, Blackwood took Freud to a cocktail party at her mother's house in Hans Crescent. The other guests included Sir Winston Churchill's son Randolph, an alcoholic lout. When he saw Freud, he asked in his booming voice, "What the bloody hell is Maureen doing—turning her house into a bloody synagogue?" (Aronson, p. 146).

Ann Rothermere wrote to Cecil Beaton in February 1953 describing Freud's visit to her son Lord O'Neill at his Irish home, Shane's Castle. "Lucian . . . was in pursuit of Lady Caroline and was socially a disaster in that parish pump border state and of course I am blamed for encouraging tartan-trousered eccentric artists to pursue virginal Marchionesses' daughters." When Maureen Dufferin left for Switzerland, Caroline went to stay at Shane's Castle where she "was discovered with Lucian on the hearth-rug beneath dimmed lamps" (Mark Amory, ed., *The Letters of Ann Fleming*, 1985, pp. 122–123). After various confrontations, Blackwood left Hans Crescent to live with Freud in Paddington and then eloped with him to Paris. There she met Picasso, who drew on her hands and fingernails: she did not wash for three days afterward. She sat for several of Freud's finest portraits, notably "Girl in Bed," for which she posed in the Hôtel de la Louisiane above the Buci market in Paris, and "Hotel Bedroom." These paintings testify to her out-

standing allure, but capture her alarmed looks. A Freud portrait of Caroline with her sister Perdita never advanced beyond one eye without its lashes. "I minded the boredom of posing for Lucian," she told an interviewer in 1984. "The boredom was unbearable" (Taylor, p. 11).

Blackwood married Freud, in December 1953, at the Chelsea Registry Office in London. It was never a conventional match. "I somehow knew that you simply don't have a baby with Lucian," Blackwood recalled. "You have a love affair with him if that's what you want to do, you go to Paris with him, but he hated responsibility and it would have been crazy to have children with him" ("Lady Caroline Blackwood," *Daily Telegraph*, 16 February 1996). The Freuds lived in a Georgian house in Dean Street, in the heart of seedy Soho; the Colony Room and the Gargoyle Club, raffish Soho drinking clubs, became her haunts. She attracted many men, including the critic Cyril Connolly, whose sentimental lechery grew so obtrusive that Freud ambushed him in a street and kicked his shins. Blackwood was impressed by the ruthless vision of Freud and of their friend Francis Bacon: her later fiction was a literary version of their view of humanity. Freud's pitiless nude portraits can remind the spectator of visiting a hospital patient, whose dressing gown falls open, revealing genitalia that it would be polite to ignore and yet to which one's eyes keep returning. Blackwood's literary treatment of human vices is equally embarrassing, insistent and arresting. Although her books show compassion toward sufferers, she wrote in *For All That I Found There* that "sympathy [is] rather like a fur-coat offered to one on a scorching day" (p. 66).

A NEW YORKER

After the disintegration of her marriage, she moved in 1957 to New York, where she studied acting at the Stella Adler school. She became involved with the Anglo-American screenwriter Ivan Moffat, the Harvard-educated son of the English actress Iris Tree, and followed him out to Hollywood. As a GI in 1945 Moffat had married Nathalie Sorokine, who had previously lived in a sexual trio with Simone de Beauvoir and Jean-Paul Sartre (she is "Natalie" in Beauvoir's 1972 psychosexual novel *L'invitée*). Blackwood's marriage to Freud was dissolved in Mexico in 1958. If she disliked the West Coast, it was unimpressed by her. At a drunken dinner party in 1958, where the film actress Shelley Winters was a fellow guest, Christopher Isherwood noted, "Caroline was round eyed as usual, either dumb or scared" (in Katherine Bucknell, ed., *Christopher Isherwood Diaries,* vol. 1, 1996, p. 768). At another drunken dinner party given by Isherwood, in 1959, attended by the English actors Laurence Olivier, Richard Burton, and Emlyn Williams, Isherwood thought her "a frost" (in Bucknell, p. 814). As one of Blackwood's characters in *For All That I Found There* reflects, "Passivity—even a rather disgruntled and critical passivity—can be quite solid . . . like a wall, and you can twine yourself on to it like a strand of dusty ivy" (p. 63).

Blackwood appeared in an Italian film, modeled for *Vogue,* and enjoyed an intimate friendship (which she denied was consummated) with the famous photographer Walker Evans, who was twenty-seven years older. Then, in Yonkers in August 1959, Blackwood married Israel Citkowitz, a composer who suffered from a creative block and was more than twenty years her senior. After the birth of her first daughter, Natalya, in 1962, Blackwood suffered postpartum depression: elements of her experience appear in her short story "The Baby Nurse" in her collection *For All That I Found There.* A second daughter, Eugenia, was born in 1964. After the birth of a third child, Ivana, in 1966, her marriage to Citkowitz was effectively over. During this decade she was entangled with several men. She had a brief affair with the English editor Alan Ross, whose *London* magazine first published "The Baby Nurse." In the mid-1960s she was involved with Robert ("Bob") Silvers, founder in 1963 and coeditor of the *New York Review of Books.* Although her marriage to Citkowitz finished in 1966, he continued to live near her and served as her gentle nanny-duenna until his death in 1974.

Meanwhile, Blackwood had begun to write for publication. The English poet and critic Sir Stephen Spender, who was coeditor of the political, cultural, and literary monthly magazine *Encounter,* had the excellent impulse to commission her to write an account of the California beatnik scene. This was the true beginning of Blackwood's literary career, although she had long hankered to write. "I always knew I was a writer," she recalled. "But I hadn't any proof of it. I didn't put things in drawers as some writers do. I just started when I started" (Taylor, p. 11). Christopher Isherwood and Don Bachardy accompanied her on a research visit to beatnik bars in March 1959. "Caroline was dull," Isherwood noted afterwards, "because she is only capable of thinking negatively. Confronted by a phenomenon, she asks herself: what is wrong with it?" (Bucknell, ed., *Isherwood Diaries,* p. 803).

She published her long article "Portrait of the Beatnik: Letter from California" in the June 1959 issue of *Encounter* under the name of Caroline Freud. This deadly accurate, dismissive essay was later reprinted in her first book, *For All That I Found There.*

> The Beatnik is simply a bourgeois fantasy that has become incarnated and incarcerated, in a coffee-house and a "pad"; he is merely the Bohemian in every American businessman that has got out. He is a luxury product, the revolutionary who offers no threat, the nonconformist whose nonconformity is commercial. He shocks and scandalises without causing anxiety; he is the rebel not without cause, but the rebel without repercussions.
>
> (p. 88)

Blackwood found the beatniks posturing and phoney; the Beat poet Lawrence Lipton, known as the "Grand Lama" of Venice West, whom she interviewed, seemed to her despicable. She was not impressed by the beatniks' supposedly liberated sex lives, which seemed to reflect American puritans' mistrust of pleasure and joy:

> The Beatnik, in his rejection of the popular American concept that Success equates with Manhood, stresses a non-virility often mistaken for homosexuality. He is essentially a-sexual. Once again the ideal of the "cool" precluding the personal commitment demanded by sexual activity. He has, however, no particular objection to sexual inter-

course as long as it is conducted quickly, clinically, and above all wordlessly.

(p. 90)

Another revealing essay by Blackwood, "The Mystique of Ingmar Bergman," was published in *Encounter* in April 1961 but never reprinted in book form. The anti-intellectualism of Bergman's films, she thought, impressed only foolish people. She believed that Bergman—compared with the painters she knew like Bacon and Freud—was cowardly. Bergman wavered while they were unblinking in confronting the horror of human experience.

> Once he has successfully painted a hideous Lutheran world where evil is rampant, human misery irrevocable, knowledge futile, and blind faith the only guide, he always lacks the courage to carry his conception to any necessary bitter conclusion. He is then forced to resort to the classical Hollywood ending. Good young lovers go galloping off on wagons over hopeful horizons at the end of *The Magician, Smiles of a Summer Night,* and *The Seventh Seal.* In *Brink of Life* the unmarried mother, on seeing the error of her ways, is allowed to go galloping back to her own unexpectedly all-forgiving mother. The Magician is finally sent for by a corny and unconvincing king. The cold, callous Professor of *Wild Strawberries* is ultimately not only honored by the State, but a most unlikely Swedish Beatnik says she loves him best of all.

(pp. 54–55)

Although Blackwood's reportage is elegant, minutely observed, and sometimes wickedly funny, it can seem overly negative. Reportage felt to her to be a fertile source of ideas and moods for her fiction. Thus an article, "A Big House in Ireland," which she contributed to the British Broadcasting Corporation's weekly magazine *The Listener* (12 December 1974), was a source of ideas for her novel *Great Granny Webster.*

In April 1970, after returning to London, she began a relationship with the American poet Robert Lowell, fourteen years her senior. Their son Sheridan Lowell was born in September 1971, and after obtaining divorces from their spouses in Santo Domingo, they married in

October 1972. She was still magically beautiful: Lowell's friend Grey Gowrie, an Anglo-Irish poet and politician with a passionate interest in the opposite sex, considered her "one of the most beautiful women of her generation (a more intense and fascinating version of the film star Michelle Pfeiffer, I found)" ("Lady Caroline Blackwood," *Independent,* 15 February 1996). Blackwood had inherited her father's intelligence and was attracted to men with intellectual passion. She relished serious conversation, in which she would seize upon a point and worry it like a terrier—a trait in her novel writing too. "I like men you can talk to, even when they aren't gay," she said. "Lucian and Israel and Lowell were all like that. Whether it was important or trivial, they saw the point" ("Lady Caroline Blackwood," *Daily Telegraph,* 16 February 1996).

Lowell suffered from bipolar disorder, and Blackwood was distressed and confused in her reactions to his manic episodes. She felt useless during his attacks, and feared their impact on her children. Her anxiety, volatility, and drunken late night tirades aggravated his condition. The turmoil and tension of their relationship were aggravated by the chaos of their domestic arrangements. There are clues to her personal chaos in the production of her first book, *For All That I Found There.* Neither Blackwood nor the publishers remembered to add page numbers to the table of contents; some sections are dated and others are not; her "Portrait of the Beatnik," which had been published in 1959, is described as having been written in 1964. She misspells the name of an Irish neighbor, Lady Mairi Bury, as Lady Mary Berry.

The sequence of poems in Lowell's *The Dolphin* (1973) provides a vivid, intimate narrative of his involvement with Blackwood, to whom the book was dedicated. Among other poems, "Fall Weekend at Milgate" evokes their life together at her manor house in Kent, while the sequence "Marriage" recounts her pregnancy and the birth of their son. "Ivana" is addressed to Blackwood's daughter after her accidental burning. The book was partly Lowell's way of excoriating pain. "Everything is real until it's published," he wrote

CAROLINE BLACKWOOD

in "With Caroline at the Air-Terminal" (p. 72). There are also powerful poems about Blackwood, Citkowitz, and their children in Lowell's grueling, posthumously published collection *Day by Day* (1978).

During 1976–1977 the marriage disintegrated. As a result of punitive taxation leveled by the Labor government, Blackwood left England for Ireland in 1977 and took an apartment in the great Georgian house of Castletown in county Kildare, which was convenient for Guinness family parties. After an emotionally hectic period, Lowell hurriedly left Castletown in September 1977 and died in the backseat of a New York taxi, clutching a Freud portrait of Blackwood, on his way to resume life with his second wife, the novelist Elizabeth Hardwick. This death was followed by perhaps a more demoralizing blow. Blackwood's love of children had impressed Elizabeth Bishop, although she was sometimes a difficult mother. She was badly hit by her eldest daughter's death at the age of sixteen, in 1978, after a party.

The English author James Lees-Milne noted her "chain-smoking, churchyard cough, beautiful blue staring eyes, raddled complexion" when they met in 1980. "A difficult girl," he wrote, with whom conversation was hard going: "no comeback, no return of the ball" (Lees-Milne, p. 101). A few years later Blackwood wrote a characteristically discomforting tribute to her friend Julian Jebb, entitled "Suicide" (in Tristram and Georgia Powell, eds., *A Dedicated Fan: Julian Jebb 1934–1984*, 1993), recalling their discussions of "the most perfect place for us both to kill ourselves." It was a beach on the Isle of Wight.

> He described it so vividly and with such enthusiasm that I still think about it with a morbid fascination. He claimed that it was the most depressing beach in the whole world. It had sand which was dirty grey and very soggy. It always seemed to be raining there, a slow but relentless drizzle. The whole coastline was built up with the most hideous examples of modern British architecture. The water was very shallow on this dreaded beach and floating with stinking seaweed. We would both have to wade and wade before it became deep enough to drown ourselves. But it would be worth it because we

would hear the desolate sounds of seagulls screeching and one would feel that there was nothing on this odious spot to draw one back to life. Julian told me the name of this horrendous beach but I've deliberately forgotten it because he made it sound too attractive.

(p. 161)

Jebb's suicide in 1984 made her recall lines from Lowell's poem "For Sheridan," their son:

> Past fifty, we learn with surprise and a sense
> of suicidal absolution
> that what we intended and failed
> could never have happened—
> and must be done better.

(*Day by Day*, 1978, p. 82)

Blackwood loved her brother Sheridan Dufferin, who in 1963 had opened an art gallery in Bond Street, London, with the dealer John Kasmin as his business partner. Sheridan Dufferin subsequently sat on the Arts Panel of the Arts Council of Great Britain and served as a trustee of the National Gallery. He was an attractive, amusing man whose kindness, gentleness and laconic humor were disarming and admirable. Around 1986 Dufferin developed AIDS and endured his illness for nearly two years with a characteristic mixture of fortitude and fatalism. During 1987 (accompanied by her friend Marguerite Littman) Caroline Blackwood attended a weekend workshop in Kent organized by the London Lighthouse, a hospice and counseling service for people with AIDS, to which her brother and his wife were generous benefactors. She spoke sensibly and solidly of his illness and of her fear that her surviving children in the course of their lives might be exposed to HIV.

Blackwood returned to the United States in 1987, settling in Sag Harbor, Long Island, in a house that had once belonged to President Chester Arthur. Increasingly her circumstances came to resemble those of a character in her final novel, *Corrigan* (1984):

> Sabrina's floor was constantly cluttered with clothes, records, cassettes, magazines, jewellery and make-up. Old bottles of wine and whisky and milk

7

would also be lying around together with various cans which had once contained Coca-Cola or beer. . . . Nadine was shocked to see the remnants of uneaten food lying in dishes that had somehow got perched on top of a pile of underwear or valuable furs. She would shiver when she caught sight of a slice of ham or Camembert into which someone had stubbed their cigarette.

(p. 46)

Drinking and smoking remorselessly, Blackwood would sit up with friends talking late into the night, sometimes outrageous, embarrassing, or too outspoken, but often hilarious and seldom boring. Her love of the grotesque and macabre were irrepressible. In 1995 family discord about the settlement of trust funds brought some British newspaper publicity, which exaggerated and misrepresented the problem. Journalists increasingly fastened onto the most hackneyed and uninteresting aspects of her life, which perhaps had advantages. As the widow of a famous painter reflected in a story in *For All That I Found There,* "one always delights to find oneself described in clichés. It's like being so well wrapped up in thick wads of cotton-wool padding that one becomes invisible" (p. 64).

Although her powers were depleted by alcoholism, her occasional writings—including a vivid memoir of Francis Bacon for the *New York Review of Books* (24 September 1992)—remained exceptional. Blackwood's partial self-portrait, Angelica, in *Good Night Sweet Ladies* (1983) is ruled by "the dark, cruel vision that came from her paranoia" (p. 132), but Blackwood's fearful, semi-paranoid outlook was redeemed by her jokes. Her life, though, was incorrigibly disorganized. The British reference book *Who's Who* made several attempts during the 1980s to include her in its columns, but she always failed to complete or return the necessary questionnaire. The journalist Valerie Grove waited in vain for more than two hours in the cocktail bar of the Carlyle Hotel in New York for Blackwood to show for an interview. They finally met in London. "She still has huge, avid, black-ringed blue eyes which often wear an anxious, even frightened, gaze," Grove recorded. "Her voice . . . is smoky, throaty, grand and like the Mitford girls, a voice from the past" (Grove, p. 14).

Blackwood was pleased that after the belated publication of her final book, *The Last of the Duchess* (1995), the *Sunday Times* of London began to use her as a book reviewer. They chose her to review such books as Dawn Langley Simmons's macabre, gruesome autobiography, *Dawn: A Charleston Legend.* It was a shrewd match of book to reviewer. Simmons had been identified by an ignorant midwife as a male and physically abused in her working-class family; after recovering her true gender, she had married an abusive husband with monstrous habits and cruelty. (See Blackwood, "A Crisis of Identity," *Sunday Times,* 10 September 1995, sec. 7, p. 5). But Blackwood was already mortally ill with cancer, from which she died on 14 February 1996, in New York.

BLACKWOOD'S BOOKS

From an early age Caroline Blackwood wanted to write novels, but it required the encouragement and advice of Lowell to give her confidence. Through her characters, she depicted and analyzed obsessive behavior, terminal self-absorption, female fury, and the anguish of the isolated. Many of her protagonists behave with cruelty or inflict steady, long-term pain on those in their power, but although Blackwood showed sympathy for human suffering, the passivity of some of her victims is treated as irritating and disagreeable. Blackwood's prose was relentless, spare yet eloquent; she had a taste for the macabre and could be very funny. Her dark humor was more often nervous than joyful.

FOR ALL THAT I FOUND THERE

It was Lowell who encouraged her to assemble her first book, *For All That I Found There* (1973), a collection of stories, reportage, and meditative pieces, with a title from an Ulster Protestant marching song. Lowell thought its mixture of genres made it resemble a fragmented novel. The book contains five short stories, four items of reportage, three autobiographical fragments recalling her early life in Ulster, and a concluding essay on the sectarian unrest in Northern Ireland. The book is a hotchpotch: its prevailing temper is of apprehensive despair.

The five short stories feature frustrated or scared people who are being overwhelmed by their hostile environment. These are not among her most important writings. "Please Baby Don't Cry" is the story of a California woman who has entered the hospital for plastic surgery. The hospital staff seems sadistic while the surgical results are calamitous. Her eyelids are destroyed so she can never close her eyes again. "Who Needs It?" is set in a down-market beauty salon. Its proprietor resolves to fire an elderly employee, who had been branded on the arm with a serial number while in a Nazi concentration camp, because the tattoo is too sordid and depressing for the clients. "The Baby Nurse" depicts an opinionated, meddlesome, greedy governess whose employer is suffering from postpartum depression. "The Interview" features a lonely, tipsy painter's widow being interviewed in a plush, sordid hotel bar by an importunate journalist. The interview moves from intrusive, tactless questioning into an implacable, self-centered monologue by the widow. The final story, "How You Love Our Lady," contains a New Yorker's memories of her Irish girlhood with a hysterical, ultimately suicidal mother.

The reportage begins with an account of the uproar following a theatrical performance at the Open Space Theatre in London in 1971. Sonia Orwell, widow of the author of *Animal Farm,* has been asked to chair a panel of liberal women journalists discussing the play with the audience. But radical hecklers overwhelm the panel's well-mannered democratic optimism: the playwright Jane Arden, who wrote *A New Communion for Freaks, Prophets and Witches* and founded the Holocaust Theatre, screams, "everything you have all been saying is just bloody bourgeois shit" (p. 84). The piece is a mordant, deadpan description of infantilized militant self-indulgence.

In addition, a reprint of Blackwood's "Portrait of the Beatnik," the book contains damning reportage on her visit to a Harlem Free School. Her observation of her time there—surrounded by violence, pandemonium, sexual aggression, ignorance—constitutes a claustrophobic account of what happens when sentimental visionaries and complacent idealists obtain authority in educational systems. It is a terrible indictment of the inner-city education available to black Americans in the early 1970s and does not shrink from the ugliness of what she saw. It is one of her most searing pieces of writing, which retains its power to shock and outrage. "In escaping the tyranny of dull traditional disciplined education, had all these black students not simply become victims of another equally oppressive tyranny— the tyranny of their own aimlessness and anarchy?" (p. 106). The theme of *For All That I Found There,* indeed, concerns people with vacuous, disordered lives desperately trying to survive in brutalizing circumstances.

The reportage concludes with Blackwood's coruscating memoir of her daughter's treatment in a burn unit after a domestic accident. It contains a highly characteristic passage of daydreaming about the plastic surgeon Sir Archibald McIndoe. "He saw sympathy as a very wretched substitute for skill . . . even the coldest and most impersonal curative action was less inhuman than sentimental and empathizing inaction." What his patients "feared was not callous impersonality" but "the twin cruelties of pity and horror" (p. 113).

The Ulster section of this book includes Blackwood's memoir of the pedophile jockey McAfee. Its final few pages, entitled "Memories of Ulster," were written in 1972. She felt that the people of Northern Ireland, rent by sectarian violence between Catholics and Protestants, were "interned by the gloom of her [the province's] industrialised provinciality, by her backwaterishness, her bigotry and her tedium" (p. 138). She suggested that the vacuity and boredom of Ulster life contributed to the civil war: the province's inhabitants felt "perverse and destructive terror of sinking back into a humdrum and peaceful obscurity" (p. 143).

CAROLINE BLACKWOOD

THE STEPDAUGHTER

Blackwood's first novel, *The Stepdaughter* (1976), is a concise, gripping monologue by a rich, self-pitying woman who is tormenting her fat, neurotic, thirteen-year-old stepdaughter. Like much of her fictional writing, it has a claustrophobic emotional intensity as it demonstrates how a selfish woman's emotional state distorts her perception and treatment of other people. *The Stepdaughter* has Blackwood's hallmark exactitude, wit, and sensitivity as well as the relentless tone of resentment characteristic of her narratives. Its frustrated female fury is oppressive. "Women have become paralysed," one woman tells another. "It's the culture that has made us all lose the courage to be ourselves when we are hurt—to really yell and scream" (p. 100). *The Stepdaughter* is an account of harrowing pain and relentless emotional rejection written with a dark humor reminiscent of the early novels of Evelyn Waugh. Its ruthless scrutiny of human nastiness recalls the pictures of Freud and Bacon.

The Stepdaughter is set in a spacious, overheated luxury penthouse, with commanding views of Manhattan's splendor and squalor, occupied by J. She is raging and distracted, after being abandoned by her rich international lawyer husband, Arnold, and projects her pain onto her stepdaughter, Renata. She is also callous to her own little daughter, Sally Ann, and persecutes Monique, their young French nanny. "Monique is like a person who is being kept in solitary confinement in this apartment. When she tries to communicate with Sally Ann, it's with the desperation of some prisoner in an ancient dungeon who tries to save his sanity by talking to the rats" (p. 11). In a series of coldly miserable, almost demented letters written in her head to imaginary correspondents, J. chronicles the claustrophobic unhappiness of the four women confined in the hellish luxury of the apartment. "Squalor, corruption, disease, cruelty, desperation and violence—I see no sign of these things, looking down from the height of my view. If they are anywhere they seem to be confined exclusively within the walls of my fine apartment" (p. 51).

The chief cruelty is directed at Renata, whom Blackwood pictures in words recalling her own miserable pubescence.

> She had a tense, half-apologetic, half-defiant expression on her face, which made one think that she herself felt that she had some kind of vital deficiency, which made it unlikely that anyone would ever want her. The thing that Renata lacked so painfully was the very smallest grain of either physical or personal charm. . . . Her face was pudgy with lost, fat-buried features, and her skin was bad, as if she had always lived on a diet of ice-cream and starch.
>
> (pp. 18–19)

Eventually the greedy, unlovable, self-destructive Renata runs away and is never found—searching, J. thinks, "in the cold savage streets of New York for the undesirable accident" (p. 110).

GREAT GRANNY WEBSTER

The tone in much of Blackwood's fiction is that of a prodigious and observant child: alert, aware, unhappy, and helpless in the power of cruel, devious, or emotionally suffocating adults. This temper is conspicuous in her second novel, *Great Granny Webster* (1977), which is partly based on her own miserable childhood. This short, mordant book had critically the most favorable reception and was short-listed for the Booker Prize. Lowell celebrated its composition in his beautiful poem "Runaway" (published in *Day by Day*).

Its narrator is sent in the mid-1940s to convalesce with her great-grandmother after a minor operation. The latter lives in a large, somber, fusty, and uncomfortable house at a coastal resort, although the narrator never makes it to the beach. The food is unpalatable, the only books are about fishing, and central heating is anathema to the austere old woman. Mrs. Webster has created for herself a hermetically sealed loveless vacuum in which to live. Self-centered, arid, and charmless, she views everything with sour displeasure and spoils the lives of everyone close to her. She bullies her old servant into a living death, drives her daughter mad, and creates an atmosphere of such deadening lovelessness that her granddaughter Lavinia pursues a life of forced gaiety and sexual adventures until her abrupt suicide. Aunt Lavinia is an attractive but vulnerable character (based on Blackwood's Aunt Veronica) who is too frantic in her social and sexual lives. She gives good, although sometimes insincere, advice to her niece, the narrator, including this semiautobiographical comment:

> I'm afraid, darling, [people] have found you rather odd in the way you sit there at parties looking so goggle-eyed and tongue-tied. When you are with strangers you are so withdrawn that everyone finds your presence rather alarming. You just sit there staring at everyone in that intense, tormented way. You really must try to stop doing that, because it makes people nervous. They wonder if you've got something gravely wrong with you. They wonder if you are quite all right in the head . . . once you reach your early thirties I've always had the strong suspicion—and to this I must add, God help you— you'll probably be very much like me.
>
> (pp. 60–61)

The narrator's father, like Basil Dufferin, drank too much port when young and has been killed in action in Burma. She remembers little of him except "that he had once told me to read Shakespeare because when I grew up and was very unhappy I would find every kind of human unhappiness perfectly expressed there" (p. 69). The narrator's mother is excluded from the narrative and discounted as ruthlessly as Maureen Dufferin. The narrator's grandmother, Lady Dunmartin, is closely based on Brenda Dufferin, Blackwood's disturbing grandmother who thought she was a fairy and that her children were evil changelings. The cumulative family misery, resentment, grief, and despair cannot be palliated.

THE FATE OF MARY ROSE

Blackwood's third novel, a misanthropic psychological thriller, *The Fate of Mary Rose* (1981), was underrated by some critics but ranks among her best. She sometimes named it as her favorite among her novels and hoped it would be adapted for the cinema, but its subject matter was considered too gruesome by the studios.

A ten-year-old girl, Maureen Sutton (who shares her first name with Blackwood's resented mother), vanishes from a dainty Kent village called Beckham. An occasional visitor to the village is the novel's narrator, Rowan Anderson, a distinguished historian in his thirties, selfish, ambitious, and unhappily married to Cressida, whose obsessive interest is the overprotective and panicky mothering of their timid, dull, six-year-old daughter, Mary Rose. Cressida's child-centered existence is both shallow and unbalanced.

The center of Anderson's emotional life is his lover in London, Gloria, who (like Blackwood) is a beautiful woman with unfocused literary ambitions and prone to scathing tirades. His weekend visits to Beckham make him feel persecuted and result in his whisky-sodden claustrophobic attacks. When Maureen's corpse is eventually found raped, mutilated, and stabbed, Cressida's excessive motherly love develops into an exultant mania of protectiveness for little girls. Her ghoulish interest in the crime disturbs Mary Rose, whom she insists on taking to Maureen's anguished funeral; afterward mother and little daughter keep a long freezing vigil together by the grave. Cressida begins pestering Maureen's parents and confides disgusting details of the crime to an increasingly traumatized Mary Rose. A neighbor warns Anderson that Cressida is unfit to have charge of the child. He is desperate to avoid his responsibilities—repelled by his wife's cruelty, but scarcely liking his daughter—while vigilante mobs try to catch and castrate suspects. When Cressida becomes deluded that her husband is the murderer, he abducts Mary Rose, hoping to save her, but is chased in his car by the police. After a crash, he is detained, and the little girl (who has fallen from the car at high speed) is taken away. The book ends with him wondering "if she would ever manage to escape from the demon-infested murky world of her mother, if for Mary Rose the plunge towards the tarmac would not always seem safer than life" (p. 206).

This fast-paced, exciting, and ultimately horrifying book is terse, elegant, and skillful in all its effects.

GOOD NIGHT SWEET LADIES

Good Night Sweet Ladies (1983) is a collection of five short stories. They are altogether more polished and emphatic than those in *For All That I Found There*. Blackwood's depiction of annihilating egotists who are variously bullying, reclusive, vain, or self-deceiving is so implacable that the reader can feel as overwhelmed as Lowell did by her late-night tirades. The stories' power and emotional precision are, however, undeniable.

"Matron" describes an intimidating hospital tyrant who punishes any infraction of her rules and examines "the violence and explosive rage that permanently seethed somewhere deep down within the confines of Matron's psyche" (p. 19). After Matron insists that Mrs. Appleseed, a meek old lady who has sat at her husband's bedside for three days and three nights, should eat something, junior nurses provide regular trays of food. But Mrs. Appleseed cannot face the glutinous vol-au-vent, pink blancmange, and other nasty dishes. Her husband's continuing survival is so unexpected that physicians flock from other hospitals to marvel at the patient. The constant sight of Mrs. Appleseed with a tray of untouched food lying on her knee, uneaten in defiance of Matron's orders, destroys discipline and morale on the ward. When the old man finally dies, Matron, disgusted by her weakness and failure, resigns.

"Taft's Wife" describes a social worker who dislikes emotional commitment, scenes, or recriminations in his sex life. "As a lover he merely 'obliged.' He was never the hunter. He was promiscuous not out of excessive lust but out of excessive passivity" (p. 44). Like the character in Oscar Wilde's *The Importance of Being Earnest* who invented an imaginary friend, Bunbury, to provide him with emotional alibis, Taft claims to his sexual partners that his love for the memory of an invented dead wife makes it impossible for him to commit. He invokes this fantasy wife to save himself from the overtures of an unhappy, drunken woman with whom he is obliged to eat Sunday lunch. Although Taft's lunch is ghastly, there is an even more gruesome dinner party in the next story, "Addy," which describes a lonely divorcée going out for dinner despite realizing that her old border-sheepdog, Addy, is dying.

"Olga," the title character of another story, is a seventy-year-old woman, strong willed and pleasure-loving, whose terminal illness obliges her to live with her son Oliver. He is embarrassed when she comes to talk to his friends at the cocktail hour, and jealous of her energy, which makes her so attractive to his friends. Olga's famous beauty has been wrecked by disease. "Her eyes were very round and they still had the gaze of a little girl and the childishness of their expression was disturbed because of the unhealthy darkness in the sockets" (pp. 80–81).

An even more personal story, "Angelica," describes a flamboyant, aging, self-obsessed professional society beauty walking in Brompton Cemetery, a few yards from Blackwood's London house. Other people exasperate her. "Lately her feeling of generalised free-floating boredom had become so sharp that she often felt that it was drilling through her like an instrument of torture" (p. 94). Angelica resembles "a person who continued to suffer from the results of ancient injuries . . . someone who had all the rage and malevolence of the cripple (p. 111). Her depression has been accentuated by breaking up with a younger lover, Jason, a shallow, vain, greedy creature.

> Her moods tended to deteriorate and become fouler and more petulant in the very pleasant circumstances where she had hoped they might improve. Sitting, unhungry, at dinner parties she would stare at all the expensive foods that seemed to flow on and off her plate in great tidal waves of courses. She viewed her fellow guests with paranoid rage and horror. . . . She found their kindness as distasteful as all the rich sauces that smothered the fish and the meat that her hostesses kept trying to feed her.
> (p. 95)

There is some self-portraiture in this "woman with bitter, exhausted eyes, whose beauty was now something that was clumsily stencilled on the corrugated surface of her face with make-up aids" (p. 128).

CORRIGAN

Blackwood's final novel, *Corrigan* (1984), was a near miss—not a failure, but her least successful. It depicted the effects on Devina Blunt, a depressed elderly widow, of a charming, energetic, handsome Irishman less than half her age who arrives at her house in Wiltshire in a wheelchair collecting money for a charity. He claims to be psychic, talks in beguiling blarney, and is manipulative.

Until Corrigan's appearance, Mrs. Blunt lives in inarticulate grief waiting for the miracle of her husband coming back to life. She scares and irritates her daughter Nadine, who is married to a smug, disapproving journalist, with her indifference and her morbid introspection. Corrigan's physical and philosophical courage however imbue Devina Blunt with renewed confidence and hope. She passes her driving test, buys a cumbersome van, raises money for Corrigan's hospital, St. Crispin's, opens a market garden, hires laborers, deals in antiques, starts painting and sells her pictures. Most controversially, she adapts her house so that Corrigan can move in. He encourages her to drink champagne while they talk elatedly of Pascal, Joyce, and Kafka. Nadine loathes Corrigan, and after Mrs. Blunt dies of heart failure, with a bottle of champagne beside her, she snubs him at the funeral. When she seeks him out to apologize, St. Crispin's Hospital is revealed to be a cheap pancake house, and Corrigan is discovered to be a con man with working limbs. Mrs. Blunt, it emerges, had seen through his trick, but had not minded, because he made her so happy. "He was my wine and my walnuts" (p. 268).

Some revelations in the denouement are somewhat fatigued and awkwardly handled, but in a cleverly twisted ending, Nadine is inspired by the now vanished Corrigan to walk out of her bad marriage.

BLACKWOOD'S REPORTAGE

In 1980 the novelist Francis Wyndham, then commissioning editor on the *Sunday Times Magazine* of London, sent Blackwood to Paris with the photographer Lord Snowdon (ex-husband of Princess Margaret) to write an investigative piece on the gruesome old age of the duchess of Windsor. The duchess was the former Maryland beauty and divorcée Wallis Warfield Simpson, for whom King Edward VIII had renounced the British throne in 1936 so that he could be free to marry her. After his death in 1972, the duchess (who had been given fabulous royal jewels by her abject and infatuated husband) became ill and confused and fell into the clutches of a cunning Paris show business lawyer, Maître Suzanne Blum.

Blackwood obtained three interviews with Blum in her expensive, disagreeable Paris apartment. She also interviewed other old men and women who had known the Windsors in the 1930s and put together a macabre and muddled book, full of mordant humor and observations, that was too defamatory of Blum to be published in the lawyer's lifetime. It was eventually issued as *The Last of the Duchess* (1995), a wickedly entertaining book that one reviewer reported would be enjoyed by readers who like to linger at the scenes of nasty accidents. Gruesome and farcical by turns, *The Last of the Duchess* is written in a deceptive tone of simple schoolgirl innocence which, coupled with various inaccuracies and solecisms, only increases the disorienting sense of bizarre and mounting horror. In a reader's note, Blackwood declares at the outset that she has written "an entertainment, an examination of the fatal effects of myth, a dark fairy-tale." She alleged that the duchess was kept alive by cruel and unusual methods; her body, supposedly, had shriveled and turned the color of a prune. Having reported that the duchess could only take sustenance through a nose drip, Blackwood visualizes the lonely captive being fed a delicious, feather-light soufflé through her nose. Blum implausibly claimed to Blackwood, by contrast, that the duchess was gay, winsome, and still listening to Cole Porter songs.

CAROLINE BLACKWOOD

Most of the book describes Blackwood's three interviews with Maître Blum. Blum is shown to have been a foul-tempered bully who used legal threats both to enforce her lies and to indulge in small-time extortion from publishers and journalists. On one occasion Blum actually threatened Blackwood's life. Blum was alternately servile and vicious in her dealings. Greedy for fame and power, she is bloated with self-infatuation and cankered with peevish malice. There are strong suspicions of financial chicanery and a certainty that she is confining the decrepit old duchess as a semi-captive in a palatial Paris house. In the summary of King Edward VIII's discarded mistress, the marchesa Casa Maury, laughing between huge gulps of Dubonnet, it is the story of a "horrible old lady locked up by another horrible old lady" (p. 213).

When Blackwood was interviewing people for her research, it could seem that she was oblivious to what was being said, but in fact she was acutely alert. Her credibility could never be doubted in her reportage, although she might make the atmosphere seem more grotesque or sinister.

In March 1984 Blackwood visited the nuclear protest camps encircling the United States cruise-missile air base at Greenham Common in Berkshire at the request of an American magazine, which had commissioned an article on the Women's British Peace Movement. For over two years, women protesters had been camped around the base's perimeter fence. The result was her book *On the Perimeter: Caroline Blackwood at Greenham Common* (1984). From the outset, as she described,

> I was very curious to meet the Greenham women, for the press had decorated them with such loathsome and frightening adjectives, they had been made to sound almost mythical in their horror. They'd been described as "belligerent harpies," "a bunch of smelly lesbians," as "ragtag and bobtail" and "the screaming destructive witches of Greenham." They'd been described as "a lot of silly women with nothing better to do," a merely contemptuous description. They'd been accused of being "sex starved," which sounded a lot more deadly because it made them sound so dangerous.

They were also described as being in the Soviet Union, and it was said that many of them were Russian spies.

(p. 1)

She reported the violent misogyny and sexism of the soldiers charged with defending the base:

> Many of the soldiers were under the impression that all the peace women were only camping round the base because they wanted to sleep with them. This was such a vain and deluded assumption, it was comic . . . they often hardly seemed like men, they seemed more like dangerous beasts. They were figures to be feared for their cruelty, but this gave them no erotic charisma. The foulness of their language as they shouted at the peace women befouled *them* rather than the women. They seemed besplattered with their own oaths and soiled by their own sordid fantasies.

(p. 14)

The book is a study of misogyny, and of the antilesbian propaganda of the Thatcher government. A passage in which Blackwood wrote of her shock when American soldiers mooned her from a bus led to a class-conscious, laboriously facetious, ill-written attack on her in the London *Times* (see Bernard Levin, "Baying at the Moon," 11 March 1984, p. 8).

Blackwood used a similar mixture of vignettes, anecdotes, and interviews to write her personal account of hunting and hunt saboteurs, *In the Pink* (1987). In this lovely, disturbing book she uses her power of depicting obsessive personalities to anatomize both fox hunters and animal rights activists. She analyzed the bigotry of the activists and the nostalgia of their opponents—and found violence everywhere.

For the hunters the excitement of the chase lies in its violent accidents, with their attendant danger of brain damage, paralysis, blindness, disfigurement, or death. The activists are horrified by the violence of hunting, with its accidental injuries to horses and hounds, and by the blood-crazed dogs tearing exhausted foxes to pieces. Yet they prove equally impelled to violence as they poison hounds, use trip wires to upset horses and throw riders, and plot to send the duke of Beaufort's severed head to Princess Anne. At their worst, the hunting fraternity emerges from *In the Pink* as boorish, cruel, and anachronistic; arrogant, snobbish, ignorant, and unimaginative. Their opponents are no less unreasonable, unsympathetic, and ill-educated. The embattled antagonists have much in common, especially loutish violence and lack of proportion. One master of the foxhounds claimed to Blackwood that horsewhipping a hunt saboteur was a private matter rather like beating one's wife.

The book begins with a character sketch of the tenth duke of Beaufort (1900–1984), perhaps England's most passionate twentieth-century huntsman. Then she visits the Southwark headquarters of the League Against Cruel Sports, and next an animal sanctuary with the inapt name of "Little Heaven." Its proprietor, a vegan called Tim Morgan, tells her that he so despises hunters' cruelty that he would gladly kill one. Yet to Blackwood the animals in "Little Heaven" seemed neglected, and she concluded that animal rights activists were more committed in their loathing of fellow human beings than in their love for animals.

Many British people follow the hunt not on horseback but in motor cars. Blackwood gave a mordant account of car hunting with the Quorn and the Pytchley hunts. She spent the day stuck in traffic gridlock in narrow country lanes or shivering as she strained through prickly hedges waiting to glimpse the hunt thunder past. Blackwood made the mistake of telling her host (a gnomelike old man who venerated English traditions) that she had been too myopic to see the one fox he had glimpsed in full flight. He resolved that she could not go home until she had seen a fox and was thus condemned to more freezing boredom. The boredom, futility, and frustration became claustrophobic and like a microcosm of human existence.

Blackwood had the British aristocracy's supreme admiration for fortitude, both physical and emotional. This was at the root of her reluctant sympathy for their wayward self-destruction.

More people are brain-damaged, paralysed, blinded, disfigured and killed while fox-hunting than pursuing any other perilous or unnecessary activity—skiing, boxing, or motor-racing, for example. The range of possible accidents offered by the hunt is enormous. The unpredictable behaviour of other horses and riders, the rabbit hole, the hidden tree stump, the wire in the fence, the treacherous patches of bog, all can produce fatalities.

(p. 52)

The etiquette of fox-hunting required more discipline and stoicism than army life, she judged.

If riders fall and sustain injury, they are not meant to let it be known that they are hurt, for then the other members of the hunt will have to attend to them and it will spoil the "run." . . . A second rule of etiquette also creates unnecessary casualties. The fallen rider should never let go of the reins. The hunt does not enjoy having a riderless horse galloping in its midst. The horse has to be caught before it causes another accident and this again ruins the run . . . many riders are dragged horribly after a fall, which can sometimes bring the horse down on top of them, so they are crushed under its weight or kicked in the face.

(pp. 52–53)

Together with Anna Haycraft (the novelist Alice Thomas Ellis) she compiled a cookbook for the expeditious, *Darling, You Shouldn't Have Gone to So Much Trouble* (1980). "The book was Caroline's idea," according to Haycraft in 1991. "She hates cooking even more than I do. She got absolutely pig-sick of spending hours in the kitchen. When she was a bride she used to go all over London looking for special herbs and all that sort of stuff. After a while you think better of it" (Michael Bateman, "A Cheat's Guide to Posh Nosh," *Independent on Sunday,* 10 March 1991). Written in the belief that cookery is drudgery, which too often subordinates and defeats women, Blackwood's cookbook offers shortcuts that avoid the time-consuming but possibly satisfying tasks of baking, marinating, chopping, peeling, grating, parboiling, leavening, or basting. Its recipes, which rely on canned ingredients and ready-made sauces, were described with distaste by the English novelist Anita Brookner as *"cuisine grosseur* with a vengeance" ("Cuisine menteur," *Times Literary Supplement,* 14 November 1980, p. 1282).

Caroline Blackwood's novel *Great Granny Webster* failed to win the Booker Prize for Fiction because one of the prize's judges, the poet Philip Larkin, insisted that no book so evidently autobiographical could be treated as fiction. It is undeniable that her novels and stories insistently, reiteratively told tales of her own emotional life from different starting points and obverse angles. The self-centered and destructive women in her fictions were differently colored versions of her mother or herself. There were some aspects of her experience of which she did not write—her alcoholism, for example, or her exciting but disordered love life—because she disdained people who were abject, confessional, or craved pity. She admired emotional fortitude, honored people who were reticent in their crises, and wished she could be more stoical. Aunt Lavinia in *Great Granny Webster*, who was based on her aunt, Lady Veronica Blackwood, exemplifies the "near-religious belief that it was wicked to inflict one's personal despair on others. Any display of self-pity or self-dissatisfaction she saw as a social cruelty that was very nearly criminal. Having been plagued all her life by a terror of ennui and seeing human unhappiness as a condition so commonplace as to be boring, she stubbornly refused to burden other people with her own" (p. 130).

This was a model that Caroline Blackwood tried to emulate in her life and idealized in her books. Like many of the finest short stories of Henry James, Blackwood's fictions were studies of character in particular—often static, constricted—situations. There is seldom much outward action in her short stories, which explore inner turmoil rather than describe external movement. Her novels *The Stepdaughter* and *Great Granny Webster* are studies of character with only perfunctory plots. *The Fate of Mary Rose* has an almost dizzying plot, which climaxes with a sudden burst of movement—its narrator's part in a high-speed car chase—that ends in calamity. *Corrigan*'s story line is implausible and uneven in places.

Blackwood's characters, though, are authentic and compelling, with voices, eccentricities, and gestures that endure. *Great Granny Webster* ends with the old woman's cremation, and the scattering of her ashes. A harsh wind blows some specks of the incinerated woman into the eye of one of the few mourners, a pathetic, tremulous servant whom Mrs. Webster had bullied and humiliated for years—one final vindictive act by someone still causing pain from beyond the grave. Blackwood's protagonists will not go away; they are painful grit in one's eye, spreading discomfort that nothing can ease or amend.

SELECTED BIBLIOGRAPHY

I. FICTION. *For All That I Found There* (London, 1973; New York, 1974); *The Stepdaughter* (London and New York, 1976); *Great Granny Webster* (London, 1977; Boston, 1979; New York, 2002, with intro. by Honor Moore); *The Fate of Mary Rose* (London and New York, 1981); *Good Night Sweet Ladies* (London, 1983); *Corrigan* (London, 1984; New York, 1985 and 2002 with afterword by Andrew Solomon).

II. NONFICTION. *Darling, You Shouldn't Have Gone to So Much Trouble* (London, 1980); *In the Pink* (London, 1987); *On the Perimeter* (London, 1984; New York, 1985); *The Last of the Duchess* (New York, 1995).

III. BIOGRAPHY. Nancy Schoenberger, *Dangerous Muse: The Life of Caroline Blackwood* (New York and London, 2001).

IV. INTERVIEWS. Laurie Taylor, "Caroline Blackwood's Bond with the Anti-Cruise Protesters," in London *Times* (5 September 1984); Stephen M. L. Aronson, "Sophisticated Lady," in *Town & Country* (September 1993); Michael Kimmelman, "Titled Bohemian: Caroline Blackwood," in *New York Times Magazine* (2 April 1995); Valerie Grove, "In Ulster We Were Horrified by the Mix of Monarchy and Sex," in London *Times* (14 April 1995).

V. ARTICLES. Lynn Barber, "Bacons on the Wall, Vodka on the Floor," in *Daily Telegraph* (23 June 2001); Hugo Vickers, "Beautiful Blue Eyes," in *Literary Review* (August 2001); Jenny Diski, "Entitlement," in *London Review of Books* (18 October 2001); Elise Harris, "The Insatiable Fiction of Desire," in *Nation* (3 December 2001).

VI. OTHER SOURCE CITED IN TEXT. James Lees-Milne, *Deep Romantic Chasm: Diaries 1979-1981* edited by Michael Bloch (London: 2000).

NORMAN CAMERON

(1905–1953)

Helena Nelson

OXFORD UNIVERSITY IN the 1920s was seething with young writers. World War I had almost wiped out one generation of poets. Edward Thomas, Wilfred Owen, and Rupert Brooke were gone. The biggest and most influential new name was T. S. Eliot (*The Waste Land* was first published in 1922), but others were jostling for attention. Free verse had arrived; concreteness of language and imagery was being asserted in the face of Georgian tradition and sentiment. At the same time, lyric forms flourished in the poetry of A. E. Housman, Thomas Hardy, and W. B. Yeats. It was a curiously fertile time, rife with new possibility. Jazz was in the air, and the perplexing American poet e. e. cummings was the subject of lively discussion.

This was the background that awaited the young Scot Norman Cameron when he enrolled in Oriel College in 1924, aided financially by two awards: a classics exhibition and a Bible clerkship. He had come to study classical history and philosophy, but he was already writing poetry too—and it was important to him. He had won school prizes for verse in both 1922 and 1923. One of his poems had been published in 1924 in *Public School Verse,* an anthology that was circulated among aspiring poets before they even arrived at the hallowed university portals; in the same volume there was a poem by the slightly younger Wystan Auden. Cameron's Oxford years would bring him into contact with Auden, C. Day-Lewis, Stephen Spender, Louis MacNeice, and the ill-fated but gifted Clere Parsons.

Three years later, Cameron's confidence had grown considerably. He had traveled abroad, developed new interests, made lasting friendships. He was president of the Oxford English Club, having had poetry published in student publications steadily throughout his study period. Then he invited an American poet, Laura Riding, to speak about Edgar Allan Poe. She was accompanied on her visit by Robert Graves, poet and World War I survivor. At the age of twenty-two, Cameron was about to form connections that would centrally affect the rest of his life, both as man and poet.

That same year, in the seminal anthology *Oxford Poetry 1927* (edited with a manifesto-type preface by C. Day-Lewis and W. H. Auden), Cameron had six poems, more than any other contributor. Cameron's measured, musical presence asserted its distinctive claim to attention. It looked like the beginning of a successful poetic career.

But it wasn't like that. Cameron did not go on, in terms of popular acclaim, to join the "big names" of the 1930s and 1940s. When he died prematurely in 1953 he had published only one modest individual collection (*The Winter House and Other Poems,* 1935), a shared wartime volume (*Work in Progress,* 1942) with Alan Hodge and Robert Graves, and a pocket-size pamphlet (*Forgive Me, Sire,* [1950]). The total of his published poems barely outnumbered the years of his life. Yet Cameron had never ceased to write poetry or to care deeply about it. Poet friends like Dylan Thomas, David Gascoyne, James Reeves, and Robert Graves regarded him highly. Even after his death, his poems continued to find a steady trickle of passionate advocates. Of few writers can it be said, as Warren Hope asserts in his excellent biography: "Cameron is to be admired for the poems he did not write, for the kind of poet he did not become" (p. 86). Cameron's best poems still win ready supporters. But why is he not better known? Why did he start so strongly and end so quietly? The answer is not a simple one.

NORMAN CAMERON

EARLY YEARS

Norman Cameron was born in India in 1905, into a strongly Presbyterian family. His father and grandfather were both Church of Scotland ministers. Cameron's father, John, had gone out to India initially as a military chaplain. On one of his home leaves he met Isabel Macrae, the poet's mother; they corresponded for nearly a decade and a half before he finally secured a civil post at the age of thirty-eight and she traveled out to Bombay to marry him. Norman was the first born of their family of four, and from the start his health was regarded as frail.

It was possibly health considerations that lay behind the decision to send Norman and his younger brother Lewis back to Scotland to stay with their maternal grandmother. Lewis was scarcely more than a toddler; Norman was between five and seven years old when the hot streets of Bombay were exchanged for the cool gray stone of Edinburgh. Before long, however, it emerged that young Norman was at loggerheads with his grandmother, who openly preferred little Lewis. The older boy was boarded out with family friends, where he was happier. But news of their father's collapse and death reached Edinburgh when Norman was no more than eight years old. His widowed mother and her other two children returned to Edinburgh. It must have been a strange time for the young boy—people coming and going, instilling a sense of loss and uncertainty.

Shortly after this Cameron was sent away to prep school on the northeast coast of Scotland, a lengthy journey by train for a small boy on his own. But he was a survivor. Although his slight stammer betrayed a characteristic diffidence, he apparently settled well at school. Certainly his academic performance was good enough to win him a coveted scholarship to Fettes College, a highly regarded Edinburgh public school. Here too he did well, and it was partly through writing that he won friends and a distinctive identity.

At the age of thirteen Cameron published his first amusing prose piece in the school magazine, the *Fettesian*. His style was assured: he clearly enjoyed both language and performance. At the same time, he was working intensively on transla-tions of Latin and Greek poems, an early training that must have driven home an understanding of meter, scansion, and form, as well as an awareness of classical grace and compression. Cameron also wrote original verse, most of which he kept to himself. If he indulged the permissible teenage habit of pouring adolescent torment onto the page, he did not share the results. He was best known for witty prose pieces in the school magazine, like "The Art of Malingering."

FIRST PUBLISHED POEM

Cameron's early poem "Disease of the Mind," probably written when he was seventeen, strikes a new note. It provides an early indication that he struggled with private anxiety strong enough at times to resemble madness. Here the text works its way from torture to release, from "choking" mist to "clean sunshine." A deliberate contrast between syntactical complexity at the outset and sudden simplicity at the end suggests a synthesis of form and meaning available only to a developed poetic awareness. It is hard to believe that this poem was not preceded by much practice. Probably the young poet was writing— and discarding—a substantial quantity of verse. Even then, he may have had the "impossibly high" standards to which Robert Graves later referred in his introduction to the posthumously published *Collected Poems*.

OXFORD DAYS

At Oxford, Cameron was to write poems that stand among his best. His poetic gift did not fade as he got older: it assumed a steady light in his early twenties and maintained that steadiness until his death. He was fascinated at this time by poetry and its terse challenges, to the extent that other academic work suffered. During his student years he published fourteen poems, a rich harvest in Cameron terms and a sign of burgeoning creativity.

At school, writing had been an important part of the young poet's individual and social identity; he had also proved himself witty and entertaining.

NORMAN CAMERON

The same characteristics won him firm friends at Oxford (Cameron had a lifelong talent for friendship), but he maintained the ability to stand just outside any group. Oxford in the 1920s manifested a peculiar division of species: young male students tended to ally themselves with one of two main camps: the "Athletes" or the "Aesthetes." The Athletes were sportsmen; they played rugby. Fitness, brawn, and aggressive team spirit marked them out. Aesthetes were intellectual; many were homosexual (or sexually ambivalent) and associated with the arts. The historian A. J. P. Taylor, Cameron's close friend, stood staunchly outside both categories, but he accompanied Cameron to some "poets' parties," and Cameron, who had always been hopeless at rugby, was certainly more Aesthete than Athlete. Both groups, however, shared one traditional student interest—drinking. Hope's biography cites an amusing incident recalled by a fellow student. It was Cameron's task to read the Lesson in the Oriel Chapel service (one of the duties of his Bible clerkship). The poet had clearly been drinking before the service and either accidentally, or in blissful disregard of circumstances, began: " 'Here beginneth the fourth chapter of the Gospel according to St. George'; the provost barked at him from his stall: 'John, boy, John,' but Norman majestically repeated what he had said and then went ahead" (p. 27).

Cameron liked parties and made lasting friends in different colleges. Significantly, he had a sense of his own absurdity. This quality may have helped him keep the self-dramatizing practices of the Aesthete poets in perspective. In the Oxford magazine *Outlook*, March 1926, he published a short story: "The Altruistic Tenderness of Len-Wing the Poet." Clearly the whole idea of poetic sensibility was occupying his mind. In the story the central character, Len-Wing, kills himself in despair when he realizes he cannot successfully separate his true and timeless poems from the trivia he produces on demand as court poet. Even as he sets himself to write a real poem, his "poetical soul" gives "a little shriek of self-derision." Self-derision was Cameron's balancing strategy. He did not kill himself—nor despair—but neither did he compromise. He was not prepared to be a "court poet." He was either going to write true poems or none at all.

POEMS WRITTEN AT OXFORD

Cameron's Oxford poems were born of personal experience, but they did not spill intimacies—they were secret about themselves. Peter Scupham, himself a poet and one of Cameron's continuing advocates, describes this beautifully: he has "that air of disclosing a secret and keeping it in simultaneously, of telling all but telling nothing as the poet slips away leaving his Cheshire cat's smile hanging in the branches." A secret smile, not smug but curiously attractive, is one of Cameron's hallmarks.

The poems published over four years in *Oxford Poetry* all follow formal, clear, rhyming structures. No modernist influence is apparent. Three of them ("The Marsh of Ages," "Peace from Ghosts," "Pretty Maids All in a Row") employ a number of short, two-foot lines, giving the resulting text a thin rectangular look on the page. The other poems ("Nunc Scio Quid Sit Amor," "The Thespians at Thermopylae," "Decapitation of Is," "Virgin Russia," "Marine Lament," "Fight with a Water Spirit") sit squarely and are more typical of Cameron's later style. They are short poems, their ideas compressed and self-contained. The favored meter is iambic (usually a five-foot line), and it is subtly handled. The effect is restrained, unassuming, and highly controlled. However, the "secret smile" is often there, and so is an intense awareness of language.

TWO KEY EARLY POEMS

"Nunc Scio Quid Sit Amor" (Now I know what love may be), first published in *Oxford Poetry 1926,* illustrates Cameron's complex linguistic sensibility. The title and prefatory quotation are from Virgil's eighth eclogue. It is characteristic of Cameron to draw on his classical reading but to work up a minor detail, something readers might not have noticed. Here his comments on love have likely personal relevance to his own sexual experience which, according to Martin

NORMAN CAMERON

Seymour-Smith, included a homosexual encounter recalled with shame as well as possible contact with female prostitutes while on holiday in mainland Europe. But if Cameron was dogged by a sense of Calvinistic guilt, it did not prevent him from having a more complicated response to experience—a mixture of dread and delight with which it is easy to empathize. "Nunc Scio" opens with a long and carefully controlled sentence, extending over nine lines of the single twelve-line stanza. The phrases unfold an exotic image of the "outrageous foreigner" (love), which has swooped down like some exotic bird and landed on the poet's shoulder. The last three lines offer a sharp contrast. Each is an end-stopped statement, adding an unmistakable tinge of self-mockery. The "I" of the poem is no hero. He quails at Love's onslaught:

I fear you and I fear you, barbarous Love.
You are no citizen of my country.

With the odd repetition of "I fear you," language itself gives way before the assailant. And yet the poet is controlling language in a very particular way. The adjective "barbarous" draws on the poet's awareness of its original meaning via Latin from the Greek: *barbaros,* meaning foreigner, or non-Greek. Earlier, the "fierce outlander" picks up the sound and strength of "outrageous foreigner" but also echoes the German *Ausländer,* or foreign visitor.

Through rhyme too Cameron exerts conscious control. Although *Nunc Scio* is cast in traditional iambic pentameter, the rhyme scheme has a particularly interesting effect on the last line. The word "tree" in the second line carries its rhyme sound alternately right through the poem, though the other alternating rhyme varies. Each of the "tree" rhymes is a single-syllable masculine rhyme (tree, sea, me, see, free) until the very last line, which enforces a change, pushing unexpected emphasis onto the second syllable of "country." Suddenly the reader is in the world of the old Scots and English ballads, where "coun-tree" was a regularly used rhyming word and "sea/free/tree" some of the popularly recurring rhymes. It is an unexpected and resonant reversal.

"Fight with a Water-Spirit" is another key poem. It is a sonnet, traditional in some ways,

unexpected in others. The thought observes a *volta* (switch in direction) at line 9, but the rhymes span the divide in an unusual way, making a deliberate connection between form and meaning. The poem tells a brief story: the poet comes to a ford across a stream. Many others have successfully (apparently) crossed the water. The narrator alone sees a "jeering water-ghost" mocking the travelers, none of whom have really achieved "true conquest of the stream." The narrator challenges the water spirit to a fight—and wins it. But no sooner has he crossed the stream than he is scared by seeing the spirit still smiling behind him, proving the conquest was illusory. The rhyme connections reinforce the fact that the poet hasn't achieved a proper break between octet and sestet—something is pulling him back. The poet concludes that fighting with the water spirit is pointless and that he should go on "with less ambition." The imagery of water, crossing-places, boundaries, and frontiers will recur in later poems, but here conquering the stream probably represents poetic achievement. Cameron's early poems are attempts to cross a stream, to conquer a mysterious art. He realizes that all his forays have failed and that the purpose of "conquest" was misplaced all along. He is not saying other poets are better than he is—far from it. The other travelers are only more deceived in the belief that they have succeeded. Cameron continues (he has not given up the journey) in a spirit of humility and, interestingly, he gives the place "a holy name." This idea of poetry as something mysterious and holy, inimical to ordinary ambition, explains much of his later life.

THE RIDING-GRAVES CONNECTION

Cameron graduated in 1928, barely scraping through his final exams. A stroke of financial luck (a bequest) meant he did not have to find a job immediately. He did not go back to live in Edinburgh though; instead he joined his artist friend John Aldridge in a studio in London only a short walk from St. Peter's Square, where Laura Riding and Robert Graves had set up the new Seizin Press. As always, Cameron was part of a lively social circle, but poetry was the driving force. Graves and Riding were full of ideas, publishing and disseminating radical ideas about art, poetry, and life. Through them, Cameron met other poets and artists. He helped with work at the press and became a member of what he would later call "the Family." He must have participated in lively argument: Riding and Graves had high ambitions for poetry, and their circle was select. But Cameron was not writing much himself, or if he was, his poems did not see the light of day. He socialized, took friends to visit his mother in Edinburgh, went to see his brother Lewis, now a student in Cambridge, and held parties at his London studio.

Then in April 1929, the Graves-Riding enterprise hit a major crisis. A troubled situation had arisen: Graves, Riding, Graves's wife, Nancy Nicholson, and a married Irish poet, Geoffrey Phibbs, were emotionally entrammeled. The relationships were intense and intensely argued. One day, after an unsuccessful attempt among all parties to achieve some kind of resolution, Laura Riding jumped out of the window in St. Peter's Square, apparently in an attempt to kill herself. She survived the fall but with serious injuries to her hip and spine.

Cameron's loyalty was evident. He lent Graves a substantial sum toward Riding's hospital expenses. Graves and Riding moved to Majorca once Laura was well enough to travel, taking the Seizin Press with them. Cameron, now in need of an income, sailed to Nigeria, where he had secured a job as education officer. At the age of twenty-five, he had already lived in four different countries.

There is little published work from which to draw conclusions about what was going on in Cameron's mind at this time. It is clear that he was attracted to the energies of the Graves-Riding duo and was strongly influenced by the intellectual dynamism of Laura Riding (which had such a profound influence on Graves and many other poets). Riding saw poetry as the vehicle of truth; it had nothing to do with wittiness or cleverness or decorative expression. Such ideas connected well with the underlying thought of *Fight with a Water-Spirit*: to both Riding and Cameron the poetic enterprise was to be ap-

proached with "holy" awe. Perhaps Cameron was, to some extent, stuck on the bank of the stream at this time—too awed to cross, though fascinated by the water. Certainly it is odd that he did not sustain the productivity of his Oxford years; his interest in poetry was undiminished, and his attachment to Graves, Riding, and his other London poetry friends was continued through a lively correspondence. When a second inheritance allowed him to quit the Nigerian job in 1932, he went to join his friends in Deyá, Majorca.

However, it did not work out. The lives of those in the Graves-Riding entourage were fascinating and educative, but the danger of an emotional fracas was never far away. Cameron clearly expected to stay in Deyá: he invested considerable funds in building a house and also agreed to give financial support to a Riding-Graves plan for further land development. He was, for a time, one of Riding's literary disciples, participating in a kind of advanced poetry training. He worked closely with her on translating Rimbaud, a project which would continue off and on over nearly a decade.

All the same, Cameron's relationship with his mentor was a strange one. He admired, listened, and learned. But eventually the attraction was outweighed by repulsion. Once again, human interaction had become emotionally and sexually complicated—Graves had had a brief affair with a young German girl, Elfriede Faust. Cameron's relationship with Laura, though only on one occasion, had also crossed the bedroom door. He began to feel a revulsion toward her, which he described as a "sort of horror." He may also have felt sorry for Elfriede—certainly he liked her well enough to go "skinny-dipping" with her. At a party, a bitter row with Riding blew up, and Cameron left the island with Elfriede shortly afterward. In June 1933 the escapees were married in London; it may not have been a love match. The twenty-three-year-old Elfriede was in a fragile state of health, and Cameron may have wanted to help her secure British nationality. Cameron himself was twenty-eight. His last published poems had appeared five years previously, and he had never had settled employment.

The marriage with Elfriede did not last. Although Cameron visited (and liked) his wife's family, some time in 1935 Elfriede left him and went to live with Maurice Lane-Norcott, a successful comic writer for the *Daily Mail.* She was ill: within a year tuberculosis would end her life.

Meanwhile, Cameron had at last settled into a job as copywriter with J. Walter Thompson, an American advertising agency. The work suited him well. It allowed him to pursue what Graves called his "passionate exactitude" for words and phrasing, see his large circle of London friends, drop in at the pub on the way home—and even work on poems at the office in the afternoons. His circle of friends was expanding. About this time he befriended the young poet Dylan Thomas. His friendship with Geoffrey Grigson, poet and editor of *New Verse,* also flourished. Between 1933 and 1935 Cameron published seventeen poems. In some ways he must have been happier, in others assaulted by a battery of emotions associated with leaving Majorca and the breakdown of his subsequent marriage. However, at least he was writing, consciously carrying his vocation as poet forward. In 1935, at the age of thirty, he finally published his first collection.

THE WINTER HOUSE AND OTHER POEMS

The Winter House was a slender hardcover volume, issued by the London publisher Dent as part of the *New Poetry* series. Cameron chose to present the contents in chronological order, either deliberately or fortuitously choosing exactly thirty poems, one for each year of his life so far. (Later he would refer to himself as "one-poem-a-year Cameron.") Restraint, in any case, was his hallmark. When, for instance, Geoffrey Grigson, as editor of *New Verse,* conducted a survey in which selected poets were asked, "Do you intend your poetry to be useful to yourself or others?" Cameron, with typical candor, replied, "Neither. I write a poem because I think it wants to be written." In other words, he waited for poetry to demand expression. Without that inner sense of necessity, he did not write at all.

Certainly *The Winter House* contained much of Cameron's life so far in highly distilled form.

The first seven poems included some of his best from Oxford, including "Nunc Scio Quid Sit Amor" and "Fight with a Water-Spirit." Most of the other poems had appeared previously in *New Verse,* one of the few publications to greet the collection (not entirely surprisingly) with acclaim. For most reviewers, however, this set of quietly understated pieces appears to have been insufficiently attention-catching. It was not widely reviewed, and Cameron's name remained of only minor interest to the world at large. Dylan Thomas, who had by now become a kind of younger (and often troublesome) brother to Cameron, proudly asserted that all his friends (of which Cameron was one of the foremost) were failures, especially in terms of ambition. Perhaps the lack of strong response to *The Winter House* would not have displeased Cameron's self-deprecating sense of irony; perhaps, on the other hand, it made publication seem less important, especially to someone for whom literary ambition was an uncomfortable concept.

Nonetheless, this slender collection has stood the test of time. It contains many fine, succinctly memorable poems. Even today the style feels contemporary. Of the thirty poems in the volume, the longest is twenty-four lines. Only one poem occupies more than a page—more than half the contents are twelve lines or shorter. A self-contained, ironic tone dominates the group, though the title poem signals the bleak side of Cameron's life—a sense of his own wintriness, perhaps exacerbated by his return from sunnier Majorca. Certainly the poet himself is the winter house "whose phantom planks are filled / By old storm holding back against new storm." The "old storm" should not be underestimated as a passing reference. Cameron was never quite at home in himself and always preserved a sense of attack from outer forces. Despite his apparent sociability, there was something isolated and unhappy about the man, probably stemming from childhood. However, in some poems, the suggestion of onslaught is offset by a lighter irony.

"Public-House Confidence," for example, adopts the bantering voice of a man in a bar, who, after a few drinks, confesses his secret: he is masquerading at work. The workers think he is a boss; the boss thinks he is one of the workers, and so he draws "the pay of both for doing neither." The poem teases but at the same time is neatly honest. It invokes a different kind of house—a pub—where confidence is inflated by alcohol.

COMING TO TERMS WITH LOSSES

Other key poems in *The Winter House* clearly reflect Cameron's Majorcan experiences which, he later told Martin Seymour-Smith, had led him to "madness and misery." "Release from Fever" reflects both that misery and a sense of successful escape. The text evokes a moment in illness when fever breaks. This must have had a literal application—the poet in his youth was prone to feverish infections. Here, though, the fever metaphor is extended to "long, hysterical argument" leading to an "explosion" which is also "the last frantic argument and good-bye." The occasion recalled is likely to have been the final row that spurred Cameron's departure from Deyá. However, the poem certainly doesn't end in madness and misery. Instead, the reprieve is unexpectedly joyful. The poet lies down and laughs, an exuberant belly laugh of "stomach-filling mirth." The secret smile has burst out into full-blown comic delight.

Cameron's comic bent is a reflection of how seriously he took poetry, for his honest, self-appraising eye measured the potential ridiculousness of poetic posturing. On the one hand, poetry was truth—too important to be written lightly, easily, or at length. On the other hand, extreme belief in poetic truth, at the expense of other aspects of ordinary life, struck him as dangerously seductive, leading to a hysterical imbalance only correctable by spontaneous laughter. That laughter is one of the most engaging aspects of this poet—and a corrective impulse to extreme poetic intensity. It is a vital part of his contribution to the timeless debate about what poetry is, or should be.

At least three other strong poems in the collection show Cameron's deep disturbance over events in Majorca and his method of thinking them through. It should not be forgotten that although Cameron's verse was never imitative (his form and method was entirely his own), Laura Riding in particular had a powerful influence on his thought, so powerful that in later life at least one close friend thought it had proved permanently damaging. Many observers of the Riding circle spoke about her dynamic effect in terms of magic—even witchcraft. Cameron too felt there was something mysterious about her, something he was both drawn to and repelled by. All the same, his Edinburgh background and Presbyterian upbringing must have constantly asserted a note of brusque common sense. But he was aware of something he could not explain, and in "The Successor," he acknowledged it.

This short poem evokes a magic circle, where one "High Priest" takes over from another, satirically echoing the way Laura Riding adopted a series of poetic "disciples." As one went out of favor another came in, forming a kind of ritual cycle. Cameron dramatizes his own temporary role as "High Priest" in an intense, visual little narrative: there is an altar on which "rising flame" roars. The language is dramatically biblical: "And I stood forth, the new / High Priest." Words like "menace" and "menacing" leave no doubt that the situation is dangerous, but at the same time, through deliberate hyperbole, the rhetoric suggests pleasure in the drama.

The single stanza has a circular movement, the first and last of the thirteen lines being identical. The rhyme scheme (only four rhyming sounds) is close and intricate. It is an excellent example of the highly focused technique that Dylan Thomas later described to the novelist Henry Treece in 1938: "A poem by Cameron *needs* no more than one image; it moves round one idea, from one logical point to another, making a full circle" (Thomas, *The Collected Letters*, p. 281).

If there is irony in the hyperbole of "The Successor," the same is not true of "All Things Ill Done," another poem reflecting on the Majorcan experience. This nine-line piece also has a strong central image—the sea. But the mood and tone is dark. The poet feels a sense of "sinister stagnation," and the sea, a "binding-link of separation," offers him only a "blank gift." What is a "blank gift?" Perhaps here it signifies noncreation, blank sheets of paper, life itself a series of meaningless journeys and separations. Certainly this idea is also pivotal in "A Calendar-Flush," which invokes "so-many journeys," "tolls and fords and bridges." It is not so surprising that Cameron, who had been shifting from country to country since he was a child, should feel himself foundering. It is typical of his practical good humor that he talks of the attempt to put his life back together in terms of "Income, boot-leather and the building-trade."

PERSPECTIVES AND POINT OF VIEW

More than a third of the poems in *The Winter House* are in the first person, a direct (or at least apparently direct) method of reassembling personal experience. However, Cameron also habitually stands outside himself: "A Calendar-Flush" is a third-person piece, although it is clearly about personal experience. A number of poems employ first-person plural: "we" represents a whole body of people. In "By Leave of Luck," "we" are the lucky privileged classes. In "Naked Among the Trees," "we" are the pleasure-lovers who have abused love's gifts. The first-person plural is another kind of distancing method, a way of looking at things from a new angle.

Interestingly, in one poem, "Let Him Loose," the narrative voice includes both "he" and "I," switching from third person to first person in the central stanza. The poet is aware of opposite aspects of his personality: the surface man, who is by inference cool and wintry, and the splenetic "throbbing" inner man trying to get out and join the "hot world." It is a poem that expresses Cameron's sense of his own inner split as well as his curious compassion for his own uncontrolled impulses. And yet, although the language is simple, the thought, as so often with this poet, is not. The "hot" man, the "man of blood" sounds like the vital, sexual, human impulse, restrained perhaps by an intellectual or spiritual controller. But at the end of the poem, when the inner man is let loose, suddenly he is not at all carnal: "see him go / Into a cloud or traveling down some wind." It is as though Caliban has suddenly turned out to be Ariel.

"Meeting My Former Self" also introduces a dialogue between Cameron and himself. He cheerily offers his "former self" "an island in the Atlantic" and describes the delightful life he had in Majorca. The twist is very strange. Cameron had certainly once been drawn to this life. Nevertheless, in the poem it is the "former self" who is now embarrassed at the thought of such an existence. The narrator (the present self) is "weeping and humiliated" by the scorn shown by his "former self"—a complete reversal of the expected roles. Perhaps he refers to a version of himself even further in the past. Certainly he seems ironically to suggest that at one point he would have rejected an easy, island life.

Robert Graves, in his preface to Cameron's posthumously published *Collected Poems,* identified his old friend's "divided character" and ongoing dialogue with himself:

He never became a schizophrene, but learned to watch the internal drama and politely introduce the irreconcilable characters to each other, giggling: "I'm afraid you're bound to quarrel; still, please remember that you are all me—or should one say 'I'?"

Nevertheless, there is a particular resonance when Cameron writes simply as "I," without donning a complicated persona.

"THE COMPASSIONATE FOOL"

The penultimate poem in *The Winter House,* "The Compassionate Fool," captures an enduring aspect of the man who wrote it. It is typical Cameron—only a dozen lines, three quatrains of iambic pentameter—and this time it has the authority of first-person narrative. The poem concerns a meeting between the poet and his "enemy." As so often, the poet exploits features of form to reenact the movement of thought. The construction of the first stanza differs significantly from the second two. First, it rhymes alternately, instead of *abba* like the following two verses. Second, it employs a strangely contorted syntax in lines 3 and 4 (the rest of the poem runs as smoothly and simply as natural speech). The odd-ness of expression in the first stanza—impossible to ignore—reflects the transparent plot of the enemy: "His ordered chairs, he to beguile me dressed / So neatly." The inversion is Miltonic, invoking the serpent of *Paradise Lost.* Moreover, the contrast of phrase, between the ornate ("he to beguile me") and the simple ("dressed so neatly") highlights the pathos of a too-obvious plot.

The rest of the poem develops the oddly vulnerable character of the assassin. The narrator/victim stays—though he knows what will happen—simply because he can't bear the ambusher "to eat his cake up by himself." Even as he perishes under the knife, he pities his slayer. Cameron identified compassion as one of his crucial "gifts." Warren Hope's biography refers to what Cameron told Cathcrinc, his second wife: "A poet's talent is important and if I'm a poet I hope to live up to this, but being a good poet isn't my greatest ambition. If I have a really important gift, I think it's compassion" (pp. 118–119).

So compassion was pivotal, though at the same time he saw himself as the "fool." The folly he had in mind, however, was closer to King Lear's fool than any other: the perspective of a minor character who could mock in the middle of tragedy, wisely foolish—and quite unable to avert catastrophe.

THE APPROACH OF WAR

If publication of *The Winter House* marked a watershed in Cameron's poetic development, the years immediately afterward suggested he might have gone on to the expected second collection in a few years' time. He was writing, and he was publishing. Other new poems reflected on his Majorcan experience, and one of them, "Forgive Me, Sire," appeared in *New Verse,* August-September 1935. His attraction to a young actress and dancer resulted in three love poems, also published in *New Verse.* At the same time, his job as copywriter continued to prove enjoyable. He was working with words, often playfully and with delight. To relax he did crossword puzzles

or talked about poetry, politics, and life with his friends in his favorite pub. He reveled in silly verbal concoctions, but at the same time hated imprecision of thought or language on serious matters. One of his frequently used phrases was, "Translate that into what you mean."

In 1936, a reconciliation having been negotiated, he met up with Riding and Graves in London. Through them he was introduced to the poets James Reeves and Alan Hodge, both of whom were to prove permanently close friends. He continued to work on his translation of Rimbaud under the direction of Laura Riding. At the same time, his knowledge of German was extended by holidays in Germany. At Easter in 1938, Graves and Riding introduced him to the Russian-born Catherine de la Roche—a spot of matchmaking. Very quickly—perhaps too quickly—the relationship between Catherine and Norman intensified. By September of the same year they were married.

Ironically, Graves and Riding were now alarmed by the match and wanted him "rescued." At the same time, Catherine wanted to persuade Cameron to break with Riding—she thought he lost confidence in himself whenever he was near Laura. Catherine was also uneasy about Cameron's many other close friendships, particularly by his readiness to offer financial help to struggling artists and writers such as Len Lye and Dylan Thomas. The marriage, though happy some of the time, was experiencing early conflict.

Meanwhile, in mainland Europe, tensions were reaching a breaking point. Riding and Graves left for the United States as war beckoned; Cameron declined to accompany them, though his friends Alan and Beryl Hodge did go. Riding and Cameron agreed to continue their collaboration over the Rimbaud poems by post. About this time, Cameron recorded a feeling of national foreboding in "The Firm of Happiness, Ltd." In this poem, using an uncharacteristically long discursive line and the clinical tone of a newspaper reporter, he describes happiness as "an empty building." In fact "nobody knows what to do with this monstrous hulk"; one suggestion is to turn it "into a barracks." The sense of grim loss, both personal and national, is unmistakable. In September 1939, war between Germany and the United Kingdom was declared.

War brought further change and separation. Cameron took a job with the Psychological Warfare Executive writing propaganda, and by 1940 he had been moved out of London to a new secret center sinisterly known as "The Country."

Meanwhile, Catherine was increasingly keen for him to make a permanent break with Laura Riding. The editorial correspondence about the Rimbaud poems was proving less than helpful. Alan Hodge returned from America, updating Cameron on the latest emotional upheaval in the Graves-Riding relationship, which was enduring painful death throes. Cameron decided at last to sever relations with Laura and wrote to request return of his manuscripts; they would never again resume contact. The significance of this decision should not be underestimated. Of all his poetic associates, Riding had had the most powerful and pervasive effect on his understanding of poetry. His technique was no more imitative of hers than it was of Graves, but from her he learned what James Reeves would later describe as the poet's "moral attitude to poetry and to his craft." The connection with her was not easily shaken, even though he clearly had mixed feelings about its continuing value. It took two factors to move him forward. One was certainly his wife Catherine. The other was Riding's decision to leave Graves, remain in the States, and establish her future with Schuyler Jackson.

A break with Riding may have been what Catherine wanted, but it was not enough to save the marriage. Cameron managed to get a job for his wife at "The Country" so at least they could see each other. But it was no good: the relationship was in real difficulty. There was a separation, then a reunion, then a permanent separation.

Cameron was not writing many poems, but the trickle of production was at least steady despite the war: pieces appeared in *New Verse, Epilogue III,* and *Horizon.* Some of these harked back to the Majorcan experience; others reflected the wartime offensive of the Allies. Cameron had formed a close friendship with a French couple, Marie-Christine and Robert Mengin, patriots opposed to both Adolf Hitler and Charles de Gaulle, leader of the Free French Forces. For Marie-Christine he wrote a poem called "The Invader," and he included this in an unusual publication, *Work in Hand,* published in 1942.

WORK IN HAND

The thin hardback volume *Work in Hand,* printed by the Hogarth Press, marked an ongoing alliance among Alan Hodge, Robert Graves, and Norman Cameron. Graves had by now returned from the States, leaving Riding with Jackson, her new partner and future husband. Paper and publication costs were high at this time, which was probably the main reason why Graves, Cameron, and Hodge agreed to publish their work "under a single cover for economy and friendship." It was significant for Cameron, however, that even at a time of war he was consciously preparing work for publication, talking to fellow poets, furthering his ideas. One view shared by the three men was that poetry was a matter of quality, not quantity. Graves contributed the largest number (eighteen poems) to the slender volume; Hodge's contingent numbered seventeen and Cameron included eleven pieces, although in fact three separate love poems (those originally published in *New Verse*) were grouped under one title.

Cameron's contribution includes some of his most memorable work. The first of the set, "Forgive Me, Sire," is an elegantly humorous quatrain. In one sense it is an in joke, since the "Sire" addressed is none other than Graves himself, here ironically allocated the rank of God. In another way it affirms Cameron's identity as man and poet. The central metaphor is one of an army, in which Cameron, "who should command a regiment," steps out of line. Instead of becoming a leader of men, he ambles "amiably," "one of the neat ones." He is not ambitious, just cheerful and friendly. But how subtly he undermines even that description of himself: the "Forgive me, Sire" is ironic hyperbole. Cameron is wholly unrepentant.

This is even more true in "A Visit to the Dead," one of Cameron's best poems. It plays on many ideas—the idea of dead poets, the classical idea of the Underworld peopled by shades, even Laura Riding's curious idea that poets were, in a sense, dead to the world because their real lives were elsewhere, the life of the mind. Like Orpheus, the narrator makes a journey to the "dead ones' habitat." But unlike Orpheus, he is not there in search of a lost love; the purpose of the visit is to study. The first three lines of the poem make this mission sound interesting and strange; it is then mercilessly deflated in the last line of the first stanza which sums up what the narrator learned—"To twitter like a bat." This is the Majorcan experience ridiculed in new and confident guise. The form is precise and careful. Each quatrain has two five-foot lines followed by one of four and then one of three. The syllable counts are precise: two lines of ten, one of eight, one of six. The gradual shortening of the lines contributes to a satirical tone; pauses created by the shortfall allow a deliberate thinking space, a secret smile.

The poet finally escapes from the regions of the dead, not, like Orpheus, thanks to his musical ability but because of his ability to laugh. Laughter is the "innermost resource" that brings him back. Delightedly he is suddenly transformed to "Marco Polo, traveler," ready to tell his story. This is an important poem for Cameron: his travels have become an adventure and a triumph, his purpose to speak of what he has seen. He ends with an exclamation mark, a sign (as in "The Successor") of unrepentant rebellion.

Other poems in *Work in Hand* are less jubilant. "The Downward Pulse" records an impulse to self-destruction, perhaps connected with his ongoing failure to make a love relationship work. The sonnet "Now Let Me Roll" has the poet about to throw himself beneath the hooves of a "herd," though in this poem it is "ridicule" (as opposed to laughter) that can kill. In "The Shack" (perhaps written after the separation from Catherine) there is a sense that the poet regards himself as damaged beyond repair. He refers to himself as a "grey monster" with his "house in lava-dust," so dusty that the desolate habitation chokes his loved one to death. Even in the three love poems, probably written at a happier time, there is still a feeling that the poet regards himself as sullied—"smoky and soiled."

The last poem in the group, "The Invader," was the one he wrote for Marie-Christine Mengin—the only poem, he later said, that he had ever "deliberately written for a therapeutic purpose." It is a true "war poem" in that it touches on a contemporary event: the German invasion of France. At the same time, "the invader" becomes a whole character type, the person who wants everything, but in seizing valuables always misses what he really needs. The poem neatly sums up the dichotomy: the invader "lives condemned to gorge and crave," both "oppressor and . . . slave." It is confident and strongly felt, the poet in complete control of form, meaning, and movement.

DIVORCE AND CHANGE

Later in 1942, Cameron agreed to a divorce, at Catherine's request. He was working hard and drinking heavily. Soon he was sent to Algiers, where he wrote the frequently anthologized "Green, Green Is El Aghir." A sense of misery affected him at times—once again he was "exiled" from home; once again a marriage had crumbled. However, as always, he drew strength from old friendships while continuing to form new ones.

In October 1943 he was transferred to Italy, still working in propaganda: first Bari, then Syracuse, Naples, and Rome. A handful of poems marked his travels: "Steep Stone Steps" in Naples, "Via Maestranza" in Syracuse, "The Verdict" written near Imola.

Finally, in April 1945, the war with Germany was over. Cameron went with several others from his unit to Austria to work briefly on a newspaper previously edited and issued by the Russians. By the end of the year he had returned to London, sharing his studio flat with Alan Hodge. He was awarded an OBE for his services to war propaganda.

NORMAN CAMERON

AFTER THE WAR

The cessation of war left Cameron unsettled and dogged by what he later described in a radio broadcast as "a mood of black depression." His return to London did not last long. Although briefly employed by the BBC, he decided in 1946 to go back to Vienna, once again working with occupation forces. But life there wasn't easy, and the winters were bitterly cold. However, in 1947 he met a woman he could love, the Austrian journalist Gretl Bajardi. After securing the post of copywriter with Mather and Crowther in London, he asked Gretl to join him there as his wife.

On the personal front, things were gradually coming together, although so far as poetry was concerned, Cameron was despondent. In 1948 he wrote in a letter, "I myself am scarcely any longer a poet." Nonetheless, he contributed two poems to the leading magazine *Poetry Review*—one original poem and one translation.

CAMERON THE TRANSLATOR

One of the interesting puzzles of Norman Cameron's life is how he continued to write verse of such high quality when he wrote so little poetry at all. Most poets develop their skills through lesser work—there is apprentice work, then practice and more practice. In Cameron's case, only highly finished pieces survive. Perhaps at least one key to the formal quality of his writing lies in his verse translation. Even at school, this was where he had started—translating Greek and Latin poems was a labor of love for him, a way of developing the craft. Throughout the period in Majorca he had continued to study and work on Rimbaud. As another poet-translator, Charles Sisson, points out: "Translation is the best of literary exercises, perhaps the only serious one. . . . the translator can have before him a competent model, not to copy but to study and to make something of his own out of."

Certainly in the last years of Cameron's life translation played an increasingly important role. The translator's persona made complete sense in terms of his background: his life hitherto had been a series of transitions between different countries, different cultures. He had married three times—women of three different nationalities, not one of them the same as his own. Gretl did not even speak good English when she first moved to London. In "All Things Ill Done," at least a decade previously, he had conveyed the painful sense of sea and time as his own "old binding-link of separation." Through translation there was an opportunity to bring his separations into a meaningful whole.

Cameron's version of Voltaire's *Candide* was published in 1947. Between then and his premature death in 1953 he would go on to accomplish an astonishing amount of high-quality prose translation from French and German prose texts, including works by Balzac, Baudelaire, Stendhal, Deleuze, and Ivanov. He even coauthored a rendering of Hitler's *Table Talk 1941–1944* (1953).

However, it was the verse translation that allowed him not only to study poets in depth but to also practice his chosen craft. Following the publication of his Rimbaud translations, he went on to Villon. It was his habit to adhere to the original forms so far as possible, and for Villon he chose to use a "period" English (seventeenth-century) which he felt corresponded "in maturity, richness and resemblance to the modern tongue." Most importantly of all, he stressed that his "qualifications for the task of translating Villon's poems into English verse lie in whatever gifts I may possess as a poet." Although self-deprecating about his self-evident linguistic skill, he was working harder as a writer than he had ever done before, and poetry was at the heart of his concerns.

FINAL YEARS

Two years after his marriage, a series of personal tragedies struck. First Cameron's younger brother, Lewis, dropped dead in the street—probably as a result of cerebral hemorrhage. The poet's mother, Isabel Cameron, was already unwell. Later that same year she died of cancer. Cameron's own health was not particularly good—all too soon he would find out why. No doubt Lewis's unexpectedly premature death affected his sense of priorities: he decided to give up his job as copywriter to spend more time on Villon, a project close to his heart. He visited Graves in Majorca with Gretl and published a slim pamphlet of fourteen previously published poems, *Forgive Me, Sire,* the first publication (despite its modest appearance) to win him some attention in the United States.

However, bequests from his mother and brother were slow to arrive, and without a regular salary, money was an issue. Cameron decided to borrow, using the inheritances as collateral, and undertook a full medical examination to secure the money. The examination revealed dangerously high blood pressure, which resisted all attempts to reduce it. Cameron made his will, leaving all assets to Gretl except his manuscripts and copyrights, which he bequeathed to Alan Hodge, his literary executor. He was no fool: he knew he would not live to be old. His task now was to make the most of the time he had. He decided to convert to Catholicism, his wife's faith, and continued his translation apace, probably with Gretl's financial future in mind. His marriage was happy, but his circumstances were difficult: in May 1951, a fire at the flat burned his entire collection of books, but with personal values sharpened by human loss, he remarked: "Never get too much attached to property."

In 1952, three new Cameron poems were broadcast on national radio—"Punishment Enough," "Bear in Mind," and "Lucifer." None of these had been included in the 1950 pamphlet. In June of that year Cameron also recorded brief comments on a selection of his own poems in a BBC radio recording. The last in the set was "That Weird Sall Never Daunton Me," the only Cameron poem to employ Scots. In the same year, the poet published no fewer than five volumes of prose translation as well as his translated *Poems of François Villon* (1952).

In early 1953, Cameron visited his old friend James Reeves. Cameron was none too well, recovering from a recent bout of flu. However, he was preparing for a public reading he had agreed to give in London. Following the two radio airings, this very private poet was now working to develop a more public reputation.

Indeed, as Reeves later pointed out, "he valued and coveted true recognition." But the sands were running out. A week after his visit to Reeves, and before the anticipated reading, he experienced a cerebral hemorrhage—dying at exactly the same age as his father and almost certainly of the same cause. Both Norman and Lewis had inherited a genetic weakness from which there was no escaping.

POSTHUMOUS APPRAISAL

It was left to Robert Graves to bring out a posthumous full collection of Cameron's poems in 1957. It was an attractive volume, bearing a frontispiece photograph of the author and with cover recommendations from both the Poetry Book Society and the Book Society. In the preface, Graves paid warm tribute to his friend, including long extracts from personal letters. The volume was not reprinted until 1968. In the *Review,* 1971–1972, there was a brief revival of critical interest, with essays by Francis Hope, Geoffrey Grigson, James Reeves, Roy Fuller, and G. S. Fraser. Each of them recalled a man who was never less than distinctive. Even Francis Hope, who found instances of "flabby romanticism" and "hackneyed sentimentality" in Cameron's work, credited him with an interesting sort of "effortful naturalness" and regretted that his output was so small. Fuller and Reeves both supported Grigson's view that Cameron "wrote or coined poems it would be ridiculous to attack," and certainly Francis Hope's reaction to some of the verse is hard to justify.

Some critics have attempted to credit Cameron with specific kinds of influence on other writers: Fuller thought he bred imitators of his short, mythological narratives in the 1930s; Seymour-Smith suggests he influenced the "Movement" poets of the 1950s. However, it is possible that Cameron, who always operated outside both fashion and "school," influenced others more by his "moral attitude" toward poetry than by his writing technique. He hated pushiness, self-inflation, and literary ambition. Like his onetime mentor, Laura Riding, he believed a poem should be "true" and written from an impulse toward truth and for no other reason. As his friend James Reeves described him in his *Review* essay: "He was what is called a poet's poet: no poet of any standing was unaware of him, but he made no general impact, was never fashionable. . . ." Despite the best attempts of those who held him in high regard, Cameron's fragile reputation remained largely uncelebrated in both England and Scotland. It was left to an American—Warren Hope—in 1985 to secure publication (first in the United States and five years later in London) for a complete version of Cameron's works, including unpublished poems and selected translations. In 2000, Hope published the definitive biography, drawing, among other sources, on extensive interviews with Cameron's contemporaries and friends, many of them now dead.

CAMERON'S SCOTTISH IDENTITY

To what extent did Cameron, born and bred of a Scots Presbyterian family, draw from a Scottish cultural tradition? Kate Calder, writing in the Edinburgh-based magazine *Chapman* in 1991, makes a case for his Scottish allegiance. She suggests that his narrative brevity resembled the Scots ballad makers; that he shared an interest in the "fantasies of the community" with the Orkney-born poet Edwin Muir; and that finally he was strongly affected by European influences "in the best tradition of Henryson, Burns and MacDiarmid." She dismisses Cameron's only overtly Scots poem, *That Wierd Sall Never Daunton Me,* with the embarrassed disclaimer: "Worse pseudo-ballads have been written!"

However, Cameron played no part in the Scottish renaissance claimed by MacDiarmid. (It is not known whether the two men ever met.) Cameron did not write in Scots, and in his letters, his communication is not marked by a native turn of phrase. Most significantly, when approached in 1935 by Edinburgh's *Scottish Bookman* just before publication of *The Winter House* and asked to contribute a poem, he replied that poems were "too valuable to waste on provincial magazines."

So far as influence was concerned, Cameron's interests were wide-ranging. In verse translation his main emphasis was on dead authors—Villon (fifteenth century), Rimbaud, de Musset, Heine (nineteenth century)—and there is much to suggest he felt more in sympathy with period writers from many different cultures than with contemporary Europeans. He introduced David Gascoyne to the work of Allen Tate, John Crowe Ransom, and Hart Crane. He went his own way, his immediate poetry concerns shared with a small group of close friends writing in English, namely Robert Graves, Alan Hodge, and James Reeves. These writers did not form a "school." They did not coin a method or a movement. Their poems did not noticeably resemble each other, other than in a liking for lyricism and succinctness.

However, Cameron did belong inside one very particular Scots cultural tradition—the tradition of the expatriate Scot, fiercely independent and always standing just outside any other culture. When Cameron as a child arrived in Scotland from Bombay, he was "different." Throughout his lifetime he sustained that identity. As an adult working in London he would travel north with friends to visit his mother in Edinburgh, then appear in full Highland dress to startle his English companions. People who knew him in London often referred to him as a Scot, and to Gretl he referred to himself as *"der lange Schotte"* (the tall Scot), but the term mostly defined what he was not—not English, not mainstream, not typical.

His Scots Presbyterian background also had a distinct influence on his personality: a sense of guilt shadowed his footsteps. His conscience often troubled him. He was also reticent, suspicious of emotional excess, careful and accurate—all Scottish characteristics. But he did not work in a Scottish cultural tradition, and he was buried, finally, in a London cemetery.

"THAT WIERD SALL NEVER DAUNTON ME"

A final word is necessary on Cameron's Scots ballad, "That Wierd Sall Never Daunton Me." It is easily dismissed as too strange for comment: Francis Hope, sharing Kate Calder's sentiments, suggested that it would make "even devoted admirers . . . wince." However, in Cameron's radio broadcast of 1952, he chose to include it as the final piece. Clearly he did not regard it as slight or insignificant, and neither should we.

The poem's title is a line from the seventeenth-century anonymous Scots ballad about Thomas the Rhymer. A "wierd" is a supernatural being, or witch. "Daunton" means subdue. The title, then, might be translated as "That witch shall never subdue me." The strangeness of the language is immediately explained by Cameron's adherence to seventeenth-century Scots. This is not modern Scots dialect, or the Lallans used by MacDiarmid.

The story behind the poem, that of Thomas the Rhymer, or True Thomas, is also important. In one sense Cameron clearly felt it to be his own story, and perhaps that of his friend Robert Graves as well. Graves probably introduced him to the ballad—it is discussed at some length in *The White Goddess*. Thomas the Rhymer, a thirteenth-century Borders poet, claimed to have been given the gift of prophetic truth by the queen of Elfland. In the seventeenth-century ballad that tells his story, the elvish queen challenges Thomas to kiss her. He doesn't hesitate. "That wierd sall never daunton me," he declares, kisses her, and becomes her willing slave for the next seven years in Elfland. His reward is an apple that gives the gift of truth, a "tongue that can never lee."

In Cameron's version, he immediately counters Thomas's bold assertion that the wierd will "never" subdue him. Oh yes she will, Cameron says. The kiss, according to Cameron, is not the reward; it is the dangerous beginning that allows the faery lady to "daunton thee and drag thee down / In worship and despair." He is almost certainly alluding to both his and Graves's relationship with Laura Riding, the woman who, to some extent, acted as muse to both men, inspiring equal amounts of admiration and misery.

But what does Cameron do with the ballad? In some ways he is completely true to the original. In language and dramatic expression, he adheres, albeit with a certain self-dramatizing irony. But he also makes changes. The original ballad is set in four-line stanzas of uneven tetrameter. Cameron adjusts and regularizes. He chooses another traditional ballad form, tetrameter alternating with trimeter. The effect of the shorter second line is more haunting, more disconsolate. Cameron's narrative is brief. He doesn't develop the story; he simply gives Thomas a piece of sensible advice:

"If thou a wierd wilt rightly woo
Kiss not and hush thy mirth. . . .

Once again, here is a reference to Cameron's own irrepressible laughter, his inexhaustible corrective. But he seems to be saying, in ironically archaic register, "Don't laugh, whatever you do." The advice continues: if kisses are avoided, and the faery lady is allowed to accomplish the poet's resurrection into a different kind of life, then (and then only) will it be safe to woo her. Or apparently. Typically, Cameron overturns his own directive in the last stanza:

And thou canst woo her not afear'd—
Or poets thus do say.
But, ah! what suitor of a wierd
Hath lived to tell the day?"

The answer, of course, is Cameron himself. Cameron is the same "Marco Polo" who returned from the kingdom of the dead to tell all. He has the gift of True Thomas, the gift of poetry. He speaks cheekily; he speaks with a secret and companionable smile, but he never doubts his calling.

LAST WORDS

In his introduction to Cameron's *Collected Poems* in 1957, Robert Graves declared that although he had never tried to memorize Cameron's work, "a good half of it has become fixed in my head." Indeed, Cameron is extremely memorable. The combination of controlled form and elliptical thought exerts potency. He may be a minor poet, but his life and work represent something of timeless importance: an unqualified loyalty to truth, a courageous determination only to write of necessity, a lifelong study of method and form encapsulated in a slender body of excellent poems. Norman Cameron modestly stands back, stares the muse right in the eye, and grins. Such an individual is not easily forgotten.

NORMAN CAMERON

SELECTED BIBLIOGRAPHY

I. COLLECTED WORKS. *The Collected Poems of Norman Cameron, 1905–1953,* intro. by Robert Graves (London, 1957); *The Complete Poems of Norman Cameron,* ed. by Warren Hope (Edgewood, Ky., 1985); *Norman Cameron: Collected Poems and Selected Translations,* ed. by Warren Hope and Jonathan Barker (London, 1990).

II. POETRY. *The Winter House and Other Poems* (London, 1935); *Work in Hand,* with Alan Hodge and Robert Graves (London, 1942); *Forgive Me, Sire* (London and Denver, 1950).

III. WORK ORIGINALLY BROADCAST ON RADIO. "Norman Cameron on Norman Cameron," ed. by Warren Hope, in *Poetry Nation Review* 112 (November–December 1996); *Alfred de Musset's Nights,* intro. by Warren Hope (Ardmore, Pa., 1999).

IV. TRANSLATIONS: VERSE. *Selected Verse Poems of Arthur Rimbaud* (London, 1942); Philippe Soupault, *Ode to Bombed London* (Algiers, 1944); Arthur Rimbaud, *A Season in Hell* (London, 1949; repr. London, 1998); *Poems of François Villon* (London, 1952).

V. TRANSLATIONS: SELECTED PROSE. Voltaire, *Candide, or Optimism* (London, 1947); Honoré de Balzac, *Cousin Pons* (London, 1950); Charles Baudelaire, *My Heart Laid Bare and Other Prose Writings* (London, 1950); Henri Beyle, *To the Happy Few: Selected Letters of Stendhal* (London, 1952); Bernard Deleuze, *Vagabond of the Andes* (London, 1953); Adolf Hitler, *Table Talk 1941–1944,* trans. with R. H. Stevens (London, 1953).

VI. CRITICAL AND BIOGRAPHICAL STUDIES. James Reeves, "Norman Cameron," in *Commitment to Poetry* (London, 1969); Ian Hamilton, ed., *The Review: Norman Cameron Issue* (autumn-winter 1971–1972); Martin Seymour-Smith, "Norman Cameron," in *Guide to Modern World Literature,* vol. 1 (London, 1975); Kate Calder, "Norman Cameron—Unacknowledged Scot," in *Chapman* 65 (summer 1991); Peter Scupham, "Shelf Lives 7: Norman Cameron," in *Poetry Nation Review* 129 (September–October 1999); Warren Hope, *Norman Cameron, His Life, Work and Letters* (London, 2000).

VII. GENERAL BACKGROUND. A. J. P. Taylor, *A Personal History* (London, 1983); Dylan Thomas, *The Collected Letters,* ed. by Paul Ferris (London, 1985); C. H. Sisson, *On the Look-Out: A Partial Autobiography* (Manchester, U.K., 1989); David Gascoyne, *Collected Journals 1936–42* (London, 1991); Laura (Riding) Jackson, "Emmie," in *The Word Woman and Other Related Writings,* ed. by Elizabeth Friedmann and Alan J. Clark (Manchester, U.K., 1994); Robert Graves, *Collected Writings on Poetry,* ed. by Paul O'Prey (Manchester, U.K., 1995); Robert Graves, *The White Goddess,* ed. by Grevel Lindop (Manchester, U.K., 1997).

CHRISTOPHER CAUDWELL
(Christopher St. John Sprigg)
(1907–1937)

Robert Sullivan

Communism becomes an empty phrase, a mere façade, and a communist a mere bluffer, if he has not worked over in his consciousness the whole inheritance of human knowledge.

Lenin

INCREDIBLE AS IT may seem, Christopher St. John Sprigg, sometime poet, writer of books on aviation, and author of detective novels, took the above epigraph not only as a motto but also as a modus vivendi, as he transformed himself into "Christopher Caudwell," cultural theorist. Sprigg reversed the traditional pseudonymous procedure and chose his mother's maiden name for his serious work, while maintaining his original name for his potboiler and other journalistic pieces. He was killed on his first day of action, 12 February 1937, a few months after his twenty-ninth birthday, while fighting with the British Battalion of the International Brigades at the Battle of Jarama in the Spanish Civil War. Before he left for Spain in December 1936, Caudwell had submitted *Illusion and Reality* (1937), the book for which he was to become best known, to Macmillan. He had already published under his other identity six detective novels (a seventh was to appear posthumously) and five books dealing with matters of aviation. His one serious novel, *This My Hand,* the only one published under the recently adopted pseudonym, appeared in 1936. From the voluminous manuscript material he left behind (housed at the Harry Ransom Research Center, University of Texas) have come the following titles: *Studies in a Dying Culture* (1938), *The Crisis in Physics* (1939), *Poems* (1939), *Further Studies in a Dying Culture* (1949), and *Romance and Realism* (1970). A selection of other manuscript material including two volumes of short stories, a science fiction novel, a pseudo-Nietzschean philosophical rumination entitled "The Wisdom of Gautama," two dramas, and a study on biology was published as *Scenes and Actions* (1986); the *Collected Poems* appeared the same year. Remarkably, while acting as secretary to the Poplar Branch of the British Communist Party, among other duties, Caudwell turned out all his Marxist texts in just over one year, from August 1935 until his departure for Spain in December the next year.

Such productivity is astonishing, but well before his conversion to communism Christopher St. John Sprigg was no stranger to industry. He wrote to a friend in 1934 that "during the last three months [he had] written the following tripe; 1 detective novel. 1 aviation text-book. 30 aviation articles. [and] 6 detective short stories," all this while doing "4 half-days a week office work." The "tripe" that Sprigg refers to here has met the fate of all ephemeral literature, but *This My Hand,* the novel he was writing that same year as Christopher Caudwell, is still of interest as a marker of how he was attempting to align his fictional output with his newly found weltanschauung. He explained his need for some form of worldview in a letter dated November 1935, by which time he had begun his immense reading project: "Seriously, I think my weakness has been the lack of an integrated *Weltanschauung,* I mean one that includes my emotional, scientific, and artistic needs." The worldview that Caudwell eventually adopted (or adapted) was dialectical materialism, but at the time of writing this letter he had already drafted a version of *Illusion and Reality* with the working title "Verse and Mathematics." This version relied more heavily on his reading in anthropology, cultural linguistics, psychology, and the symbolic function in human evolution, surveyed along with his reading in Marxism in the bibliography to *Illusion and Reality,* which contains more than five hundred entries. The earlier version provides a clearer picture of the genesis and evolution of his vast project, before Caudwell attempted to "marxify" it in those hurried months before he left for Spain. It also helps explain some of the book's irritating inconsistencies.

There is no doubt that in those frantic last few years of his life, Christopher Caudwell intended to align his investigations into all forms of cultural production with that of his recently acquired worldview. The nature of his actions is indisputable—joining the Communist Party, selling the *Daily Worker* on street corners, volunteering for Spain—but, as with all textual evidence, his intentions as realized in his writings have been less clear. He wrote hurriedly, especially during 1936 when he was revising *Illusion and Reality* and writing many of the "Studies," most of the time at over 5,000 words per day. His manuscripts at the University of Texas attest to the urgency of his project; many of the manuscript pages have other essays scribbled on their obverse sides. Understandably enough, since there was no time for revision, his work is riven with irregularities, youthful generalizations, and enthusiastic antitheses: and, given his historical time (when Stalin's machinations had not yet come to light), Caudwell's writings are marked by a naïve historical inevitabilism, a blind "faith" in the USSR as the terminus of the socialist experiment. His Marxist orthodoxy (if there is such a thing) will continue to be debated, as is only fitting given dialectical materialism's emphasis on continual process, but what is not up for debate is Caudwell's contribution to the study of humanity's struggle with nature in all its manifestations, from poetry to physics. Christopher Caudwell was that rare thing in British intellectual history, a self-taught philosophe obsessed by what he termed "the bourgeois error" of misunderstanding the essential, mutually determining interrelationship of humanity with nature, whether in the sciences or the arts. Whatever his status in the years to come, his endeavor will always be remembered as (the words are E. P. Thompson's) "the most heroic effort of any British Marxist to think his own intellectual time."

BIOGRAPHY

Christopher St. John Sprigg's short life began on 20 October 1907. He was born in Putney, then a quiet suburb of London, and was the youngest of three children. His father, William Stanhope Sprigg, was a journalist, as was William's father. Sons Theodore and Christopher would eventually join the same profession. Stanhope Sprigg helped found the *Windsor Magazine*; for a time a literary agent, he was also the literary editor for the newly founded *Daily Express,* and was the London representative for the New York *Standard.* Christopher's mother, Jessica Caudwell ("Jessie"), a miniaturist and illustrator, came from a Catholic family out of Berkshire. Stanhope Sprigg converted to Catholicism to marry her, and his only daughter, Paula, would eventually become a nun in the convent school in which she was educated. Like his younger brother, Theodore ("Theo") would also become a prolific author, eventually forming a publishing partnership with Christopher. The family seems to have led a fairly happy and close-knit existence until Jessie Caudwell's death in the middle of the World War I, when Christopher was only six. This seemed to initiate a period of fragmentation in their family life. Around this time (1916–1917), Stanhope Sprigg moved his family to Hampstead, taking in a housekeeper (a woman he was later to marry) and her young son. As the oldest, Paula came home from her school to help run the house, but shortly thereafter she returned to the Sion Convent to take her vows, never to return to the family fold again. The year before, Theo, only fifteen years old, had joined the merchant marine and went to sea for an extended period, leaving Christopher alone with the new housekeeper and her son.

A short time later his father sent Christopher as a boarder to the Benedictine School at Ealing, the first of many temporary (and shared) accommodations that Sprigg/Caudwell would inhabit

CHRISTOPHER CAUDWELL

for the rest of his life. He did well at school, passing science "with Distinction," even if he was somewhat retiring and averse to sports. The most important aspect of his time at Ealing was the friendship he struck up with Paul Beard, a kindred spirit interested in literary matters; Beard would eventually witness the transformation of his boyhood friend into Christopher Caudwell, and would edit the posthumous *Poems* (1939). The reasons are unclear, but despite a promising academic career, Christopher left the school in 1922, when he was only fifteen. There was some talk of a disciplinary incident, but his brother Theo would later maintain that the reasons were solely financial. The young man now joined his father, who had taken up the literary editorship of the *Yorkshire Observer*. Here Christopher worked as a cub reporter and occasionally wrote literary reviews. Father and son were based in Bradford, a city as provincial as London was cosmopolitan, and there is evidence in some of the later fiction that Christopher felt something of an exile there. One of these stories, from a batch he called "Lodgings for the Night" and entitled "The Great Man," has the narrator remark that he had been "thrust down in a small provincial town, and had a mania for loving women who did not love [him], so what was there to do with that awful solitude . . . but to write." *This My Hand* (1936), the only novel permitted the sobriquet "Christopher Caudwell," has a thinly disguised Bradford as the fictional Tinford, a place where people are driven to do desperate things. It is very likely while sojourning in Bradford that Sprigg wrote a good deal of poetry, including the often revised "The Art of Dying."

After these few years in Bradford, Christopher returned to London to join his brother, who had come home from sea and was setting up business as a journalist there. Christopher at first gained some editorial experience working for the trade journal *British Malaya,* then established a publishing company with Theo called Airway Publications. Christopher thereupon began a series of books and articles on aviation subjects, the first full-length study being *The Airship* (1931), in which he called upon his knowledge of physics. Science and poetry were to be the two poles of human endeavor that Christopher Caudwell sought to unite in his investigation of cultural production, and by the beginning of the 1930s Christopher Sprigg had offered evidence of this interest. In 1927, he published his first poem, "Once I Did Think," in *The Dial* under Marianne Moore's editorship, and in 1929 an essay in the magazine *Automobile Engineer* on his design for a variable gear system, which was later patented but never manufactured. By 1930 the two brothers had become successful entrepreneurs, their business having undergone an expansion due to a legacy that both of them enjoyed. They shared a flat in London, and when Theo married Vida Devant in 1929, his younger brother moved with the couple to their Surrey home, "the Thatched Cottage," an address that was to appear later in most of the obituaries. There was no sign during these years (1926–1934) that Christopher St. John Sprigg had any left-wing political interests; indeed, on the contrary, he and his brother volunteered to help with services during the General Strike of 1926. In 1933, just as the Sprigg brothers' business was expanding, a series of loans were called in by a Machiavellian associate, and they were forced to liquidate their publishing enterprise. It has been suggested that this example of capitalism's untrustworthy nature may have turned the young journalist toward socialist principles, and although it is unlikely that this event alone sufficed, 1934 saw the start of this transformation.

Christopher St. John Sprigg, especially now after the business collapse, had to find other ways to make a living, so in 1933 he turned to writing detective novels. He published the first two, *Fatality in Fleet Street* and *Crime in Kensington* in 1933, and he continued writing in this genre even when working as Christopher Caudwell on his Marxist writings. The publication of *The Six Queer Things* in 1937 attests to how he was subsidizing his serious work what he called "potboilers," some of which he could write in a few weeks. Now that his office work had greatly diminished, Christopher turned to a rigorous reading and writing schedule, composing various short stories and poems and beginning to read the various texts that would inform "Verse and

35

Mathematics: A Study of the Sources of Poetry." He continued writing his detective fiction and other journalistic pieces, but he had embarked on his serious fiction now and was sending a series of stories to the Beards for their criticism and comment. One of these remains of particular interest with regard to both Sprigg's own intellectual and spiritual quest and that of his generation. "We All Try" (he later adapted the story as a play with the more telling title "The Way the Wind Blows"), tells of a young upper-middle-class man's search for spiritual fulfillment and a form of commitment as substitutes for a more traditional religious faith. Brian Mallock's "journey" leads him to engage in the most degrading of tasks, to join the workers' movement for a time, and even to live with a working-class girl, but all to no avail. These motifs have become part of the mythology of the 1930s, a decade in which many disenchanted intellectuals flirted with Communism because of class guilt or the search for a substitute faith. That Caudwell knew he was fictionalizing a kind of typology of the epoch is evident by his remark to Elizabeth Beard that he thought the story had captured "the Zeitgeist" of the time. In a later note, he clarified for her his true intention in the story. He tells her that she had got "the theme *wrong*" (original emphasis), that the story was not to show "the necessity of work, but the failure of idealism, as long as it was only a selfish longing for self fulfillment, and has no social roots."

In another letter to "Betty" Beard, dated 24 July 1935, Christopher wrote to tell her that their discussions on poetry and aesthetics generally had "spurred [his] poor brain to such feverish activity" that he was then "half way through a book called 'Verse and Mathematics,'" and "writing at the rate of 4–5000 words a day!" He goes on to say that he would go to Cornwall for some months to work on the book and other projects, and shortly thereafter he sent a carbon of the book he now called "Illusion and Reality," while maintaining the original subtitle, "A Study of the Sources of Poetry." Betty Beard's reply and criticisms of the manuscript prompted Christopher to reconsider and clarify some of his critiques, especially those on the concept of beauty and the

nature of religion, and this led him, he tells her, to separate "Studies" on these topics. Hence the beginning of the series "Studies in a Dying Culture." It would not be too much of an exaggeration to suggest that while in Porthleven, Cornwall, during these few months in 1935, as he was transforming "Verse and Mathematics" into "Illusion and Reality" and sketching out his "Studies," that Christopher St. John Sprigg became Christopher Caudwell. A further indication of this transition came at this time in a letter to his brother Theo, informing him that when he returned to London he would no longer live with him and his wife Vida, claiming (disingenuously, as it turned out) that he would move to the East End of London to get some "local colour" for his writing.

When he returned to London in late 1935, he moved to the militantly leftist working-class area of Poplar in the East End. He eventually joined the Poplar Branch of the Communist Party of Great Britain, soon becoming branch secretary. Although he was now writing as "Caudwell," he was known to his comrades as "Spriggy," or "John," or "Chris." Caudwell attended lectures at Marx House on literature and Marxism for a time, but apparently was not one for intellectual company, especially within the party: no one in his branch knew of his writings until after his death. He wrote numerous letters to the newspapers on party matters, sold the *Daily Worker* on street corners, and protested meetings of Mosley's British Union of Fascists. In June 1936 he was involved in a fight at one of these demonstrations, arrested, allegedly "beaten up" by the police, and then fined at a court hearing. His theoretical stance against Fascism had now taken a more practical turn, and when, a few months later, General Francisco Franco's forces decided to move against the fledgling Republican government in Spain, Caudwell volunteered to drive his branch's ambulance there. There was some ambiguity in his orders once he had reached Albacete, as to whether or not he should return home, but it became clear much later (after years of wrangling between Theo and the C.P.G.B) that his orders were to become a combatant. True to his profession, he became joint editor of the *Wall* newspaper and so competent in handling the machine-gun that he was made an instructor. From more than one account, it appears that he died heroically. At the battle of Jarama on 12 February 1937, his position was overrun by Franco's Moorish troops, causing a disorganized and hasty retreat. Caudwell and his co-gunners went back to retrieve the key from their machine-gun to render it useless to the enemy, but they were killed by grenades on reaching the position. He was one of nearly four hundred men (out of a total of six hundred in his battalion) who died in that battle, and his body was never recovered. John Lepper, one of the survivors, described the carnage in his poem "Battle of Jarama, 1937." The second stanza gives testimony:

Death stalked the olive trees
Picking his men
His leaden finger beckoned
Again and again.

It is little consolation, but it must be said that Caudwell seemed happy in Spain. His letters (see the brief selection in *Scenes and Actions*) are replete with a sense of fulfillment and hope for the newly formed Republic. As an analyst and de-constructor of the nature of illusion in all its guises, it is perhaps a sad irony that he died with his own illusions intact.

THE POETRY AND FICTION

Shortly before his departure for Spain Caudwell put his affairs in order, and although his brother had possession of his manuscripts, it was to Paul Beard that he left instructions for their disposition. He sent a kind of balance sheet of his accumulated work, with the titles on one side of the page and his comments on the other (see the reproduction of this letter in *Scenes and Actions,* p. 231). He described most of the creative work as belonging to his "dishonest sentimental past." It may be that Caudwell was Sprigg's and his own best critic. Had he survived Spain, only a very small amount of the creative work published in *Scenes and Actions* (1986) and *Collected Poems* (1986) would have appeared, and that only in modified form. The great majority of

the poems are derivative, literary in their impulse, and "smell of the library," an accusation, ironically enough, that Caudwell was to level against Eliot and the Metaphysicals. The stories in the collection "Lodgings for the Night," written in what he called his "Chekovian" manner, are of interest mainly for biographical reasons. We have already seen how two of these stories, "The Great Man" and "We All Try," help to shed light on Sprigg/Caudwell's psycho-biography. The collection entitled "The Island," containing what he called in a letter his "Kafka" pieces, are not really short stories at all, but rather ruminations on various philosophical concepts. The verse-play *Orestes* and the one serious novel *This My Hand* are of the most interest, in part because they illustrate how Caudwell was attempting to use the ideas of Marx and Freud in his imaginative work at a time when he was synthesizing their ideas for his philosophical studies.

The poems are heavily influenced by the work of T. S. Eliot (what young poet in the 1920s could escape his influence?) and Eliot's popularization of the metaphysical poets. There is also an Augustan flavor to some of the poems, and in some a strange fusion of Marvell with Donne, as in "The Hair": "Ah, when I'm bald, and love becomes disgust / (Your love will last up to that date I trust)," with the concluding couplet "Not even then, for round your ribs will be / The bare arms of my own anatomy." The whole poem is a sort of mélange of Donne's "The Relic" and Marvell's "To His Coy Mistress" (p. 119, all references here are to the *Collected Poems,* 1986). It is as if, in the vast majority of this verse, Sprigg/Caudwell had withdrawn from that "real" historical time that Caudwell analyzed so shrewdly, into some trans-historical poetic library. That this poetic sensibility's diction, syntax, and imagery were not the result of some hurried project is best demonstrated by the poem "The Art of Dying," which Sprigg reworked on and off for ten years. The perennial theme of dying young as escape from the ravages of time is expressed thus: "If you still sport youth's clear rebellious rose / When the grave's antique scissors on you close / Reflect you have some forty gustless years / Of wambling sorrow, age's easy

CHRISTOPHER CAUDWELL

tears, / Scaped by this stratagem" (p. 138–139). It would be extremely difficult to guess that this verse was written in the 1920s and 1930s.

If this summary analysis of the poetry has been overly negative, it is negative in the service of Caudwell's memory. It is indicative of how tentative he would have been to allow his new self (as opposed to that "dishonest sentimental past" self) to own one of these creations that one of the very few politically contemporary poems he did write—"Heil Baldwin," a satire on the Anglo-German naval agreement of 1935—has the signature "Christopher Caudwell" crossed out in the typescript. There are some good poems, of course, and Caudwell could have salvaged a slimmer volume had he had the chance and the desire. Such a volume would have included "Tierra del Fuego" (p. 121), "The Coal" (p. 128), "Essay on Freewill" (p. 12), and *Orestes,* among others. Some of the "Juvenilia" testify to a felt experience rather than a studied response, including "On a Dead Cat," with such lines as

You're made
Such sight as you would have distained
A matted carcase, gravel-stained.

(p. 33)

And, although we do not have the originals with which to compare, some of the translations are fine, especially "Five Translations from the Chinese," the fifth of which reads:

The leaves had fallen from the trees,
There was no moon to light our steps,
And it was long since in the rounded bowl
The wine had laughed at me,
But I was young.

Although the verse-play *Orestes* owes something to Eliot's experiments in this genre—particularly his innovations with a modern chorus and the juxtaposition of the vernacular with stylized language—this is the most successful adaptation that Caudwell attempted. It was most likely written quite late, in 1935–1936, when Caudwell was attempting to synthesize his reading of Marx and Freud. If we recall that in Aeschylus' *Orestes,* the hero complains that "The

torture of these Furies touches most the mind," it is less surprising that Caudwell's modern tragedy is set in the consulting room of Dr. Tape, the "Austrian Wizard." In this version, the cosmic drama of men and gods has moved within the theater of the self, the absolution of guilt now in the hands of the analyst, who at the play's end performs the necessary exorcism: "But as for you, you shades or Furies, go! / You're merely inhibited tendencies / And now I've analysed you, quick avaunt!" And this modern-day Orestes proclaims the psychic nature of his plight and the dilemma inherent in absolution: "Because I only did it in a dream / They cannot punish or forgive my sin." He is constantly pursued by the Furies ("Blessed be the brain that bore us and the complex / That gave us suck") regardless of whatever diversion he devises: "I drove to Wick at 60 m.p.h. / And found them curled beneath the tonneau cover / And when I flew to Moscow on the Moth / They hung head downwards from the fuselage." In part, the guilt and neurosis of Orestes and his sister Electra stem in this poem from a social cause—it is a clearly defined middle-class guilt—as well as a family murder. Although not fully realized—the social dimension of the poem needs more integration with that of the psychological—this verse experiment is certainly a harbinger of what Caudwell could have done had he come back from Spain. There is a range of feeling and verse-form in *Orestes* that suggests he was beginning to find a more mature poetic voice, almost a voice of his own.

Christopher St. John Sprigg had little regard for his "potboilers," as he called his detective fiction. In a letter dated December 1934, he classified such writing as "tripe" which had become "a sensori-motor habit, quite independent of the cerebrum." Later, as Christopher Caudwell, he criticized such writing as "the religion of today, as characteristic an expression of proletarian exploitation as Catholicism is of feudal exploitation." We will afford little or no space to these books here, except to say that they are all orthodox examples of the classic "whodunit" that flourished in the 1920s and 1930s. They are set in an atemporal social and political world as hermetically sealed from the pressing concerns of the epoch as some of the locked rooms so typical of these fictions. Caudwell's crime novel, however, is altogether another species. In a letter to the Beards (they came thick and fast during 1935–1936) dated 21 May 1935, Caudwell tells them that he has "been working at high pressure on a serious novel." He goes on to tell them that it is "about murder and sudden death; but not the Macbeth novel which [he] now [sees] is impossible." The title in fact does come from act 2, scene 2 of Shakespeare's play, when the protagonist, shortly after Duncan's murder, contemplates the magnitude of his crime:

Will all great Neptune's ocean wash this blood
Clean from my hand? No, this my hand will rather
The multitudinous seas incarnadine, Making the green
  one red.

What no doubt interested Caudwell in Macbeth, a theme that is central to *This My Hand,* is the idea of shared guilt leading to catastrophe. As with the verse-play *Orestes,* the haunting presence of Freud is evident, especially his *Civilization and Its Discontents* (1930), in which his thesis was "to represent the sense of guilt as the most important problem in the evolution of culture"; and, again like *Orestes,* the novel explores the notion of psychology as fate. "Why do we torment ourselves," protagonist Ian Venning asks. "I mean nobody wants these things and yet they happen." Salmon, another character in the novel who acts as a sort of chorus, more than once brings the Freudian subtext to the surface: "'Guilt, guilt, nothing but guilt!' said Salmon more cheerfully. 'That, in my opinion, is the modern disease.'"

Ian Venning, a shopkeeper's son who has stolen money from his former employers, is able to break through class barriers because of a friendship with the upper-class Colin Firth that he made during the war. He meets the neurotic Celia at the Firth family's home, and she is attracted to him, especially to his hands, because of a certain "coarseness" in his nature. We are given then a sort of case-history of Celia's neurasthenic past (all the characters get this psycho-biographical treatment), and when they eventually marry, Ian is "driven" to tell her of his previous theft. This

is the first link in a chain of inevitable events that leads Venning to the scaffold. Driven to madness by Celia's neurotic behavior and her threat to tell the police of his crime, the hand that she was attracted to strikes her dead. Ian now turns to Barbara Mitton, his erstwhile lover, and she helps him (somewhat like Lady Macbeth) cover up the crime. But now Ian is linked in his guilt to Barbara, and this hidden knowledge begins to drive a wedge between them. When, in despair, she commits suicide ("It was as if life said: 'There is nothing you can do, nothing at all'"), it seems for a while that Ian is free of this shared guilt. There is something within Ian Venning that desires apprehension and punishment, however, so much so that he actually befriends the detective who is investigating Celia's murder. In a way similar to Raskolnikov's anxiety in *Crime and Punishment,* he suffers "a kind of phobia as long as the policeman [is] out of his sight." After Barbara's death, Venning is driven into the arms of a young working-class girl called Mary Britain, thinking she would not "finger his soul" like the two previous women in his life. He is compelled, however, to tell Mary about his previous misdeeds, and he ends up strangling her. The last chapter, by far the best in the novel, could stand on its own as a moving indictment of capital punishment. As Venning awaits his execution, his presence is described as being "like a repressed madness . . . in the heart of the community." Compared with Venning's involuntary and impassioned killing of Celia and Mary, society's cold, clinical, revenge is figured as inhuman. The last sentence of the book describes the departure of the hangman after he has completed his task: "It looked almost as if there had been a substitution and the real murderer was escaping."

This My Hand is not a great novel, indeed it is not a very good novel, but it deserves to be read if only for the fact that there is nothing else like it in the history of the English novel, except perhaps for Godwin's *Caleb Williams* (1794). It has more of the flavor of continental fiction, a strange mixture of Zola, Camus, and Dostoevsky. It deserves to be read also because, like *Orestes,* it has the imprint of Caudwell upon it, rather than that of Christopher St. John Sprigg. It should be in print because it shares with the verse-play Caudwell's interest at this time (1935–1936) in psychology as fate, or, as he put it in a letter: "That Fate is just ourselves as ourselves: that this thing that seems compulsive and external is internal."

ILLUSION AND REALITY

Illusion and Reality is arguably the most complex book ever written in the English language on poetry's function, its characteristics, and its evolution within society. This complexity arises from at least two causally related reasons: the hurried nature of its composition (Caudwell wrote it at the rate of 4,000–5,000 words per day), and the equally hurried revisions to the earlier manuscript that he called "Verse and Mathematics." These revisions, made while he was drafting his series of "Studies," were necessary in order that he might bring his vast reading and the concomitant project—the explication of the symbolic function in human evolution—into line with his newly found Weltanschauung. The new title "Illusion and Reality" now came with an epigraph from Engels—"Freedom is the recognition of necessity"—a dictum so crucial to the studies he was now writing, but the manuscript still maintained the original subtitle, "A Study of the Sources of Poetry," which points to the book's genesis and original conception. The hurried revisions resulted in several deformations and what seem like excurses in the manuscript, adding to what already was a highly complex argument. One of the early negative reviews, written by H. A. Mason, was entitled "The Illusion of Cogency" and appeared in *Scrutiny*; in a later issue, F. R. Leavis remarked that his reviewer, Mason, told him that the book had "cost him more pain to get through than any other book he had ever tackled." This is an understandable attitude, since *Illusion and Reality* is less a book for reviewing than it is for consulting time and time again in order to profit from the many insights it affords on poetry's genesis and its characteristics. And these insights are not merely of historical interest: indeed, Caudwell's remarks

on the nature of the poetic "sign" prefigures much later work, such as, for example, Michael Riffaterre's *Semiotics of Poetry* (1978); and his notion of the "social ego," or transindividual consciousness, bears comparison with some of Fredric Jameson's ideas in *The Political Unconscious* (1982). Nevertheless, it is true that a cursory reading will not yield these important contributions to aesthetics, or at the very least some of the excurses will defuse their power. The longest and most contentious of these is the section which seeks to trace the evolution of "bourgeois poetry" (chapters 3–6), which, although providing some shrewd critical insights, seems to form a disruptive wedge between the discussion of mimesis at the end of chapter 2 and the resumption of the nature of representation in chapter 7 entitled "The Characteristics of Poetry." The epicenter of *Illusion and Reality,* and most likely the crucible of its original inception, is an investigation into poetry's function within the other great symbolic systems of religion, science, and mathematics, and how these have contributed to humanity's evolution. With this as our focus, we can now turn to a synopsis of the book's essential movement.

Caudwell begins his discussion of how "illusion grows out of reality" by relying on his voluminous reading in biology and cultural anthropology. He remarks on how, in the tribe, the "instincts must be harnessed to the needs of the harvest by a social mechanism," and, after this representation of the harvest in "phantasy" at the group festival ("the matrix of poetry"), the participants are prepared for "the labours necessary for its accomplishment." Poetry in this primitive state helps transform instinctive energy into conscious energy and thus can be termed as something "economic," Caudwell argues. These emotions which are "harnessed" for the production of the harvest are individual as well as collective, in that they remain present in the individual consciousness because the "symbolic world" is social, helping to form what Caudwell calls the "social ego." Even natural phenomena such as a sunset or "the song of the nightingale" belong to this social ego since they are "signs encrusted with social meaning." The workings of ritual and primitive art have similar functions in that both are concerned with "the adaptation of man's emotions to the necessities of social cooperation." Whereas mythology and poetry are "self-regulating" (the illusions are modified to serve the needs of the society), the advent of "true religion" arrests this development and no longer adjusts itself to these needs. "The death of mythology" brings with it the birth of class religion.

It is here in chapter 3 that Caudwell turns to his broad historical sweep of the movement of English poetry, but he returns to poetry's function and its characteristics in chapter 7, taking up again his discussion of mimesis, or representation. He sets up a hierarchy of dynamic oppositions including instinct/environment, emotion/ rationality, poetry/science, illusion/reality, music/ mathematics, and the affective versus cognitive aspects of language. Poetry in Caudwell's scheme is situated between the extreme poles of music and mathematics, poetry becoming music if all referential elements could be eliminated and we were left only with "emotional" sound. There is always, however, a dialectical relation between the object and the attitude struck towards it: "language is stamped everywhere with humanity as well as with man's environment. Just as science is near the environmental pole, so poetry is near the instinctive. . . . Science yearns always towards mathematics, poetry toward music." Here we see the vestiges of Caudwell's original thesis in "Verse and Mathematics." He is at pains in this section of the book to show that the "conscious illusion" of poetry—its construction of a mock reality, a pseudo-statement, in order to strike an emotional attitude—should not be confused with the "delusion" of dream or of true religion. The latter mixes the subjective wish with the objective reality: "It [religion] takes poetic illusions, valued and considered true for their subjective content, and demands that men give them the status of statements symbolic of external reality." The illusions of poetry, unlike religion, have a positive role in helping adapt humanity to its environment. But, Caudwell asks, if poetry's emotional attitudes are transient, what then is their value? The experience (and here we

see in essence the sociobiological stance of Caudwell's thesis) "leaves behind a trace in memory. It is stored by the organism and modifies its action."

Caudwell now moves on to the particularities of language itself, what Marx called the "great instrument" in the fashioning of consciousness, and also how poetic language is related to that of the dream. If language helps constitute reality, then it must be possible to alter reality through language. Wittgenstein is wrong in thinking that language is a "passive photograph of the universe," and while he is correct in assuming a correspondence between a statement and what it refers to, he neglects the correspondence between "the symbols and inner reality," the affective structure. There was no way that Caudwell could have avoided confronting his old mentor Freud, whose theories stand as intermediary between the explication of biological and social being. While acknowledging Freud's findings with regard to the "conflict between man's instincts and environmental reality" and his insights into the comparisons of the dream and the poem, Caudwell is careful to differentiate his theory from that of Freud's. Whereas he agrees that there is a fundamental relationship between the linguistics of dream and that of the poem—displacement, condensation, overdetermination, and latent and manifest content—Caudwell contends that the signs of dream are only, finally, explicable in terms of personal biography. Conversely, the poem is "turned out," is ex-pressed, in signs that belong to the community. And it is not only the referential aspect of the poem, the pseudo-statement, that is recognized because it belongs to a "common perceptual world," but so too is the affective aspect of the poem "recognized" by the "social ego." This latter concept is crucial to Caudwell's whole enterprise. He derives it from the "god" of early ritual and transmutes it into a form of intersubjectivity in which the social basis of consciousness allows for trans-individual emotional utterances. This is why a sunset can be a "social event." Caudwell finally summarizes the difference between the dream and the poem by suggesting that poetry is a form of "inverted dream." The "I" of the poem (the poem is always a lyric in his theory) helps adapt the instincts to the environment, whereas the "I" of the dream attempts to adapt reality to the instincts. The social basis of consciousness requires that poetry be essentially the "socialization of dream." In the final chapter of *Illusion and Reality*, "The Future of Poetry," Caudwell turns aside from his investigation of the symbolic function in human evolution and the characteristics of poetry within that function and takes up the more urgent and contemporary question of how poetry could be like its origins in the harvest festival, a "guide and spur to action." Auden had written in a poem that "poetry makes nothing happen," but it was a central desire of his generation that it could. Caudwell's grand synthesis seemed to offer such a hope.

Auden, in fact, wrote one of the first reviews of *Illusion and Reality* and spoke to such a desire: "We have waited a long time for a Marxist book on the aesthetics of poetry. . . . Now at last Mr. Caudwell has given us such a book." He concludes his review by making a shrewd comparison between Caudwell's book and the "books by Dr. Richards." He was referring to the *Principles of Literary Criticism* (1924), which Caudwell listed in his bibliography, and no doubt to *Science and Poetry* (1926), a book that the young Sprigg must have read since it was reviewed (by T. S. Eliot) in the same issue of *The Dial* in which he had published his first poem. Given his predilections at this time (1927), the very title would have been intriguing enough, let alone the central thesis of how science was displacing the primitive "magical" worldview, and how poetry must still afford an emotional stance with regard to the world. Richards's argument for humanity's need for both scientific (referential) truth as well as an emotional attitude to reality (poetry) would have caught Caudwell's attention. Another of Richards's books, this time in collaboration with C. K. Ogden, is of crucial importance to Caudwell's poetics. In a letter to the Beards, he was careful to defuse any hint of plagiarism when he remarked on the similarities between his manuscript and *The Meaning of Meaning* (1923). He goes on to say that he had "only just read their book" and it is more than likely that some

of the nomenclature and methodology—they had emphasized the importance of symbolization in the organism's adaptation to its environment—was, as Caudwell put it, "coincidental." Much of this theory he was already constructing from his own capacious reading in biology and evolutionary anthropology.

As his bibliography attests, Caudwell read widely in biology, psychology, linguistics, and especially in anthropological investigations into culture: these include works by Edward Sapir, Durkheim, Frazer, Van Gennep, Levy-Bruhl, Lewis Morgan, and Jessie Weston, among others. It would be well beyond the scope of this essay to trace the influence of how all these titles went into the making of *Illusion and Reality,* but what is clear is that they afforded an easy transition to Caudwell's eventual adoption of a Marxian explication of human development. Marx himself had planned to write a book on Morgan's *Ancient Society* (Caudwell lists it in the original 1877 edition) to show how the anthropologists had, quite independently, confirmed the materialist view of history. Engels used his notes for his *Origin of the Family* (1884). Of all Caudwell's variegated reading in this area, Jane Harrison's *Ancient Art and Ritual* (1913) offers a paradigmatic example of the theoretical alliance of cultural anthropology with Marxism. Harrison offers a comprehensive survey of the psychological and biological importance of symbolic projection in ancient art forms, and an intelligent discussion of the psycho-social function of mimesis which is close to Caudwell's own. She concludes her book with a hopeful view of the future when art may once more have a social and collective purpose: "Science," she argues, "has given us back something strangely like a World-Soul, and art is beginning to feel she must utter our emotion towards it." Throughout her discussion of how primitive man attempted to symbolize his world in the realms of religion, art and magic, Harrison stresses also how such endeavor is always driven by material needs.

As if to signal the new method he would now embrace, Caudwell wrote on the verso of a manuscript page of "Verse and Mathematics" a crucial statement by Marx on how he came to a materialist view of human history. In his preface to "A Contribution to the *Critique of Political Economy*," Marx outlined the system and Caudwell took note: "The mode of production of material life conditions the social, political and intellectual life process in general. It is not the consciousness of men that determines their being but, on the contrary, their social being that determines their consciousness. . . ." If this pronouncement had seemed to Caudwell as being a too "mechanical materialist" approach (Caudwell was nothing if not an "interactionist"), suggesting the material base as the only determining factor in human affairs, he would have found modifications in other of Marx's statements, those that incorporated the role of human agency in the construction of their reality. The Third Thesis on Feuerbach reminds us: "The materialist doctrine concerning the changing of [men's] circumstances and education forgets that circumstances are changed by men. . . ." Similarly, Caudwell would have noted that in the First Thesis Marx's critique of "all previous materialism" in which "the object, reality, what we apprehend through our senses, is understood only in the form of *object* or *contemplation*; but not as *sensuous human activity*. . . ." (Marx's emphases). These positions would have confirmed if not replicated the theories that Caudwell was already formulating in his pre-Marxist reading. Finally, another brief text, this time from *Capital*, volume 1, chapter 7 (Caudwell cites the three-volume edition) serves as a Janus-like document: it looks back to Caudwell's reading in evolutionary anthropology's stress on the imaginative function in human evolution and forward to his newly-found philosophy:

Man opposes himself to Nature as one of her own forces. . . . By this acting on the external world and changing it, he at the same time changes his own nature. . . . We presuppose labour in a form that stamps it as exclusively human. A spider conducts operations that resemble those of a weaver, and a bee puts to shame many an architect in the construction of her cells. But what distinguishes the worst architect from the best of bees is this, that the architect raises his structure in imagination before he erects it in reality.

It would be difficult to find a more concise text that speaks to the core of Caudwell's enterprise; how the imaginative process is a vital part of the ongoing dialectical process in humanity's struggle with nature. As he puts it in the last sentence of his book: "Thus art is one of the conditions of man's realisation of himself, and in its turn is one of the realities of man."

THE STUDIES IN A DYING CULTURE

In a letter dated 30 November 1935, Caudwell wrote to Elizabeth Beard from his new address in working-class Poplar, telling her that she must cease writing to him because her queries on aesthetic matters have resulted in his writing a "10,000 word study on 'Beauty and the Beautiful.'" He goes on: "As a matter of fact a book is taking shape which will consist in synthetic studies in particularly interesting aspects of modern culture." This marks the genesis of what became published as *Studies in a Dying Culture* (1938) and *Further Studies in a Dying Culture* (1949). Originally part of this group of essays, *The Crisis in Physics* (1939) and *Romance and Realism* (1970) were published as separate books. The distinction between "Studies" and "Further Studies" and their publication dates have more to do with the publishing industry than with any order of composition; "Beauty," for example, although one of the first written, was published in "Further Studies." As well as this ambiguity about the order of their composition, there has also been some debate as to their overall position within Caudwell's oeuvre. David Margolies (1969) argued for placing *Illusion and Reality* as the most mature text, written after "Studies," and thus a more representative text in the evolution of Caudwell's Marxism. E. P. Thompson (1977), on the other hand, called for a downgrading of *Illusion and Reality* as the prior text, and a corresponding elevation of "Studies" as the more cogent statement of Caudwell's Marxist theory. Since the availability of Caudwell's manuscripts at the Harry Ransom Research Center, the University of Texas, Austin, it has become clear that Caudwell was writing some of the "Studies" at the same time he was revising the manuscript "Verse and Mathematics" which became *Illusion and Reality*. (See Sullivan, 1987, especially the "Appendix," for extensive evidence for such a position.)

There is no doubt that the "Studies" are a more clearly articulated and organized set of texts, and that Caudwell's Marxism (most especially the workings of ideology on cultural production) is a less hurried and more mature version. For example, his notions of the "genotype" and the "instincts" as possible unchanging entities as articulated in *Illusion and Reality*—the main cause for the attack on him in the *Modern Quarterly* "debate" (see bibliography)—is less ambiguous in the "Studies." In "Beauty," for example, we read that "such simple responses to external or internal stimuli *change* from age to age, but in relation to the rapid tempo of social life, there is a consistency about them which leads us to separate them as *hypothetical* entities." (p. 90, *Studies and Further Studies in a Dying Culture,* 1971, italics added.) And again, in "Consciousness," he talks of "conscious mentation, sensibility," consisting of "potential instinct," which he characterizes as a "fictive conception, but methodologically useful, like the 'genotype' in heredity" (p. 196). It seems that in his set of "studies" Caudwell was attempting to refine and clarify some of the conceptual apparatus that went into *Illusion and Reality,* and in true dialectical fashion each project changed the other.

The range of topics in the studies, taking in as they do discussions of relativity physics ("Reality"), neurology ("Consciousness"), comparative religion ("The Breath of Discontent"), and theories of ethics ("Pacifism and Violence"), to select a random few, makes any full discussion of their content well beyond the scope of this essay. It is possible, however, to give a summary of the theoretical matrices informing all these essays, and to explain how these work in a representative few. Although, as stated above, the separation of the essays into "Studies" and "Further Studies" was somewhat arbitrary, the division is useful for analytical purposes. The whole set of them are indissolubly linked by the concept of causality (Caudwell's notebooks show

a sustained interest in this concept); and the question of how the notion of freedom and its relation to the "bourgeois error" of separating subject from object are related to the notion of causality. The "Studies" tend to emphasize the erroneous bourgeois concept of freedom (the key essay here is "Liberty"), whereas the "Further Studies" concentrate more on the chronic separation of the subject-object relation in bourgeois philosophy (the crucial essay here is "Reality"). Encompassing the whole analytic apparatus is Caudwell's deconstruction of "bourgeois ideology." He describes its workings in "Men and Nature," among many other places: "It is not an error in the sense that it can be isolated, as a separate mistake, from every department of culture," but rather it acts like "a pressure from outside," giving to that culture the "characteristic distortion which is not visible to those who still live within the framework of that economy." (*Further Studies,* p. 116). This is no simple "reflective" theory of ideology, in that what Caudwell is suggesting here, and throughout the studies, is that the bourgeois producers of culture, from the novelist (*Romance and Realism*) to the physicist (*The Crisis in Physics*), do not accidentally produce errors, but rather they *necessarily* produce these fabrications due to the "ideological pressure" within which they work.

For example, to take two representative figures from the "Studies," neither G. B. Shaw nor D. H. Lawrence are false prophets because of some deceptive ploy on their part. On the contrary, they are simply propagating the only "ideas" of which they are capable, given the ideological parameters in which they work. These contemporary authors (H. G. Wells, T. E. Lawrence, Shaw, and the other Lawrence) who are chosen to illustrate the illusion of freedom, the meta-illusion in Caudwell's system, are taken as examples because they are also interested in socio-economic problems. Shaw, the "bourgeois Superman," is caught in "the bourgeois intellectual heresy of believing in thought without action," that reality can be changed through "pure wisdom." His plays figure characters as "walking intellects." They are dramas in which "the actors are nothing, the thinkers are everything"; even a character such as the armorer in *Major Barbara* has to be "transformed into a brilliant theoretician before (as Shaw thinks) he can be expressive on the stage." Shaw was an early admirer of Marx's work, but because of his vestigial bourgeois aspirations he became "a good man fallen among Fabians" as Lenin described him. Fabianism allowed him a certain residual "social respectability." Such a compromise is evident (even if unconsciously) in the plays: Shaw, like Major Barbara, ends up by marrying "money, respectability, fame, peaceful reformism and ultimately even Mussolini" (p. 15).

D. H. Lawrence, seemingly Shaw's ideological opposite, actually joins him hand-in-hand when the circle of bourgeois ideology is completed. Shaw's privileging of the intellect leads to a position close to Fascism, Caudwell argues, and Lawrence's promotion of instinctual feeling leads to the same place. They cannot see that both thought and feeling are necessarily interdependent, one heightening the other. Caudwell sums it up succinctly: "Man feels more deeply than the slug because he thinks more." There is a certain sympathy for fellow-novelist Lawrence because he realized that in many ways the modernist experiment was futile, demonstrating the futility of the "pure artist" at a time when society was breaking down. Caudwell maintains that "Lawrence's gospel was purely sociological," and his notebooks record a series of Lawrence's pronouncements on this theme, of how he was "sickened" by the decay of bourgeois relations, which are described in one letter as being "like insects, gone cold, living only for money, for dirt." But what, Caudwell asks, is Lawrence's solution for the reparation of this modern dilemma? He "appeals to the consciousness of men to abandon consciousness," and he is led to this contradictory agenda because, like Shaw, he cannot unite thinking and being. Lawrence illustrates very well the Rousseauesque notion that man is born free, but is everywhere in societal chains; that he is free "in so far as his 'free' instincts, the 'blood,' the 'flesh' are given an outlet." Such an argument leads to the position that man is free "not through, but in *spite* of social relations." This argument is similar Caudwell's critique of

Freud in the study on "Bourgeois Psychology." Somewhat like Marx turning Hegel "the right side up," Caudwell accepts much of the Freudian apparatus and nomenclature, but reverses its essential claims. The psyche, the consciousness and unconsciousness, and their role in human evolution is a given, but rather than forming an "eternal dualism that cannot be resolved," Caudwell insists that this is the very dynamic that drives evolution and culture. It is less a matter of "sublimation," however, than it is "solution," or "adaptation" in this ongoing interplay. Freud cannot see the physiological consequences of his theory, Caudwell insists: the "so-called instincts . . . are unconscious, mechanical, and unaffected by experience . . . they are the material of physiology." Whereas, psychology, which "must be extracted from sociology, not vice versa" must study "all those psychic contents that result from the *modification* of responses by experience" (p. 184, original italics). Like all the other bourgeois ideologues who are critiqued in these essays, Freud suffers from the basic "bourgeois illusion that the individual stands opposed to an unchanging society which trammels him."

In the essay, "Reality: A Study in Bourgeois Philosophy," the crucial essay in *Further Studies*, Caudwell traces the vicissitudes of the subject-object split, which arose initially out of the "basic" illusion of freedom. Some of the results of this dualism are the separation of theory from practice, material from idea, and science from art. Caudwell had read Lenin's *Materialism and Emperio-Criticism* (listed in the bibliography to *Illusion and Reality*) in which phenomenalism, or positivism (what Lenin called "emperio-criticism"), is singled out as a particularly "reactionary" philosophy. Lenin argued that this philosophic position had led to an undermining of everything from common understanding to theories taken up by the "new physics," in which the very existence of matter was being questioned. Lenin's critique, not to mention Caudwell's abiding interest in science, most likely led to his study *The Crisis in Physics* (1939). The other book-length study, *Romance and Realism,* did not appear until 1970. These two seemingly disparate topics of physics and literature come in for the same treatment as the other essays, and offer further evidence of the "decay" of modern culture due to the sundering of the subject-object relation. Theoretical physics may seem the ultimate in objectivity, but it too is produced by "consciousness," as is the novel, a consciousness that is itself produced by certain ideological pressures. Caudwell quotes the scientist Max Planck to make his point: "We are living in a very singular moment in history. It is a moment of crisis, in the literal sense of that word. In every branch of our spiritual and material civilization we seem to have arrived at a critical turning point. . . ." (*The Crisis in Physics,* p. 26. Caudwell uses the same quote in his "Foreword" to the whole set of essays in *Studies in a Dying Culture.*) The "crisis" in physics is at base a philosophical problem, Caudwell argues, a questioning of the very foundations of the "bourgeois world-view"; it is essentially another example of the chronic dualism that infects bourgeois ideology. Although Einstein had addressed the problem of the subject-object relation in his relativity physics, he ultimately remained within the old Newtonian deterministic universe. Contrarily, the "new" physicists working in quantum theory, Jeans, Eddington, and Heisenberg, for example, wanted to proclaim determinism (or causality) extinct; substantiated by Heisenberg's theory of indeterminacy these scientists believed they had re-instigated free will into the universe. In Caudwell's view, both sides demonstrate the bourgeois epistemological dualism, which either manifests itself as the "mechanical materialism" of the old school, or the "idealism" of the new. But, paradoxically, Heisenberg himself proved the theory that when man "practices" on nature he changes it; in that epistemological experiment Heisenberg showed how the "observer," the subject, interpenetrates with the object, in *practice.*

It is the problem of the "observer" in fiction that Caudwell addresses with sustained insight in his study *Romance and Realism.* He had written to the Beards that *This My Hand,* his only serious work of fiction, suffered because the "impartiality" that he had sought was "impossible," and that the "problem of the observer remains the central problem of the novel." *Romance and Realism* suffers from some of the summary treatment of literature that marred *Illusion and Reality* (the Brontës and George Eliot, for example, are contained in a few paragraphs), but his remarks on the form of the novel and its evolution bears comparison with more well known theorists such as Georg Lukács. Remarking on the experimentation with point of view at the end of the nineteenth and the beginning of the twentieth centuries and its relation to the problem of the observer, Caudwell offers the following insight: "It is also not an accident that these authors [James, Hemingway, Joyce, Conrad] are each in some way alien to the culture they describe. . . ." Virginia Woolf and Dorothy Richardson are "aliens in a subtler sense" in that "bourgeois culture . . . was and still mainly is man-made." He goes on to argue that these émigrés write the "significant narrative of their time" partly as a consequence of their alien viewpoint which happens to be congruent with a culture undergoing fragmentation. Nevertheless, despite the many innovations in modernist narrative, and Caudwell cites the "subtlety and complexity" of Henry James, "bourgeois modernism," as Lukács was to call it some years later, suffers from the lack of a critical perspective, a subjective attitude working on an objective reality. The search for the most appropriate point of view is associated with the search for various degrees of detachment, and this stems from the same error that was at the same time afflicting physics. The bourgeois novelist is always striving after "the closed world of physics, independent of the observer." This search for a "closed world of story, reflecting society and yet completely self-determined, and the impossibility of ever succeeding . . . because it is self-contradictory, is really the history of the bourgeois novel" (*Romance and Realism,* p. 57).

In that final, hurried letter to Paul and Elizabeth Beard dated 9 December 1936, a matter of days before he left for Spain, Caudwell described the "Studies" as "imperfect—hasty sketches." Most of them, he goes on, will "have to be rewritten and refined in some way. . . ." Unfortunately, he

CHRISTOPHER CAUDWELL

never had this opportunity, but the work he did leave to us continues to reward reading and rereading.

SELECTED BIBLIOGRAPHY

Works are differentiated here, as in the British Museum Catalogue, under the authors Sprigg and Caudwell. Different editions are cited only if a significant introduction or commentary accompanies the text.

I. AS CHRISTOPHER ST JOHN SPRIGG "Once I did Think." ("The Ecstasy"), *The Dial* (1927); *The Airship: Its Design, History, Operation and Future* (London, 1931); With Henry D. Davis, *Fly with Me: An Elementary Textbook on the Art of Piloting* (London, 1932); *Crime in Kensington* (London, 1933); *Fatality in Fleet Street* (London, 1933); *Pass the Body* (American title of *Crime in Kensington*), (New York, 1933); *British Airways* (London, 1934); *Death of an Airman* (London, 1934); *The Perfect Alibi* (London, 1934); *The Corpse with the Sunburned Face* (novel) (London, 1935); *Death of a Queen: Charles Venables' Fourth Case* (London, 1935); *Great flights* Illustrated from photographs. (London, 1935); (Editor) *Uncanny Stories.* (London, 1936); *Let's Learn to Fly* With Photographs and Drawings. (London, 1937); *The Six Queer Things* (London, 1937)

II. AS CHRISTOPHER CAUDWELL *This My Hand.* (London, 1936); *Illusion and Reality* (London, 1937; New York, 1947; Berlin, 1973); *Studies in a Dying Culture.* With an Introduction by John Strachey. (London, 1938); *The Crisis in Physics.* Edited with an introduction by Professor H. Levy (London, 1939); *Poems* (London, 1939 and 1965); *Further Studies in a Dying Culture.* Edited with a preface by Edgell Rickword. (London, 1949); *Illusion and Reality.* With a biographical note by George Thomson. (New York, 1955); *The Concept of Freedom.* With an introduction by George Thomson. This includes some of the essays from *Studies in a Dying Culture* and some chapters from *The Crisis in Physics.* (London, 1965); *Romance and Realism.* Edited by Samuel Hynes (Princeton, N.J., 1970); *Scenes and Actions* (unpublished prose). Edited with an introduction by Jean Duparc and David Margolies (London, 1986); *Collected Poems.* Edited with Introduction by Alan Young. (Manchester, U.K., 1986); *Studies and Further Studies in a Dying Culture.* With an Introduction by Sol Yurick. (New York, 1971)

III. BIBLIOGRAPHIES AND ARCHIVAL COLLECTIONS. There is no comprehensive bibliography of Caudwell's work, but there are extensive bibliographies in Pawling (1989), in Sullivan (1987), and in Young and Munton (1981), the details of which are given below. Caudwell's manuscripts are housed in the Harry Ransom Center, The University of Texas, Austin. Some of this material was published in *Scenes and Actions* (1986), and *Collected Poems* (1986), but a vast amount of manuscript still remains unpublished.

IV. CRITICAL STUDIES. Jane Harrison, *Ancient Art and Ritual* (New York, 1913); Scott Buchanan. *Poetry and Mathematics.* (New York, 1929); Sigmund Freud. *New Introductory Lectures on Psycho-Analysis,* trans. W. J. H. Sprott (New York, 1933); N. B. Bukharin, "Poetry, Poetics, and the Problems of Poetry in the USSR," in *Problems of Soviet Literature: Reports and Speeches at the First Soviet Writers Congress.* (London, 1935); Paul Beard, "Some Recent Novels," *The New English Weekly* (1936); W. H. Auden, Review of *Illusion and Reality. New Verse* (1937); Paul Beard, "Views and Reviews: *Illusion and Reality,*" *The New English Weekly* (1937); H. A. Mason, "The Illusion of Cogency," *Scrutiny* (1938).

Louis Harap, "Christopher Caudwell, Marxist Critic, Poet and Soldier," *Worker* (1946). Sigmund Freud, *Delusion and Dream: and Other Essays,* ed. and introd. Philip Rieff (Boston, 1956).

Sigmund Freud, *Civilization and Its Discontents* (New York, 1962); Sigmund Freud, *The Future of an Illusion,* ed. James Strachey (Garden City, N.Y., 1964); Frederick Benson, *Writers in Arms: The Literary Impact of the Spanish Civil War* (New York, 1967); George Moberg, "Christopher Caudwell: An Introduction to his Life and Work." Ph.D. Dissertation, Columbia University, (1968); Margolies, David, *The Function of Literature: a study of Christopher Caudwell's Aesthetics* (New York, 1969).

Georg Lukács, *The Meaning of Contemporary Realism,* trans. John and Necke Mander (London, 1972); Sir James George Frazer, *The Golden Bough: a study in Magic and Religion* (abridged edition). (London and Basingstoke, 1976); Stanley Hyman, *The Armed Vision.* (New York, 1955); Samuel Lynn Hynes *The Auden Generation* (London, 1976); B. Bergonzi, *Reading the Thirties* (Pittsburgh, 1978).

Fredric Jameson, *The Political Unconscious* (Ithaca, 1982).

Leonard Jackson, *The Dematerialisation of Karl Marx.* (London, 1994)

V. MODERN QUARTERLY DEBATE ON CAUDWELL I. A. Richards, *Science and Poetry.* (London, 1926).

John Strachey, *The Coming Struggle for Power.* (London, 1934); Stephen Spender, "Review of *Illusion and Reality.*" (1937); Stephen Spender and John Lehmann (eds.). *Poems for Spain,* introd. Stephen Spender (London, 1939).

George Thomson, *Marxism and Poetry.* (New York, 1946); Alick West, "On *Illusion and Reality*" *Communist Review* (1948); George Thomson, *Aeschylus and Athens, a Study in the Social Origins of Drama.* (London, 1949).

Alan Bush et al. "On Caudwell and Marxist Aesthetics," *Modern Quarterly* (1951); "The Caudwell Discussion," *Modern Quarterly* (1951); George Thomson. "In Defense of Poetry," *Modern Quarterly,* (1951); Oscar Thomson. "The Poetic Instant," *Modern Quarterly* (1948); Maurice Cornforth, "Caudwell and Marxism," *Modern Quarterly* (1950–1951).

I. A. Richards, *Principles of Literary Criticism* (London, 1967); Alick West, *One Man in His Time: An Autobiography* (London, 1969); Ludwig Wittgenstein, *Tractatus Logico-Philosophicus* (London, 1969).

C. K. Ogden and I. A. Richards, *The Meaning of Meaning: A Study of the Influence of Language Upon Thought and of the Science of Symbolism, with Supplementary Essays by B. Malinowski and F. G. Crookshank* (London, 1972); Maynard Solomon (ed.), *Marxism and Art: Essays Classical and Contemporary* (New York, 1973); Francis Mulhern, "The Marxist Aesthetics of Christopher Caudwell," *New Left Re-*

CHRISTOPHER CAUDWELL

view (1974); Eileen Sypher, "Towards a Theory of the Lyric: Georg Lukács and Christopher Caudwell," *Praxis* (1976); E. P. Thompson, "Caudwell." *The Socialist Register* (London, 1977); Raymond Williams, *Marxism and Literature.* (Oxford, U.K. 1977); Michael Riffaterre, *The Semiotics of Poetry* (Bloomington, 1978); Robert C. Tucker (ed.), *The Marx-Engels Reader* 2nd ed., (New York, 1978).

A. Young and A. Munton, *Seven Writers of the English Left: A Bibliography of Literature and Politics, 1916–1980* (New York, 1981); Helena Sheehan, *Marxism and the Philosophy of Science.* (Atlantic Highlands, N.J., 1985); Robert Sullivan, *Christopher Caudwell* (London, 1987); Christopher Pawling, *Christopher Caudwell: Towards a Dialectical Theory of Literature* (New York, 1989).

BRUCE CHATWIN

(1940–1989)

Thomas Wright

IT IS DIFFICULT to define a man who spent his life trying to avoid such definition. Complex, reticent, and endlessly evasive, Bruce Chatwin's personality was a colorful collection of masks and bizarre contradictions. He never stayed in one place or adopted one pose or intellectual position long enough to be given a label: he was always traveling somewhere else, always on the move.

As an author, Chatwin is no less elusive. Within his works the boundaries between fact and fiction and intellectual disciplines are dissolved, and each of his books seems to contradict its predecessor. Chatwin even regarded the most open-ended label of "writer" with annoyance: every kind of classification was a shackle.

Yet despite this, it is possible to broadly define Chatwin as an energetic and ambitious intellectual adventurer who used the genres of travel writing, the journalistic essay, the short story, and the novel to explore his favorite preoccupations and ideas. Is the life of the nomad or the life of the settler more congenial to our nature? Is there an alternative to Western materialism? What is the relationship between language and the earth? These are a few of the vast questions addressed in his books.

We can also identify certain recurring patterns and typical characteristics within Chatwin's writing that make his books fairly homogeneous despite their generic diversity. One of his favorite devices is to juxtapose and forge connections between apparently disparate subjects and ideas. In the "From the Notebooks" section in *The Songlines* (1987) Chatwin brings together Bedouin and Moorish proverbs, quotations from arcane texts, lines from poets such as Charles Baudelaire and William Blake, and excerpts from his own traveling diaries to illustrate the theme of man's innate restlessness.

This intellectual habit reveals the generalizing and fundamentally Platonic nature of Chatwin's thinking: he is always looking for the archetype beneath a series of examples. In every culture, he suggests, men have understood the restlessness of their species: although Buddha and Blaise Pascal lived at different times and in different places, they were essentially talking about the same thing. Chatwin was always trying to identify universal themes and ideas: he thought that all stories are, at bottom, traveler's tales and that the history of the world is the struggle between the settler (Cain) and the nomad (Abel). With characteristic ambition, he searched for a language with which to discuss human nature as it exists outside of history.

Chatwin was a brilliant amateur and a polymath: he drew on science, literature, mythology, and countless other branches of learning in order to create that language and to illustrate his theories. He has been likened to a nineteenth-century synthesizer of knowledge, but the best comparison is perhaps with men of the late English Renaissance. Like Sir Thomas Browne, Robert Burton, or Jeremy Taylor (all of whom are mentioned in his works), Chatwin thought that knowledge consisted of finding correspondences between things; he also believed that there was no fundamental difference between the arts and the sciences. In his writings, which employ characteristic Renaissance techniques and conceits such as the metaphor and the microcosm, Chatwin tries to return to their world: a lost Eden before the division and specialization of intellectual disciplines.

It is hardly surprising that Chatwin's work has frequently been criticized by specialists and experts, who argue that it lacks scholarly rigor and a sound scientific foundation. This, however, is to misunderstand the nature of Chatwin's endeavor, which was utterly opposed to the inductive method of modern science. Chatwin was not interested in the patient accumulation and examination of facts: he begins with a poetic idea and then searches for evidence to prove it (which, officially at least, is the opposite of scientific method). He thought that, in themselves, facts did not amount to much; indeed, without a theory or a story to sort and shape them, he believed them to be meaningless.

It is in this context that we can appreciate another essential characteristic of Chatwin's authorship: his fondness for myths and stories. Chatwin believed that stories conferred meaning on the chaos of experience: the history of a particular place gave it significance; the facts of a person's life only made sense when they could be grasped as a narrative. His writings are crammed full of stories, anecdotes, and fragments of folktales; he also frequently dramatizes scenes in which a storyteller enthralls a listener. Chatwin, who was himself a great raconteur, has a similar relationship with his readers: the experience of reading his books is rather like listening to a traditional storyteller or a dazzling Socratic mentor.

As many of his friends remarked, Chatwin did not really care whether a story was true or not, only that it was interesting. He exaggerated and embellished the tales he heard on his travels, and in his books he continually conflates fact and fiction. On being asked to identify the line between fact and fiction in his works, he once confessed: "I don't know where it is. I've always written very close to the line" (Ignatieff, p. 24). This is an aspect of Chatwin's work that has troubled many critics and readers, but it is entirely consistent with his poetic and unscientific attitude to reality. He favored the Kantian notion that the world outside cannot be understood, or unveiled, by human reason: we can only ever project onto it the ideas and fantasies of our minds.

Chatwin was, then, a gifted maverick intellectual and a marvelous fabulist. To fully understand the power and appeal of his books, however, we must consider a third attribute of his authorship, without which he would perhaps be little

more than a second-rate writer. Chatwin was also a prose stylist of genius. His lapidary prose, which has been variously described as "pared down," "laconic," and "chiseled," provides the perfect counterpoint to his extravagant and abstract speculations. While his theories operate at a highly generalized level, Chatwin's style brings details into sharp focus: like his photography, it vividly evokes landscapes, characters, and scenes and brilliantly captures colors, patterns, textures, and surfaces. What is special about Chatwin's writing is this relationship between the generalized ideas and the intensely specific style: when there is harmony between them, Chatwin can convince you of anything, and when there is friction it creates a kind of intellectual fire.

LIFE

Charles Bruce Chatwin was born in Sheffield, in northern England, on 13 May 1940, the son of Margharita and Charles Chatwin, a lawyer from Birmingham. Although most of his ancestors were solid middle-class "Birmingham worthies," he could also number among them a desert traveler and a sailor. After a nomadic childhood spent, for the duration of the war, with various members of his family, the Chatwins settled first in the Birmingham suburbs and then in a farming village outside of the city.

In his youth, Chatwin attended the prestigious English public school Marlborough College, where he was, he later remarked with characteristic exaggeration, "considered to be a dimwit and dreamer . . . and was bottom of every class" (*Anatomy of Restlessness,* 1995, p. 10). Far more important to him than the education he received there was the reading he did alone. A local bookseller gave him an anthology that contained extracts from the works of Baudelaire, Arthur Rimbaud, John Aubrey, and Sir Thomas Browne; he also read Robert Byron's travel book *The Road to Oxiana* (1937). These writers exercised a great influence over Chatwin, and he came to regard Byron's work as a sacred text.

Unlike most of his school contemporaries, Chatwin did not attend university. Instead he began full-time employment as a porter at

Sotheby and Co., the fine-art auctioneers. Within seven years he was appointed head of the Impressionist Department and soon after became one of the youngest directors in the firm's history. Despite his spectacular success, the work bored him and wore him out. In 1966 his eyesight started to suffer, and he resigned. Although the older Chatwin was always intensely critical of the art world and of his younger "capitalist" self, his experience at Sotheby's was important for his writing. He learned to weave elaborate stories around objects, and he encountered a variety of interesting and eccentric collectors, some of whom appear in his books. Susannah Clapp (1997) has also suggested that Chatwin's laconic and intensely visual prose was influenced by Impressionism and by his experience as a Sotheby's cataloger.

Chatwin, who was a bisexual man, married Elizabeth Chanler in 1965; the couple settled in Edinburgh, where, after a period of traveling, Chatwin decided to take a university course in archaeology. His brief experience of academia was not a happy one: he never completed his course and left after a few rather dismal years. "Penniless, depressed, a total failure at the age of thirty-three" (*Anatomy,* p. 13), he was rescued by Francis Wyndham, an assistant editor at the *Sunday Times Magazine,* who offered him a job there as arts adviser. This led to a successful career as a freelance journalist, which ended, or so the story goes, when Chatwin sent a telegram to the magazine composed of the words "Gone to Patagonia." There he would research the book that launched his career as a writer, a career that produced six books and lasted only twelve years. Chatwin died of AIDS in 1989; he was forty-eight years old.

Childish, energetic, camp, seductive, chameleonlike, ambitious, lonely, melodramatic, restless, inspired, inspiring—these are a few of the epithets that have been used to describe Chatwin's personality. One thing that all observers agree on is that his character was inherently contradictory. He was an ascetic aesthete, a cosmopolitan Englishman, and a husband who enjoyed several gay affairs. Most people also agree that his contradictoriness manifested itself in his books.

These are often ambiguous and open-ended, and they dramatize his inner conflicts (such as that between the ascetic and the aesthete). His fondness for paradoxes, non sequiturs, and juxtapositions could also be mentioned here.

Other aspects of Chatwin's personality and biography have a strong bearing on his writing. The fact that he was thoroughly middle-class is significant. In one interview he remarked "If you travel, you escape being labelled with class stereotypes. [As] I come from a very middle-class family . . . travel was an immense relief" (Ignatieff, p. 32). It has often been said that he was on the run from the homosexual side of his nature (an interpretation that was anathema to Chatwin, who disdained the label of "gay man" and dismissed the idea that one's sexuality determined one's character). It is equally plausible to suggest, however, that he was trying to escape his social background, something that was (and still is) a far more important indicator of character in England than sexuality. It is interesting to note that Chatwin was addicted to telling tales about himself and his origins: it was as though he was trying to invent for himself a new personality.

Chatwin was also probably fleeing from his nationality, as he admitted to being very uneasy about his Englishness. Like many English writers, such as Norman Douglas and Lord Byron, he traveled in order to get away from the rather claustrophobic atmosphere of English society. Many characteristics of Chatwin's writing appear distinctly, almost deliberately, un-English, such as his boundless enthusiasm and his passion for ideas. Yet other attributes of his writing reveal a thoroughly English cast of mind: his lack of interest in his own or in others' psychology and his tendency to focus on ideas or objects rather than on people. It has been said that it is the Englishman's dream to be always busy: to never stand or pause to reflect; Chatwin realized this dream.

Other attributes of Chatwin's character that are important for his writing are his gifts as a storyteller, conversationalist, and actor. He was, Salman Rushdie wrote, "a magnificent raconteur of Scheherazadean inexhaustibility" (*Imaginary*

Homelands, p. 237), and his books are full of tales, anecdotes, and character sketches. They also contain numerous examples of "oral" forms such as the dialogue and the anecdotal set piece. Chatwin's skills as an actor and a mimic were legendary: at school he excelled in women's roles, and his impersonations were so good and so camp that he earned the nickname "Chatwina." These skills are often on display in his books, particularly when he reproduces the voices of other people. Finally, we should remember that Chatwin was an autodidact because it explains the highly original and unsystematic nature of his thinking.

EARLY WRITINGS

While studying at Edinburgh, Chatwin started to write a book on nomads with the provisional title *The Nomadic Alternative.* This ambitious work, which was to have been part popular science and part polemic against Western materialism, was never completed although Chatwin struggled with it for several years. Sections of the book did appear, however, in articles that Chatwin wrote in the early 1970s (these have been republished in his two collections of posthumous miscellaneous pieces *What Am I Doing Here* (1998) and *Anatomy*). These pieces give us an idea of the content, scope, and style of Chatwin's unfinished magnum opus.

Inspired by the desire to comprehend his own restlessness, Chatwin set out to understand what it was that made men travel. His characteristically bold and universalizing conclusion is that we have a natural instinct to move; he illustrated his theory with "evidence" plundered from books on history, literature, science, and anthropology. In the polemical part of the book he suggests that nomads are morally and physically superior to settlers and that their societies have proved to be more enduring. According to Chatwin, men who stay still tend to become violent and insane; he argued that these, and most other afflictions, could be cured by a walk: one of his mottoes was *solvitur ambulando*—it is solved by walking. *The Nomadic Alternative* was a combination of abstract theorizing, wild speculation ("Footballers

are little aware that they too are pilgrims. The ball they boot symbolises a migrant bird." *Anatomy,* p. 106) and long catalogs of quotations and illustrations gathered together from thousands of sources. It had neither scholarly rigor (academics openly derided Chatwin's ideas) nor the fluency and accessibility of writing intended for the general reader: Chatwin was unsure of both his audience and his style.

While his ideas sounded impressive when he discussed them in conversation with friends and publishers (he was commissioned to write the book by the publisher Jonathan Cape), he lacked the necessary experience as a writer to express them or give them a coherent form. As Chatwin himself later commented, "It was so much a young man's book, with a tendency to . . . cram everything in. I finally consigned it to the dustbin because it was absolutely unreadable" (Shakespeare, p. 219). Fortunately Chatwin's wife retrieved the manuscript and miraculously produced it when he came to write *The Songlines.* That work includes several passages from the manuscript, and it is the closest he came to writing his great nomad book.

Chatwin's writing improved enormously during his time as a journalist for the *Sunday Times Magazine.* He learned how to express his ideas pithily and persuasively and how to evoke a place or a character with an epigram and a couple of vivid images. He also acquired the skill of spotting a good story from stray pieces of information and of simplifying complicated intellectual concepts. He was at his best interviewing people with whom he felt a natural sympathy: his profile of André Malraux—"a talented young aesthete who transformed himself into a great man" (*What Am I Doing Here,* p. 114) is perhaps his finest piece. Malraux, he tells us, is an artist in life and an intellectual who "is unclassifiable, which in a world of -isms and -ologies is also unforgivable" (p. 119). In his books, Chatwin would prove himself to be a master of the short, vivid character sketch; it was an art that he perfected as a journalist.

Journalism forced Chatwin to write concisely, quickly, and accessibly. It also encouraged him to develop an authorial persona, something that his early nomadic writings lacked. Having acquired these skills and attributes, Chatwin soon tired of journalistic work and looked to express himself in other genres. He continued, however, to write journalistic pieces right up to his death; some are collected in *What Am I Doing Here* and *Anatomy of Restlessness*.

IN PATAGONIA *(1977)*

Chatwin was commissioned by the *Sunday Times Magazine* to write a piece on the legendary outlaw Butch Cassidy, who had sought refuge for a few years in Patagonia. *In Patagonia* grew out of this assignment although Chatwin, being Chatwin, later claimed that it had been a spur-of-the-moment decision made during a conversation with a friend in Paris. Seeing a map of Patagonia on her wall he had remarked "I've always wanted to go there." "So have I," the friend replied, "go there for me," and Chatwin went. (*Anatomy,* p. 14).

As we learn from the opening pages of the book, Chatwin was also inspired to go to Patagonia by the story of the life of Charley Millward, his grandmother's cousin. Millward had found there the carcass of a brontosaurus (actually it was a mylodon or giant sloth, but the young Chatwin was convinced that it was a dinosaur), and Chatwin wished to revisit the sight of his relative's remarkable discovery. Thus he could describe the book as a Romantic quest: "the oldest kind of traveller's tale . . . in which the narrator leaves home and goes to a far country in search of a legendary beast" (*Patagonia Revisited,* with Paul Theroux, 1985, p. 17).

During this pilgrimage to his family's past, Chatwin came across a dazzling variety of tales and curiosities: stories concerning Cassidy and other outlaws, the intriguing history of the principality of Araucania and Patagonia, everyday episodes that capture the history of South America in miniature, and fascinating languages that link the Patagonian Indians to their soil. Along the way there are characteristic speculations about literature, Western materialism, and the nature of man; we also encounter a huge cast of marvelous characters.

Chatwin tends to see the Patagonians as archetypal figures (we meet an "English Gentleman" and a number of "tipo Gauchos"), and he paints them with one or two broad strokes: "The driver was a cheerful tough, his feet smelling of cheese. He liked Pinochet" (p. 100). He also offers us several racial types: we meet a Russian and a Scot who apparently embody the spirit and the essential characteristics of their native countries. These and other characters are exiles that live both in Patagonia and (in their imaginations) their native countries. They populate the sparse and empty South American landscape with memories and images from "home"; if they didn't do this, one senses that the emptiness of Patagonia would drive them insane. Their stories are sad and deeply moving; they give the book its slightly melancholy and elegiac atmosphere.

In Patagonia is loosely held together by the story of Chatwin's personal quest and by certain recurring themes and preoccupations, such as his meditations on restlessness and the idea of home, and on the influence of landscape on the human character. Like Osip Mandelstam's *Journey to Armenia* (English edition, with introduction by Chatwin, 1980) and Ernest Hemingway's *In Our Time* (1924)—two books that Chatwin took with him in his rucksack—it is organized into short, impressionistic chapters (ninety-seven in all). Critics have compared the arrangement of the book to a cubist painting or a constructivist "assemblage." Another comparison could be with those multicolored computer-generated fractal patterns in which a shape is repeated endlessly, because each of the chapters reads like a microcosm of the whole.

Despite the book's affinity with the quest romance, its chapters are not linked by a conventional linear narrative. The book is more digressive than progressive, and it proceeds at a measured pace. It can be compared to Edgar Allan Poe's *The Narrative of Arthur Gordon Pym* (1838), a book that is mentioned by Chatwin; to a slow-moving Western; or to a rambling and fragmentary road movie. There is something hypnotic about its unhurried pace: it generates its own momentum and carries the reader along with it.

The book's slow flow evokes the Patagonian landscape itself: an empty, inhospitable and waterless place in which little moves or grows. Chatwin brilliantly conjures up the scenery in short, clipped sentences: "The landscape was empty. The hills went gold and purple in the setting sun. . . . Round the shacks broken bottles glinted" (pp. 66–70). His style owes a great deal to Hemingway, Mandelstam, and Flaubert; one important stylistic influence that has not previously been identified is that of the Argentinian writer Jorge Luis Borges. Laconic lines such as the following could have come from any of Borges's gaucho tales: "One night a knife flashed on an empty street, but the blade hit the watch in his waistcoat pocket and the hired killer fled" (p. 133).

Chatwin's prose can also be compared to his photography. He has a wonderful knack of focusing on a significant detail and of capturing a striking and memorable image; he also lingers long and lovingly on surfaces and textures: we can almost touch the corrugated iron, tin, glass, granite he describes. His imagination was intensely visual and he aspired to "pure description": he attempted to turn the intrusive authorial "I" of the conventional travel writer into the "eye" of the detached photographer. "The eye" is a phrase used in the art world to describe those who immediately recognize the beauty and genuineness of an artwork: Chatwin had "the eye" in this and in many other senses.

In Patagonia won the Hawthornden Prize and the E. M. Forster award, and it received lavish praise from reviewers. Some critics confessed, however, to being rather bewildered by it. While much of its matter was typical of a conventional "travel book" it was unorthodox in, among other things, its failure to mention the more mundane details of Chatwin's trip such as how he had traveled around. Its style too is sometimes closer to a work of fiction: some of the scenes border on the fantastic, and many of the characters are caricatures. In fact, the real people on whom Chatwin's characters are based, as well as subsequent travel writers, have accused Chatwin of making up a great deal of *In Patagonia.*

This confusion about the generic nature of the book derives from an ignorance of the history of travel writing and a misunderstanding about Chatwin's art. While it is true that from the seventeenth century onward travel writers set out to observe foreign lands with scientific detachment and to relate useful and accurate information to their readers, there is an older tradition of travel writing that is much closer to romance fiction. In this tradition, authors such as Marco Polo and Sir John Mandeville instinctively blend fact with fiction and offer readers a poetic and mythical rather than a scientific understanding of the world. Chatwin revived this ancient tradition partly because he was drawn to the marvelous and the fantastic and partly because he favored the Kantian notion that the world outside cannot be revealed by human reason. As reality cannot be laid bare, it must be created: the word precedes the world, the land is called forth by the song.

Bound up with this notion is Chatwin's idea that Patagonia is not just a geographical entity—an endless desert to be mapped out scientifically—but also an invisible country that exists in people's minds. And this is the country that his book describes: the Patagonia that lives in the imagination of its exiled inhabitants and in the imagination of the world. He discusses, for instance, the Western "idea" of Patagonia as the outer limit of the human world and writes about the country's representation in literature. Chatwin later described himself as a "literary traveller" who was excited as much by a literary reference as, for instance, a rare animal (*Patagonia Revisited,* p. 7). *In Patagonia* bears this out.

Readers who travel to the "real" Patagonia expecting to find a world similar to that of Chatwin's book will therefore be disappointed. Yet the fact that they will go out in search of it, and the fact that they will read the country through his eyes, demonstrates the poetical power of his writing. For countless readers, Chatwin's invisible Patagonia has replaced reality, and thus is the famous Romantic claim justified: poets really are the unacknowledged legislators of the world.

In the writing of *In Patagonia,* Chatwin sought to avoid other elements of the conventional travel book: exoticism, purple prose, dull historical chapters, and what he called "the cheap ironic asides that are the stock-in-trade of the travelling writer" (Introduction to Sybille Bedford's *A Visit to Don Octavio,* London, 1990, p. 12). However, despite the fact that the book was hailed as an "original" masterpiece on its publication, it also has a number of twentieth-century precursors. English travel writers of the 1920s and 1930s such as Graham Greene, D. H. Lawrence, and Robert Byron compiled miscellaneous, fragmentary, and essayistic works in which they continually leaped back and forth over the line that divides fact from fiction. Like them, Chatwin was drawn to the genre because he found it capacious enough to accommodate his endless curiosity and his fertile imagination.

THE VICEROY OF OUIDAH *(1980)*

Chatwin's second book disappointed the expectations of those who were waiting for another *In Patagonia,* and it is a book that continues to surprise many of his devotees. As Chatwin explained in a preface to the first edition, he had originally intended to write a biography of the book's hero, the Brazilian slave trader Dom Francisco de Souza, who traveled to the West African country of Dahomey at the beginning of the nineteenth century. Chatwin's research in Africa was interrupted when he became caught up in a military coup (an account of which can be found under the title "A Coup: A Story" in *What Am I Doing Here*) and, in any case, the material he had collected was too patchy for a biography. Convinced, however, that Dom Francisco's story was worth telling, Chatwin wrote it as a novel.

That story is easily summarized. Having arrived in Dahomey, Dom Francisco helps to depose the king. For this act, he is rewarded by the new king with wealth, the title "viceroy of Ouidah," a monopoly over the slave trade, and a

seraglio of women. In old age, however, he loses both the king's favor and his sanity. On his death, he leaves around a hundred children whose descendants gather together at the beginning of the novel to mark the anniversary of his decease.

Dom Francisco is a nomad who believes "any set of four walls to be a tomb or a trap"; he prefers "to float over the most barren of open spaces" (p. 56). A hard, ruthless man not unlike one of the "tipo Gauchos" from *In Patagonia,* he leaves those he encounters with the sensation that they have brushed with death. Dom Francisco's great mistake is to settle down and become a man of property in Dahomey. Chatwin vividly evokes his claustrophobia and his burning desire to escape that country, a desire that in the end drives him mad. Africa too is to blame for his demise. "Gradually [it] swamped him and drew him under. Perhaps out of loneliness, perhaps in despair of fighting the climate, he stepped into the habits of the natives" (p. 79).

In the novel, Chatwin again focuses on the visual rather than the psychological. He presents his story as a "sequence of cinematic images . . . strongly influenced by the films of Werner Herzog," who would eventually direct a film based on the novel called *Cobra Verde* (*What Am I Doing Here,* pp. 137–138). Chatwin's prose is sparse and economical. The opening pages are as laconic as a medieval chronicle, and the dryness and emptiness of Dom Francisco's native Brazil are evoked in terse sentences that might have come from *In Patagonia:* "Then the clouds went away. The sun quivered in a blue metal sky. The mud cracked" (*Viceroy,* p. 49).

A number of French influences on Chatwin's style have been identified: Jean Racine, Honoré de Balzac—whose *Eugene Grandet* (1833) gave Chatwin the idea of producing a book without chapter divisions—and, in particular, Gustave Flaubert. Francis Wyndham has noted how similar Chatwin's single-sentence paragraphs (while revising the book Chatwin condensed a page of prose into a single line) are to those of Flaubert's. It was also to Flaubert that Chatwin turned for inspiration when he wrote the exotic African scenes of his novel, many of which read like translations of Flaubert's *Salammbô* (1862).

"There were," Chatwin writes of a meal, "phallic sweetmeats of tamarind and tapioca, ambrosias, bolos, babas, and piles of golden patisseries." Here is Chatwin's portrait of Dahomey's "new" king: "His fingernails curled like cocks' feathers. His loincloth was purple and his sandals were of twisted gold wire. At his feet were the heads of a boy and girl. . . . (pp. 84–85).

As this last quotation suggests, Chatwin's exotic style, which also owes a great deal to the King James translation of the Bible, is particularly effective at evoking scenes of horror and barbarity. *The Viceroy* is full of such scenes: we are told, for example, that the "new" king "drank from skulls [and] spat into skulls. Skulls formed the feet of the throne, the sides of his bed and the path that lead to the bed-chamber" (p. 98). As Nicholas Murray has pointed out in his excellent book on Chatwin, writers such as Alfred, Lord Tennyson and Sir Richard Burton had already established Dahomey "as a place in the literary imagination which functioned as an image of extreme barbarism" (*Bruce Chatwin*, p. 52); Chatwin continued this tradition.

Although the novel was greeted with almost universal acclaim, Chatwin thought that its detached baroque language and its terrifying scenes of violence and excess repelled many people; what readers have found particularly disturbing is the combination of the two. Like his protagonist, Chatwin seems to view "each fresh atrocity with a glassy smile" (p. 97): he gazes at it dispassionately and then paints it in gorgeous jeweled prose. He refrains from passing moral judgment on the scenes he describes here and indeed in the vast majority of his books. His amoral attitude to writing was not unlike that of Flaubert or a late-nineteenth-century aesthete: he is reported to have remarked of the hideous scenes in *The Viceroy* "it's all color eventually."

Soon after its publication, Chatwin said that the book was probably the best he would ever write; few of his readers have agreed. It failed to match the success of *In Patagonia,* and it has always been the least popular of Chatwin's books. This is partly because of the dark subject matter and Conradian pessimism but also because it belongs to a tradition of French writing that is unfamiliar and alien to many English and American readers.

ON THE BLACK HILL *(1982)*

In the early 1980s, Chatwin was still widely known as the highly original "travel writer" of *In Patagonia.* The label irritated him so much that he "decided to write something about people who never went out" (Ignatieff, p. 27). He was also inspired to write *On the Black Hill* for deeper and more personal reasons. "No man can wander without a base," he once remarked in an interview, ". . . [and I regard] the Welsh border . . . as what Proust calls the soil on which I still may build" (Shakespeare, pp. 375–376). The reference to Proust is apposite because in the novel Chatwin brings the world of childhood, and of a child's attachment to a particular place, to vivid and magical life. We see the world of the Welsh borders through the eyes of the novel's heroes, the twins Benjamin and Lewis Jones; by the end of it, we feel that we know their world as well as we know our own. This is a considerable achievement for a writer who was famously uneasy about the idea of home.

The rhythm of life on the Welsh borders is regulated by the changing seasons. Time moves slowly and in a cyclical pattern: it is completely out of synch with the linear movement of history. While the novel is in part a microcosmic chronicle of the twentieth century in the manner of Anthony Burgess's *Earthly Powers* (1980), history is something that happens elsewhere: in London, Nagasaki, and in the newspapers. The borderers understand the world they inhabit, and the movement of time within it, through the King James Bible, which is quoted throughout the book. As V. S. Pritchett remarked, their imagination "is mythical and Biblical": they see themselves "as travellers to the 'Abiding City' of God." They also display attributes of what Chatwin called a Celtic sensibility: a reverence for nature and a fondness for curious superstitions that demonstrate their belief that the universe is enchanted and alive. Like Chatwin's Patagonian exiles, their invisible or "mythical world lives side by side with reality" (Pritchett, *Lasting Impressions,* pp. 42–46).

Curiously it is the mythical world of the borderers' imagination that draws them extremely close to nature and connects them to their soil. Chatwin's language too brings their landscape close to us: "a carriage-drive looped downhill through stands of oaks and chestnuts. Fallow deer browsed under the branches, flicking their tales at the flies . . . human voices scared them, and their white scuts bobbed away through the bracken" (pp. 45–46). In passages such as this a rich exchange is set up between the world of nature and the world of words, an exchange that is one of Chatwin's great themes; after reading the book, we start to see the natural world in high-resolution detail. It has been said that it is the task of poets to restore the natural world to us, a world from which we have been separated by science and post-Descartian philosophy. This is precisely what the prose of *On the Black Hill* achieves; it is Chatwin's great song of the earth.

Chatwin establishes a vital connection between words and the world not through naturalism or realism (the literary equivalents of objective scientific analysis) but through a number of "artificial" fictional devices. The most obvious of these is his use of the myth of the doppelgänger, or double. Although the relationship between Chatwin's twins (or "Chat's twins") is certainly not as antagonistic as that between Frankenstein and the monster or Doctor Jekyll and Mr. Hyde, Lewis and Benjamin are distant literary descendants of such figures. Each of them knows when the other is worried or in pain, and they converse without uttering a word. Typically their intimacy is evoked with a striking image: "if either twin caught sight of himself . . . he mistook his own reflection for his other half. So now, when Benjamin poised his razor at the ready and glanced up at the glass, he had the sensation of slitting Lewis's throat" (p. 87).

Although the novel was very well received, certain commentators criticized Chatwin for writing a sentimental and unrealistic fairy tale of modern life and of inventing a remote and quaint rural land called "Chatwinshire" that would appeal to metropolitan readers. It is obvious, however, Chatwin never intended to write a realistic work. He did not believe that realism was the most effective way of evoking "reality," particularly the "reality" of a group of people who live both on the land and in the imagination. The novel was awarded both the James Tait Black Prize and the Whitbread Award for first novel (the judges either forgot *The Viceroy* or regarded it as a work of nonfiction). The book's tremendous critical and popular success was enhanced by its adaptation for both the stage and the cinema a few years after its publication. It remains one of Chatwin's best-loved books.

THE SONGLINES *(1987)*

In 1984 Chatwin traveled to the Central Australian desert. He wanted to explore there the aboriginal concept of the "Songlines," a concept that struck him as the most fascinating he had ever come across. His "novel" is a chronicle of his physical journey through Australia and his intellectual journey toward an understanding of the Songlines and their significance. The narrator (who is called Bruce) is the reader's representative within the book: his struggle to comprehend the Songlines becomes our own.

In the novel, the Songlines are defined in various ways by different characters: the closest that Chatwin ever came to a concise definition was in an interview he gave at the time of the book's publication. "The Songlines," he explained, "are a labyrinth of invisible pathways which stretch to every corner of Australia. Aboriginal creation myths tell of the legendary totemic ancestors . . . who create themselves and then set out on immense journeys across the continent, singing the name of everything that crosses their path and so singing the world into existence. . . . The whole of Australia can be read as a musical score" (Ignatieff, pp. 30–31). While this occurred in a distant period of the past known as the "dreamtime," contemporary Aborigines still remember the songs of their ancestors. They use them to navigate their way across the country and to prove their ownership of pieces of land.

Bruce's (and the reader's) first response to the Songlines is absolute wonder, a sensation that is expressed in the joyous early chapters of the book. One of these is written as an ecstatic prose poem containing the line: "calling all things into being and weaving their names into verses. The Ancients sang their way all over the world. They sang the rivers and ranges. . . . They wrapped the whole world in a web of song" (p. 73). After the sense of wonder subsides, narrator and reader are left to consider the implications of the "Songlines." We immediately think, for example, of Chatwin's long-standing interest in the relationship between the world and words, and between traveling and writing. "Bruce" is soon off and running on an ambitious intellectual trek; he moves and talks so quickly on the way that the reader is sometimes in danger of being left behind.

First he makes the characteristic suggestion that the Songlines may be universal: "it struck me," he muses, "that the whole of Classical mythology might represent the relics of a gigantic 'song-map' " (p. 117). At the end of the book, he has a vision of "the Songlines stretching across the continents and the ages . . . wherever men have trodden they have left a trail of song" (p. 280). He then returns to his great theme of nomadism and, using the example of the Aborigines, explores many of the ideas contained in his first, unfinished book, *The Nomadic Alternative.* During the writing of *The Songlines,* Chatwin reread and plundered his early manuscript, and it was evidently a great relief to him to finally dispose of themes and speculations that he had been carrying around with him for years.

Chatwin holds up the Aborigines as an example of a nomadic people who have a harmonious relationship with their environment. They walk lightly over the earth and are not obsessed by wealth or possessions, which, the iconoclast in Chatwin believed, fill men with fear and in the end possess them. These and many other reflections in the book are directed specifically at Chatwin's Western readers. *The Songlines* is in fact his most sustained and impassioned polemic against Western materialism, and this is surely one of the reasons for its extraordinary success. His final theoretical leap in the book is perhaps the most daring of all (certainly it has proved too

daring for several scientists who have dismissed it as a fantasy). He advances the idea that man was, at some distant point in his evolutionary history, preyed upon by a catlike beast. It is sometimes difficult to follow the development of this particular argument, however, or to grasp its relationship to the rest of the book.

Chatwin described *The Songlines* as a "novel of ideas," a genre established by French writers such as Denis Diderot at the end of the eighteenth century. Chatwin originally intended to write it as a dialogue between "Bruce" and "Arkady," the other main character in the book. Arkady and Bruce were to have sat beneath a tree and discussed the idea of the Songlines, like characters in a Platonic dialogue. Chatwin's models were to have been the *Symposium* and the *Apology.* "I've never seen anything like it," he commented, "in modern literature, a complete hybrid between fiction and philosophy" (Shakespeare, p. 416).

This comment suggests something of Chatwin's enormous ambition and also the extent to which he was prepared to experiment with the conventional novel form. In its published form, *The Songlines* is a dazzling collage of fragments: there are character sketches, conversations, prose poems, essays, and book reviews. The most original section of the book in stylistic terms is perhaps "From the Notebooks." Here Chatwin reproduces quotations, speculations, and diary excerpts from the notebooks he carried around with him on his travels. Modeled on Edith Sitwell's *Planet and Glow-worm* (1944), an anthology of English literature Chatwin had loved as a child, this section displays his ability to connect stray quotations and extraneous pieces of information. It offers us the image of the world of contemporary learning as a ruined labyrinth, a labyrinth that only a poetic genius such as Chatwin can navigate.

The Songlines was enthusiastically received by reviewers and readers. It became an instant best-seller and, to Chatwin's amusement, it was nominated for both fiction and nonfiction prizes. There were, however, a number of people who strongly disapproved of the book. Among these were the white Australians of the Aborigine Land

Rights movement in Alice Springs portrayed by Chatwin in the novel. They accused him of stealing their ideas, of caricaturing them, and of presenting "dated" theories that were politically conservative and inherently imperialistic.

The Songlines is by no means the most stylistically accomplished of Chatwin's books: the prose is less polished than that of his other writings, and the structure is so loose that he could, with some justice, refer to the published book as a first draft. It is, however, the most intellectually and emotionally satisfying and stimulating of his works: while readers inhabit its world they are utterly enchanted and inspired. It has the flavor of an intellectual epic or a saga; an eccentric and intensely personal work, it has been accurately described as Chatwin's own "songline."

UTZ *(1988)*

The eponymous hero of Chatwin's final novel is based on a collector of Meissen porcelain figures he had met while working for Sotheby's in Prague in the late 1960s. Chatwin described the man as an obsessive who "could not leave the collection and it ruined his life." In this way, however, "he managed to shrink his horizons down to the world of commedia dell'arte figures" and "blocked out the horrors of . . . the Second World War and the early years of Stalinism" (Shakespeare, p. 478). While this description suggests how close the fictional Utz is to the original, Chatwin's hero is in fact a composite figure made up of a number of collectors he encountered.

Despite his occasional outbursts of iconoclasm, Chatwin had always been intrigued by objects and in particular by the stories that could be woven around them concerning their provenance, creators, and collectors. *Utz* is an exquisitely crafted tale inspired by the 1,200 or so pieces in Utz's Meissen porcelain collection. Utz is presented as the archetypal collector: he believes that public museums are no place for art and that every fifty years their collections should be looted and returned to private circulation. Like the characters in *On the Black Hill,* he believes that the great events of history are irrelevant to his concerns or are of consequence only insofar as

"Wars, pogroms and revolutions offer excellent opportunities for the collector" (p. 18). Yet one of the themes of the novel is that there can be no escape from history. Utz's apartment in Prague has been bugged by the Communist authorities, and he has been forced to leave his beloved collection to the state in his will.

After a few of the short, fragmentary chapters (reminiscent of those in *Black Hill* and *In Patagonia*), we are introduced to countless stories, myths, and intellectual speculations surrounding Utz and his collection. In a series of dialogues between Utz and the detached and faceless narrator, we are given a brief history of porcelain and its relationship to alchemy and to the Jewish myth of the golem. While discussing the golem legend, which concerns the creation of an artificial man from clay, Utz admits that in some sense he believes his porcelain figures to be alive. Chatwin's fiction had always been concerned with ideas, and in the novel he teases out every possible philosophical implication from his story. He meditates on the nature of things ("the changeless mirror in which we watch ourselves disintegrate," p. 93) and raises what one reviewer called the "dirty great issues of life and creativity."

Utz is a rare foray into metafiction for Chatwin. The narrator frequently confesses his difficulties in remembering his hero's character (he is not even sure whether he had a mustache) and expresses doubts about the veracity of parts of Utz's story. The conclusion of the novel is open-ended: around the time of Utz's death his collection disappears, and the narrator offers us a number of theories to account for this. Had Chatwin taken this self-conscious and self-reflexive writing any further he would perhaps have laid himself open to the charge of being unfaithful to his artistic motto, which was: "Never let anything artistic stand in your way" (*What Am I Doing Here,* p. 366).

Chatwin once described himself as a miniaturist, and Utz is like a delicate little portrait by the English Renaissance miniaturist Nicholas Hilliard. Written in his tightest lapidary style ("The room was almost in darkness. . . . On the carpet, the animals from the Japanese Palace shimmered like lumps of phosphorescence," p. 93), it is the work of the fastidious aesthete who on one occasion remarked that a perfectly crafted Japanese snuffbox encapsulated everything that he was and believed. Reading the novel immediately after *The Songlines* is like entering a tiny baroque church at the end of a long walk through a vast and inspiring romantic landscape.

Utz received almost universal praise from reviewers; it sold extremely well and was short-listed for the Booker Prize. Unfortunately it was to be the last fictional addition to Chatwin's box of literary treasures. Within a year Chatwin, who had been becoming increasingly ill for some time, died of AIDS. The saddest thing about the novel, in the opinion of many, including Salman Rushdie, was that it suggested that Chatwin was "beginning [a] new, light-spirited phase of flight" (*Imaginary Homelands,* p. 235).

WHAT AM I DOING HERE *(1989)*

In the final year of his life, Chatwin compiled an anthology of journalism and miscellaneous writings dating from every period of his career. Also included in the volume are a few previously unpublished pieces on the art world that are among the last things he wrote. As he edited the anthology, Chatwin knew that he would soon die: the volume constitutes, therefore, a kind of memorial volume as well as a microcosm of his oeuvre.

What Am I Doing Here is a fittingly personal book; at times it has the ease and intimacy of a volume of table talk. Salman Rushdie wrote about it in exactly these terms: "one of its chief delights is that it contains so many of the author's best anecdotes, his choicest performances" (*Imaginary Homelands,* p. 237). It is, Rushdie went on, "a sort of autobiography . . . an autobiography of the mind" (p. 239). This is of course the only kind of autobiography that Chatwin could have written, for he believed that what was important and essential about people was their intellectual passions rather than their emotional concerns.

Oscar Wilde once remarked that people are most revealing when they speak about ideas or other people: that it is only when they wear a

mask that they reveal the truth about themselves. Chatwin's anthology bears out this idea because he is at his most revealing and personal when he describes his heroes (aesthetes such as Ernst Jünger, sages such as André Malraux, and eccentric and ambitious autodidacts such as the Austrian-American botanist and explorer Joseph F. Rock.) or when he discusses an idea. Meditating on the subject of the yeti in "On Yeti Tracks," he comments: "I still have no idea what these 'Yeti tracks' were. My whole life has been a search for the miraculous: yet at the first faint flavour of the uncanny, I tend to turn rational and scientific" (*What Am I Doing Here,* p. 282).

Chatwin's boundless curiosity and his restlessness are revealed in the variety of subjects touched on in the volume, which is a sort of brief guided tour of his chief preoccupations. There are pieces on nomadism, travel, art collecting, the alternatives to Western materialism, and the limitations of science and conventional scholarship. Such qualities are also embodied in the diversity of the styles Chatwin employs: here we find anecdotes, short stories, prose poems, memoirs, critical introductions, travel pieces, political journalism, folktales and character sketches. Chatwin demonstrates his mastery of a variety of styles; in the very best articles, such as the travel piece "The Volga," he also shows that he is the master of a terse and cinematic style that is his own. "Soldiers in top-boots were striding about as if they had saddles between their legs. Then a slender young man stepped ashore carrying a single stalk of pampas grass" (p. 173).

On its publication a few months after Chatwin's death, the book was enthusiastically reviewed except by those who expected him to answer the question "What am I doing here?" by explaining the emotional motivation behind his restlessness. It was praised as an epitome of Chatwin's career and as the perfect companion to his other writings (it contains a number of pieces directly relating to his earlier books). It gave critics the opportunity of evaluating Chatwin's achievement as a writer. In the *London Review of Books* the travel writer Colin Thubron spoke of Chatwin's "obsessive quest for stories" and brilliantly identified the distinctive character of his genius as a "cinematographic sense . . . married to its apparent opposite—a questing abstract imagination."

OTHER POSTHUMOUS WRITINGS

Reviewers of *What Am I Doing Here* and Chatwin's obituarists speculated on what he might have written had he lived on. When he died on 18 January 1989 he had a number of works either in progress or in their embryonic stage in his mind. These included a book on healing called *The Sons of Thunder,* an opera on the life of Rimbaud, and a "Russian novel" on an American subject entitled *Lydia Livingstone.* None of these was ever finished or anywhere near completion. The little information we have of them, however, is extremely tantalizing, and it is likely that some or all of them would have added to Chatwin's reputation.

Volumes that have not, in the opinion of certain critics, significantly added to Chatwin's reputation are those that have been published in the years following his death. *Anatomy of Restlessness,* an anthology of uncollected writings edited by Jan Borm and Matthew Graves and published in 1996, is certainly nowhere near as interesting or satisfying as *What Am I Doing Here.* Indeed it could be described as a collection of pieces that Chatwin deliberately omitted from that earlier volume.

It does, however, contain some interesting and characteristic pieces. The reviews of a travel book by Wilfred Thesiger and a biography of Robert Louis Stevenson are revealing and excellently written, as is the pen portrait of the "two Timbuctoos": one "the administrative centre of . . . the Republic of Mali," the other "the Timbuctoo of the mind—a mythical city in a Never-Never Land" (*Anatomy,* p. 27). But overall the volume is of more interest to the student or biographer of Chatwin than to the general reader. While there is much about the sources of his inspiration and the ideas that inform his books, there is little that can stand by itself as good writing. Reading the sections on "The Nomadic Alternative" and "Art and the Image-Breaker" after *The Songlines* and *Utz* makes one realize not only how much Chatwin developed as a writer but also the

wisdom of his decision to abandon theoretical writing for a more visual and stylish prose.

Photographs and Notebooks (1993), edited by Francis Wyndham and David King, is a far more interesting book. According to Wyndham's excellent introduction, Chatwin left behind fifty of his famous French moleskin notebooks at his death. These contain fragmentary meditations, pen portraits, and photographs taken on his travels, and the kind of quotations and speculations that were reproduced in the "From the Notebooks" section of *The Songlines.* It has also been suggested that among Chatwin's papers there are more conventional diaries, of a highly confessional and sensational nature. No such entries are reproduced in *Photographs and Notebooks,* however, and the truth about this will only be known in 2010, when the embargo on the Bodleian Library's Chatwin archive is lifted.

Wyndham is conscious that "the contrast between the unconsidered [notebook] entries and [Chatwin's] finished work is extreme"; he also concedes that "artless spontaneity was among the qualities that [Chatwin] least desired to express" (p. 13). He suggests, however, they give us a valuable glimpse of the sources of Chatwin's inspiration and offer the kind of mundane details whose absence from Chatwin's published books many critics bemoaned. "God, what have I let myself in for?" Chatwin writes in one entry. "I am the last passenger, the ultimate miracle in overstuffing an African bus. First Class in the train after this" (p. 74). In others he meditates on the posterior of a camel and his own sore and curiously deformed feet.

As Wyndham suggests, the notebook entries also give us a very strong impression of the nature of Chatwin's visual appetite. They include some wonderful character sketches (Chatwin always brings a character to life through close attention to its appearance) and countless vivid evocations of scenes in which his focus is always on the surfaces, textures, and colors of things. "The afternoon I spent examining the market—a close emplacement of shacks, wood and corrugated iron, often made with a deliberate collage of many-coloured pieces. Rauschenberg could not do better" (p. 44).

BRUCE CHATWIN

Chatwin's focus is exactly the same in the marvelous photographs that are reproduced in the book, and it is these that really make the volume a genuine addition to the Chatwin canon. Along with a delight in surfaces, textures, and colors, his dry, detached, and rather spartan photographs display his eye for perfect composition and for geometrical patterns. This emphasis on color, pattern, and form has led critics to compare the photographs to abstract art, and certainly content is the least important thing about them. Yet they are not entirely devoid of life and sensuality either, nor are they "closed" or unambiguous images inhospitable to a variety of interpretations.

It will be obvious from the above description that Chatwin's photographs offer us the perfect visual equivalent of his prose style. He himself emphasized the connection by reproducing his photographs both inside his books and on their covers. Other attributes of the photographs are also interesting in this context: for example, Chatwin's habit of making striking juxtapositions (an abandoned car in a forest, a train in the desert) and his fondness for metaphorical images that just about manage to avoid slipping over into the didacticism of conceptual art. The absence of people in many of his pictures is also suggestive: when they do appear they are often dwarfed by infinite and empty landscapes or made to fit into a structural pattern of color and architecture.

Further examples of Chatwin's artful (but never arty) photography have been published. In 1999 Roberto Calasso introduced and edited *Winding Paths: Photographs by Bruce Chatwin,* which includes many more images than its predecessor and reproduces them along with a number of sage quotations from Chatwin's works. Although it is more comprehensive than the earlier volume it is far less satisfying: the pictures are reproduced in a smaller format that fails to do them justice.

CONCLUSION

Chatwin has enjoyed an extraordinary posthumous fame. His books have sold enormously well throughout the world, and as the preservation and reproduction of his literary relics suggests, he himself has become a cult figure. He has inspired a line of travel clothing and is quoted in pop songs; he has also become a sort of patron saint of Western backpackers.

His enormous popularity is of course due to the quality of his writing; it is also a result of his remarkable character and biography. Chatwin's life, as he said of André Malraux's, is one of his masterpieces: he regarded it as a kind of artistic performance and filled it with grand gestures and theatrical scenes. He was a writer of the self-dramatizing variety, and like his hero Rimbaud, he consciously tried to give his biography the outline and resonance of a myth. He did this by telling lies, or rather by inventing "truths," about himself: a famous example of this is his claim that his name derived from the Anglo-Saxon word Chettewynde, meaning "winding path." Chatwin's comment on Robert Louis Stevenson is relevant to his own case: "Whether his acts [or claims] were genuine or faked is beside the point. The events of his life and the circumstance of his death have a mythic wholeness common to figures of heroic legend . . . and he managed to attract a great deal of publicity for them" (*Anatomy,* p. 132).

Chatwin's biography does indeed have a mythic structure and resonance. A handsome middle-class boy from the provinces, he came to London and invented a marvelous persona, he traveled everywhere, did everything, wrote a handful of original and immediately popular books, then died tragically young, at the height of his literary powers. It is hardly surprising that Nicholas Shakespeare's authorized biography of Chatwin was an enormous popular and critical success on its publication in 1999. Even if it had not been as brilliantly written as it is, it would surely have caused a great sensation.

Despite his distaste for autobiographical revelation, it is clear that Chatwin himself understood the importance of creating a distinctive personality, and the process of self-fashioning and self-projection goes on throughout his works. The authorial persona he invented can in fact be described as his greatest character; in a way that reminds us of writers such as Walt Whitman, Oscar Wilde, or Lord Byron, Chatwin is the true hero of his books. Some believe that the Chatwin cult is in danger of overshadowing his books, yet in the end, it may be that his life and personality, and their relationship to his writing, ensures their continuing popularity.

SELECTED BIBLIOGRAPHY

I. PRINCIPAL WORKS. *In Patagonia* (London and New York, 1977; repr. London, 1998); *The Viceroy of Ouidah* (London and New York, 1980; repr. London, 1982); *On the Black Hill* (London, 1982; New York, 1983; repr. London, 1988); *The Songlines* (London, 1987; New York, 1989; repr. London, 1998); *Utz* (London, 1988; repr. London, 1998); *What Am I Doing Here* (London and New York, 1989; repr. London, 1998).

II. OTHER WORKS. *Patagonia Revisited,* with Paul Theroux (Salisbury, U.K., 1985; Boston, 1986; as *Nowhere Is a Place: Travels in Patagonia,* San Francisco, 1992); *Photographs and Notebooks,* ed. by David King and Francis Wyndham (London, 1993); *Anatomy of Restlessness. Uncollected Writings 1969–1989,* ed. by Jan Borm and Matthew Graves. Published in the United States as *Anatomy of Restlessness: Selected Writings, 1969–1989* (London and New York, 1996); *Winding Paths: Photographs by Bruce Chatwin,* ed. by Roberto Calasso (London, 1999).

III. BIOGRAPHICAL WORKS. Susannah Clapp, *With Chatwin: Portrait of a Writer* (London, 1997); Nicholas Shakespeare, *Bruce Chatwin* (London, 1999; New York, 2000).

IV. CRITICISM AND INTERVIEWS. Karl Miller, *Doubles: Studies in Literary History* (Oxford, 1985); Michael Ignatieff, "An Interview with Bruce Chatwin," *Granta* 21 (spring 1987); V. S. Pritchett, *Lasting Impressions* (London and New York, 1990); Salman Rushdie, *Imaginary Homelands* (London and New York, 1991); Nicholas Murray, *Bruce Chatwin* (Bridgend, U.K., 1993); Patrick Meanor, *Bruce Chatwin* (London and New York, 1997).

ANNE FINCH

(1661–1720)

Tom Jones

OVER THE LAST century, the poetic reputation of Anne Finch, countess of Winchilsea, has grown tremendously. While just one of a number of women authors of the Augustan period (approximately 1660–1760) whose works have been rediscovered and reevaluated by scholars, critics, students and general readers, Finch has perhaps found the most regard as a poet. There are many possible reasons for her recent reception: she led a relatively secluded life, so her biography fails to detract attention from her work; the interest her poetry shows in the condition of women in her time is pronounced, but not strident enough for her to be treated merely as an example of early feminist thought and writing. The most obvious reason is that she simply is the most interesting of the women poets whose reputations and influence are being reconstituted.

Yet study of Finch's work is still in its early stages, and is limited by many of the constraints operating on the study of women's poetry in general. Much traditional literary scholarship focuses on a poet's reading, and how and by whom he or she was read. Finch's education, as with most women of her time, was not as extensive as that of her male contemporaries. There has been little work done, and it is presumed there would be little point, in searching for allusions and references to classical authors in her work, as she did not have the standard classical education of her male contemporaries. Very little has been done even in identifying allusions and debts to English poets in her work. And even less has been done, perhaps more justifiably, in identifying the contribution her poems made to English literary culture: all of them but those contained in the 1713 *Miscellany Poems, on Several Occasions,* and one or two appearing in other anthologies, remained unpublished until the twentieth century. The rest of the poems could have influenced only those people of Finch's acquaintance who might have read them, and though this includes such figures as Alexander Pope and Jonathan Swift, it still does not amount to full participation in the public dialogue that has traditionally been the main concern of literary studies. The main object of writing on Finch, then, has recently been and for the time being reasonably remains to illuminate the main thematic concerns and literary techniques of her work, while expanding a sense of her position in literary history and her relation to an established literary canon. A look at exemplary poems in several of the many genres in which she wrote will show the sophistication of her work in relation to two principal themes of Augustan poetry in general: politics, particularly political exclusion and opposition; and the relationships between a poet and his or her language, and that language and the external world.

BIOGRAPHICAL SURVEY

Relatively little is known of Finch's life, and most of that recorded by Barbara McGovern in *Anne Finch and Her Poetry: A Critical Biography,* on which the following brief account relies. Anne Finch was born Anne Kingsmill in April 1661 in Sydmonton in Hampshire, southern England. She had a sister, Bridget, and a brother, William. Her parents, Sir William Kingsmill and Anne Haslewood, both came from established families of Royalists in the civil wars that had divided supporters of parliament and supporters of the monarchy through the middle decades of the seventeenth century. Her father died when she was five months old, and her mother in 1664. Finch's early life was disrupted by legal disputes over profits from estates that her father had left to provide an education for her and her sister in two separate court cases in 1664–1665 and 1670–1671. Anne spent most of the period in between these two disputes living with her paternal grandmother, Lady Bridget Kingsmill, in Charing Cross, London. When Lady Bridget died in 1672, Anne went to Northamptonshire, where she was reunited with her brother. She spent ten years here, brought up and educated among family and neighboring friends, until her brother died in 1682, and she moved to London to become a handmaid to Mary of Modena, the wife of James, duke of York, later James II. In this sophisticated, and Catholic, court environment, Anne would have had the opportunity to meet other courtiers, including the poets Anne Killigrew, who was also a handmaid to Mary, and John Dryden, who wrote a famous Pindaric ode on the death of Anne Killigrew. Here she might have developed a sense of the strategy and connivance that is traditionally associated with courtly life, as well as picking up some of the intellectual polish and easy refinement that go along with it.

One of the courtiers she definitely did meet was her future husband, Heneage Finch. They probably met in 1683, the year in which Heneage was made a gentleman of the bedchamber to James. They were married on 15 May 1684, in the Chapel Royal at St. James's Palace, and remained married and childless until Anne's death in 1720. John Middleton Murry, editor of a selection of Finch's poems, says, perhaps hyperbolically, "There can have been, in the whole history of love, few happier marriages than this one" (p. 8). Heneage and Anne were both extremely loyal to the monarch they served. James became king in 1685, and ruled for three years, attracting criticism for autocratic behavior, using the dispensing power of the monarch (the right to dispense with ordinary laws of the land) to appoint bishops of his own Catholic religion. His position eventually became untenable, and in 1688 he left the country for exile in Saint-Germain, France. In legal documents it was decided to call his flight an abdication, and William of Orange, who became William III, was invited to accept the throne. These events became known as the Glori-

ous Revolution, and were thought to have enshrined the principle of the monarch's responsibility to the people over whom he reigns, the principle of elective monarchy, and to have settled the much vaunted balance of power within the English constitution. Heneage and Anne, however, never subscribed to these opinions, maintaining instead that James and his son were the rightful successors to the throne, a position known as Jacobitism. Both Heneage and Anne were non-jurors, that is, they refused to take the oath of loyalty to William III, and as a result were politically disenfranchised. Heneage's support for James extended to his making an attempt to leave England and join the exiled court in France in April 1690. His attempt failed, and he and Anne settled in Eastwell in Kent, living a relatively retired life, with Heneage dedicating himself to antiquarian studies, and Anne suffering from occasional but severe bouts of depression, known in contemporary medical discourse as melancholy or the spleen.

The events of the late 1680s are extremely important to an understanding of the political aspects of Finch's poetry, and, as with so much Augustan poetry, its political aspects are intimately related to its religious, personal, and even apparently purely descriptive aspects: without some sense of the language of political allegiance it is very difficult to read Augustan poetry. Finch had moved from centrality at the court of the monarch she supported and believed to have an inalienable political right to rule, to marginality, living away from London, politically disenfranchised, in a society she believed had sacrificed its sense of loyalty to certain immediate political conveniences. The political tone of her work is sometimes nostalgic and forlorn, sometimes more bitingly regretful, but always carries a sense that principles have been abandoned, a right to rule usurped, an older and better order passed away.

The Finches lived at Eastwell for most of the next two decades. By 1708, they began to spend more time in London, buying a house in Cleveland Row around 1710 or 1711. On 4 August 1712, Charles Finch, the count of Winchilsea, died, leaving Heneage to inherit the title and estate, and making Anne countess of Winchilsea.

ANNE FINCH

While this event must have increased the couple's prestige, it does not seem to have done them much financial or political good: as a non-juror Heneage was unable to take up the seat in the House of Lords to which the inheritance entitled him, and most of the estate was tied up in a legal dispute. But at the same time Anne was becoming well acquainted with London literary life, exchanging poems with other writers, men and women, and having poems placed in anthologies for publication by Alexander Pope and Delariviere Manley. The only collection to be published in her lifetime, *Miscellany Poems, on Several Occasions,* emerged in 1713, although it was no great public success. Anne Finch died on 5 August 1720 in Cleveland Row, and is buried at Eastwell.

It is easy to place Finch's poetic work in the context of her life. Her poems often indicate and discuss her sense of political alienation and nostalgia. They dwell on the pleasures of retirement in the country as a response to this alienation. They deal with the joys of married love, the difficulty of coping with mental disorder, and the consolation of religion. They testify to the importance of literary friendships, and the difficulties involved in writing as a woman in a predominantly male literary world. Finch's poems, however, are of far more than documentary interest; they do much more than reveal a set of concerns specific to a certain order of Augustan aristocratic and literary lady. They are among the most thoughtful and reflective poems in the canon of Augustan poetry, setting about some of the dominant themes of Augustan writing in a distinctive and impressive manner.

LYRICS, SONGS AND SHORTER POEMS

Among the many kinds of lyric poetry Finch practiced is an interesting group of poems that have a slight, trivial, or occasional subject, and are concerned to question the relationship of the poem itself to that subject. These poems are quite often amorous, or relate to the exchange of letters or presents between friends, and were particularly popular in the later seventeenth century. "A Sigh" is one of these poems, and in it Finch asks what kind of sign an amorous sigh is.

> Gentlest Air thou breath of Lovers
>   Vapour from a secret fire
> Which by thee itts self discovers
>   E're yett daring to aspire.
>
> Softest Noat of whisper'd anguish
>   Harmony's refindest part
> Striking whilst thou seem'st to languish
>   Full upon the list'ners heart.
>
> Safest Messenger of Passion
>   Stealing through a croud of spys
> Which constrain the outward fashion
>   Close the lips and guard the Eyes.
>
> Shapelesse Sigh we ne're can show thee
>   Form'd but to assault the Ear
> Yett e're to their cost they know thee
>   Ev'ry Nymph may read thee here.

The sigh is a sign of love, "a secret fire," that does not yet know it exists, because the amorous fire only discovers itself by means of the sigh. The sigh does not simply point to love—it is part of love, essential to love, because it alerts people, including the lover herself, to the existence of love.

The sigh is a strange composite: it is both powerful and vulnerable. It is the "Softest Noat of whisper'd anguish" (l. 5), but it is a safe messenger, steals through crowds of spies, strikes upon the lover's heart and assaults the ear. It is slight, yet effective; it communicates while having no obvious form. Finch emphasizes the formlessness of the sigh: "Shapelesse Sigh we ne're can show thee" (l. 13). There is no way of representing the sigh orthographically; one cannot spell it, but somehow the poem has managed to capture the sigh: young nymphs may read it "here," in the poem, in order to preserve themselves from the dangerous coquetry of the love game. The poem moves towards an apparent contradiction: it is impossible to represent the sigh, yet the poem has represented it.

Finch is participating in a common form of poetic play that asks how one can represent or write about things that seem constantly to be changing, as things so often change and vary in love games, perhaps more than in any other field of life beside politics. Alexander Pope, for example, in his *Epistle to a Lady,* has much to say about these topics, emphasizing the changeability of women to the point of absurdity at which it becomes impossible to represent them at all. Once involved in this kind of play, poets often start to question the role of the poet. If things are so changeful and difficult to represent, can it be the role of the poet to memorialize and record, or to show things as they really are? Charles H. Hinnant's book *The Poetry of Anne Finch: An Essay in Interpretation* (1994) recognizes this doubt about the capacity of the poet to represent a presumed outward reality as one of Finch's recurrent themes, and discusses "A Sigh" as a poem that expresses doubt in the capacity of linguistic signs adequately to represent the things or ideas to which they are supposed to refer (pp. 55–56). A slightly different reading to Hinnant can be shown by looking first at an example of Finch doing something similar in this brief poem titled "Adam Pos'd".

Cou'd our First Father, at his toilsome Plough,
Thorns in his Path, and Labour on his Brow,
Cloath'd only in a rude, unpolish'd Skin,
Cou'd he a vain Fantastick Nymph have seen,
In all her Airs, in all her antick Graces,
Her various Fashions, and more various Faces;
How had it pos'd that Skill, which late assign'd
Just Appellations to Each several Kind!
A right Idea of the Sight to frame;
T'have guest from what New Element she came;
T'have hit the wav'ring Form, or giv'n this Thing a
  Name.

The variability in the behavior of a fashionable lady would have made it impossible for Adam to exercise his divinely granted power to give all things he saw appropriate names. The nymph threatens the descriptive power of language. She also threatens poetry in particular because poets have so often been compared to Adam in respect of their ability to see new things and describe them in fitting and new ways: poets are always trying to claim that they have something in common with Adam because they have mysterious linguistic skills, although it is evidently a more complicated matter for a female poet, as Finch shows in this poem that seems to attack her own gender. Again, the amorous world questions what

language and poetry might be able to represent and to do.

ODES AND LONGER POEMS

Such moments of questioning occur also in some of Finch's evidently more ambitious poems: "To the Nightingale" and "Upon the Hurricane" both end by pointing out the limitations of the poetic voice.

> Thus we Poets that have Speech,
> Unlike what thy Forests teach,
>   If a fluent Vein be shown
>   That's transcendent to our own,
> Criticize, reform, or preach,
> Or censure what we cannot reach.
>> ("To the Nightingale," lines 30–35)

> . . . as our Aspirations do ascend,
> Let every Thing be summon'd to attend;
> And let the Poet *after God's own Heart*
> Direct our Skill in that sublimer part,
>   And our weak Numbers mend!
>> ("Upon the Hurricane", lines 299–303)

"The Spleen" also has a moment of poetic doubt.

> O'er me alas! thou dost too much prevail:
>   I feel thy Force, whilst I against thee rail;
> I feel my Verse decay, and my crampt Numbers fail.
>> (lines 74–76)

A number of superficial and attractive explanations for these moments of poetic doubt offer themselves. Firstly, one might suggest that Finch is expressing some kind of female uncertainty. If she were a male poet she would confidently claim to meet all the challenges her subjects set her. She meekly admits to not being up to the task. This kind of view is presented by Dorothy Mermin in her 1990 article "Women Becoming Poets: Katherine Philips, Aphra Behn, Anne Finch." A second explanation is that she has serious doubts about the poetry in general, believing it is unable to represent or adequately capture the things it sets out to describe, a view more like Jennifer Keith's in "The Poetics of Anne Finch" (1998).

Neither of these positions is quite right. The length and range of these poems make it clear that Finch is extremely ambitious. Two of them are Pindaric Odes, traditionally grand forms about which I shall say something shortly. Also, the theology of these poems will not allow one to pin a form of proto-deconstructive thinking onto them. If there is indecision and gloom, it is a human indecision and gloom, born out of a failure to see God's will at work in the world in the appropriate manner. The end of the poem "Upon the Hurricane" explicitly calls for God's help in achieving this feat, at least as far as the poet is able. The moments of doubt about the capacity of the poet and poetry in general to represent things and present adequate explanations should be considered as a traditional Christian form of sceptical humility in the face of God's providence. Finch is not humble about her poetry just because she is a woman, or just because she doubts the effectiveness of language, though both these suggestions are partly true. She also acknowledges that not even the highest human endeavor is capable of seeing through and presenting God's providence in a clear and comprehensible manner.

Finch's ambition is evident from her choice of the Pindaric Ode. *The Princeton Encyclopaedia of Poetry and Poetics* calls the Pindaric Ode one of the most formal, complex, and ceremonious forms of lyric poetry. The form is derived from the work of Pindar (522–442 B.C.), whose odes were written to be performed with music and dancing on occasions of public celebration. They employ abrupt shifts in tone and imagery to evoke a state of high poetic inspiration and attest to the importance of their occasion. The Pindaric Ode in English was popularized by Abraham Cowley, who wrote many paraphrastic translations of the odes of Pindar. The form remained popular throughout the later seventeenth century and the eighteenth century, practiced by John Dryden, among others. One reason against attributing Finch's poetic humility to her position as a woman or to a presumed scepticism about the capacity of language to do its job is that in such a grand and extravagant form as the Pindaric Ode many poets felt themselves in danger of failure. Abraham Cowley himself felt such

trepidation. Here is an extract from the preface to his *Pindarique Odes* of 1656:

> The digressions are many, and sudden, and sometimes long, according to the fashion of all *Lyriques,* and of *Pindar* above all men living. The *Figures* are unusual and *bold,* even to *Temeritie,* and such as I durst not have to do withal in any other kind of *Poetry*: The *Numbers* are various and irregular, and sometimes (especially some of the long ones) seem harsh and uncouth. . . .
>
> (p. 69)

Cowley, as an ambitious male poet, has his doubts about the appropriateness of his language in these poems. A form of poetic humility is almost traditional when writing in such an extravagant form as the ode. Cowley compares himself humbly to Pindar: "alas, my *tim'erous Muse / Unambitious* tracks pursues" ("The Praise of Pindar"). Finch is employing a grand public mode, one that was current, popular, and ambitious, and one that brought with it a diffidence about the kind of poetry being produced and the poet's success in it. Finch is not being particularly timorous in her moments of poetic self-doubt.

The poems are ambitious even for Pindaric Odes. "The Spleen" develops its inquiry of a physiological condition into an investigation of human weakness and limitation—or fallenness, if one wants to take a theological view. Likewise, "Upon the Hurricane" turns a meteorological oddity into the basis for a study of God's providence. The enquiry into the inscrutable wisdom of God's providence is a common genre in the Augustan period, both in poetry and prose. People at this time were interested in the origin of evil and the nature and function of suffering in a divinely created world. Pope's *An Essay on Man* (1733) and William King's *On the Origin of Evil* (1733) are clear examples of this genre, which Voltaire's *Candide* (1759) parodies. The most clear poetic example of this kind of work in the period immediately preceding Finch's writing career is John Milton's *Paradise Lost* (1674) which famously attempts to justify the ways of God to man. Finch is tackling one of the grandest subjects available to poets in the early eighteenth century, and one that had just been treated by one of the greatest poets in the language.

Finch's technique in "Upon the Hurricane" is grand, ambitious, and suitable to her theme. Lines 11–60 treat the effect the storm has on trees. Finch's images are copious. She gives many examples of different species of trees that are affected by the wind: the shrub, the beech, the oak, the pine, and so on. This copiousness comes with repetition, inversion, and variation of syntactical patterns, playing out the continuity of the argument and examples, and also their subtle differences one from another.

In vain the *Shrubs,* with lowly Bent,
Sought their Destruction to prevent;
The *Beech* in vain, with out-stretch'd Arms,
Deprecates th'approaching Harms;
In vain the *Oak* (so often storm'd)
Rely'd upon that native Force,
By which already was perform'd
So much of his appointed Course,
As made him, fearless of Decay,
　　Wait but the accomplish'd Time
Of his long-wish'd and useful Prime,
To be remov'd, with Honour, to the Sea.

(lines 11–22)

The shrub, beech, and oak all act in vain, but each is described in a different posture; the pine joins in their ambition. Finch uses periphrasis: the trees become the "num'rous Brethren of the Leafy Kind." Periphrasis is one way of attaining easily a Miltonic grandeur of style, an expansiveness and abstraction of expression that indicates poetic importance and achievement. The traditional form of periphrasis involves metonymy, using one part of a thing to represent the whole, followed by an implicit personification. This formula describes such stock phrases as "the finny tribe" (meaning fish) as well as Finch's trees. The trees are described in human terms, most notably in the early part of this passage by being given desires and wills. The oak wants to be cut down and to be used in the construction of naval vessels. It is as if the trees perceive their own social and military utility, and want to contribute to the well-being of the country.

The activity of nature also serves Finch's grand theological purpose. The personification of the trees is not simple; it is not just that the trees are being described as if they were people. Nature as nature (rather than nature seen as human) is being given some sort of purpose towards which it strives. This fiction of an active, purposive, motivated nature (if it is a fiction) underlies many of the seventeenth- and eighteenth-century genres of natural description in literature. Nature is shown constantly to exhibit signs of a divine will at work. The workings of this divine will are often convenient to specific political aims: because the world is the expression of God's will, the oak desires to become part of the ship-building scheme of Britain's navy, which itself, by extension, is part of God's providential scheme. Providence is often used to justify pre-existing political schemes or to suggest that certain political schemes are part of God's will. The passage on the trees goes on to exemplify poetic ambition and grandeur by making a sustained comparison between contemporary Britain and the Middle East of biblical times. Comparing Britain and Judea also gives the impression that God has a particular regard for Britain, as he did for the people of Israel: if God sends the storm as a warning, he is at least bothered enough about the inhabitants of the place to warn them. Finch here taps into a strain associated with Milton, suggesting that the English are God's chosen people.

One ought to ask how far Finch succeeds in this poem of theological justification, just as one ought to ask whether Milton manages to justify the ways of God to man in *Paradise Lost.* The poem does not want to justify the ways of God in the same manner as an epic. While Milton employs the sublime and intends to rouse awe in his readers, he also offers exemplary narratives, protracted debates, and even brief allegories in the service of his argument. He uses an epic mode. Finch's ode is more concerned to juxtapose images of frightful devastation in order to arouse feelings of awe towards God. The relative disconnection of these images serves her purpose. God's will in this case is inscrutable. To know precisely why God chose to punish certain people at this time is to reach above one's limited human position. Rather, God's action on this occasion should be taken as a warning: all people deserve this kind of treatment from God, and those who have actually received it are intended as examples.

Finch does not hint at reasons for God's actions, but God's punishments are generally aimed at human vanity, pride, arrogance and presumption. Finch sees these sins in specifically political terms. The hurricane has removed political distinction: "the rash Contender," the politically ambitious and divisive person, no longer calls people either Whig or Tory. It is implied that God punishes the British for their political division, squabbling, factions, and party rage, an idea that appears frequently in eighteenth-century poetry, in which political dissent is a very important theme. Alexander Pope, for example, believed dissent to be at the heart of the action of Homer's *Iliad,* saying in his poetical index to that work, "The great *Moral* of the Iliad, that *Concord, among Governours, is the preservation of States, and Discord the ruin of them.*" God punishes Britain for its recent political revolutions and upheavals.

From what is known of Finch's political allegiances, however, one might look for something more partisan in this punishment. Finch was loyal to the Stuart line, and may have been suggesting that capitulation to the regime of William III was sinful. Finch may well be pushing a party line as if it were a detached and disinterested view of the political scene. She presents her objections to specific political pursuits as if they were objections to vanity and ambition in general:

> What art Thou, envy'd *Greatness,* at the best,
>   In thy deluding Splendors drest?
> What are thy glorious Titles, and thy Forms?
> Which cannot give Security, or Rest
> To favour'd Men, or Kingdoms that contest
> With popular Assaults, or Providential Storms!
>
> (lines 289–294)

There are hints of nostalgia here. The Stuart monarchs are the favored men who have not been able to weather providential storms, and must resign themselves to God's will. If this is a Jacobite poem, it is not a particularly virulent one: the Stuarts must accept what has transpired as providence, and so, if even the rightful monarchs must resign themselves to God's will and give up the honors and glories of this world, then so should, and so must, all other people.

Finch is not backing out of important political and poetical arguments and commitments in this poem. She is not being humbly feminine, nor doubting the capacity of poetry to deal with important questions. She is simply dealing with a difficult poetic topic that requires a writer to confess a lack of complete knowledge and relies on the production of awed and sublime feelings in its readers.

FABLES

Finch must have been strongly attracted to the fable as a genre, working with it as she did consistently throughout her life. As Jayne Elizabeth Lewis has shown in *The English Fable: Aesop and Literary Culture, 1651–1740,* fable was a popular and relevant poetic mode in late seventeenth- and early eighteenth-century Britain. Its didactic potential gave it particular power as an instrument of political argument. The tendency of fable to turn things such as animals or household objects into symbols made it attractive to writers interested in the nature and function of language, particularly poetic language. The fable, then, might have appealed to Finch both as a medium for political argument and as a means of reflecting on her own practice as a poet, two topics in which her other work demonstrates a clear interest.

Finch opens her 1713 collection with a prefatory fable "Mercury and the Elephant." In this piece Mercury, the messenger god, meets an elephant while he is on one of his errands. The elephant detains the god and asks him to adjudicate a dispute with a wild boar. The elephant claims to have won a fight with the boar by fair means, but says that the boar has been accusing him of foul play, using his size to hinder the boar before he was ready to fight. The elephant hopes that Mercury will settle the dispute, but all the god does is to express surprise that a creature as unwieldy and presumably as gentle as the elephant fought at all. Finch goes on to make a comparison between the elephant and the female poet. The female poet might well set about excusing the imperfections of her work and anticipating the objections of critics, only to be met with incredulity that she has written at all. The poem closes with a reflection that it is better to await the event of publication with equanimity than to be anxious about one's reception.

As is the case with many fables, the meaning of the poem seems fairly simple and clear until one looks closely at the comparisons the poem employs. Finch would seem to be having a little joke, saying that it does not matter how she prefaces this volume of poems, or what extravagant lengths she goes to in order to anticipate critical objections, as (male) readers will merely be surprised that she has written at all. Part of the joke here is that she is writing an extravagant preface while acknowledging that extravagant prefaces will do her no good. The fable is much more extravagant than it might sound. The comparison between the female poet and the elephant is remarkable for its inappropriateness. One would expect a female poet to be small, polite, civilized, humble, and many other things. But Finch picks out an animal as the vehicle for her fable that seems to have the opposite qualities. The elephant is an "unwieldy Brute" (l. 7) and seems to be rather belligerent. The elephant is also reporting a battle, and the battle that the elephant has had must stand in for Finch's own work or for her defense of her own work, her attempt in this fable and in the introductory poem that follows it to justify her literary endeavor. This implicit comparison brings out a rather martial element to Finch's attitude to her work: she seems to regard her writing as a form of battle.

The comparisons that Finch employs or implies are, then, unexpected, or somehow comically inappropriate. It is worth asking how and why they are inappropriate. It might be said that the comparison of the female poet to the elephant is in some way humble or self-effacing, that Finch suggests her writing is clumsy and inelegant in order to pre-empt her critics. Yet Finch could have chosen many more traditional images to achieve this effect, such as the bird that has not

yet learned to fly. There is something absurd in the selection of the elephant as the figure of the female poet, but it is an absurdity that refuses to let Finch appear trivial in her own work: if she is strangely inelegant, she is so in an imposing manner. Similarly, the aggressive implied comparison between writing and battle is unexpected and even absurd, but simultaneously hints at the seriousness with which Finch regards her own practice. The final paragraph of the poem produces a more serious tone out of the absurdity of the fable itself, having the tone of a dour moral. Finch asserts with assumed indifference that she writes for herself and not for the male readers who may so easily become disbelieving critics. She describes the female poet, "Betray'd by Solitude to try / Amusements, which the Prosp'rous fly" (lines 45–46). One would expect solitude to be the friend of the poet, but here the moments of isolation in which poetry is composed become the poet's enemy. Finch also suggests that she is led to poetry by a lack of prosperity. Finch cannot mean here that she was led to writing by a desire to make money, which was certainly true of many of her contemporaries: her social position prevented any such need. She must mean that she is not prospering in some other sense, the two most likely candidates being that her depression was affecting her, or that she felt politically alienated (prosperity often means political success at this time). Either way, Finch suggests that she is writing a poetry of complaint, whether it is personal, political, or, most likely, both. Finch's fable reveals some very complex attitudes to her own work, and the job of writing poetry in general, through a disturbing comedy of disjunction.

Finch deals with similar themes in "The Miser and the Poet," a poem described as a tale, but one that has the form of a fable: the miser in question turns out to be Mammon himself. In this piece a poet leaves the city on a vacation, loses his way, and meets Mammon "in a Pit with Thorns grown over" (l. 24). The poet chides Mammon for digging for gold, and Mammon responds that poetry is now seriously outmoded, and that the poet should be about making money instead, giving examples as he talks of the many and various recent poets, including Finch herself under her pen-name "Ardelia," who have not been rewarded as they should have been for their poetical labors. The poet is to some degree convinced and decides to hide his verses in Mammon's pit until such time as poetry is again the topic of polite conversation. He closes by admitting that Mammonists have surpassed poets, and the Bank of England grown bigger than Parnassus.

Finch is opposing recent changes in British political and economic life in this poem. The arrival of William III in 1689 began a revolution in government economic policy as William sought ways to fund the wars he was conducting. In the two decades between the accession of William and the date of this poem, 1709, many of the institutions of modern finance were put in place: the government began to borrow money at far higher levels, instituting national debt; the Bank of England was established; various new forms of credit and stock-market speculation were practiced. Opponents of William's regime often focused their criticism on the financial practices that were popularized during his reign, arguing that the new power of stocks, shares, credit, investments, and money was destroying the traditional forms of wealth made possible by the ownership of land. These opponents of William often also believed that new money was destroying the forms of social organization that went along with land ownership, and threatened the cultural life of the nation at large. This is a political poem, but one that extends its opposition to particular political practices into the cultural sphere by questioning the relationship between political decisions, here in the realm of economics, and the life of a poet. It is an extended and witty treatment of the commonplace idea that poets live a life of penury in the context of revolutionary financial change.

As in "Mercury and the Elephant," however, Finch's poem reveals complexities. She is not simply claiming that cultural achievements are no longer rewarded appropriately as they were in the late Stuart period after the Restoration in 1660. Her description of the poet is rather too equivocal to suggest that he is really worth rewarding:

A Wit, transported with Inditing,
Unpay'd, unprais'd, yet ever Writing;
Who, for all Fights and Fav'rite Friends,
Had Poems at his Fingers Ends;

(lines 1–4)

The poet is not praiseworthy, he is deluded ("transported") by his own writing, and uses his work to serve whatever purpose he is personally interested in at the time. When the poet upbraids Mammon for digging for gold, the poet appears a little absurd: he believes he can sustain himself on "high Reflections" (l. 28), as if one could live on poetical inspiration alone and did not need money. Mammon, in fact, looks almost as reasonable as the poet. His description of the court of Charles II,

When all was Riot, Masking, Playing;
When witty Beggars were in fashion,
And Learning had o'er-run the Nation,

(lines 32–34)

is equivocal too. Charles's court was famously elegant and well educated, but it was also famously debauched, obscene, and unfaithful. One could only look back on that time with a qualified nostalgia. Mammon seems even to have good taste. When he lists the poets who are worth rewarding and yet received no reward, he actually lists good poets, poets that Finch admired—and even Finch herself. Mammon seems to know what good poetry is, and to think even that it might be worth rewarding, but sees that, because it is not rewarded, it is not worth pursuing. He appears to be a miser through realism rather than through a deluded passion for gold.

The poem never gives in to a complete ironic reversal of the expected support of the poet. Mammon takes on a rather more sinister tone toward the end of his argument with the poet, echoing the words Iago uses in *Othello* when he is persuading his dupe Rodrigo to get some money: "put Money in your Purse" (l. 83). Although Mammon's words here seem light enough, and Iago's words when he speaks them are comic, there is the suggestion that Mammon's words will lead on to a tragic action in the same way that Iago's lead on to the tragic action of the later parts of Shakespeare's play. As with Iago, it is part of the danger of the miser that his arguments seem so reasonable. It is difficult to know how to take the poet's final capitulation:

I here submit to your Discourses;
Which since Experience too enforces,
I, in that solitary Pit,
Your Gold withdrawn, will hide my Wit:
Till Time, which hastily advances,
And gives to all new Turns and Chances,
Again may bring it into use;
Roscommons may again produce;
New *Augustean* Days revive,
When *Wit* shall please, and *Poets* thrive.
Till when, let those converse in private,
Who taste what others don't arrive at;
Yielding that Mammonists surpass us;
And let the *Bank* outswell *Parnassus.*

(lines 90–103)

Some parts of the vision of the future the poet presents are hopeful: there will be a time when poetry is again publicly valued, when monarchs and people of position are again patrons of the arts. Yet the poet's actual vision is not necessarily as hopeful as it might seem. There is a suggestion that literary and cultured people should give up on public life, should "converse in private," a sense that parallels Finch's political experience, in which those right-minded people loyal to the Stuarts had to retire from public life and keep their opinions to themselves. The poem is related in this way to Finch's poems of retirement from public life. It withdraws from an ideal of public culture at the same time as announcing one. And the poet's action, placing his wit in the pit whence Mammon draws his gold, also seems rather hopeless. Gold really is drawn from the earth, but poetry only ever flourishes by practice. The poet seems to give in to Mammon's way of thinking by hiding his wit in the earth: he announces hope for the future while pursuing a course of action that makes that future far less likely. The characters in Finch's fables behave in slightly unexpected ways, producing complex morals and revealing a thoughtful anxiety about the relationship between the poet and public life.

DRAMAS

Finch's two heroic dramas, "The Triumphs of Love and Innocence" and "Aristomenes: or, The Royal Shepherd," deal more explicitly with questions of public importance than any of her other works, and yet are, paradoxically, among her most private pieces. Both of them deal with kingship, what it is to be a successful and legitimate monarch, in ways that connect them very closely to Finch's politics. Yet the plays are perhaps the least read and least discussed works of her various output, for many reasons. The heroic drama of the Restoration and Augustan period has never enjoyed a critical vogue, the comedy of the period taking the greater share of attention. Its heroism is of a very measured kind, and seems cold and artificial next to Shakespeare. There are also reasons more specific to Finch. She states of her two plays in an advertisement to "The Triumphs of Love and Innocence" that "a more terrible injury cannot be offer'd me, then to occasion, or permitt them ever to be represented." Although she included "Aristomenes" in *Miscellany Poems,* it seems she never intended either play for public performance. It may be that the plays were written as closet dramas, that is, plays to be read privately among friends. Pope describes in a letter having visited the Finches and hearing a play read, and it is possible that this was one of Finch's plays, and that they were composed with just such occasions in mind. The important paradox to be grasped is that Finch's most overt treatment of public themes should necessarily be found in her most private work. Her loyalty to the Stuarts demanded a degree of secrecy from her on the topic of legitimate monarchy, and just as her manuscript poems have been found to be more overtly political than her published work, so the plays she wished never to be staged are her most overt utterances on public themes.

"The Triumphs of Love and Innocence," the play Finch chose not to publish, is also the most politically explicit. The play is set in Rhodes, and its main action concerns the restoration of the queen of Cyprus to her throne. She has been deprived of her position by the Venetian government and has been exiled to Rhodes. The action of the play begins with the arrival of the governor of Cyprus, the respected soldier General Lauredan, arriving in Rhodes as a representative of the Venetian government to ask for the queen to be handed over to him. The play immediately begins to employ the political vocabulary used to describe the removal of James II from the throne and the installation of William III in his place: the monarch placed on the throne of Cyprus is called a "bold Vsurper" (I.i.8). There is a very clear connection between the rightful monarch of Cyprus, exiled in Rhodes, and the rightful monarch of England, exiled in France and Italy. Finch makes the allusion to contemporary British politics less explicit and more interesting by making her rightful monarch a queen. Not only does this difference in gender mask the allusion a little, it also brings to the fore problems of the relative powerlessness of women in politics, which Finch must have felt strongly, and also makes the final amorous resolution of the play possible.

The play is an investigation of honor in the political and amorous spheres. It employs a conventional double plot in order to bring together the question of political loyalty to the exiled queen and the amorous loyalty of various couples, including, eventually, the queen and Lauredan, onto whom the throne of Cyprus turns out to have devolved. The argument of the play seems to be that these two forms of honor are inextricable, and that honesty and honor in any sphere of life require loyalty to those who have a natural right to govern. The play is careful subtly to defend the Stuarts. When Lauredan makes his request for the queen to Aubusson, the Great Master of Rhodes, Aubusson rejects him outright, apparently without consultation with his advisers or the people. Aubusson here is in danger of looking like an autocrat, a monarch who makes rash political decisions without consultation and against the will of the people, something that Charles II and James II were accused of, and which led to the abdication of James. Aubusson defends himself so:

Think not my Lord, because you hear dissension
That 'tis my arbitrary will prevails
But know, that ere your vessel loos'd from Venice,

Fame, with her thousand tongues, had told your purpose.
And 'twas the states, th' assembl'd states decree,
That it shou'd instantly be thus rejected
Least, that a secret, and obscure debate
Might make itt thought, we were dispos'd to yield,
And only held our honour at a price
Above, what your commission was to offer.

(I.i.95–104)

Aubusson's announcement looks like autocracy, but it is in fact the considered opinion of the whole state presented in an apparently autocratic manner for the sake of loyalty.

The play makes a number of Shakespearian allusions, most notably to *Othello*. Finch's play shares its geographical and imperial setting with Shakespeare's, and also has two characters very much like Iago, the Lord Riccio and Rivalto, who ruthlessly dupe their acquaintance and attempt to sabotage the various love plots that are transpiring. Rivalto at one point also appears like Angelo, the precise duke of *Measure for Measure,* who, when tempted by Isabella, gives in to his sensual appetites and tries to force her into submitting to him. Rivalto in Finch's play tries to win Marina over to marrying him, and then reverts to force. Finch's drama is poetically as well as politically allusive.

Aristomenes, the published play, is less explicit in its politics. It deals with the liberation of the Messenians from Spartan tyranny by means of the heroic actions of a father and son, Aristomenes and Aristor, and a foreign Prince, Demagetus. Themes of monarchic right, loyalty, and usurpation are present here, but the play is a perhaps more concerned to displace public concerns into a pastoral setting. In a prologue Finch claims she writes from a position of rural retirement, and that her play cannot be expected to be as sophisticated as those performed in London. Finch is again expressing alienation from public life. A similar alienation is seen in the character of Demagetus, who is forced in the early stages of the play to keep his disguise as a shepherd, Climander, and refrain from entering battle. A prince is unable to express his nobility, and must instead retire to the country. There is some sense of frustration at the exile of monarchs here, but any possible Jacobite allusions are

ANNE FINCH

veiled: it is not his own country the prince seeks to liberate. *Aristomenes* is a more forlorn play than *The Triumphs of Love and Innocence*: Messenia is liberated, but its young hope Aristor and his new Spartan bride, Amalintha, are both killed. There is little hope of the establishment of some future dynasty, and the play closes with a conventional recognition of the terrible vicissitudes of human life.

RECEPTION

An account of the reception of Finch's work ought to begin with the notice taken of it by her more famous contemporaries. One of her songs, "Love, thou art best of Human Joys," was set to music by Henry Purcell, possibly the greatest British composer. Jonathan Swift and Alexander Pope both wrote poems to her. Swift's "Apollo Outwitted" jokingly suggests that she has won the gift of poetry from Apollo only to be cursed to remain the first amongst modest poets, never claiming the fame that is her due. Pope was her friend throughout the last decade of her life, and must have read her work closely: he borrows and adapts a line from "The Spleen" in his grand philosophical poem *An Essay on Man*. Pope's friendship with Finch may well have had a political aspect. Pope remained at least sentimentally loyal to the Stuart line, and associated with many prominent Jacobites and Jacobite sympathizers, including Matthew Prior, the poet and politician. Myra Reynolds notes an attribution to Finch of a poem addressed to Prior, and suggests that they might have become acquainted through Elizabeth Singer (*The Poems of Anne Countess of Winchilsea*, introduction, p. liii). The contemporary reception of Finch and her work presents a picture of a successful and esteemed poet at ease in a group of poetically and politically like-minded writers.

As Barbara McGovern and Charles H. Hinnant point out in the introduction to their edition of the Wellesley College manuscript poems, Finch's poems were not reprinted in her lifetime, as the works of some of her female contemporaries were. She is nonetheless one of the few female poets of the Augustan period to have received

sustained critical notice over the last two centuries. Much of this is due to William Wordsworth's admiration of her poetry of natural description. He stated in his supplementary essay to the preface to *Lyrical Ballads* that Finch's "Nocturnal Reverie" was one of the only new descriptions of external nature in the period between the publication of Milton's *Paradise Lost* and James Thomson's *The Seasons*. Consequently, and perhaps at the expense of the rest of her very varied work, Finch has been consistently admired as a nature poet, a precursor of the Romantic fashion for verisimilar descriptions of external nature and reflection on the mental and spiritual consolation available from contemplation of the landscape. Wordsworth himself selected passages from poems by Finch for an album presented to Lady Lowther, a relative of Wordsworth's patrons. This selection, which was printed in the early twentieth century, puts thirty pages of Finch's poems first in a selection of little-read eighteenth-century poetry.

Anthologization of Finch's poetry over the ensuing century and more has been deeply influenced by Wordsworth's assessment. Her "Nocturnal Reverie" is perhaps the most often selected poem, appearing in many anthologies throughout the nineteenth century. Oscar Wilde, reviewing one such anthology, quotes Wordsworth's assessment of Finch and states himself "it must be admitted that the simple naturalism of Lady Winchilsea's description is extremely remarkable" (*Woman's World,* November 1887, p.199). The first, and still the only, scholarly edition of Finch's poems appeared in 1903, edited by Myra Reynolds, as one of the centennial publications of the University of Chicago. This edition prints all the poems from *Miscellany Poems* and also poems from manuscripts, one of which was formerly owned by Edmund Gosse, an academic and admirer of Finch's work. Reynolds's admirable introduction does a very important job in establishing Finch in a literary milieu, identifying allusions to her in the work of other writers, and developing a sense of her relation to the body of Augustan poetry.

John Middleton Murry published a selection of Finch's poems in 1928, with the simple statement

76

that her poems had given him much pleasure that he now wanted to share with other readers who might not want to deal with Myra Reynolds' scholarly edition that had preserved Finch's original spelling. Murry also suggests that at least half of Finch's work is bad, and needs to be removed to allow the reader access to what is valuable in her good poetry. There is an unusual attitude of simultaneous admiration and condescension in Murry's introduction. He regards Finch as a true poet, but a fatally inconsistent poet. He says that her phrases are extremely feminine, that they "linger like fragrance in the memory. They are a woman's phrases; and they have a peculiar perfection of femininity" (p. 14). Yet at the same time he sees in her a refusal of, or at least a distaste for, male dominance in the world of poetry: "Modesty was thrust upon her by a masculine convention. She accepted the convention, but she did not like it" (p. 18).

To a great extent, the experience of reading Finch is still conditioned by the assumptions and preferences of this earlier group of readers and critics. Barbara McGovern in *Anne Finch and Her Poetry* (1992) has suggested that

> Wordsworth's praise has been a mixed blessing. It resurrected Finch's name from the obscurity that befell any pre-nineteenth-century English woman writer. But for nearly two hundred years it has distorted the general perception of her as a poet and thwarted recognition of the depth, the quality, and the diversity of her work.
>
> (p. 79)

Denys Thompson's selection of her poems, published as part of a series of neglected English poets, makes a relatively predictable set of choices as to which of her poems deserve to be represented. Larger and more general anthologies of eighteenth-century poetry do something to alter this presentation of Finch's work. Roger Lonsdale's landmark 1989 anthology *Eighteenth-Century Women Poets* presents some less familiar pieces, and furthers Reynolds's work by expanding on the literary context of Finch's writing. David Fairer and Christine Gerrard select "Upon the Hurricane," "The Spleen," and "The Nightingale," three of Finch's more ambitious pieces, for their *Eighteenth-Century Poetry: An Annotated*

Anthology, as well as using a piece from the Wellesley College manuscript. This anthology, primarily aimed at the university market, may significantly alter the way in which Finch is perceived by a generation of readers by returning her grander works to the center of her poetic project.

The most significant advances in the reception of Finch's poetry were the publication of the Wellesley College manuscript poems and the development of a critical discourse around her work. The Wellesley College poems, owned in the early twentieth century by Edward Dowden, a Shakespearian critic, were published in a private edition in 1988 in Italy, but have recently been made more generally available in McGovern and Hinnant's edition. This addition to the canon of Finch's work allows the reader to see the more intensely political and reflective nature of her poems in their private state, showing, as Carol Barash had remarked of the 1713 *Miscellany Poems,* how Finch tones down her politics for publication (*English Women's Poetry 1649–1714: Politics, Community and Linguistic Authority,* p. 282). Hinnant and McGovern have also been instrumental in broadening the critical discourse surrounding Finch's work, developing the work of Ann Messenger and others. Study of Finch's poetry is now for perhaps the first time possible without entering into apology for her work as minor, or inconsistent, or worthy of consideration primarily on account of having been written by a woman. The variety, intelligence, reflectiveness, and relevance of her work is now recognized, and she is being worked into the history of Augustan literature.

SELECTED BIBLIOGRAPHY

I. WORKS. *The Spleen* (London, 1709) (Pamphlet edition, published anonymously); *Miscellany Poems, on Several Occasions.* (London: J.B., 1713); *Pope's Own Miscellany: Being a Reprint of "Poems on Several Occasions," 1717* (Edited by Norman Ault, London, 1935) (Pope put eight of Finch's poems in this miscellany, more than any other poet except himself and John Buckingham—Ault's reprint is the most accessible version of this text); *The Anne Finch Wellesley Manuscript Poems: A Critical Edition* (Edited by Barbara McGovern and Charles H. Hinnant, Athens and

ANNE FINCH

London, 1998) (Edition of the large Wellesley College folio containing many poems written after Finch's 1713 collection).

II. MODERN SELECTIONS. *Eighteenth-Century Poetry: An Annotated Anthology*. Edited by David Fairer and Christine Gerrard (Oxford, U.K., 1999); *Eighteenth-Century Women Poets*. Edited by Roger Lonsdale (Oxford, U.K., 1989); *Poems by Anne, Countess of Winchilsea, 1661–1720*. Edited and introduced by John Middleton Murry (London, 1928); *Poems and Extracts Chosen by William Wordsworth for an Album Presented to Lady Mary Lowther Christmas, 1819*. Introduced by Harold Littledale (London, 1905) (Contains an extremely influential selection of Finch's descriptive poetry); *Selected Poems*. Edited by Denys Thompson (Manchester, U.K., 1987).

III. COLLECTED. *The Poems of Anne Countess of Winchilsea*. Edited by Myra Reynolds (Chicago, 1903) (Citations in the text are to this edition).

IV. OTHER WRITERS' WORKS. Abraham Cowley. *Poetry and Prose*. Edited by L. C. Martin (Oxford, U.K., 1949); Jonathan Swift. *The Complete Poems*. Edited by Pat Rogers (New Haven, 1983).

V. CRITICAL AND BIOGRAPHICAL STUDIES. Reuben A Brower. "Lady Winchilsea and the Poetic Tradition of the Seventeenth Century." *Studies in Philology,* 42: 61–80 (1945)

Katharine Rogers. "Anne Finch, Countess of Winchilsea: An Augustan Woman Poet," in *Shakespeare's Sisters: Feminist Essays on Women Poets*. Edited and introduced by Sandra M. Gilbert and Susan Gubar (Bloomington and London, 1979) Pp. 32–46.

Anne Messenger. "Selected Nightingales: Anne Finch, Countess of Winchilsea, et al.," in Anne Messenger, *His and Hers: Essays in Restoration and Eighteenth-Century Literature* (Lexington, Ky., 1986) Pp.71–83).

Jean Mallinson. "Anne Finch: A Woman Poet and the Tradition," in *Gender at Work: Four Women Writers of the Eighteenth Century*. Edited and introduced by Ann Messenger (Detroit, 1990) Pp. 34–76); Dorothy Mermin. "Women Becoming Poets: Katherine Philips, Aphra Behn, Anne Finch," *English Literary History,* 57: 335–355 (1990); Barbara McGovern. *Anne Finch and Her Poetry: A Critical Biography.* (Athens and London, 1992); Charles H. Hinnant. *The Poetry of Anne Finch: An Essay in Interpretation* (Newark, London, and Toronto: 1994); Carol Barash. *English Women's Poetry, 1649–1714: Politics, Community and Linguistic Authority* (Oxford:, 1996) (Suggests that Finch is the first poet to think of herself reflectively as an English woman poet); Jayne Elizabeth Lewis. *The English Fable: Aesop and Literary Culture, 1651–1740* (Cambridge, 1996); Jennifer Keith. "The Poetics of Anne Finch," *Studies in English Literature 1500–1900,* 38: 465–480 (1998).

Ann Messenger. *Pastoral Tradition and the Female Talent: Studies in Augustan Poetry* (New York, 2001).

ALASDAIR GRAY

(1934–)

Gavin Miller

SCOTTISH LITERATURE UNDERWENT a period of rebirth in the early 1980s. Glasgow, in particular, was a focus for new writers. Preeminent among them was Alasdair Gray. Although he had published little, Gray was an accomplished visual artist and playwright and had been writer-in-residence at Glasgow University. His first published novel, *Lanark: A Life in Four Books* (1981), had an extraordinary impact upon Scottish literature and released a dam burst of new writing from authors such as James Kelman, Janice Galloway, Tom Leonard, and Liz Lochhead. After the success of *Lanark,* Gray went on to produce further novels and collections of short stories. His fiction frequently mixes contemporary Scotland with bizarre and outlandish fantasy, moving easily from personal experience to other worlds of science fiction or inner worlds of imagination. As well as producing fiction and drama, Gray has written collections of poetry, ventured into literary criticism, and intervened in Scottish politics with pamphlets advocating independence. He has also maintained a parallel career as a visual artist specializing in murals, portraiture, and book design. This expertise is quite apparent in Gray's books: they are marvels of typography complemented with his own pen-and-ink illustrations.

LIFE

Alasdair James Gray was born to Alexander and Amy (née Fleming) Gray in Glasgow on 28 December 1934. Alexander Gray worked in a box-making factory. Amy was a shop assistant for a clothing firm. Though working-class, the family lived in a modern and well-designed housing scheme quite unlike the extreme deprivation of neighborhoods such as the Gorbals. Gray's childhood security was soon broken by World War II. Bombing raids on Glasgow forced the family to evacuate to various locations outside the city. They finally settled in Yorkshire, where Alexander Gray worked as a hostel manager. The family returned to Glasgow after the war, and it was there that Alasdair would complete his education.

Throughout his schooling Gray distinguished himself as a precocious writer and artist. While at high school, he had stories published in *Collins Magazine for Boys and Girls* and read his verse on BBC Radio. The utilitarian emphasis of the Scottish educational system, however, was not to his taste. In a biographical piece from the collection *Ten Tales Tall & True* (1993), Gray recalls, "Compound interest, sines, cosines, Latin declensions, tables of elements tasted to my mind like sawdust in my mouth: those who dished it out expected me to swallow while an almost bodily instinct urged me to vomit" (p. 156). The psychosomatic connection is no exaggeration: Gray regularly suffered asthma attacks and eczema from early childhood until after graduation from art college. His psychological stress (with its physiological consequences) was also intensified by the death of his mother in 1952, while he was still a teenager.

Despite these problems, Gray successfully completed high school. Although his family did not have enough money to support his education, Glasgow School of Art arranged quite exceptional financial support in order that Gray could attend. He specialized in design and mural painting but continued writing throughout college, working on early sections of what would later become *Lanark.* He graduated in 1957 and began a journey through Spain funded by a travel scholarship. This abortive journey would later be recounted in "A Report to the Trustees of the

Bellahouston Travelling Scholarship" collected in *Lean Tales* (1985).

Gray returned to Scotland and, while supporting himself as a part-time high school teacher, worked on various mural projects for the remainder of the 1950s. In 1961, during a stint as a scene painter for the Edinburgh Festival, he met his first wife, Inge Sørensen. They married in the same year and had a son, Andrew, in 1963. Gray briefly brushed with fame in 1964, when he was the subject of a BBC TV documentary, *Under the Helmet.* Payment from this program allowed Gray to support himself in various artistic ventures. He further supplemented his earnings by writing radio and TV plays; these commissions would provide a regular source of income throughout the 1960s and 1970s.

In 1972, Gray joined a creative writing group run by Philip Hobsbaum, a literature professor at Glasgow University. There Gray met other Glaswegian writers such as Tom Leonard, James Kelman, and Agnes Owens. Five years later, his steadily increasing literary profile led to an appointment as writer-in-residence at Glasgow University. During this period, which ended in 1979, *Lanark* was accepted for publication by Canongate. Its eventual appearance in 1981 was Gray's impressive debut on the literary scene.

In the 1980s, due to the success of *Lanark,* Gray no longer needed to earn a living from activities outside of art and literature. He published two collections of short stories: *Unlikely Stories, Mostly* (1983) and, with James Kelman and Agnes Owens, *Lean Tales* (1985). As well as producing another novel, *1982 Janine* (1984), Gray continued to write scripts, publish poetry, and develop earlier work into prose fictions such as the novelistic collage *Something Leather* (1990).

Gray, who had separated from his first wife in the late sixties, married again in 1991 to Morag McAlpine. In the following years he published two novels, *Poor Things* (1992) and *A History Maker* (1994), as well as a collection of short stories, *Ten Tales Tall & True* (1993). Gray also entered the political arena with *Why Scots Should Rule Scotland,* a pamphlet advocating Scottish independence written for the 1992 general elec-

tion and later revised and republished for the general election of 1997. After the publication of *Mavis Belfrage* in 1996, Gray produced little original literature. Much of his time was occupied in artistic activities or in his long-standing project to compile an annotated anthology of literary prefaces.

Gray's publishing history shows an usually long time lag between composition and publication. Parts of *Lanark,* for example, were written in the 1950s. He also frequently reworks plays into prose fiction: *The Fall of Kelvin Walker* (1985), *McGrotty and Ludmilla* (1990), and *Something Leather* all reemploy scripts from Gray's early career. In the epilogue to *Something Leather,* Gray is disarmingly frank about the homogeneity of his work:

> A few years ago I noticed my stories described men who found life a task they never doubted until an unexpected collision opened their eyes and changed their habits. This collision was usually with a woman, involved swallowing alcohol or worse, and happened in the valley of the shadow of death. I had made novels and stories believing each an adventurous new world. I now saw the same pattern in them all—the longest novel used it thrice.
>
> (p. 232)

Gray's published work therefore rarely shows a pattern of chronological progression—rather, like motifs in a musical composition, the same themes and issues are varied and elaborated throughout his writing.

LANARK

Lanark: A Life in Four Books (1981) casts a long shadow over the rest of Gray's work. Most authors build up to their magnum opus. Gray's delayed entry into the literary marketplace meant, however, that his first published work was his largest and most significant. Its impact upon the Scottish literary scene is hard to overestimate. Allan Massie in the *Scotsman* declared *Lanark* was "a quite extraordinary achievement, the most remarkable thing done in Scottish fiction for a very long time. It has changed the landscape" (p. 3).

ALASDAIR GRAY

Lanark consists of four books. Books 1 and 2 recount the life of Duncan Thaw, a narrative which in many ways follows Gray's own biography. The protagonist is born into a working-class Scottish family before World War II, excels at art and literature, and lives a life divided between humdrum reality and vivid fantasy. Unlike Gray, Thaw fails at art school and eventually commits suicide by drowning. Book 3 begins with a protagonist arriving in a mysterious city by train, unable to recall his past or even his identity. He assumes the name Lanark and enters a nightmarish world where people are afflicted by mysterious diseases that distort and transform their bodies. He is cured of his own disease—"dragonhide"—by taking refuge in an underground hospital-like institution. There he consults an oracle and learns of his previous existence as Duncan Thaw. Lanark eventually leaves the institute for the city of Unthank in a quest for sunlight. On his arrival there, accompanied by his lover Rima, he is seduced by the idea of representing this city at an international summit—a task which he fails to carry out effectively. While at the summit, though, he is introduced to the "author" of *Lanark*, "Nastler," a figure modeled closely on Gray. Nastler explains to Lanark his position in a fictional world, outlines his powerlessness, and explains that his failure as a delegate will drive him back to Unthank in defeat. The story ends with Lanark contemplating the city of Unthank from a vantage point as it lies half-submerged by flood. He watches in foreknowledge of his own death the next day, at last a "slightly worried, ordinary old man but glad to see the light in the sky" (p. 560).

Lanark introduces themes that recur throughout Gray's work. In particular, it introduces a certain character type: that of an individual who inhabits an imagined inner life of greater vivacity than the objective, outer world. This psychic withdrawal was very much a part of Gray's existence as he grew up. In "Mr. Meikle: An Epilogue" from *Ten Tales Tall & True*, Gray recalls how, as a disaffected high-school student, "My body put on an obedient, hypocritical act while my mind dodged out through imaginary doors" (p. 156). The same condition afflicts Duncan Thaw in *Lanark*, for whom "apparent life was a succession of dull habits in which he did what was asked automatically, only resenting demands to show interest. His energy had withdrawn into imaginary worlds and he had none to waste on reality" (p. 157). For Thaw, like Gray, much of this withdrawal can be traced to the demands of his schooling, in which art and literature take a distant second place to math and science.

Gray avoids, though, the temptation to present his protagonist simply as the heroic victim of an unsympathetic environment. Thaw is egotistical and insensitive. Much of his imaginative energy is expended not in the creation of art but in the production of sadomasochistic fantasies. He also regards himself as elevated beyond the ethical standards of his community. Earlier generations of Scotsmen contained the Calvinist "Elect"—Protestants who were so assured of their predestined salvation that they would commit sin without fear of damnation. This self-serving attitude was the object of satire in James Hogg's *The Private Memoirs and Confessions of a Justified Sinner* (1824). Thaw is something of a modern-day justified sinner. He exploits his father and bullies his sister in order to further his artistic career. Even his short-lived romance at art college is infected with this attitude. His girlfriend, Marjory, is but a means to an end:

> He stopped and gripped her arm. "Marjory, can I draw you? Naked, I mean?"
>
> She stared. He said eagerly, "I won't be embarrassed—my picture needs you."
>
> (p. 286)

Her nakedness, Thaw implies, would be important not because he loves her sexually but because it would further his artistic career. Unsurprisingly, Marjory declines his invitation, and the couple soon separate. As "Nastler," the "author" of *Lanark*, comments, "The Thaw narrative shows a man dying because he is bad at loving" (p. 484). Thaw's inner imaginative life may protect his artistic inclinations, but it also cuts him off from meaningful human relations with the real people around him.

To regard the story of Thaw, though, as wholly biographically informed would be a mistake. There is a neglected context of Scottish thought that is as influential upon Gray as French existentialism is upon the work of Jean-Paul Sartre or Albert Camus. A part of this intellectual environment is the work of the psychiatrist R. D. Laing (1927–1989). Laing was, like Gray, a Glaswegian. Not only did the two meet in the 1980s, but also, as Laing's biographer, John Clay, reveals, "Gray had been an admirer of Laing's books since they first came out in the 1960s. [Gray:] 'I found them stimulating because agreeable. When one writer finds a second agreeable it is most certainly because number one has translated number two into number one's terms'" (Clay, p. 228). The title of Laing's most significant book, *The Divided Self* (1959), provides a clear indication of this influence. Laing sets out his theory of the "schizoid self." Such a personality retreats from relations with other people by building a barrier against them—a disavowed, outer, "bodily" self that takes on the duties of everyday life. The schizoid feels that his or her real self is an inner being who leads an imagined life of greater vivacity and apparent freedom. One of Laing's case studies neatly exemplifies this character type. He describes a patient who, because of this psychic split, could not properly have sexual relations with his wife. The patient experienced intercourse as a relation of his body to hers, a connection of which his "true," mental self had no part. This individual could only find satisfaction by imagining himself making love to his wife at the same time as his body was having sexual relations with her. An intensified version of the same problem afflicts the unnamed Glaswegian comedian in Gray's novel *Something Leather:* "when we made love I imagined other women *instead* of Donalda, and other men instead of me. I could not ejaculate without imagining . . . a tyrant with a harem of captured brides, a cowboy sheriff with a jail full of deliciously sluttish prostitutes" (p. 196). In Laing's theories, as in Gray's narratives, the divided self is fundamentally unhealthy. Although the inner self is preserved, the defensive measures take their toll—the "false," bodily self is a barrier through which love cannot communicate.

Laing's account of the futility of an inner fantasy life fits well with the generic characteristics of *Lanark*. When Thaw is reborn as Lanark, he finds that his previous life persists in a fantastic, imaginatively transfigured form. The people he meets are echoes of those he formerly knew in his life as Thaw and are now afflicted with fantastic diseases which, as Gray remarked in an interview with Mark Axelrod, are "metaphors for bad mental states, like the tortures in Dante's *Inferno*" (Axelrod, p. 109). Lanark himself has "dragonhide," a condition that turns his skin into a hard, insulating armor. When he was Thaw, he cared little for friends and family—at best, other people were there to be exploited as part of his glorious destiny. Lanark's illness turns this psychic condition into a fantastic physical metaphor. His armored skin and crablike pincer parallel the callousness and cruelty of his earlier existence. The generic shift in *Lanark* to fantasy provides no respite for its protagonist. Even a new world of the imagination remains obsessively bound to the reality Thaw has tried to escape.

Lanark, though, is freed from his dragonhide when he descends to the Institute. This paradoxical establishment is dedicated to helping those who suffer from disease, while at the same time sustaining itself with the energies of those who succumb to their condition. Those who die of dragonhide release tremendous quantities of energy that can be used for power; other diseases provide food and raw material for circuitry. Lanark's spell in the institute has its biographical parallel in the events described in "A Report to the Trustees of the Bellahouston Travelling Scholarship" in *Lean Tales*. Gray's hospitalization during his attempt to travel through Spain seems to have cured him of the unexamined compulsions that restricted his personal growth: "I was afraid of losing the habits by which I knew myself, so withdrew into asthma. My tour was spent in an effort to avoid the maturity gained from new experiences" (p. 207). Gray, like his creations Thaw and Lanark, finds release from a shell of deadened conformity that has outlived its initial protective function.

The remainder of Lanark's narrative, however, recapitulates Thaw's failures. Lanark reassumes a kind of spiritual dragonhide when he is offered an opportunity to represent his city at the General Assembly. Like Thaw, Lanark represses his spontaneous emotional life and withdraws from engagement with his loved ones. His feelings when he leaves his son, Alexander, exemplify this re-creation of a divided self: "Lanark felt tears behind his eyes and realized his mouth was straining to girn [groan] aloud. He felt it would be horrible for a boy to remember a pitiable father and turned his face away and hardened the muscles of it to keep the grief inside" (p. 463). Although Lanark leaves for the assembly full of heroic daydreams, he fails abysmally in his duties: when he is needed most, he has been imprisoned, under arrest for drunkenly urinating in the street. He only finds a degree of happiness again when he returns to Unthank and is reunited with Rima and Alexander.

Lanark's literary impact was due largely to its transplantation of a local setting into a contemporary form and style that had not previously been attempted in Scottish writing. Despite its modishness, though, *Lanark* is a traditional moral fable that subverts the myth of the artist or writer as an extraordinary, heroic outsider. It tells the same story three times: that of a man who substitutes dreams of power for the love he cannot find and who suffers accordingly until he is released catastrophically from his mental imprisonment. The best commentary upon the aims of *Lanark* comes perhaps from Gray's fictional author, "Nastler," who intrudes upon the text in order to tell Lanark that "an illusionist's main job is to exhaust his restless audience by a show of marvellously convincing squabbles until they see the simple things we really depend upon. . . . Perhaps the best thing I could do is write a story in which adjectives like *commonplace* and *ordinary* have the significance which *glorious* and *divine* carried in earlier comedies" (p. 494).

1982 JANINE *AND* SOMETHING LEATHER

Gray's second published novel, *1982 Janine* (1984), is the object of some controversy. It presents the first-person narrative of Jock McLeish, an expert in security systems, who is staying the night in a small Scottish hotel. Jock's drunken stream of consciousness constitutes the first half of the book as he indulges in sadomasochistic fantasies involving a cast of characters such as "Superb," "Big Momma," "Helga," and "Janine." His effort to marshall his sexual fantasies, though, is repeatedly interrupted by memories he would rather ignore. Driven to desperation by these intrusions from the real world, he takes an overdose of barbiturates. Fortunately for Jock, this suicide attempt fails; it seems, in fact, to precipitate a spiritual rebirth. Gray employs his design expertise to represent this process: as the drugs take effect, the text splits into multiple columns running in various directions to parallel the fracturing and multiplication of Jock's internal monologue. After Jock regurgitates the pills, he resolves to tell the story of his life in chronological order. This narrative train of thought occupies the second half of the book. Jock recalls the humdrum oppressiveness of his family life and the brutality of his schooling—circumstances that drove him to prefer a life lived in erotic fantasy. His greatest failure of his life was to have abandoned Denny, his first love, for Helen, his eventual wife. From this decision, and the death of his friend Alan, came Jock's imprisonment in a loveless marriage and a tedious job.

The most troubling aspect of this novel, to many, is Gray's depiction of sadomasochistic sexual fantasy. A small sample gives the flavor of Jock's imagination: "Helga, Big Momma, Superb and Janine stand in a row wearing very tight shrinkfit jeans. . . . Ropes tie their wrists high above their heads but they do not hang from these although they would have to do so if someone pulled off their steep wedgesoled sandals with, ah, eight-inch high heels" (p. 116). Gray's later novel *Something Leather* (1990) presents a similar problem with its depiction of sadomasochistic sex in a fictional reality (as opposed to a fictional imagination such as Jock's). In one scene, June, a lonely divorcée, is handcuffed in high heels, photographed, caned, and later shaved and tattooed, by a trio of women.

Curiously, in an age of sexual liberation, there has been no serious attempt to cast such material as innocuous sexual deviation. This is undoubtedly because of a perceived association between sadomasochism and sexual violence. Criticism of this aspect of Gray's sexual politics varies in pertinence and acuity. Undoubtedly some of the ire directed against *1982 Janine* and *Something Leather* is actually aimed at the author. Gray has been frank in his admission that such material gratifies his own predilections. In "Critic Fuel: An Epilogue" in *Something Leather,* he admits that "while writing the first chapter of this book I enjoyed a prolonged cold-blooded sexual thrill of a sort common amongst some writers and all lizards" (p. 234). A more pointed, less ad hominem, objection is that Gray's work may in some way legitimate sexual violence against women. In particular, June's ordeal in *Something Leather* is vulnerable to this criticism: in Gray's narrative, her experience liberates her from the conventions of her society, rather than, for example, traumatizing her in the way normally experienced by rape victims.

To defend *Something Leather* against the charge that it descends into pornography is indeed difficult. However well intentioned (and even accurate) Gray's presentation of sadomasochistic psychology may be, the essentially unrealistic tone of June's narrative places it in a pornographic realm. The reader is invited to a make-believe world where sadomasochistic lesbian foursomes occur at the drop of a hat and where psychologically complex sexual experiences require no explicit consent and are entirely free of risk. In Gray's defense, it may be argued that readers perceive this generic shift as surely as the switch to a fantasy world in *Lanark* and are just as unlikely to regard the narrative as literally realistic.

1982 Janine is rather easier to distinguish from pornography. Jock's fantasies are rarely continuous enough to be read for any kind of gratification. They are also quite clearly Jock's attempt to distract himself from his own misery: "I now, in perfectly cold blood, return to my Superb who is being raped up the arse by Charlie. Since the best whisky in the world cannot fill my mind with happy memories I must get back to a fantasy and keep control of it this time" (p. 86).

These fantasies are not even, as one might presume, images of Jock's frustrated desires. Jock himself comes to understand that his daydreams reflect his own predicament: they concern a "woman [who] is corrupted into enjoying her bondage and trapping others into it. I did not notice that this was the story of my own life. I avoided doing so by insisting on the *femaleness* of the main character" (pp. 193–194). Peculiar though it may sound, there is something realistic about Jock's daydreams. As Stephen Bernstein notes in his literary study *Alasdair Gray,* Jock's fantasies of sexual exploitation represent the way he has sold himself out to the expectations of his society: "Jock tacitly suggests that he had been forced to prostitute himself throughout adult life. Prostitution and the internal division it implies go on to become central metaphors. . . . For Jock the basic transaction of a body rented out for the pleasure of others encompasses vast areas of personal, class, and institutional behaviour" (p. 67). *1982 Janine* resembles *Lanark* in this use of fantasy. When Thaw commits suicide he is translated into a fantasy world that merely repeats—in bizarre metaphors made real—the reality he has tried to escape. Jock McLeish also tries to retreat into a world of fantasy, but he too finds himself pursued there by the real world he would rather ignore.

1982 Janine also complements *Lanark* in its study of a divided self. Like Thaw, Jock has been driven into a fantasy world by a life where he can find no emotional engagement. Scottish traditions of corporal punishment play a part in creating this psychic division. Jock is beaten at school by his teacher, "Mad Hislop":

"Hold out your hands, and double them."

I did so in a daze of astonishment. Did I cry out at the first blow? Almost certainly, but afterward I did not flinch and certainly did not weep. . . . I glared at him with a rigid grin I can feel on my face at this very moment, and I stepped toward him and raised my hands till they almost touched his chin and I whispered, "Again!"

(p. 85)

Rather than supply a spontaneous human response such as tears, terror, or rage, Jock armors himself with the dragonhide of cultivated indifference. A similar pattern is described in the novella *The Fall of Kelvin Walker* when the protagonist is humiliated by an encounter with his father during a live television show: "Kelvin had tied his body in a knot for two reasons. One was to shield it from the flaying glance of the studio audience and of those extra millions who were surveying him through the cameras, the other was to protect a precious core of certainty from the shattering contempt of his father" (p. 134). This response is linked to the beatings Kelvin received as a child: "He heard his father say that his condition was not new—he had always gone like that after a good thrashing, and always took ten or twelve minutes to recover" (p. 134). That Jock should base his fantasies around sadomasochistic rituals is therefore quite appropriate. Like his obsession with prostitution, this is an echo of the world he is attempting to evade: ritualized beating stands for a whole series of chastising and chastening circumstances that force the self into an inner life detached from outer, bodily existence.

Jock's fantasies, though, also go beyond his personal life. They have a political meaning: "if a country is not just a tract of land but a whole people then clearly Scotland has been fucked. I mean that word in the vulgar sense of *misused to give satisfaction or advantage to another*" (p. 136). During the 1992 general election, Gray published a political pamphlet, *Why Scots Should Rule Scotland,* in which he advocated Scottish independence. In the revised edition, published in 1997, he makes explicit his reasons for this political position. Gray's nationalism grows out of his disaffection with the British Labour Party and what he sees as its failure to consolidate the egalitarianism imposed, by necessity, during World War II. He recalls a scene from Frank Capra's motion picture *It's a Wonderful Life* (1946), in which Jimmy Stewart's character is shown his home town as it would have been without him:

It has become a garish Las Vegas glittering with adverts for strip shows and gambling, the streets full of conspicuously wealthy folk in flashy cars beside beggars and a prostitute in whom he recognizes the faces of old school friends and the girl next door—the values of the rich money lender have prevailed. That is how I feel about modern Britain.

(p. 105)

The sexual content of Gray's work is not usually prurient or gratuitous. Taken in isolation, certain scenes may seem pornographic or offensive. When read in context, though, the sexual subject matter of novels such as *1982 Janine* and *Something Leather* is rarely titillating. Gray's presentation emphasizes the psychological complexities of sadomasochism and frequently exploits the figurative and metaphorical potential of such behavior.

POOR THINGS

Poor Things (1992) is perhaps Gray's most successful novel after *Lanark* and *1982 Janine.* The text presents a series of documents which Gray, the volume's "editor," claims were found among the records of a now-defunct firm of Glaswegian solicitors. The longest narrative is "Episodes from the Early Life of a Scottish Public Health Officer," written, we are told, by Archibald McCandless, M.D. McCandless tells of his involvement at Glasgow University's medical school with the mysterious and malformed surgical genius Godwin Baxter. Baxter introduces McCandless to Bella, a woman in her mid-twenties with the mentality of a child. Baxter explains that she has been created by resurrecting the body of a suicide, within which he has planted the brain of a child. As he later reveals to McCandless, the brain is that of the suicide's own unborn daughter. Baxter keeps this knowledge from Bella by telling her that she is an amnesiac orphan. Bella, whose mind matures rapidly, maintains an engagement with McCandless while simultaneously "eloping" with an unscrupulous lawyer, Duncan Wedderburn. The pair travel around Europe and North Africa. Bella comes back changed by the brutal realities of the world; Duncan returns mad, convinced that Bella is the Scarlet Woman described in the Book of Revelation. Upon Bella's return, she and McCandless arrange to marry, but their wedding is interrupted by one General Aubrey Blessington, who reveals that he is Bella's husband (or, at least, the husband of her body.) Blessington's threats are futile, though. Bella, who worked in a Parisian brothel during her time abroad, identifies him as "Monsieur Spankybot," a regular visitor to the "dungeon." He withdraws his claim on Bella and later commits suicide.

Following this narrative is a more sober account by Victoria McCandless, M.D., wife of Archibald. She insists that McCandless's incredible tale was concocted as he lay dying of multiple sclerosis. The facts of her life are, she insists, very different. Her first husband was indeed General Blessington. She left him voluntarily, however, soon after she met Godwin Baxter, who had been asked to surgically remove her clitoris. Baxter had refused to do so, and she divined that he might provide a place of refuge for her. After fleeing to Baxter's house, she fell in love with him, but he refused to marry her. She therefore consented to a marriage of convenience and companionship with McCandless.

To these two narratives are appended notes by Gray in which he purports to demonstrate the authenticity of McCandless's story. These notes emphasize the central, and undecidable, dilemma of the book: What is the status of McCandless's narrative? Of course it is fictional: no such person exists, no such events take place. But what is its standing within the world of *Poor Things*? Is it a (fictional) fantasy? Or a (fictional) reality? The reader is left unable to decide whether McCandless is a deluded fantasist or whether Victoria is attempting to cover up her mysterious origins.

The ambiguous status of McCandless's story is more than mere playfulness on Gray's part. For all the sanity and moderation of Victoria's narrative, there is something missing in the reality which it calmly and optimistically portrays. Victoria is unable to feel with more intensity than that dictated by universal benevolence. She recalls her attendance upon her dying husband: "I stayed beside him though I could have done more good at other bed-sides. Never mind. I may want company during my own last days, so am glad I did not refuse it to him" (p. 255). Victoria

later comes to understand the effects of this absence of feeling. Her two youngest sons join the army to fight in World War I and are killed in the Somme, while her eldest son works as a propagandist for the "Department of Imperial Statistics." She eventually concludes that what led to their blind obedience was an unspoken belief that their own lives were worthless. Her inability to love them uniquely meant, she concludes, that "I did not give them the self-respect to resist that epidemic of self-abasement" (p. 307). The foregoing quotation is given in Gray's "Notes Critical and Historical"; it is, we are told, from Victoria's postwar pamphlet *A Loving Economy,* in which she advocates greater tenderness between parents and children as a way of endowing the latter with self-respect.

In light of his wife's later insights, McCandless comes off better. In response to his memoirs, Victoria is forced to admit "My husband practised what I preached": "I, the fearless advocate of homely cuddling and playful teaching, was kept out of the house by my clinical work" (p. 252). McCandless's story of his wife's origins may or may not be the literal (albeit fictional) truth. However, the idea that his wife was not born until the twenty-sixth year of her life is certainly a figurative truth. Her upbringing in an affection-starved household and her subsequent finishing school education left her, she admits, "a rich man's domestic toy" (p. 258). That she should be "born" with the mind of a child after encountering Godwin Baxter is, at worst, a distortion of the facts by McCandless to better express the reality of his wife's existence. This kind of truth, though, cannot be conveyed in the practical, down-to-earth scientific thought patterns employed by Victoria. For that, one requires an imaginative transfiguration of reality like that employed by her husband. The mingling of fantasy and reality in *Poor Things* therefore functions much like that found in *Lanark* and *1982 Janine*: McCandless's overheated imagination (or, perhaps, his faithful account of a bizarre scientific experiment) communicates figuratively aspects of reality that are overlooked by straightforward realism.

ALASDAIR GRAY

A HISTORY MAKER

Poor Things was lauded by Elizabeth Young in *The Guardian* as "a bibliophile's paradise of postmodern precision" (p. 23). Young clearly meant this as both an accurate description and as a compliment. There is, though, significant debate over whether the term "postmodern" should be applied to Gray's fiction, and what, indeed, this would mean. *A History Maker* (1994) provides Gray's most explicit engagement with this concept. This short novel tells of a world in which history seems to have ended. The invention of "powerplants" in the twenty-first century has peacefully revolutionized all societies. These devices provide energy and can synthesize all manner of organic and inorganic materials. Communities are now small, self-sufficient matriarchies that communicate via a global "open intelligence network." The menfolk occupy themselves with televised battles fought between rival clans using archaic weapons. Death in battle is uncommon: the powerplants can grow new organs, limbs, and even brains for injured soldiers.

Like *Poor Things, A History Maker* marshalls a variety of fictional sources. The central narrative is that of Wat Dryhope, a renowned Scottish warrior of the Ettrick clan. He is approached by the mysterious "Delilah Puddock," who attempts to exploit his nostalgia for the days of historically effective mass warfare. Delilah is really Meg Mountbenger, a conspirator in a plan to destroy the powerplants using a specially designed virus. She drugs and infects Wat, who then unwittingly passes the infection to other people and their powerplants. The reader is informed of Meg's secret agenda in the "Notes Explaining Obscurities" which follow Wat's narrative. These reveal that the conspiracy is foiled by the wise matriarchs who govern the world. They quickly divine Meg's actions and arrange for the quarantine of both Wat and the infected powerplants. The notes are written by Wat's mother, who also provides a prologue to the tale in which she warns: "*A History Maker* shows that good states change as inevitably as bad ones, and should be carefully watched" (p. xv).

Any understanding of *A History Maker* must deal with the status of the future society envisaged by Gray. To what extent is this a genuine utopian vision of a "good state?" There is certainly much to admire in this society. War is limited to a spectator sport, the ecology of the planet is stabilized, and work is fulfilling instead of abstract and specialized. Gray himself provides an introductory acknowledgment of the anthropologist Margaret Mead, "whose *Coming of Age in Samoa* provided the form of a kindlier society than her critics thought possible" (p. ii). The novel may indeed present a technologically advanced matriarchy as a desirable future.

On the other hand, very little of the fantasy or science fiction in Gray's work is straightforwardly visionary. *A History Maker* might also reflect features of our own society—one in which war is putatively "limited" and might even be said to exist (to Western eyes) as a media spectacle. The gender relations of the future also resemble our own—Wat confronts his Aunt Mirren with the fact that he was unattractive to women until he became a soldier. Furthermore, Wat's nostalgia for past warfare is a longing for a time in which history was real: "a period," as he says, "of excitement when folk thought they were making a better world" (p. 28). Ironically, Wat's present resembles one of the historical periods described by his mother in her notes. This future past is our own present—a time that has been referred to as "postmodern." Kate Dryhope's analysis probably conveys much of Gray's own attitude to this term:

Postmodernism happened when landlords, businessmen, brokers and bankers who owned the rest of the world had used new technologies to destroy the power of labour unions. Like owners of earlier empires they felt that history had ended because they and their sort could now dominate the world for ever. This indifference to most people's wellbeing and taste appeared in the fashionable art of the wealthy. Critics called their period *postmodern* to separate it from the modern world begun by the Renaissance when most creative thinkers believed they could improve their community. Postmodernists had no interest in the future, which they expected to be an amusing rearrangement of things they already knew.

(pp. 202–203)

A History Maker may be a vision of a genuine utopia, or it may be a fantastic reflection of our present-day political complacency—the question cannot be easily settled. Nonetheless there can be little doubt about Gray's scepticism toward postmodernist thought. In the postscript to *Sixteen Occasional Poems 1990–2000* (2000), Gray mentions a conference he attended in the United States where a speaker discussed postmodernism:

> His energetic speech led to a discussion that said nothing about the links between vision and word and ignored description of an intricate universe and how well or badly we live in it. . . . The chaos theory was mentioned with enthusiasm by one who seemed to think it a liberation from logical constraint instead of a logical way to solve problems.

(p. 29)

Gray has also distanced himself from the application of the term "postmodern" to his own writing. Stephen Bernstein quotes Gray on the superficiality of this classification: "one convenient way of dealing with Gray's work is to label it postmodern and analyze it accordingly. . . . Yet Gray's rancor at being called a postmodernist is evident in several places. He complains of 'critics—however friendly—who are so interested in what is sometimes called my *ludic* writing . . . that they forget half my writing is not like that' " (p. 28).

Literary postmodernism—as opposed to the sociological or philosophical trend—constitutes a genre of novels with a certain "family resemblance." The appearance of the author as a character, an analogy between the creation of fictional worlds and the "construction" of our everyday reality, and similar self-reflexive devices tend to recur in "postmodern" writing. Certainly they can be found in Gray's work. For instance, the "author" of *Lanark,* "Nastler," appears to his protagonist and informs him that "Your survival as a character and mine as an author depend on us seducing a living soul into our printed world and trapping it here long enough for us to steal the imaginative energy

which gives us life" (p. 485). Notwithstanding Gray's own disavowal of the label "postmodern," the point and significance of such features in his work has been the object of some dispute. One possibility is the understanding of postmodern literature developed by critics such as Brian McHale. This approach takes its inspiration from the sociology of knowledge. We like to think of knowledge as a rigorous progression—"the march of science"—from evidence to hypothesis to theory, all the time converging on the truth. This ideal, though perhaps a necessary one, is undoubtedly a fiction. A host of accidental, human factors—from institutional politics to research grants—undermine the pretense that our knowledge of the world is wholly disinterested and impartial. In this sense, our world might be said to be "socially constructed." McHale sees Gray's fiction in this light: as an attempt to draw our attention to the fictionality of the "real world."

Other readers have been less certain of Gray's supposed status as an (unwilling and unwitting) postmodernist. William Boyd in the *Times Literary Supplement* concluded that "*Lanark* on the whole owes little to post-modernist fiction. Barth's *Giles Goat Boy,* Pynchon's *Gravity's Rainbow* and other huge exercises in quasi-allegorical fiction belong to another literary department" (p. 219). The problem remains, though, of how to reconcile Gray's apparently playful formal innovations with the frequently didactic tone of his fiction. An analogy with Bertolt Brecht's theory of drama may be appropriate here (and has been suggested by the critic Randall Stevenson). Brecht wrote plays that drew attention to their own artificiality. The purpose of this "epic" theater was to direct the audience's attention to the world outside the stage: one which, Brecht believed, could be transformed by their neglected capacity for historical agency. Gray's apparent playfulness may have a similar function. A useful illustration may be provided by the peculiar relation between the narration of *Lanark* and the events it describes. The narrative of *Lanark* is actually a tale that is told to Lanark when he is resident in the underground institute. Any narration of what happens to him after he leaves the institute is actually a prediction by its narrator, the disembodied "oracle." Lanark's abandonment of his son, and his failure as a delegate, are, in truth, all events that may (or may not) happen after he has heard them narrated. Like Brecht's drama, Gray's writing here gestures toward our capacity to shape the future. The text of *Lanark* points to a fictional future—Lanark's life outside the institute—which, like the reader's own future, remains as yet undecided.

The debate over "postmodernism" both as a historical category and as a literary genre is highly involved and still ongoing, and even the relevance of the term to Gray's fiction is arguable. Any reading, though, must, as Gray himself demands, take account of the full range of his work from the playful and decorative to the engaged and didactic.

SHORTER FICTION, DRAMA, AND POETRY

Gray has supplemented his major novels with forays into short stories, plays, and poetry. He has also published two novellas: *The Fall of Kelvin Walker* (1985) and *McGrotty and Ludmilla* (1990). *The Fall of Kelvin Walker* is typical Gray material. The protagonist renounces his Calvinist religion and leaves his small hometown of Glaik for the bright lights of London where he bluffs his way into job interviews by pretending to be Hector McKellar, a renowned Scottish broadcaster. Kelvin eventually comes to the attention of McKellar, who arranges for his employment as a television interviewer. Kelvin's increasing political agenda, however, leads McKellar to arrange his destruction: Kelvin's father is planted in the studio audience and confronts his son on national television over the theft of forty pounds and some jewelry. Kelvin is humiliated and returns to Scotland with his father, where he is eventually ordained as a minister. *McGrotty and Ludmilla* centers upon a similar character. Mungo McGrotty arrives in the heart of British government as a token provincial and is manipulated into stealing "The Harbinger Report," a secret document that has driven its author insane. Knowledge of the report gives McGrotty virtually unlimited powers of blackmail, for it reveals a worldwide organization that

bestows eternal life upon its few, elite members. Assisted by Ludmilla, daughter of the minister for social stability, McGrotty coerces his way into parliament and is eventually made prime minister, where he continues to shield the conspiracy that has served him so well. Like Thaw in *Lanark,* both Kelvin and McGrotty owe much to Scotland's Calvinist inheritance. For all Kelvin's disavowals of his upbringing, his faith in his own ability to succeed, and in the righteousness of his methods, is little more than the self-confidence of a justified sinner. Where Kelvin fails in his atheistic Calvinism, however, and so returns to the theistical variety, McGrotty succeeds and attains a kind of secularized redemption. As one of those who are in fact granted eternal life, he belongs to a secular version of the Calvinist Elect.

Although Gray has written a number of plays for various media, only one script is readily available in published form. *Working Legs: A Two-Act Play for Disabled Performers* (1997) was written for the Birds of Paradise theater company, and is intended to be performed by wheelchair users. The protagonist, Able McMann, exists in a society where the majority prefer to use wheelchairs instead of their legs. Able is ostracized and unemployed because of his fondness for walking, running, and dancing. Although he eventually suppresses these "hypermanic" tendencies and is able to find work and love, he cannot contain them indefinitely and soon ends up unemployed and facing homelessness. In a rage, he wrecks a pub and is arrested by police (in wheelchairs), who beat him unconscious. The story has a "happy" ending: Able is in a coma for seven months; when he awakes he is paralyzed from the waist down. Although this play is superficially concerned with bodily disability, it shows the influence of R. D. Laing's challenge to notions of normality and deviance—indeed, the theater company takes its name from Laing's book *The Bird of Paradise* (1967). The wheelchair-using majority are not physically incapable; rather, they have been socially conditioned not to use their legs. Able is categorized as ill because he deviates from this cultural norm. A psychiatric vocabulary of denigration is applied to his pathological overuse of his limbs—he is "hyperactive," "hypermanic," or even a "hypermaniac."

Unlikely Stories, Mostly (1983) was Gray's first collection of short fiction. The volume brings together a number of stories, most of them originally published in small periodicals. The earliest, "The Star," was published while Gray was still at high school. It foreshadows the blend of realism and fantasy that marks his later work. A young boy discovers a fallen star in the back garden of his tenement block. He takes it to school, where it is mistaken for a marble by his teacher. But before it can be confiscated, the boy swallows the star and ascends into the heavens. Many of the other stories employ this mix of mundanity and myth. "The Problem" provides an explanation for Glasgow's overcast skies: the sun rarely visits because the narrator has unwittingly offended her by mentioning her spots and by seeing other planets behind her back. Other stories include a riveter who splits in two like an amoeba ("The Spread of Ian Nicol"), and a man who turns, inadvertently, into a mythic archetype on his wedding night ("The Comedy of the White Dog"). As with Gray's longer fiction, the fantasy sections are not merely playful exercises in the creation of fictional worlds. In "The Great Bear Cult," a craze for dressing up as bears sweeps 1930s Britain. This comical tale, though, alludes to the rise of prewar British fascism in the form of the "brownshirts" and the "blackshirts." When the human bears attack Labour party buildings, "The police remain aloof until the riots are nearly over and most of the people they arrest are left-wing and furless" (p. 60).

The three longest stories in the volume return to Gray's concern with politics. "Five Letters from an Eastern Empire" and the pair of stories "The Start of the Axletree" and "The End of the Axletree" are fantastic parables on imperial government. The axletree stories tell of the rise of a monoglot empire founded on a project to build a tower to the sun. Things fall apart, however, when it is discovered that the sky is a solid barrier. An attempt to penetrate it shatters the tower, and the empire collapses. "Five Letters from an Eastern Empire" is a warning about the

naïveté with which artists may portray political events. The state-sponsored poet Bohu is deceived into composing a poem on the destruction of the old imperial capital. He writes this piece in the belief that this catastrophe has already happened; in fact, his poem is a piece of propaganda for an event that has yet to take place. The aesthetic virtues of his poem are such that this contingent future is presented, to the delight of his masters, as "a simple, stunning, inevitable fact" (p. 132).

Gray's contribution to the collection *Lean Tales* (1985) is less impressive. Lacking sufficient material for an entire volume of short fiction, Gray suggested to his publishers that it also include material by James Kelman and Agnes Owens, whom he knew from Philip Hobsbaum's Glasgow writing group. Whatever the merits of his collaborators' work, Gray's selection of stories is rather insubstantial. The longest is a biographical memoir, "A Report to the Trustees of the Bellahouston Travelling Scholarship," which tells of his disastrous attempt to travel through Spain after graduating from art college. The most substantial piece of fiction is "The Story of a Recluse," where Gray completes Robert Louis Stevenson's unfinished tale. The ending is typical of Gray's work. Rather than rescuing and marrying the object of his affections, the hero is betrayed by her—she is loyal to her seeming captor, and, Gray suggests, finds little of interest in her dull, self-appointed rescuer. Most of the remaining "tales" are rather slight, and several are straightforward advertisements for the neglected talent of other Scottish writers and artists.

Ten Tales Tall & True (1993) was Gray's next volume of short stories. Ron Loewinsohn in the *New York Times Book Review* commented that the stories continued "one of Mr. Gray's persistent themes: our escapes almost always lead us only to another prison" (p. 11). In the story "The Trendelenburg Position," a dentist proposes a technological escape route from misery and poverty. He suggests that everyone be given a virtual-reality suit with which they can imagine they are living happily on a sunny, unspoiled island. This little piece of science fiction outlines metaphorically the dilemma that faces Gray as an artist. What if

ALASDAIR GRAY

his fictional escape routes are mere escapism, serving only to consolidate oppression? In "Fictional Exits" the narrator tells the parable of an imprisoned artist who draws a door on the wall of his cell, a door so realistic that he can walk through it by power of belief. This, the narrator tells us, is how "new arts and sciences, new religions and nations are created" (p. 93). In contrast, though, stand the imaginative solutions of the police in Glasgow, who claim in court that when they have *"stitched up"* a suspect this really means, in police jargon, *"properly arrested with no hint of falsehood or perjury in the procedure"* (p. 94). Without some kind of imaginative vision, though, we are trapped like the characters of "Near the Driver," where Gray again uses science fiction to outline what he sees as the condition of present-day Scotland. His characters are trapped in a Scottish train controlled by a centralized computer system based in England. The train is on a collision course, and not even the driver has the power to stop it: his duty is to securely restrain the passengers in case they interfere with the smooth running of the system.

The didactic tone of *Ten Tales Tall & True* continues in Gray's next volume of short fiction, *Mavis Belfrage* (1996). Although it is subtitled *A Romantic Novel with Five Shorter Tales,* the outside cover admits "this book should be called *Teachers: 6 Short Tales.*" Like *Something Leather,* the collection is marred by a careless recycling of earlier materials. "Mavis Belfrage" is a reworked television play from the 1970s and exploits Gray's favorite theme of an "unexpected collision" between a man and woman—in this case, an affair between Colin Kerr, an inhibited college lecturer, and his former student, Mavis Belfrage. Although Colin is eventually betrayed by Mavis, he is so transformed by the experience that he emigrates to Africa and marries a local woman. The remainder of the tales is a mixture of fictional pieces and biographical reminiscence. Indeed, the slightness of the collection, and its rather raw reemployment of earlier work, led John Sutherland to conclude in the *Times Literary Supplement* that *Mavis Belfrage* "continues the curious diminuendo in Alasdair Gray's career

since the monumental achievement of *Lanark*" (17 May 1996).

Gray has also published two volumes of poetry: *Old Negatives* (1989) and *Sixteen Occasional Poems: 1990–2000* (2000). Of these, the former is more substantial. The poems in *Old Negatives* are grouped in four periods: "In a Cold Room 1952–57," "Between Whiles 1958–61," "Inge Sørensen 1961–71," and "To Lyric Light 1977–83." The collection begins with Gray's sometimes overwrought adolescent verse. "Statement by an unceilinged blood" gives the flavor of this period:

IN THE BEGINNING WAS THE CAVITY:
EYESOCKET IN NO SKULL, WOUND IN NO FLESH,
THE FACELESS MOUTH, THE COATLESS POCKET.
THIS GOT SUCH HORROR AT ITS OWN VACUITY
IT TRIED AT LENGTH TO SCREAM, AS WHO
 WOULD NOT?

(p. 20)

The volume moves away from this nihilism toward increasing hopefulness and reconciliation, concluding with "End," which reflects upon this progression:

The grave colours of earth
brighten toward
an
open book
of
light unstained
by
word

(p. 67)

"Cowardly" from "Between Whiles 1957–61" analyzes what has hindered this personal development:

I do not live by hope, but certainty,
I hold stones tight: these are the things I know.
I build a tower of them.
I do not grow.

(p. 39)

Like many of Gray's novelistic characters, the speaker in *Old Negatives* cannot grow because he is imprisoned by a rigid wall of habits. He must move away from such cowardice toward the faith and confidence created by love: "A growing tree contains both rock and sun, / A loving man has made his facts catch fire" (p. 39).

Sixteen Occasional Poems is a slim volume of pieces, the majority of which are ad hoc responses to particular circumstances and events. Gray addresses topics as diverse as the end of apartheid, the death of Princess Diana, and the ideology of genocide. One piece, written as a commentary upon the reunification of Germany, contrasts this geopolitical change with Gray's recurrent tendency to inertia:

what in Berlin east or west
can break chains of habit & guilt letting me see
things wholly themselves
things not smeared with me?

(p. 10)

Perhaps, suggests Gray, he is too old to yet again lose the habits by which he is imprisoned:

am 55 my best work done
having promised too many too much
& running (no)
flying away

(p. 9)

It might be responded, however, that Gray's worst habit is literary self-castigation. His "best work" is a landmark in contemporary writing that fully justifies his current standing as an elder statesman of Scottish literature.

CONCLUSION

Alasdair Gray's career as an author seems to be drawing to an end. The frequency and volume of his publication has gradually declined in the two decades since the initial impact of *Lanark.* Gray's latest work is *The Book of Prefaces* (2000), a compilation of famous literary introductions annotated by Gray and a variety of collaborators. In his postscript, Gray describes it as "a memorial to the kind of education British governments now think useless, especially for British working class children. But it has been my education, so I am bound to believe it one of the best in the world" (p. 631). This scholarly volume anticipates Gray's appointment in 2001 to a chair of creative writ-

ing at the University of Glasgow. He shares the professorship with James Kelman and Tom Leonard, two writers whom he has known since his membership in Hobsbaum's creative writing group in the 1970s. There can be little doubt that this belated recognition is well deserved. Gray's work has been at the forefront of Scottish literature and has inspired many of the latest generation of Scottish authors. In particular, the scope of his writing is admirable. Although the setting of his work rarely strays outside Scotland, he manages to bring global political issues into a small, domestic stage—even, indeed, into the private lives and fantasies of his characters. That Gray can do this without hectoring or preaching to his audience is all the more remarkable.

SELECTED BIBLIOGRAPHY

I. NOVELS. *Lanark: A Life in Four Books* (Edinburgh, 1981; New York, 1981); *1982 Janine* (London, 1984; New York, 1984); *The Fall of Kelvin Walker: A Fable of the Sixties* (Edinburgh, 1985; New York, 1986); *McGrotty and Ludmilla; or, The Harbinger Report* (Glasgow, 1990); *Something Leather* (London, 1990; New York, 1990); *Poor Things: Episodes from the Early Life of Archibald McCandless M.D., Scottish Public Health Officer* (London, 1992; New York, 1992); *A History Maker* (Edinburgh, 1994; San Diego, 1996).

II. STORY COLLECTIONS. *The Comedy of the White Dog* (Glasgow, 1979); *Unlikely Stories, Mostly* (Edinburgh, 1983; New York, 1984; rev. ed., Edinburgh, 1997); *Lean Tales,* with James Kelman and Agnes Owens (London, 1985); *Ten Tales Tall & True: Social Realism, Sexual Comedy, Science Fiction and Satire* (London, 1993; New York, 1993); *Mavis Belfrage: A Romantic Novel with Five Shorter Tales* (London, 1996).

III. POETRY. *Old Negatives: Four Verse Sequences* (London, 1989); *Sixteen Occasional Poems: 1990–2000* (Glasgow, 2000).

IV. PLAYS. *Dialogue* (Kirknewton, U.K., 1971); *Working Legs: A Two-Act Play for Disabled Performers* (Glasgow, 1997).

V. NONFICTION. *Why Scots Should Rule Scotland: Independence* (Edinburgh, 1992), rev. as *Why Scots Should Rule Scotland, 1997: A Carnaptious History of Britain from Roman Times Until Now* (Edinburgh, 1997); *A Short Survey of Classic Scottish Writing* (Edinburgh, 2001).

VI. OTHER WORKS. Memoir, *Alasdair Gray* (Edinburgh, 1988); as editor, *The Book of Prefaces: A Short History of Literate Thought by Great Writers of Four Nations from the 7th to the 20th Century* (London and New York, 2000).

VII. ARCHIVE MATERIAL. Collections of Alasdair Gray's manuscripts and other papers are held in the Mitchell

ALASDAIR GRAY

Library, Glasgow; Glasgow University Library; and in the National Library of Scotland, Edinburgh.

VIII. CRITICAL STUDIES AND INTERVIEWS. William Boyd, "The Theocracies of Unthank," in *Times Literary Supplement* (27 February 1981); Alan Massie, "Glasgow Will Never Be the Same After *Lanark*," in *Scotsman* (28 February 1981); Randall Stevenson, "Alasdair Gray and the Postmodern," in Robert Crawford and Thom Nairn, eds., *The Arts of Alasdair Gray* (Edinburgh, 1991); Elizabeth Young, "Glasgow Gothic," in *Guardian* (3 September 1992); Ron Loewinsohn, "Dominance and Submission," in *New York Times Book Review* (6 March 1994); Mark Axelrod, "An Epistolary Interview, Mostly with Alasdair Gray," in *Review of Contemporary Fiction* 15, no. 2 (1995); John

Sutherland, "Night Off in Glasgow," in *Times Literary Supplement* (17 May 1996); Stephen Bernstein, *Alasdair Gray* (Lewisburg, Pa., 1999); Gavin Miller, "Literary Narrative as Soteriology in the Work of Kurt Vonnegut and Alasdair Gray," in *Journal of Narrative Theory* 31, no. 3 (fall 2001); Phil Moores, ed., *Alasdair Gray: Critical Appreciations and a Bibliography* (Boston Spa, U.K., 2002).

IX. FURTHER READING: CONTEXT AND IDEAS. R. D Laing, *The Divided Self: An Existential Study in Sanity and Madness* (Harmondsworth, U.K., 1965); Brian McHale, *Postmodernist Fiction* (New York, 1987); John Clay, *R. D. Laing: A Divided Self: A Biography* (London, 1996); Cairns Craig, *The Modern Scottish Novel: Narrative and the National Imagination* (Edinburgh, 1999).

93

DERMOT HEALY

(1947–)

Amanda Fields

SINCE THE PUBLICATION of his first book of short stories in 1982, Dermot Healy has produced novels, poetry, plays, screenplays, and a memoir. His writing is fiercely Irish, steeped in the tumultuous divisions that have plagued Irish identities, and engaging the political, social, and economic history of Ireland in the twentieth and twenty-first centuries. As an Irish writer, Healy has also confronted the decline of Irish traditional culture, particularly the Irish Gaelic language. His work explores the emotional disassociation and confusion that follow cultural loss. In Healy's case, this loss is centered in language. Healy's characters often confront the inadequacies of language as a conveyor of meaning. His work also explores the nature and uses of memory, as well as the cycle of life and mortality.

Few critical assessments of Healy's work, and no book-length study or comprehensive biography, exist in 2003; thus Healy's writing must be examined in relation to the work of his contemporaries and the study of Irish history and culture in general. For biographical context the reader may also attend to the revelations put forth in Healy's memoir, *The Bend for Home* (1996), and how the memoir offers insight into the characters, themes, and events in his fiction and poetry.

Dermot Healy was born in Finea, County Westmeath, Ireland, on 9 November 1947, just two years before the Republic of Ireland was declared, establishing Ireland's independence from Great Britain and separation from Northern Ireland, which remained part of the United Kingdom. In Healy's youth, his family moved to County Cavan, where his mother, Winnie Slacke Healy, worked in the family bakery. His father, Jack Healy, a member of the civic guard, died after a long illness when Dermot was fifteen. A few days after this event, Healy began to keep a journal, which he eventually edited for inclusion in his

memoir, *The Bend for Home*. While growing up he spent much of his time among the women who owned the bakery on his mother's side of the family. He was often truant from his Catholic school, which resulted in a strained relationship with his strict Aunt Maisie, a woman he portrays with affection and humor in *The Bend for Home*. Aunt Maisie and Healy's mother play a key role in the memoir when Healy observes them in old age and reflects on the loss of his father as a role model during his adolescence. In 1974, Healy married Anne Mari Cusack, a designer and cook. They have two children.

In addition to his writing Healy has been active as a director and performer. In 1980 he was the winning director in the All-Ireland Drama Festival with his production of Samuel Beckett's *Waiting for Godot*. In May 1994 he performed with the musician Fintan Vallely in *The Humours of Balleyconnell,* a production of his poetry, with songs and flute music. Healy also played the lead in Nichola Bruce's 1999 film adaptation of Irish emigrant life, *I Could Read the Sky*. In the film, an elderly Irish laborer, played by Healy, remembers his past in layered fragments of memory, developing a theme involving the inevitable passage of time and emotional wounds that never heal.

Healy's efforts have also extended toward the creation of two respected literary journals in Ireland. He established the literary arts magazine *Drumlin,* serving as its editor from 1978 to 1979. In 1989 Healy was a cofounder of *Force 10,* a journal featuring the work of established and emerging artists. It publishes fiction and nonfiction, interviews, photographic essays, poetry, sketches, and prints, documenting life in the Sligo region of Ireland, where Healy has lived. Healy has been the recipient of many awards for his writing, including two Hennessy Literary Awards

DERMOT HEALY

(1974 and 1976) and the 1983 Tom Gallan Award for his story "The Tenant," which is included in the collection *Banished Misfortune* (1982). He won the 1995 Encore Award for *A Goat's Song* (1994), which was also short-listed for the Booker Prize. Healy's 1996 memoir, *The Bend for Home,* was short-listed for Esquire/Apple/Waterstone's Nonfiction Award. Healy is also honored as a member of Aosdána, an affiliation of artists selected as outstanding contributors to the arts in Ireland.

The most lauded and widely available works by Healy are *A Goat's Song* and *The Bend for Home.* This essay will focus attention on these two works, while also discussing Healy's 1999 novel *Sudden Times,* his first collection of short stories, *Banished Misfortune,* and two major poetry collections, *What the Hammer* (1998) and *The Reed Bed* (2001).

A GOAT'S SONG

A Goat's Song contains many of the themes that consistently appear in Healy's fiction. The title of the novel derives from Greek language and myth, a choice that reflects the profusion of mythological allusion in the story. The novel's protagonist, Jack Ferris, is a self-proclaimed writer of "goat songs" or tragedies. He explains the derivation of the phrase this way: "Tragedies. Tragos—goat. *Oide*—song. From the Greek" (p. 227).

In the novel, Healy focuses on three main themes: the love affair between Jack Ferris and Catherine Adams; the often violent schism between Catholicism and Protestantism in Ireland; and the search for language that meaningfully describes these things. The novel's characters reveal the various perspectives of political and identity-driven conflict. Catherine's family is from Northern Ireland, while Jack is from the Republic. The novel tends to fluctuate between these borders.

A Goat's Song is divided into four sections, each containing eight to nine chapters. The opening section, "Christmas Day in the Workhouse," dovetails from the novel's final scene, in which Jack Ferris waits on a bridge in Belmullet for his estranged lover, Catherine Adams, who in a letter

indicated to Jack that she wanted to get back together. If one were to read only the final scene of the novel, one might conclude that there is hope for the relationship between Jack and Catherine. However, Healy structures the novel so that at the end, readers will understand that Jack is misguided in his thinking at this point, and that Catherine is not coming back. The opening section of *A Goat's Song* introduces us to Jack, a playwright, pining away in the West of Ireland for Catherine, an actress who is currently playing the lead in the Belfast production of Jack's play. After attempting to see Catherine and discovering that he is not even welcome at the rehearsals of his play, Jack falls into a lovesick, drunken, depressive haze.

In the midst of his alcoholic binges, Jack admits himself into a mental ward, where he begins to record the oral histories of the other patients. As he becomes energized through the writing process and stories of others, Jack is inspired to craft a fact-based history of Catherine Adams and her family. This narrative takes the story in a new direction; the novel becomes more active, a poignant story of Catherine's family and the initial meeting of Catherine and Jack. In envisioning this narrative, Jack articulates a new purpose: "to enter a new story. She must be imagined. He opened a spiral-bound notebook and thought, Here it begins" (p. 84).

In the next section, "The Salmon of Knowledge," comprising Jack's narrative, readers are introduced to Jonathan Adams, Catherine's father. Jonathan is a Protestant, a sergeant of the Royal Ulster Constabulary (RUC), established after the founding of the new Northern Ireland state. He is sent to the city of Derry to keep the peace during a civil rights march on 5 October 1968. Despite a ban by William Craig, the minister of home affairs in Northern Ireland, the planned civil rights march goes on. As a result, the police and the Catholic marchers begin a conflict that escalates into rioting and violence. After the march, which turns violent, Jonathan witnesses footage of himself on television, ruthlessly beating people with a baton. The image, played repeatedly throughout Ireland, fills him with shame and guilt. As more violence breaks out and members of the RUC are targeted, Jonathan has difficulty rationalizing the intense paranoia he feels. The only comfort he can find is in interactions with his Catholic neighbor, Matti Bonner, who never mentions the incident that it seems everyone has seen on television. When Jonathan gets married, Matti Bonner is the best man at his wedding. But this intimacy with Matti is short-lived, and Jonathan feels implicated when his friend commits suicide by hanging himself from a tree, halfway between the local Protestant and Catholic churches. In an attempt to distance themselves from the conflict, Jonathan and his wife, Maisie, who is originally from the South, buy a weekend house on the Mullet peninsula near Belmullet, located in the Irish Republic. After these events, Jonathan retires from his station, in Fermanagh, and spends more and more time at the Belmullet home.

As Jonathan becomes more accustomed to the culture and context of the South, he is both drawn toward and resistant to the Republic, and this ambivalence manifests itself in his study of the literature and history of the area. His intensive reading and research is unexpected due to his initial discomfort with the Republic. Prior to buying the house in Belmullet, Jonathan strongly opposes the reading of fiction because he felt that "the language of the imagination offered licentious freedom" (p. 114). Yet after Jonathan acquires the property in Belmullet, he is in need of information: "The South was a museum in which Jonathan Adams, at least, wandered as a stranger" (p. 147). Jonathan voraciously reads about the history and mythology of the area. He begins to write a religious history of Belmullet, but eventually burns it. He then turns to fiction, and, "For the first time in his life he felt that literature might open the door that politics had closed on him" (p. 163). Literature, then, provides Jonathan with a new way of perceiving the world, just as moving to the Republic challenges his perceptions.

Jonathan also begins to teach himself the Irish language. He hires a tutor to teach Irish to his now teenaged daughters. As a result of these actions, "The North was silenced" (p. 174). The pain, violence, and guilt of the North are muffled by this foreign place. Soon Jonathan becomes ill, and, as he dies, Catherine reads him a version of the myth of the Salmon of Knowledge, an Irish myth told in many versions. In Jonathan's version, two men, Aengus and Fionn, capture the Salmon and prepare it for Aengus to eat so that he may gain its knowledge of life. After accidentally touching the fish as it cooks, Fionn gains the knowledge instead of Aengus. Fionn then transforms into a woman whom Aengus becomes obsessed with. To escape, Fionn transforms into a bird. By gaining the Salmon's knowledge, Fionn is able to discover what his journey in life should be. He discovers "What language was—a bridge between the flesh and the spirit" (p. 197). In the meantime, Aengus meets a man who informs him of the many shapes of the Salmon myth—a discussion of the myth within the telling of the myth itself.

At this point the story collapses into scenes of Jonathan, who fluctuates between hallucination and clarity on his deathbed. He imagines the origins of language and has a vision of the Tower of Babel, comparing the division of language to the split in Ireland. Ultimately, Jonathan realizes that all journeys begin and end cyclically.

Jonathan Adams might be seen as the most complex character in the book. He is torn between the fluidity of myth and the oppositional nature of religion and politics. However, it must be remembered that Jack Ferris is imposing his interpretation on a man he has never known; Catherine's father had died before Jack met her. It is really Jack Ferris who is the most complex character in *A Goat's Song,* given his capacity to imagine the complexities of another's mind and experience. The reader is left to wonder which of Jack's assertions are actual pieces of Catherine's life and which are only imagined. The act of imaginative writing about the "reality" of Catherine's life lends itself to thoughts on the nature of intimate relationships, what people know and do not know about each other, and how one might develop a genuine knowledge of another person through a layering of contexts.

Healy also creates character complexity by focusing on the crossing of borders, both geographical and imaginative. For example, both

Jonathan and Jack are at one time in the novel displaced persons, Jonathan in the South and Jack in the North. The existence of borders, and the act of crossing borders, creates a tension that forces characters to confront crucial questions of identity, their own and others'.

Through Jack's imagining of the Adams' story, and Jonathan Adams' interest in writing and literature within Jack's story, Healy intertwines layers of text. In *A Goat's Song,* several characters use writing to break through barriers. For Jack, writing is a way to "enter a new story" with Catherine. Jonathan Adams uses writing to ease the sense of guilt he feels for contributing to the turmoil of his country. And Catherine Adams writes letters to Jack Ferris during their estrangement, an action that breaks down emotional barriers: "It was as if the act of writing itself negotiated a middle ground" (p. 345). Language is of particular importance in "The Salmon of Knowledge." Before becoming a policeman, Jonathan trained to become a priest, but he discovered that he could not translate his spirituality into words spoken in front of a congregation. Eventually, Jonathan must come to grips with the limitations of language; he has difficulty watching his brother, a minister, preach because he feels that his brother's approach appeals more to the emotions rather than the intellect. In this way Healy explores the question of how meaning is transmitted through language, and how meaning can be interpreted differently depending on different contexts and points of view. In addition, Healy demonstrates how the language of popular and visual culture affects meaning, through the repetition of images such as the television scene in which Jonathan Adams beats rioters.

"The Hares," the third section of the novel, begins after Jonathan Adams' death. Jonathan's wife, Maisie, and two daughters, Catherine and Sara, move permanently to the house in the West. Catherine, an actor, meets Jack Ferris, a playwright, and they begin a love affair that spirals into alcoholic bingeing and jealousies. During this time, Jack writes scripts for Catherine and Catherine performs in the roles he creates. It is only when Catherine begins to write letters that she experiences the kind of thrill that Jack does when he writes. She defines their intimate relationship through her writing, revealing the ambivalence and malleability of meaning conveyed through language. In the fourth section, "The Musical Bridge," Jack moves to Belfast with Catherine and experiences what it is like to be the outsider; his accent and religion are unwelcome in the North. It is not long before he feels endangered. He returns to Belmullet, without Catherine, whose career is blossoming as the star of Jack's play. At the end of the novel, Jack readies the old Adams house for Catherine's return. The reader understands that Catherine is not coming back, since the beginning of the novel picks up where the end leaves off. In *A Goat's Song,* Healy uses distinctive stories, viewpoints, and texts to express the ambiguous nature of truths in political and religious strife. As a result, Healy raises questions about character motivation and psychology. For example, where does Jack Ferris's account of the Adams family end and the "real" account begin? The truth becomes muddled, as politics and history, as the conflict between Protestant and Catholic, becomes muddled.

Perhaps the main theme of *A Goat's Song* is the confrontation of seeming opposites and irreconcilables. Matti Bonner's suicide explicates this point. In Jonathan's hometown in the North, services at the Protestant and Catholic churches are meticulously arranged so that the members of each congregation do not have to encounter one another. Matti's suicide forces them to come out of their respective churches at the same time. As the Protestants and Catholics try to fathom Matti's death, they are curious about each other, attempting to discover whether their assumptions will prove supportable. At the funeral, Catholics scrutinize Jonathan Adams as he comes to pay his last respects. The suicide has enabled contradictory impulses to collide and coexist, if briefly. In enacting such collisions in *A Goat's Song,* Healy pays homage to human complexity.

THE BEND FOR HOME

In a prefatory note to his memoir, *The Bend for Home,* Healy translates the Irish phrase *Corr baile*

(Irish) as "The bend for home, which gives rise to many place names in Ireland, as for example Corballa, Corbellagh, etc." The memoir then opens with the tale of a birth, which the reader is purposely misdirected to believe is the birth of Healy.

At the beginning of the story, the local doctor is called to the Healy household. He examines Healy's mother, decides that she has many hours before she will give birth, and heads to the local pub. When the doctor returns, he crawls into bed beside Healy's mother and falls asleep. Then a midwife comes to perform the delivery. Healy concludes the tale with the following:

> Where the doctor was during these proceedings I don't know. As for the child, it did not grow up to be me, although till recently I believed this was how I was born. Family stories were told so often that I always thought I was there. In fact, all this took place in a neighbour's house up the road, and it was my mother, not Mary Sheridan [the midwife], arrived on her bike to lend a hand.
>
> (p. 3)

With this opening passage, Healy establishes his theme of the fragmentation and limitation of memory and language.

The Bend for Home is a memoir about growing up in 1950s Ireland, the relationship of a son to his parents, the retrieval of written records from the past, and reflections about that past and of the aging process. The book is also a meditation on memory, storytelling, and truth. Healy acknowledges the difficulty of accurately recollecting the past, as well as the need to craft a viable story from the piecing together of fallible memories. Later in the book's first section, Healy writes, "What happened is a wonder, though memory is always incomplete, like a map with places missing. But it's all right, it's entered the imagination and nothing is ever the same" (p. 33).

In the memoir's first succinct vignette, Healy reminds readers of the imperfect nature of memory; although the birth story is essentially true, in claiming the story as his own experience, its truth or meaning shifts. Because, while a child, Healy listened frequently to family members tell the story, it became real and present to him; he internalized it as his own.

In *The Bend for Home* memory is frequently conflated with the process of writing; storytelling effects a transcending of experience, an imaginative coloring of the facts. Imaginative language allows for a richness of expression, of exaggeration, of a departure from the "truth." Of his first piece of writing, about the rain, Healy states,

> It is hard for me to remember my first lie, since I've told so many. . . . It was a combination of lies and a fondness for words started me. I can still remember the liquid feel of those words for rain. How the beads were blown against a windowpane, and glistened there, and ran. The words for rain were better than the rain itself. I wanted to type up the words.
>
> (p. 57)

The Bend for Home is broken up into five distinctively structured books. The first book, "The Bridge of Finea," is about Healy's childhood; it is told in a series of vignettes about the people he grew up with and his admiration for his father. Book 2, "The Sweets of Breifne," details scenes of the family's move from Finea to Cavan and his father's impending illness. In Cavan readers are introduced to Aunt Maisie, Healy's mother's sister, a dominating figure in Healy's life through her elder years. Maisie operates the bakery and sweet shop owned by her family, and the Healys move into an apartment connected to the shop.

In "Out the Lines," book 3, Healy's father is ill, and Healy spends much of his time sitting by his father's bed, reading. Healy's father dies at the end of this third book, which marks a major shift in the memoir. In fact, *The Bend for Home* might be divided thematically into two parts— the first half concentrates on Healy's relationship with his father, while the latter half focuses on his developing relationship with his mother. When Healy's father dies, he begins to keep a daily journal, employing the coded language of a teenager. The first entry of the journal, written a few days after his father dies, helps conclude the third book of the memoir.

DERMOT HEALY

Book 4 is titled "Sodality of Our Lady: A Version of a Diary 1963." Healy presents images of his adolescent self, fumbling with sexuality and frequently truant from school. Readers are also introduced to his writing voice at that age, as well as his perceptions of his mother and Aunt Maisie as they live and work together in the bakery and sweet shop. Healy gives the impression here that the memoir is being written as he cares for his elderly mother and Maisie. During this time, the journal is given to him by his mother, who has dug it out of storage. Of his adolescence, Healy writes,

> It annoys me to remember those days. I would rather attribute them to some fictional character who would later be given some understated moral retribution. But those acts, follies, thieving, are me.
>
> But what awfulness do we leave out as memory defends its terrain? What images are locked away that only imagination can release? Beyond those wild sexual arousals are other plainer moments, disguised as clichés, hiding from the language of elation. They are the mundane everyday that memory does not espouse.
>
> (p. 101)

Through revelations such as these, Healy seems to be appealing to readers, asking them to commiserate with him in the challenges of recollecting the past. In using the phrase "a version of a diary" in the title of book 4, Healy also once again leads readers to question the veracity of the narrative. The word "version" indicates that Healy has edited and perhaps changed the presented entries; readers would have no idea whether the editing consisted of small instances of stylizing or entire re-creations of events.

Finally, book 5 is about Healy's relationship as a caretaker to his mother and Aunt Maisie. In this section Healy observes his two aunts, Nancy and Maisie, and his mother, Winnie, telling stories of the past. Their overlapping and sometimes clashing accounts illustrate the problematic nature of memory that is his subject. Just as he read by his dying father's side, Healy now reads and writes at his mother's side as she suffers from dementia. Healy writes that his Aunt Maisie "tries to remember for her [Healy's mother] a past

which is quickly escaping. . . . Looking after Mother is like watching language lose its meaning" (p. 280). Again, Healy confronts the malleable nature of language and the gaps created when language no longer attaches itself to what was once thought of as tangible meaning. One way that Healy deals with what is happening to his mother's memory is by recording the process of loss. After she falls and hits her head, Healy records the effect of the experience on his mother's memory:

> I fell on the fender, she says quietly. It was dark. That's what happened. She touches the white cap on her scalp. But now I'm fine.
>
> The time she fell on the fender she was sixteen. But the two blows to her head—the fender and the radiator—have become mixed up.
>
> (p. 246–247)

Each story his mother tells reveals a discrepancy in memory, and Healy parallels his mother's loss with his own memory gaps.

As with much of Healy's fiction, *The Bend for Home* comprises multiple points of view and perspectives: Healy as a middle-aged man taking care of his elderly mother; Healy as a fiction writer writing nonfiction; Healy's childhood memories; Healy's adolescent journals; Healy's attempts at coming to grips with the deaths of his parents. Like many memoirists, Healy meditates in the text on the process of accumulating and relating one's memories, as well as the memories of others. From the beginning anecdote of birth, memory is celebrated and scrutinized as a distinctly human, and therefore inherently complex, vehicle for imaginative truth.

SUDDEN TIMES

In his writing Healy often displays a photographic conception of scenes in time and space. His 1999 novel, *Sudden Times,* illustrates the snapshot-like quality that Healy can bring to a work. *Sudden Times,* which began as a short story published in 1989 by the literary journal *Cyphers,* reflects a culture of suspicion and paranoia amidst silences. The narrator of the story, Oliver ("Ollie") Ewing, an Irish laborer, is not a conventional storyteller, so readers must collect information that is often contradictory and try to piece together what has occurred.

As in *A Goat's Song* and *The Bend for Home,* in *Sudden Times* Healy connects themes of memory, storytelling, and truth. Ollie Ewing is trapped somewhere between truth and lies. Jobless, he moves from Sligo to London to work construction with his best friend, Marty. (Incidentally, Healy lived in London for fifteen years and had experience working at construction sites.) Shortly after Ollie moves into Marty's trailer, Marty disappears. Rumors of protection rackets and drug deals heighten Ollie's belief that a man named Silver John is responsible for Marty's disappearance. When Ollie finds Marty's burned body and bones in the back of a truck, he is convinced that Silver John is the murderer, though his evidence is slim. He accuses Silver John and his associate, Scots Bob, of the murder and is promptly pummeled by them in public.

Each day after discovering his friend's body, Ollie waits to be chosen from the crowd of men vying for construction work. Many people had warned Ollie not to get involved with Silver John; he takes this seriously only after his beating. But it is too late. After his encounter with Silver John, no one will hire Ollie, until Silver John himself shows up and hires him. Ollie feels as if he has no other option than to take the work that Silver John offers.

Shortly thereafter, Ollie's brother, Redmond, comes to London to seek construction work. Later, Ollie and Redmond throw a party, during which Scots Bob and Silver John show up. Scots Bob kills Redmond after a fight over a woman named Meg. At Scots Bob's trial for the murder of Redmond, Ollie takes the stand as a witness. The section is composed of a lengthy passage of dialogue between the barrister and Ollie. By the end of the section, if readers thought they knew the real story, they are back to square one, for Healy infuses the scene with a sense of fragmentation and ambiguity.

To enhance disorientation, Ollie's story is visually structured in well-spaced, brief vignettes, each with subject headings (for example, "the price of a can," "I'll start again," and "ducks"). If the vignettes are seen as photographic in nature, then these subject headings could be translated as captions. Since the vignettes are brief and out of order, and the prose style is extremely spare, readers must actively piece together the chain of events.

In the beginning of the novel, Ollie lives in a crowded artists' home in Sligo. He works various low-paying jobs, such as a cart collector at a supermarket. During this time, Ollie is paranoid that someone is after him; before the character of Scots Bob enters the narrative, readers learn that someone by that name will be let out of prison soon. Eventually, Ollie returns to London to see his father, who has not forgiven him since Redmond died. Much like *A Goat's Song,* the story then cuts away to the past, both reviewing and adding to Ollie's story thus far.

At the end of *Sudden Times,* a party in memory of the deceased Marty and Redmond is thrown at a Sligo pub. Readers will realize that, after this party, Ollie will experience the story as told from the first half of the book. This sort of structure is similar to that of *A Goat's Song,* where the impendent nature of events issues from the reader's knowledge of what has gone on before. Still, just as readers may not be sure of Jack Ferris and Catherine Adams's ultimate relationship to each other in *A Goat's Song,* readers of *Sudden Times* are left uncertain about the fate of Ollie Ewing. Scots Bob, convicted of Redmond's death, will be out of prison soon. Ollie is still paranoid, still convinced that "they" are after him. Readers do not know what will happen to Ollie, or even if his paranoia is well-founded. This sort of organization lends itself to the question of what is important in each of these novels; a sense of closure does not seem significant.

The disorderly structure of the book creates an unconventional narrator. From the beginning, Ollie's reliability as a narrator is in question; however, this unreliability becomes more evident as the text proceeds. Readers may be caught between Ollie's seeming paranoia and the search for the truth of all that has happened to him relating to the death of his friend and his brother.

DERMOT HEALY

In addition, there is a political current in this novel; the English and the Irish are mentioned frequently, as a people divided from each other. As in *A Goat's Song, Sudden Times* fluctuates between borders, except this time the border is between England and Ireland. The theme of division has much to do with loss, and the loss of the Irish language seems to be a poignant subtext in the novel. Ollie hardly recognizes the Irish language. In one instance, he speaks in Irish to a woman about her singing, after he recognizes pieces of Irish song lyrics. But he is seen as a fraud, a mere dabbler in the language. In the same scene, a man tells him, "You should be ashamed of yourself to have no Irish" (p. 178).

The suggestion is that native inhabitants of the country who do not fully embrace or know the language cannot be truly Irish. In another scene, a German psychiatrist asks Ollie, "Vot is it like to speak in the language of the conqueror?" (p. 37). This loaded question confronts the subjugation of British colonialism and the proliferation of the English language; culture and language, then, become difficult to separate in the storyline of *Sudden Times*.

In another instance, at the party that results in Redmond's death, Ollie and his friends speak about *Murphy Agus A Chairde* (Murphy and His Friends), a television show that aired when Ollie was a child. This brief interchange becomes fodder for the lawyers at Scots Bob's murder trial, who claim that Ollie and his friends were speaking in Irish as they furtively planned to attack the Englishmen (Scots Bob and Silver John). The trial becomes openly political through this focus on nationality. Ollie claims throughout the novel that he is not political, but perhaps one of Healy's themes is that if one claims Irish identity, or any nationality, one cannot, and indeed must not, escape politics.

Another indication of the loss of the Irish language can be seen in Ollie's dream of a third eye attached to his forehead:

> Then I saw the child's eye. It was stuck onto my forehead by the sucker behind the pupil. I could put my finger in behind the socket and it moved freely. I wanted to tear it off immediately but instead I found I was looking through it at myself in the mirror.
>
> The other eyes were seeing normal things but this eye was seeing something else, something I myself didn't want to see.
>
> (p. 329)

This third eye indicates the mental stress and illness undergone by Ollie, as well as the loss of language as an instrument of Irish identity:

> Then the thing with the words happened. The words for the things escaped me.
>
> Escaped me.
>
> I thought I should have a word with the authorities but something told me to leave it.
>
> As I stood there I knew there was a certain loss, of that I was certain. And yet somehow this was to my benefit. But still and all it was sad to know the loss.
>
> (p. 319)

Healy's invention of the third eye serves multiple purposes. For example, one might interpret the eye as extrasensory perception. Or the eye may be hallucinatory, since Ollie has the ability to see things that no one else believes— men chasing him, a sniper, the murder of his friend Marty. One might also read this third eye as foreseeing Irish cultural loss. Perhaps the use of a child's eye indicates that a child's memory is the least tainted by ingrained cultural and political expectations. Readers might observe that Ollie's childlike persona appears elsewhere in the fragmented, disorganized vignettes.

A child might also be unable to articulate what he or she has seen or heard in a way that is suitable or acceptable to adults. And if Ollie's articulations are seen as childlike, one could read into the parent-child relationships in the novel— from Ollie's mother and father to the way Ollie is treated by his peers. For instance, the barrister at the trial treats Ollie like a naughty child, attempting to confuse him and trip him up in a lie. It may give one pause to compare this treatment of Ollie by the English barrister as a reflection of past relations between Ireland and England. In addition, the disdainful treatment toward class and nationality in the novel is difficult to ignore.

The title *Sudden Times* may put one in mind of the contemporary feeling that random events occur suddenly, that one never knows what to expect. The disordered structure of the novel is mastered by Ollie Ewing's bursts of remembered images that are difficult to piece together. The scenes are snapshots compiled slowly for meaning, though one never really knows what has happened or who to believe. For instance, Silver John and Scots Bob could either be minor punks or serious thugs. Readers know Silver John and Scots Bob lie about the incidents at the party, but it is not clear which of the threats to Ollie is true, if any.

Healy's decision to create an unreliable narrator in *Sudden Times* is reminiscent of his approach to the question of reliability in perspective in other works. In *A Goat's Song,* for instance, Jack Ferris writes the history of Catherine Adams's family from an imagined perspective, while Catherine writes letters to craft a version of events that does not quite translate into her reality. In *The Bend for Home,* Healy continues to explore the line between fact and fiction. Mirrors appear frequently in both *Sudden Times* and *The Bend for Home*; Ollie experiences great discomfort when confronted by any sort of vision or reflection of himself. Since Ollie cannot fathom really looking at himself, his credibility is again called into question. It may also be worth noting that Ollie is a much different character than Jack Ferris, who is constantly trying to analyze the psychological motivations of himself and others. The characterization of Ollie Ewing and Jack Ferris seems to dictate the prose styles of the two novels while still maintaining focus on similar themes. Jack's ability to imagine the complexities of others suits the denser style of *A Goat's Song,* while Ollie's limited ability to articulate himself fuels the simple flashes of prose in *Sudden Times. Sudden Times* expands upon many of the themes that Healy consistently presents in his work. As alluded to by its title, *Sudden Times* explores the role of individuals in both collective and random anguish through a compilation of unexpected events and disordered revelations. Thus, it is difficult to leave Healy's

fiction with the sense that his characters have the capacity to achieve resolution.

BANISHED MISFORTUNE

Banished Misfortune is a collection of twelve short stories with varying points of view. Several of the stories contain themes of social and economic stratification in Ireland and England, themes explored elsewhere in Healy's work. The four stories discussed here most aptly reflect these themes, although the collection as a whole comments on a wide range of subjects, including sexuality and degrees of love, the natural world, politics, abortion, and homelessness.

"The Curse" is a traditionally structured story in which the experience of a young, unnamed boy results in his epiphany about the class system that will rule the opportunities granted him in the future. The boy's realization is an adult realization, thrusting him momentarily into an adult world with set rules and codes of conduct. In the opening scene of "The Curse," the boy and his friends are swimming in a canal. Ted Webster-Smith, well known for his power and prestige in the horse-racing world, and his right-hand man, Pat Wheelan, arrive at the canal and decide to get in the water themselves. The boy considers this a good time to approach Webster-Smith about a job, since he dreams of becoming a jockey. Webster-Smith tells the boy that he will give him a job if he does him a favor. The favor involves delivering a verbal message to a certain woman: the "curse" of the title refers to a profanity that Webster-Smith instructs the boy to shout at the woman. When the boy climbs into the car with Webster-Smith, he notes, "The seat is filled with crops and other riding gear, and so big it is impossible to sit still, as we swing up and around the bridge, the radio, like a miracle, bursting forth with the turn of the ignition, and I know I am in a different world when so much can happen at the same moment in time" (p. 24). Already, the boy senses the clear distinctions between the world he lives in and the world of the man who owns the car.

Soon after, the boy delivers the message to the woman, who is tending bar at a pub, and returns to another pub where Webster-Smith is waiting. The boy soon realizes that Webster-Smith has no intention of offering him a job, stating, "I wait. I can taste there in the air the sweet smell of weakness and failure" (p. 26). The boy feels as if he has failed an opportunity, even though the opportunity held out to him was false; Webster-Smith takes advantage of the boy's naivety, and he is the type of man who is constantly approached by people interested in finding success in his professional field. But this sense of failure observed by the protagonist is also apparent in the men who surround Webster-Smith. In the pub the boy observes deferential treatment toward Webster-Smith, who is consulted for opinions that others obviously do not really seek. Those who defer do so in tacit acknowledgment of a class-driven code of conduct.

When the boy realizes that he is not going to get the job, he in turn curses Webster-Smith and races away. At the end of the story, the boy walks with a man who is speaking about horse racing. In a traditional epiphany, the boy relates, "I decide that there is no use crying over the number of doors closed to me in that town from then on, so I accompany him, pretending, for today at least, to be other than I am, and much more besides, while he, thinking he knows me, talks of superior breeds in the sprinting world" (p. 27). The boy sees that there are limitations to empowerment in the world he lives in. The often intangible lines of class have been drawn quite clearly for him on this day.

Similarly, "The Tenant" demonstrates the tension that can arise from codes of class conduct. The story has two protagonists: Mr. Franklin is a new cashier at the Bank of Ireland in Dublin in the 1960s, while Mick Johnson is a porter at Swann's Hotel, where Franklin will be staying. From the beginning encounter between Franklin and Johnson, class distinctions are made obvious through small actions. For instance, the porter shows Franklin to his room, and when Franklin asks if hot water is available all day, the porter runs the water until steam rises, rather than simply stating yes. By responding in unconventional silence to Franklin, the porter demonstrated a disdain that he cannot voice due to their class differences. Franklin is presented as a meticulous, soft-spoken, "democratic" man who quickly and patiently establishes himself at the bank. "At best it was expected of him that he should have irregular habits and the eccentricities of the educated. But his gait was purposeful and only the frequent pinch of his fingers told remotely of an inner life" (p. 85).

The bank itself is undergoing technological and structural changes. Franklin spends time "sorting out new business without resort to the old class distinctions" (p. 88). In addition, women will soon be employed at the bank. Franklin's opinion is that "it would be on his bachelor's shoulders and prematurely grey head the burden of approaching modernity would sit, meaning that he must like women and like machines that were programmed to undermine his domain by calculation and grievances beyond telling" (p. 89). With this revelation of Franklin's apparent dislike for change, Healy creates another dimension to his established persona. It seems that submission to tradition is a matter of dignity for Franklin.

Similarly, the general concepts of class and property are matters of pride in this story. The Johnsons own a hastily built suburban home in which Franklin becomes a tenant; around the same time, Franklin is put in charge of the Johnsons' account at the bank. After Mrs. Johnson searches Franklin's room and discovers that Franklin keeps a briefcase locked, Franklin begins to leave the briefcase open for her, which "demoralized Mrs. Johnson," who then desires to find out this man's fallibilities in order to humiliate him (p. 92). Then Franklin befriends the Johnsons' son, Ronnie, who begins to treat his father as if he is inferior, which prompts the Johnsons to decide that they must evict Franklin. Episodes such as this abound in the story, where the lines between class and pride are set against the conflict between the desire to be worldly and the habits of gentility.

The Johnsons and Franklin each hold certain powers over each other based on occupational roles, property, and expectations. Franklin's role as a tenant creates a reversal of superiority; the Johnsons begin to lose respect for him, and their pride is hurt by his acquisition of their accounts as their cashier. Finally, Franklin leaves for Christmas at the Johnsons' request, not intending to come back. In the final scene, Franklin and Moran, the owner of the bank, are in the bar of the hotel in which Franklin is once again staying. The situation is already made awkward for Franklin because his superior has stooped to visit the hotel bar and have a drink. Ronnie Johnson comes in and, out of place, expresses anger at his parents' decision to evict Franklin. Franklin is embarrassed in front of Moran, for Ronnie does not realize that everything has been restored to normal—Franklin, no longer a tenant, will again be served by Ronnie's father, the porter. By approaching Franklin without the proper code of deference, Ronnie has acted inappropriately. Furthermore, Moran, to whom Franklin shows deference, develops a lower opinion of Franklin once he discovers who Franklin has been associating with. The characters' realizations of class distinctions, then, are both important and fragile in this story.

Another story, "Blake's Column," introduces a character engaged in these class themes through the use of more than one text. The story is told from the point of view of Blake, an opinion columnist who makes a career out of being condescending. Healy writes, "Like all others of his creed he was superficially hardened toward unhelpful criticism, but especially anxious over praise which he had not earned" (p. 29). At the beginning of the story, a herd of cattle stares through Blake's window and suddenly leaves; the narrator speculates that they leave because of Blake's "lack of sympathy" (p. 28). The columnist is unpopular in public, and he seems to have little realization of the effects his writing has had on others' perceptions of him.

One of the themes of "Blake's Column" is the idea of ethics and purpose related to the occupation of writer. Friends and family worry about Blake's pompous approach to the column and his criticisms. People do their best to minimize conversation with him. All Blake has left, then, are his unpopular columns, which are being rejected by the editor, as well as other methods of writing. He keeps a journal, writes opinion

pieces that do not get published, works on chapters of a novel, writes book reviews, and writes critiques of socialism and Ireland. All of these texts distance Blake from the human element that writing does not provide. By the end of the story, however, Blake resolves to feel more concern for others: "He bewailed writers undone by fawners, who in their need sought religious or spiritual advantage, ravaging the emotions of their families, rather than deal with what their uncomplicated senses told them" (pp. 41–42). This realization seems to imply that Blake is trying to come to terms with himself as a writer, and perhaps readers will be inspired to meditate on the craft and purposes of writing. But Blake's resolve to change also seems unconvincing, undermined by the pompous style in which he articulates it.

Healy also raises the question of what must be explicitly stated and what can be absented from a story. A sentence referring to Blake's wife and son reads, "Sheila and Ben had left him a year and a half ago. Because. Because" (p. 33). Blake's personal failings have been revealed through the inclusion of various texts of his, so readers might easily guess why his wife would leave him. "Because" implies that the reason has already been established, but the repetition of the sentence also lends a sense of fatigue to the mood of "Blake's Column," a disseminating quality that hovers around many of the characters in this collection.

The title story of *Banished Misfortune* also presents this kind of lonely fatigue through the depiction of the McFarland family, a family of traveling musicians in the South that were driven from their home in the North out of poverty. They arrive in Galway, where "slates littered the streets," and "the scene was obscenely familiar to the family from the north who felt for a moment slightly superior in their ability to deal with chaos, death, laughter at death" (p. 103). As the family attempts to adjust to constant displacement, they reflect upon the acquisition of their farm in the North through ancestral work on the railways in the United States. The McFarland parents consider the influence of history and context on themselves and the differing cultures of the South, and they have difficulties discovering, "a sense of other realities than being Irish" (p. 109). Again, the fierce hold of Irish identities is at play in Healy's writing.

HEALY'S POETRY

The language of Healy's poetry is concise and spare; the poems' abstract meaning is conveyed through simple, concrete images. The poetry can be seen as a natural extension of Healy's prose writings, covering familiar territory in a new vehicle. *What the Hammer* (1998) and *The Reed Bed* (2001) share many of the same themes, and it is to the advantage of readers of Healy's poetry to examine the interconnection between them.

Healy's verse often focuses on the sea or uses the ocean as a backdrop, no doubt reflecting Healy's place of residence during their writing—a house by the sea near Sligo. In *What the Hammer,* Healy continually evokes the vastness and power of the sea, envisioning it as a life force. The storms coming from the sea are a frequent motif, and Healy evokes the lush, wet, gusty climate of Ireland in rendering the journey of life that is a thematic connection in *What the Hammer.* In the first poem, "Sea-Sand," Healy reminds readers of the indivisibility of land and sea and the constancy of transformation. In the poem, as a sea storm moves onto land, even the sand that is part of the structure of the homes yearns to return to the water.

In the other opening poems of the book, Healy emphasizes the circular pattern of life and death, progressing, in "July Storm," to a version of a creation story in which the sea is the autonomous creative force. After a great flood ("For three days the sea blooms / in every crevice") and the appearance of land (Ireland's Benbulbin takes the place of Mount Ararat from the Christian creation story), language is born ("The *S* in sea rows out to *E.* / The *O* in ocean soars"). Healy continues to focus on natural forces in the title poem of the collection, "What the Hammer," a meditation on earth, air, fire, and water. Of the last of these he writes, "I've seen you lift the splashing / rocks without a sound" (p. 28), another nod toward the strength of the sea and the elements of the natural world. In the midst of these elemental things a speaker emerges in the poems, a narrator preoccupied with mortality. Death comes in the form of a house pet in "Death, the Cat," appearing in the doorway to collect a life. At the end of the poem, the narrator speculates about new lives who will experience the world the narrator knew before death, and how the cat/death will be part of their experience as well. Although death only comes once to each individual, it is an experience shared by all. In the last stanza, Healy writes, "And with a sort of relief / I suddenly realise / even the cat will be his."

As this collection moves from birth to death, it also moves from the encompassing sense of the worldly to the more specific concerns of the individual. In "A Dream," Healy writes about Maisie, his aunt, who is a major character in the memoir *The Bend for Home.* As an elderly Maisie waits patiently for someone to come and attend to her needs, Healy remarks on her enduring faith that eventually someone will come. And someone does. Healy also concentrates on the death of someone called Jimmy Foley—from a dream about Foley's death, to Foley's philosophy about loneliness, to Foley's funeral. In each of these poems, Healy speculates on his own mortality. In "Travelling," he writes, "and there's nearly too much to remember / and there's not too far to go." The apparent subject is train travel, but the placement of the poem, directly after several poems about death, works to put the reader in mind the things one attends to before death and the final scenes of life. This speculation turns to the encompassing fears that can occupy the solitary mind.

Healy writes about this concern most succinctly in "My House Is Tiny." Here is the poem in its entirety:

My house is tiny
and my sorrow
is the smallest
at this end of the country.
And yet the whole sea
at my back
can fit into
the most frightened
human mind.

DERMOT HEALY

This poem examines the paradox of the solitary consciousness that constitutes the "everything" of human experience, and the sense of smallness that can overwhelm one when thinking in relative terms.

What the Hammer then shifts back to the enduring power and wisdom of the natural world. Birds and plants frequently appear as wizened gatekeepers of knowledge. Cuckoo-pints mate in a ritualistic dance. Cormorants stand at the entrance to hell as Healy alludes to Ulysses and Lethe. "The Litany of the Wagtail" details quick movements of life through the dance of birds. In these poems, the birds and plants represent natural events, rhythms, and cycles—birth, ritual, death. These themes, served by the metaphors of the natural world, are reiterated in Healy's next collection, *The Reed Bed.*

The narrative voice of *The Reed Bed* is similar to that of *What the Hammer,* although in this collection Healy seems to take a direct approach to the issue of globalization and its effects. In "When They Want to Know What We Were Like," Healy writes, "And everything they find will have been / somewhere else to start with. / How far have the cereals been blown / from the field in which they were sown?" In this poem Healy posits the question of roots and the homogenization of peoples through products. *The Reed Bed* might also be compared to *Sudden Times* in its concerns; poems in this collection often focus on the contemporary anxiety brought about by sudden and massive conflicts.

Healy also draws a comparison between this anxiety and an inability to fully conceive of the sensory world; many of the poems alternate in tone between paranoia and fear and a benign detachment from the suffering of others. Once Healy delineates a lack of clarity in human comprehension, he progresses to "The Wall I Built," which comments on the instability of the future.

The wall I built
the sea took.
The stones I gathered
the sea scattered.
Falling asleep I look
left, right,

because, you see,
they don't make
tomorrow like
they used to.

The narrator's preparatory construction of the wall is scorned by the sea. Attempting to sleep in a fit of anxiety, the narrator realizes that stability is an illusion; walls tumble without warning.

As in *What the Hammer,* Healy shifts in *The Reed Bed* between the global and the individual, and the speaker of the poems often conjures memories of the past. In "The West End," the narrator compares wild times living in London's Piccadilly in his thirties to his current, calm abode in the West of Ireland. In "The Hallway" the narrator is surprised that a normally pleasant memory of being a youth becomes a nightmare at an older age. These poems convey acceptance and humor as if familiarity with the aging process has reconciled the speaker, who at one point refers to himself as "an old fogey," to mortality. In "Away with the Birds," the narrator meditates on the excitement of youthful ventures from the vantage point of a homebody, settled and content: the poem begins, "Just before a long journey / I get so homesick / that I can hardly talk, / or think, or eat." Near the end of the poem the speaker comments on his change of perspective: his mature stance is "not like in the old days / when I couldn't wait / to enter / the vast strangeness."

CONCLUSION

Healy's work can be seen as participating in the ethos of contemporary Irish literature in its exploration of sociopolitical themes, its concern with the nature of identity, storytelling, memory, and mortality, and its focus on the function and use of language. Examine, for instance, the unreliable narrator Ollie Ewing in relation to Patrick McCabe's serial killer Pat McNab in *Emerald Germs of Ireland* (2001). The male child's perspective, and the fragmentation of memory and storytelling that characterize much of Healy's fiction, are also present in Roddy Doyle's *Paddy Clarke, Ha-Ha-Ha* (1994) and Patrick McCabe's *The Butcher Boy* (1992). Setting Healy's work in the context of Irish writing of the late twentieth and early twenty-first centuries is a useful starting place for a critical approach to his oeuvre. Critical endeavors concerning Irish literature typically rely on a keen sense of the Irish history and culture from which the works emanate, since it is difficult to separate these entities from the literature. In this respect, Dermot Healy's writing is no exception.

SELECTED BIBLIOGRAPHY

I. PROSE WORKS. *Banished Misfortune and Other Stories* (London and New York, 1982); *Fighting with Shadows; or, Sciamachy* (London and New York, 1984); *A Goat's Song* (London, 1994; New York, 1995); *The Bend for Home* (London, 1996; New York, 1998); *Sudden Times* (London and New York, 1999); *After the Off,* photographs by Bruce Gilden (Stockport, U.K., 2000).

II. POETRY. *The Balleyconnell Colours* (Dublin, 1992); *What the Hammer* (Oldcastle, Co. Meath, Ireland, 1998); *The Reed Bed* (Dublin, 2001).

III. CRITICAL STUDIES. Tim Pat Coogan, *Ireland Since the Rising,* repr. (Westport, Conn., 1976); Homi K. Bhaba, "Of Mimicry and Men: The Ambivalence of Colonial Discourse," in *October* 28 (1984); Terrence Brown, *Ireland: A Social and Cultural History, 1922 to the Present* (Ithaca, N.Y., 1985); D. P. Doumitt, *Conflict in Northern Ireland: The History, The Problem, and the Challenge* (New York, 1985); Terrence Brown, *Ireland's Literature: Selected Essays* (Mullingar, Ireland, and Totowa, N.J., 1988); Terrence Brown and Nicholas Grene, eds., *Tradition and Influence in Anglo-Irish Poetry* (Totowa, N.J., 1989); Terry Eagleton, Fredric Jameson, and Edward W. Said, *Nationalism, Colonialism, and Literature* (Minneapolis, Minn., 1990); T. W. Moody, and F. X. Martin, eds., *The Course of Irish History,* rev. ed. (Lanham, Md., 1995); Theo Dorgan, ed., *Irish Poetry Since Kavanagh* (Dublin, 1996); Thomas MacDonagh, *Literature in Ireland* (Tipperary, Ireland, 1996); Robert Welch, ed., *The Oxford Companion to Irish Literature* (Oxford, U.K., and New York, 1996); Christina Hunt Mahony, *Contemporary Irish Literature: Transforming Tradition* (New York, 1998); Liam Harte, and Michael Parker, eds., *Contemporary Irish Fiction: Themes, Tropes, Theories* (London and New York, 2000); David Pierce, ed., *Irish Writing in the Twentieth Century: A Reader* (Cork, Ireland, 2000); Brian Griffin, Graham Davis, and John Newsinger, eds., *Ireland and the Union: Questions of Identity* (Dublin, 2001). Rudiger Imhof, *The Modern Irish Novel* (Dublin, 2001)

REGINALD HILL

(1936–)

John Lennard

CRIMES FILL THE earliest myths and epics, and the narrative arc from criminal motives to aftermath is a staple of classical tragedy and the Bible alike. Elaborated with victims' innocence (or complicity), suffering, and revenge (or forgiveness); criminals' defiance (or remorse), trial, and freedom (or punishment); and communities' need to restore balances disturbed by crime, such plots are perennial in Renaissance drama, early novels, and nonfiction forms including ballads, *The Newgate Calendar,* and journalism. Yet a distinct burgeoning is visible from the mid-nineteenth century, fueled by mass-market periodicals and symbolized by Sherlock Holmes, created in 1886.

There were great flowerings of the crime short story before 1914 and the novel in the 1920s and 1930s, a "Golden Age" of works by Fitzgerald, Faulkner, Christie, Sayers, Allingham, Chandler, and Hammett. Some were Modernist, some anti-Modernist, but all thrived in the new paperback format. Since 1945, inventive variegation at all lengths, intense symbiosis with film and TV, and proliferation of hardbacks, (trade) paperbacks, and omnibuses have led bookshops to develop crime sections of unprecedented size and range. Yet much literary criticism, especially in England, remains snobbishly aloof from popular fiction, and scholarly analysis is dogged by untenable generic classifications—"American," "hard-boiled" "crime writing" versus "English," "soft-boiled" "detective fiction," and so forth—rationalizing personal tastes and prejudices while ignoring wider literary and cultural contexts.

The need for a comprehensive approach is evident in the career of Reginald Hill, famous as the creator of Yorkshire policemen Andrew Dalziel (pronounced "Dee-ell") and Peter Pascoe, and among the most wide-ranging, skilled, and literary British crime writers. Hill's work sharply engages with the world he and his readers inhabit yet seamlessly involves the many traditions on which he draws, and the Crime Writers' Association Cartier Diamond Dagger, awarded in 1995 for "lifetime achievement," has rarely been so well-deserved. Since 1970 he has published fifty novels and collections of stories under four names: about half concern Dalziel and Pascoe, and their evolution, with the social topography of "Mid-Yorkshire," is of primary interest, but interacts with thrillers, spy novels, ghost stories, and the wild, bittersweet world of serendipitous black P.I. Joe Sixsmith. Attention to chronology is also needed, for Hill's best work confronts head-on the profound social and political changes which his Britain has suffered and celebrated.

LIFE AND LITERATURE

Reginald Charles Hill was born in 1936 in West Hartlepool. His father, Reg (1907–1961), played soccer for Hartlepool United; sports-players were then ill-paid, and Hill's background was "very ordinary working class" (Muller, "Interview," p. 33). His mother, Isabel (née Dickson, 1907–1998), a factory-worker, read Golden Age writers such as Agatha Christie (1890–1976), and Hill discovered the crime sections of local libraries while borrowing books for her.

In 1939 the family moved to the Lake District, and from 1947 Hill attended Carlisle Grammar, an ancient foundation which excelled academically after the war. An avid reader, Hill was a teenage crime-writing addict, but found through school a love of canonical literature, which necessarily displaced crime writing; in 1955 he won a place at St Catherine's College, Oxford, to study English. He first did National Service—two years in the Border Regiment, ending as a Lance-

Corporal—and matriculated in 1957. The Oxford course then began with Anglo-Saxon and covered the high canon from 1300 to the later nineteenth century; weekly essays were required. He graduated in 1960, and promptly married Patricia Ruell, a childhood friend.

After a year in Edinburgh working for the British Council, Hill became an English teacher at a school in Essex (1962–1967), then at Doncaster College of Education, where he rose to Senior Lecturer. In 1981 he became a full-time writer. Professionally engaged with canonical literature from the ages of 24 to 45, he is exceptionally well-read, but also faced daily exposure to an entrenched literary snobbery disdaining genre fiction as déclassé and unliterary. He had returned to crime reading after graduating, and in the late 1960s began to write crime novels and thrillers himself: irritation with snobbery and love of the great nineteenth-century novelists, from Austen to Dickens, to whose standards he aspired, induced a determination to erase in practice the false distinction of crime writing from literature. An ambition magnificently fulfilled, his mature work exhibits a profound intertextuality to complement his own powers of description, analysis, and narration.

FIRST NOVELS, 1967–1974

Hill completed his first novel in 1967, and immediately began a second. By 1974 he had completed fourteen, of which ten had been published, and four were in press: eight under his own name, including four Dalziel & Pascoe books, four by "Patrick Ruell," and two by "Dick Morland." At first glance the volume of work suggests quality stretched thin, and the pseudonyms indicate his publishers' attempts to categorize by genre (Hill—crime; Ruell—thrillers; Morland—science fiction) to protect the sales-image of each byline. In fact the volume of work betrays only a ferocious self-discipline of daily composition, maintained throughout his career, and the variety disguised by pseudonyms indicates systematic exploration of fictional territories. In retrospect, the first two novels established a working method Hill would apply

for thirty years.

The first completed (second published) novel was *Fell of Dark* (1971), a crime thriller whose protagonist, Harry Bentinck, is on the run in the Lake District, wrongly but reasonably suspected of a double rape-murder; the second completed (first published) novel was *A Clubbable Woman* (1970), introducing Detective Superintendent Andrew Dalziel and Detective Sergeant Peter Pascoe of Mid-Yorks CID. The title *Fell of Dark* is from a poem by Gerard Manley Hopkins (1844-1889) which passionately imagines despair, but in the Lake District, where mountains are "fells," the phrase becomes a grim jest; *A Clubbable Woman,* where "clubbable" means both "companionable, popular, hence likely to be elected to a club" and "of a kind to invite being clubbed to death," is equally double-edged, and invokes Dr. Johnson (who famously called Boswell "a clubbable man"). Such enjoyable allusions and a simultaneous unease in juxtaposing civilized literature with uncivil behavior, both harnessed to the richer telling of the tale in hand, are a hallmark of Hill's work. The sexual aspect of the crimes in both books, handled explicitly without prurience and feelingly without flinching, also signaled a persistent concern, and northern English settings, real or archetypal, were tellingly exploited for land- and streetscapes, and for the voices, minds, and malted wit of their peoples.

Fell of Dark, moreover, opens with a credo Hill has never ceased to explore:

> I possess the Englishman's usual ambivalent attitude to the police. They are at once protectors and persecutors. They tell you the way, but they make you feel guilty for asking.
>
> (p. 9)

Bentinck's fears form an important part of the narrative, when the threats of slab-fat Inspector Copley make him panic and run: with the novel complete Hill found himself still pondering Copley, and recast him as the even fatter and heavier-handed Andrew Dalziel. Violent bulk run to seed suggests, in any English policeman of Dalziel's generation, a history of playing rugby (there are many police teams), so a local rugby club became

REGINALD HILL

central to an investigation, and provided a title. But to investigate Dalziel at work required narrative "police procedural," not personal "thriller," and in creative contrast, as foil and antagonistic apprentice, the slim build, university education, and official politeness of Peter Pascoe. Few authors with one complete novel promptly attempt something so different in style and structure, but for Hill the process of contrasting composition was valuable. Dalziel & Pascoe jelled, Mid-Yorks thickened, and further D. & P. novels were irresistible: but with remarkable wisdom Hill determined always to write at least one nonseries book between returns to Mid-Yorks—a resolution he kept until 1999.

Hill's writing from 1969 to 1974 shows this alternation clearly. Further D. & P. novels appeared in 1971, 1973, and 1975, and four thrillers by "Patrick Ruell" between 1971 and 1975. There were also three literary crime thrillers published under his own name, and two novels as "Dick Morland." Though set in a near-future U.K., and built on fantastical premises, both Morlands are satirical dystopias closer to Orwell than Asimov: *Heart Clock* (1973; later *Matlock's System*) postulates state regulation of death, with an annual budget determining life-expectancy, while *Albion! Albion!* (1974; later *Singleton's Law*) imagines England ruled by soccer clubs and tribal fans. These premises aside, both are political thrillers, pleasantly twisty but most interesting in their engagement of plots, characterization, and dialogue to scathing satires of British attitudes toward authority and personal identity.

The three Hill novels explore intertextuality, and reveal rich and structural comedy. *A Fairly Dangerous Thing* (1972) ironically misquotes Pope's famous *Essay on Criticism* ("A little learning is a dangerous thing"), and backs its irony with the tale of Joe Askern, a schoolmaster who is drawn by his roving eye, blackmail, and the villainous father of a troublesome student into the attempted burglary of a stately home. When the burglars encounter an orgy abetted by corrupt councillors and a local pornographer, things look catastrophic, but in a set of delightful twists all works out well, and Joe's judgements of himself and others (especially women) are shown to have

been as mistaken as the critics whom Pope rebuked. The joke is richest knowing Pope's original, for the verse-paragraph (lines 215–232) beginning "A little learning . . ." ends with the line "Hills peep o'er hills, and Alps on Alps arise!": the rebuke to latter-day critics is wittily unanswerable, and to read Hill's novel against Pope's poem is to find a book far beyond most thrillers—but the wit is lightly worn, never interfering with the genial tone or properly comedic ending (Joe engaged to much-fancied fellow-teacher Maggie Cohen).

A Very Good Hater (1974) is another title from Dr. Johnson ("Bathurst was a man to my very heart's content . . . he was a very good hater"), but its relevance is far more uneasy. At a regimental reunion, two wartime pals, Goldsmith and Templeton, who survived captivity together as many of their unit did not, are disturbed by Templeton's belief that he has seen a fugitive SS officer, Nikolaus Hebbel, whom both have cause to hate. Shadowing the suspect, Goldsmith finds himself complicit in the man's death, which may or may not have been an accident, and tries to ease his conscience by proving the man to have been Hebbel. The outcome, comedically shaded by Goldsmith's relationships with his girlfriend and Hebbel's widow, is unexpectedly dark, casting doubt on how he and Templeton survived as POWs and the real nature of his desires; a brief second part, set seven years later, reveals him as a successful politician and the best hater of the lot. Dr Johnson's phrase is in context fairly genial, but Hill mines it (within a gripping tale that ponders revenge in general) for its poisonous core, leaving a well-entertained reader distinctly queasy.

Despite a killer both casual and calculating, *Another Death in Venice* (1976) is a vigorous comedy of manners following a package-tour group from Rimini to Venice and into the depths of Thomas Mann's novella of death and romantic passions. A sensuous enjoyment of more colorful settings than northern England affords gives a lush touch, but the plot remains taut and the characterization spiced with awareness of things unsaid; the surprising dénouement invokes Visconti's BAFTA-winning film *Morte a Venezia*

(1971) as well as Mann. Clearest is the comedy, both of individual sentences—"[St Mark's] square was like a giraffe—absurd, impossible, and beautiful beyond comprchension, as if Michelangelo, Christopher Wren, Walt Disney and God had sat in committee to build it" (p. 118)—and as an assumed ground against which much darker elements are set in relief. Both Aaron Sorkin and David Chase, creators respectively of TV shows *The West Wing* and *The Sopranos,* have said that they could only sustain the moral concerns of those series on a base of comedy, and Hill's use of that base for related reasons was central to the development of Dalziel and Pascoe.

DALZIEL AND PASCOE, 1970–1987

W. H. Auden (1907–1973) proposed in "The Guilty Vicarage" (1948) that murder-mysteries in a closed setting (like the archetypal village Colin Watson dubbed "Mayhem Parva") are related to Athenian tragedy. Despite the inconveniences of being found dead at the beginning or arrested at the end, victim or killer may be the tragic protagonist, and preoccupations with premature death, revenge, and purgation make Auden's suggestion logical, but Hill's mature work achieves tragic stature by methods quite other than Auden envisaged.

One strand of *A Clubbable Woman* (1970) is overtly comedic, a consummated courtship between Jenny Conlon, the victim's daughter, and boyfriend Antony Wilkes. The death of Mary Conlon, the "clubbable woman," turns out to have been grimly farcical, but husband Sam, hauntingly unable to mourn, provides a melancholy theme whose attendant clowns are Dalziel and Pascoe, closest not to the staple "good cop/ bad cop," nor clever Holmes and slow Watson, but to Laurel and Hardy and the long tradition of productively paired straight-men and jokers.

The counter-comedic balance, beyond their grim work and need for black humor, is their depth of contrast, embodying profoundly conflicting concepts of policing. Dalziel, older, stronger, and fatter, is street-smart beyond compare, but lacks higher education and all modesty, detecting by a well-informed intuition he cannot be bothered to justify. A lowland Scot raised in Yorkshire (so doubly hard-headed), he is a drinker, and a Northerner to the marrow, gimlet-eyed for the main chance, closed-mouthed yet free with half-genial insults, harping on stereotype and delighted to put one over on anybody, especially the posh or Southern. Pascoe, quite contrary in his youth, neatness, fondness for literary allusion, and trained reliance on forensic data and reasoning, is recognizably a post-1960s breed, a naïf with a sociology degree who thinks policing should defer to egalitarian convictions. In crude form their contrast is familiar from B-movies and TV shows, but they have a real community of citizens to police, among whom they must live and on whose behalf cooperate in the Queen's name. Behind the badinage grows an understanding that these opposites represent a debate about the civility of the society that we, Hill's readers, inherit and must pass on.

A Clubbable Woman is enlivened by Pascoe's eye for a date and shaded by Dalziel's memory of being left fifteen years before by his wife, who informed him of her decision by telegram:

> He'd often thought since of his wife in some post office writing those words down, then passing the form to some clerk to count them up. Had he said anything? Had there been an expression on his face as he counted? Was there a query perhaps?
>
> It must have cost her a packet.
>
> But, he thought now, with a self-irony which had only developed of later years, but, he thought as he looked down at his tightly clenched fist, it had been money wisely spent.
>
> (*A Clubbable Woman,* p. 78)

One reason for the divorce was that "In [Dalziel's] league of gross appetites, sex had always come a very poor third to whisky and food" (*Ruling Passion,* p. 198), and his sexuality could be deferred, absorbed by his physicality and habitual, sensual scratching of his own bulk. Pascoe's could not, and in *An Advancement of Learning* (1971) and *Ruling Passion* (1973) he courted his onetime girlfriend, Ellie Soper, now lecturing at a teacher-training college and trying to write novels. Contact was lost after Pascoe joined the police, through geography and irregular hours but also because Ellie and other student friends scorned the authoritarian conservatism and eager violence of the police deployed against them at demonstrations. Cocooned in academia, Ellie's liberal convictions have gone untested, but the discovery of human remains in the college grounds, a student's murder, and a lecturer's suicide put convictions of all kind at a premium, and bring into her disturbed world a daylight nightmare, the gross figure of Dalziel, and a lifeline, Pascoe.

The difficulties, as the investigation develops, of squaring personal and professional fidelities are as important as the case (incidental in many ways, as cases must be to policemen). The compromises Peter and Ellie make hurt, but sexual attraction and the summer sun that heats the novel see them through. In *Ruling Passion* an autumn weekend with four friends from student days is to be "something of a proving ground" (p. 110)—and proves savage, for on arrival they find three friends dead and the fourth missing. Beyond shock and horror, there is for Peter the frustration of being a witness without official standing, and a welling rage that makes physical force (supposedly Dalziel's vice) come easily to him; and for Ellie the pain of suspecting the missing friend, as the police must, and of watching Peter racked by the same dilemma. Back home, she must also cope with Dalziel's clumsy concern for his subordinate, and the womanly support he wants her to provide. As the murder-case and Pascoe's less glamorous burglary and fraud investigations in Mid-Yorks proceed, much comes to the boil (including, memorably, Dalziel in an antique shop); by the end it is clear that Peter and Ellie, however intellectually and morally prickly, nevertheless offer one another loving friendship and sanctuary. Ellie proposes marriage, and Peter gladly accepts.

In transferring the integrity of successive novels from the episodic details of crime to the evolving domesticity of the investigator, Hill followed Dorothy Sayers (1893–1957), in whose *Gaudy Night* (1935) and *Busman's Honeymoon* (1937) Lord Peter Wimsey finally persuades Harriet Vane to marry him, and discovers on a

honeymoon troubled by a corpse how difficult it is to reconcile intimate trust with a necessarily merciless pursuit of truth. The echoes are loud: *Gaudy Night* is set in Oxford, an elite grove of academe whither Harriet has retreated, *An Advancement of Learning* at Holm Coultram College, a less elite enclave which also finds the scurrilities and baseness of the world have broken in; and the novels share an intense, Renaissance epigraphy, Sayers prefixing to each chapter passages from a rich variety of Tudor sources, Hill quotations from the marvellous essay by Bacon whose title (changing "The" to "An") he borrowed. In *Gaudy Night* Sayers mapped the smug isolation of "Mayhem Parva" onto Oxford's "dreaming spires," inward-looking colleges, and social snobbery, at once objectifying a sense of isolation and breaking the hermetic seal to let in the bustle of the university and the shadow of the world beyond. Her epigraphs, allusive dialogue, and comedy of manners sustain a literary self-consciousness allowing rich metafictional (hence readily polygeneric) composition. She extended her breakthrough in *Busman's Honeymoon*, subtitled "A Love Story with Detective Interruptions," by remapping the world she had achieved directly onto the marriage of Peter and Harriet, the precious territory of their honeymoon becoming the sanctuary violated by their need to solve a crime, but thereafter pursued Christian work and translation. Hill, driven by background, circumstance, and political conviction to choose the ordinary over the elite, bourgeois policemen over an aristocratic sleuth, was able to begin developing to its full potential the serial crime novel in which series characters provide a comedy of manners grounded in the trials of love and friendship, while the burden of each case (and death) enacts in bas-relief the figure of tragedy.

Ruling Passion (another title from Pope) ends with Pascoe's autumn engagement; *An April Shroud* (1975) begins with Dalziel's speech at his spring wedding, and with the Pascoes on honeymoon Hill turned overdue attention to Dalziel, whose gargantuanism, though enriching the narratives, had shielded him from scrutiny. Saving his telegraphic divorce, readers learn little intimate until a health-scare in *Ruling Passion* takes him to the doctor for an intimidating check-up: "Dalziel came from behind the screen with all the demureness and probably the total volume of Gilbert's three little maids from school" (p. 127). Despite the humour Dalziel is inwardly fearful of his chest-pains, as an obese, choleric, heavy-smoking hard-drinker should be, and as we all would be—a humanizing connection with the fat man for every reader, developed by placing him in unfamiliar circumstances and allowing readers to see them through his eyes.

Ellie's parents live in Lincolnshire, and the wedding (to which Dalziel leads a Yorkshire deputation) follows a week of heavy rain. For Dalziel it is the start of a rare holiday, a fortnight of unstressed touring prescribed for its physical benefit but as much a psychological necessity, a chance to shake off a fatalistic lassitude induced by intimations of mortality—the "melancholy fit" which in Keats's "Ode on Melancholy" "hides the green hill in an April shroud." Dalziel's wanderings are curtailed by floodwaters, and he finds himself marooned in . . . an isolated country-house occupied by an unlikely family whose pater familias has just died in mysterious circumstances! The lively parody of hermetic murder mysteries keeps matters amusing, and this time Dalziel is the witness without official standing, while Bonnie, a larger-than-life widow, is cheerfully willing to seek solace in his arms and substantial enough to give him a run for his money. Dalziel in love is an intriguing proposition, but Bonnie's purpose may be distraction, and Dalziel knows her need for investors in the family business makes his own savings account uneasily relevant. Two further deaths make a positive outcome impossible, and the novel is in many ways as bleak as it is watery, but the climactic mock-medieval banquet, where the returned Pascoes are blessed with a vision of Dalziel dressed as Henry VIII, re-establishes his comedic resilience to wives while preserving a complex humanization.

Ruling Passion and *An April Shroud* left Mid-Yorks, but the next six installments stuck to home territory. Pascoe's engagement coincided with promotion to Inspector, and in *A Pinch of Snuff* (1978) his underling role is taken by Sergeant Edgar Wield, as impossibly ugly as Dalziel is fat, whose intriguing reticence and dry wit soon established him as a full series character. The novel deals with locally produced pornography (bruited in *A Fairly Dangerous Thing*) and the horror of snuff films, but also with police corruption; both subjects feed the Pascoes' marital debates, and Hill poses the sexual exploitation of children against the announcement of Ellie's pregnancy. Related motives dominate *A Killing Kindness* (1980), in which the "Yorkshire Choker" is strangling fiancées to "protect their innocence" and claiming responsibility in telephone-calls quoting misogynistically from *Hamlet*. Between these novels came a novella, *Pascoe's Ghost* (1979), with atmospheric chapter-epigraphs from Edgar Allan Poe, and a companion story, "Dalziel's Ghost," which comically debunks the supernatural. As seeming ghost stories both tales flirt with the great modern crime-writing taboo, a supernatural agency invalidating reason and forensic science, and both pave the way to *A Killing Kindness,* which begins with a séance and ends with supernatural vengeance—but despite the bravura execution, this strange twist can for horribly real reasons be thought a rare failure of Hill's.

The D. & P. novels afford wide-angle and wide-ranging views of the area their protagonists help to police, from the detail of local cinemas, fairs, parks, and housing to patterns of residence, travel, class, wealth, old-boy networks, mercantile back-scratching, and private collusions. The emergent city resembles Doncaster (where Hill was living), a mix of elegant older architecture, low-quality council housing, dereliction, small businesses, and redeveloped industrial estates and malls, somewhere in coal country with Leeds, Bradford, and the dales to the north, Sheffield to the west: but it is never named, and like the designation "Mid-Yorks" is archetype, not portrait. This approach generally works well—but the real North was terrorized in 1978–1981 by Peter Sutcliffe, the Yorkshire Ripper, who killed thirteen women and reduced the whole country to bewildered rage before being caught, while Hill's "Yorkshire Choker" is a literary construct in whose deeds the stranger-stranger element that makes serial killing so terrifyingly incomprehensible is thinned away. Hill was writing before *The Silence of the Lambs* (1988) popularized psychological analyses of serial killers, but his use of supernatural elements to execute justice, if formally excellent, tacitly admits failure to comprehend within Mid-Yorks the social disturbance and self-loathing suspicions that Sutcliffe inflicted in reality, and that Thomas Harris (in a different literary mode) caught in Hannibal Lecter and Clarice Starling.

If *A Killing Kindness* is a qualified failure, *Deadheads* (1983) is Hill's first masterpiece, a superb novel in which elements of the case and the serial development of character are fused. For accountant Patrick Aldermann, owner of local mansion Rosemont and tender of its magnificent rose gardens, the smooth course of life owes much to the happy frequency with which those who block his upward way die accidental deaths. For his well-bred wife, Daphne, growing friendship with Ellie Pascoe is tested by Peter's professional interest in Patrick's strange good fortune. The titular motif of deadheading, lopping blooms past their prime to let buds develop, extends through section-epigraphs (canonical writers on roses) to the chapter-titles and -epigraphs, names and catalogue-descriptions of roses richly applicable to the chapters that follow: "1 / MISCHIEF / *(Hybrid tea, coral and salmon, sweetly scented, excellent in the garden, susceptible to black spot)*" (p. 9). The intellectual gamesmanship is matched by an uncertainty, maintained to the last, as to whether any crime has been committed, and the whole is a substantive meditation as well as an absorbing adventure.

Such titles and epigraphs extend Hill's gift for analogy, through which Dalziel's humor and grotesque bulk are promoted, and his character extended:

Andy Dalziel, according to much of his acquaintance, had a very simplistic approach to life. He saw everything as either black or dark blue. In this they were mistaken. Life was richly coloured for the fat man; full of villainy and vice, it was true, but with shifting shades and burning pigments, like Hogarthian scenes painted by Renoir.

Pascoe understood this. "He detects with his balls," he had once told Ellie gloomily.

A Killing Kindness, p. 48

Wield's physiognomy is similarly treated—"[his] ugliness was only skin deep, but that was deep enough" (*A Pinch of Snuff*, p. 26)—but his rocky façade conceals a dangerous secret for a policeman: homosexuality. The end of a long-term relationship and the attractive grace of Police Cadet Shaheed Singh (introducing themes of racism and minority policing) trouble Wield in *Deadheads*, and in *Exit Lines* (1984) and *Child's Play* (1987) the ramifying problems faced by any closeted homosexual in a homophobic service are persistently explored. *Exit Lines* uses as chapter-epigraphs famous last words, and by implicating Dalziel in possible drunk-driving and manslaughter charges introduces the command corridor, where public relations and cover-ups are managed—a heightening of the narrative overview that maintains Pascoe's relative ignorance despite promotion and growing experience, framing difficulties of detection with problems of politics and the practical uses of the need-to-know principle. *Child's Play: A Tragi-comedy in Three Acts of Violence With a Prologue and an Epilogue* turns on acting in every sense, mixing a cunningly disguised plot with general concern about motives for deception. Both novels develop significant minor characters—idiotic Constable Hector, ambitious Detective Constable Seymour, canny solicitor Eden Thackeray, and exotic theater-director Eileen Chung—but their deepest concern is Wield's impossible position, which finally becomes untenable, his secret conflicting with the professional dedication he uses to contain his emotions.

Chastity having failed, and his new lover having been murdered, a dazed Wield has no choice but to confess:

Dalziel's face across the table looked about as sympathetic as a prison wall. But it was not sympathy he wanted, Wield reminded himself. It was the right to be himself. He thought of the effect saying this was likely to produce on Dalziel and felt his courage ebb. He had to admit it—the man terrified him! Here before him in awful visible form, was embodied all the mockery, scorn, and scatological abuse which he had always feared from the police hierarchy. At least, to start with Dalziel was to start with the worst.

He drew a deep breath and said, "I want to tell you. I'm a homosexual."

"Oh aye," said Dalziel, "You've not just found out, have you?"

"No," said Wield, taken aback. "I've always known."

"That's all right, then," said Dalziel equably. "I'd have been worried else that I'd not mentioned it to you."

Child's Play, p. 259

For readers whom Dalziel's knowledge and pragmatic tolerance surprise, as for Wield, there is much reassessing to be done, not least in measuring Dalziel against Neville Watmough, a politically ambitious superior who is both bigoted and opportunistic. For Pascoe too, heart-searching is needed:

After [Dalziel] had finished, there was silence in the room. Even Dalziel's scratchy serenade was allowed to fade away as he observed the younger man's reaction with interest.

At last [Pascoe] spoke.

"Wield's queer?" he said incredulously. "Bugger me."

"Best be careful what you say," said Dalziel and roared with laughter.

Pascoe looked at him with undisguised distaste and Dalziel stopped laughing and said with a sigh, "All right. What's up?"

"Nothing. I just don't think it's a laughing matter, that's all."

"What do you think it is, then? A hanging matter?"

Pascoe flushed and said angrily, "That's not what I meant at all and you know it. I reckon I'm a damn sight more . . ."

His voice tailed away as he saw the fat man's sly amusement.

"Liberal, is that the word? Some of your best mates are gay? Well, here's another to join the merry throng!"

Pascoe took a deep breath and said, "All right. Sorry. Let's start again, sir. You go easy on the jokes and I'll go easy on the righteousness."

"Sounds fair," said Dalziel.

Child's Play, p. 268

Ellie also knew what Peter had missed in a colleague and friend, so there is humble pie to be eaten as well as chagrin to be endured—but Pascoe's balance is restored in the epilogue, revealing a twist even Dalziel had missed. More importantly, Pascoe's recovery in this conversation ("You go easy on the jokes") and Dalziel's acceptance of it mark a new give-and-take in their relationship, a mellowing with age and depth; with Pascoe's later conversations with Wield, re-establishing friendship, the series itself reached a humane maturity that would require new challenges to develop further.

PATRICK RUELL AND OTHERS, 1971–1991

The eight novels by "Patrick Ruell" fall into clear groups of four, published 1971–1975 and 1986–1991. Between the groups come (besides D. & P. work) two novels by "Charles Underhill," and five nonseries novels, a collection of stories, and some articles published in propria persona.

The early Ruells are comedic spy-thrillers, deftly plotted and increasingly literary. In *The Castle of the Demon* (1971; later *The Turning of the Tide*), Emily Follett is the first of several female protagonists who find themselves caught in governmental ructions caused by their husbands' secret lives, and seek new love among those exposing the secrets. Once Emily's blindness to her husband's deceit ends, passivity must give way to initiative, and a reader's satisfaction comes from that development amid a burlesque of romantic clichés—a dark stranger on a horse, and an ice-breaking friendship between a most independent-minded cat and a great lolloping dog. *Red Christmas* (1972) celebrates the familiar Yuletide Dickensiana of Mr. Pickwick and Dingley Dell, all crisp snow, jolly carols, and hot punch, but combines it with a country-house murder-mystery and the vicious terrorism spawned at that time by the Cold War. *Death Takes the Low Road* (1974; later *The Low Road*) sees one William Blake Hazlitt chased through the Scottish highlands and islands by British and Russian agents of indistinguishable morality; the lively narrative, switching between Blake's flight and pursuits by assorted agents and his American lover, ignorant of his intelligence connections, deals in romance and the romantics, with an underpinning of Boswell's proto-romantic *Tour of the Hebrides* (1785). The last and oddest of this group, *Urn Burial* (1975; later *Beyond the Bone*), deals like *Red Christmas* with a dirty side-show of the Cold War, but takes its title and epigraphs from the great archaeological and metaphysical essay by Sir Thomas Browne (1605–1682): their intellectual weight over-matches the plot, despite thick flavors of the oc-cult and a lively satire of rural development. Never uninteresting or badly written, the novel tries to make too much of too many ingredients, and thereafter Hill seems briefly to have pulled back from this mode to reassess what he wanted to do with it.

Supernatural and antiquarian elements resurface in the Underhill novels, *Captain Fantom* (1978) and *The Forging of Fantom* (1979), but (as in *Pascoe's Ghost,* 1979) under far tighter control. Carlo Fantom was a seventeenth-century Croat-ian who fought on both sides of the English Civil War, and got himself into *Brief Lives* by John Aubrey (1626–1697) as a speaker of thirteen languages, an inveterate "ravisher," and a "hard-man," one whom a secret herb makes impervious to lead bullets. Hill was fascinated by Aubrey's sketch of Fantom, and though imitative of the romping *Flashman* novels (1969–) by George MacDonald Fraser (b. 1925)—hugely popular in the late 1970s—Hill's imaginations of seventeenth-century military life suggest substan-tial research and fine-grained historical scruple, presenting a period mind as well as period detail. The "hard-man" legend, though debunked by Fantom himself, becomes more ambiguous, an enticingly dangerous form of self-confidence that, like inordinate lusts and the vagaries of war, makes for alarming instability. A mock-scholarly preface suggests a Fantom series was planned, but *The Forging of Fantom,* a prequel imagining Fantom's youth in Croatia and Venice, is Hill's only book not to find a U.S. publisher, and there

have been no more Underhills. The brief appear-ance of this third pseudonym may nevertheless mark a successful test by Hill of his ability to earn by writing, anticipating his 1981 decision to resign from teaching to write full-time.

Another view is that with the supernatural dif-ficulties of *A Killing Kindness* (1980) Hill's inter-est in the paranormal reached a further impasse, and his next three nonseries novels reverted firmly to the romantic spy-thriller format pio-neered as Ruell. *The Spy's Wife* (1980) has the most direct version of the betrayed female protagonist, Molly Keatley, whose husband, Sam, one day leaves as usual and next contacts her from Bulgaria, en route to Moscow. Disciplined and low-key—Sam is a fellow-traveling journal-ist, not a master-spy—the novel achieves consid-erable psychological depth and a memorable, painfully ironic ending. *Who Guards a Prince?* (1982) is a more straightforward thriller, again tightly controlled but venturing toward Bond ter-ritory: the plot involves an English prince, a Boston Irish dynasty, the U.S. presidency, and a dogged, dangerous (ex-)policeman from the prince's protection detail, Douglas McHarg—a cipher (as such heroes tend to be) capable nevertheless of tragic loss and qualified romance. *Traitor's Blood* (1983) is the funniest of the three, revelling (like *Another Death in Venice*) in lush Italian settings, and, unusually for Hill, running up the body-count sufficiently for tragedy to explode; the darker theme is the tangled family misunderstandings and betrayals underlying the mayhem, and a painful set of questions about the places of nature, nurture, and self-deception in the inheritance of a treacherous disposition.

In the mid-1980s D. & P. novels achieved maturity, and higher standards are evident in Hill's other work from this period. *No Man's Land* (1985) fulfills the promise of the Fantom novels as researched historical imaginations, but deals with the recent, catastrophic past of World War I, especially a concern that would become a major issue for Pascoe:

Britain declared war on Germany on August 4th, 1914. The British Army killed its first German soldier on August 22nd near Mons. Seventeen days later on September 8th, near the Marne, the British Army killed its first British soldier, a 19-year-old private condemned for desertion. Thereafter, for the duration of the war, it continued to condemn them to death at the rate of 60 per month and execute them at the rate of 6 per month. These figures are approximate. Some months were better than others.

(p. 9)

Even now Her Majesty's Government refuses to apologize for its savagely bigoted treatment of British Other Ranks on the Western Front, and Hill's novel is driven by humane rage. It centers on a legend of the Great War, that deserters of many nationalities found refuge in "the Desolation," an area up to twenty miles deep so pulverized by entrenchment, mining, and bombardment during the battle of the Somme in 1916 that when the front line shuffled forward a few miles it became an enclosed wasteland behind the British positions. An adult version of Golding's *Lord of the Flies* (1954), with deserters as the schoolboys and the ruinous horror of the Desolation as the island, *No Man's Land* tempers anger with compassion and pity with admiration, twining personal narratives and wider view through three movements: "Dissolution," "Desolation," "Resolution." Hill's aesthetic and human desire for a comedic ending (resolution) is partly indulged, but an epilogue revealing the lives of survivors is set in September 1939 (resolution), and the final sentence bitingly extends the famous closing image of the butterfly in Lewis Milestone's film of *All Quiet on the Western Front* (1929):

> For a moment [the butterfly] fluttered outside the still open door of the farmhouse. Then it rose out of the shaded yard and let the explosion of heat from the baking tiles carry it skywards, as if it would not stop soaring till its tiny wings were shrivelled in the burning heart of the sun.

(p. 352)

The underlying image is of Icarus, the hope of an ordinary, unshelled French countryside conceived as an impossible hubris, and the following novel, *The Collaborators* (1987), though freestanding, extends the bleakness of 1939 into the grim occupation that followed. Structured as a flashback illuminating a widow's guilty plea to one of the courts, half-official, half-kangaroo, that tried collaborators in 1945, the novel passionately imagines moral complexities and hoping-against-hope compromises that Anglo-American historians and novelists have largely ignored, and reflects knowledge of continental European fiction and scholarship. The two novels form a diptych, and deserve far more critical attention than they have had.

In the same year Hill published his second collection of short stories, built, like *Pascoe's Ghost,* around an eponymous novella. *There Are No Ghosts in the Soviet Union* (1987) beautifully solves the clash between the essence of the ghost story and the tenets of crime writing by making those tenets an imposition of the state: it really is a ghost that dunit, but in the USSR a rational explanation is required, however absurd an evasion of what characters have seen; readers thus find themselves (contrary to detective training) rooting for the supernatural as the truer version of events. It helps that the underlying plot is that of *Don Giovanni,* with a most vengeful ghost in the role of the statue—but the novella handsomely repays its literary debts. The shorter stories include the first appearance of Joe Sixsmith ("Bring Back the Cat!"), a whimsical D. & P. story ("Auteur Theory"), a savage World War I tale ("The Bull Ring"), and a scurrilous continuation of Jane Austen's *Emma.* Besides the D. & P. collection *Asking for the Moon* (1994) and the limited-edition *Brother's Keeper* (1992), there is no subsequent collection of stories, but Hill continues to publish them, and many are very good indeed (as two CWA [Crime Writers' Association] awards testify); some are ideas too tightly twisted to seed a novel and at home in short fiction, but many relate to longer work as a form of artist's cartoon, trials in light and composition.

Hill's increasingly analytical practice of his craft was marked from the late 1970s by some historical and critical essays. A friend of Julian Symons (1912–1994), Hill never criticizes *Bloody Murder* (1972), Symons's influential, theorized history of detective fiction, but the scholarly thrust of his work on Early Modern crime-writing and his broad understanding of the form are wholly counter to Symons's paradigms. The disagreement is explicit in "Looking for a Programme" (1986), Hill's most extended and theoretical argument of his craft and a personal statement of preferences and influences: the key issue is his refusal to accept the isolation of crime-writing from literature and concomitant pragmatism (anti-essentialism) about genre. The essay, like Hill himself, is self-deprecating, wry, modest, funny, and beneath all these passionate: but having abandoned the classroom for his desk Hill prefers to let his novels speak for themselves, and has never collected his essays or published critically.

The late Ruells began with *The Long Kill* (1986), a perfect tragedy. The plot, now more familiar than in the 1980s, is the assassin who wants to retire, but the novel's force comes from the intense familial loves and hatreds that are the mainsprings of action, and their engagement with the titular motif—a sniper's preference for a longer-than-necessary line of fire, an annealing distance blessed with clarity and enabled by a hand and eye as sure as they are hidden. The ending is devastating, in not only its deaths but its survivals, lives now to be lived with knowledge, in the emptiness of betrayals that steal the past and losses that gut the future. *Death of a Dormouse* (1987) begins more simply, with a man's death in his car, but his widow, Trudi Adamson, is another betrayed woman, and the novel revisits *The Spy's Wife* with a criminal rather than Cold War flavor and superb epigraphs from Burns's "To a Mouse":

Thou saw the fields laid bare an' waste,
An' weary winter coming fast,
An' cozie here, beneath the blast,
  Thou thought to dwell,
'Till crash! the cruel coulter past
  Out thro' thy cell.

        (p. 79)

A coulter is the upright shank of a plough, supporting the ploughshares into which swords may be beaten: Burns's image is of total loss, and Hill's seems to be, as Trudi's security, comfort, and belief are destroyed by the revelations of her widowhood. But Hill's comedic impulse runs strong; the dormouse in Trudi may have to die before the lioness in her can emerge, and romance, or at least sexuality, tries to flourish—but the ending is irresolute, and intimate trust is not to be hired.

Similar ambivalences fill the last Ruells. In *Dream of Darkness* (1989) Sairey Ellis is at eighteen the youngest of Hill's betrayed women, and the betrayal is familial; the action provokes the recovery of traumatic personal memories about her mother's death in Uganda, but also of traumatic political memories—the still largely suppressed details of Britain's post-imperial scramble to get out, get even, and get on, all at once and without being seen to do anything. The betrayals of Sairey, past and present, unfold in tandem as she works to remember; a single act of kindness by her last betrayer grants her some security in a world laid waste, but healing will take a lifetime. Though cleverly constructed, morally enraged, and sharply ashamed of Britain's malevolent, self-interested baseness and foot-shuffling, the novel never engages (as title and plot suggest it might) with Conrad's *Heart of Darkness* (1899) or the underlying racist metaphor of Africans being as dark of soul as of skin; the psychotic presence of Idi Amin Dada (b. 1925), the Army strongman whom the departing British helped to seize power in Uganda, sketches a form such engagement might have taken (Francis Ford Coppola viewed America in Vietnam through Conrad's lens in *Apocalypse Now*), but the very tightness of the plot, admirable in itself, impedes its fuller development.

That the problem might be the extent to which Hill is a novelist of place is suggested by the taut perfection of *The Only Game* (1991), largely set in urban England. Soon-to-be-ex-Inspector "Dog" Cicero, once an undercover Army officer in Northern Ireland and now, scarred by failure and bereavement, CID in Romford (a rough bit of London), sees the case of a missing child attract "funny buggers"—the Police Special branch who, as IRA terrorism blurred policing and counterinsurgency, became the local arm of the secret services. His own attention is attracted by the child and its mother, in whom he finds hope of personal redemption: she is another of the betrayed, her supposedly dead husband a thieving Noraid bagman whom both IRA and security services now pursue. The novel weaves its title with Dog's unlikely nickname, a form of "underdog" used in gambling parlance to state odds: a fast-shuttling plot binds the "great game" of espionage to the bitter, lasting games of schoolyard malarkey and "the only game [in town]" in many senses—all metaphorically unified through poker, taught to Cicero from early childhood by his world-champion Uncle Endo. The high roller's bluff, counter-bluff, assessments of odds, baiting to enlarge the pot, and need to be poker-faced are used to pattern a relentless thriller: if Dog is to win at all he must win everything, and in the end *The Only Game* rejects the tragedy with which it flirts for tough-minded comedy that does not suppose resolutions to come cheap, even in fiction, and knows well that the only experience close to winning the lot is losing it.

After 1991 Hill published only under his own name, and pseudonymous work was reissued to benefit from the televised popularity of Dalziel and Pascoe. As often with pseudonyms, it is publishers who create and destroy—but "Ruell's" eight novels form a clear corpus including first-rate tragedy and comedy; their place in Hill's writing deserves study as a creative tactic, not simply as a marketing function.

DALZIEL AND PASCOE AFTER 1988

In 1983 Hill started a D. & P. centered on mining, a major part of Yorkshire life, but the miners' strike (a year of violence pitting mass pickets against policemen from all over the U.K.) forced a pause. When it was over, a program of pit-closures and asset-stripping began that left swathes of the industrial north destitute and moribund. In this growing wasteland, pocked with virtual no-go areas for the uniformed police, Hill found a Yorkshire in which general disempowerment, and the highly politicized role of women during the strike, had undermined an entrenched chauvinism to leave the ground shifting beneath everyone's feet.

Under World appeared in 1988, Hill's second masterpiece and the best fiction yet published on the social consequences of the strike; that so few works even mention them (*Billy Elliot* is another honorable exception) underlines his unfashionable, compelling, and Dickensian practice of the social novel. True to his convictions about civil society, there is anti-Thatcherite irony, but *Under World* is centrally concerned with futures neither union nor police could protect. In a pit-village, Burrthorpe, a man dies underground; investigation stirs a pre-strike trauma, the disappearance of a little girl, conveniently blamed by Watmough on a pedophile who left an ambiguous suicide note. In broadening complication, deep disharmony and adulterous temptations bloom within the Pascoes' marriage—but what of their young daughter Rosie, and needs for one another? The novel masterfully deploys motifs, contrasting, for example, pit-head winding-gear that lowers men into the coal and returns them blackened to the light, with the infamous paternoster (an open, cyclical elevator) at Sheffield University, lifting students from their roots and lowering them back as strangers to their parents' world. Ellie, teaching an extramural course attended by a young Burrthorpe miner in desperate need of rescue, finds that for middle-class socialism, as for liberal policemanship, Burrthorpe is perilous, the more so as emotional confusions drag her into the tense police investigation. It takes Peter's near-fatal injury in an underground rockfall to clarify her priorities: the conclusion leaves no one unscathed, and neither damage nor healing can be confined to one book.

Later D. & P. novels have more extended multi-novel plots and themes than earlier ones, and *Under World,* with epigraphs from Dorothy Sayers's translation of Dante's *Inferno,* is followed by two purgatorios and a paradiso in a sweeping movement from tragedy to comedy. The Pascoes' purgatorio is *Bones and Silence* (1990), a title from Virginia Woolf for a plot twining a friend's suicide, a Teflon murderer, and Dalziel's appearance as God in a processional performance of the York Mystery Cycle (whence section-epigraphs). Dalziel's purgatorio is *Recalled to Life* (1992), modeled on *A Tale of Two Cities* (whence title and epigraphs), in which the secret services try to snip a loose end dating from the 1963 Profumo scandal by blaming a miscarriage of justice on the late Wally Tallantyre—Dalziel's police mentor. As honor took Dickens's Dorsay to Paris, so Dalziel's quest takes him to Washington, with unpredictably enlightening and qualified results: if Tallantyre's memory is protected only uncertain poetic justice is done, and Dalziel, like Dorsay and the Pascoes before him, is forcefully reminded of mortality. Hill's only series venture outside the U.K. draws on the Cold War attitudes anatomized in nonseries work and is pungently satirical, but the genial gusto of Dalziel's rogue-elephantine progress through cupboards crammed with CIA skeletons romps an upward way. The paradiso, *Pictures of Perfection* (1994), is Wield's: with title and epigraphs from Jane Austen, Hill's third masterpiece transplants the village of Enscombe from Austen's Hampshire to Mid-Yorks as a delightful hybrid of Arcadia and Brigadoon, inflicts an apparent spree-killing (as at Hungerford in 1987), and ends, as Austenite comedy should, with emotional magic and true love. Wield's lasting cohabitation with antiquarian bookseller Edwin Digweed in Enscombe has subsequently given the series a permanent home for whimsy, and a vibrant source of pastoral.

Hill's domestication of magic realism, at once glitteringly intellectual, achingly funny, and so grounded that even whimsies lock into place, makes *Pictures of Perfection* the most joyous of all D. & P.s, surpassing Sayers's *Gaudy Night* in utterly reinventing "Mayhem Parva," and standing beside Eco's *The Name of the Rose* (1980) in the modern pantheon. But Wield's happiness is not Dalziel's—or Pascoe's. Despite physical recovery from his injuries, promotion to Chief Inspector, and a repaired marriage, Pascoe becomes uncertain of himself and his job as never before, and in *The Wood Beyond* (1996), enraged by learning of his great-grandfather's 1917 execution: an irruption into Mid-Yorks of material from *No Man's Land.*

The Wood Beyond is a pastoral with abattoir, framed by the journey of Enscombe sheep to a continental slaughterhouse. The title abbreviates *The Wood Beyond the World* (1894), a fey fable by William Morris (1834–1896); sections with epigraphs from Marvell's "The Nymph complaining for the death of her Faun" name other fine-sounding woods—Sanctuary, Glencorse, Polygon, and Wanwood, the first three destroyed with a million men in the criminally ill-conceived battle known as Passchendaele, and the last, within the plot a desecrated Mid-Yorks location, a coinage by Hopkins to express autumnal desolation ("Though worlds of wanwood leafmeal lie"). Connecting World War I material and Pascoe's family history to a present case of animal-rights violence pushes coincidence towards fantasy, but the class structures that made prejudiced execution of Other Ranks lawful were and are real, while sympathy with Pascoe's rage and Enscombe's ability to contain the unlikely, however wild, allow the plot to run its tragedic risks successfully. There is also a comedic counterweight in Dalziel's pastoral role as a satyr transfixed by a substantial faun, Amanda "Cap" Marvell, once the Hon. Mrs. Pitt-Evenlode and still establishment-connected, but galvanized by her son's putative death in the Falklands-Malvinas War, and a decade of divorced radicalization, into a grand animal-rights crusader. Tragedy qualifies comedy, and the novel ends with romance suspended by a quarrel—but "Cap" Marvell has since been a regular presence and occasional source of titbits about Dalziel's childhood.

Peter's crisis continued in *On Beulah Height* (1998), a return to *Under World* making of one masterpiece a greater:

> Thou shalt no more be termed Forsaken; neither shall thy land any more be termed Desolate: but thou shalt be called Heph'zi-bäh, and thy land Beu'lah: for the LORD delighteth in thee, and thy land shall be married.

From this origin in Isaiah 62:4 (a context to consider) Beulah became, in *Pilgrim's Progress,* the land before Heaven, and in Mid-Yorks a crag above Dendale, drowned with its village fifteen years before in creating a reservoir, at the end of a long, hot summer during which three little girls vanished and even Dalziel could find no trace. Now, in another long, hot summer, falling waters expose the ruins, and in nearby Danby, Lorraine

Dacre, daughter of a resettled Dendale girl, goes missing; compounding Dalziel's revisited agony is the virtual loss of Pascoe, pacing with Ellie beside the hospital-beds where Rosie, now seven, and a schoolfriend fight meningitis for their lives.

Hill handles the machinery of searching and the journeys of the Dacres and Pascoes from guilt-ridden terror to crippling grief or haunted joy with great skill and tact, and *On Beulah Height* is another superbly responsible social novel. It also confronts Mahler's *Kindertotenlieder* ("songs for dead children") with stunning demotic translations by a Dendale girl turned singer of the libretti, poems by Friedrich Rückert (1788–1866) fraught with the vulnerability of children and the legend of the Erlking. As a cover for her CD, to be sold at the Danby Music Festival, the singer provides a drawing which is also a clue, and the creative breadth which led Hill to translation led also to draftsmanship: besides the CD cover, there are Wield's plan of Dendale and an illustrated text of *Nina and the Nix*, a Yorkshire fairytale of child-snatching published by Digweed, given by Wield to the Pascoes, adopted by Rosie as a favorite and configuring her brainsick dreams. The rich mix ferments through iterated anagnoresis to full catharsis; as in *Under World*, the missing dead are recovered, and such closure as tragedy permits the living is claimed through epic melancholy and biblical resonance, but once again no one is unscathed.

Arms and the Women: An Elliad (2000) is by contrast a relieved romp, visiting with Ellie, W.D.C. Shirley "Ivor" Novello, and other women an encounter with terrorists, but granting Ellie publication of a novel and featuring an inset-tale casting Dalziel as Odysseus and Peter, still struggling with demons, as pious Aeneas. The whole is wreathed in Shakespeare and Hopkins, very un-Virgilian, and despite many deaths sees the women save everyone who matters (including a trussed Dalziel and Pascoe), while the "funny bugger" who endangered them is landed right in it.

Dialogues of the Dead (2001) and *Death's Jest-Book* (2002) form a diptych and, written consecutively, broke Hill's formative resolution. A third

straight D. & P. has been announced, and judgement must wait. The diptych returns to serial killing, replacing the slightly over-literary "Yorkshire Choker" of *A Killing Kindness* not with a development of the more realistic pedophile killer in *On Beulah Height* but with the utterly literary "Wordman." The metafictional self-consciousness generated by illustrations, translations, and inset-narratives, all present throughout, bulks length and reaches a new intensity, becoming an explicit part of a metaphysical dance of death. Openly subtitled a "word game," *Dialogues of the Dead* (titled after satirical fantasies by George Lyttelton, 1709–1773), like *A Killing Kindness,* offers a giveaway clue so absurdly early that even forewarned readers sail past, and blends the gruesome and facetious so smoothly that moral purchase is hard to come by. *Death's Jest-Book* (titled after a play by T. L. Beddoes, 1803–1849) is explicitly a *danse macabre,* using illustrations by Holbein: it turns on cliché as richly as Shakespeare, and closes the book on the Wordman, but not, quite, on the sly malice and putative redemption of Franny Roote—whom Pascoe arrested in *An Advancement of Learning,* and who now, released from jail, begins to write him letters. The long-term consequences of the violent ending are known only to Hill, but cannot be easy for any Pascoe.

An interim conclusion is that Hill tactically inflated the humor and literariness that make the purblindness of serial killing alien to Mid-Yorks. The decision reacts against the hit BBC TV series *Dalziel & Pascoe,* approximately faithful to Hill's novels but inevitably simplifying plots and character, and perhaps against David Peace's *Red Riding Quartet* (1999–2002), which portrays Sutcliffe and the policemen who took so long to catch him in a nightmare of the damned. A stunning, bilious read, Peace's fractured prose finds tragedy as impossible as comedy or canonical allusion: its success, unsustainable at series length, is irrelevant to the fictional achievement of Mid-Yorks save in relieving Hill of any felt obligation to confront Sutcliffe directly. The jury remains out on Hill's inflationary approach to his own literariness, but given his triumph in *Pictures of*

Perfection over the related perversion of spree killing, it would be unwise to bet against him.

Consecutive writing also activates a latent problem mocked in *One Small Step* (1990), a novella celebrating D.'s & P.'s twentieth anniversary: that while Mid-Yorks travels in time with Hill, Dalziel and Pascoe age too slowly. By now Dalziel should have retired and Pascoe be at least a Chief Constable—or even Eurofed Police Commissioner, as he is when in *One Small Step* he raises Dalziel from gouty retirement to solve a murder on the moon. Kinder to Dalziel (who joins the 250,000 Mile High Club) than to politicized Pascoe, the novella is a splendid gift to fans, but the time-lag problem becomes significant with increasing length and continuous plots: Pascoe must soon be promoted, and as the rank of Chief Superintendent has been abolished, logic suggests he might leapfrog Dalziel into the command corridor. To keep him in Mid-Yorks, if breaching police rules, would be extremely interesting, as would the reactions of Ellie and fast-growing Rosie to Peter's nominal superiority over the comedic, righteous, and side-splitting force majeure of Andy Dalziel. Whatever he does, Hill will not disappoint.

JOE SIXSMITH

A redundant black lathe-operator turned PI, Joe was conceived in the 1970s for a film script, born and raised in short stories of the 1980s, and matured in four novels that alternated with Mid-Yorks from 1993 to 1999. As a note to the first explains:

> This book is set in a town called Luton in Bedfordshire. This should not be confused with the town called Luton in Bedfordshire, which the author has never been nearer to than the airport.
>
> (*Blood Sympathy*, p. 5)

In interview Hill cheerfully explains that he could not face researching the real Luton, but his zestful invention of a mildly fantastical Luton (anticipating magical Enscombe) is in the spirit of Sixsmith, a fine man with a fine cat and a Wodehousian aunt bent on matchmaking, who

rarely knows what he's doing but has the gift of serendipitously solving multiple cases by mixing them up. Joe's adventures in *Blood Sympathy* (1993) allow Hill's comedic gifts a southern, interracial arena and freer reign than any D. & P. save *Pictures of Perfection* (1994), a pattern sustained in *Born Guilty* (1995) and *Killing the Lawyers* (1997), though Luton's mean streets get steadily meaner. But *Singing the Sadness* (1999) moves close to the Mid-Yorks of *On Beulah Height* (1998), driven by the crimes against children that so often dominate the news.

Joe's favourite haunt in the first three novels is the Glit, a theme-club dedicated to 1970s pop-icon Gary Glitter—the stage-name of Paul Gadd, convicted early in 1999 of multiple offenses relating to Internet child-porn and sexual assaults on minors. Unmentioned in *Singing the Sadness,* where Joe is on a church-choir tour of Wales, the new shadow of the Glit is pervasive as he stumbles into civic corruption, echoing another real case involving systematic abuse and prostitution of children in care. Joe and his serendipity do what they can, and their comedy has force, but pedophile corruption cannot be solved or extirpated, and among Joe's musical heritages are, besides Glitter and Gospel, the Blues of endurance without relief. The results are humanely irresolute, and the series has since been in abeyance.

Though unfortunate and coincidental, Gadd's impact on Joe's Luton and Hill's response is a measure of how close to the wind he sails. In his concerns for betrayed women, for Ellie Pascoe as a first-generation modern feminist and Wield as a gay cop, and for the many children and adolescents whose abuse and deaths he has contemplated, as in his robust satire of the incivility evident in Thatcherism and Blairism, Hill has repeatedly shown himself a novelist and citizen of the greatest responsibility. His aggressive intertextuality is a hallmark of postmodernism, but his aesthetic and formalist brilliance has never bypassed the demands of the quotidian or vile, and his work as a whole has a moral probity and coherence quite lacking in many contemporary writers of "literature" whom critics uncritically praise. Hill is a self-effacing comedian, acute observer, and pungent stylist: Dalziel is one of the great creations, bulbously alive and confoundingly unpredictable, and Hill's later work includes some of the finest English comedic and tragic novels of the 1990s, as comprehensively literary as they are dedicated to literature's business with crime.

SELECTED BIBLIOGRAPHY

I. NOVELS AS REGINALD HILL.

THE DALZIEL & PASCOE SERIES: *A Clubbable Woman* (London, 1970; Woodstock, Vt., 1984); *An Advancement of Learning* (London, 1971; Woodstock, Vt., 1985); *Ruling Passion* (London, 1973; New York, 1977); *An April Shroud* (London, 1975; Woodstock, Vt., 1986); *A Pinch of Snuff* (London and New York, 1978); *A Killing Kindness* (London, 1980; New York, 1981); *Deadheads* (London, 1983; New York: , 1984); *Exit Lines* (London, 1984; New York, 1985); *Child's Play: A Tragi-comedy in Three Acts of Violence with a Prologue and an Epilogue* (London and New York, 1987); *Under World* (London and New York, 1988); *Bones and Silence* (London and New York, 1990); *One Small Step* (London, 1990); (a novella, subsequently included in *Asking for the Moon*—see "Short Stories" below); *Recalled to Life* (London and New York, 1992); *Pictures of Perfection: A Dalziel and Pascoe Novel in Five Volumes* (London and New York, 1994); *The Wood Beyond* (London and New York, 1996); *On Beulah Height* (London and New York, 1998); *Arms and the Women: An Elliad* (London and New York: Delacorte, 2000); *Dialogues of the Dead: or Paronomania! an AGED WORM for WEPT ROYALS a WARM DOGE for TOP LAWYERS a WORD GAME for TWO PLAYERS* (London, 2001; New York, 2002); *Death's Jest-Book* (London, 2002; as *Death's Jest Book,* New York, 2003); *Good Morning, Midnight* (London, 2004). (There is one Dalziel & Pascoe collection, *Asking for the Moon,* and five strays: "Auteur Theory," "Where the Snow Lay Dinted," "A Candle for Christmas," "Brass Monkey," and "A Gift for Father Christmas." See "Short Stories" below.)

THE JOE SIXSMITH SERIES: *Blood Sympathy* (London, 1993; New York, 1994); *Born Guilty* (London and New York, 1994); *Killing the Lawyers* (London and New York, 1997); *Singing the Sadness* (London and New York, 1999). (There are three stray Sixsmith stories: "Bring Back the Cat!" in *There Are No Ghosts in the Soviet Union,* and the uncollected "The Running of the Deer" and "The Cancellation." See "Short Stories" below.)

NONSERIES NOVELS: *Fell of Dark* (London, 1971; New York, 1986); *A Fairly Dangerous Thing* (London, 1972; Woodstock, Vt., 1983); *A Very Good Hater* (London, 1974; with the sub-title *A Tale of Revenge,* Woodstock, Vt., 1982); *Another Death in Venice* (London, 1976; New York, 1987); *The Spy's Wife* (London and New York, 1980); *Who Guards a Prince?* (London, 1982, and as *Guardians of the Prince,* Fontana, 1983; as *Who Guards the Prince?* New York, 1983); *Traitor's Blood* (London, 1983; Woodstock, Vt., 1986); *No Man's Land* (London and New York, 1985); *The Collaborators* (London, 1987; Woodstock, Vt., 1989). (*The*

Four Clubs, dated 1997, appears in some bibliographies, though Hill has never heard of it. It was probably an alternate title considered by Severn House for *Albion! Albion!* accidentally publicized and surviving as a net-ghost when *Singleton's Law* was preferred. See Novels as Dick Morland below.)

II. NOVELS AS PATRICK RUELL. *The Castle of the Demon* (London, 1971; New York, 1973; as *The Turning of the Tide* by Reginald Hill, Sutton, U.K. and New York, 1999); *Red Christmas* (London, 1972; New York, 1974; with a foreword by Robert Barnard, London, 1995); *Death Takes the Low Road* (London, 1974; New York, 1987; as The Low Road by Reginald Hill, Sutton, U.K. and New York, 1998); *Urn Burial* (London, 1975; Woodstock, Vt., 1987; with a foreword by Peter N. Walker, London, 1993; as *Beyond the Bone* by Reginald Hill, Sutton, U.K. and New York, 2000); *The Long Kill* (London, 1986; Woodstock, Vt., 1988); (filmed for U.S. TV by MCA Universal in 1993 as *The Last Hit,*; with the plot relocated to New Mexico); *Death of a Dormouse* (London and New York, 1987); *Dream of Darkness* (London, 1989; Woodstock, Vt., 1991); *The Only Game* (London, 1991; Woodstock, Vt., 1992).

III. NOVELS AS DICK MORLAND. *Heart Clock* (London, 1973; as *Matlock's System* by Reginald Hill, Sutton, U.K. and New York, 1996); *Albion! Albion!* (London, 1974; as *Singleton's Law* by Reginald Hill, Sutton, U.K. and New York, 1997).

IV. NOVELS AS CHARLES UNDERHILL. *Captain Fantom: Being an Account of Sundry Adventures in the Life of Carlo Fantom, Soldier of Misfortune, Hard-man and Ravisher* (London, 1978; New York, 1980); *The Forging of Fantom: Being an Account of the Formative Years in the Life of Carlo Fantom, Soldier of Misfortune, Hard-man and Ravisher* (London, 1979).

V. SHORT STORIES. *Pascoe's Ghost and Other Brief Chronicles of Crime* (London, 1979; New York, 1989) (Comprises "Pascoe's Ghost," "The Trunk in the Attic," "The Rio de Janeiro Paper," "Threatened Species," "Snowball," "Exit Line," and "Dalziel's Ghost," the first and last also appearing in *Asking for the Moon*); *There Are No Ghosts in the Soviet Union and Other Stories* (London, 1987; Woodstock, Vt., 1988; as *There Are No Ghosts in the Soviet Union: A Novella and Five Stories,* New York, 1989) (Comprises "There Are No Ghosts in the Soviet Union," "Bring Back the Cat!" [Joe Sixsmith], "The Bull Ring," "Auteur Theory," [Dalziel & Pascoe], "Poor Emma," and "Crowded Hour,"); *Brother's Keeper* (Helsinki, 1992) (Comprises "Brother's Keeper," "The Worst Crime Known to Man," "Poor Emma," and "Crowded Hour"); *Asking for the Moon* (London, 1994) (A Dalziel & Pascoe collection, comprising the novellas *One Small Step* and *Pascoe's Ghost,* and the short stories "Dalziel's Ghost" and "The Last National Serviceman,"); "The Thaw" (1973), in Martin Edwards, ed., *Northern Blood 3: An Anthology of the Best in Northern Crime Writing* (Birkenhead, U.K., 1998). Pp. 84–99; "A Shameful Eating," in *A Suit of Diamonds* (London, 1990; New York, 1991). Pp. 97–114; "Urban Legend" (1989), in H. R. F. Keating, ed., *Crime Waves 1: The Crime Writers' Association's Annual Anthology* (London, 1991), pp. 104–109; "The Running of the Deer," in Charlotte Macleod, ed., *Christmas Stalkings: Tales of Yuletide Murder* (New York, 1991). Pp. 31–58 (Joe Sixsmith); "The Man Who Defenestrated his Sister," in H. R. F. Keating, ed., *The*

Man Who . . . (London, 1992). Pp. 99–119; "Market Forces," in Martin Edwards, ed., *Northern Blood: An anthology of the best in Northern crime writing* (Manchester, U.K., 1992). Pp. 121–143; "Proxime Accessit," in Maxim Jakubowski, ed., *New Crimes 2* (London and New York, 1992). Pp. 156–173; "Realpolitik," in Patricia Craig, ed., *Julian Symons at 80—A Tribute* (Helsinki, 1992). Pp. 15–26; "Stonestar," in Liza Cody and Michael Z. Lewin, eds, *1st Culprit: A Crime Writers' Annual* (London, 1992). Pp. 221–229; "True Thomas," in Liza Cody and Michael Z. Lewin, eds, *2nd Culprit: A Crime Writers' Annual* (London, 1993). Pp. 80–102; "Where the Snow Lay Dinted," in Martin Edwards, ed., *Northern Blood 2: A Second Collection of Northern Crime Writing* (Newcastle upon Tyne, 1995). Pp. 79–93; "The Cancellation," in Maxim Jakubowski, ed., *No Alibi: The Best New Crime Fiction* (Manchester, U.K., 1995). Pp. 145–162 (Joe Sixsmith); "The Italian Sherlock Holmes," in Martin H. Greenberg, Jon L. Lellenberg, and Carol-Lynn Waugh, eds, *Holmes for the Holidays* (New York, 1996). Pp. 230–256; "The Perfect Murder Club," in Martin Edwards, ed., *Perfectly Criminal: The Crime Writers' Association's Annual Anthology* (Sutton, U.K. and New York, 1996). Pp. 90–103; "On the Psychiatrist's Couch," in Martin Edwards, ed., *Whydunit? Perfectly Criminal II: The Crime Writers' Association's Annual Anthology* (Sutton, U.K. and New York, 1997). Pp. 66–82.; "A Candle for Christmas," in *Ellery Queen's Mystery Magazine* (January 2000). Pp. 4–29; "Castles," in *Ellery Queen's Mystery Magazine* (July 2000). Pp. 122–134; "John Brown's Body," in P. D. James and Harriet Harvey-Wood, eds, *Sightlines* (London, 2001). Pp. 201–223; "A Gift for Father Christmas," in three parts in the *Daily Express* (London, 2002); "Brass Monkey," in *Ellery Queen Mystery Magazine* (January 2003). Pp. 38–54; "The Boy and Man Booker," in John Harvey, ed., *Men From Boys* (London, 2003).

VI. POETRY AND PLAYS. "Morning Ride," in *The Poetry Review* LV.2 (Summer 1964), pp. 75–76; "Dénouement," in *The Poetry Review* LIX.1 (Spring 1968), pp. 30–31; *An Affair of Honour* (1972) (An unpublished television play); *Ordinary Levels* (1982) (An unpublished radio play).

VII. ESSAYS AND ARTICLES. "The Educator: The Case of the Screaming Spires," in Dilys Winn, ed., *Murder Ink: The Mystery Reader's Companion* (New York, 1977), pp. 470–472 (An idiosyncratically organized volume of short essays); "Desmond Bagley" and "Michael Kenyon," in Klein *et al.,* eds, *St James Guide to Crime and Mystery Writers* (4th ed., 1996), pp. 36–37, 597–598; "Holmes: The Hamlet of Crime Fiction," in H. R. F. Keating, ed., *Crime Writers* (London: British Broadcasting Corporation, 1978), pp. 20–41 (Accompanies a BBC TV series of the same name); "A Pre-History: Crime Fiction Before the 19th Century," in H. R. F. Keating, ed., *Whodunit? A Guide to Crime Fiction* (London and New York, 1982), pp. 20–25 (Hill is also credited as one of three collaborators with Keating in producing the major reference section, "Writers and their Books: A Consumer's Guide," pp. 109–248); "A Little Talent, Lots of Practice," in *The Writer* (Boston), November 1985; "Looking for a Programme," in Robin Winks, ed., *Colloquium on Crime* (New York, 1986), pp. 149–166; "Serial Rites," in *The Writer* (Boston), December 1988; "The Plot's The Thing!" in *The Writer* (Boston), November 1995, pp. 11–14; "Foreword," in Michael Kenyon, *The Whole Hog* (1967; London, 1996), pp. 1–2;

"Introduction," in Hillary Waugh, *Last Seen Wearing . . .* (1952; London, 1999), pp. vii–x; "The uneventful life and quiet times of Reginald Hill," in *Reginald Hill: Your FREE guide to the works of Britain's finest crime writer* (London: , 2000), pp. 5–7; (A small pamphlet to celebrate 30 years of Dalziel & Pascoe, with a cut version at "Message from the Author," is at http://www.randomhouse.com/features/reghill); "Lord Byron (1788–1824)": http://www.twbooks.co.uk/cwa/hillonbyron.html.

VIII. INTERVIEWS Rosemary Herbert. "Reginald Hill," in *The Fatal Art of Entertainment: Interviews with Mystery Writers* (New York and Toronto, 1994). Pp. 194–223; "Reg Hill in conversation with John Seeley," *A Shot in the Dark* 7 (Spring 1996): 38–43; Adrian Muller. "Interview: Reg Hill," *Crime Time* 2.3 (1998): 32–43); Phil Penfold. "Solitary origins of Dynamic Duo," in *The Stage,* 14/10/1999, p. 20; "Why Hale and Pace were no laugh playing my detectives: The Truth about the origins of Dalziel and Pascoe," *Mail on Sunday* (London), 30 July 2000 (Though presented as an article by Hill, a piece written up by a *Mail* journalist from an interview with Hill); Natasha Cooper. "Inside the mind of a crime writer," in *The Times* (London), 30/9/2000; Huw Richards. "College Dropout Loves Life of Crime," in *The Times Educational Supplement* 4447 (21/9/2001). P. 36. (There are entries on Hill in Murphy's *Encyclopedia,* and in the *Oxford Companion, St James Guide,* and *Mammoth Encyclopedia,* all listed as "Useful Reference Works" below.)

IX. CRITICAL STUDIES. Auden, W. H., "The Guilty Vicarage" (1948), in *The Dyer's Hand and other essays* (1963; London, 1975), pp. 146–158; Binyon, T. J., *'Murder Will Out:' The Detective in Fiction* (New York, 1989); Chernaik, Warren, Swales, Martin, and Vilain, Robert, eds, *The Art of Detective Fiction* (London and New York, 2000); Freeling, Nicholas, "Dorothy L. Sayers" (1992), in *Criminal Convictions: Errant Essays on Perpetrators of Literary License* (London, 1994); Friedland, Martin L., ed., *Rough Justice: Essays on Crime in Literature* (Toronto, 1991); Hanks, Robert, "Unlikely Partners in Crime," in *The Independent* (London), 15/3/96, Television p. 7l; Lennard, John, "The Redeemed Vicarage," *London Review of Books* 16.9 (12 May 1994): 30–31; "The Gold in Them Thar Hills," *Threepenny Review* 67 (Fall 1996): 20–21; Symons, Julian, *Bloody Murder: From the Detective Story to the Crime Novel: A History* (London, 1972; as *Mortal Consequences,* New York, 1972; with revisions, Harmondsworth, U.K., 1974; 4th ed., London, 1994) (A hugely influential and pioneering history, in many ways invaluable, but often tendentious and felt to embody a misguided approach).

X. USEFUL REFERENCE WORKS. Mike Ashley, ed., *The Mammoth Encyclopedia of Modern Crime Fiction* (London, 2002) (Restricted to work after 1950, but very full within that limit;, with a substantial section dealing with films and TV, and useful appendices, including the most comprehensive listing of award-winners available); Robert Chesshyre. *The Force: Inside the Police* (London, 1989; London, 1990); Julian Earwaker and Kathleen Becker. *Scene of the Crime: A Guide to the Landscapes of British Detective Fiction* (London, 2002); Rosemary Herbert, ed., *The Oxford Companion to Crime and Mystery Writing* (Oxford and New York, 1999); Kathleen Gregory Klein, Jay P. Pederson, and Taryn Benbow-Pfalzgraf, eds. *St. James Guide to Crime & Mystery Writers* (Farmington Hills, Mich., 1996)

(A detailed and comprehensive guide, with full bibliographies and in many cases brief comments by the subject as well as a short critical essay); Bruce F. Murphy, *The* *Encyclopedia of Murder and Mystery* (New York, 1999); Ian Ousby. *The Crime and Mystery Book: A Reader's Companion* (London, 1997).

PATRICK MCCABE

(1955–)

James P. Austin

ONE OF IRELAND'S newest and brightest literary voices, the writer Patrick McCabe is best known outside Ireland for the novel that made him famous, 1992's *The Butcher Boy.* That novel encapsulates many of the themes, settings, and auxiliary elements that characterize McCabe's writings as a whole and help us to understand what he means when he draws characters that are, among other things, thirteen-year old murderers, schizophrenic mama's boys, transvestite prostitutes, and alcoholic headmasters. The effect is darkly comedic, often campy, and whimsical at points. But in McCabe's works these skewed characters are not simply entertaining; they are also the expression of the author's considerable and singular vision of his homeland. For in Patrick McCabe's Ireland, these characters, their hopes and desires consistently dashed, are emblematic of what can be termed an inherent and inescapable "Irishness." This term, never used by McCabe or his characters, nevertheless encapsulates the characters' constant preoccupation with getting "outside" what they perceive as their own inferior identities, an inferiority always linked to being Irish. Most often this means leaving Ireland behind for England, as happens in *Carn* (1989) and *Mondo Desperado* (1999). Or, McCabe's characters become attached to American popular culture icons or retreat into their own fantasies of betterment, as in *The Butcher Boy* and *Breakfast on Pluto* (1998). However, something always brings them back to themselves, their attempts at reinvention stall or explode in their faces, a disappointment McCabe renders with both darkness and humor. And each character deals differently with his or her newfound preoccupation with Irish identities. In McCabe's work being Irish and being proud of it do not go together: The men and women in the pages of his novels want to slough off their rural Irish roots like a husk, to step into something more glamorous, more promising, and less Irish, as being Irish is "associated irremediably with the local, the secondary, the menial" (Herron, p. 173). It is this desire, and the inevitable inability to consummate this desire, that drives the characters, tells their stories, and informs us just what it means to be born into the Ireland of Patrick McCabe. The characters in McCabe's work do not typically understand the origin of their anxieties, much less can they articulate them, but the consistency of anxiety and insecurity throughout McCabe's work, and how he links these emotions to his characters perceptions of themselves as inferior, is the theme linking his work.

BIOGRAPHY

Patrick McCabe was born in 1955 in Clones, Ireland, in County Monaghan, near the Northern Ireland border, the second of five children. For much of McCabe's childhood he was obsessed with those elements of the non-Irish that would later appear, with much greater exaggeration, in his fiction. His interests then included American comic books and Hollywood movies.

Unlike some of his more unfortunate characters, McCabe made the transition to a successful vocation when he was trained as a teacher in Dublin. In 1985, McCabe, his wife, and their two children moved to London so that McCabe could take a teaching job there. He began to write in his spare time, and in 1986 he published his first novel, the obscure *Music on Clinton Street,* titled after a Leonard Cohen song. His second novel, *Carn,* was published in 1989 and earned modest praise if not mainstream readership and success.

PATRICK MCCABE

It was not until the 1992 publication of *The Butcher Boy,* McCabe's masterwork, that his status as a new and urgent voice in Irish letters was recognized, a fair amount of fame was earned, and the freedom to write full-time was secured. He and his family returned to Ireland in the late 1990s and as of 2003 resided in Sligo.

EARLY WORK: CARN

One of the least well-known of Patrick McCabe's novels, *Carn* (1989) was printed in America only after the considerable success of *The Butcher Boy.* The novel primarily follows the fortunes of two residents of Carn, an Irish city on the border with Northern Ireland: Josie Keenan, who leaves Carn and Ireland in search of dreams that never materialize; and Sadie Rooney, who dreams of life outside her rural town but who never actually gives herself the opportunity to experience such a life. McCabe also treats the downtrodden city of Carn itself as a character, as we watch it disappear along with the railway industry that had marked the city's boom era, only to be briefly revitalized when an ambitious businessman Americanizes certain aspects of the city and opens a meat-processing plant. By telling the stories of Josie and Sadie, McCabe offers two possibilities of life for the Irish in the 1960s. Both Josie and Sadie aspire to be something "more" than they are—that is, something other than the spawn of Ireland. Josie does indeed leave Ireland behind but finds life in England harsher than she could have imagined, and the adventure and opportunity that England seems to promise continually eludes her. Sadie stays in Carn, despite her constant daydreams of American icons like Elvis Presley and Steve McQueen, and finds herself trapped in the struggle between Ireland and Northern Ireland with a husband who collaborates with the North. By weaving these two stories together with the brief rise and eventual fall of Carn, McCabe offers a dim view of the possibilities for the Irish during this time. Like so much of McCabe's subsequent work, the novel tells a story of Irish "shame," using the characters and setting to help the reader understand Irish identity.

The novel opens with the closing of the railway in Carn, an event that plunges the city into economic ruin: the storefronts are empty and dilapidated, the unemployment figures high. The city's primary claim to fame is the shooting death of Matt Dolan years before at the hands of the Irish Republican Army (IRA). Carn clings tightly to this man, revering him, and producing another anti-IRA patriot in his son Benny Dolan, who eventually marries Sadie and whose murder of a prominent politician dramatically secures Sadie's place as inescapably Irish.

The closing of the railway in Carn is a challenge met by James Cooney, who sets about revitalizing the city by opening the meat-processing plant and pumping money into businesses such as the Turnpike Inn, a local pub. But the resurgence is, almost from the beginning, an ephemeral one: the Turnpike Inn is decked out in all things American, an imitation that fuels the city but cannot last in a place so ardently Irish. Carn's desire to establish within itself something vastly different from itself, and the inherent instability of such a wish, is reflected also in Josie and Sadie, whose stories intertwine and eventually dovetail as the novel progresses.

Josie's mother dies young, and her father, delirious with grief, dies not long after, leaving Josie at the mercy of a local orphanage. The misery of her life at the orphanage fosters in her the desire to flee, to dress herself up in a new identity, to cross over to England where things, she thinks, are always better than they are in Ireland. When she does eventually arrive in Liverpool, Josie finds work as a waitress and a prostitute—hardly the version of English prosperity she had envisioned but a life that nonetheless helps her recognize the one true power she feels she possesses—power over men who will pay her for sex.

Sadie also dreams of a non-Irish life, preoccupied with the romance and glamour of American popular culture. One of her initial romantic experiences, with an English boy named Dave Robinson, turns out badly when the boy is seen around town with another girl. Through this humiliation she "learns her place" as an Irish girl: she is unfit for an English boy, just as she had been told by friends and elders who warned her that the romance would come to no good. This rejection causes Sadie to embrace her "shameful" identity and to concern herself with things related to Carn and Ireland. As a result she marries Benny Dolan, the son of the town's dead hero, embodiment of the very Irishness Sadie had grown up wanting to escape.

Sadie's and Josie's stories intertwine when Josie, broke and without prospects in England, is forced to return to Carn. To help soothe her sense of failure, Josie plies her trade of prostitution with Pat Lacey, one of Carn's esteemed politicians. In so doing, Josie not only exacts a measure of vengeance against the town, as personified by Lacey, but a measure of control as well through Lacey's ashamed yet passionate visits.

She meets Sadie at a wedding reception and the two strike up a friendship. By this time Sadie has fully implicated herself in the life of the city she had wanted so desperately to leave, raising the children she and Benny have had as he becomes embroiled in tensions between Ireland and Northern Ireland. He is employed by the "Northmen" to help smoke out a man suspected of holding weapons for the IRA. Benny is the lookout while the northmen search the house for IRA weapons, and he spies Pat Lacey as he races toward the house to seek help for Josie, who he had left at his nearby house in a suicidal fit. Benny sees him approaching but cannot identify him and he panics, shooting Lacey dead. His legacy as a failure is sealed: "[The northman] turned to Benny and spat, 'You bastard—you stupid bastard! Now you've done it good and proper!'" (p. 215). The northmen attempt to cover their tracks by setting the house on fire, which Josie notices and begins running toward. While it is never explicitly stated by McCabe that Josie runs into the fire in a naïve attempt to save Lacey, he does note that Lacey has a large funeral while Josie is buried "in an unopened coffin" (p. 224). Thus Benny, whose father was a hero, turns out to be a poor replica. Instead of dying a hero's death, Benny is sent to prison in shame, the murderer of a politician. The Dolan name, once a source of pride for a community starved for it, is

soiled by Benny's bungled attempt to perpetuate the family honor. As a result, Sadie becomes an outcast from the only community she has ever known, one she had hoped to leave behind all along.

The ending of the story sounds a theme common to McCabe's other major works. The Ireland of the 1960s is a place where nothing can possibly go right, where an attempt to escape one's Irishness leads to dire consequences (in this case, death); where the desire for escape turns into forced alienation from the very community you had wanted independence from in the first place; and where imitative attempts at heroic acts can only fail and ruin the once proud family name. The novel's concluding events coincide with James Cooney's decision to close the meatpacking plant, thus ending Carn's brief resurrection. And so the city of Carn and its residents all suffer a similar fate. Behind Carn's ephemeral boom is the reality that, in McCabe's version of rural Ireland in the 1960s, there is little hope for change—either for the characters or for Carn itself.

THE BUTCHER BOY

In 1992 McCabe published his most famous and widely acclaimed novel, *The Butcher Boy,* which was nominated for the Booker Prize the following year and adapted into a movie of the same name directed by Neil Jordan in 1997. Many readers and critics consider *The Butcher Boy* McCabe's major opus, as it effectively encapsulates the primary and recurring themes in his fiction. *The Butcher Boy* explores—in inimitable fashion—Irish identity, particularly in contrast to the more powerful forces of Western popular culture and middle-class British society. In *The Butcher Boy* these forces are observed by Francie Brady, son of an alcoholic father and suicidal mother and resident of a small, depressed (both economically and spiritually) village in rural Ireland. The village represents the downtrodden aspect of Irish society: the country's politicians have at various points tried to "renovate" its denizens into more upstanding citizens, and it is the kind of place that more economically developed segments of Western society have traditionally treated with contempt. When Francie is ultimately unable to alter the fixed signification of his identity and "takes his place in the world" as the murderous Butcher Boy, he also discovers that his place "was always already ordained by history and family circumstances" (Herron, p. 173). It is this sense of powerlessness in the face of the immovable force of extrinsic influence that confirms for Francie his essential "Irishness," an identity he embraces with homicidal aplomb.

The story comprises Francie's first-person account of the events of "twenty or thirty or forty years ago [when] I lived in a small town where they were all after me on account of what I done on Mrs. Nugent" (p. 1). "Mrs. Nugent," it turns out, is the mother of the young newcomer Philip Nugent and the wife of the ardently middle-class Mr. Nugent. The Nugents represent to Francie that which he both desires and hates. At the beginning of the novel the Nugents move to Francie's town, fresh from a successful stay in England. They carry with them all the markers of a stability Francie can only dream about. They own a nice home and the latest appliances. Philip has attended a British prep school, Mr. Nugent does not drink alcohol, and Mrs. Nugent carries herself with a faux-aristocratic dignity largely unknown to Francie. Part of her behavior includes regular humiliation of Francie, who makes several early attempts to befriend her and her son but is rebuffed each time.

Francie is acutely aware of the Nugents' status—he notices Philip's new belongings, for example—but his fascination with them quickly sours when Mrs. Nugent refers to Francie and his family as pigs—a derogatory term often directed toward the Irish by the British. At this point the contradictory nature of Francie's interest in the Nugents becomes more explicit. He revels in his role as "pig," first by standing guard at certain spots around town to demand from Philip and Mrs. Nugent a "Pig Toll Tax" for access to the village.

At the same time, Francie still wants to feel connected to the world outside the village, a connection that is represented by Uncle Alo, a successful family member returning home for the holidays. "Successful" to Francie and his family is defined as having acquired non-Irish traits. Uncle Alo has left Ireland behind entirely by relocating to London. He has even acquired a British accent, which Francie quite admires. Francie boasts to his friend Joe that his Uncle Alo has "ten men [working] under him" (p. 21).

Alo's visit causes quite a stir—Francie cannot sleep due to the anticipation, and Francie's mother spends days baking cake after cake in over-preparation for his arrival. Francie fantasizes about treating the Nugents as snobbishly as they have treated him, assuming that Mrs. Nugent will be intrigued by encountering one of her own "kind" walking through the village with Francie. Once he has her attention, he dreams, he can go about the business of the middle class—namely, alternately humiliating and ignoring the lower classes. But Uncle Alo's visit does not go as Francie hoped. At a family gathering, Francie sees that Alo's prosperity is indicated by the "gold tiepin and polished nails, the English voice" (pp. 26–27). Thus class is defined through belongings and through the voice of the non-Irish, which conspire to create a certain effect that the Irish family members—excepting Francie's father—can only admire from a distance. To Francie, that air of the middle class and his proximity to it is almost enough to make him happy, albeit ephemerally. But Francie's father is threatened by the presence of Alo. The result is that Francie's mother and father argue at length in front of the entire family, including Alo, effectively ruining the evening. The night ends when Francie's father drinks himself to sleep and passes out in his armchair.

This scene is significant in that it confirms for Francie the inescapable truth of his circumstances and reminds him that his life more closely resembles his father's than that of Uncle Alo. His first response in light of this is to attempt an escape. The morning after the disastrous gathering with Uncle Alo, Francie runs away from home, heading directly for Dublin. In so doing, he initiates a sequence of events that will entirely break apart his already tenuously structured family and result ultimately in the acceptance of his role as an Irish boy, as a "pig," and his transformation into the crude, insane, and murderous Butcher Boy.

Francie's stay in Dublin is brief, but when he returns, his marginal family structure has begun its dramatic and sudden collapse. Carried over the edge by Francie's disappearance, his mother drowns herself in a lake, but Francie does not know this until he arrives home to face his father:

> I don't know how long da was standing there staring at me. There were red circles round his eyes and I could smell him. *You,* was all he said. I didn't know what he meant. . . .
>
> O you didn't hear? He says with a bitter smile. Then he told me they had dredged the lake near the garage and found her at the bottom of it, and says I'm off to the Tower I might be back and I might not.
>
> (p. 43)

Francie's response to the news is to spy on the Nugents, peeking in their windows and climbing the gutter to have a glimpse of the life that seems more impossible than ever to attain: "They had a butter dish with a special knife, all these things they had. It was as if just by being the Nugents it all came together as if by magic not a thing out of place" (p. 44). Thus with the news of his mother's demise, the considerable gap between himself and the Nugents, those standard-bearers of middle-class virtue, has grown so wide as to be nonnegotiable. Things go right for the Nugents as if "by magic" and end in disaster for Francie; more than ever, Francie feels it is some intangible quality beyond his control that has created people like the Nugents and like himself. Despite his resistance, Francie is finding himself increasingly "fixed" as a poor Irish boy, and his mother's death begins the process of his acceptance of this role: "As long as I walked the streets under them stars there'd be only one thing anyone could say about me and that was: I hope he's proud of himself now, the pig, after what he did to his poor mother" (p. 44).

As Francie gradually accepts his place, his projection of blame onto the Nugents becomes more protracted and his hatred of their status more dangerous. He pays the Nugents a visit that ends with Francie on the floor of their kitchen,

on his hands and knees, squealing like a pig. The encounter ends, however, when Philip gives him a look "more sad than frightened" (p. 55), indicating to Francie that his attempt to frighten them by imitating the "pig" to which Mrs. Nugent compared him has instead turned out pitifully: "I think it was him looking at me with them sad eyes that made me get up and say that was a good laugh but I think it's about time I was back at the farmyard" (p. 56).

At the same time, he still deeply desires access to the Nugents' lifestyle and, against the advice of his only remaining friend, Joe, Francie invades the Nugent home again only days later, when the family has left town. As the contrast between his life and the Nugents' becomes more defined, Francie's attempts to both imitate and reject the Nugents' lifestyle grow more starkly disturbing. Alone in the Nugents' home, Francie fantasizes a reversal of the roles he and Philip play, assuming a position as Mrs. Nugent's new son:

> Then I heard Philip Nugent's voice. . . . You know what he's doing here don't you mother? He wants to be one of us. He wants his name to be Francis Nugent. . . .
>
> Mrs. Nugent was standing over me. Yes, Philip, she said. I know that. I've known it for a long time.
>
> Then slowly she unbuttoned her blouse and took out her breast.
>
> Then she said: This is for you Francis.
>
> (p. 60)

But Francie's dream of suckling the maternal breast of Mrs. Nugent is accompanied by a nightmarish vision of his own mother. For, despite his deep desire to join the Nugent family and thus enter the middle class and leave his own broken conditions behind him, he cannot in good conscience leave behind that which he knows is rightfully his own: his family, his heritage, and his culture—in other words, his "shameful" Irishness.

Realizing this, Francie rejects the breast and reverts to his now-familiar role as pig, attempting to gain satisfaction by inscribing onto the Nugents *his* role rather than the other way around.

He writes "PHILIP IS A PIG" on the wall with Mrs. Nugent's lipstick and imagines teaching the Nugents in his "pig school" how to behave like real pigs, complete with Mrs. Nugent on all fours, squealing. Francie completes his vengeful act by defecating on the floor of the Nugents' home, because "pigs are poo animals and they simply will cover the place in it no matter what you do" (p. 61). In so doing, Francie not only leaves a tangible remnant of his presence, but his soiling of the middle-class home with lower-class excrement confirms the very role that Mrs. Nugent has assigned to him: as a filthy, slovenly pig, an Irish boy. Thus Francie irrevocably distances himself from his deep wish to join the Nugent family and also rejects his desire for a stable mother figure.

The Nugents return home while Francie is still inside; horrified, Mr. Nugent phones the police, who escort Francie to a reform school. He watches from the car as the Nugents reenter their home: "Mrs. Nugent was still crying when I left but Mr. Nooge put his arm around her and led her inside. When the silent films are over sometimes this hand comes out of nowhere and hangs up a sign with THE END on it. That's what it was like" (p. 64). While Francie is hardly finished with the Nugents, the scene does place an exclamation point on the disastrous events of the day and effectively ends any illusions Francie had for being any kind of boy other than the one he is.

Francie is hauled off to a reform school renowned for taking in bad boys and returning them to society somehow better off. But for Francie, who is by now well on the road to becoming the insane adult narrating these events to the reader, even this attempt at reform goes awry. Indeed, as the police drive him to the reform school, one of them reminds him that he is beyond reform: "By Christ if you were mine I'd break every bone in your body, he said. Then he wiped his mouth and muttered: Not that you could be any different" (p. 64).

During his six months in the reform school, Francie begins to experience anxiety about his friend Joe developing a friendship with the Nugents—an anxiety that is brought fully to bear when he receives a letter from Joe saying that

"Philip is OK Francie. . . . He really is OK. He doesn't want any trouble with anyone" (p. 71). Francie's isolation increases, as does his hatred of the Nugents. His experience at the reformatory is also marred by the advances of an amorous administrator, whom Francie dubs "Tiddly" and who makes proclamations of matrimonial love. As with his experiences in the outside world, Francie both welcomes and is disgusted by this pedophilic experience and further confirms that the only sort of love he deserves revolves around those things that make him Irish: "He'd give me as many Rolos as I wanted if I told him the worst bad thing I ever did. I told him things about the town but he kept saying no no worse than that and I could feel his hand trembling under me. No matter what I told him it still wasn't bad enough" (p. 82). Thus Francie's bad acts—his acts of stereotypical "pig" Irishness—are appealing to the man but also insufficient.

With this in mind, Francie ends his stay at the reform school and returns home to find that things have dramatically changed for the worse. His first discovery is of his father, dead in his armchair, having drunk himself to death. Desperate to go back to the way things were before the Nugents moved to town—matters are now so dire that even the depressing landscape of his bygone familial situation seems appealing—Francie does not notify anyone and keeps his father's rotting corpse where he found it; he speaks to his "da" as if he were still alive.

Another change involves his friend Joe, who avoids Francie and is clearly nervous when Francie does eventually corner him. Eventually Francie learns that Joe and Philip Nugent have become friends, as have their parents, and that Joe will soon be attending the very same prestigious preparatory school as Philip. So Francie, having suffered the loss of his parents, now has to bear the loss of his best friend to the Nugents and what they represent.

Francie's response is to surround himself with all that he thinks of as shamefully Irish. He takes a job at the local butchery, where it is his job to butcher baby pigs—thus becoming the embodiment of the Butcher Boy, the murderer of Irish "pigs." Francie's complete failure to assume a new identity leaves him only the option to symbolically murder that which he has failed to shed. It is an expression of self-hatred that gradually consumes both Francie and the Nugents.

But he is not content only to wallow in this state; Francie's mind is constantly churning with thoughts of the loss of his friend, even as he reinforces the distance between himself and the Nugents by slaughtering baby pigs. The slaughtering of the pigs helps Francie realize the extent of his self-hatred, a hatred he quickly projects onto the Nugents, who are the distant embodiment of everything Francie wishes he could be but has learned he will never become. Finally Francie is left with only one option that seems viable to him, and that is to murder Mrs. Nugent, a task which he gruesomely completes. In Francie's mind this act completes and resolves the events of the story. A moment before the murder, Francie explains to Mrs. Nugent just why he feels compelled to do it: "You did two bad things Mrs. Nugent. You made me turn my back on my ma and you took Joe away from me." Afterward, "I opened her up and stuck my hand in her stomach and wrote PIGS all over the walls of the upstairs room" (p. 195). He hides her body in a cart he uses for work and hauls her through the village, stopping along the way to buy cigarettes. Then he returns home and sets the house afire in a botched suicide attempt.

The novel ends with Francie arriving at the mental hospital from which he has narrated the events of the novel as a middle-age man. The police who escort Francie to the hospital show him all the newspapers that covered his story, and all the headlines make reference to Francie Brady as pig: "*Brutal pig killing . . . Francis Brady is a pig*" (p. 212). And so it happens that the only place for a true "pig" in *The Butcher Boy* is a place separated from the rest of the world, where he can be observed and studied and no longer be a danger. The "pig" Francie Brady is a boy who orients himself according to the only identification he is allowed, and the anger resulting from this revelation of Irish shame is an anger best kept under lock and key.

THE DEAD SCHOOL

McCabe's follow-up to *The Butcher Boy* was 1995's *The Dead School,* a novel that ranges from the mid-1910s to 1979. Underscoring two separate historical and political periods of Ireland, it follows two separate story lines that become one late in the novel.

The novel opens with the boyhood of Raphael Bell, who leads a happy enough life in rural Ireland until his father is brutally murdered by Black and Tans (English recruits into the Irish constabulary) while tending his farm. This horrific event is witnessed by young Raphael, and the Black and Tans advise him to keep it in mind if he ever considers becoming a patriot for Irish independence as his father had been. But Raphael's response to his father's murder is to cling more tightly to his father's values and to his pride in Ireland. This becomes the impetus for Raphael's life of high achievement, which is built around certain supposedly infallible beliefs in the quality of Irish heritage.

At the same time, McCabe narrates the events of Malachy Dudgeon's childhood, which takes place a generation later than Raphael Bell's. Malachy too grows up in rural Ireland. But unlike Raphael, who leads what is primarily a happy, pastoral existence—and whose father, even in death, was a man to be admired—Malachy leads a life that is anything but rosy. His father, Packie, is the town drunk, a man worth deploring, and his mother is carrying on with a family acquaintance, Jemmy Brady—an infidelity Malachy discovers but does not share with his father, who shortly thereafter drowns himself in a nearby lake. Malachy's response to his father's death, which is not at all the hero's death of Raphael's father a generation earlier, is to virtually ignore his mother, a choice that will haunt him at the end of the novel when his mother suffers from a debilitating mental disorder as an elderly woman.

Eventually, but at different times, Raphael and Malachy arrive at St. Patrick's Training College to become teachers. Raphael begins his attendance in 1930, after a successful career as a prep student at St. Martin's College, where he was reminded by his Uncle Joe just how much of the family pride—and, in a way, the pride of

Ireland—Raphael carries with him to St. Patrick's. Indeed, for Raphael there is a direct correlation between honoring his father's memory and upholding strict traditions, both nationally and at his university. His entire life is built upon these principles, and they serve him well for a time. Eventually Raphael graduates from St. Patrick's and becomes the headmaster at St. Anthony's, a staid preparatory school where it seems at first Raphael will live out his days, happily protecting and perpetuating his love of things Irish.

Years later, when Malachy enters the school, matters have changed. The place is no longer staid, and Raphael "would have had a heart attack if he had seen what was going on; the place was swarming with women and all you could hear was rock music blaring out of the canteen" (p. 61). The school that Raphael had found so hallowed and steeped in tradition a generation earlier had become a shadow of itself—an objective correlative for Ireland as a whole, according to Raphael. Malachy embodies this diminishment, which will later become more pronounced when he takes a job teaching at the school where Raphael is the headmaster. Malachy's path to the university, and to the preparatory school Raphael runs, is far less focused than Raphael's similar path. Malachy arrives at these places arbitrarily, it seems, without Raphael's nationalism and tragic patriotism to guide his way. As a result, Malachy's experience at the university is also less focused on Ireland itself than Raphael's had been. He spends much of his time watching American movies and admiring American film stars like Jack Nicholson and Dustin Hoffman.

The eventual meeting of Raphael and Malachy—and the fallout of that meeting—is made more significant by the stillborn death of Raphael's son, Maolseachlainn. Malachy's name, it turns out, is a shortened and distinctly less "Irish" version of Raphael's son's name. When the two meet, and Raphael hires Malachy to teach at St. Anthony's, the older man is reminded of his dead son even as his pride and nationalism are offended by Malachy's chopped-up, inferior name.

These sensibilities are further offended, and ultimately corrupted, as the culture Raphael has so closely guarded begins to change before his very eyes. His favorite television show, *The Walton Programme,* which discusses the nationalistic pride upon which he has built his identity, quickly becomes less popular than the salacious *Terry Krash Show.* His school's yearly visit to Kilmainham Jail, a landmark of the Irish struggle for independence, is replaced as an annual destination by Waterworld, a theme park.

Malachy's incompetence as a teacher only exacerbates the threat Raphael feels to his sense of national identity and thus to his own father. What was important a generation ago is being swept away by trashy television programs or water parks, and in Raphael's eyes this generational inferiority is embodied by Malachy. As a result, Raphael's sense of identity begins a dramatic drift. By the end of the novel his school has been closed, and Raphael, now a broken, alcoholic ex-headmaster, goes inside the empty building and hangs himself from a ceiling fan.

Malachy, meanwhile, who has only a brief stint as a teacher, eventually seeks to shed his rural Irishness—the very thing of which Raphael was so proud—by disappearing into the urban underground of Dublin, in the process losing his fiancée and becoming a drug addict. He is "rescued" from this urban fate, to which he does not rightly belong, when he is given news of his mother's severe illness. He returns home only to find his mother mentally dysfunctional and on the verge of death. He remains at home to care for the mother he had shunned in his youth, thus claiming for himself a more direct share of his own father's identity within the family. This return to the family, carried out only after his forays into teaching and urban underworlds have revealed Malachy to be unsuitable for anything *but* a return to the family, confirms "the pathetic limitations of his attempt to escape his cultural conditioning and positioning" (Herron, p. 183). Here, then, is another variation on McCabe's recurring theme: a rural boy like Malachy belongs only where he came from because there is indeed something unchangeable about his Irishness and no amount of city living or teacher training will wash it away. *The Dead School* communicates the hopeless scenario of being born Irish with a combination of dark humor and a current of determinism. The story arrives by illustrating the manner by which Malachy causes the downfall of Raphael and his values. The new—the inferior—eclipses and destroys Raphael's pastoral take on Ireland, leaving both their lives in shambles and destroying the novel's most redemptive image: St. Patrick's Training College.

BREAKFAST ON PLUTO

Breakfast on Pluto (1998) is titled after a 1969 chart hit by Don Partridge, and this fact is mentioned before the novel itself actually begins. This provides some indication of the wild ride ahead: The story of "Pussy" Braden is as bizarre and unlikely as an actual breakfast on Pluto, and foreshadows Pussy's preoccupation with American popular culture. In it, McCabe introduces us to yet another of his cunningly original small-town Irish characters, Patrick "Pussy" Braden, in a narrative that takes the form of writings by Braden to his therapist Terence. As with other McCabe characters, Patrick Braden's small-town Irish heritage contributes to his desire to leave Ireland behind for the bright lights of the big city: in his case London and Belfast, where he becomes associated with the IRA during a heightened period of terrorist activity in the 1970s and very nearly winds up dead more than once.

The novel's structure-within-a-structure and some relevant facts about Braden himself are revealed in two brief prologue chapters. We learn that Braden was "a high-class escort girl" (p. 1), a line that hints at his later misadventures as a transvestite in both Ireland and London, and we discover that the meat of the story is actually a first-person account written by Braden himself, at the urging of his therapist Terence, entitled "The Life and Times of Patrick Braden." This embedded structure appears in McCabe's work again in *Emerald Germs of Ireland* (2001).

Like *The Butcher Boy*'s Francie Brady, Patrick Braden comes from a severely fractured family.

Born in the small town of Tryeelin, he is the bastard son of the town's priest, who refuses to acknowledge the boy. His mother leaves him at the front steps of the local church when he is an infant and then vanishes. Braden blames his father for forcing his mother to run away in order to keep the relationship between the supposedly chaste priest and his son a secret. Like Francie Brady, Braden wishes for a "normal" family, but when he finally recognizes that this is not possible, he begins seeking familial love and acceptance in unlikely places. Having dressed with increasing femininity and longed for "a vagina all [his] own" (p. 36) as he grew up, by his teenage years Braden is having relationships with a number of older men, in part seeking the father he never had. The first of these men is a local politician named Eamon Faircroft, who "Pussy" Braden carries on with in secret until the married man dies, leaving Braden feeling alone and unloved by another father figure. It is this death that spurs his departure for London, where he takes his place among the transvestite prostitutes in Piccadilly Circus.

Braden's purpose in becoming a prostitute is twofold. First of all, it puts him in contact with men, typically older men, who are breathlessly attracted to him—as with Eamon Faircroft, these men provide the attention his own father never provided. This dynamic is disrupted when one of his customers attempts to choke him to death, causing Braden to shut down his "escort service" because it no longer provides him with paternal love. His other purpose is that prostitution provides him ample street time to search for his absentee mother, and he often mistakes strangers for her: "How many times did that one happen?" he asks himself, "Why, hundreds, dearest, hundreds!" (p. 5).

Eventually Braden returns to Tryeelin to be with friends, to feel safe, and to confront his father, which he does while the priest is busy with confession. When his father, horrified at the sight of this transvestite in his church, requests that he leave, Braden's confrontation becomes an injured litany of insults, and he pledges "never will I forgive you! Never never never!" (p. 177).

Surprisingly, however, *Breakfast on Pluto* ends on a hopeful note, which separates it in this regard from McCabe's other, sometimes nihilistic, work. Arriving one day for his usual appointment with Terence, Braden is informed that the doctor has gone away and will not return. For him this is truly the last straw: "I bawled my eyes out and was in such a state . . . I was on the verge of burning everything I'd written for him and everything to do with him" (p. 197). But unlike Francie Brady, Braden does not suffer a psychotic break after this last, bitter disappointment. Braden, for all his problems, is a character of stronger mettle than Francie. This earnest desire for a family is not eclipsed by his bitterness at not finding one. The novel ends years after the events of the 1970s, which comprise much of the novel's bulk, after Braden has permanently shelved his prostitution career and seems to have arrived at a peaceful, if not entirely happy, state of being. He never found his mother, but he seems resigned to it. Nevertheless, Braden still dreams of someday feeling the sense of wholeness he associates with being an accepted part of a family—though perhaps not *his* family. This fantasy of an unattainable wholeness—and of having something you can see all around you but never have yourself—has echoes of Francie Brady, but Braden represents a finer, more textured version of a familiar McCabe character.

MONDO DESPERADO

Following on the heels of *Breakfast on Pluto,* McCabe's short-story collection *Mondo Desperado* (1999) distinguishes itself by being, in the words of one reviewer, even "stranger and campier." In an "editor's note" by Simon Mitchell that prefaces the stories, we are informed that they are all written by one "Phildy Hackball," whose works "permit us a glimpse . . . into a world which is truly desperate" (p. x). Of course, both editor Mitchell and author Hackball are McCabe's own inventions. McCabe utilizes this method to further imbed the stories within the strange town of Barntrosna. This desperation seems embodied in the small Irish town of Barntrosna, where most of the characters in the stories come from. Barntrosna's residents are typically enticed by the promise of something famous or respectable or by the possibility of escape to the big city, namely London. In the comedic "My Friend Bruce Lee," for instance, the narrator claims that the famous martial arts expert is a friend of his and even that he is an occasional visitor to the small Irish town. The reader rightly suspects this is a complete fabrication: throughout the story, while the narrator recounts events and speaks to Bruce Lee, the movie star himself never seems to respond—his speech is never dramatized. The end result is both silly and heart-rending, as the narrator is revealed to be desperate to make his insignificant corner of Ireland somehow more than it is.

Desperation takes on a different form in "I Ordained the Devil," in which the bishop of Barntrosna tells us about the time he unwittingly ordained into the ministry Packie Cooley—who is, the bishop claims, the devil himself. The "desperation" in the story can be read two ways. First, the fact that the town's bishop—himself supposedly a representative of goodness and stability—can presume that the devil has infiltrated not only the temporal earth but this village in particular also presumes a fated posture for the town—that, of all places, the devil would be in his element in a rural Irish village. A second reading suggests that it is the bishop's *assumption* that the devil would find Barntrosna a suitable place, more than the factual reality of the devil's presence, that illustrates the contagious outlook that Barntrosna, and by extension all of Ireland, is fated, and not in a good way. Either way, the end result of "I Ordained the Devil" is an aged bishop constantly punishing himself for what may or may not have been the actual ordainment of the devil.

Perhaps the story that says the most about desperation is the long, final story, "The Forbidden Love of Noreen Tiernan." In it, Noreen is characterized as a happy, relatively well-adjusted young woman, a bright spot among the blights of Barntrosna. Since this is McCabe's Ireland, it is not surprising that Noreen desires something more than what she has in Barntrosna and departs for nursing school in London.

It is notable that Noreen is the only main character in *Mondo Desperado* who is permitted to leave the confines of the city, and it is this departure, and what happens when Barntrosna's best and brightest character interacts with the world at large, that allows *Mondo Desperado* to intersect with McCabe's other works. The beautiful and pure Noreen enters nursing school only to be co-opted and defiled by her roommate Stephanie, a husky, heavy-set woman who leads Noreen into a demanding lesbian relationship that very nearly kills her. Ultimately Noreen is forced to return to Barntrosna, and the message is clear: no matter how ambitious or promising or virtuous, people from Barntrosna should never, ever leave.

This last story returns us to a familiar theme in McCabe's work—the use of dark humor and outrageous scenarios to narrate the Irish and their place in the world. This dark humor is evident in the neurotic ramblings of Francie Brady and the sad, flamboyant narrative of Pussy Braden, and is symptomatic of the irreverence of *Mondo Desperado,* a collection that narrates dreams of stardom, disappointment, and failure.

EMERALD GERMS OF IRELAND

Emerald Germs of Ireland (2001) both continues and diverges from themes and storytelling techniques of previous novels and story collections. Like *The Butcher Boy, Carn,* and *The Dead School, Emerald Germs of Ireland* ascribes to the Irish an inherent quality of fractured national, familial and personal identity. As the novel begins, the protagonist, Pat McNab, has already fully arrived at a psychotic and seemingly schizophrenic break. The novel's serial structure—wherein each chapter is a story unto itself, gradually filling in the relevant facts of McNab's upbringing—reflects not only the fractured nature of Pat McNab as a person but also the dead-end, rural Irish identity he so strongly embodies and, not unlike Francie Brady, eventually revels in.

At the same time, the novel's structure also reveals a strong and somewhat predictable symmetry. Early on we discover that McNab has

not only just recently murdered his nagging mother—whom he then misses terribly throughout the rest of the novel—but has apparently murdered scores of others and buried them in his garden. *Emerald Germs of Ireland* then commences with the narration of these "murders," the verisimilitude of which are gradually called into question. The first "victim" is Mrs. Tubridy, the nosy neighbor McNab murders when she will not stop asking when McNab's mother is due to return from America, where he claimed she had gone.

As McCabe attempts to illustrate the fractured nature of both Pat McNab and the country that produced him, he unwittingly guides the reader into a predictable set of expectations. Indeed, each of the novel's fourteen chapters ends with McNab murdering someone, ranging from a woman who reminds him of an old girlfriend to his own father, in a poignant story told as flashback from McNab's childhood.

While this predictable structure ultimately muffles much of the novel's overall dramatic impact, the individual chapters/stories themselves are intriguing, particularly as we begin to suspect that these tales of murder are only a figment of McNab's imagination. We learn in "The Little Drummer Boy," for instance, that McNab murdered his father only after much urging by his toy drummer boy, which spoke to him. As in many of McCabe's novels, the father is a domineering presence, always looming, always threatening the son and challenging his manhood. Pat McNab's father also bullies his wife, and it is this brutality that leads to his murder at the hands of his son.

But the unreliability of the story, as evidenced by the talking drummer boy, complicates the issue, making it impossible to say with finality that these events are anything more than Pat McNab's ardent and most clandestine wishes, a permanent psychosis caused by his father's humiliation of him and brutality toward his mother. It is also possible, however, that McNab's murder of his father in boyhood is the only "actual" murder that takes place, and that the animation of the drummer boy as a speaking character is the young

PATRICK MCCABE

McNab's first foray into the near-schizophrenia within which he resides in the novel.

McNab's crumbling mental state and its bearing on the reliability of these narrated events is linked directly to his father's alcoholic and frustrated behavior, by now a familiar trope in McCabe's work. In the case of Pat McNab, he is so traumatized by his father's brutality and eventual death that he grows into a highly paranoid man, living with his mother (whom he ultimately "murders") in a highly infantile domestic arrangement. His paranoia manifests itself either as murder or as murderous fantasies, in which anyone who transgresses the tightly constructed borders of his personality or condescends to him in any small way is subject to his wrath.

The reliability of McNab's perceptions, and of the narration as a whole, is most directly called into question in the final chapter, "Twenty-one Years." McNab is at Sullivan's, the local pub—nearly the only place McNab visits in the novel outside his home—when he is visited by Sergeant Foley. The interaction between Foley and McNab reveals gaps between what is said in dialogue and what McNab sees for himself. For example, at one point Foley informs McNab that the police station has burned to the ground, but when McNab goes to see for himself, the police station is still there. Foley also hints at several points that he is aware of McNab's murderous tendencies, then claims that he is only kidding. McNab's paranoia results, naturally, in his murder of Sergeant Foley, but the interaction between the characters reveals the space created between McNab's perceptions and reality and calls into question whether his murder victims ever existed at all except as figments of a schizophrenic mind. In this regard, then, Sergeant Foley functions as a figure of conscience and guilt within McNab's deranged mind, and his interactions with McNab reveal the distinct possibility that McNab has imagined the novel in his head.

CONCLUSION

Viewed as a whole, the major works of Patrick McCabe reveal the development and repetition of themes that characterize the odd workings of McCabe's Ireland. For example, Sadie Rooney and Josie Keenan of *Carn,* Raphael Bell of *The Dead School,* the inimitable Francie Brady of *The Butcher Boy,* Pussy Braden of *Breakfast on Pluto,* and Pat McNab of *Emerald Germs of Ireland,* all exist in different towns and quite often at different periods of twentieth-century Ireland. Their eccentricities and mental illnesses are many and varied, and as such it cannot be said that the characters are too similar, their stories too much the same. And yet the evident commonalties reveal an Ireland that has lost something of value: a sense of itself. The stodgy Raphael Bell, for instance, bemoans the lost nationalistic vigor of his youth and is so appalled by what he sees of late-twentieth-century Ireland that he too succumbs to the irresistible force that pervades McCabe's work, that his Ireland has lost something essential about itself, something perhaps unrecoverable.

McCabe's characters thus busy themselves with trying to ride the coattails of people and places more fully formed and worth participating in. Pussy Braden, Josie Keenan, and Noreen Tiernan make haste for the bright lights of London, where they see promising futures as a condition of the place, in the same way that they perceive Ireland as a shameful backwater worth leaving behind. But the manner in which these temporary expatriates interact with London is not at all the same as that of lifelong Londoners, who feel entitled to the opportunities and promises of their city. Indeed, the McCabe character in London is more alienated than he or she was in the Ireland left behind. Once their forays into the world at large prove to be unmitigated failures, these three find refuge back in the safe confines of their home country, the place that is both their fate and their birthright, whether they like it or not.

In other cases, McCabe's characters cannot view Ireland as a ruefully safe haven, perceiving it instead as a claustrophobic, inescapable prison, both physically and mentally. Raphael Bell of *The Dead School* dies for this very reason, so alarmed is he at the shameful state of Irish national identity and the co-opting of that identity by offensive television programs and glib school

PATRICK MCCABE

vacations. Francie Brady, perhaps the most severely disturbed of McCabe's characters, descends gradually into madness and murder because his attempts to connect and interact with the Nugents are clumsy, unsuccessful, and ultimately unbearably humiliating. This humiliation at the hands of the "other"—an other that is richer, more stable, and seems to have in its hands all that Francie Brady ever wanted—is linked to the humiliations and defilements of Pussy Braden, Josie Keenan, and Noreen Tiernan. For when McCabe's Irish come into proximity with what they desire, the impossibility of that desire, and the gulf between being Irish and being an "other," is starkly illuminated.

In still other instances, the desire for otherness as an escape from downtrodden Irishness expresses itself as a protracted infantalization: if you can't change your lot in life, you can attempt to remake your family into a better image or simply return to the womb and start again. Pussy Braden dreams of knowing the mother who deserted him, as if the correction of that desertion—which marked him as undesirable and "broken" in the first place—will lead to a wholeness he has never known. Pat McNab remains faithfully attached to his mother's house, fending off the "intruders" who threaten to upset the stasis he has so carefully constructed, even if the intruders are only figments of an overactive, schizophrenic mind. Even Francie Brady's crazed mind has a method. His attempts to interact with the Nugents are matched by a charming, if horribly executed, attempt to remake his incredibly dysfunctional family in a more positive light.

What conclusions can we draw from this analysis? In the skewed version of Ireland drawn in McCabe's pages, the country and its citizens represent, as Tom Herron puts it, "a myth of failure and betrayal"—a failure to live up to Ireland's long history and thus a betrayal and shame of one's self. It is the inescapable nature of this interlocked dissemination of failures and betrayals that marks the characters as having a place in McCabe's Ireland, a country that cannot seem to right itself, about which there is an inherent quality of "the secondary [and] menial" (p. 173) that surrounds both the place and its people.

SELECTED BIBLIOGRAPHY

I. NOVELS AND SHORT STORIES. *Music on Clinton Street* (Dublin, 1986); *Carn* (London, 1989); *The Butcher Boy* (London, 1992); *The Adventures of Shay Mouse* (Dublin, 1994); *The Dead School* (New York, 1995); *Breakfast on Pluto* (New York, 1998); *Mondo Desperado* (New York, 1999); *Emerald Germs of Ireland* (New York, 2001).

II. FILMS AND PLAYS. *Frank Pig Says Hello* (Co-Motion Theatre, Dublin Theatre Festival, 1992); *The Butcher Boy,* screenplay by Patrick McCabe and Neil Jordan (Warner, 1998).

III. INTERVIEWS. John Kelly, "Interview with Patrick McCabe," *Irish Times* (16 May 1998); Joe Jackson, "When Love Hurts," *Irish Times* (3 June 2000).

IV. CRITICAL AND BIOGRAPHICAL STUDIES. Rüdiger Imhof, "The Fiction of Patrick McCabe," *Linen Hall Review* (Autumn 1992); Patrick Brennan, "From Britpop to Yeatspop," *Irish Times* (7 February 1997); Clare Wallace, "Running Amuck: Manic Logic in Patrick McCabe's *The Butcher Boy,*" Colin Lacey, "Patrick McCabe: A Comedy of Horrors," *Publishers Weekly* (16 November 1998); *Irish Studies Review* (August 1998); Tom Herron, "ContamiNation: Patrick McCabe and Colm Toibin's Pathologies of the Republic," in Liam Harte and Michael Parker, eds., *Contemporary Irish Fiction: Themes, Tropes, Theories* (New York, 2000); Tom Gilling, "Patrick McCabe's Murderous Protagonist Likes to Sing His Multiple Victims to Death," *New York Times Book Review* (18 March 2001); James M. Smith, "Remembering Ireland's Architecture of Containment: 'Telling' Stories in *The Butcher Boy* and *States of Fear,*" *Eire-Ireland* (fall-winter 2001).

BRIAN MOORE

(1921–1999)

Robert Sullivan

SHORTLY BEFORE HIS death, on 10 January 1999, Brian Moore was at work on his twentieth novel. This was to have been another "historical" fiction, in part based on the life of the poet Arthur Rimbaud, and would have extended Moore's consistent output over the years of publishing a novel every two to three years. Such publishing history started with the novel *Judith Hearne* in 1955 and ended with *The Magician's Wife* in 1997, but it does not include the pulp fiction that Moore wrote under pseudonyms when he first started his career as a journalist after emigrating to Canada after the war, nor his "faction" *The Revolution Script* (1971) depicting the events surrounding the kidnapping of James Cross and Pierre Laporte by young FLQ members in Montreal. He was often referred to as a "writer's writer" (Graham Greene called Moore his "favourite living novelist," a remark that later came to haunt Moore), and his novels garnered many prizes. As if in testament to his ambiguous national identity, Moore was considered twice for the U.S. National Book Award until it was discovered that he was not an American citizen. It is perhaps because of this ambiguity of identity (one of Moore's favorite themes) that his reputation as one of the foremost contemporary novelists writing in English has suffered. A Canadian citizen until his death, and at first claimed as "one of the truly distinctive voices in Canadian fiction," Moore lived at first in Montreal, then New York City, and from 1966 until his death in California. Ultimately it matters less whether Moore is a Canadian, Irish, or American writer. What is crucial is that his oeuvre records an unswerving regard for "humanity's capacity to endure," a remark from William Faulkner's Nobel acceptance speech that Moore often cited. This necessity for endurance is caused for the most part by a despair brought about by the lack of (and the need for) some form of belief in an increasingly secular world. In many of his novels, a substitute faith is discovered in the miraculous power of love.

BIOGRAPHY

Brian Moore (his family used the Irish pronunciation "Bree-han") was born into a middle-class Catholic family in Belfast on 25 August 1921, a short time after the treaty was signed that would divide Ireland. His father, Dr. James Bernard Moore, an eminent surgeon at the Belfast Mater Hospital, married Eileen McFadden, one of his nurses and twenty years his junior. Brian was one of nine children, six of whom were girls. Two aunts were also frequently present, making the household a very feminine one, a state of affairs that no doubt helped lead to one of Moore's hallmarks—the representation of a female consciousness. His father, a Nationalist who sympathized with Franco and later supported Ireland's neutrality during the war, much to his son's chagrin, served as the model for Professor O'Neill in *Judith Hearne* and Gavin Burke's father in *The Emperor of Ice-Cream* (1965). His mother was no doubt the model for the sympathetic portrayal of Mrs. Tierney, mother of the selfish Brendan Tierney in *An Answer from Limbo* (1962), and the whole family, including aunts and friends, is cast as the accusatory ensemble that put on trial the eponymous writer-protagonist in *Fergus* (1970). In 1940, lacking the qualifications for university, Moore joined an Air Raids Precautions unit in Belfast and saw some horrific sights as he helped coffin bodies after a series of German raids in 1941. Moore's father died a year after the air raids, due to the severe strain put on him by his work in the hospital.

Mainly due to his academic success in French, Moore was recruited to serve with the British Ministry of War Transport as a port official in Algiers. He served also in France and Italy. In 1945, Moore took up an appointment with the United Nations Relief and Rehabilitation Administration and was stationed in Warsaw for a period of time. It was here that he filed his first journalistic pieces, articles on the transitional conflicts between church and state, experience he would call upon many years later for his ecclesiastic thriller *The Color of Blood* (1987). But it could be argued that it was a more personal experience during these years that had the most long-lasting effect on Moore's life and work. It was during his sojourn in Poland that Moore met a Canadian journalist called Margaret Swanson, and the repercussions of this affair changed his life. Although short-lived, this was Moore's first mature romance and he has stated that it was one of the main reasons that he chose to emigrate to Canada in 1948. He settled at first in Toronto and then moved to Montreal in 1949, eventually securing a job on the Montreal *Gazette,* at first as a proofreader (like his protagonist Ginger Coffey), then as a reporter. He consolidated his new life in Canada by marrying Jacqueline Sirois, a fellow journalist, in 1951, and in 1953 his only son, Michael, was born. Moore took out Canadian citizenship the same year, a nationality he was never to relinquish even though he lived for more than half his life in the United States.

Moore now settled into a rigorous writing schedule, contributing stories to *Weekend* magazine and eventually writing pulp fictions under the pseudonyms "Michael Bryan" and "Bernard Mara," titles that would help buy him the time to write his first serious novel. That "time" became more urgent when he was struck by a motorboat when swimming alone in a lake in the Laurentian Mountains. He had gone there to work on *Judith Hearne,* and after the accident he realized that (as he put it much later) he did not have "an eternal ticket." After the accident, Moore had trouble speaking for some time (he had suffered severe trauma to his skull), but when he began to write again he found a sure fictional voice for *Judith Hearne,* which was published by André

Deutsch in 1955 to excellent reviews. It also won the Author's Club of Great Britain First Novel Award and when published in the United States the next year was afforded a similar successful reception. Now that he had "returned" to Belfast for his first novel, Moore remained there for his second, turning out *The Feast of Lupercal* (1957) in under a year. This time he returned to his old school St. Malachy's College (St. Michan's in the novel) to dramatize the pathetic life of Mr. Diarmuid Devine, one of its teachers. Apparently publication was held up due to the fear that the school might sue, but as Moore was fond of relating years later, the principal's response was: "This boy is merely biting the hand that birched him."

Moore now began *The Luck of Ginger Coffey,* his "Montreal novel." Originally entitled "The Mirror Man" (mirrors were to become a recurrent motif in his fiction), Ginger is a Dubliner who, like Moore, was a new Canadian seeking a job as a reporter. Moore completed the novel in Amagansett, Long Island, where he was now residing, recently the recipient of a Guggenheim Fellowship. Published in 1960, *The Luck of Ginger Coffey* made its debut as a film in 1964, with a script by Moore and starring Robert Shaw and his wife, Mary Ure. Moore now embarked on his most ambitious project to date, both thematically and formally, with the writing of *An Answer from Limbo.* Moore felt with this novel that he had begun to carve "a little niche in [literary] history," as the first Irish-born novelist to write believable American characters. But the novel's critical reception (in 1962 in the United States and spring 1963 in the United Kingdom) was a big disappointment to him, even though it was nominated for a National Book Award.

The novelist now turned to a project he had consciously avoided when he had at first contemplated a writing career, the writing of what comes closest to his bildungsroman. In *The Emperor of Ice-Cream* (1965), Moore turned to his own youth and his experience in the Air Raid Precautions unit during the blitz. During the writing of this book, while living alone in a Manhattan apartment, Moore met and fell in love with Jean

Denny, originally from Nova Scotia, who was to become his second wife. Moore's future success (and his fate) took a crucial turn at this time when he was contacted by Alfred Hitchcock, the legendary director. Hitchcock, who was the recipient of a Catholic schooling, had read *The Feast of Lupercal* and was aware of Moore's reputation for writing from a woman's point of view.

The director had in mind the notion to make a film about the Soviet agents Guy Burgess and Donald MacLean, told from the perspective of MacLean's wife, but when Moore and his new partner, Jean, arrived in California the project moved in a different direction. The movie that was made, *Torn Curtain,* starring Julie Andrews and Paul Newman, was released in 1966 and, as Moore predicted, was a flop. However, there were positive consequences to this venture, not the least of which was the financial reward that bought Moore the time to write his next novel. The film experience with Hitchcock also allowed Moore to hone his narrative skills, particularly the techniques of montage and flashback, so evident in his next two novels, *I Am Mary Dunne* (1968) and *Fergus* (1970). Another consequence of this sojourn with Hitchcock and Hollywood was Brian and Jean's decision to live permanently in California, at first in various rental properties and then eventually settling into a remote house along the Pacific Coast Highway overlooking Zuma Beach. He wrote to a friend that it seemed a good spot for writing novels and, indeed, although he and Jean traveled extensively every year, Moore began a writing regime here that would produce fifteen novels over the next thirty years.

After the completion and publication of *Mary Dunne* (1968), Moore worked on a film script of the novel as well as a script for *The Lonely Passion of Judith Hearne,* which was to star Deborah Kerr. Neither project came to fruition, but Moore was paid for these tasks and this helped finance his divorce and the private school that his son, Michael, was now attending. Such work, personal and professional, kept him busy in the next year or so, but he had already made notes on another circadian fiction, this time the day of

crisis in the life of a budding novelist who had been drawn into the movie business. After the completion of *Fergus,* Moore was at work on yet two other fictional possibilities based on a dream he had had in Carmel, California, up the coast from his own home. These early sketches were both to come to fruition as *The Great Victorian Collection* (1975) and *Cold Heaven* (1983). However, he turned first to writing his only novella after a visit to his wife's home in Nova Scotia, where he was surprised to overhear the Mass delivered in the vernacular. *Catholics* (1972) turned out to be the tautest of Moore's fictions, written in concise, sometimes poetic prose and only 102 pages in length. Published at first in the United States in the *New American Review,* the novella eventually won the W. H. Smith Award in the U.K. and became a well-made film.

During this period (1970–1973), Moore was somewhat diffident about the nonrealistic "turn" his fiction was taking (*Fergus* had received some negative reviews because of its "fantastic" premise, especially by a writer known for, as he put it himself, "telling the truth"), and he no doubt welcomed the invitation to do a "journalistic" job that was as close as he could get to a documentary truth. Written only months apart, *Catholics* and *The Revolution Script* (1971) are the most disparate (all the more so because contiguous) of Moore's, albeit multifarious, output; one is a futuristic rumination on the foundations of the Catholic faith, the other a very contemporary and factual account of a revolutionary cell. Yet they share an element that is essential to both (as does *The Great Victorian Collection,* the novel that follows them), a phenomenon that intrigued Moore at this time— the role of the media, particularly television, in shaping the outcome of events. *The Great Victorian Collection,* a multilayered fable about creation in which a young professor of history (a Victorian specialist) dreams of a vast collection of Victoriana and awakes to find it a reality, is the most complexly allegorical of all Moore's novels and for him was the most risky to date. Publication was delayed by events other than Moore's procrastination caused by the "turn" his fiction was taking, most particularly his appointment as a visiting professor at UCLA. The novel was finally published in the United States and Canada in June 1975 and in the United Kingdom a few months later. Although the reviews were less than enthusiastic, the novel won for Moore his second Governor General's Award in Canada and the James Tait Black Award in the U.K.

Moore now turned to the much surer ground of *The Doctor's Wife* (1976), a book that many critics felt returned to the strengths of his very first novel—the writing of realistic narrative from a woman's point of view. *The Doctors Wife* turned out to be Moore's most lucrative fiction, and although it failed to win the Booker Prize for him, it was said to have netted $500,000 in paperback and film rights, certainly enough to allow him to experiment now with whatever fiction he chose. Always one to have ideas for a new novel jotted down in one of his notebooks, Moore had already drafted out the beginnings of *The Mangan Inheritance* (1979) during the successful reception and publicity (he and Jean were written up in *People* magazine) surrounding *The Doctor's Wife.*

This novel was greatly delayed (indeed, it was almost never finished) by another near-death experience suffered by Moore. In 1977, while attending a dramatic adaptation of his earlier book *The Emperor of Ice-Cream* at the Abbey Theatre in Dublin, Moore succumbed to the often recurrent bouts he suffered from bleeding ulcers. A problem since the 1950s, this malady now almost proved fatal. He was operated on in Dublin and, when he was fit enough to travel, again in Los Angeles in 1978. He was keenly aware once more of his mortality, just as he had been after the boating accident, and, as always, Moore was not one to let an experience escape a possible fictive transformation. *Cold Heaven* (1983), a book that he referred to in his notes as his "Lazarus" novel, begins with a boating accident and the presumed death of Dr. Davenport, who "miraculously" comes back to life. Miracles, especially the miracle of love, a concern in Moore's fiction since *The Lonely Passion of Judith Hearne,* became in these years (the 1980s) a dominant theme. Among the many reviews collected in his

papers at the University of Calgary is one on the book of a friend about the bringing up of his mentally challenged son, Noah. Moore remarks that the book is a "testament to endurance" and a "true story about love." For whatever reasons—most likely his ruminations of the selfless nature of authentic love—Moore set aside the composition of *Cold Heaven* and turned to one of his strangest tales, *The Temptation of Eileen Hughes* (1981), a pivotal book in the Moore canon, both in its form and content. A story of idolatry (a working title was "The Girl Who Was God"), it is the first fiction in which the author mixes a philosophical or moral parable with the driving narrative force of the thriller form, a mixture that would characterize the remainder of his work.

In 1982, Moore reestablished his Canadian roots when he became writer-in-residence at the University of Toronto. During this time, while putting the finishing touches to the manuscript of *Cold Heaven,* he was asked to write the film script for a French-Canadian production based on Simone de Beauvoir's *Le Sang des autres* (The Blood of Others) to be directed by Claude Chabrol. His sojourn in Canada, conjoined with the coincidental reading of Graham Greene's discussion of the Jesuit *Relations,* led Moore on to his next fiction, *Black Robe* (1985). After the publication and success of *Black Robe* (the one disappointment being its failure to be nominated for the Booker Prize), Moore became the subject of a Canadian National Film Board documentary on his life and writing entitled "The Lonely Passion of Brian Moore." The opportunity to visit his past life both in Ireland and elsewhere—literally and mnemonically—during this period was no doubt a major factor in the composition of Moore's next novel, *The Color of Blood* (1987). Moore's imaginary country in *Color* is a thinly disguised Poland where he had served after the war, but he had in mind also contemporary Northern Ireland, where he had recently witnessed similar kinds of roadblocks and armored vehicles. *The Color of Blood* was nominated but did not win the Booker, but Moore had sufficient compensation that year when he was lauded with an honorary doctorate of letters from Queen's University, Belfast, the very same institution he failed to enter more than forty years earlier. Moore's next fiction was virtually thrust upon him at this time. While staying at the Wellington Park Hotel, a short walk from Queen's University, Moore and the other residents had to be evacuated because of a bomb scare. This event, plus a "story" he had heard about a similar circumstance, led him to pen the thriller *Lies of Silence* (1990). In an unpublished interview with Robert Sullivan conducted at his home in Malibu in January 1992, Moore commented on why he had decided to write *Lies of Silence* despite having stated on more than one occasion that he would not deal with the "Troubles" in Northern Ireland. In doing so, he also summarized his vocation at this late stage in his career:

> Well, I've been a professional writer now for over thirty years, and one thing I would like to say to you—and it goes back to some of the things touched on earlier about politics—is that despite an early interest in politics (as you know I was in Eastern Europe just after the war), I've always felt that writing about politics was a dangerous thing, because of the topicality of it. Something written in 1960 with a political basis might be incomprehensible today. If you want to write novels that will be remembered it is a better choice to write about character, about people's dilemmas, that people can identify with. I would hope that *Lies of Silence,* even twenty years from now, is something that people will be able to identify with, because it's an ordinary person's dilemma. Another thing that has happened to me is that I look now for some sort of moral dilemma that interests me, but at the same time I want now as I never did before—as I never quite so consciously did before—I want to hold the reader's attention.

In the same interview, Moore, who had turned seventy in 1991, remarked on the less autobiographical direction his fiction had taken and was to take in the 1990s: "But eventually, if you hope not to repeat yourself, you realize that you've used up your own life, your own experience, so you begin to think in terms of—for the want of a better word—more intellectual novels, novels that will pose a moral problem." Thus, Moore now looked to historical and/or contemporary events on which to base his fiction, taking a "true

story" and universalizing it into some philosophical or moral drama. The first of these was inspired by the rise of the priest-leader Jean-Bertrand Aristide in Haiti, which Moore transformed into *No Other Life* (1993). Later he became interested in the reports in France on the trial of Paul Touvier, a member of the Milice who was accused of personally overseeing the murder of fourteen Jews during the Occupation. In Moore's fiction, Pierre Brossard, twice condemned in his absence for "crimes against humanity," is haunted throughout the narrative until his assassination at the novel's close. The "statement" that is pinned to his body concludes thus: "After forty-four years of delays, legal prevarications, and the complicity of the Catholic Church in hiding Brossard from justice, the dead are now avenged. The case is closed." But because of some intricate plotting that would be unfair to reveal here, this is a morally ambiguous closure to say the least. *The Statement* was published in 1995, the same year the Moores were able to move into the house they had built near Jean's original home in Nova Scotia.

It was here and in Malibu that Moore wrote his last completed novel, *The Magician's Wife* (1997), a tale of faith and illusion set in nineteenth-century France and Algeria. It is a mark of the consistency of his project that his final novel, the narrative of which is once again filtered through a woman's consciousness, should explore the meaning and trappings of faith. Like *Black Robe,* it sets French imperialism (and the religion that subtends it) against indigenous beliefs and customs. Henri Lambert, a French magician, is sent to Algeria to work his "miracles" and pit his power against the native marabout Bouz-Aziz, a holy man, in order to weaken his power and defuse a possible jihad against French occupation. His wife, Emmeline, however, is much impressed by the "mysterious sense of sainthood" that surrounds Bouz-Aziz and the "intensity of belief" that she witnesses among his followers: "It was a force at once inspiring and terrible, a faith with no resemblance to the Christian belief in Mass and the sacraments, hellfire and damnation, sin and redemption, penance and forgiveness" (p. 208) It is Emmeline who ultimately denounces her husband's "miracles" as a sham, and although this does not prevent the French conquest the following year, she is able to live with her conscience because she had not "kept silent about the truth of these events." In 1998, Moore, now seventy-seven years old, embarked on yet another novel set in nineteenth-century France, a fiction that had the poet Arthur Rimbaud as a character. No doubt this fiction would have been yet another testament to how Brian Moore, with every novel, set out to do something new so that he would never have to "repeat" himself.

THE BELFAST NOVELS

Although not written in chronological order, there is a strong case for examining *The Lonely Passion of Judith Hearne* (1955), *The Feast of Lupercal* (1957), *The Emperor of Ice-Cream* (1965), *The Doctor's Wife* (1976), and *Lies of Silence* (1990), as a group of novels that represent Moore's prolonged argument with his native city. He was fond of quoting François Mauriac's remark that "for the novelist, the door closes at twenty," and it could be said that Moore left Belfast, but Belfast never left him. These books depict a set of circumstances in which the characters must confront a harsh social climate, a space in which a great deal of personal resilience is needed to overcome atavistic habit, religious prohibition, and societal pressure. The five novels form a kind of graph of aspiration, which finds its nadir in *Judith Hearne,* its apex of hope in *Emperor,* then drops again into tragic despair and desperation with *The Doctor's Wife* and *Lies of Silence.*

Judy Hearne is the most pathetic of the main characters portrayed in these books, with the least opportunity for changing her sad existence. When we are introduced to her in the first few pages of the narrative we learn how she is fully entrenched in those atavistic habits, those social and religious restraints of which she is victim and which she helps perpetuate. The key elements in her life—her aunt's picture and the oleograph of the Sacred Heart, representing her reliance on the past and her subordination to the Church—are once again set out in her new lodgings. The fact that her aunt's photograph ("looking down at her, stern, reminding her of her behaviour") and the oleograph ("wise and stern and kindly") are again set in their place at the very end of the novel (after her breakdown and removal to a nursing home), signifies the cruel stasis that is her life. It seems, at least for a while, that her life might change when she meets at one of her boardinghouses the recently returned exile James Patrick Madden. But this turns out to be a tragedy of errors: he sees in Judy a more gentile and affluent version of the typical boarder, and he has her in mind as an investor in a business venture. She sees in him her last desperate chance for love, more urgent now as her faith wanes. Judy's desire is enormous, her hope burgeoning, and now her disappointment is terrible. She turns for solace to the place she had sought companionship so many times before: "No one. The church an empty shell, nobody to hear, no reason to pray, only statues listen. Statues cannot hear. . . . And if I am alone?" It is this constant aloneness that drives Judith Hearne to alcoholic despair, degradation, and a life without hope. Many of Moore's later protagonists are able to put their "faith" in love when their belief fails them, but even this is denied to the lonely spinster.

There is some hope for Diarmuid Devine in *The Feast of Lupercal.* The title *A Moment of Love* in one paperback version has its own significance, since Devine (a virgin, Catholic schoolmaster teaching at his old school) is offered a "moment" when resolute character and a brave decision could very well change his life. Unlike the lonely spinster, he has a genuine chance for love and affection in what is otherwise a sterile life, but because of both the restrictive social forces in which he lives and his own innate weakness he is unable to act. Like Judith Hearne, he is responsible for reproducing these social strictures, but unlike her he should be more conscious of this fact: "It was the education in Ireland, dammit, he had said it many a time" (p. 12).

His opportunity comes when he meets Una Clarke, a younger, vibrant, and, more ominously, Protestant girl. But, characteristically, Devine lets the "moment" pass. At the end of the novel he has, like Judy Hearne, come full circle, and like her he associates his chance for love with the religious conscience that has held him in check: "To fail to sin, perhaps that is my sin" he ponders to himself. Devine is made to suffer greatly, ironically enough, for this failure to sin; the whole school gets to know of his "affair" with Una Clarke when he is written up on the lavatory wall and caned by a fellow master (Una's uncle) in full view of the school. In a final interview with Una, when she remarks on this beating, the irony is not lost on Devine when he remembers that he has been teaching *Julius Caesar,* the first scene of which enacts the fertility rites of Lupercal, a ritual in which barren women are symbolically whipped in order to make them fertile: "It's a form of expiation, I suppose," he tells her (p. 217). In that same interview at the close of the novel, some words that Devine had uttered earlier in a "moment" of confidence come back to haunt him: "I could change . . . and damn the consequences," he had told her. But in virtually the last words of the book, Devine realizes his true predicament: "She was right, he couldn't change" (p. 218). The possibility of change in such a deterministic universe would be difficult for the most daring of characters, but for the irresolute Judith Hearnes and Devines it is impossible. That Moore had in mind deterministic and implacable forces at work in this fictional universe is clear from some notes he made for "Mr. Devine" (a working title): "Show how the forces of Ireland, religion, conventional middle-class morality and finally, the Catholic Puritanism toward sex, prevented this honourable and well-intentioned man from attaining his due in life—Una."

It is a more youthful and a more resolute Gavin Burke in *The Emperor of Ice-Cream* who is able to break out of this syndrome of despair and stasis, but at the cost of the almost literal—emphatically symbolic—destruction of the environment in which he is trapped. A much slighter novel than the previous two (if albeit a much less dark one), Gavin Burke's resolve is almost dictated by the events of history, and he is, as it were, "conscripted" into action when he helps rescue the victims of German air raids on Belfast: "And

in that moment, within Gavin, there started an extraordinary elation, a tumult of joy. . . . The world and the war had come to him at last. Tonight, in the Reichchancellery of Berlin, generals stood over illuminated maps, plotting Belfast's destruction" (p. 199). For much of the novel Gavin, a young college dropout, seems destined for the same circular fate as his older predecessors as he suffers continually the premonition that nothing would ever change in the stasis that is Belfast during the "phony war" of the early 1940s. "Nothing would change. Out there, in the world, governments might be overthrown, capitals occupied, cities destroyed, maps redrawn, but here, in Ireland, it made no difference" (p. 135). Guided by fragments of modern verse, especially the poem by Wallace Stevens that gives the book its title, Gavin Burke is able to seize his "moment," to "let be be the finale of seem," and to break free of those forces that held Judith Hearne and Diarmuid Devine in check. He jettisons the hold that religion has had on him (the statue of the Divine Infant of Prague), abandons the schooling that enforces such adherence, and, in a somewhat contrived closure to the novel, the very house that has held him captive for so many years is "condemned." Now speaking with a more mature voice, in the novel's final paragraphs he notes the enormous changes that have taken place, how "his father's world was dead," and how, now, his own "grown-voice . . . would tell him what to do."

If the three novels just discussed figure Belfast as a site of denial, an obstacle to desire, then *The Doctor's Wife* and *Lies of Silence* continue this concern with some variations. A crucial difference that the two novels share is that the two protagonists, Sheila Redden in *The Doctor's Wife* and Michael Dillon in *Lies of Silence,* make important decisions and take important steps to change their lives, when, in the words of Sheila Redden, they realize that "The future is forbidden to no one. Unless we forbid it ourselves" (p. 49). However, although these two protagonists escape the confines of Belfast, both literally and ideologically, they are tracked down eventually by Belfast's representatives, and their freedom is cut tragically short. In *The Doctor's Wife,* Moore uses the violence of Belfast as a counterpoint to the serenity of his heroine's sojourn in France. Sheila Redden had gone there to revisit her youth and is disappointed when her doctor husband is detained in Belfast, attending to the victims of bombings there. When she meets a young American, however, she becomes aware of an opportunity, albeit a frightening one, to change her life. Sheila Redden is a more sophisticated and liberated human being than her Belfast counterparts (her consciousness and sexual desire are more akin to Moore's North American women), but despite her resolve she is unable to fly by those nets that hold back Belfast souls, or if she does it is at a terrible price. Belfast continually breaks into her romantic sojourn, either as memories of the bombings there or, more brutally, when her husband comes to take her home and ends up raping her. Eventually she is able to break free of her husband (and the young American), but we leave her at the novel's close living anonymously in a London bed-sitter, somewhat like Judy Hearne.

Lies of Silence (1990) is written in Moore's thriller mode, the narrative driven forward by the twin plots of a terrorist action and a thwarted love story. Michael Dillon is the hotel manager who must drive the IRA bomb to his own hotel, threatening the lives of many innocent tourists, or sacrifice the life of his estranged wife, who is being held captive by the same terrorists. The moral dilemma is complicated by his ongoing affair with a younger woman, with whom he eventually "escapes" under police protection (he had managed to safely evacuate the hotel) to London. However, in a way similar to Sheila Redden, Belfast's representatives follow him and deny absolutely any future happiness he and Andrea might have foreseen. Shortly before he is shot by an IRA bullet, the tragic irony is underscored for us (especially if we remember the desire for change by Dillon's Belfast forebears Devine and Gavin Burke), when he remarks after arriving "safely" in London: "She was right. They were here. Everything had changed. Everything" (p. 177). *Lies* was to be Moore's last chapter in the long debate with Belfast, and it has at times the ring of a summation about it, as in this

observation early in the novel when Dillon ruminates on his native city:

> Dillon felt anger rise within him, anger at the lies which had made this, his . . . birthplace, sick with a terminal ignorance of bigotry and injustice, lies told over the years to poor Protestant working people about the Catholics, lies told to poor Catholic working people about the Protestants, lies from parliaments and pulpits . . . and, above all, the lies of silence from those in Westminister who did not want to face the injustices of Ulster's status quo.
> (p. 50)

Whoever is to blame, the conclusion that these two novels seem to reach is that the "sickness" endemic to Belfast kills love if it cannot deny it.

THE FRAGILITY OF SELF

The protagonists in five novels of Moore's middle period—*The Luck of Ginger Coffey* (1960), *An Answer from Limbo* (1962), *I Am Mary Dunne* (1968), *Fergus* (1970), and *The Mangan Inheritance* (1979)—all of them estranged from their roots in one way or another, learn that to jettison former social and religious taboos will most likely land them in a limbo of dislocation and despair. This theme of the fragility of identity begins with *Ginger Coffey,* reaches a paradigmatic climax with *I Am Mary Dunne,* and ends in the gothic search for selfhood of Jamie Mangan.

Ginger Coffey, a Dubliner recently arrived in Montreal, a more buoyant figure than his Belfast countrymen, is the victim of an incurable optimism. Despite being a "B.A. failed, something in a distillery, a noncombatant in the war," Ginger is always sure that his "ship would come in" and disregards his wife's constant pleas that a measure of reality is needed in their economic and marital situation if they are to survive in the New World. Eventually, after attempting to bluff his way into a newspaper job as a desk man, he accepts the lesser post of proofreader, indicating that at least he is beginning to recognize the reality of his situation, but it is too little too late. Vera, his wife, has already decided to leave the "sad imposter" and take up with an old family friend. Ginger then slips into the drunken netherworld of his fellow proofreaders (all losers in one way or another), until, forced to relieve himself in doorway, he is put on trial on the exaggerated charge of indecent exposure. In order to protect his family, James Francis Coffey supplies a fictitious name in court, symbolizing his newfound responsibility, not to mention identity. For a great deal of the novel it looks as if the title would turn out to be totally ironic, but Ginger is lucky at last when an understanding judge dismisses the charge. A police officer remarks: "Twenty years on the force. . . . And I never saw a judge give a guy a break like you got. Luck of the Irish it must be, eh Irishman?" (p. 234). When eventually Ginger is reunited with his repentant wife, we feel that in many ways he deserves it. The frightening anonymity he suffers in the course of his separation from wife and family, not to mention from his own sense of a secure self, is depicted at the very heart of the novel; at his lowest ebb, Ginger ponders this sense of fragility: "He had no one. He was three thousand miles from home, across half a frozen continent and the whole Atlantic ocean. . . . Would anyone ever know him again?" (p. 169).

Ginger Coffey is more tragicomedy than tragedy and is the least dark of these identity novels, mainly because of Ginger's disposition and his willingness to accept "humble circs." Not so for Moore's next North American character of Irish descent. Brendan Tierney, the Belfast-born "artist" who is driven by a narcissistic desire to revenge himself on his Belfast past (Moore published a story on this theme entitled "Preliminary Pages for a Work of Revenge" in 1961, which is incorporated into the novel), both sacrifices his mother (literally) and himself (figuratively) because of this narcissistic rage.

When we meet him in the novel, Brendan, living with his sexually frustrated wife, Jane, and his two children, has hit upon a scheme to bring his widowed mother over from Belfast so that his wife might work full-time and he can give himself over to the great novel that he believes is in him. But things do not work out as planned. Moore's experiment with a triadic point of view (Brendan's, his mother's, and Jane's) allows him to contrast Brendan's selfish goals with his wife's

sexual fantasies and, most importantly, his mother's genuine concern for this "pagan" family in which her own grandchildren have not been baptized. Mrs. Tierney's interference in her daughter-in-law's affairs (she performs a secret baptism on the children) leads eventually to her removal from the Tierney household and to the empty apartment of a cousin. Through a series of deft narrative juxtapositions, we witness her suffering a stroke and her fear of dying "alone in the limbo of a strange apartment" while waiting for her son to call. But Brendan's commitment to his novel is by now all consuming, and as his mother lies dying he worries about the cuts his publishers have asked him to make in his book. His mother's last words are "Love me?" But even at her graveside Brendan is preoccupied more with the stuff of his next novel than with his mother's lonely fate. Time and time again throughout the novel Brendan ponders on the person he once was and the person he is becoming. In the last two sentences of the book he speaks from a limbo of despair as he realizes too late just how far he has changed: "I have altered beyond all self-recognition. I have lost and sacrificed myself." *I Am Mary Dunne* stands both chronologically and thematically at the center of these novels dealing with the transformations (and deformations) of self. Its working title, "A Woman of No Identity," accentuates this concern and its eponymous heroine, mainly because she is a woman, suffers most emphatically from these shifting senses of self. The novel is a brilliant dramatization of a day of crisis in the life of a woman who has had to change her name three times and who, on this particular day (partly because of the tensions she is undergoing due to a premenstrual condition), forgets her present identity when asked for it at a beauty salon. The first-person narrative is told from Mary's point of view as she lies in bed "waiting to bleed" and reviews her day, a day when friends and incidents bring up a lifetime of different lives and identities. Married three times, her name and in a sense her identity "subject" to male hegemony (including her maiden name "Dunne," which is given to her by her father), Mary seems to have found a stable haven with her third husband, Terence Lavery. But a meeting with an old girlfriend, her biological condition, and that lapse of memory at the beauty salon sets in motion a reexamination of her life. *"Memento ergo sum* (we are what we remember) is both Mary's motto and her burden, forced as she is to recall painful events in her life, including what she terms the "Juarez dooms," Juarez being the site of her most recent divorce. The novel is circular in nature, and the narrative brings us back to Mary's mnemonic odyssey. ("And so, here in the dark, I closed my eyes and went back sixteen years.") She seems to have reached a form of stability when in the final words of the novel she repeats "I am Mary Dunne, I am Mary Dunne, I am Mary Dunne," but this is perhaps more of a desire than a confirmation.

Written immediately after *I Am Mary Dunne, Fergus* (1970) could be considered a further installment in an autobiographical impulse that Moore began with *The Emperor of Ice-Cream.* One day of crisis in the life of the eponymous protagonist (this time male), this circadian fiction continues as well the conflict of values and generations that was introduced in *An Answer from Limbo.* Fergus Fadden, the self-exiled novelist from Belfast, is living by the Pacific Ocean, working on a film adaptation of his second successful novel and living with a beautiful woman "young enough to be his daughter." In an uncharacteristic move into fantasy thus far in his fiction, Moore has Fergus's father "appear" to him on the second page of the novel. He is only the first of a series of "apparitions" that include Fergus's mother, his sister, and many other family members and friends. It is as if an older Brendan Tierney is put on trial for the selfish pursuit of his art. Many of these "visitors" from Fergus's Belfast past have appeared in previous Moore fictions, including younger versions of Fergus himself in the guise of Gavin Burke and Brendan Tierney, but in this novel Moore brings the past and present into collision, not by a flashback technique such as in *Limbo* and *I Am Mary Dunne* but by having the past present itself en masse in Fergus's house. His sister is representative when she questions Fergus's's substitution of art for conventional religion: "Your trouble is, you can't

be sure of anything. You have no laws, no rules, no spiritual life at all" (p. 55). When, at the end of the novel, Fergus is able to "release" the motley crew that had come to interrogate him, he is able to do so only because it was he who summoned them in the first place. In this sense, *Fergus* is a fictional allegory of the self being put under scrutiny by its own conscience.

The final novel to be examined in this group of fictions that deal primarily with the erosion or fracture of self-esteem or self-image, *The Mangan Inheritance* (1979), figures this theme literally. Moore had as his working title "The Family Album," and the narrative is replete with images of one kind or another. In an ironic reversal of the usual gender stereotype, when Jamie Mangan's wife leaves him for another man, she takes his "image," his sense of self, with her. Beatrice Abbot is independently wealthy, a successful actress, and so much the power in this relationship that Jamie is often referred to as "Mr. Abbot." Crushed by her desertion of him, he remarks to his father that, since his wife left: "It's as if I—the person I was—your son—the person I used to be—it's as if there's nobody there anymore" (p. 43). However, he finds among his father's papers a daguerreotype that could be the image of Ireland's *poete maudit* James Clarence Mangan; since there is a striking resemblance, Jamie takes this as a "sign" that he should resume his vocation (he once had a poem published in *The New Yorker*), while at the same time tracing his poetic roots in Ireland. In the meantime, as if by some fateful design (there are various hints of predetermination at work in this novel), his wife is killed in an automobile accident before she has had time to change her will.

Now Jamie Mangan is affluent enough to travel to the west of Ireland in search of his poetic ancestors, and it is here, in the second, long section of the novel, that the narrative turns into a gothic tale of incest and a parable of psychic quest. After much degradation and revelation, Jamie Mangan comes face to face with another legatee of the Mangan inheritance, his double, Michael Mangan, who had been castrated by his own daughter Maeve after an incestuous relationship with her and the molestation of his niece

BRIAN MOORE

Kathleen, the same Kathleen with whom Mangan has had a sexual fling. Sickened by the dung heap of perversity he has uncovered while digging for his roots, Mangan returns to his father's deathbed in Canada. The short third section of the novel closes on a note of ambiguity, when we learn that Jamie Mangan's young stepmother is pregnant with a son, suggesting perhaps that the Mangan inheritance may yet have another legatee.

THE SILENCE OF GOD

In Moore's very first book, at the end of her harrowing ordeal, Judith Hearne is driven to distraction by the need for some assurance that there is some presence behind the signifiers of her faith: "Why do you torture me, alone and silent behind Your little door? Why?" (p. 209) she cries as, in her desperation, she makes an attack upon the tabernacle door. Always at the very least a subtextual concern in Moore's fiction, this theme of God's inscrutability is foregrounded in the novels of the 1980s, beginning with *The Temptation of Eileen Hughes* (1981) and *Cold Heaven* (1983), and running through the "clerical" novels *Black Robe* (1985), *The Color of Blood* (1987), and *No Other Life* (1993). The theme of the cleric who sacrifices himself for the greater love of his followers begins with *Catholics* (1972), and that novella is best considered along with the priestly novels just mentioned. These books share also the notion of how love might function as a "substitute" faith and also how this faith must be tested if this love is to be found truly "miraculous."

The notion that spiritual love can act as a replacement for a more traditional faith is figured most directly in *The Temptation of Eileen Hughes,* the working title of which was "The Girl Who Was God." In this novel, a young Irish girl is "adored" by her rich employer Bernard McAuley, who sees in the virgin Eileen an index of the spirituality that is lacking in his materialistic life. For a long time Bernard worships Eileen secretively, but on a trip to London he confesses his obsession when he reads some things she says as a "sign," an "epiphany." He explains the nature of his ecstasy to the incredulous Eileen in the

following way: "But love isn't like [desire]. When you fall in love with someone, really fall in love, it's a sort of miracle, it's almost religious. The person you love is perfect. As God is perfect" (p. 76) But Eileen does not remain "perfect" for too long after this moment, when she loses her virginity to a young American on vacation in London. Bernard then comes to realize that "Love is a religion whose God is fallible" and attempts to kill himself. It is no coincidence that Bernard McAuley once contemplated becoming a priest but felt rejected by God. Now that he is again spurned by the spiritual love he thought would sustain him, he eventually dies a broken man.

Toward the end of *The Temptation of Eileen Hughes,* when Eileen is relieved of her burden and we read that she walks down the McAuleys' driveway to "her freedom," it foreshadows Marie Davenport's release in Moore's next novel of involuntary "sainthood." On the last page of *Cold Heaven* we read: "It was over. She had been returned to ordinary life, to its burdens, its consequences." The ordinary, quotidian life that Marie Davenport refers to here had been suspended for most of the narrative because she had been an unwilling witness to a vision of the Virgin and had refused to "testify." Her husband, Alex, who she had intended to leave, is struck by a motorboat exactly one year later on the anniversary of the sighting and is presumed dead until, Lazarus-like, he disappears from the morgue. Marie now takes this as the first "sign" of her punishment by those implacable forces of the "cold heaven" that oversees her every movement. The narrative is full of "signs" and/or coincidences that seem to lay bare some predetermined plan to make her tell her story and take up her assigned place in the history of Mariology. She believes that her husband, who eventually turns up in a comatose state, is being held in a kind of suspended animation until she acquiesces in the divine plan. One of the more manipulative servants of this plan, a Father Niles, who pursues Marie like some vindictive representative of the Old Testament, remarks of her plight that she is the "sinner pursued by God, so to speak." Fortunately for Marie, his wrath is superseded by

151

the mystical love of an old nun, Mother St. Jude, who (ironically, given the vision vouchsafed to the unbeliever Marie) is in despair because of the periodic absences of faith that she suffers. It is her love and understanding ("Marie looked into those dark eyes, filled mysteriously with love for her") that eventually leads to a younger novice, Sister Anna, witnessing the Virgin. This allows Marie to return to that "ordinary, muddled life of falling in love and leaving her husband and starting over again" (pp. 264–265).

The two women in the novels just discussed are tested, each in her own way, because of the seeming inscrutability of God's will. The clerics in *Catholics, Black Robe, The Color of Blood,* and *No Other Life* also suffer because of God's silence and/or inscrutability, but they each find solace in their sacrificial love for others. Apart from the individual crises that afflict these clerics—the severe testing of their faith and their terrible doubts about God's presence—these novels are concerned also with the realpolitik of the Church, a topic that Moore would take up again with a different emphasis in his novel *The Statement* (1995).

Catholics is set sometime in the future, at a time when the Ecumenical movement has reached a stage when Catholicism is merging with other faiths and it has been decreed from Rome that there shall be no more Masses in Latin and no more private confessions, among other edicts. But on the remote island of Muck, off the west of Ireland, the abbot and monks still adhere to these practices, and they have drawn thousands of visitors and television crews from all over the world. James Kinsella, one of the new breed, comes as a plenipotentiary from Rome to put a halt to these "heresies," and the political plane of the novella turns on his and Abbot O'Malley's debate on these issues. Kinsella sums up the new theology thus: "I suppose the Mass to me, as to most Catholics in the world today, is a symbolic act. I do not believe that the bread and wine on the altar is changed into the body and blood of Christ, except in a purely symbolic manner. Therefore, I do not, in the old sense, think of God as actually being present, there in the tabernacle" (p. 67). When the abbot remarks, "I

think I was born before my time," he speaks for the whole cast of characters in Moore's fiction who agonize over the mystery of the tabernacle. A central irony of the book is that the abbot has doubted God's presence in the tabernacle for some time, and has, as he puts it himself, been running the abbey as a "sort of foreman," avoiding prayer (which means the confrontation with his own doubt) and entering that dreadful state he calls "null." Now, when Kinsella leaves, his mission accomplished, Abbot O'Malley must convince his recalcitrant monks that the true miracle is prayer and must, at the book's close, sacrifice himself for their sake: "He bent his head. 'Our father, Who art in Heaven,' he said. His trembling increased. He entered null. He would never come back. In null."

The Jesuit Father Laforgue in *Black Robe* suffers a very similar fate when, at the end of his arduous journey—a spiritual journey within the self as well as the literal journey through the wilds of seventeenth-century Canada—he decides to baptize the "savages," who do not believe and who call the ritual a "water torture." Afflicted time and time again throughout his spiritual odyssey with his own doubt about the meaning of the sacrament, his faith in the redemptive power of love saves both him and the Hurons. When pressed by the Huron leader to baptize his people in the hope of saving them from the plague that is afflicting them, Laforgue ponders their sincerity and his own recent "statement of belief. " He remarks: "Had that statement of belief in God any more meaning than Taretande's promise to do God's will? What *was* God's will? He looked at the tabernacle. He felt the silence" (p. 245). But he remembers the Huron leader's crucial question and his reply: "Do you love us. Yes." It is these same words that afford the narrative its closure. In a similar way, Cardinal Bem in *The Color of Blood* has traveled through the wilderness of doubt concerning the true nature of God's will, and he confronts his own death while administering Holy Communion. The novel closes thus: "The silence of God: would it change at the moment of his death? He held up the Host as though to give it to her. He saw her finger tighten on the trigger. And heard that terrible noise." These "ecclesiastical" novels have their political dimension as well as their depiction of personal doubt. In *Black Robe,* this is the colonial assault on Canada by the twin forces of French commerce and the Jesuit mission to civilize the "savages," as the native Indians are called. Laforgue's personal crisis and the juxtaposition of the belief systems of the colonizer and the "savages" they wish to subjugate—the personal and the political—are brought neatly together in the following passage:

> He looked at the empty eyes of the statuette [of the Virgin] as though, in them, some hint might be given him of that mystery which is the silence of God. But the statuette was wooden, carved by men. The hosts in the tabernacle were bread, dubbed the body of Christ in a ritual strange as any performed by these Savages.
>
> (p. 242)

The political thrust of *The Color of Blood* revolves around the efforts of the peace-loving Cardinal Bem to stop some of his right-wing extremist archbishops from inciting the population to rise against the government in a country that is Poland in everything but name. Although he is assassinated at the novel's close there is the hope that his sacrifice will stem further bloodshed.

When Bem remarks at one point in the narrative that his people are "using religion now as a sort of politics," he points toward Moore's next novel of political intrigue and personal religious crisis. *No Other Life* is perhaps Moore's darkest book when it comes to the enigma of faith. In this novel, the twin strands of political action and personal doubt are conjoined through two characters, Father Paul Michel, originally from northern Quebec, now a resident of the Caribbean island of Ganae (modeled on Haiti) for thirty years, and one of his adopted pupils, Jean Cantave. The narrative is in the form of a memoir, as the old and now retired priest sets down for posterity how he adopted the young village boy who would eventually go to the Sorbonne and would return to his island to free his people from the bondage of a corrupt regime. Jean Cantave (his initials underscoring the frequent references to him as the "Messiah") carries the political element in

this novel; he is a "revolutionary priest" much like the historical Jean-Bertrand Aristide who decides to step down as president in order to save his people from the inevitable bloodshed that would follow his arrest by the military. In a sermon against violence, similar to that of Cardinal Bem, Cantave tells his people (he preaches in blank verse): "When you can no longer see me, / When you can no longer find me, / I will be with you" (p. 201). To his puzzled friend and mentor Father Paul Michel he remarks: "Christ was a leader who did not lead" (p. 208), suggesting, rightly as it turns out, that the people's faith would be premised on his absence and promised return. But as a counterpoint to this political "faith" in their redeemer, there is the parallel narrative of Father Paul Michel and his chronic doubts about redemption in any form. He relates at one point in his memoir how he is summoned to his mother's deathbed in Quebec and how she tells him something of which he already has a suspicion, that after death there is "no other life." It is indeed a pessimistic closure to this novel when eventually Father Michel learns that Jean Cantave, unheard of for some time but still the keeper of his people's faith, has actually been dead for some time. It is indeed a dark epitaph when we read the following closure: "I knelt down by the unmarked grave but not to pray. I touched the muddied earth in a useless caress as though, somehow, he would know that I had come here. I wept but my tears could not help him. There is no other life."

THE CRITICAL RESPONSE

Understandably enough, the first sustained critical work on Moore came from Canadian critics, although Christopher Ricks wrote an appreciative and influential piece in 1966. Hallvard Dahlie was the pioneer with his 1969 monograph dealing with the novels up to *I Am Mary Dunne* and outlining how Moore had adopted a "broader vision" after *The Luck of Ginger Coffey.* Dahlie published another monograph in 1981, accounting for the novels up to *The Mangan Inheritance* and offering a valuable discussion of some of the nonfiction and a selection of the short stories.

John Wilson Foster, in his book *Forces and Themes in Ulster Fiction* (1974) forwarded understanding when he documented how Moore's novels up to *Fergus* shift from a pattern of "ritual failure" to one of "ritual displacement," but the strongly ethnological approach is less useful for Moore's later period. Similarly, Jeanne Flood's excellent reading of some of the novels in her 1974 monograph is hindered for other books because of her desire to reduce all the novels to disguised psychobiographies. Thus, in a later review article on *Black Robe* (1990), we read that Moore "is writing neither about Jesuits nor about Native Americans . . . [but rather] the ancient impasse between father and son."

The most valuable set of essays so far are those collected in the *Irish University Review* special issue (1988), published as a consequence of Moore's honorary doctorate from Queen's University. Mainly by Irish scholars, these essays offer revised readings of most of the novels and generally bring a more theoretical and philosophical light to bear upon them. Robert Sullivan's monograph (1996) extended this treatment, subjecting various groups of Moore's books to various theoretical approaches. His study is perhaps most useful for its innovative reading of *The Great Victorian Collection* as a "metatext" for all Moore's work. The best analysis of Moore's stylistic choices, especially the manipulation of narrative voice, is provided by Jo O'Donoghue's book (1990), which takes also the transformation of Moore's relation to faith and belief as a central investigative principle. Denis Sampson's "unauthorized" biography is a welcome addition to Moore studies. His central premise of how the "chameleon" Moore disguises himself in his various fictions is perhaps less interesting than the fullest chronology we have to date of Moore's life. We await with great anticipation the forthcoming authorized biography by Patricia Craig.

SELECTED BIBLIOGRAPHY

I. NOVELS. *Judith Hearne* (London, 1955; Boston and Toronto, 1956), retitled as *The Lonely Passion of Judith Hearne* (New York, 1956); *The Feast of Lupercal* (Boston and Toronto, 1957; London, 1958), retitled *A Moment of Love* (New York, 1966); *The Luck of Ginger Coffey* (Boston and Toronto, 1960); *An Answer from Limbo* (Boston and Toronto, 1962; London, 1963); *The Emperor of Ice-Cream* (New York, 1965; London, 1967); *I Am Mary Dunne* (London and New York, 1968); *Fergus* (New York, 1970; London, 1971); *The Revolution Script* (New York, 1971; London, 1972); *Catholics* (London, 1972; New York, 1973); *The Great Victorian Collection* (London and New York, 1975); *The Doctor's Wife* (London and New York, 1976); *The Mangan Inheritance* (London and New York, 1979); *The Temptation of Eileen Hughes* (London and New York, 1981); *Cold Heaven* (London and New York, 1983); *Black Robe* (London and New York, 1985); *The Color of Blood* (New York, 1987), as *The Colour of Blood* (London, 1987); *Lies of Silence* (London and New York, 1990); *No Other Life* (London and New York, 1993); *The Statement* (London, 1995; New York, 1996); *The Magician's Wife* (London, 1997; New York, 1998).

II. SELECTED SHORT STORIES. "Sassenach," in *Northern Review* (October-November 1951); "A Vocation," in *Tamarack Review* (autumn 1956), repr. in Devin A. Garrity, ed., *The Irish Genius* (New York, 1960); "Lion of the Afternoon," in *Atlantic Monthly* (November 1957); repr. in Desmond Pacey, ed., *A Book of Canadian Stories*, rev. ed. (Toronto, 1962); "Next Thing Was Kansas City," in *Atlantic Monthly* (February 1959); "Grieve for the Dear Departed," in *Atlantic Monthly* (August 1959), repr. in John Pudney, ed., *Pick of Today's Short Stories* 12 (London, 1961); "Uncle T," in *Gentlemen's Quarterly* (November 1960), repr. in Norman Levine, ed., *Canadian Winter's Tales* (London and Toronto, 1968); "Preliminary Pages for a Work of Revenge," in *Midstream* (winter 1961), repr. in Irish Academy of Letters, *The Dolmen Miscellany of Irish Writing* (Dublin, 1962) and in Mordecai Richler, ed., *Canadian Writing Today* (Harmondsworth, U.K., 1970); "Hearts and Flowers," in *Spectator* (24 November 1961); "Off the Track," in Robert Weaver, ed., *Ten For Wednesday Night* (Toronto, 1961), repr. in Giose Rimanelli and Roberto Ruberto, eds., *Modern Canadian Stories* (Toronto, 1966).

III. NONFICTION. *Canada*, with the editors of *Life* (New York, 1963); "The People of Belfast," in *Holiday* (February 1964); "The Expatriate Writer," in *Antigonish Review* 17 (1974); "The Writer As Exile," in *Canadian Journal of Irish Studies* 2, no. 2 (1976); "Old Father, Old Artificer," in *Irish University Review* 12, no. 1 (1982).

IV. BIBLIOGRAPHIES AND ARCHIVAL COLLECTIONS. Richard Studing, "A Brian Moore Bibliography," in *Eire-Ireland* 10 (1975); Brian McIlroy, *Brian Moore: A Bibliography*, in *Irish University Review* 18., no 1 (spring 1988); The Brian Moore Papers, First Accession and Second Accession: An Inventory of the Archive at the University of Calgary Libraries, comp. by Marlys Chevrefils and ed. by Jean F. Tenerand and Appollonia Steele, with bi-critical essay by Hallvard Dahlie (Calgary, 1987). A description of the recently acquired but as yet uncataloged archive of Moore's papers at the Harry Ransom Center, University of Texas, Austin, can be accessed online at: http://www.hrc.utexas.edu/news/press/2000/bmoorenr.html.

V. CRITICISM, BIOGRAPHICAL STUDIES, INTERVIEWS. Jack Ludwig, "A Mirror of Moore," in *Canadian Literature* 7 (winter 1961) and "Brian Moore: Ireland's Loss, Canada's Novelist," in *Critique: Studies in*

Modern Fiction (spring-summer 1962); Philip French, "The Novels of Brian Moore," in *London* magazine (February 1966); Christopher Ricks, "The Simple Excellence of Brian Moore," in *New Statesman* (18 February 1966); Hallvard Dahlie, "Interviews Brian Moore," in *Tamarack Review* (winter 1968); John Wilson Foster, "Crisis and Ritual in Brian Moore's Belfast Novels," in *Eire-Ireland* (autumn 1968); Hallvard Dahlie, *Brian Moore: Studies in Canadian Literature* (Toronto, 1969); Michael Paul Gallagher, "Brian Moore Talks to Michael Paul Gallagher," in *Hibernia* (10 October 1969); Richard B. Sale, "An Interview in London with Brian Moore," in *Studies in the Novel* (spring 1969).

James Simmons, "Brian Moore and the Fallacy of Realism," in *Honest Ulsterman* (March 1970); George Woodcock, "Brian Moore's Poor Bitches," in *From Odysseus Ever Returning* (Toronto, 1970); John Wilson Foster, "Passage Through Limbo: Brian Moore's North American Novels," in *Critique: Studies in Modern Fiction* 13 (1971); Michael Paul Gallagher, "The Novels of Brian Moore," in *Studies* (1971); Murray Prosky, "The Crisis of Identity in the Novels of Brian Moore," in *Eire-Ireland* (fall 1971); John P. Frayne, "Brian Moore's Wandering Irishman—The Not-So-Wild Colonial Boy," in Raymond J. Porter and James D. Brophy, eds., *Modern Irish Literature*: *Essays in Honor of William York Tindall* (New Rochelle, N.Y., 1972); Jeanne Flood, *Brian Moore* (Lewisburg, Pa., 1974); John Wilson Foster, *Forces and Themes in Ulster Fiction* (Dublin and Totowa, N.J., 1974); Tom Paulin, "A Necessary Provincialism: Brian Moore, Maurice Leitch, Florence Mary McDowell," in Douglas Dunn, ed., *Two Decades of Irish Writing* (Cheadle, U.K., and Chester Springs, Pa., 1975); Derek Mahon, "Webs of Artifice: On the Novels of Brian Moore," in *New Review* 3, no. 32 (1976); Robert Sullivan, "Brian Moore: A Clinging Climate," in *London* magazine (December 1976/January 1977); Patrick Rafroidi, "The Great Brian Moore Collection," in Patrick Rafroidi and Maurice Harmon, eds., *The Irish Novel in Our Time* (Villeneuve-d'Ascq: L'Universite de Lille III, 1976); David Staines, "Observance Without Belief," in *Canadian Literature* 73 (1977); J. H. Dorenkamp, "Finishing the Day: Nature and Grace in Two Novels by Brian Moore," in *Eire-Ireland* 13 (1978).

Allen Shepherd, "Place and Meaning in Brian Moore's *Catholics,*" in *Eire-Ireland* 15 (1980); Hallvard Dahlie, *Brian Moore* (Boston, 1981); Paul Goetsch, "Brian Moore's Canadian Fiction," in Heinz Kosok, ed., *Studies in Anglo-Irish Literature* (Bonn, 1982); Jeanne Flood, "*The Doctor's Wife:* Brian Moore and the Failure of Realism," in *Eire-Ireland* 18, no. 2 (summer 1983); Kerry McSweeney, "Brian Moore's Grammars of the Emotions," in *Four Contemporary Novelists: Angus Wilson, Brian Moore, John Fowles, V. S. Naipaul* (Kingston and Montreal, 1983); Raymond J. Porter, "Diarmuid Devine and Ginger Coffey: Entrapment and Escape," in James D. Brophy and Raymond J. Porter, eds., *Contemporary Irish Writing* (Boston, 1983); Terence Brown, "Show Me a Sign: The Religious Imagination of Brian Moore," Brian Cosgrove, "Brian Moore and the Price of Freedom in a Secular World," Patricia Craig, "Moore's Maladies: Belfast in the Mid-Twentieth Century," John Cronin, "The Resilient Realism of Brian Moore," Hallvard Dahlie, "*Black Robe:* Moore's 'Conradian' Role and the Quest for Self," Seamus Deane, "The Real Thing: Brian Moore in Disneyland," Michael Paul Gallagher, "Religion as Favourite Metaphor: Moore's Recent Fiction," and Patrick Rafroidi, "The Temptation of Brian Moore," all in *Irish University Review* 19, no. 1 (spring 1988).

Jo O'Donoghue, *Brian Moore*: *A Critical Study* (London, Montreal, and Buffalo, 1991); Robert Sullivan, unpublished interview with Brian Moore (Malibu, Calif., 3 January 1992); Robert Sullivan, *A Matter of Faith*: *The Fiction of Brian Moore* (Westport, Conn., 1996); Denis Sampson, *Brian Moore: The Chameleon Novelist* (Toronto, 1998).

VI. FILMOGRAPHY. *The Luck of Ginger Coffey,* directed by Irvin Kershner, screenplay by Brian Moore (1964); *Torn Curtain,* directed by Alfred Hitchcock, screenplay by Brian Moore (1966); *Catholics* (a.k.a. *The Conflict*), directed by Jack Gold, screenplay by Brian Moore (1973); *Le Sang des autres,* directed by Claude Chabrol, screenplay by Brian Moore (1984); *The Lonely Passion of Brian Moore,* documentary, directed by Alan Handel, written by Brian Moore (1986); *The Lonely Passion of Judith Hearne,* directed by Jack Clayton, screenplay by Peter Nelson (1987); *Black Robe,* directed by Bruce Beresford, screenplay by Brian Moore (1991); *Cold Heaven,* directed by Nicolas Roeg, screenplay by Allan Scott (1991).

EDWIN MORGAN

(1920–)

Chris Jones

EDWIN MORGAN HAS been one of the most prolific poets working in Britain since the end of World War II. His *Collected Poems* (1990), a selective collection of his poetry up to that time, runs to some six hundred pages. By 2002 he had published five additional volumes containing new poetry, and this is to say nothing of his prodigious activities as a dramatist, translator, essayist, and editor.

Quantity is no guarantor of quality, of course, but Morgan's work has not been short of admirers. His work is popular with both critics and nonspecialist readers. In 1982 Robin Hamilton wrote that "Edwin Morgan now seems to many to be the most exciting and adventurous writer at present working in Scotland" (p. 9), a view shared by many critics and academics. Morgan's poems are often studied in British schools, ensuring for them a wide audience. As the corpus of his work has grown, Morgan has steadily accumulated official accolades, honors, and prizes. Among these are the OBE (officer of the Order of the British Empire), which Morgan received in 1982, thirty years after his first poetry publications. In 1997 he was awarded the Order of Merit of the Republic of Hungary for his services to Hungarian literature as a translator. After the death of Ted Hughes in October 1998 there was much speculation in the press about whether the post of poet laureate might be offered to Edwin Morgan, but as a gay man, and as a supporter of Scottish political independence with known Republican sympathies, Morgan was considered too radical and controversial; the post was offered instead to Andrew Motion. The people of Glasgow, Morgan's hometown, responded by creating the poet laureateship of Glasgow, and on National Poetry Day (4 October) 1999, Morgan became its first incumbent. This was followed in April 2000 with Morgan being awarded the Queen's Gold Medal for Poetry, perhaps as a consolation for not getting the official laureateship. Since then Morgan has been made a Fellow of the Royal Scottish Academy of Music and Drama and in 2001 was awarded the Weidenfeld Translation Prize for his version of Racine's *Phaedra* (2000).

Both in terms of its formal resourcefulness and its subject matter, Morgan's poetry has great range. *From Glasgow to Saturn,* the title of his 1973 volume, effectively proclaims the ambitious reach of his oeuvre. Morgan is, by turns, a local poet celebrating his hometown and its inhabitants; a national poet writing with a confidence about his country that earlier Scottish poets could not so easily take for granted; an internationalist who appropriates from other cultures and literatures; and a futurist who incorporates into his poetry the language of space-age technology and the fantasies of science fiction. Morgan has written love poetry, poetry about the urban dispossessed, nature poetry, war poetry, and poetry both about space travel and about the journey of a sperm toward the egg it is to fertilize. He has written in English and, occasionally, in Scots, the literary medium of the great eighteenth-century Scottish poet Robert Burns. Formally, Morgan's poetry encompasses the sonnet sequence, heroic couplets, the dramatic monologue, and free verse, as well as more experimental verse such as concrete poetry and what he has termed "emergent" poems. This range can seem bewildering, but Morgan's pluralism is a major part of his attraction, for whatever one's tastes there is likely to be a Morgan poem to suit. Morgan is championed both by advocators of what might be termed the poetic mainstream in Britain (the more conservative traditional end of the poetry establishment, supported by government arts councils and major publishing houses) and by those associated with an avant-garde poetic counterculture (typified by an antiestablishment experimentalism and promulgated mainly by independent small presses). So in 1994 we find Morgan being interviewed with respect and admiration in *Angel Exhaust,* a subversive journal dedicated to radical postmodernist writing, and three years later he receives the same treatment in *Dark Horse,* a magazine committed to "the New Formalism" and the revival of traditional form and meter. Such an embracing of normally mutually antagonistic positions is rare among contemporary British poets.

Despite this wide acceptance and admiration, criticisms have been raised against his work. He has been accused of being too curious about the intricacies of the everyday. Morgan would freely admit this; his 1978 work for radio, "The Demolishers" (in *Collected Poems*), propounds that "Whatever men do is interesting. / The interest is in the detail." Yet Morgan's detractors might argue that such interest in detail comes at the expense of intellectual depth, that Morgan's poetry lacks the note of basso profundo. Likewise, some readers find Morgan's more playfully inventive poems simply whimsical; not so much experimental as mere experiments. It is significant that fans of Morgan often enjoy certain kinds of his poetry (the sonnets, for instance, or perhaps the concrete poems) far more than others. Some prefer poems that support a specific point of view rather than accepting the whole oeuvre on its own terms. In his poetry Morgan has set himself a task that can be formulated into a simple question: Is it possible to write poetry which is both formally and linguistically challenging and, at the same time, popular? To engage with the problems Morgan's work raises in this respect is to engage with one of the most pressing unresolved issues left to contemporary British poets by the early-twentieth-century modernists.

LIFE

Morgan was born on 27 April 1920 in the West End of Glasgow, Scotland, the son of Stanley Lawrence Morgan and Margaret Mckillop Arnott Morgan. Growing up in nearby Pollokshields and Rutherglen, he was moved by the poverty he saw in his native city, and by the sporadic violence its inhabitants endured and perpetrated on each other. Glasgow became both the setting and the subject of many of his most famous poems, such as "In the Snack-bar," "Glasgow Green," and "King Billy" (all included in his 1968 collection *The Second Life*). Morgan's father was a clerk in a company of iron and steel merchants, and he succeeded in inculcating in his son an almost Victorian passion for industrial machinery. Morgan has recalled how family summer outings on the steamers of the River Clyde would result in his being dragged to the engine room by his father, who would then explain in detail the workings of the boat and how it powered itself across the water. Morgan remarked in 1983 that before his father's lesson, "the engines would have only a sort of hypnotic functional beauty," but that subsequently "the whole industrial process remained human, despite all its problems, and I was never able to become a Luddite" (quoted in Crawford and Whyte, pp. 1–2).

For small boys growing up in the industrial heartland of Britain before World War II, this kind of experience was not uncommon. W. H. Auden (with whom Morgan shares a number of poetic interests and qualities) described how the romance of gasworks and mine shafts cast a similar spell over him as a young boy. One can see how this might be; the heavy industries of areas like Clydeside were renowned around the globe, and until their postwar collapse Britain was an economic superpower. Industrial technology was associated with the ideal of progress; environmental dangers were poorly understood. However "unpoetic" it might seem, and however much it challenges the clichéd stereotypical view of what poetry reflects (which would, in itself, please Morgan), this fascination with technology, machinery, and scientific endeavor has permeated Morgan's mature work. One is far more likely to find a poem by Morgan about Britain's greatest builder of suspension bridges ("Construction for I. K. Brunel," in *The Second Life*), about space travel to escape the destruction of the Earth ("In Sobieski's Shield," in *The Second Life*), or about high-tech learning ("The Pleasures of a Technological University," in *From Glasgow to Saturn*), than about a host of golden daffodils or similar scene of natural beauty. With respect to subject matter, at least, Morgan might be termed anti-romantic, although his relationship with poetic tradition will require more serious consideration, and be returned to at the end of this essay. What must be noted here is that boyhood enthusiasms anticipate the concerns of his later poetry, just as a certain boyish, restless energy animates them.

At seventeen, Morgan went to Glasgow University to study English literature, although he also took courses in several other subjects, including French and Russian. At university he widened his already omnivorous reading habits and was introduced to modern poetry in English and other European literatures. However, in 1940, with the war in Europe intensifying, Morgan was called up for military service before his studies were complete. To his parents' alarm, Morgan first registered as a conscientious objector. While waiting for the tribunal which would consider his case as an official "conchie" (in contrast to World War I, genuine conscientious objectors were not forced to fight during World War II), Morgan came to believe that the forces of fascism must be resisted and consequently changed his stance. Due to his strong commitment to pacifism, he requested that he might serve in the Royal Army Medical Corps instead of as a frontline combatant. This was granted and as a result he spent the rest of the war in the Middle East with the Forty-second General Hospital. Morgan saw service in Palestine, Lebanon, and Egypt, and he witnessed the human cost of the German general Erwin Rommel's nearly decisive offensive on Alexandria in 1942.

In many ways the war shattered Morgan's optimism and youthful faith in progress. His early poetry is often dark and fearful; it is not until the 1960s that his work recovers from the trauma of the late 1930s and the 1940s and becomes imbued with the exuberance that his boyhood promised; the title of his 1968 collection, *The Second Life,* refers to this sense of a new, belated beginning. All of which is not to say that his early poetry is primarily concerned with the war, although one can detect its shadow occasionally. Morgan

almost deliberately avoided writing about his experiences in the desert until 1977 and his volume *The New Divan*. Here he finally recorded how "I dreaded stretcher-bearing, / my fingers would slip on the two sweat-soaked handles" and how he could not forget "the easiest trip of all," carrying a dead officer who, drained of blood from an amputated leg, was "light as a child" (no. 99). The fact that he twice faced up to his responsibilities (first in the desert and then in his writing) surely argues against the view that there is no solemnity to Morgan.

After the war, Morgan returned to his studies and graduated with a first-class honors degree in 1947. Subsequently, the department of English at Glasgow University offered him a lectureship, a post which he accepted and remained in until his retirement in 1980.

In considering the relationship between Morgan's life and his work, one must also discuss his sexuality. In 1990 Morgan used his seventieth birthday as the occasion to come out publicly as a gay writer. For those who had read Morgan's poetry carefully, this was no surprise; *The New Divan* describes how the speaker's lover would come to him furtively by night, "till you were posted far off. / I was innocent enough / to think the posting was accidental" (no. 98). Homosexuality, although forbidden by British military law, was not punished by court-martial during the war, for fear of the effect on both civilian and service morale. Rather, if discovered, one of the "offending" parties was discreetly posted away; the message in the poem is clear for anyone who is willing to hear it. What Morgan's birthday revelation may reenact quite nicely for the more naive reader is the same ironical gap between the young, innocent soldier and the older, more knowledgeable poet: the same sense of revisiting earlier incidents (here poems rather than life events) with a new sense of understanding or revelation. This is in fact the declared reason for Morgan's coming out; to "record the truthful emotional basis of the poetry" (as quoted in Walker, p. 302). Given this motivation, one might understandably ask why it took Morgan as long as it did to publicly confirm his position as a gay poet. The truth is that postwar Britain was an extremely homophobic society. Alan Turing, the mathematician who cracked the German Enigma code and was therefore the Briton who individually did most to aid the Allied war effort, was removed from his university post after being entrapped into revealing his sexuality to the police; he subsequently committed suicide in 1954. (Morgan gives Turing a place in heaven in his poem "Section 28," in the 2002 collection *Cathures*.) Morgan might rightly have feared for his own post and his position in society for much of his working life, although by 1988 he had the confidence to proudly declare in the title of a poem from the collection *Themes on a Variation,* "'Dear man, my love goes out in waves.'"

EARLY WORK

The year 1952 was a significant one for Morgan. It saw the publication of his first book of poems, *The Vision of Cathkin Braes,* as well as the publication of his verse translation of *Beowulf,* his important essay "Dunbar and the Language of Poetry," and the completion of the manuscript "Dies Irae" (for which he could not find a publisher, but which he later included at the start of his *Collected Poems*). These works are interesting to the student of Morgan, for they anticipate a number of his preoccupations and attributes as a mature poet, not least his prolific output.

In the prefatory note to the *Collected Poems,* Morgan writes of the collection "Dies Irae" that "it was intended as a complementary volume to *The Vision of Cathkin Braes*—rather like the tragic and comic masks of drama" (p. 15). Some critics have found "Dies Irae" mannered and overblown in style. It is true that several of the poems display a torturous, ambiguous syntax. This is due, in part, to the influence of the Welsh poet Dylan Thomas and the extravagant excess of the writers of "the Apocalypse," a loose grouping of poets popular in the 1940s but not much read or admired now. Yet the apocalyptic bombast is, in this case, not gratuitous or superfluous, for Morgan's subject is Judgment Day, when Christ will come again to Earth to judge the living and the dead at the end of the world (the Latin title means "Day of Anger" and is a moniker for Judg-

ment Day). The title poem itself forms a powerful opening to the poet's oeuvre, imagining the anger of God, directed toward the individual mortal soul, as a terrible maelstrom unleashed on a helpless, solitary sailor, and is therefore a reworking of the traditional, medieval allegory of the journey of the soul toward heaven being like that of a ship toward safe haven. It is written in blank verse (unrhymed lines of iambic pentameter, although Morgan uses the line with a degree of flexibility), heavily patterned with alliteration and assonance; the effect achieved is curiously somewhere between that of Milton and Anglo-Saxon verse. (Sometimes called Old English, Anglo-Saxon is the earliest form of the English language and formed a substantial part of Morgan's studies as a student at Glasgow University.)

The Anglo-Saxon note is sounded more fully elsewhere in the collection, for it contains translations of a number of relevant poems from the Anglo-Saxon canon. "The Seafarer" and "The Wanderer" both develop the same allegory of the Christian soul as trouble-beset navigator which Morgan had reworked for the title poem "Dies Irae," and, together with "The Ruin," a poem which describes the weather-crumbled remains of buildings of a once-great civilization (often taken to be the ruins of the Roman city of Bath), these poems represent the Anglo-Saxon genre of the heroic elegy. All three poems lament the passing of the material trappings of former ages, and some Anglo-Saxon scholars have seen them as an expression of millennialism (they are often dated to the tenth century A.D.), the fear that the end of the world, and God's subsequent judgment, might be approaching as the year 1000 loomed. Certainly "The Wanderer" contains a passage which is commonly accepted to present an image of the apocalypse and which Morgan translates as follows:

The wise man perceives how terrible is the time
When all the wealth of the world lies waste,
As now scattered throughout this earth
Walls are standing where winds howl round
And hoarfrost hangs, in crumbling courts.
Wine-halls are sinking, kings are at rest

Bereft of joy, all the flower of men
Has fallen by those walls. . . .

Since Anglo-Saxon has no future tense, its present tense may be translated to give either a future or a present meaning. Morgan has here chosen the present to make the imagined scene more immediate; the "double updating" of passages, like this one, dating from the earliest part of the English tradition, brings the ancient past into conjunction with the contemporary, and past, present, and future cease to have their normal values, as would be the case on Judgment Day. The collection ends with a modernization of an Early Middle English poem, "The Grave," which tells the reader, "your dwelling was doomed before you were born." Etymologically, "doom" means "judgment"; the last repose of our mortal remains has been decided by God's judgment from the beginning of time. The relationship of these terms underscores the collection's cohesive unity.

The comic companion volume to "Dies Irae," *The Vision of Cathkin Braes,* seems, in some ways, less well-knit a collection, despite having been more successful in finding a publisher. It too makes use of medieval tradition; its title piece is reminiscent of medieval dream vision and it introduces a procession of farcical comic dancers, including Mary, queen of Scots, Salome, and William Wordsworth, seeming to take as its model "Dance in the Quenis Chalmer" by the Scottish medieval poet William Dunbar. The collection also includes "Ingram Lake, or, Five Acts on the House," a satirical, semidramatic poem, each act of which is supposed to have been written by (and as a part parody of) a different, thinly disguised contemporary dramatist, whose number includes "William Tennissippi" (Tennessee Williams) and "Soûl-Jeûn Parterre" (John-Paul Sartre). "Verses for a Christmas Card" arrests the reader's attention with its Edward Lear– or Lewis Carroll–like use of seeming nonsense words, but it is hard to detect a thematic unity to these poems. Closing the collection is "A Song of the Petrel," a translation from the Russian of Maksim Gorky, in which the tenacious seabird is depicted enduring a terrible storm, referring the reader back to the opening of "Dies Irae."

Together the two collections certainly seem richer than if taken independently and while it is perhaps overstating the case to suggest that they form a poetic diptych, nevertheless it is hard to see what early readers made of *The Vision of Cathkin Braes* without being able to compare it to "Dies Irae."

Morgan's translation of *Beowulf,* published in 1952 but completed during the 1940s, shows that his commitment to Anglo-Saxon poetry during this period of his career was far from cursory; the earliest English epic is over three thousand lines long and Morgan's translation, reprinted in 2002 for its fiftieth anniversary, is thought by some scholars of the subject to be the best attempt yet made to render the poem into modern English. An important introductory essay sketches out the scope of the problem faced by a translator of a poem such as *Beowulf,* with all its shifts in pitch, intensity, and focus, and of the need "to collaborate with the greatness of the original when it is great, and to allow it to speak with varied voices" (p. xxxiv). Translation is itself a creative act, but one that more explicitly demands that the ego of the artist be subsumed by the demands imposed by the original work. Translating *Beowulf* enabled Morgan to dramatize and ventriloquize voices other (quite radically "other") than his own. Morgan's introduction also carefully traces the gradual reintroduction of something like the "native" Anglo-Saxon line (based on accent rather than syllable count) into English poetry during the first half of the twentieth century (giving examples from T. S. Eliot and Auden) and relates this to the need to find more flexible rhythmical patterns, closer to those of spoken language, positioning the essay in the same tradition as William Wordsworth's preface to the *Lyrical Ballads.* Morgan's *Beowulf* is, then, a craftsman's apprenticeship, but it is much more than this. Morgan has spoken about how the translation was his unwritten war poem, and this assertion must be borne in mind as a qualification to the often expressed view that Morgan did not write about his war experiences until 1977 in *The New Divan.* That this ancient heroic epic, dealing with bloody, internecine tribal conflict, monstrous attacks on civilian communities, and the responsibilities of a strong leader toward his people, resonated with a young poet who had recently served during World War II should not surprise any who knows the poem well. Even Morgan's 1952 introduction more or less spells the point out: "Grendel is a superstitious embodiment of danger among peoples whose struggling civilization and amenity are only a stockade in a hostile . . . environment" (p. xxxv). The concerns of a writer and the anxieties of an age can find expression in oblique ways, refracted unexpectedly through material other than that of the author's own, original devising. These lessons were important to Morgan's development as a mature poet writing with a strong sense of social commitment.

Morgan's 1952 essay on William Dunbar was first published in the scholarly journal *Essays in Criticism* and reprinted in Morgan's collection *Crossing the Border: Essays on Scottish Literature* (1990). Dunbar was a poet in the fifteenth-century Scottish court whose work is characterized by its variety of attempted subject matter and a correspondingly large repertoire of formal techniques. Morgan clearly admires Dunbar's range as well as his energy, arguing that Dunbar's verbal copiousness is shaped and restrained by his formal control and that Dunbar represents a kind of poetic "middle way," negotiating the twin dangers of expressing energy without the discipline of order (Morgan's example of this kind of poet is Walt Whitman) and writing with empty formal perfection (as exemplified, according to Morgan, by Robert Bridges's sonnet-sequence *The Growth of Love*). Instead, Morgan thinks that for Dunbar energy is felt as order. It is often the case that when poets write critical prose on other poets' work, they either write deliberately about their own poetry, but by subterfuge, or unconsciously reveal more about their own poetic preoccupations than about those of the ostensible subject (Eliot's criticism is the classic example of this phenomenon). Attracted by the qualities of Dunbar which he praises in this essay, Morgan clearly wishes to emulate them himself. This essay sees him claiming one of the most significant poets of a burgeoning, independent Scottish literary culture as his poetic forefather, and one

whose example he intends to follow; variety and ordered energy do come to be defining characteristics of Morgan's body of work.

Other insights into Morgan's poetic character are to be found in this essay. "Display of poetic energy" is valued over what Morgan calls the "distillation of poetic situation, in personal emotional encounters" (p. 46). This sublimation of the artist's personal concerns to the greater requirements of the art form reminds us of Morgan's discipleship to the *Beowulf* poet and illustrates the degree to which his aims and achievements, his theoretical and practical poetics, are both consistent and, to a considerable extent, worked out, even at this early juncture. Significantly, the criticisms which can be made of Dunbar's work—that it is not sincere, that it is not serious enough—are sometimes leveled against Morgan, but Morgan's articulated awareness of Dunbar's limitations in this essay is also a measure of his self-awareness of these potential dangers.

These four 1952 works, then, laid down markers for the territory which Morgan's work would more substantially occupy later in his career. As Morgan's prefatory note in the *Collected Poems* indicates, "Dies Irae" and *The Vision of Cathkin Braes* established his intention to sound both tragic and comic notes in his poetry, treat themes with high seriousness and playfulness, record the savagery of the universe as well as its farce. So it is no surprise to find the *Instamatic Poems* of 1972 directly confronting the violence of two youths pushing a young couple into a plate-glass shop window in Glasgow in order to loot the shop ("Glasgow 5 March 1971"), or of a woman in a cemetery being knifed by a bored youth while she tends her mother's grave ("Glasgow October 1971"). The power of apocalypse that is asserted in the collection "Dies Irae" is given a more explicitly postnuclear expression in "Computer Error: Neutron Strike" (in the 1984 collection *Sonnets from Scotland*), in which the destruction of Aberdeen, Scotland, is imagined. But the near-nonsense of "Verses for a Christmas Card" anticipates Morgan's experiments with sound poetry, a form in which the phonemic qualities of language take precedence, and which Morgan often exploits for comic effect. So, in "The Loch

Ness Monster's Song" (in *From Glasgow to Saturn* [1973]), a language is invented for the monster to speak, a language partly imitative of aquatic noises, but which remains amusingly impenetrable, as is true of the legend of the monster. Moreover, "Five Poems on Film Directors," from *The New Divan* (1977), resurrects the method and structure of "Ingram Lake," with a similar dose of healthy cheek. "The Mummy" (first published in *Collected Poems,* under the heading "Uncollected Poems 1976–1981"), in which the embalmed Rameses II is sedated to prevent him from breaking his own stitches while trying to seduce his Parisian curator, displays the same taste for high farce as "The Vision of Cathkin Braes," which engineers an intimate dance between Salome and the sixteenth-century Scottish religious reformer John Knox.

Taking the four important 1952 writings together, we see the foundation of Morgan's career as a translator laid; the pedigree for his technical profuseness established; the tendency to self-abasement in service of the poem anticipated; the ability to dramatize voices other than his own practiced; the method of plundering the past in order to contemporize it developed; the integration of Scottish figures and traditions with universal themes and materials explored: in short, we see the mature Morgan in an embryonic state.

MORGAN'S SECOND LIFE

We first become aware of the full range of Morgan's mature gifts in the watershed collection *The Second Life,* published in 1968. The 1960s were liberating years for Morgan, as they were for many Britons. Memories of wartime suffering had receded enough to permit a sense of optimism about the future, to which Morgan's true, underlying character could once again respond without shame or disguise. This sense of liberation developed a personal dimension in 1963 when Morgan met John Scott, with whom he was romantically involved until Scott's death in 1978. Although their relationship was not a public one (they never lived together), privately Morgan felt a happiness and self-confidence which, on the

evidence of his earlier poetry, was formerly lacking.

During the 1960s, British society as a whole was experiencing a vibrant renaissance of brash, confident popular culture against which background many of Morgan's experimental poems of the period are best read. *Newspoems* (written between 1965 and 1971, but not published as a collection until 1987) are "found poems" constructed out of the headline typeface of contemporary newspapers and magazines, with Morgan editing and cutting and pasting to reveal "hidden messages" in the ephemera of a superabundant, but disposable, daily media. So in block capital letters the 1966 "Notice in Hell" commands "HALT," and, on a new line and displaying an un-inked horizontal crack through the newspaper type, it continues "COMMIT ADULTERY," while in its counterpart poem, "Notice in Heaven," the descending and indented typography informs the reader that "You can / SING / here." This technique of finding and revealing unexpected meanings in pregiven material is also central to Morgan's 1967 collection *Emergent Poems,* in which lines from other texts are broken up into their separate letter-forms, which are in turn scattered down the page, in apparently random patterns (although carefully contrived to generate words and phrases which contribute to the poem's effect) before coming to rest in the final line, the complete original sentence. For example, "Manifesto" takes the last line from Karl Marx's *The Communist Manifesto* in Russian (which is usually translated as "workers of the world unite!") and finds in it English words such as "rise," "stand," "learn," "protest," and "print," and eventually the sentence "proletarians in every land are one," although these words are fractured into sublexical units by white space and take some time to discern. The visual effect of these "emergent" poems is of gazing at the frenzied motion of atomic or molecular particles colliding and rebounding across the page, making fortuitous "chance" associations before stabilizing in form into the final sentence (although the extent to which significant structures are produced by chance, or are inevitable, is something that these poems ask of both linguistics and particle physics).

Such verbal games and methods of composition may seem throwaway, but this was the era in which the Beatles were demonstrating that pop music, conventionally assumed to be disposable aural wallpaper, could have lasting artistic qualities on its own. Also around this time, Andy Warhol was making pop art out of whatever commercially produced images came to hand. Morgan's unconventional work from this period at least deserves to be judged as belonging to part of a new cultural phenomenon. What is perhaps most remarkable about these poems is that they are not the work of a young, rebellious artist trying to overthrow the conventions of his elders, but the result of enthusiastic engagement by a university don in his late forties with the emergent counterculture of a much younger generation, a generation with whom he shared a sense of rebelliousness and radicalism.

Whatever value one places on these experimental poems, which were published during the 1960s only in small print runs by independent presses, in *The Second Life* these modes are deployed alongside more traditional forms and pieces with a more direct emotional appeal. The title of the collection is one of Morgan's favorite phrases; it occurs in "In Sobieski's Shield" and was later used in "Instructions to an Actor" (in "Uncollected Poems 1976–1981," in *Collected Poems*), a monologue spoken by Shakespeare to the boy in his company who is to play Hermione in *A Winter's Tale,* instructing him to show forgiveness, described as being "like a second life." It resurfaced in "Junkie," a poem from the 2002 collection *Cathures.* For the poet, who was forty-seven at the publication of his first major book and who had felt at thirty that "life had passed me by" ("Epilogue: Seven Decades," in *Collected Poems*), the significance of the title phrase is obvious, but the sense of celebration of new life after death is also embodied in many of the poems throughout the collection.

Opening the volume are three poems each dealing with the tragic death of an iconic figure of the twentieth century; the American writer Ernest Hemingway, the American actress Marilyn Monroe, and the French chanteuse Edith Piaf. Taking a Hemingway title as its own, the first poem, "The Old Man and the Sea," conflates Hemingway with the character in his story, and describes the sea captain shooting himself to avoid being engulfed by an encroaching white mist, just as Hemingway notoriously committed suicide to avoid being overtaken by the effects of old age. The Hemingway/sea captain character therefore deprives himself of the kind of second life which Morgan is currently enjoying, but the poet makes little intervention in this scene, merely noting that it raises questions but few answers. As Morgan had earlier learned to imitate the style of other writers with his adaptations and translations of medieval poetry, so he here mimics Hemingway's voice, using an additive, nonhierarchical syntax in which straightforward clauses are loosely linked to each other by commas, or the most basic conjunctions of all, "and" (frequently) and "but" (once). Consequently, the movement of the verse drifts steadily onward, enacting the expansive travel of the mist at the syntactic level. Like the end of "The Old Man and the Sea," the use of "And" as the first word of the first poem in the collection also raises questions without answers. What is it that comes before "And"? The "first life," perhaps? Hemingway's first life is scarcely alluded to in the poem, and Morgan's, too, is obscured to the reader. There may be a sense in which Hemingway's suicide is used here as a ritualized obliteration of the youthful Morgan, which the poet no longer wishes to carry within himself into his second life. In any case, more destroyed first lives are yet to raise more unanswered questions in this collection.

"The Death of Marilyn Monroe" is written in clear imitation of Allen Ginsberg, with its long, runover line full of rhetorical questions, exclamations, use of "America" as an addressee, and anaphoric repetitions. Monroe becomes the symbolic victim of the Los Angeles cult of celebrity and the poem finishes by asking Los Angeles whether it will be followed around now by Monroe's hearse. This question, of course, also finds no answer and the poem leaves us wondering about the opportunities and perhaps even freedoms that a second life might have held for Monroe. But, unlike Hemingway, Monroe could exercise no decision-making power over whether or not she would participate in, or withdraw from, those potentialities.

"Je ne regrette rien" differs from its two companion poems in that its subject, Piaf, is given her own voice. This simple technical fact prevents her from remaining the victim that Monroe does, or the enigma that Hemingway becomes, in the previous poems. Baldly the singer recounts the sufferings she has endured: blindness, prostitution, teenage motherhood, the loss of her child to starvation, the surgery she has undergone, the lovers who have been and gone. Yet the speaker is defiant, proud, unsubdued. She regrets nothing. At forty-five she is able to begin a new love affair with undiminished passion and enthusiasm; her past is no inhibition to her ability to live in the present, for, in a line that might be a motto for Morgan, she states, "I don't keep the past in my pocket." The ability to change, and to accept change, and not to wish in vain for beauty to endure unchanged, is something Morgan greatly admires. In "The Domes of Saint Sophia" the speaker ultimately rejects the as-yet-still-preserved sites of St. Sophia, St. Paul's, and the Taj Mahal for monuments of civilizations that have already fallen into disrepair or ruin. The beauty of the former is admitted, but theirs is a beauty only for the eye, "and they give no grip / to the searching mind / in its trouble." In effect, a ruined building acknowledges that it belongs to the real world of change and mutability, and this pleases the poet who prefaced his 1974 collection of essays with the declaration, "CHANGE RULES is the supreme graffito." The poem is an explicit clarification of what had earlier attracted Morgan to the Anglo-Saxon poem "The Ruin"; a kind of imaginative free space is opened up by the ruin, a capacity for awe and wonder which the building in its "perfect" form does not permit. At the time that Morgan was writing *The Second Life,* extensive construction programs started to be carried out in Glasgow. Old tenements were demolished so that modern housing could be put up, a process alluded to in "To Joan Eardley" and "The Second Life." Far from being critical of the rapid refashioning of his city, Morgan thoroughly approved of it, as his 1978 piece "The Demolishers" makes clear. Glasgow itself is plainly one of the targets of the title of this collection.

One of the most powerful examples in the collection of a transforming change being wrought during the passage into a second life is found in "Message Clear." Formally this is one of Morgan's "emergent" poems; indeed, it is the most famous of the emergent poems, although it was not published in the volume of that name. Its final bedrock line at the base of the page reads "i am the resurrection and the life." The message then, is that of the Gospels and the speaker is Christ. But, as is typical of an emergent poem, the message is far from clear to begin with, making an irony of the title. What we see, or perhaps hear, are snatches of Christ's message, coming to us gradually. Alerted by the title to the importance of this text as a message, we are conditioned to receive, to concentrate on picking up the fragments of, the signals that are being broadcast. It is as if Christ's voice is trying to reach us from the spirit world, but the material world is disturbing its transmission. The message slowly grows clearer as phonemes form words, words form phrases, and eventually the coherent sentence is formed. This might be intended to mime several similar processes, perhaps Christ's own body becoming steadily more corporeal as he appears before the disciples after his resurrection, or the growth of the disciples' faith in his physical embodiment after death (Thomas of course doubts the corporality of Christ at first sight), or even our own ability to open ourselves to the possibility of hearing Christ's message (making Thomases of us all). To enjoy the opportunities of a second life one has to be aware that one has been offered a second life.

Several other poems in this collection remain among Morgan's best loved and most widely read, but the scope of this introductory essay necessitates that Morgan's whole body of mature work be considered, however briefly. To that end the remainder of the essay will move from a straightforward chronological account of Morgan's publications to a brief treatment of four key areas of Morgan's poetic practice, drawing examples from the breadth of his corpus in an attempt to sketch out something like the full range of the work.

MORGAN AS CONCRETE POET

Concrete poetry was an international avant-gardist movement which developed in the 1950s and 1960s, in part fueled by structuralist and poststructuralist linguistic theory, which teaches that linguistic signs are arbitrary and connected to their referents only by convention. In a sense, concrete poetry sets itself the goal of closing that gap between the sign and its referent, of reinvesting the sign with some of the actual properties of its referent in order to make language seem more than arbitrary. It attempts to make the physical manifestation of the poem (the typography and spatial arrangement of the letter forms on the page) carry the meaning—for the poem to be the object of its own attention rather than to signify an absent external reality. As concrete poems are often sparing in their use of language and present themselves as almost pictorial minimalist images, the movement can also be seen as a reaction against the trivial and even meaningless language used in advertising slogans, posters, and jingles as part of the marketing campaigns of a consumerist society. Concrete poetry responds with precise essentialism in language. "Silencio" by the Swiss poet Eugen Gomringer is a good example of this; the repeated word "silencio" completely fills the boundaries of the poem in a closely printed block, apart from one gap of white in the dense typescript, the exact size of a missing "silencio." This of course enacts the silence of the poem's title far more effectively than any word can, although it needs the noise of surrounding language to make its point.

During the 1950s Morgan became a regular correspondent of Augusto and Haroldo de Campos, two Brazilian brothers who were leading exponents of the style. Morgan soon started making his own concrete poems, and together with Ian Hamilton Finlay, another Scottish poet working within these new conventions and helping to define them, Morgan founded and coedited a short-lived but influential 1960s journal, *POOR.*

OLD. TIRED. HORSE. This publication aimed to introduce concrete poetry and other forms of innovative writing (especially American Black Mountain school poets) into Britain. That Scottish concrete poetry has earned international respect as well as an audience at home, while the equally vibrant English branch of the movement has languished largely unnoticed in the critical doldrums, is largely due to Morgan's continued efforts to popularize and explicate; the teacher in Morgan helped create a taste for this new and potentially challenging form of poetry.

Although Morgan has not produced any concrete poems since *Themes on a Variation* (1988), they form a major constituent of his oeuvre. "Siesta of a Hungarian Snake" (in *The Second Life*), reprinted in its entirety below, is one of his most well-known concrete poems; note how the snake's shape is suggested by the use of upper- and lower-case type. The phonemic combinations "sz" and "zs" are common in the Hungarian language, as well as being onomatopoeic in this context:

s sz sz SZ sz SZ sz ZS zs ZS zs zs z

Another good example of Morgan working in this genre would be "The Chaffinch Map of Scotland" (also in *The Second Life*), which lays the several Scottish dialect words for "chaffinch" on the page to make a pictorial representation of Scotland, each word positioned according to the location where it is used; the result is a diagrammatic dialect map in which the chaffinch sings itself into existence by a performative act of self-naming. Readers wishing to explore how Morgan constructs linked sequences from such experimentation should refer to his 1970 collection *The Horseman's Word.*

MORGAN AS SONNETEER

Despite his penchant for the new and the innovative, Morgan is equally at home with the most traditional and enduring of European forms, the sonnet. Nevertheless, it would be naive to imagine that the form does not undergo some transformation at Morgan's hands. Since Petrarch (several of whose sonnets Morgan has himself transformed into English), the sonnet has primarily been a vehicle for the expression of love. Morgan's contribution to the form's history has been to make it a medium for history, real and imagined. His 1984 sequence *Sonnets from Scotland* tells the narrative of his homeland from its primeval formation, in "Slate" and "Carboniferous," into its future and a time when tectonic drift has made it an island and carried it into the mid-Atlantic ("Outward Bound"), before it is eventually found "On Jupiter." Along the way, the inevitability of change is typically celebrated. "Theory of the Earth" delights in the Scottish geologist James Hutton's realization that even the hardest granite was once molten rock. In the sonnet, Hutton's work proves to Robert Burns that his famous affirmation of the permanence of his love, that it will last "Till a' the seas gang dry, my dear, / And the rocks melt wi' the sun," is no guarantee of love's immutability:

> They died almost
> together, poet and geologist,
> and lie in wait for hilltop buoys to ring,
> or aw the seas gang dry and Scotland's coast
> dissolve in crinkled sand and pungent mist.

Twenty-two sonnets later we see that this wait has been brought to an end and Morgan brings some of Hutton's predictions to fulfilment in "The Desert." By this point in the imagined future, "everything was sand." With ironic reference back to Burns's lyric, the speaker reflects, "They had their rough strong songs, rougher belief." The songs of a poet are no defense against the forces of time, as Morgan knows well; he even directs the irony at himself. For in between "Theory of the Earth" and "The Desert," the sonnet "North Africa" describes several Scottish poets being sent to the Middle East during the war; "Why did the poets come to the desert? / They learned the meaning of an oasis." Inserting himself into the poem, the sonneteer writes, "Morgan ate sand, slept sand at El Ballah." First the poets of Scotland visit the desert, later the desert visits the poets of Scotland. Despite learning the meaning of an oasis, their rough strong songs do not prevent the encroachment of the sands and now, in this imagined future, Morgan's

mouth is permanently filled with sand. Characteristically, Morgan is untroubled by this idea of his own transience. The penultimate poem of the sequence, "A Golden Age," simply notes:

> Perhaps it did not last. What lasts?
> The bougainvillea millenniums
> may come and go, but then in thistle days
> a strengthened seed outlives the hardest blasts.

As in the key poem of *The Second Life* dealing with Edith Piaf, all that matters is that there are no regrets. In general, Morgan prefers the Italian sonnet form of his translatee Petrarch, with its eight- and six-line division around the "turn" or *volta,* to the so-called English sonnet with its three quatrains and final couplet. The first form clearly suits Morgan's temperament. He is more interested in twisting or changing a poem's argument, turning it in a new direction, than he is in summarizing what he has already developed. The scope of the present essay prevents further consideration of Morgan's use of the sonnet sequence, but interested readers are directed toward his "Glasgow Sonnets" in *From Glasgow to Saturn.*

MORGAN AS A LOVE LYRICIST

That Morgan's often erotic love lyrics are among his most popular poems and often selected for inclusion on school syllabuses is ample demonstration of the fact that they are not exclusively gay love poems, any more than Burns's lyrics are exclusively heterosexual. Indeed, as love is a universal emotion, a love poem cannot easily be limited by the sexuality of its author. Many of Morgan's poems encourage this ease of general appropriation by deliberately eschewing the third-person, gender-specific pronouns "he" and "she", and instead resorting to "you," opening them up to both gay and straight reader. That they are almost without exception written in free verse, rather than in traditional, formal patterns, can be said to reflect the liberty and freedom from restraint which the poet feels in love.

Both *The Second Life* and *From Glasgow to Saturn* contain a deliberately orchestrated sequence of love poems at their core, and the reader will find these poems more rewarding if read in those sequences. In general the earlier sequence is joyous and optimistic, while the second series explores an unhappier, less communicative relationship. Even within the *Second Life* poems, however, there are a few indicators of the coming pain expressed in *From Glasgow to Saturn*. The speaker of "When You Go" describes how his lover fell asleep in his arms until woken by the sound of rain; "I asked if you heard the rain in your dream / and half dreaming still you only said, I love you." The scene is certainly a touching one, but the speaker's pleasure in it is not as secure as it might be. A semiconscious avowal of love could be construed as less meaningful or committed as a fully cognizant declaration, but more importantly, this memory is being articulated as a remedy for despair in the possible eventuality of the speaker's lover leaving him. That possibility is stated as a certainty in the first line of the poem ("When you go"), before being modified into a conditional in the second line ("if you go"); a modification which itself smacks of an attempt to convince the speaker as much as anyone else. The very utterance of the first line betrays a lack of confidence on the speaker's part about the longevity of the relationship. Read in this way, the distance from "When you go" to *From Glasgow to Saturn*'s "The Milk-cart," in which the speaker ruefully remarks, "it is hard / to wish for you, harder to sleep, useless to weep," does not seem so very great.

MORGAN AS TRANSLATOR

To translate a poem is, inevitably, to change it, but we have seen that change is not something Morgan shies away from. The paradox about translation is that while much is transformed, an essential core of the poem must somehow be preserved if the translation is to be judged any kind of success. For Morgan the integrity of the original poem most not be violated, but preserving that integrity can call for unusual tactics. His much-lauded 1972 collection *Wi the Haill Voice* (With the Whole Voice) is a case in point. Morgan translates twenty-five poems by the Rus-

sian futurist poet Vladimir Mayakovsky, but unexpectedly he does so into Scots. Mayakovsky was often denounced by members of the Communist Party for being elitist in his use of modernist defamiliarization tactics to make familiar subjects appear strange, but at the same time he strove toward a voice which would be accessible to the working man. Revoicing the Russian poems into Scots curiously preserves these tensions in which the original poems existed, although it does displace them somewhat. Scots is a more demotic or vernacular medium than Standard English and one traditionally used by what a communist might term "the Scottish proletariat"; to those who speak Scots these translations are linguistically direct and accessible. It is true, however, that for the majority of Morgan's readers, the Scots translations are themselves defamiliarizing and require some effort of attention to decode. A futurist horse-song, "A Richt Respeck for Cuddies," presents us with:

Bleezed in the blafferts,
wi ice-shoggly bauchles,
the street birled and stachert.
The cuddy cam clunk,
cloitit doon doup-scud,

Here, the farm-laboring Scot might find the Russian futurist speaking directly to him, but most of us probably need some help from a glossary to make out something like "Hit in the gusts / with ice-shaky old shoes / the street spun and staggered. / The horse came clunk, / fell down with a thump on its buttocks." It is the working man's voice which actually becomes the strangeness and creates the distancing effects in Morgan's translations. If we are still confused, we can console ourselves with what Morgan had to say on precisely this problem in his essay "The Translation of Poetry" for the journal *The Scottish Review*:

> It is important to remain faithful to these shocks and splashes of impact. . . . For example, long before one fully understands a difficult poem by Eugenio Montale, his world stirs and reveals itself. . . . At this stage, too, most poems yield more

unmistakable pleasure than they do at any later moment of understanding.

(quoted in Crawford and Whyte, p. 101).

Morgan's encyclopedic ambitions and his verbal copiousness, his desire to incorporate as much of the universe into his poems as possible, is amply demonstrated in his translation of the *Altus Prosator,* a sixth-century Latin poem, traditionally attributed to Saint Columba, the Irish missionary who converted the Picts to Christianity (it is included in Morgan's 1996 text *Collected Translations*). Translated by Morgan as "The Maker on High" ("maker" in Scots can also mean "poet"), the piece is a praise-poem to God and has an "abcedarian" structure; that is, it consists of twenty-three stanzas, each beginning with the correct letter of the Roman alphabet (no *j, u,* or *w*). Morgan's version starts, "Ancient exalted seed-scatterer whom time gave no progenitor," and ends, "Zabulous burns to ashes all those adversaries / who deny that the Saviour was Son to the Father." As the poem's range of reference runs from the divine creation of the universe to its destruction, this poem also includes Christ's resurrected second life, as well as a *dies irae* (the Latin phrase is used untranslated). For Morgan, as it seems for Saint Columba, to order language into a logical structuring is to reveal the structure of divine order.

Interesting effects are created when the idea of translation spills over into Morgan's original poems; the aforementioned "Loch Ness Monster's Song" demonstrates this, although "The First Men on Mercury," published in 1973 in *From Glasgow to Saturn,* is a more compelling example. The poem begins with the Earthling astronauts introducing themselves to the Mercurians in English, and asking, in time-honored science fiction tradition, to be taken to their leader. The Mercurians reply in their own language, "Bawr stretter! Bawr. Bawr. Stretterhawl?" At first there is no communication, only mutual unintelligibility; clearly there is a need for translation. As the two communities continue to talk to each other, however, that is exactly what starts to happen; translation in its etymological sense of being a "carrying across" as well as its literal sense of an interface between languages.

English loanwords start to creep into Mercurian speech and vice versa. A creole seems to develop, but by the end of the dialogue complete reversal has taken place, for the Mercurians tell the Earthlings that they must return to their planet. "Stretterworra gawl, gawl" reply the Earthlings before the Mercurians have the last word: "Of course, but nothing is ever the same, / now is it? You'll remember Mercury." A genuine cultural and linguistic exchange has taken place and each speech-community has left its indelible imprint on the other as a souvenir of that exchange. It is a comically accelerated and exaggerated model of exactly what happens when two literary cultures come into contact, as when a translator such as Morgan introduces the poems of the Russian Boris Pasternak or the Hungarian Attila József to his readers. As Earth is much larger than Mercury, the poem might also be read as a kind of political allegory of what happens when a large state like England imposes itself on a smaller state like Scotland. Morgan does not adopt the easily assumed posture of the victimized Scot; he knows that the smaller state may leave its mark on the larger just as effectively. Both parties are changed by the encounter, and this is what interests Morgan.

CONCLUSION

Morgan's range and variety is a clear challenge to the reader, although one that was laid down as long ago as 1952. How successful he is judged to be may ultimately depend on how broad-minded the reader is prepared to be in admitting the validity of all of Morgan's activities and the sincerity with which he is felt to have approached them. More fundamentally, Morgan's work raises the question of what the proper place of past literary tradition is to be in a poetry of the twentieth and twenty-first centuries, which has to compete with countless verbal messages transmitted via a variety of technological media.

Morgan is impatient with artists who do not accept the modern world as a fact and incorporate it within their work, and he is mistrustful of the idea of past tradition predetermining present writing. Yet at the same time we have seen him translating from ancient languages and incorporating writing from other texts within his own poems; his 1988 collection *Themes on a Variation* includes poems "reconstructed" from pieces by Shakespeare, Milton, Pope, Byron, and Tennyson. If Morgan is so suspicious of the past, why is he so keen to use earlier literature as a material for his avowedly contemporary poetry? The key to this paradox is the graffito "CHANGE RULES." The past may be appropriated if it is already felt as the present. There is not the same need for Morgan, as there was for Ezra Pound, to "make it new"; "it" is still in pristine condition and available to the artist in the present moment. One is reminded of Eliot's motto that all pasts are present, but for Eliot this notion was tinged with nostalgia, and one always has the sense of past literary tradition pulling Eliot's poetry back from the twentieth century, whereas in Morton there is no incongruity in reimagining the arrival of Saint Columba in Scotland in a collection titled *From Glasgow to Saturn,* which includes poems about space travelers. Saint Columba is envisioned as a kind of space voyager or discoverer; he bustles about his business with a practical energy that we would associate with the modern world:

Where's Brude? Where's man?
There's too much nature here,
eagles and deer,
but where's the mind and where's the soul?
Show me your kings, your women, the man of the
 plough.
And cry me to your cradles.
It wasn't for a fox or an eagle I set sail!

("Columba's Song")

Throughout his life, Morgan's program has been to try and synthesize the experimentalism of the early modernists with the tradition of more direct, conventional poetry. His achievement, if it may now be claimed, is that he has created an anti-elitist version of modernism, a formally challenging and complex poetry which yet can communicate with both immediacy and depth to the uninitiated. It is a modernism formally similar to the work of Ezra Pound or T. S. Eliot, but without the right-wing, reactionary politics. It is a forward-looking, rather than backward-looking

modernism (perhaps for once the term "postmodern" is appropriate here?). It is a poetry that unites public and private concerns, which will not shy away from past literary tradition but refuses to lionize that tradition or sink beneath its burden. It is as tolerant and catholic a body of poetry as one can expect to find from a single author, and in 2003, with Morgan in his eighties and struggling to fight cancer, it is also a most courageous poetry, as the sequence "Demon," the closing poem of *Cathures,* testifies:

I know you can still hear me. Before I vanish:
You must not think I'll not be watching you.
I don't come unstuck. I don't give up.
I'll read the writing on the wall. You'll see.

("The Demon at the Walls of Time")

SELECTED BIBLIOGRAPHY

I. COLLECTED WORKS. *Collected Poems* (Manchester, U.K., 1990); *Collected Translations* (Manchester, U.K., 1996).

II. POETRY. *The Vision of Cathkin Braes* (Glasgow, 1952); *Emergent Poems* (Stuttgart, 1967); *Gnomes* (Preston, U.K., 1968); *The Second Life* (Edinburgh, 1968); *The Horseman's Word* (Preston, U.K., 1970); *Glasgow Sonnets* (West Linton, U.K., 1972); *Instamatic Poems* (London, 1972); *From Glasgow to Saturn* (Cheadle, U.K., 1973); *The New Divan* (Manchester, U.K., 1977); *Sonnets from Scotland* (Glasgow: 1984); *Newspoems* (London, 1987); *Themes on a Variation* (Manchester, U.K., 1988); *Hold Hands Among the Atoms* (Glasgow, 1991); *Sweeping out the Dark* (Manchester, U.K., 1994); *Virtual and Other Realities* (Manchester, U.K., 1997); *Demon* (Glasgow, 1999); *Cathures* (Manchester, U.K., 2002).

III. OTHER WORKS. *Beowulf* (Aldington, U.K., 1952, repr. Manchester, U.K., 2002); *Wi the Haill Voice: Twenty-five Poems by Vladimir Mayakovsky, Translated into Scots* (South Hinksey, U.K., 1972); *Essays* (Cheadle, U.K., 1974); *Crossing the Border: Essays on Scottish Literature* (Manchester, U.K., 1990); *Nothing Not Giving Messages: Reflections on Work and Life,* ed. by Hamish Whyte (Edinburgh, 1990); *Jean Racine's Phaedra: A Tragedy: A New Verse Translation of Phèdre* (Manchester, U.K., 2000).

IV. INTERVIEWS. Michael Gardiner, interview with Morgan in *Angel Exhaust* 10 (spring 1994): 52–63; Gerry Cambridge, interview with Morgan in *Dark Horse* 5 (summer 1997): 34–43.

V. CRITICAL AND BIOGRAPHICAL STUDIES. Robin Hamilton, *Science and Psychodrama: The Poetry of Edwin Morgan and David Black* (Frome, U.K., 1982); Robert Crawford and Hamish Whyte, eds., *About Edwin Morgan* (Edinburgh, 1990); Marshall Walker, "Poets of the Scottish Renaissance from Hugh MacDiarmid to Edwin Morgan," in his *Scottish Literature Since 1707* (Harlow, U.K., 1996).

MARY RENAULT

(1905–1983)

Nikolai Endres

MARY RENAULT'S HISTORICAL novels—fast paced, meticulously scholarly, often critical of academia—paint a vivid picture of a world long past yet still alive: from Demosthenes to Darius, Phaedra to Phaedo, Xerxes to Xenophon. Spurred by late-nineteenth-century archaeological discoveries of the ancient world, including Heinrich Schliemann's excavations of the ruins of what is believed to be Troy and Sir Arthur Evans's momentous diggings at Crete, Renault imagines in her fiction fabulous beauties and beasts, lovers and losers. Renault's perspective as a lesbian and historian has shaped her work. A scholar in the traditionally male domain of antiquity, her books are often used in the classroom in the context of both Greek mythology and gender and gay studies.

LIFE AND LETTERS

Mary Renault was born Eileen Mary Challans in London on 4 September 1905. Her father, Frank Challans, was a physician; her mother, Clementine Mary Baxter Challans, was a traditional housewife. Her parents had a stormy marriage and led increasingly separate lives after Mary's birth. She was aware of their marital problems and would characterize her childhood as unhappy.

Her formal education began at Romford House School in London, where she soon discovered the allures of literature: the *Chanson de Roland,* François Villon, Sir Thomas Malory, Jean Froissart, Edmund Spenser, John Milton, Lord Byron, Charles Dickens, Rudyard Kipling, and other Victorians and Edwardians. After World War I she continued at Clifton Girls' School in Bristol. There she studied Latin, engaged in close friendships with other girls, and wishfully pretended to be an Indian in the Wild West. In 1925 Renault

went to St. Hugh's College in Oxford, an intellectual world that her mother considered unsuitable for women. She studied languages, mythology, philosophy, and history. The classical and medieval were held in check: "Plato was for the spirit; for adventure she still turned to knights and troubadours" (Sweetman, p. 37). Her favorite professors were J. R. R. Tolkien, author of *The Lord of the Rings* trilogy (1954–1955) and editor of the *Oxford English Dictionary,* and Gilbert Murray, a renegade classical scholar who investigated "the barbaric and tribal elements underlying Hellenic civilization, a revolutionary view at a time when the ancient world was most often depicted as classically Aryan" (Sweetman, p. 36). Renault liked to go beyond the syllabus, reading noncanonical and "taboo" works.

In 1928 she graduated with a degree in English. The obvious professional path was teaching, but Renault refused to follow a prescribed career. After holding a number of minor jobs and furthering her interest in the theater, she decided to train for a nursing career at the Radcliffe Infirmary, Oxford, not having enough money to study medicine. In 1933 she met a fellow student, Julie Mullard, who became her lifelong partner. They would negotiate "a sort of marriage that, because of its transgressive nature and the independence and bisexuality of both women, could rely on no established precedent" (Zilboorg, p. 69). While working as a nurse in a neurosurgical ward, Renault wrote her first novel, an instant bestseller; the pseudonym "Renault" was taken from Thomas Otway's Restoration drama *Venice Preserv'd.* During World War II, Renault provided medical care to soldiers and civilians alike, spent hours in shelters, and lived in London during the blitz. In 1947 she won an MGM prize, formerly awarded by the Hollywood movie studio to the authors of books that might be made into movies; the prize secured her financial independence. That same year, the British royal family undertook a trip to South Africa, celebrating the Commonwealth and putting the former colony on the map. Renault and Julie soon followed suit. They lived in Durban and eventually settled at the Cape. Like many emigrants, they escaped "the misery of austerity Britain, in the hope of finding a new life in the sun" (Sweetman, p. 117). Though they received dual passports, they never returned to England.

Soon, Renault reached a logical decision about the direction her work would take; she wanted "to compare the dilemmas of the present with those of the past, to try to sort out the universal, basic stuff of human nature from the ephemeridae, sometimes overwhelming in their momentary impact, of the particular society and environment" (quoted in Zilboorg, p. 139). Numerous shipments of books arrived in Camps Bay, an area on the beach in Cape Town, where Renault established "the best private classical library in sub-Saharan Africa" (Sweetman, p. 244). She used mostly the Loeb Editions, which contain Greek or Latin originals with facing translation. After diligent research on how Plato, Xenophon, Herodotus, Thucydides, Plutarch, Diogenes Laertius, Macrobius, Athenaeus, and others reconstructed the world of Socrates—her "patron saint"—and other classical personages, the seed of Renault's first historical novel was planted. After so much immersion, it was time to see Greece for herself. In 1954 she and Julie set out for a trip to the Mediterranean. Traveling as tourists and scholars alike, they investigated archaeological excavations, admired ancient architecture, breathed in the clear air of spring, marveled at the rugged geography, ate traditional foods, and drank deeply from Renault's new world. The itinerary included locations of the greatest significance: Piraeus, Athens, Crete, Delos, Knossos, and Marathon. Eight years later, they returned to a more commercial and prosperous Greece, adding Delphi, Corinth, and Epidaurus to their repertoire. But traveling put a physical strain on Renault, making this their last journey to region that so fed her imagination, indeed their last voyage ever. Renault never crossed the Atlantic for the United States, although she was invited for lectures.

Back in South Africa, Renault was active in the Progressive Party and in Black Sash, the women's movement at the forefront of the fight against nonwhite disfranchisement. She was elected a Fellow of the Royal Society of Literature and served as president of the South African chapter of PEN, where she came in conflict with the writer Nadine Gordimer in Johannesburg over whether standards for admitting black members should be lowered (Renault believed in a meritocracy) and over Renault's refusal—some would say failure—to address in her writing the volatile political situation of her time in favor of "escapist" classical fiction. The latter criticism Renault explicitly objected to as censorship. Nevertheless, her partner's assessment, "Mary always said her best weapon was the pen—or the typewriter" (quoted in Zilboorg, p. 173), is euphemistic at best. Renault died on 13 December 1983, aged seventy-eight. A work in progress about the Middle Ages—crusaders in twelfth-century France, the medical order of the Knights of Saint John, and their settlement on Rhodes—remained unfinished. Fittingly, Julie scattered Renault's ashes over Ceres in the Cape Mountains, a final tribute to the fruitfulness of the past.

FACT AND FICTION

Renault wrote fourteen novels, eight of which deal with classical antiquity. Her first five works of fiction, mostly out of print now, are "nurse romances" set in Great Britain and seen by many critics as her apprentice novels. *The Charioteer* (1953) can be described as an academic novel. *Purposes of Love* (1939), published as *Promise of Love* in the United States, introduces the world of the hospital. The British title recalls the nurses' prayer: "and forward Thy purposes of love" (p. 34; page references to Renault works are to the first U.S. edition of texts, unless stated otherwise). Vivian Lingard has an affair with the pathologist Mic Freeborn, who is really in love with Vivian's brother Jan. Androgynous names and references to Aristophanes' famous myth of double-sexed creatures create gender slippage. According to the myth, human beings were originally round, with four hands and legs and two faces. Because they were powerful, they attempted to overthrow the gods. For this blasphemy, the gods punished them by cutting them in two. Now each "half" is in search of his or her other half or "twin." For matters of sexuality studies, Aristophanes is tracing the fantastic origins of same-sex love, which is the search for one's other half with the consequence of three antagonistic types of sexual orientation: homosexuality (male half-male half), lesbianism (female half-female half), and heterosexuality (male half-female half, female half-male half). Aristophanes' rudimentary creatures lost their wholeness as the result of hubristic behavior toward the gods, yet if unity and wholeness are found, something wonderful happens: "the two are struck from their senses by love, by a sense of belonging to one another, and by desire, and they don't want to be separated from one another, not even for a moment" (*Symp.* 192 B.C.).

Jan is Vivian's "twin" and look-alike, but because of moral constraints he can be loved only through his female half. Such erotic sliding results in tragedy. Jan is killed in a car crash, once again split in half like Aristophanes' harmonious circle-men before the fall. This love triangle further involves absent partners and other parties, notably the senior staff physician Donald Scot-Hallard, a clear contrast to Mic, whose "growth was like that of a plant in darkness, which, unless light is given in time, soon turns to etiolation and death" (p. 305). Renault also introduces her first fictional "lesbian" (her sexuality is not explicitly stated), Colonna Kimball, who is an avid reader of cowboy stories, dresses like the epicene Lord Byron, feels at home in the intellectual aristocracy of "Bloomsbury," and enjoys Christopher Marlowe's *Edward II,* a play about the king's love for the courtier Piers Gaveston. At the same time, she refuses to be pigeonholed: "There was an inevitable attraction about people who overlapped categories and threw down walls in the mind" (p. 47). One of the hallmarks of Renault's oeuvre is that her characters defy labels.

Another anticipatory topic is the body, actually two bodies: the "dressed," anonymous, sterile, ugly, diseased body versus the "undressed," liberated, fertile body. Ironically, although nurses and doctors often save lives, emotionally they are stunted—not on the battlefield, but by the jail-like wards (all named after battlefields), soldier-like uniforms, and monotonous routine of the hospital:

> [The nurse's] apron-strings held back her shoulders, her high round collar kept up her chin, like a scold's bridle; her cap, rigidly pleated, circumscribed the movements of her head. A white stiffened belt, whose constriction she could feel whenever she tried to breathe deeply, gripped her waist. . . . [The costume's] purpose was partly that of a religious habit, a reminder of obedience and renunciation; partly, as such habits generally are, a psychic sterilizer, preventing the inconvenient consciousness of personality. In it, all gestures of expression automatically died, leaving only a few of servant-like relaxation, folding the arms, or setting them akimbo.
>
> (p. 111)

Color is injected into this drabness by visits to the countryside or the ballet; by allusions to the venerated world of the past, "the lament for Ammon and Osiris, for Lesbia's sparrow, for Lycidas and Adonais, for the flowers of the forest" (p. 129); and by making theatrical expressions of love. At Jan's burial, Mic glorifies him by evoking ancient legends: "There should have been fire for Jan; an olive-wood pyre, or a raft of pine burning on the water." The Christian tomb oppresses: "the enclosing boards, the earth's weight, the smug encumbrance of the stone" (pp. 360–361). What *are* the purposes of love, a promise, merely? Thanks to Jan's sacrificial death, Mic and Vivian make up, and at the end Mic looks ahead to a bright professional future, but their love life remains ambiguous with endless possibilities of disaster.

Kind Are Her Answers (1940) reveals Renault's fascination with superstition and medicine, prudishness and promiscuity. Christopher "Kit" Anderson, a young doctor, is married to Janet, a hypochondriac who is recovering from a miscarriage and a hysterectomy, for which she blames her husband. Janet hates all men and sex and joins an Oxford religious society, humbly called The Group, which is satirized for its stock creed, vicarious asceticism, and mock charitable zeal. After a mission trip to Africa, Janet stays on as a governess and moves in with a woman. Kit, on one of his rounds, falls in love with Christie Heath, an actress at the Brimpton Abbey and great-niece of and nurse to Miss Amy Heath, an ailing Miss Havisham in a gothic mansion named Laurel Dene, attended to by a creepy maid called Pedlow. Unlike the frigid Janet, Christie is sensual, silly. An un-British openness about sex heightens Kit and Christie's fling: *"This is insanity. . . . Her mouth was still smiling, distant and dreamlike, as he closed it with his own"* (p. 41). Christie offers her love (and body) like a "lollipop," insinuatingly: "Would you like me to be more mistress-like, darling? Would I fascinate you more if I wore teagowns and black lace vests? And diamond garters?" (p. 92). Peter Wolfe effectively describes the excesses of their affair: "She feeds him éclairs, Turkish delight, coffee creams, and coconut biscuits in her zeal to sweeten an intrigue already sultry and overly sticky" (p. 50). The staunch Christian Pedlow blackmails Kit and Christie with poison-pen letters but actually prevents Christie from a foolish marriage and thus reunites the couple, leading to the book's cliché ending: "You're never going to be unhappy any more" (p. 287). The critics were less than kind: Rosamond Lehmann wrote about *Kind Are Her Answers,* "Miss Renault is, I feel, at a dangerous cross-roads in her career. Popular she will be. It is to be hoped that nothing and no one will persuade her to pour herself out in an unstemmed flow of fiction during the next few years." (Lehmann, 1940, p. 758). *The Friendly Young Ladies* (1944), published as *The Middle Mist* in the United States, begins with the seventeen-year-old Elsie Lane unhappily coming to grips with her parents' estrangement. They do nothing but quarrel, and she is a constant bone of contention: "you're afraid even to *be* anything, you just go on one day after another, making yourself smaller, and flatter, and duller" (p. 80). To drown her misery, like Emma Bovary or Don Quixote, she seeks refuge in romantic fiction. Finally she runs away to her sister Leonora. The

boyish, butch, and bohemian "Leo," who models herself on Huck Finn and writes westerns under the nom de plume Tex O'Hara, lives with her lover Helen Vaughan in a literally fluid erotic bond on the floating houseboat *Lily Belle* on the Thames. Erin G. Carlston (1996) remarks of this setting that "boats can be taken as a symbol of the insularity and instability of the homosexual relationship; the houseboat is always in danger of sinking, for example, so the bilge has to be pumped out constantly" (p. 167). Leo is up to something special—exploring her true sexual identity. A doctor suggests to Elsie: "Don't you think, knowing your parents as you do, that perhaps the reason they don't talk about her is that they haven't a word for love?" (p. 35). A ménage à trois ensues that includes Leo, Helen, and Joe Flint, an American writer who lives on an island, far away from mediocrity but also exiled from reality. At the close, Elsie, a criminal in the eye of the law, foolishly turns herself in to the police in order to assuage the supposed grief of her parents, who have moved from Cornwall to London, which she misreads as their quest for a prodigal child.

Just how "friendly" are the characters in *The Friendly Young Ladies*? A passage from Plato's *Lysis* (included in the novel) about *philia,* the public manifestation of *eros* (erotic love or desire) as friendship, signals the conflict of the novel. A "true friend" offers the termination of all lesser affections, representing a love sought not merely in satisfaction of physical pleasures (called "the enemy"), but for its own sake. A wonderful notion, but does it work? Leo longs "to be a man with his friend, emotion-free, objective, concerned not with relationships but with work and things, sharing ideas" (p. 164), but there is no "middle mist." Peter Bracknell (whose name is a witty tribute to Lady Bracknell of *The Importance of Being Earnest*), a dashing physician/psychologist and Elsie's sweetheart if she had her way, thinks he has the solution to everything, but his smugness only emphasizes the polarity between *amicitia* and *amor* (friendship and love). He lecherously covets *all* these friendly young ladies, but not *one* in particular. The Wildean line "all men kill the thing they love" (p. 239) sums up his futile quest. The ending is unsatisfactory—Leo leaves Helen for Joe—and Renault herself, in an afterword composed forty years later, calls the story "silly." However, considering her acknowledgment that Radclyffe Hall's *The Well of Loneliness* (1928), the first lesbian novel, inspired her, the ending leaves room for a subversive reading (Leo opting for Helen): Carlston remarks that "the most [Renault] could do was gesture in the direction of conventionality, and leave the lesbian reader to imagine the improbable, but far more interesting, alternatives" (p. 175).

Return to Night (1947) derives its title from a Laurence Binyon poem: "Return, you dreams, return to night / My lover is the armed light." Hilary Mansell, a doctor, falls in love with a trauma patient, the much younger Julian Fleming. Spectacularly beautiful, he is a Greek god, "the flower of Sparta brought back from Thermopylae on a shield" (1971, p. 19). But his inordinately good looks—*too* good—are also a curse, for in his family, male beauty is associated with sexual decadence. After graduating from Oxford, Julian lives with his unsympathetic mother (the father is absent), who criticizes his predilection for theatricality. (She had married a flamboyant Canadian actor/soldier, and when she found out he was a bigamist, she mercilessly reported him to his commander.) Julian needs to rid himself of this Freudian trap of a clutching mother to fulfill Hilary spiritually and sexually and to accept her as an equal rather than a mother surrogate, mistress, or Madonna. The narrative is further complicated by Hilary's lesbian tendencies (she has a crush on her landlady, whose husband is a traveling journalist covering the war abroad); her frustration at incompetent colleagues, archaic surgery equipment, sexist stereotypes, and unaccommodating administrators; her professional ethics which interdicts affairs with patients; Julian's effete and affected world, a player "striking attitudes with a painted face" (p. 269); and his morbid hatred of his own beauty, bordering on self-mutilation.

For one moment, their beings truly intermingle: "This was not like the kisses he had given her, violent and bewildered; this he waited for her to give, and received it as if it had the power to put a soul into his body. She felt as though it was taking the soul from her own" (p. 186). However, erotic reciprocity in *Return to Night* echoes a histrionic rehearsal of magic and mystery modeled on Eros and Psyche, Hero and Leander, Mark Antony and Cleopatra at Actium, Lancelot and Guinevere, Don Quixote and Sancho Panza, Faustus and Helen, Alice in Wonderland. Sections from Shakespearean plays both heighten the novel's artificiality and provide an outlet for one's true nature, both disguise the self and lay it shockingly open:

> Not being taken seriously was obviously the way to live. . . . Provided one did it well enough—if one's technique had the polished surface which gave invulnerability—one could get away with anything on the stage. If the disguise were really impenetrable, one could get an emotional response from other people honestly, without loss of self-respect; one could become real.
>
> (pp. 116–117)

Julian performs the roles of Caliban, Oberon, or Hamlet, always creating (dis)illusions. The ending in Mott's Cave represents a primordial and archetypal emergence from the Platonic cave to a world devoid of curtains or chains. Hilary arrives just in time to prevent Julian from suicide. The dreams return to night. Although this was the novel for which Renault received the MGM Award, the book was never filmed. Its settings and trappings indeed make it cinematic, as the critic Thomas Sugrue (1947), in listing its atmospheric attributes, attests: "An English town in the Cotswolds, a tense scene in the operating room, upper middle class country house interiors, Romeo and Juliet love scenes by the dozen, tea every afternoon, rain or shine, and masses of old wartime tweed." (Sugrue, p. 16).

North Face (1948) contains unique imagery of mountain climbing and features an eerily named gothic hotel in Devonshire, Wier View. Guests on vacation, Miss Searle, an Oxford don, and Miss Fisher, a nurse, collide like rocks over their worldviews, language, hang-ups, urbanity, dress, and physicality. When Miss Fisher is knitting, her ball of wool falls to the ground. She and Miss Searle reach for it simultaneously:

The hand of a scholar, meticulous, with fineness but no strength in the bone, taut veins blue under the thin skin at the back, the nails ribbed, brittle and flecked here and there with white; the other broad-palmed and short fingered, with the aggressive smooth cleanliness that comes of much scrubbing with antiseptic followed by compensating cream, the nails filed short and round, their holiday varnish spruce.

(p. 12)

The humanist has safely anesthetized herself against emotional turmoil; the scientist has aestheticized unpleasant feelings. In contrast, Neil Langton, the "North Face" from Scotland, and Ellen Shorland successfully cope with their psychological aberrations; they come, so to speak, to shore and land. Ellen did not act on a declaration of love—until her pilot lover was shot down over the English Channel. Now she has chained herself to him by wearing his insignia as a necklace; its removal at the book's end breaks her bondage. Neil, a former teacher of classics, is a guilt-ridden drug addict, scarred by horrendous losses and haunted by an awful marriage (like Aeneas and Dido). Sadomasochism, incest, and voyeurism (like Actaeon and Diana) is tactfully hinted at. A climax occurs when Neil and Ellen discover a corpse in the water, a scene similar to that in William Golding's *Lord of the Flies,* which prompts a reflection on the war's atrocities: "Only now it *is* normal; it's trivial even. Someone who'd been tortured at Dachau, or crawled around the ruins of Hiroshima with their bone marrow rotting away, would say I didn't know what trouble meant" (p. 125). At the same time, their courtship remains awkward: "Like all first kisses, it tried to do too much: to explore and explain, demand and persuade and reassure; to satisfy the spirit and the blood" (p. 171). During a perilous climb and high above an abyss, Neil reaches the peak of personal insight:

Not in search of death, but of life, he had gone to the rock; to be measured in seconds perhaps, perhaps to be bought with death as soon as realised; life, and reality, none the less. . . . [Ellen] had drawn him like an unclimbed face which promises difficulty and exposure at every pitch; but at the summit the realisation of oneself and of the mountain,

union and release, a sky whose spaces humble, but no longer humiliate or appal.

(p. 256)

He grasps that he cannot live without Ellen, nor she without him; in keeping with the conventions of the romance, they get married.

HOMOSEXUALITY AND HEROISM

In *The Charioteer* (published in 1953 in England but not issued in the United States until 1959 due to its homosexual content) Renault transitions from the medical milieu of her nurse romances to the ancient world, the setting of her best-known works. Bernard Dick notes that in many ways, Renault's characters are "Hellenic souls imprisoned in modern bodies" (1972, p. 6). The sixteen-year-old Laurie Odell meets Ralph Lanyon, a nineteen-year-old head prefect who is about to be expelled from school for a homosexual liaison. Laurie "is lifted into a kind of exalted dream, part loyalty, part hero-worship, all romance. Half-remembered images moved in it, the tents of Troy, the columns of Athens, David waiting in an olive grove for the sound of Jonathan's bow" (p. 31). The image of the title is drawn from the allegory of the charioteer in Plato's *Phaedrus.* The black horse represents sexual gratification; the white one embodies virtue. The charioteer must restrain the black steed; however, in order to lift up a heavy burden, both horses must have the same force, and it is for this reason that the charioteer feeds, indiscriminately, both horses with ambrosia. Such tension characterizes modern gay experience: as one of Renault's biographers notes, "Homosexuals were outcasts in 'straight' society, struggling to adjust to a sexuality which could not offer the support of a traditional ethic—the struggle symbolized by the chariot in the *Phaedrus*: one horse heaven bent, the other plunging earthwards" (Sweetman, p. 139).

Laurie volunteers to fight Ralph's expulsion, but Ralph puts a stop to his campaign. Nevertheless, through a sense of shared connection, the Platonic turmoil is harmonized: "In a mingled exaltation, pride, and sheer consuming interest, [Laurie] smiled back into Lanyon's eyes" (p. 31).

As Paul Hammond (1996) points out, "Renault understands the importance of the glance, the hint, the allusion in eliciting recognition" (p. 230). Soon after, Laurie is injured at Dunkirk and recovering in a hospital. He was rescued by the captain of his boat, Ralph. It is as a patient that Laurie needs to come to terms with his physical disabilities and the hospital's "climate of shabbiness, dejection, and failure" (p. 174), and with his social "stigma." Laurie falls in love with the attractive but repressed and inhibited Andrew Raynes, a conscientious objector, Quaker, pacifist, and chaste medical orderly with a Socratic tutor. Finding it difficult to express his feelings, Laurie has recourse to the *Phaedrus,* but he falsifies the text with his denial of eroticism at the expense of rhetoric, never managing to lure Andrew into his realm. Renault next has the reader attend a "gay" party, "something between a lonely hearts club and an amateur brothel" (p. 311), complete with bitchiness and backbiting, cattiness and camp, Bims and Bunnys. Fortunately, Ralph joins Laurie. They make love and renounce melodrama, complying with Alan Sinfield's assertion that "queer heroism . . . involves invalidating queerness" (1994, p. 144), especially as the "queer" milieu sows discord, villainy, and self-destructive behavior.

The ending is well known:

> Quietly, as night shuts down the uncertain prospect of the road ahead, the wheels sink to stillness in the dust of the halting place, and the reins drop from the driver's loosened hands. Staying each his hunger on what pasture the place affords them, neither the white horse nor the black reproaches his fellow from drawing their master out of the way. They are far, both of them, from home, and lonely, and lengthened by their strife the way has been hard. Now their heads droop side by side till their long manes mingle; and when the voice of the charioteer falls silent they are reconciled for a night in sleep.
>
> (p. 347)

What reads temptingly as a quotation from Plato is actually a radical reworking of the *Phaedrus.* In Plato's dialogue, the charioteer sees his boy, glimpses Beauty, and bids farewell to society. The couple takes off while "their wings are bursting to sprout" (*Phaedrus* 256d); the soul literally ejaculates: "It looks upon the beauty of the boy and takes in the stream of particles flowing into it from his beauty . . . , when it is watered and warmed by this, then all its pain subsides and is replaced by joy" (*Phaedrus* 251c). However, *eros* eventually fails because of impracticability. What is recounted in the *Phaedrus* "doesn't exist anywhere in real life," Ralph reminds Laurie, "It's just a nice idea" (p. 32). Socrates' philosophy has too little appeal and even less "sex-appeal." Even his teacher Diotima in the *Symposium* questions the feasibility of her ladder of love: "Even you, Socrates, could probably come to be initiated into these rites of love . . . [but] I don't know if you are capable of it" (*Symposium* 209e–210a). Her lofty ascent proves too high, too exacting. In the *Theaetetus,* in a moment of facetious self-inspection, Socrates mentions Thales of Miletus, who was studying the stars and gazing aloft when he fell into a well. In the *Phaedo,* Socrates recommends that a philosopher abstain from food, drink, sex, shoes, clothes, and ornaments. Few can or *want to* succumb to these ascetic toils.

In Renault, the horses are reconciled and grounded (though only momentarily), while in Plato the heaven-bound struggle continues. If at all, the turmoil is reconciled at the expense of the black horse. It is hard to imagine that in Plato both the black and the white horses' "long manes mingle." Generally, although Plato in the *Phaedrus* views human sexuality as something more complicated than he did in his middle dialogues (the *Symposium,* for example) and imbues intellect with receptivity and motion, Socrates' philosophy neglects the physical and tries to sublimate the sexual instinct. Channeling the desire into spiritual procreation sounds like a wonderful idea—if only it worked. All this is relevant for the *Charioteer* because several characters valorize chastity (Andrew in particular) and—vainly—suggest that sexual desire (or, for that matter, the homosexual instinct) can be suppressed. Laurie and Ralph, I think, try to tread a middle ground between the sexual promiscuity of the gay scene (similar to Plato's black horse) and Socrates' lofty ascetic ideals. In short, by balancing the black horse and the white one they embody the charioteer that Renault's title refers to.

MYTH AND MYTHOLOGY

In her re-creations of the past, Renault is at her best, boldest, and brightest, skillfully combining fact and fiction and her insights into human character in the creation of a compelling narrative. Renault's historical novels will be discussed here chronologically, according to the historical and cultural periods they portray rather than by date of publication. Note that in her novels Renault does not latinize proper names (using Herakles for Hercules and Hekate for Hecuba, for example). In this discussion, Renault's spelling is retained when referring to the fictional characters but otherwise the more common transliterations are used. In all of her historical novels, Renault gives information on the historical background of the period in which the narratives are set through such elements as maps, timelines, author's notes, outlines, glossaries, bibliographies, and character lists.

The King Must Die (1958) is set in the Bronze Age, ca. 1450 B.C., when the palace at Knossos was wrecked in an earthquake, approximately 250 years before the Trojan War. The Mycenaean cult of the Earth Goddess required human sacrifices, including the king as the supreme victim, to ensure the rain that would sustain the life-giving crops. Theseus manages to lift the Navel Stone in the Grove of Zeus, under which he finds a sword and sandals that reveal who sired him.

Theseus was a national hero of Athens. As with many legends, there is no proof that there is a real person behind the myth. Renault thus re-creates his story. She recalls how Theseus was conceived in her brain:

> the first Linear B decipherments were appearing, with their glimpses of feudal Mycenaean kingdoms; along with some dramatic discoveries of royal tombs. There began to be descried a mainland culture different from the mannered elegance of the Minoan. Here with their skeleton hands still folded over their long gold-pommeled swords, lay the tall princes whose descendants took Troy; beside their domed tombs had stood the great stone walls of their fortress-palaces, the gates with their huge lintels, lifted no one knows how, and their lion-carved capstones. The written tablets shadowed a warlike society, well organised, aristocratic and art-loving, but primitive and barbaric by the standards of Crete's millennial sophistication.
>
> ("Notes on *The King Must Die*," pp. 82–83).

All this was exciting news. Moreover, in distinction to his cousin Herakles, who conquers folk-tale monsters, Theseus destroys *human* enemies of travelers, which makes him a particularly fitting subject for original fictionalization, especially for a first-person narrative. (Renault is always more interested in humans, not gods; or, to be more precise, in humans with god-like attributes.) Sources Renault mentions are Plutarch's *Life of Theseus* (the Greek biographer) and probably the mythographer Apollodorus (second century B.C.); modern scholarship includes Robert Graves' *The Greek Myths,* M. I. Finlay's *The World of Odysseus,* and M. Ventris and J. Chadiwick's *Documents in Mycenaean Greek.*

In Sophocles' *Oedipus at Colonus,* Theseus and Oedipus meet—in one of the great encounters of classical literature. Oedipus, after finding out that he killed his father, Laius, and slept with his mother, Jocasta, was exiled from Thebes. After many years of unrest and right before he expires, he meets Theseus and warns him of impending danger:

> Oh Theseus,
> dear friend, only the gods can never age,
> the gods can never die. All else in the world
> almighty Time obliterates, crushes all
> to nothing.
>
> (Sophocles, *Oedipus at Colonus*, lines 685–689)

Human confidence amounts to little more than ignorance. Oedipus thought he knew everything and was found desperately wanting. He did not even know who his parents were! Having finally acknowledged his human limitations and the power of the gods, Oedipus, with the help and protection of Theseus, finds peace. He dies, to use Renault's terms, "consenting" and in accordance with his *moira*.

Theseus grasps what it entails to be king: "To do justice, go to war for one's people, make their peace with the gods" (p. 60). In Eleusis, under the guidance of Queen Persephone, he wrestles and slays the Year King Kerkyon. Then he arrives in Athens, where he outwits the jealous witch Medea. He is thus recognized as the heir of King Aigeus. With hissing sounds, Medea prophesies Theseus' destiny: "Theseuss of Athens. You will cross water to dance in blood. You will be King of the victims. You will tread the maze through fire, and you will tread it through darkness. Three bulls are waiting for you, son of Aigeus. The Earth Bull, and the Man Bull, and the Bull from the Sea" (p. 130). Theseus voluntarily includes himself in the tribute to the Minotaur; half man and half bull, this creature is hidden in a hermetic labyrinth crafted by Daedalus and feeds on seven youths and seven maidens from Athens. With the help of sea nymphs, Theseus retrieves a ring for Asterion, King Minos's son and pretender to the throne, and establishes his royal claim as the son of Poseidon. Through his skill as a bullfighter, Theseus saves the lives of a group of bull dancers, the Cranes, who, as their name implies, manage to perform impossible tasks by becoming larger than life. According to Plutarch, the Crane is also a dance imitative of the twistings and windings of a labyrinth. The Cranes realize that their only hope is a democratic coexistence: "We were comrades, men and girls, and sharers in a mystery, and craftsmen bound by our craft" (p. 203); "limbs of one body" (p. 212); and even on their way home from Crete, "one kindred still" (p. 312).

Though often supremely strong, like his cousin Herakles, Theseus is physically human and needs to rely on his wits to achieve his heroic deeds. In Renault's account, Theseus actually failed to raise the Navel Stone the first time; it is only when he returns with a fulcrum and lever, instruments requiring cunning, that he succeeds. Eventually, Theseus fells the leper Minos and slaughters Asterion. It is the apex of his mission:

I swung Labrys back. . . .

From the Throne Room above I heard the cry of the Cranes; and from the porch the din of rout, as the news reached the defenders. But I stood still, seeing through the crystal a small bright image, such as a god may see who looks down from the sky, far down and back a thousand years to men who lived and suffered in ancient days; and in my heart was a long silence.

(pp. 307–308)

The House of the Ax vanishes from the face of the earth, by the trembling of Poseidon. Theseus' helpmate is Ariadne, who falls in love with him, saves his life with a spool of thread to mark his escape route from the labyrinth, and returns with him to Athens. However, when the ship stops in Naxos, Ariadne takes part in savage orgiastic rites and dismembers the king. To Theseus' horror, these revelers are reminders of the old barbaric religion that he hoped had been defeated with the destruction of the Minotaur. He abandons Ariadne and sails home. Renault is exploding the romantic myth of a forlorn, pining Ariadne dumped by a womanizing Theseus. Right before his arrival, Theseus does not change his black sail for a white one to indicate to his father his safety. Was it an honest oversight, divine interference, or a calculated, premeditated act? Overcome by grief, Aigeus precipitates himself into the sea now named after him.

As his father's successor, Theseus must live within the bounds of his *moira*. His grandfather Pittheus defines *moira* as follows: "The finished shape of our fate, the line drawn round it. It is the task the gods allot us, and the share of glory they allow; the limits we must not pass; and our appointed end. Moira is all these" (pp. 15–16). The sacrifice of the King Horse, Theseus' first rite of passage, illustrates this elusive concept: "How he reared up like a tower . . . ; the scarlet cleft in the white throat, the rank hot smell; the ruin of beauty, the fall of strength, the ebb of valor; and the grief, the burning pity as he sank upon his knees and laid his bright head in the dust" (p. 11). Crucially, the horse dies "consenting," with conviction. Theseus reflects on his *moira*, wondering "how far a man can move within his moira, or, if all is determined, what makes one strive" (p. 222). *Moira* is not predestination but a gift humans need to prove themselves worthy of. In Sophocles' *Antigone,* the chorus celebrates man and endorses his perfectibility:

And speech and thought, quick as the wind
and the mood and mind for law that rules the city—
all these he has taught himself. . . .
Man the master, ingenious past all measure
past all dreams, the skills within his grasp—
he forges on, now to destruction
now again to greatness.

(lines 395–409)

Life seems full of insurmountable obstacles—and faced with destruction one might conclude that life is not worth living. But there is also the matter of greatness. In the end, Theseus grasps the significance of *moira* and the restrictions it imposes: "Better then not to question the Immortals, nor when they have spoken to grieve one's heart in vain. A bound is set to our knowing, and wisdom is not to search beyond it. Men are only men" (p. 332).

In *The Bull from the Sea* (1962), the sequel to *The King Must Die,* Theseus catches a loose bull from Crete, Podargos, and brings all Attica under the rule of law, an unparalleled peace. Other dramatic episodes are Theseus' defeat of Procrustes, a savage who fits his prisoners to his bed; his reconciliation with the pirate Pirithoos, the leader of the Lapiths, with whom he undertakes journeys to terrae incognitae, such as the marvelous land of the Centaurs; the settlement of Megara and the Isthmus; and a dramatic encounter with Oedipus—another man who (unwittingly) killed his father—an old man with "a face like Fate itself. Beyond sorrow, beyond despair; with hope and fear forgotten" (p. 82). Renault effectively fictionalizes Sophocles' account. In *Oedipus at Colonus,* Oedipus comes as "someone sacred, someone filled / with piety and power, bearing a great gift" (lines 312–313). Theseus offers him protection as "a fellow-citizen with full rights" (line 724). At the end of the play, the gods speak directly yet miraculously to Oedipus; for once, they bridge the tremendous gap between the human and divine realms. In *The Bull from the Sea,* after the violent deaths of Antigone,

Polyneices, Eteocles, and Creon, Theseus ends the fratricidal strife of the House of Laius:

> The people sang me as judge and lawgiver of Hellas, and shared the pride of it. And indeed, from that time on wronged folk from all the clans of Attica would come to sit on my threshold: slaves with cruel masters, widows oppressed or orphans disinherited; and not even the chiefs dared murmur when I saw right done. . . . I saw it as an offering to the gods.

(p. 176)

Previously, one night in Crete, Theseus ran into a girl who asked for a lock of hair as a token of eternal affection: Phaedra. Now Theseus sails off to wed Minos's youngest daughter.

On his way, Theseus is detained by the Amazons, a community of self-sufficient women and warrior priestesses of Artemis, goddess of chastity. He engages in competition with their leader, Hippolyta (whose sister is Antiope in myth), and has a son with her, Hippolytus. Together, as man and wife and king and queen, they defeat a horde of invading Scythians. Theseus expects to die in combat and approaches his end "consenting." Instead, Hippolyta is killed in action. He bestows highest honors on her: "She had taken my death, lover for lover; she had been a woman at the last. She who was once a king should have known that only a king can offer for the people" (p. 234). The book concludes with erotic doom. Phaedra falls in adulterous and incestuous love with Hippolytus, who adamantly refuses sex. Jealous and rejected, Phaedra stages a rape, leading Theseus to curse his son by evoking the wrath of Poseidon (while earlier he eradicated monsters to *save* humans). It is only after Hippolytus is swallowed by the bull from the sea that Theseus determines his son's innocence and his wife's guilt. He strangles Phaedra and stages a suicide. A paralyzed Theseus then gloomily reviews his life, with *moira* still utmost on his mind: "Why not be content to curse? But while man is man he must look and think; if not forward, back. We are born asking why, and so we end" (p. 324). In his Ulyssean restlessness, has he overstepped his *moira*? In Pontos, he obediently declared: "The laws of the gods are beyond our knowing" (p. 201). In old age, the already fine line between choice and predetermination has blurred: "Fate and will, will and fate, like earth and sky bringing forth the grain together; and which the bread tastes of, no man knows" (p. 319). The monster/bull in Theseus is gaining ground. The book ends literally elliptically, with Theseus returning to his father: "The tide comes in. A swelling sea, calm, strong and shining. To swim under the moon, onward and onward, plunging with the dolphins, singing . . . To leap with the wind in my hair . . ." (p. 331; ellipses in original).

At the end, the king must die; like his father, Theseus falls from a high rock. Landon C. Burns Jr., observes that at the end of every section in Renault's Theseus stories, a king "dies": The King Horse in Troizen, Kerkyon in Eleusis, Theseus in Athens, Minos in Crete, Aigeus in Naxos, Oedipus in Marathon, Hippolyta in Pontos, Hippolytos in Epidauros, Theseus in Skyros. Similar to Aeschylus' *Oresteia* trilogy, where the Furies hound Orestes but in the end are placated by Athena, the two books trace the development from anarchy to stability, from archetypal retribution to the Areopagitic maxim *in dubio pro reo* (when a defendant's guilt is in doubt, the court shall rule in his favor), from matriarchy to patriarchy. Renault's Theseus, however, hastens this transition, neglecting the nurturing Mother. "Apollo made me a man, and Zeus a king. There is not much woman in me," he says to his mother, Aithra, who tries to purge him of his sin of profaning a sanctuary and who gently corrects him: "Apollo, who understands all mysteries, says also, 'Nothing too much.' He is knowledge, Theseus; but She is what he knows" (*The Bull from the Sea*, pp. 47–48). Earlier, Theseus hinted at their wondrous symbiosis:

> There is a measure in all things. . . . Just as it takes man and woman to make a child, so it needed gods and goddesses to make the world. The Mother brings forth the corn. But it is the seed of the undying god that quickens her, not a mortal man doomed to perish. Wouldn't that be the greatest of all shows, to make them a wedding?
>
> (*The King Must Die*, p. 141)

But words fail to translate into action. Theseus fails to cherish the feminine qualities in himself and thinks he can survive on brutal masculinity alone.

HISTORY AND HAGIOGRAPHY

The Praise Singer (1978) begins at a crucial time in Athens's history. After Draco's institution of harsh legislation, Solon (630–560 B.C.) becomes archon and abolishes serfdom. The tyrant Pisistratus (605–527 B.C.) favors the expansion of Athenian interests. In 508 Cleisthenes instigates democracy, with all freemen enjoying the right to vote. With tremendous enthusiasm, the Acropolis is rebuilt.

The rhapsodist Simonides is doubly handicapped by his ugliness in a society that values androgynous beauty in boys and as one of Renault's exclusively heterosexual characters: "The old nobility of Attica, like that of Sparta, looked back to the Sons of Homer. Women were for pastime; but your young friend must be someone you meet in the gymnasium, not the whorehouse" (p. 105). But Simonides possesses great artistic talent coupled with political acuity. He bluntly realizes that "praise-singing is like love. . . . You do it from the heart, or you're a whore" (p. 95). Sycophancy versus courtesy poses a constant threat to his integrity as a poet. In the course of the novel, Simonides follows a sign from Apollo to travel the Greek world— Keos, Samos, Athens, the Sacred Way, Sicily—in pursuit of a voice uncontaminated by flattery. He is empowered by the fictional bard Kleobis, who teaches him Homer. At the court of Pisistratus and his sons Hipparchos and Hippias, he finds a center of cultural excellence. Simonides meets such illustrious figures as his fellow poet Anakreon (but not his greatest rival, Pindar), the tragedian Aeschylus, and the tyrant Polykrates. A visit to "mad" Pythagoras offers insight into the workings of the mind of a genius: scrolls, writing tablets, mathematicians' toys, cubes, cones, spheres, cylinders, squares, triangles; music is the manifestation of a celestial design. A parallel development is the love story between Harmodius and Aristogiton. As Renault proposes in her author's note, she is not interested in these historical figures as famous tyrant-slayers (they murdered Hipparchos but were unsuccessful in killing Hippias) and fighters for democracy, but in how history received and distorted them for political ends. Of course, here she is casting light on her own fictional method. *The Last of the Wine* (1956) is set against another climax in Athenian history, the reign of Pericles (495–429 B.C..). However, the sweet wine is about to perish to sour vinegar. Alexias, a fictional noble Athenian, and his lover Lysis take part in athletics, fight in armor on the battlefield and at sea, hunt for boar, pour libations to the gods, avoid starvation during the Spartan siege and ensuing famine of the Peloponnesian War (431–404 B.C.), heal each other's wounds, make love, and engage with Socrates in philosophy, to "wonder at the visible world; to know the causes of things; and to feel the sinews of [their] mind[s]" (1975, p. 326). Alexis narrates his views of contemporary controversies, which Renault links to the modern experience of military annihilation. Foremost is the outcry, on the eve of the megalomaniac excursion to Sicily in 415, over the Athenian general and politician Alcibiades, who was accused of mutilating statues of Hermes and profaning the Eleusinian Mysteries. The Athenian citizen loathed tyranny as a political lifestyle diametrically opposed to democratic principles, but deep down he too may have wanted to live a life of wanton luxury, arousing admiration and envy. Alcibiades' eyes are "speaking":

> I am the wish sprung from your heart, and if you wound me your heart will bleed for it. Your love made me. Do not take it away; for without love I am a temple forsaken by its god, where dark Alastor will enter. It was you, Athenians, who conjured me, a daimon whose food is love. Feed me, then, and I will clothe you with glory, and show you to yourselves in the image of your desire. I am hungry: feed me.
>
> (p. 48)

Exhortation and intimidation, feeding and forcing build up to a rhetorical climax. Alcibiades has it all, only to squander his potential and fail at practical reason. Political aspirations, when unchecked, prove dangerous and ultimately self-defeating. Needless to say, Hitler, Stalin, Mussolini, Franco in Europe, and Hendrik Verwoerd in South Africa, were less than distant memories in the late 1950s, when Renault wrote this book. In contrast, the Stoic Socrates, "the image of the Silenos painted on the big wine-mixer at home, with his snub nose, wide thick mouth, bulging eyes, strong shoulders and big head," improves his disciples as if they "had been directed by a god" (pp. 12–14).

Renault is intrigued by another crisis. In Virgil's *Aeneid,* in a central passage in Augustan literature, Aeneas' father Anchises predicts the fate of his descendants:

[The Greeks] will cast more tenderly in bronze
Their breathing figures, I can well believe,
And bring more lifelike portraits out of marble;
Argue more eloquently, use the pointer
To trace the paths of heaven accurately
And accurately foretell the rising stars.

But for Rome the task is to reign an empire: "To pacify, to impose the rule of law, / To spare the conquered, battle down the proud" (*Aeneid,* book 6, lines 1145–1154). In *The Last of the Wine,* at the Pankration, an athletic event for wrestlers and boxers, Lysis fights the wrestler Sostratos: "This monstrous creature . . . a hideous fellow . . . a mountain of gross flesh, great muscles like twisted oakwood gnarling his body and arms; a neck like a bull's; his legs . . . seemed bowed by the weight of his ungainly trunk" (pp. 204–205). Greek athletes, once agile, temperate, swift, foreshadow the brute, warped Roman gladiator. Greek wine and philosophy would yield to Rome's bread and circuses; the Greek Palaestra would give way to the Roman Arena. "We were of an age to feel the present our own, and to suppose it would never outstrip us" (p. 326), but now sculptors no longer adhere to Protagoras' golden mean and experiment with modern outrages. Renault uses the starkest measure possible to underline Athens's decay. When the Thirty, Sparta's puppet regime, pass a law prohibiting the teaching of logic, Alexias expresses disbelief: "Who can forbid logic? Logic is" (p. 390).

The Greek setting allows Renault for the first time to depict same-sex love in a celebratory context. The title alludes to *kottabos,* the practice of tossing the wine remaining in a cup in order to form the name of a sweetheart or to augur omens. Alexias' uncle takes hemlock when his lover Philon is dying from the plague: "The cup was standing on the floor beside him; he had tipped out the dregs, and written PHILON with his finger, as one does after supper in the last of the wine" (pp. 4–5). The elite of ancient Greece cherished the asymmetrical relationship between an *erastes,* a mature man, and an *eromenos,* the beloved *pais* or boy who derived from his mentor educational values and often offered his body for the gratification of the *erastes'* sexual needs. In this tradition, the pederastic relationship is preferable to heterosexual marriage; it does not exclude the physical; and the older man loving a minor is a sign of civic duty. This is the erotic milieu here, while in *The Charioteer,* deviation from conventional sexual roles results in "shutting you away, somehow; roping you off with a lot of people you don't feel much in common with" (p. 152). In *The Last of the Wine,* gone is the clinical world that attaches the odor of sickness to homosexuality; gone is the world of "Englishness" and cant; gone is the world of the Criminal Law Amendment Act that outlawed "gross indecency" between male persons in public or private until 1967, when the Wolfenden Report led to the decriminalization of homosexual acts between consenting adults in private. In *The Mask of Apollo* (1966), after Socrates' execution, several wars diminish Athens's prevalence, although the city is able to shake off Spartan hegemony. Nikeratos ("Niko"), a fictional actor, never travels without a mask of Apollo, which takes on the role of his conscience (similar to the portrait in Oscar Wilde's 1891 novel *The Picture of Dorian Gray*), a mask with a face "more for a temple than a stage" (p. 19). The mask is a relic of a heroic, golden age that survives only in art:

> Once men deserved such gods. And where are they now? They bled to death on battlefields, black with flies; or starved in the siege, being too good to rob their neighbors. Or they sailed off to Sicily singing paeans, and left their bones there in sunken ships, or in the fever swamps or the slave-quarries. If they got home alive, the Thirty Tyrants murdered them. Or if they survived all that, they grew old in dusty corners, mocked by their grandsons, when to speak of greatness was to be a voice from the dead.
>
> (p. 42)

Niko visits Delphi, the site of Apollo's shrine that counsels man to "Know thyself." He soon becomes enmeshed in the political and cultural turmoil of the day. As an actor, he must contend with Plato's reservations about mimesis—although he is not banned from the philosopher's ideal state as depicted in the *Republic.* Ironically, in his youth, Plato himself was driven by an Odyssean wonder—"I was full of images and fantasies; they had only to knock and I would open; only to ask, and I would feed and clothe them" (p. 56)—before he turned into the affable but austere critic known to posterity. Plato is joined by two female pupils in men's clothing: Axiothea and and Lasthenia. Axiothea is determined to stand her (or his) own: "Equality! I hope I need never sink so low. That poppy syrup!" (p. 74). Plato next gets involved in setting up a reign of philosopher-kings in Sicily under the tutelage of the love of his life, Dion, a man Niko feels tremendously enchanted by: "I had met a man I would gladly die for" (p. 65). However, only a god can be philosopher and king at once.

As the title alerts, the novel centers around the Nietzschean agon, or struggle between reason and passion, between Apollo and Dionysus. In Euripides' *Bacchae,* a dramatic investigation of life's cacophony, of the heart's hysteria, a cult of maenads, both sacred and murderous, both pious and mad, reveals that what must be achieved is a balance of sobriety and ecstasy. In the play, Tiresias, the blind seer, warns Pentheus, king of Thebes, not to neglect Dionysus' world. Demeter/ Earth provides the vital harvest, which tastes even sweeter with wine. Pentheus heaps contempt upon Dionysus challenging a divine order, but heaven is not mocked. The chorus speaks:

> He who in wild delusion refuses
> To worship the gods . . .

But the gods creep up
By stealth in the creeping of time
On the irreligious man.
To know or to meddle beyond
The divinely established norm
Is utterly wrong.

(*Bacchae,* lines 885–893)

A terrible doom is visited upon Pentheus, his physical integrity ripped apart by his mother, Agave. In *The Mask of Apollo* Renault reveals the play's unsettling message that human reason unmodified by instincts of earth/body leads to destruction:

> It is from the man's own soul that the god with the smiling mask will draw his power, enchanting Pentheus with the hubris in his own secret heart. Once drunk on this sweet poison, he will know himself the one sane, righteous man in a wicked world. He has refused the little madness, to choose the great.
>
> (p. 193)

In the insurrection for supremacy, Dion fights, on behalf of Apollo, against his adversary, the archon Dionysios. Niko witnesses a crucible of havoc, all hell breaking loose in Syracuse and the citadel of Ortygia. The temple of Apollo is defiled. The Avenging Furies of Aeschylus' *Eumenides* occur to Dion in a dream, without the Apollonian promise of Athena pacifying them. Similar to Agamemnon's execution by his wife Clytemnaestra, Dion is hideously murdered, "like a king in tragedy, treading upon purple to the axe behind the door" (p. 356).

An author's note passage suggestive of the Greek historian Herodotus ends the book: "The perpetual stream of human nature is formed into ever-changing shallows, eddies, falls and pools by the land over which it passes. Perhaps the only real value of history lies in considering this endlessly varied play between the essence and the accidents" (p. 370). The facts are illustrated in the textbooks, but it is the Aristotelian *mythos* (myth, plot, and story), the lacunae of history, the details that have been lost, the offenses that have been expurgated, the images that have been eradicated or diminished, the voices that have been silenced that Renault resurrects with such bravura.

BIOGRAPHY AND BLISS

Renault's crowning achievement is her trilogy fictionalizing the life of Alexander the Great (356–323 B.C.). *Fire from Heaven* (1969) relates Alexander's youth. Early on, Alexander advocates, to use a modern term, a multicultural society: he learns different languages, adopts regional dresses, and consults the oracles of various denominations; he tames the horse Thunder and baptizes it "Oxhead," semidivinely imposing order on the raw forces of nature: "Men had not mastered [the horse]; but it would go with the god" (p. 139); he immerses himself in Herodotus' *Customs of the Persians*; he chooses his erotic partners on the basis of love, not expediency; he learns from his mistakes and apologizes, when, for example, he gives the Persian queen mother Sisygambis a parcel of wool for weaving, which, unlike in his household, is done by slaves there; and he shows remarkable restraint in an honor-and-shame culture in which justice is defined as helping one's friends and harming one's enemies. To Renault, the seed of his greatness lies in these character traits. His parents present different worlds: Philip, his Macedonian father, with "Greek schooling, reason, civility," versus the outlandish Olympias, his Greek mother, who is perceived as a sorceress, "a back country, snake-dancing, howling mystagogue" (p. 12). Leonidas brings Alexander up on a Spartan diet and regime, followed by the mental nourishments of Aristotle. Alexander seems to have reached manhood when he saves his father's life, but shortly afterwards things escalate when Philip takes a new wife, exiles Olympias, and strives to set up alliances by giving away his children in wedlock. A humbled Alexander asks his father for clemency. After Philip's assassination by his commander in chief in 336, Alexander ascends to the throne.

The novel is firmly situated in the historical controversy over the ancient kingdom of Macedon's imperialistic vision. The demagogue Demosthenes embodies Athens's resistance. In an encounter between him and Alexander, the orator comes across as lecherous, virulent, cowardly, and vituperative. In addition to Demosthenes,

Renault draws a portrait of Aristotle and his workings:

> [He and his students] talked of ethics and politics, the nature of pleasure and of justice; of the soul, virtue, friendship and love. They considered the causes of things. . . .
>
> Soon a whole room was full of specimens: pressed flowers and plants, seedlings in pots; birds' eggs with their embryos preserved in clear honey; decoctions of medicinal herbs. . . . They noted winds and mists and the aspect of the clouds, and learned to prognosticate storms. They reflected light from polished bronze, and measured the angles of refraction.
>
> (pp. 160–161)

Then the novel elaborates on a central philosophical rift. In Raphael's famous mural *The School of Athens* in the Vatican, Aristotle's concern is with this world, while Plato's index finger points upward, to a transcendent *eros*. As expounded in Plato's *Symposium,* the greatest love can only be made by the soul. It is by means of this very dialogue (in addition to Aeschylus' *Myrmidons,* the lost play about Achilles and Patroclus) that, to Aristotle's dismay, Alexander and his companion Hephaistion seduce each other, recalling the Theban Sacred Band, an army of male lovers who pledged never to desert one another (but which Philip defeats utterly at Cheironeia). Later in Troy, Alexander and Hephaistion celebrate their commitment by honoring the tomb of Achilles and Patroclus, whose ashes were mingled in one urn: "Not even a god could sift the one from the other" (p. 55).

In *The Persian Boy* (1972) Bagoas, a youth of noble birth, witnesses acts of unimaginable cruelty: hearing his sisters being raped, riding next to his father's decapitated head, seeing his mother's skull crack open. Sold into slavery as a piece of property at auction, Bagoas is then castrated. His narration can be seen as both therapeutic to himself and as the perpetuation of his lost seed: as Ruth Hoberman (1996) states, "Bagoas must learn that procreating dreams is as satisfying as procreating sons" (p. 291). As the eunuch of Darius, the king of Persia, he is treated kindly, gently, courteously, but the Great King is betrayed and deposed: "Disaster after disaster,

failure on failure, shame on shame; friend after friend turned traitor; his troops, to whom he should have been as a god, creeping off like thieves every night" (1998, p. 84). Finally, Bagoas is given as a gift to Alexander and conveys a picture of Alexander, a *primus inter pares* (first among equals), and of his court with rampant freedom of speech. He is especially troubled by its informality and irreverence, nakedness and naturalness. Eventually, Bagoas falls in love with Alexander, a state of paradise: "The living chick in the shell has known no other world. Through the wall comes a whiteness, but he does not know it is light. Yet he taps at the white wall, not knowing why. Lightning strikes his heart; the shell breaks open" (p. 130). He now gives and takes love. Bagoas' account is thus of great interest to gay and lesbian studies: As Caroline Zilboorg observes, Bagoas' "subject position—as narrator of Alexander's story and Renault's text—and his object position—as Alexander's boy—problematizes not only gender but sex itself" (p. 225). It is a story told by someone who usually has no voice, by an illiterate creating a narrative, by a Persian recollecting a stranger. Yet Bagoas is never oblivious of his sexual handicap: "I was like one who can play for the dancers, yet not dance" (p. 26).

Bagoas' happiness is clouded by his jealousy at Alexander's similar devotion to Hephaistion and at the threat posed by Alexander's Sogdian wife, Roxane, the "Little Star," who attempts to poison him. Too, Bagoas laments Alexander's once immaculate body that, through constant warfare, is now maimed and stigmatized, emaciated and emasculated. In the Indus valley, after victory and triumph, the sky seems the limit: "[Alexander's] eyes were turned, as they always were, to the next horizon. What he lived for now was to make the march to Ganges, follow its shores, and reach the Encircling Ocean; his empire a finished work from sea to sea, crowned with a marvel" (p. 289). Alexander, however, faces his first collapse, an exhausted army, longing to go home, and he turns back—a march of devastation. The marriage of Alexander and Macedonian noblemen to Persian ladies is only doom deferred. Among splendid games, Hephaistion dies—to Alexander's immense grief, driven as he is to bouts of madness and a near deification of his lover. Inauspicious omens, such as the plundered tomb of Kyros (Cyrus), Alexander's idol, signal his own departure. Bagoas bids farewell with a tearful elegy:

> Go to the gods, unconquered Alexander. May the River of Ordeal be mild as milk to you, and bathe you in light, not fire. May your dead forgive you; you have given more life to men than you brought death. God made the bull to eat grass, but the lion not; and God alone will judge between them. You were never without love; where you go, may you find it waiting.
>
> (p. 411)

Ominously, the novel ends on a high note of dysfunctionality, the conundrum over Alexander's corpse: "The wars for the world had started; these people were fighting to possess him, as if he were a thing, a symbol, like the Mitra or the throne" (p. 411).

In *Funeral Games* (1981), Alexander is alive in Babylon at the beginning, hovering between life and death, but the people, priests, and soldiers are anxiously awaiting word of his fate. His wife Roxane dreams a dreadful nightmare:

> Alas, alas! The light is fallen from the sky, the lion of men is fallen. When he lifted his sword, a thousand warriors trembled; when he opened his hand, it shed gold like the sands of the sea. When he rejoiced, it gladdened us like the sun. As the storm-wind rides the mountains, so he rode to war; like the tempest that fells great forest trees, he rode into the battle. His shield was a strong roof over his people. Darkness is his portion, his house is desolate. Alas! Alas! Alas!
>
> (p. 27)

Taking up the power vacuum created by Alexander's oversight to designate an heir, the novel, with the revealing working title *Hot Embers,* emphasizes the erosion of Alexander's world: numberless armies, countless locales, nonlinear time sequences, uncontainable chaos. Unable to agree on a competent successor, the Macedonian Assembly proclaims Alexander's bastard brother Arridaios—an idiot—king. Of course, nobody is up to the task of governing an empire from the Adriatic to the Indus and from the Caspian Sea to the Nile. The dim-witted Arridaios, now King Philip II, suffers his ultimate humiliation when he is unmanned by his wife Eurydike. Intriguingly, Eurydike in drag commands her husband's soldiers as the warrior queen, but at a formidable moment she fails to address the Assembly because she is soiled with her own menstrual blood. Roxane, Alexander's Baktrian spouse, poisons Alexander's Persian wife Stateira, who is pregnant with her husband's child and miscarries before she collapses: "The four-month manikin, already human, the sex defined, even the nails beginning. One of the fists was clenched as if in anger, the face with its sealed eyes seemed to frown. It was still tied to its mother" (p. 105). Diminution, abortion, imprisonment—here is the keynote of *Funeral Games*. At the same time, Renault stresses stagnation, blockage, gridlock, returning to her favorite medium, the theater: "Thus the drama dragged, the action sagged; the audience fidgeted, coughed and yawned, began fingering its apple-cores and half-bitten onions and crusts, but was not quite ready to throw them at the actors" (p. 216). Roxane does bear a male heir, dark-eyed, bushy hair, fine bones—an Alexander in the making? Expectedly, his potential is vitiated by a goblet of poison.

Toward the close, Renault wraps up loose ends. Queen Olympias is still an enigma and oxymoron, "a Bacchic Ariadne, waiting the embrace of a Dionysos who never came . . . in tears, in savage mirth, in blazing anger and sometimes in regal grace" (p. 256). After she has Philip and Eurydike put in a stinking pigsty among excrement and vermin and executed, Olympias is memorably stoned by a mob but expires in grand style, elusive even in mortality:

> Alone in the circle, she stood with her head up while the first stones struck her. Their force made her stagger, and she sank to her knees to prevent an unseemly fall. . . . Her eyes began to swim, their images doubled; she felt her body breaking under the stones, but it was more shock than pain; she would be gone before the real pain had time to start. She looked up at the whirling effulgent cloud, and thought, I brought down the fire from heaven; I

have lived with glory. A thunderbolt struck from the sky and all was gone.

(p. 315)

Renault then revisits the charioteer, a struggle as unresolved as in her novel written thirty years earlier. For Laurie, the *Phaedrus* epitomized "confusion and uncertainty and pain and compassion, and all the tangle of man's mortality" (*The Charioteer,* p. 214). Two millennia earlier, in Renault's rendering, people were similarly torn apart by forces beyond their grasp and control: "All those great men. When Alexander was alive, they pulled together like one chariot-team. And when he died, they bolted like chariot-horses when the driver falls. And broke their backs like horses, too" (*Funeral Games,* p. 330). Jealous detractors immediately tried to nullify Alexander's achievement. Kassandros, who hated Alexander at first sight (and vice versa) and who is probably responsible for exterminating the royal line, bends the facts with the help of Theophrastos, Aristotle's successor at the Lyceum: "*[Alexander] made his victorious generals fall down to the ground before his throne. Three hundred and sixty-five concubines, the same in number as Darius had, filled his place. Not to speak of a troop of effeminate eunuchs, used to prostitution. As for his nightly carouses . . .*" (p. 317; ellipsis and italics in original). Whose account is objective, if indeed there is historical objectivity? No doubt, Renault wants to set the record straight; metafictionally, there is a book in the book, a history written by Ptolemy, Alexander's loyal friend, reputed half-brother, and ancestor of Cleopatra.

RENAULT IN THE CLASSROOM

Renault's mature novels have been translated into the world's major languages. Rivaling books by Robert Graves such as *The Greek Myths* and *I, Claudius, The King Must Die* and *The Bull from the Sea* are helpful and provocative complements to works read in a Greek mythology class, with profound portraits of some of its most famous figures: Theseus, Medea, Jason, Ariadne, Orpheus, Achilles, and Oedipus. *The Last of the Wine* and *The Mask of Apollo* offer a detailed view of the Socratic circle: the "traitors" Alcibiades and Critias; the title characters of many Platonic dialogues: Euthydemus, Menexenus, Charmides, Phaedo, and Lysis; the playwrights Agathon, Aristophanes, and Euripides; the historian Xenophon, the orator Lysias, and the star actor Theodoros; and Anytus, Socrates' chief accuser. *The Praise Singer* and *The Mask of Apollo* add to our understanding of the Greek aesthetic experience. The former details the status of odes, hymns, and oral dissemination, and such fascinating topics as ancient patronage, public recognition, and "corrupt" art. In the latter, Renault pays careful attention to the trappings of the theater, masks, the stage, props, technique, actors' guilds, rehearsals, and the religiosity of plays; she literally takes us backstage, into the audience and into the mind of an actor, and she chronicles the hard life of touring companies: the endless mending of costumes, daubing on of paint, and sleeping at raunchy inns with hard straw mattresses infested with bugs. Renault's early novels make excellent primary sources in women's studies and gay and lesbian fiction classes. For example, in conjunction with the *Symposium* and *Phaedrus,* Petronius' *Satyricon,* Oscar Wilde's *The Picture of Dorian Gray,* E. M. Forster's *Maurice,* Thomas Mann's *Death in Venice,* André Gide's *Corydon,* Gore Vidal's *The City and the Pillar,* and Marguerite Yourcenar's *Memoirs of Hadrian, The Charioteer* reads fruitfully in a course on Platonic love. Similarly, the first two Alexander novels complement Achilles and Patroclus in Homer's *Iliad,* Nisus and Euryalus in Virgil's *Aeneid,* and Greek and Roman homoerotic poetry.

SELECTED BIBLIOGRAPHY

I. NOVELS. *Purposes of Love* (London, 1939), repub. as *Promise of Love* (New York, 1939; repr. 1974); *Kind Are Her Answers* (London and New York, 1940; repr. 1974); *The Friendly Young Ladies* (London, 1944; repr. with new afterword, London and New York, 1984), repub. as *The Middle Mist* (New York, 1945); *Return to Night* (London and New York, 1947; repr. 1971); *North Face* (London and New York, 1948); *The Charioteer* (London, 1953; New York, 1959; repr. 1993); *The Last of the Wine* (London and New York, 1956; repr. 1975); *The King Must Die* (London and New York, 1958); *The Bull from the Sea* (London and New York, 1962; repr. 2001); *The Mask of Apollo* (London and New York, 1966; repr. 1988); *Fire from Heaven* (London and New York, 1969); *The Persian Boy* (London and New York, 1972; repr. 1988); *The Praise Singer* (London and New York, 1978); *Funeral Games* (London and New York, 1981).

II. OTHER WORKS. Afterword to Charles Kingsley, *Theseus: A Greek Legend Retold* (New York, 1964); "Amazons," in *Greek Heritage* 1, no. 2 (1964); *The Lion in the Gateway: The Heroic Battles of the Greeks and Persians at Marathon, Salamis, and Thermopylae* (New York, 1964), children's book; "A Man Who Survived Transition," in *New York Times Book Review* (15 August 1965), book review; "Notes on *The King Must Die*," in *Afterwords: Novelists on Their Novels,* ed. by Thomas McCormack (New York, 1969); "The Horse from Thessaly," in *The Twelfth Man,* ed. by Martin Boddey (London, 1971), short story; "History in Fiction," in *(London) Times Literary Supplement* (23 March 1973); "Shakespeare and Xenophon," in *(London) Times Literary Supplement* (12 July 1974); Introduction to Sir Arthur Conan Doyle, *Sir Nigel* (London, 1975); *The Nature of Alexander* (New York, 1975); "The Fiction of History," in *London Magazine* 18 (March 1979); "According to Celsus," in *Women Writing: An Anthology of Short Stories,* vol. 3, ed. by Denys Val Baker (London, 1980); Greg Gatenby, ed., Introduction to "A Letter from Pliny the Younger," in *Whales: A Celebration* (Boston, 1983).

III. CRITICAL STUDIES. Rosamond Lehmann, "Kind Are Her Answers," in *The Spectator* 164, no. 5840 (1940); Thomas Sugrue, "A Modern Love Affair," in *New York Herald Tribune Book Review* 23, no. 35 (1947); Jeannette H. Foster, *Sex Variant Women in Literature* (London, 1958; repr. Tallahassee, Fl., 1985); Kevin Herbert, "The Theseus Theme: Some Recent Versions," in *Classical Journal* 55 (1959–1960); Landon C. Burns Jr., "Men Are Only Men: The Novels of Mary Renault," in *Critique* 6, no. 3 (1963); Peter Wolfe, *Mary Renault* (New York, 1969).

Anne G. Ward, et al., eds., *The Quest for Theseus* (New York, 1970); Bernard F. Dick, *The Hellenism of Mary Renault* (Carbondale and Edwardsville, Il., 1972); Paul G. Kuntz, "The Labyrinth," in *Thought* 47 (1972); Bernard F. Dick, "The Herodotean Novelist," in *Sewanee Review* 81 (1973); Julian N. Hartt, "Two Historical Novels," in *Virginia Quarterly Review* 49 (1973); Carolyn G. Heilbrun, "Axiothea's Grief: The Disability of the Female Imagination," in *From Parnassus: Essays in Honor of Jacques Barzun,* ed. by Dora B. Weiner and William R. Keylor (New York, 1976).

Margaret Crosland, *Beyond the Lighthouse: English Women Novelists in the Twentieth Century* (London, 1981); Donna Mae Miller, "Images of Ancient Greek Sportswomen in the Novels of Mary Renault," in *Arete* 3 (fall 1985); Neil McEwan, *Perspective in British Historical Fiction Today* (Wolfeboro, N.H., 1987).

Claude J. Summers, *Gay Fictions, Wilde to Stonewall: Studies in a Male Homosexual Literary Tradition* (New York, 1990); Robert Aldrich, *The Seduction of the Mediterranean: Writing, Art and Homosexual Fantasy* (London and New York, 1993); Bruce Bawer, *A Place at the Table: The Gay Individual in American Society* (New York, 1993); Terry Castle, *The Apparitional Lesbian: Female Homosexuality and Modern Culture* (New York, 1993); David Sweetman, *Mary Renault: A Biography* (New York, 1993); Kevin Kopelson, *Love's Litany: The Writing of Modern Homoerotics* (Stanford, Calif., 1994); Frank N. Magill, ed., *Great Women Writers: The Lives and Works of 135 of the World's Most Important Women Writers, from Antiquity to the Present* (New York, 1994); Alan Sinfield, *The Wilde Century: Effeminacy, Oscar Wilde and the Queer Moment* (New York, 1994).

Julie Abraham, *Are Girls Necessary? Lesbian Writing and Modern Histories* (New York, 1996); Paul Hammond, *Love Between Men in English Literature* (New York, 1996); Erin G. Carlston, "Versatile Interests: Reading Bisexuality in *The Friendly Young Ladies*," in *RePresenting Bisexualities: Subjects and Cultures of Fluid Desire,* ed. by Donald E. Hall and Maria Pramaggiore (New York, 1996); Ruth Hoberman, "Masquing the Phallus: Genital Ambiguity in Mary Renault's Historical Novels," in *Twentieth Century Literature* 42 (summer 1996); Joyce Moss and George Wilson, eds., *Literature and Its Times: Profiles of 300 Notable Literary Works and the Historical Events That Influenced Them,* vol. 1 (Detroit, 1997); Alan Sinfield, *Gay and After* (London, 1998); Julie Abraham, "Mary Renault," in *Gay Histories and Cultures: An Encyclopedia,* ed. by George E. Haggerty (New York, 2000); John Gilgun, "Mary Renault's *The Charioteer*: The Boys in the Theban Band," in *International Journal of Sexuality and Gender Studies* 5 (January 2000); Caroline Zilboorg, *The Masks of Mary Renault: A Literary Biography* (Columbia, Mo., 2001); Lisa L. Moore, "Lesbian Migrations: Mary Renault's South Africa," in *GLQ* 10, no. 1 (2004).

IV. CLASSICAL SOURCES. Euripides, *Three Plays of Euripides: Alcestis, Medea, The Bacchae,* tr. by Paul Roche (New York, 1974); Sophocles, *The Three Theban Plays,* tr. by Robert Fagles (Harmondsworth, U.K., 1982); Virgil, *The Aeneid,* tr. by Robert Fitzgerald (New York, 1990); Plato, *Complete Works,* ed. by John M. Cooper (Indianapolis, 1997).

RUTH RENDELL

(1930–)

Rebecca Berg

"I AM A frightened person," Ruth Rendell told fellow mystery writer P. D. James in a 1989 interview. There are, she said, two kinds of people: those who like getting mail and those who fear what it will bring. "I don't like the post when it comes," Rendell said. "I feel a kind of tightening of the muscles." Fear, she told James, must be why she writes. Indeed, fear informs her cozy Inspector Wexford mystery series as well as her menacing psychological thrillers and the more free-ranging novels she writes under the pseudonym "Barbara Vine." The engagement with this emotion, though, often takes impersonal forms. Fear is as likely to manifest in narrative structure as in the experiences of a frightened protagonist. "It is suspense and the build-up of fear which has always interested me most," Rendell told journalist Sue Corrigan in 1998. Her inspiration, in other words, has become her method.

That method is also intensely intellectual, almost scientific, experimenting with themes as if they were hypotheses, trying them on upside-down and inside out. This is a writer who, having told journalist William Leith in 1999 that she suffers from a mild case of agoraphobia, came out in 2000 with *Grasshopper,* whose protagonist has claustrophobia.

What kind of fictional universe results from this systematic observation of self and others? Reviewers have often classed Rendell as a psychological realist. Her avowed habit of consulting psychological research supports that view. So do the precision of her characterizations and the care she takes with dialogue. Nevertheless, Rendell's work also has been described, notably by Susan Rowland and Cyndy Hendershot, as gothic in sensibility. Outbursts of exoticism, terrifying coincidences, and concatenations of unfelicitous circumstances spring up frequently in Rendell's fiction, breaching realism and shattering illusions of safety. Her characters' tendency to suffer from delusions and obsessions, as Sarah Lyall has noted, or to commit "a single misstep that spirals out of control," also suggests a darkly unforgiving, almost magically hostile universe.

The biographical roots of this vision—if, indeed, its roots are primarily biographical—may always remain obscure. Rendell has never cozied up to reviewers and journalists with confessional self-analysis. If the funny, brutal roasting of reporters in her later work is any indication, she is wary of sharing personal details with representatives of this profession to which she once belonged. *Harm Done* (1999) and *Adam and Eve and Pinch Me* (2001), for instance, see in the media a toxic mix of schadenfreude, mischief-making, and unscrupulous self-interest. Would-be biographers therefore face a choice between reiterating the bare-bones accounts of Rendell's life that can be gleaned from interviews and the riskier business of inferring from her work the themes and motives of her life. Still, there have been hints that the dark worlds of the fiction in some way reflect childhood experiences. To James, in whose respect for personal boundaries she perhaps trusted, Rendell mentioned that she had "a fairly unhappy childhood" that "just made me rather frightened." Other interviewers have pressed unsuccessfully for details.

Some things are known. Ruth Rendell was born Ruth Barbara Grasemann on 17 February 1930, the only child of Arthur and Ebba Elise Grasemann. She was raised in Essex, on the eastern edge of London. Both parents, who were teachers, knew significant hardship. Arthur Grasemann grew up poor, began working in dockyards at the age of fourteen, and eventually found his way into a university. Ebba Grasemann was an immigrant. Born in Sweden and raised in Denmark, she seems to have encountered people in

England who—if the many xenophobes populating Rendell's novels are any indication—greeted foreigners with less than open minds and open arms. Shortly after her daughter's birth, Ebba Grasemann began to suffer from multiple sclerosis. The disease was not diagnosed for some time, and it was thought that she was simply clumsy. She died while Rendell was still a girl. In light of the dangerous universe that emerges in the non-Wexford thrillers, it is worth noting that what Rendell may have perceived as a character flaw in her mother—albeit a minor one—ultimately resulted in death.

Rendell speaks of both parents with sympathy. Her mother, she has told Corrigan, was "misunderstood." Her father she describes as "endlessly patient, loving and kind." Still, the would-be biographer might cautiously register Rendell's comment to Lyall: "I'm inclined to think that most families don't work out, and that most trouble does begin in families." Perhaps also worth noting, although Rendell has never suggested a connection with her own life, is the recurrence in her fiction of overprotective, morally rigid, or fanatically tidy aunts and foster mothers. According to Marha DuBose (2000), though, the most frightening feature of Rendell's childhood was the emotionality of her parents; Rendell describes them as fighting, crying, ex-pressing themselves, and engaging in a level of strife that "from a very early age" gave her "a sense of doom."

Rendell began working as a journalist when she was eighteen, first for the *Chigwell Times,* then, until 1952, for the *Essex Express and Independent,* where she met her future husband. She has expressed regret about not attending a university. Two years after marrying Don Rendell, she stopped working. The accounts of how and why, though various, are not mutually exclusive: According to Moira Reynolds (2001), she quit journalism to be a mother (she has a son, Simon, who studied psychology and became a social worker in Colorado). Or she quit because she was "no good at journalism," as she put it to Emily Bearn (2002). Or she quit, according to Michael Neill (1995), because she wanted to be able to "rearrange the endings." Most colorfully, she quit, in DuBose's account, because she had written up a tennis club dinner in advance, chose

not to attend, and consequently omitted mentioning in her article that the guest of honor had dropped dead in the middle of his speech.

Once free of journalism, Rendell began in to write fiction. She wrote for about a decade before publishing and produced six books, none of them very good, she warned in a 1994 interview with Steve Moore, and all of them "lost and gone." They were not crime novels; the first manuscript Rendell submitted to a publisher was a comedy of manners. It was rejected, but the editor asked to see something else. Rendell sent *From Doon with Death (1964),* a mystery she had written, according to Reynolds, "really for fun."

The official first novel has received only glancing notice from critics, perhaps because it exemplifies a tendency of the Inspector Wexford series to be, as DuBose puts it, "contemporary rather than timeless." In 1964, this tale in which lesbian love figures as sexual dysfunction may have had something of the cutting edge about it, a whiff of shock. To twenty-first-century readers, it is likely to seem dated. Rendell herself, in her interview with Moore, has dismissed *From Doon with Death* as "a very small book" that received "tiny nice little reviews."

Nevertheless, the first Inspector Wexford novel is recognizably Rendell's creation. Rendell's career is shaped by the exploration of two phenomena that present themselves simply and starkly in the early work. The first might be called imagination, the second failure of imagination. Although Rendell's interest in both these forces reveals itself in both the mysteries and the thrillers, the early Wexford novels offer the easiest approach to the terrors of imagination; the terrors of its absence dominate the early thrillers. An ini-tial thematic exploration of imagination and failure of imagination will provide a vocabulary with which to later discuss the way the novels fall into what reviewer Dennis Drabelle (1992) calls "product lines": Wexfords, thrillers, and Vines.

SEDUCTIVE TERRORS:
THE LITERARY IMAGINATION

From Doon with Death presents Chief Inspector Reginald Wexford, along with his assistant and foil, Detective Inspector Michael Burden, investigating the murder by strangulation of Margaret Parsons. The victim is a dowdy, emotionally insipid, intellectually vapid housewife whose life has produced just one interesting artifact: an attic trunk full of nineteenth-century poetry in expensive editions. Each book bears a lover's inscription from "Doon." Who is Doon? The circle of suspects is small, including the victim's husband (a man who reads only crime novels), Helen Missal (liar and adulteress), and Douglas Quadrant ("a slim detached tom-cat of a man" [p. 113] who is sleeping with Helen Missal). Douglas Quadrant has an old-fashioned house, a beautiful wife, and a library full of poetry and novels. He is the prime suspect, but his wife, Fabia, turns out to be the one who has idealized Margaret Parsons beyond all recognition and is finally revealed to be "Doon."

The novel declines to be scornful of romantic delusion. Rendell guides readers toward compassion by contrasting Wexford's tolerant reaction to Doon with that of the less less literate Inspector Burden. Even more marked is the contrast between Wexford and Helen Missal, a shallow woman who calls Doon's infatuation "disgusting . . . revolting" while kicking a book across the room. (As Susan Parr [1989] notes, "The values of Rendell's characters are revealed through their attitudes toward books.") Wexford picks up the book, showing respect for beauty and learning, and says of Doon's infatuation, "This was love. . . . It wasn't disgusting or revolting. To Doon it was beautiful" (p. 174).

The pattern of violence established in this first novel—and reiterated with variation in many novels to come—comprises a killer with a romantic obsession, a victim unworthy of the killer's imagination, and a shock of disillusionment. Dullness, insensitivity, and poor taste precipitate murder. In *A Sleeping Life* (1978) Wexford explains the motivations of a woman who commits murder when the man she loves turns out to be a woman and badly dressed to boot: "She saw . . . a travesty in the true meaning of the word, and she stabbed to death an abomination" (p. 179).

Like a true romantic, Wexford respects the lover's projection; in *From Doon with Death,* the murderer's delusion is far more attractive to him than is the unimaginative victim. Wexford makes his arrest with sorrow and compassion—and with an ambiguous gesture that is protective, almost possessive, of the sobbing Fabia Quadrant: "She fell against Wexford and gasped into his shoulder. He put his arm around her hard, forgetting the rules, and closed the window" (p. 176).

"Rendell has said," writes DuBose, "that as a matter of her faith she believes in an ideal love." If romantic idealization is one of the great terrifying forces stalking the Rendellian universe—if it is always seeding violence—it is also an attractive force, perhaps more unnerving for that reason.

Some Lie and Some Die (1973) explores the attraction of this danger in more detail. Zeno Vedast, a rock star worshipped by thousands, embodies romantic projection writ large. Rendell's prose invites the reader to share in the transport:

> In the pale rosy light, the soft kind light, Vedast looked very young. . . . He stood in a corner of the room, resting his bare elbows on a shelf from which rose-buds hung, young, fresh rose-buds dead before they opened from dehydration. He waited in the silence of the evening, the silence of the forest which surrounded them. The first word came loud like a note vibrating from a string, then the clear, light voice dropped a little, filling the room with sweet bitterness.
>
> (p. 168)

In its rhythmically paired modifiers ("soft, kind," "young, fresh," "clear, light,"), in its lyrical substitution of adjective for adverb ("came loud"), in its use of simile and paradox, this passage heightens the moment, insisting on the emotional pleasures of illusion. Vedast's charismatic presence speaks to the longings of his audience and makes him the object of obsession on the part of two women who are more personally involved with him. Wexford points out that "anyone may become the object of such love" (p. 168). The object of fascination expresses not his own qualities but someone else's yearning for broader horizons, for experiences that transcend the mundane—in short, for poetry.

The link between idealization and poetry is perhaps most apparent in *Speaker of Mandarin* (1983), which along with the 1981 *Put on by Cunning,* might be considered to inaugurate a middle period for Rendell's detective. The first half of the novel, in which Wexford travels to China, is itself an urgent escape from the confines of Kingsmarkham, the fictional Sussex town that by now has been the setting for almost twenty years of Inspector Wexford novels. Wexford is haunted by a waking vision while he is in China, seeing everywhere he turns the figure of an ancient woman with bound feet. This rendering of China as disorienting, foreign, menacing, and inscrutable—traditional tropes of exoticism—has earned rebuke from critic Tony Giffone (1991). He makes an example of *Speaker of Mandarin*—not, he insists, because it has "any especial literary merit," but because it is "emblematic of what Edward Said calls Orientalism." Questions of merit aside, *Speaker of Mandarin* is in fact stylistically remarkable, startlingly divided down the middle. The language in the first half of the novel is heightened, lovingly descriptive. With Wexford's return to England, Rendell's prose reverts abruptly to workmanlike functionality, as if writer and detective both are resignedly returning to their regular jobs. Back in England, the world is so dreary that the motive for murder is simply (and, for the early Rendell, uncharacteristically) money.

Wexford, longing for richer experiences, projects exoticism onto a beautiful woman whose name—"Pandora Vinald"—suggests mythical status: "Her hair was . . . cut now with a fringe that curved symmetrically down into a page-boy, the Egyptian queen look. Her mouth was as red as cinnabar and her eyelids painted jade" (p. 123). In his eager mixing of imagery evoking easternness—whether the easternness of ancient Egyptian hair styles or the easternness of Chinese jade does not matter to Rendell's chief inspector—Wexford is reaching for something beyond what he knows. He is using Pandora Vinald as a stimulus for his imagination in a way that Rendell associates with enraged violence, as we have

seen, but also with the impulse to poetry. As usual, the projection is more vibrant than its object. Pandora Vinald calls herself "not poetical," and the "twang" in her voice compels Wexford reluctantly to agree. Still, he insists that "any man would have wanted to write a poem to or about her" (p. 124).

That stubbornness is a microcosm of the wary romanticism that characterizes *Speaker of Mandarin.* The novel is not so naïve that it fails to recognize its exoticization of China as a projection. Wexford ultimately attributes his "haunting" in China to stress, and he proves himself more open-minded about cultural differences than many of his fellow Westerners. Still, even in formulating an alternative to a countryman's attack on Chinese culture, Wexford clings to romantic projections: "The truth never really is known about China," he says, making his own state of not knowing a function of the thing not known. Likewise, the novel as a whole insists on the value of projection even as it also knows better. Wexford's ability to have an aesthetically informed romantic perception of other people gives him breadth of imagination and is at the heart of his intelligence. As Rowland argues, "It is precisely Wexford's vulnerability to imaginative genres versus dirty realism that makes him, at first, the murderers' stooge, and then enables him to intuitively reconstruct their modus operandi."

REPELLENT TERRORS: FEARSOME HOUSE-KEEPING AND THE STRUCTURE OF DREAD

If the poetic impulse can be murderous, might an absence of poetry be more appalling? Which is more dangerous—to read or not to read? In her psychological thrillers, Rendell has engaged that question with an intensity not possible inside the strict conventions of the detective novel. *Make Death Love Me* (1979) and *A Judgement in Stone* (1977) are perhaps exemplary, juxtaposing readers with nonreaders. Here it is not the romantics who commit murder, but the illiterate.

Make Death Love Me opens with Alan Groombridge fingering money. He has illicitly removed £3000 from a safe in the bank where he works.

By bank standards, the amount is small, and Alan's ambitions are correspondingly small; he does not even intend to steal the money. The bank itself is small, and it is located in a small village. In fact, the scope of Alan's whole life is so small that £3000 represent, as Jane Bakerman (1981) puts it, "utter freedom." His colleague, Joyce, exemplifies the predictability of this world, expressing herself in clichés. Alan's wife, Pam, is "a pretty woman of thirty-seven who had a job for only one year of her life and had lived in a country village for the whole of it" (p. 6).

Alan experiences this narrow world as a prison because he is different from his fellow inmates. He reads. Literature, which he discovered at the library in his twenties, has heightened his "powers of perception" (p. 25). *Make Death Love Me* suggests that intelligence, the ability to respond on an emotional level to beauty, even the ability to be in love, are not intrinsic to human nature. Human experience has not created literature; literature has created human experience. "Fiction," writes Rendell, "had taught Alan Groombridge that there is such a thing as being in love. Some say that this, indirectly, is how everyone gets to know about it. Alan had read that it had been invented in the Middle Ages by someone called Chrétien de Troyes, and that this constituted a change in human nature" (p. 23).

The world Alan inhabits supports this thesis (which, one can surmise, he has found in C. S. Lewis's *Allegory of Love*). No one Alan knows has been in love—all his acquaintances are "as dull as he and as unredeemed" (p. 23). Nevertheless, his emotional range is expanding. One evening he goes into his yard to look at "the snowdrops and the little red tulips" that he is now able to perceive as "exquisitely beautiful at this violet hour," and he experiences a "strange little pain in his heart" (p. 11).

Despite his reading regimen, Alan's knowledge of the world is small enough to keep his dreams petty; he plays with the bank's £3000, walks around the office with the notes in his pockets, and counts out money "into an imaginary hand" (p. 1).

By contrast, the two men who actually commit armed robbery—Marty Foster and Nigel

Thaxby—are an unromantic pair. Marty is "a realist" whose aspirations are "a bit of fun with easy pickups" until he is about thirty, when he will "settle down with some steady and get married and live in a semidetached" (p. 122). Nigel does have dreams, but they are unimaginative dreams inspired by pornography and automobile advertisements. After these two botch the robbery and end up with Joyce on their hands as a hostage, Alan Groombridge seizes the opportunity to disappear with £3000 they have not found because it is in the pockets of his raincoat.

Narrowness of experience makes all three of these men remarkably unresourceful criminals. Each of them delivers himself into circumstances whose boundaries close in on him over the course of the story. Marty and Nigel shut themselves, with Joyce as their prisoner, into an apartment whose dimensions become the limits of their world. This is a no-exit situation with rules: They cannot release Joyce because she can identify them. They cannot leave her alone in the apartment, for fear she will make noise or escape. They do not have the nerve to kill her. Nor will the money they have stolen last forever. Soon Nigel is thinking about sending Marty out to work to support the three of them in the apartment for life. Another rule of the situation is that Marty and Nigel have to maintain a majority of two against Joyce's one if they are ever to sleep, go to the bathroom, or shop for groceries. Marty, however, contracts hepatitis and ends up in the hospital, leaving Nigel alone with Joyce. Now the situation constricts further. When food runs out in the apartment, Nigel and Joyce begin to starve.

Meanwhile, Alan's situation is bounded by its own set of rules. He is presumed captured or killed by the robbers, so he must not be seen by anyone who might recognize him. He learns that it almost impossible to rent an apartment without bank references—or to open a bank account without an identity and an address. Eventually he finds Una, an earnest, bookish woman who rents to him without references because, she says, "anyone who likes *Eminent Victorians* is all right" (p. 101). When he and Una fall in love, Alan runs into another rule of his situation—for him the most terrible: He cannot start a new life without keeping secrets about his identity and thus cannot have a real relationship. Also, a literature-inspired sense of chivalry gives him a conscience about Joyce, whom his flight has left in the hands of the bank robbers.

The suspense in this novel has two sources: the systematic elimination of options for the protagonists, along with the sense that process brings of impending disaster, and the reader's hope that the earnest Alan Groombridge will in some way be spared. In the end, Rendell metes out fierce but proportional justice: Joyce, who has done nothing worse than speak in clichés, is wounded and survives. Marty is caught by the police. Nigel, on the run, is badly beaten in a street fight and stripped of car, money, gun, and his plans for an escape to South America—everything "except the desire to live." Rendell makes him crawl "round and round in feeble circles. . . . mumbling . . . 'You wouldn't let me die, you wouldn't let me die'" (p. 240). Then she strips him of life, too. Alan also dies, but he does so in the course of protecting Joyce from gunfire and therefore at peace with his conscience. The policeman who finds his body looks "in wonder at the contentment in the man's face, the mouth that almost smiled" (p. 236).

Reading and not reading are both sources of terror. Imagination and failure of imagination both carry the potential for violence. *Make Death Love Me* nevertheless chooses between the two. As Parr argues, Rendell is suggesting that "illiteracy stifles humanity" and "literacy can provide life with meaning."

In *A Judgement in Stone,* published two years earlier, the point is made even more ferociously. "Eunice Parchman," announces the opening sentence, "killed the Coverdale family because she could not read or write." That sentence typifies much of the tour de force storytelling in this novel, which often mimics the voice of a documentarian reporting on a famous incident. The device allows Rendell's narrative to expand into social commentary and philosophical reflection without sacrificing dramatic effect—and to introduce concepts and terminology from the field of psychology: "Illiteracy had dried up her sympathy and atrophied her imagination. That, along with what psychologists call *affect,* the ability to care about the feelings of others, had no place in her make-up" (p. 42).

Like *Make Death Love Me, A Judgement in Stone* contrasts the evils of narrow experience with those of the overactive imagination and finds the former infinitely more grim. As Bakerman has pointed out, the highly educated Coverdales who employ Eunice as a housekeeper are her foils as well as her victims. Through their character flaws, they collude in the creation of the circumstances that culminate in their deaths. The Coverdales are interferers. Also, Jacqueline Coverdale hires Eunice because she likes the contrast between her own good looks and Eunice's dowdy appearance: "Two factors decided [Jacqueline]," the narrator reports, "her vanity and her snobbishness" (p. 8). Her husband's attitude toward Jacqueline also contributes; he fails to question her sudden enthusiasm for Eunice not only because he loves his wife, but also because that love is patronizing: "He loved her for her impulsiveness which in his eyes made her seem young and sweet and feminine" (p. 11).

A Judgement in Stone punishes these petty sins with violent death; the punishment reserved for the murderer, however, is more terrible. When Eunice is caught, her only sensitivity, a compulsive need to hide her illiteracy, is violated. She becomes an object of horror to thousands. "Literacy is one of the cornerstones of civilization," explains the merciless narrator. "To be illiterate is to be deformed. And the derision that was once directed at the physical freak may, perhaps more justly, descend upon the illiterate" (p. 1). The narrator joins in the shaming of Eunice, calling her "an atavistic ape disguised as a twentieth-century woman" (p. 1).

That verdict, so different from Inspector Wexford's compassionate arm around the shoulders of a murderer who has killed out of disappointed love, suggests that the two terrors of Rendell's universe summon very different responses: For romantic passion, there is sympathy. For failure of imagination, there is intense dislike, apparent even in the Wexford novels. Thus,

RUTH RENDELL

Wexford's investigations frequently encounter witnesses or suspects whose point of view is so narrow that they cannot imagine someone else not knowing what they already know. "Brian went to Australia, didn't he?" Mrs. Chowney snaps at Wexford in *Kissing the Gunner's Daughter* (1992). She speaks in a tone "she might have used to ask Wexford if the sun had risen in the east that morning" (p. 278).

In both Wexford and non-Wexford novels, housekeeping habits often are symptoms of a narrow life. Grubby houses indicate neglect deriving from indifference and inertia. Fanatical neatness indicates misplaced priorities and a constricted imagination. Despite Rendell's description of herself to Bearn as "compulsively tidy," the neat end of the spectrum is associated with particularly dangerous pathologies. In *A Demon in My View,* "Auntie Gracie's" insistence on "elbow grease" as a moral imperative produces Arthur Johnson, a serial strangler who never leaves a dirty dish in his sink. In *Adam and Eve and Pinch Me,* another "Auntie" raises a mentally handicapped girl with such superstitious strictures about the dangers of uncleanliness that "Minny" learns to "shudder" at the thought of perspiration, take two baths a day, and stab men she mistakes for ghosts. *A Sight for Sore Eyes* (1998) is an interesting inversion of the notion that aesthetic sensibilities and romantic projections broaden the moral imagination. Protagonist Teddy Brex, reacting to the squalor in which is parents have raised him, becomes a craftsman whose passion for beauty manifests in painstaking artistry, compulsive tidiness, and a willingness to kill anyone who stands in the way of his aesthetic vision.

WRITER'S PLEASURE: THE THRILLERS

It is a consistently remarkable feature of Rendell's thrillers that they render dreary lives in ways that prohibit the reader from putting the book down. In these books, suspense arises not out of the reader's desire to know what will happen next, but out of fear—the knowledge of what is likely to happen and the desire that it not happen. Sometimes that knowledge derives from a character's demonstrated potential for violence;

sometimes, as in *A Judgement in Stone,* the end-point is telegraphed from the beginning. This is the structure of dread, and the non-Wexford novels could be said to constitute a genre of their own, one whose rules Rendell has invented and refined. Bakerman calls them "inverted mysteries."

They are not universally popular. Rendell has made it clear that she prefers writing thrillers to writing Wexford novels, but "there are a lot of people," she said in an interview with Susan Clark (1989), "who won't read the non-Wexford Ruth Rendell." They would prefer, she told P. D. James, that "I only wrote the Wexfords." It is tempting, perhaps, to dismiss such readers as pleasure-seekers with no stomach for the intellectual challenge of the non-Wexfords. In fact, the Wexford novels are every bit as brainy as the thrillers, if not always as carefully written. It may be relevant here to recall that the experience of writing a novel and the experience of reading it can be very different. When Parr describes the Rendell thrillers as "distressing" and "disturbing," she is referring to the effects on readers. When Marion McCormick (1992) writes that "nobody matches [Rendell] when it comes to turning the screw that raises tension to the level of pain," she means *readers'* pain. That is not to say that Rendell's thrillers are inaccessible or unrewarding. They offer elegantly written character studies, the fascination of evil, stylistic virtuosity, and a compulsive read.

Sometimes, too, readers may find themselves laughing. Extended passages, given over to protagonists' struggles with recalcitrant physical objects, are grimly slapstick in effect. In *A Sight for Sore Eyes,* for instance, Teddy Brex attempts without success to pave over the street-level manhole opening of a coal cellar in which he has hidden two dead bodies. He ends up slipping and falling in himself. Because he has bricked up the basement entrance to the cellar, with great attention to detail, he is trapped. When someone on the street unwittingly replaces the manhole cover, shutting him in for good with the fumes from his victims' bodies, he suffocates.

"Nothing I write distresses me," Rendell told James, although other people's books "distress

RUTH RENDELL

me terribly." Something about the process of writing makes fearsome subjects pleasurable. In the interview with James, Rendell connected this process with her tidiness: "Having a lot of confusion, a mess, and gathering it all together . . . is something I do physically as well." The translation of this pleasure into writing involves "reading about types of psychopathology and madness and putting them on paper."

The fact that Rendell "doesn't write to please everybody," as she told Neill, but "to please me," may partly explain why these novels are experienced as chilly by many readers. Another reason may be the insistence on justice. As DuBose remarks, innocent victims are not so innocent in the thrillers; if they sometimes seem to be chosen by an "accident of fate," that accident "nevertheless reflects their own choices and weaknesses."

These books prove that it is possible to inhabit a character's mind without actually being in sympathy with it. The narrative voice surveys its characters from godlike heights; sometimes it descends into their points of view to show readers the mental machinery at work, but it always maintains its reserve. The filtering consciousness is not the protagonist but the narrative voice itself. Omniscience renders it almost invisible, but this entity is nonetheless a powerful presence that readers might call "reality" or "the narrator" or "God" or, as Bakerman suggests for *The Lake of Darkness* (1980), "Fate." Whatever its name, it orchestrates, moving characters around like pawns, bringing strangers from unconnected walks of life into collision for reasons beyond their knowing. It also dispenses punishment. Presumption and greed are put in their place. Petty vanities, bad parenting, poor housekeeping—or excessive cleanliness—bring grief. Deep moral failings are punishable by death. This might just be the nature of reality, Rendell seems to say, this universe as censorious as any "Auntie Gracie."

Absolute rule invites rebellion, and not all readers have accepted the workings of fate as right and good. Reviewer T. E. D. Klein (1988), commenting on Rendell's collected stories, complains of misogyny and sees "a fondness for poetic irony of the most facile sort." His characterization of irony as a kind of habit in Rendell's

work—almost a reflex—is partially supported by the description Rendell herself gave Moore of her early unpublished work: "Always about people in some situation . . . with some irony or some twist somewhere." Not everyone finds that a bad thing. Bakerman argues that ironic contrasts bring "depth and meaning" to stories that might otherwise devolve into sensationalism. One might add that irony imparts a structural tightness to these books, an aesthetic cohesion that constitutes a very significant artistic achievement.

In her introduction to *The Reason Why* (1995), a collection of other people's stories about murderers, Rendell quotes Madame de Stael—"To understand all is to forgive all"—and suggests a revision: "To understand" (and that is one of the accomplishments of Rendell's investigations into psychopathology) "is to understand" (p. xi).

READERS' PLEASURE: WEXFORD

Like his creator, Chief Inspector Wexford concludes, in *Harm Done,* that "*to understand all is to forgive all* ought to be changed to *to imagine is to understand* and leave off the forgiving bit" (p. 54). Wexford functions as a kind of judge as well as a policeman in the series novels, playing a role parallel to the superego function of the omniscient narrator in Rendell's thrillers. But there is a difference. While Rendell writes the thrillers to please herself, she has repeatedly said that she finds more drawbacks than pleasures in writing Wexford: "A series character," she told Peter Robertson in 1992, "is a liability to any author. It's certainly great for the reader, but the author is stuck" (p. 126). Wexford readers have had some scares, as Rendell has rebelled against the yoke. After *Kissing the Gunner's Daughter* came out in 1992, a comment Rendell made at a conference launched a rumor that Wexford was being retired.But *Simisola* (1994) came out only two years after that, relieving fears. Two more books, *Road Rage* (1997) and *Harm Done,* appeared, and Rendell began once more to voice her restlessness. "I'm writing another Wexford now," she told Stephen Arable in 2002. "It may be the last, and it may not."

In fact, Rendell could be said to have been trying to escape Wexford almost from the beginning. In that desire, Thomas Leitch suggests she is like every other mystery novelist, all of whom, he argues, "disavow" their genre, insisting on their exceptionality and inventiveness against an ostensible generic norm—"just another whodunit"—that has never existed. In Rendell's case (as perhaps in that of other mystery novelists), the phenomenon might be better described as an escape attempt than as disavowal. It is not so much that Rendell wants to write a detective novel while taking credit for "inverting or subverting or deconstructing the genre" as Leitch puts it, as that she wants not to write detective novels. Barring the fulfillment of that desire, she seems to want to *appear* to write detective novels. The claim of exceptionality to which Leitch reacts so skeptically does hover around Rendell's work—but it is a claim made by publicity machines, reviewers, and critics. The claim even has been applied to Rendell's obviously traditional efforts, those one might now cite as foils for later books. Thus, the first-edition flyleaf of *From Doon with Death* reads: "This subtle first novel departs from the well-trodden paths of crime to pose a problem which in its bizarre solution calls for compassion rather than condemnation."

Far more daring departures have been carefully camouflaged. In a 1999 article, Barbara Fass Leavy convincingly uncovers in *Some Lie and Some Die*—published twenty-six years earlier—parallels to Hindu folklore tales and allusions to Hindu holy scripture. Given Rendell's encyclopedic reading habits and her intellectual curiosity, it should come as no surprise that she might sneak an apparently unconnected interest into the English country village setting of the Wexford series. As Fass Leavy notes, however, "Ancient folklore has not merely been transplanted onto a modern setting." Rather, elements of the folkloric narrative have been worked into the central desires and conflicts of the characters. In the process, Rendell's vacation from her mundane Wexford assignment is rendered invisible.

For Rendell is no revolutionary. Over the years, the Wexford novels have, it is true, transformed the village atmosphere of Kingsmarkham: The town grows into a small city, Wexford travels abroad, and the motivations for crimes move away from disappointed love. Still, the approach to social issues—especially to gender—has been tentative. A necessity for circumspection arises partly from the presence of Wexford as the governing consciousness of the novels; Wexford as a moral center is the key to readers' pleasure. By the second novel in the series, he is, as Parr argues, "fully identified with 'the law incarnate' as a man totally incorruptible who radiates strength." Wexford is thus both human and always right. His is an encompassing intelligence, "always intuitive," Rendell writes in *From Doon with Death,* "sometimes even lyrical," but also capable of being "coarse" (p. 87). He is, in other words, neither uncultured nor prissy, occupying an ideal location on the spectrum of possible behaviors. This is the omniscient filtering consciousness made flesh.

If Wexford is God brought to earth, he is also an idealized father figure. According to DuBose, Rendell was not conscious of his resemblance to her own father until her son pointed it out. "Wexford is me and he is my father," Rendell has told Moira Reynolds. This adsorption of the female writer to her male creation and thence to her father is perhaps at the heart of the way the Wexford novels sacrifice writer's pleasure to reader's pleasure. Although Wexford is the "law incarnate," he is also a man worried about his age, a husband, and a father, with consequent concerns and biases. For the suspension of disbelief to function, his reactions to a daughter's feminism, say, or to the blandishments of an attractive female murder suspect, must reflect a point of view that seems plausible for his demographic profile. Over the course of almost forty years, the range of plausibility has shifted.

In other ways, too, the Wexford novels suppress Rendell's interests in order to accommodate readers. "I don't think most readers want to read about old people," Rendell said in her interview with Robertson. "And the temptation as you yourself grow older is to start making your characters middle-age. . . . Eventually they're very old, and nobody wants that." There is a diligent emphasis on contemporaneity in these novels whose protagonist is fifty-two in 1964

RUTH RENDELL

when the series opens, and Wexford's aging does not correspond to the passage of years in real time. In novels published nearly forty years later, he appears to be in his sixties, not approaching ninety. Almost from the beginning, though, the books are self-conscious about his age. Wexford himself is gracious about the youthfulness of others. In *Some Lie and Some Die,* when he and Burden chance on a couple from a nearby rock music festival making love in "a grassy basin" (p. 16), Wexford sees the scene as a kind of pastoral dream, a paradise from which he has been exiled, but toward which he still yearns. This response contrasts starkly with that of Burden, who acts the part of the traditional policeman and takes very bourgeois, middle-aged offense. "Times have changed," Wexford chides Burden in *A Guilty Thing Surprised* (1970) (p. 103).

The emphasis on staying up-to-date means that Wexford's opinions about social issues—and therefore the value system of the narrative as a whole—change over the course of the series. In 1967, in *A New Lease of Death* (*Sins of the Fathers*), Wexford is surprised when the daughter of a servant who has killed his employer does not grow up to be "an anonymous manual worker with perhaps already a couple of petty convictions" (p. 34). Sixteen years later, in *Speaker of Mandarin,* Wexford is critical of an upper-class snob who suggests that a brutal crime involving a shotgun at close range must be the work of a thug from the working classes: "Murder is by no means confined to the working class. And, you know, Mike, it ill becomes him to have said so, it was a fault of character in him that he could say that and it makes me feel his guilt more likely" (p. 153).

The inconsistencies that result from Wexford's evolution are indicators of the fine tuning and hard work that go into maintaining his consciousness as a cocoon of comfort for readers. He is always right, but what is right changes over time; and Wexford's point of view must never sound either wild-eyed or diehard.

For the same reason, the plot elements must seem contemporary. In 1992, *Kissing the Gunner's Daughter* updates Wexford's world by

acknowledging the influence of television on the genre. The murders are committed American-style, with handguns. The murder scene is far more graphically described than in previous Wexford novels; multiple victims lie in copious amounts of blood, suggesting mass criminality. Wexford is interviewed on television and reminds himself to think of his interviewers as "the media" rather than "the press" (p. 58). The effort to stay up-to-date is explicit in other ways, too. When Burden suggests that one of the suspects has no alibi, Wexford replies: "You know, Mike, something rather strange has happened to alibis in recent years. It's getting progressively more difficult to establish hard and fast ones. It's got something to do with people leading more isolated lives" (p. 263). In 1997, *Road Rage* notes the effect of word processors on traditional methods of tracing anonymous letters: "No spelling mistakes anymore, no capitals in error for lowercase, no slipped letters, no chipped digits" (p. 69).

The result of these efforts to stay current is a sort of archaeological record of the past four decades. Perhaps it is not surprising that geographer Lisa Kadonaga (1998) would be attracted to the sense of place in the Wexford novels, noting that the landscape of Kingsmarkham registers the "physical and social processes" that have transformed it. A large country house becomes a social services agency. The landscape is littered with the ruins of other country houses, and still other country houses have been replaced with public housing towers or "converted to trout farms."

The late period is also far more overtly political than Rendell's previous work. Idealization as a motive for murder has all but disappeared from the Wexford series. The emergence of social issues as a theme is not entirely surprising; as DuBose notes, Rendell's work has always been conscious of class issues. Nevertheless there has been significant evolution. In the early and middle work, class inequities serve as a backdrop to the story, providing ostensibly realistic touches that signal the storyteller's skill and the reliability of the world she creates. In *Simisola, Harm Done,* and *Road Rage,* social issues have become the thematic center. The ultimate source of murder in

RUTH RENDELL

Simisola is a law, the Immigration Act of 1971, and the loopholes in the law that make abuse possible.

Still, it is worth asking why Rendell calls only these last three novels "the political Wexfords." Why not include *An Unkindness of Ravens* (1985), in which Wexford investigates the members of a radical feminist organization? The short answer is that in *An Unkindness of Ravens,* it is not social issues that are at the heart of the crime, but the stridency of people who insist on making an issue of social issues. A longer look at this distinction shows the constrictive effect the Wexford persona has had on Rendell's voice and sheds more light on her attempts to escape.

Wexford is open-minded enough to recognize that ARRIA, or Action for the Radical Reform of Intersexual Attitudes, is not entirely unjustified in its complaints about gender inequities. But the narrative distances itself, by way of an emphasis on the unreasonableness of ARRIA members, from the noisiness of protest. Gender issues have of course surfaced in the Wexford novels before, indicating an interest on Rendell's part. ("I think that all women, unless they are absolutely asleep," Rendell told Libby Brooks (2002), "must be feminists up to a point.") There has always been a determined evenhandedness, though. A too forward-looking Wexford would too clearly be his female creator's mouthpiece, thus shattering the illusion on which readers' enjoyment of these novels depends. *A Sleeping Life* notes the frustrations of a talented woman denied schooling because of her gender, but "balances" that point with an unsympathetic account of the complaints Wexford's daughter Sylvia has about her life as a housewife. "In a moment bound to distress Wexford's feminist admirers," Parr says of this book, "the chief inspector suggests it's nice to be a woman because men will stop and help her if she has a flat tire." Robert Barnard (1983) has complained that Rendell's "level of comment" on gender issues is embarrassingly superficial.

Have the critics been unfair? Rendell has for a number of years been visibly involved in sensitive political issues, calling for women bishops, supporting a movement to increase the number of women in parliament, campaigning for education on the dangers of clitoridectomy, joining antinuclear protests, protesting animal testing. It seems unlikely that the politically cautious tone of her early and middle-period novels can be attributed to personal cowardice or lack of passion.

Critic William Stowe (1986) refers to "a liberal internal censor" at work in *An Unkindness of Ravens* that prevents the novel from completely reinforcing readers' prejudices about feminists. Just as apparent is an internal censor that requires Rendell, despite her own interest in women's issues, to maintain an objective distance from those issues, not to seem to advocate, and, above all, to avoid being like "them." As a result, a great deal of narrative energy is devoted to distinguishing a correct position apart from radical feminism. In the early and middle novels, Wexford's daughter Sylvia bears the brunt of this distancing strategy. A softening of Sylvia's shrillness and unreasonableness in the later books, a rapprochement with her father, and, finally, passages narrated from her point of view in *Harm Done* mark the shifting cultural norms with which the Wexfords are always aligned.

The Wexford novels, including the late ones, are not works of the avant-garde, as Stowe writes, nor should they be expected to be. Stowe describes them as quintessentially "liberal" works that move relatively new ideas into the cultural mainstream. That task, he observes, is undertaken at a price: "Rendell's writing is clear to a fault: her prose aspires to a transparency that contemporary literary theorists find naïve." This kind of "transparent window" onto Wexford's point of view necessitates, he points out, "the careful repression of Rendell's own voice."

A THIRD WAY: BARBARA VINE

Comments Rendell has made about the origins of her pseudonym suggest that under her own name she has found it hard to escape the accumulated habits and obligations of her two narrative personas. Both of those personas could be characterized as superego voices, stylistically brilliant in one case, comfortingly paternal in the other. Between her publishing obligations to

RUTH RENDELL

Wexford fans and the rules of the suspense genre she herself has created, expectations of Ruth Rendell are so firmly in place—a manhole cover, one might say, or a bit of bricklaying worthy of Teddy Brex—that there does not seem to be room for the full expression of her broad-ranging imagination. What about the everyday anxieties of people who do not harbor pathological urges to violence? What about women's concerns—especially childbearing—on which a female author might have an inside track, but at which the narrative consciousness of Wexford must look from the outside?

"I wanted to let readers know to expect something different," Rendell told James. To Sarah Lyall, she has characterized the Vine novels as "softer and more feminine" than those she writes under her own name. There has never been any question of using the Barbara Vine name to obscure authorship. Both names appear on the Vine book jackets.

Ostensibly the source of the pseudonym is straightforward: Barbara is Rendell's middle name; Vine is her father's grandmother's maiden name. But another part of the story, recounted by Parr, suggests that there may be more than convenience in the choice of this name—that "Barbara" may not be a pseudonym at all. Rendell's mother called her by her middle name—Barbara. Her father called her Ruth, although he eventually capitulated and switched to Barbara. Rendell has continued to have two names in her private life, and Parr sees in this duality an explanation of the different world views, "hopeful" and "bleaker," apparent in the work. Leith wonders if "Vine is the self she struggled to suppress" and reports her as admitting, "I couldn't have written the Vines under the name Rendell, and I can't account for that." Certainly the name "Barbara Vine" is appropriate to the material, not only because under the identity assigned by her mother, Rendell writes "more feminine" books than under the identity given her by her father, but also because, as Nicola King points out, the "doubling and disguise of name and identity is a central trope" in the Vine novels. From these hints about the power of a name, it is possible to conclude that the Vine pseudonym serves Rendell, paradoxically, as a mask that makes it possible to drop her other, more concealing masks: omniscient narrator and trustworthy Wexford.

Most of the Vine novels have first-person narrators. Often the narrators are writers themselves—researching the origins of some traumatic event, delving into family secrets, or writing an ancestor's biography. The self-referential style of these books is a far cry from the transparency of the Wexford prose Stowe calls naïve. The storytelling is often tricky and unreliable. The diaries that are the centerpiece of *Asta's Book* (1993) exemplify this tendency, functioning, as King puts it, "both to conceal and to reveal the truth, offering transparency whilst also practicing concealment." Asta herself comes to see these maneuvers as inevitable:

When I first started writing this diary I told myself I'd write down only the absolute truth. Now I understand that's not possible. It wouldn't be possible for anyone, not just me. All I can do is be honest about what I feel, I can do that, what I feel and what I believe in. Total openness about the facts I can't manage.

(p. 59)

The change in Asta's approach to writing parallels the evolution of Rendell's own writing career—the progress from novels featuring cool observation and avoidance of bias to novels with feeling and point of view. In the comparatively safe space behind the Barbara Vine mask, it seems, there is room to risk subjectivity and bias.

The stylistic difference is apparent in the way two passages, the first from *A Sight for Sore Eyes,* by Ruth Rendell, the second from *The Blood Doctor* (2000), by Barbara Vine, use the verb "to be." Rendell writes:

There *are* people in this world with very good brains and astute minds who at the same time have no common sense whatever. Bad judges of character and situation, unable to take the long view, they *are* both very clever and very unwise. Richard Hill *was* one of them.

(p. 35, emphases added.)

This omniscient narrator thoroughly knows the minds of minor characters and knows the world at large just as absolutely. He (it seems reasonable to say "he" of this narrator) uses the verb "to be" to describe reality.

Vine writes:

> *I'm not sure* if I'd have liked him [the great-grandfather being researched], and up till now *it's been essential* to me to like, or at least admire and respect, the subject of the biographies I write. Perhaps, this time, *it's* only going *to be necessary* for me *to be interested* in him. And that won't *be difficult. It's only because* I found out he kept a mistress.
>
> (p. 1, emphases added.)

Every instance of the verb "to be" has a predicate that is descriptive of the narrator's personal preferences or state of mind. The passage is about the origins of his ("his" is explicit in the case of this narrator) perceptions, and its focus is perception rather than reality.

Some readers see the disorderly Vine world as more fearsome than the universe of Rendell's other work. Tracing Vine's influence in the later Wexfords, particularly in the sprawling structure of *Harm Done,* Leith suggests that Kingsmarkham, is "looking darker, more frightening." Perhaps, though, Leith conflates complexity and fearsomeness; the Vine novels, while often advertised as novels of suspense, are not primarily novels of pain. Secrets rather than situations tend to unravel over the course of the narrative tale. In the Rendell thrillers, suspense derives, as Bakerman puts it, from "the readers' knowledge of the horrors to come." In the Vine novels, the horrors lie mostly in the past, and the mechanism of suspense is gradual revelation of a story rather than anticipation of disaster.

Fear is not banished in the Vine novels. It is transformed into guilt or anxiety; clinical psychosis has become neurosis. These books, says Reynolds, quoting Rendell, are about "ordinary people under extraordinary pressure." They are different enough from each other that, while it is possible to identify recurring tropes and themes, no formulation critics have arrived at covers all the books. According to DuBose, the Vine novels explore past acts, or "sins," that reach through time and generations. King finds a common element in the exploration of childbirth, maternity, children's biological identities, and authorship— or, as a childhood friend of the narrator puts it in *A Dark-Adapted Eye* (1986),

> "It's all babies, isn't it? There was Elsie's baby that never was and now there's your aunt's and there was the baby that disappeared. Have you done *MacBeth* at school? . . . *MacBeth* is full of babies and milk. . . . It's really strange that a play like that which is full of horrors should have all that babies-and-milk stuff, isn't it?"
>
> (p. 130)

The narrator, Faith, promises to look at the play because the story she is telling is "full of babies and milk too." One might suspect that by citing the Shakespearean precedent, Rendell, as Barbara Vine, is giving herself permission to write books full of milk and blood.

The introduction of ambiguity, subjectivity, and problems of maternity allows Rendell as Vine to revisit and transform some of her lifelong themes. The dangers and attractions of imaginative idealization, a theme that by the turn of the century is almost absent from the Wexford series, resurfaces in several Vine novels. In *A Fatal Inversion* (1987), for instance, disillusioned romantic love ultimately leads to murder, but not of lover or beloved. The victim is a bystander to the drama, a woman whose honesty would ensure her survival in a Rendell thriller but who is here punished for her virtues.

The phenomenon of imaginative failure also is revisited, perhaps most thoroughly in *A Dark-Adapted Eye.* "Vera," the narrator says of an aunt who eventually commits murder, "used to become disproportionately excited over trivial things. The point was that to her they were not trivial" (p. 40). Once again, bourgeois pettiness is associated with a failure of empathetic imagination. Vera and her sister Eden often behave like the witnesses who expect Chief Inspector Wexford to know the details of their lives as well as they do. In Vera and Eden, this solipsism takes the form of

> assuming you knew exactly whom they meant when they referred to someone or other. . . . When you confessed your ignorance. . . . they became very

RUTH RENDELL

scathing. . . . And this assumption that the rest of the world was completely *au fait* with their ways extended to custom and habits, so that without being told, one was expected to know what time to get up, when to use the bathroom, where the back-door key hung, when the milkman came, who was Eden's best friend, what subjects she was taking, . . . the vicar's name, and have by heart the timetable of the Colchester bus.

(p. 44)

As in the Rendell and Wexford books, failure of imagination ultimately amounts to murder. The difference is that Vera, who starts out as repellent as any narrow-minded character in Rendell's oeuvre, has by the end won the reader's sympathy without also winning a judge's pardon. The law, it seems is not subtle enough to discern that in this case the murderer is her victim's victim.

Disproportionate punishment, misdirected punishment, and mercy for the truly guilty are common when Rendell writes as Barbara Vine. In the broadest terms, then, it is possible to make the generalization that in these novels Rendell is trying out another hypothesis, one very different from the hypothesis explored in the thrillers: Instead of an unforgiving universe, she posits an ambiguous one. It is worth taking a look at the shape and scope of ambiguity in *A Dark-Adapted Eye* because this first of the Vine novels sets a precedent the others follow.

A central issue is the identity of the narrator's cousin Jamie—not only his paternity, but also his maternity is in question. Is Faith's aunt Eden his mother? Or is Vera, who seems to have adopted Jamie to protect Eden from the social consequences of bearing a child out of wedlock, after all his biological mother? Almost universally, critics and reviewers have concluded that the novel deliberately leaves the question open. This reading relies heavily on a passage near the end of the book in which Faith weighs the arguments for and against Vera, for and against Eden, and finds herself unable to choose. Before the conclusion is reached that both women are equally likely mothers, though, it is worth recognizing that Faith has a bias in the matter, a preference for Vera. The evidence adduced for Vera as mother is mostly speculative, answering the more concrete evidence that exists for Eden. "Certainly

[Eden] became pregnant sometime in the summer of 1943," Faith admits (p. 261). Eden also disappears from the Women's Royal Naval Service from 1943 to 1945, more evidence that she actually carried a baby to term. Most tellingly, her name appears on Jamie's birth certificate.

Against these facts, Faith brings to bear all her creative powers. Eden has had a miscarriage, and Faith attributes it to an ectopic pregnancy (although earlier in the novel she admits that "there was no real reason to believe this" [p. 186]). The ectopic pregnancy, she argues, may in turn have been caused by a botched abortion—in other words, Eden never brought a baby to term after all. That would leave Vera as the biological mother. How would Vera have become pregnant while her husband was overseas fighting a war? Faith speculates that Vera may have encountered "some old boyfriend." Then she worries, "Is this too farfetched? Am I being absurd? Perhaps" (p. 261). Still, she returns to the charge. "Vera suckled Jamie, she fed him at her own breast. I saw it. I can't be mistaken here" (pp. 261–262). Or can she? Earlier, Faith admits that "memory is an imperfect function" and recognizes that "it is the knowledge, imparted to us by unshakable outside authority, that an incident we remember never took place, which we find so hard to accept" (p. 257). She applies that understanding of fallible memory to the grown-up Jamie's insistence that he was present at the scene of Eden's death and that her blood "had flown at him." The scene he remembers so vividly is impossible, Faith knows. Jamie had been removed from the room before Vera attacked her sister. Faith does not, however, apply these insights about memory to her own vivid memory of seeing Vera with Jamie in her arms and a drop of milk falling from her nipple.

The gestures at even-handedness—on the one hand Eden, on the other hand Vera—are belied by the unequal weight of the evidence Faith brings to bear on the two sides of the issue. With the preponderance of evidence pointing to Eden, Faith still insists that "so it goes on, round and round in perpetual motion without ever coming to rest on Eden's square or Vera's" (p. 263) and in doing so, betrays her own wishes. Because, in the course of her acquaintanceship with the adult Jamie, she has acquired a sympathy for his fervent belief that Vera is his mother, because she admires Vera's passionate attachment to Jamie and is appalled by Eden's dislike of children, because Eden after all only reclaimed Jamie to serve as an heir, Faith wants to believe in Vera's claim. Perhaps she is not quite the "reliable, detached and more-or-less objective" narrator King sees in her.

In fact, Faith partakes in the Longley family traits she sees as the root of the problem. "The quintessence of Longleyism," she says, is "to ask petty, pointless, rhetorical questions when up to one's neck in trouble." She demonstrates this tactic herself: Left alone to baby-sit Jamie, she finds herself unequal to the task, and as Jamie throws a tantrum, answers the door to Eden and a fiancé:

"They're all out," I said, shouting above Jamie.

"All?"

How was it I seemed to know, even then, that she was acting? Perhaps because she was no actress.

"Didn't you know Vera was here?"[Faith's question.]

"Vera? Here?" . . .

"Well of course. This is Jamie. Don't you recognize him?" [Faith's question]

(pp. 140–141)

Faith's analysis of this interaction emphasizes the pretense Eden makes of not knowing that Vera is in London visiting Faith's family. Indeed it is a pretense, because Eden and Vera have arranged to meet. But when Faith answers the door, she has no way of knowing about that arrangement, and her question illustrates the Longley habits of going on the offensive when in trouble and assuming that "the rest of the world" should be "completely *au fait*" with her life.

The narrator of *A Dark-Adapted Eye,* in other words, features neither absolute self-knowledge nor absolute honesty. The subtle treacheries of her voice are an essential ingredient in the experience of suspense the novel creates. Her storytelling mentions names and alludes to incidents, just as Vera and Eden do, without explaining them to

outsiders. In the course of the first chapter, for instance, the reader has to gradually piece together the information that Vera is Faith's father's sister—Faith's aunt—and that she has been hanged.

The teasing release of information is typical of Barbara Vine. In some of the novels, as reviewer Michael Dirda (1989) points out, "such storytelling is completely artificial." In the most tightly constructed Vine novels, however, the effect is attributable to the narrative persona itself. The structural method—the withholding of information—ties thematically into the events narrated. As King puts it, "The fascination of Vine's plots is a function of the gap between the *szujet*—the events *referred to* by the narrative—and the *fabula*—the way the events are *reconstructed* by the narrative" (King's emphases). In *A Dark-Adapted Eye,* one might say, there is not as much ambiguity of *szujet* as critics have thought and much more ambiguity of *fabula.*

Nothing inherently ties this method of suspense to crime, or, for that matter, to fear. In later Vine novels, the prominence of murder as an engine of suspense is reduced. Murder makes a sort of cameo appearance in *Grasshopper,* but it does not directly involve the main character. The foundational trauma whose details the story gradually unfolds is not a crime at all. The crimes committed in *The Blood Doctor* occur three generations back. Other issues loom in the foreground. Will the wife of the narrator realize that her husband does not share her longing for a child? Will she stop having miscarriages? Will he overcome his aversion to baby-sitting, or will it tear the marriage apart? The suspense in this novel derives as much from these everyday conflicts as from the narrator's quest to uncover sins committed by an ancestor.

THE END OF FEAR?

Inconsistencies, paradoxes, and offhand comments trigger the investigations Vine protagonists undertake. Suggestive facts are known, but not their emotional context. Invariably, the seekers of context encounter obstacles, not only external obstacles (the inadvertent destruction of family letters, say), but also obstacles internal to the personalities involved. Secrecy and ingrained reticence play a structural role in these books, and all promises to the reader are kept. The investigation always turns something up, some secret, some foundational trauma.

Would a thorough look into the author's life yield such discoveries? It has been a busy life, with more than fifty books published and many awards. Rendell also has engaged with social problems and politics; in 1997, she was made Baroness Rendell of Babergh, a Labour life peer in the House of Lords. Facts are known, then, but not their emotional context. Rendell's reluctance to publicly account for herself, perhaps understandably, matches the reticence of her characters. What does "unhappy childhood" mean? Does it mean the immigrant experience, nasty schoolmates, emotional stress? Or is there a darker story there? What about Rendell's relationship with her husband, whom she divorced in 1975 and married again in 1977? If there is a story *there,* it is jealously guarded. Perhaps, after all, the hints that have so intrigued journalists are, like the terrors explored in the fiction, dramatic formulations. Perhaps, in other words, one should not take Rendell's description of herself as "frightened" too literally. Her current life, she insists, is placid. Since her husband's death in 1999, she has lived alone in London. As she told reporter Emily Bearn in 2002, she is not worried about crime. Burglars have dropped by, she said, but "I am not fearful."

SELECTED BIBLIOGRAPHY

I. WORKS OF RUTH RENDELL (All page numbers given in citations to works by Rendell refer to the first American editions of those works unless otherwise noted.)

NOVELS. *From Doon with Death* (London, 1964; first American edition: Garden City, NY, 1965, 1964. In-text citations refer to the Long edition. Wexford series.); *To Fear a Painted Devil* (London, 1965; first American edition: Garden City, NY, 1965); *Vanity Dies Hard* (London, 1966; first published in the United States as *In Sickness and in Health,* Garden City, NY, 1966); *A New Lease of Death* (London, 1967; first American edition: Garden City, NY, 1967—also published in the United States as *Sins of the Fathers,* New York, 1967, 1970; in-text citations refer to the Ballantine Books edition; Wexford series); *Wolf to the Slaughter* (London, 1967; first American edition: Garden City, NY: 1968; Wexford series); *The Secret House of Death* (London, 1968; first American edition: Garden City, NY, 1969); *The Best Man to Die* (London, 1969; first American edition: Garden City, NY, 1970; Wexford series).

A Guilty Thing Surprised (London, 1970; first American edition: Garden City, NY, 1970; Wexford series); *One Across, Two Down* (London, 1971; first American edition: Garden City, NY, 1971); *No More Dying Then* (London, 1971; first American edition: Garden City NY, 1972; Wexford series); *Murder Being Once Done* (London, 1972; first American edition: Garden City, NY, 1972; Wexford series); *Some Lie and Some Die* (London, 1973; first American edition: Garden City, NY, 1973; Wexford series); *The Face of Trespass* (London, 1974; first American edition: Garden City, NY, 1974); *Shake Hands Forever* (London, 1975; first American edition: Garden city, NY, 1975; Wexford series); *A Demon in My View* London, 1976; first American edition: New York, 1977); *A Judgement in Stone* (London, 1977; first American edition: Garden City, NY, 1978); *A Sleeping Life* (London, 1978; Garden City, NY, 1979; Wexford series); *Make Death Love Me* (London, 1979; first American edition: Garden City, NY, 1979).

The Lake of Darkness (London, 1980; first American edition: Garden City, NY, 1980); *Put on by Cunning* (London, 1981; published in the United States as *Death Notes,* New York, 1981; Wexford series); *Master of the Moor* (London, 1983; first American edition, 1982); *Speaker of Mandarin* (London, 1983; first American edition: New York, 1983; Wexford series); *The Killing Doll* (London, 1984; first American edition: New York, 1984); *The Tree of Hands* (London, 1984; first American edition: New York, 1985); *An Unkindness of Ravens* (London: 1985; first American edition: New York, 1985; Wexford series); *Live Flesh* (London, 1986; first American edition: New York, 1986); *Talking to Strange Men* (London, 1987; first American edition: New York, 1987); *The Veiled One.* London, 1988; first American edition: New York, 1988; Wexford series); *The Bridesmaid* (London, 1989; first American edition: New York, 1989).

Going Wrong (London, 1990; first American edition: New York, 1990); *Kissing the Gunner's Daughter* (London, 1992; first American edition: New York, 1992; Wexford series); *The Crocodile Bird* (London, 1993; first American edition: New York, 1993); *Simisola* (London, 1994; first American edition: New York, 1995, 1994; Wexford series); *The Keys to the Street* (London, 1996; first American edition: New York, 1996) *Road Rage* (London, 1997; first American edition: New York, 1997; Wexford series); *A Sight for Sore Eyes* (London, 1998; first American edition: New York, 1999); *Harm Done* (London, 1999; first American edition: New York, 1999; Wexford series).

Adam and Eve and Pinch Me London, 2001; first American edition: New York, 2001).

NOVELS WRITTEN UNDER THE NAME BARBARA VINE. *A Dark-Adapted Eye* (London: 1986; first American edition: New York: 1986); *A Fatal Inversion* (Middlesex, England: 1987; first American edition: New York: 1987); *The House of Stairs* (London: 1988; first American edition: New York: 1989, 1988; all page citations refer to the American edition); *Gallowglass* (London, Penguin Books Ltd., 1990; first American edition: New York: Harmony Books, 1990); *King Solomon's Carpet* (London: 1991; first American edition: New York: 1991); *Asta's Book* (London: 1993; published in the United States as *Anna's Book,* New York:

1993); *No Night Is Too Long* (London: 1994; first American edition: New York: 1995); *The Brimstone Wedding* (London: 1995; first American edition: New York: 1995); *The Chimney Sweeper's Boy* (London: 1998; first American edition: New York: 1998); *Grasshopper* (London: 2000; first American edition: New York: 2000); *The Blood Doctor* London: 2000; first American edition: New York: 2002).

NOVELLAS. *Heartstones* (London: 1987; first American edition: New York: 1987); *The Strawberry Tree* (London: 1990).

STORY COLLECTIONS. *The Fallen Curtain and Other Stories* (London: 1976; New York: 1976); *Means of Evil and Other Stories* (London: 1979; first published in the United States as *Means of Evil: Five Stories by an Edgar Award-Winning Writer,* Garden City, NY: 1980; Wexford stories); *The Fever Tree and Other Stories* (London: 1982; first American edition: New York: 1982) *The New Girl Friend and Other Stories of Suspense* (London: 1985; first American edition: New York: 1985); *The Copper Peacock and Other Stories* (London: 1991; first American edition: New York: 1991); *Blood Lines: Long and Short Stories* (London: 1995; first American edition: New York, 1996; includes the novella The Strawberry Tree); *Piranha to Scurfy and Other Stories* (London: 2000; first American edition: New York: 2000).

OTHER WORKS. *Ruth Rendell's Suffolk* (London: 1989); *Undermining the Central Line* (London: 1989; co-authored with Colin Ward); "A Voyage Among Misty Isles" (May 16; the impression the Alaskan coast made on Rendell also is apparent in No Night Is Too Long).

COLLECTIONS EDITED BY RENDELL. *A Warning to the Curious: The Ghost Stories of M. R. James* (London: 1987); *The Reason Why: An Anthology of the Murderous Mind* (London: 1995; first American edition: New York: 1995).

EDITIONS FOR WHICH RENDELL HAS WRITTEN INTRODUCTIONS. Trollope, Anthony: *Barchester Towers* (London: 1995, 1857); Trollope, Anthony: *Doctor Thorne* (London, New York: 1991, 1858); *The Epistle of Paul the Apostle to the Romans* (Edinburgh: 1999).

INTERVIEWS AND BIOGRAPHICAL PROFILES. John Mortimer, "Well-Known Cemeteries: Ruth Rendell," in *Character Parts* (Harmondsworth, U.K., 1986). Pp. 139–143; Susan L. Clark, "A Fearful Symmetry" (*Armchair Detective,* 22(1989): 228–235; P. D. James, *Ruth Rendell* (Video no. 78 in the series *Writers Talk: Ideas of Our Time,* Northbrook, Ill., 1989); Peter Robertson, "Ruth Rendell" (*Booklist,* September 15, 1992). Pp. 126–127; Steve Moore, "A Conversation with: Ruth Rendell." *In Word* 1994, http://www.womankindflp.org/newletter/interviews/rendell.htm; Sarah Lyall, "Mysteries, of Course, but Ruth Rendell Also Sees Real Evil" (*New York Times,* April 10, 1995, p. C9); Michael Neill, "To Make the Skin Crawl" (*People Weekly,* December 18, 1995). Pp. 65–66; William Leith, "Creeping Vine" (*Independent,* September 5, 1999); Stephen Anable, "PW Talks with Ruth Rendell" (*Publishers Weekly,* January 28, 2002, p. 275); Emily Bearn, "The Prime of Baroness Rendell" (*Daily Telegraph* (London), June 20, 2002); Emily Bearn, "Being Ruth Rendell" (*Sunday Telegraph* (London), June 23, 2002); Libby Brooks, "Dark Lady of Whodunnits." (*Guardian,* August 3, 2002); Jane Jakeman, "Ruth Rendell: 'If I Were to Kill Wexford, There'd Be an Outcry.'" (*Independent,* June 15, 2002).

CRITICAL WORKS AND BOOK REVIEWS. Bakerman, Jane S.: "Explorations of Love: An Examination of Some Novels by Ruth Rendell" (1978); Bakerman, Jane S: "Ruth Rendell," in *10 Women of Mystery,* ed. Earl F. Bargainnier (Bowling Green OH: 1981, pp. 124–149); Barnard, Robert: "A Talent to Disturb" (1983); Corrigan, Sue: "Explorer of the Psyche's Darkness" (April 18, 1998, p. 11); Dirda, Michael: "Ruth Rendell: Chills and Fevers" (August 6, 1989, p. X7); Drabelle, Dennis: "Rendell's Deft Story Factory" (May 19, 1992, p. B2); DuBose, Martha Hailey: "Ruth Rendell: Triple Threatening," in *Women of Mystery: The Lives and Works of Notable Women Crime Novelists* (New York: 2000, pp. 362–373); Giffone, Tony: "Disoriented in the Orient: The Representation of the Chinese in Two Contemporary Mystery Novels," in *Cultural Power/Cultural Literacy,* ed. Bonnie Braendlin (Tallahassee: 1991, pp. 143–151); Hendershot, Cyndy: "Gender and Subjectivity in Ruth Rendell's 'The New Girlfriend'" (Fall–Winter 1994); Kadonaga, Lisa: "Strange Countries and Secret Worlds in Ruth Rendell's Crime Novels" (July 1998); King, Nicola: "Myths of Origin: Identity, Memory and Detection in Barbara Vine's *A Dark Adapted Eye* and *Asta's Book,*" in *Memory, Narrative, Identity: Remembering the Self* (Edinburgh, Scotland: pp. 93–118), Kirsch, Jonathan: "Trapped in a Crumbling World of Passion and Betrayal: *The Crocodile Bird* by Ruth Rendell" *os Angeles Times* January 5, 1994, p. E3); Klein, T. E. D. "Ruth Rendell's Thirty-Eight" (May 15, 1988, p. X9); Leavy, Barbara Fass: "A Folklore Plot in Ruth Rendell's Wexford Series" (Fall 1999); Leitch, Thomas M: "Not Just Another Whodunit: Disavowal as Evolution in Detective Fiction" (Spring 1999); McCormick, Marion: "Is Ruth Rendell Disposing of Her Long-Serving Inspector?" (May 9, 1992, p. J5); Parr, Susan Resneck: "Ruth Rendell," in *Dictionary of Literary Biography, Volume 87: British Mystery and Thriller Writers Since 1940,* ed. Bernard Benstock and Thomas F. Staley (Farmington Hills, MI: 1989, pp. 305–327); Rance, Nick: "'Victorian Values' and 'Fast Young Ladies': From Madeleine Smith to Ruth Rendell," in *Varieties of Victorianism: The Uses of the Past,* ed. Gary Day. (London: 1998; New York: 1998, pp. 220–235); Reynolds, Moira Davison: "Ruth Rendell," in *Women Authors of Detective Series: Twenty-One American and British Writers, 1900-2000* (Jefferson, NC, and London: 2001); Rowland, Susan: "The Horror of Modernity and the Utopian Sublime: Gothic Villainy in P.D. James and Ruth Rendell," in *The Devil Himself: Villainy in Detective Fiction and Film,* ed. Stacy Gillis and Philippa Gates (Westport, CT, and London: 2002, pp. 135–146); Stowe, William W.: "Popular Fiction as Liberal Art" (November 1986).

The Popular Culture Library at Bowling Green State University, Bowling Green, Ohio, has two boxes of materials related to Rendell's work. The materials include a cassette recording of an interview with Rendell; typed manuscripts of *A Demon in My View, A Judgement in Stone,* and *Make Death Love Me*; and uncorrected printers' proofs of *The New Girlfriend and Other Stories* (Pantheon edition) and *The Secret House of Death* (both the Hutchinson and the Doubleday editions).

FILM AND TELEVISION ADAPTATIONS OF WORKS BY RUTH RENDELL. *Alias Betty* (produced by Annie Miller, Yves Marmion UGC YM, Les Films de la Boissière, Go Films, and France 2 Cinéma; released in the United States by Wellspring, 2002, directed by Claude Miller, based on the novel *The Tree of Hands*); *An Affair in*

Mind (BBC: 1987, directed by Colin Luke, based on The Face of Trespass); *Carne Tremula* (*Live Flesh*) (produced by Augustín Almodovar; released in the United States by MGM: 1997, directed by Pedro Almodovar, based on the novel *Live Flesh*); *La Cérémonie* (*The Ceremony*) (produced Martin Karmitz: 1996, directed by Claude Chabrol, based on *A Judgement in Stone*); *A Dark-Adapted Eye* (BBC: 1996, television adaptation directed by Tim Fywell); *Dead Lucky* (BBC: 1991, television adaptation of *Lake of Darkness* directed by Barbara Rennie); *A Fatal Inversion* (BBC: 1992, television adaptation directed by Tim Fywell); *Gallowglass* (BBC: 1993, television adaptation directed by Tim Fywell); *The Housekeeper* (Warner Studios, 1986, film based on *A Judgement in Stone,* directed by Ousama Rawi); *Innocent Victim* (Academy Entertainment, Inc.: 1990, film based on *Tree of Hands,* directed by Giles Foster); *The Ruth Rendell Mysteries* (ITV: 1987–, series based on Rendell's thrillers and Wexford novels, various directors).

IAIN CRICHTON SMITH

(1928–1998)

Gerry Cambridge

AT HIS DEATH in October 1998 at the age of seventy, Iain Crichton Smith was not only a literary figure held in virtually unanimous affection in Scotland, but also widely regarded as one of the most significant Scottish poets of the twentieth century. An immensely prolific writer—his friend and contemporary, the Scottish poet Norman MacCaig, once humorously professed concern that Iain "hasn't had a new book out . . . for days"—Smith published nineteen books of verse in English, eleven novels, and six collections of short stories, as well as plays and literary criticism. His essay "The Golden Lyric" is one of the seminal critical discussions of the poet Hugh MacDiarmid, written with the urgency of a writer who was also elucidating his own aesthetic.

English was not Smith's first language. He grew up speaking Gaelic, Scotland's oldest language, spoken only, according to the 1991 census, by some sixty-six thousand native speakers, predominantly in the Outer Hebrides, an island group in the Atlantic Ocean west of Scotland. Smith wrote in Gaelic too, yet it is for his work in English, understandably enough, especially the poetry, that he received international recognition. Smith wrote in sonorous free and formal verse in a style which crossed an often Latinate elegance of diction with a sensibility that at times waged an aesthetic war against the dogmatic Presbyterian religion of his island childhood. While in this mode he can seem a grave and somewhat humorless writer, the work is also marked by startling perceptual leaps, when the movement of his mind is like a bright bird flitting from one unexpected place to another; the movement in his poetry is toward transcending his own difficult biography.

LIFE

Iain Crichton Smith was born on New Year's Day 1928, in Glasgow—though it is often stated, erroneously, that he was born on the Hebridean island of Lewis. He was the middle son of three. His father, John Smith, a merchant seaman, died of tuberculosis when Iain was two. His mother, Christina Campbell Smith, returned to her native Lewis with her charges shortly afterward, settling in the small township of Bayble, whose inhabitants were crofters, customarily tenants of smallholdings that they farmed in addition to other employment.

It was a forbidding environment. Lewis, some six hundred square miles in extent, the largest island in the Outer Hebrides, is magnificent but barren. Relatively few trees can grow there owing to prevailing Atlantic winds. Lewis in the late 1920s and 1930s was both a classless society in which no one bothered to lock doors—crime was nonexistent—and a primarily Gaelic-speaking community governed by the Free Church of Scotland, an extreme Calvinist offshoot of the Church of Scotland. The Free Church strictly observes the Sabbath, and has so dominated the island that Sunday commercial airline travel to it was prohibited until as late as 2002; in that year there still was no Sunday ferry service. The "Wee Frees," as members of the Free Church are colloquially called, believe in what one poet-critic, Ian McDonough, writing in the journal *The Dark Horse,* has referred to as the "paradoxical twin tenets of predestination and Original Sin" (p. 68). Smith's mother adhered fervently to the faith. She formed a model for many of the stark old women who populate Smith's poems and fiction.

Smith's childhood was fundamentalist and circumscribed. The family was poor—his mother

207

survived on a widow's pension of around £1 a week. The annual one-day visit to the island's main town of Stornoway—"a lustrous city" to the little boy—just seven miles away by bus, was a huge adventure. Smith was bookish and, socially, relatively isolated, a condition that his mother encouraged, fearful that her son's bronchitis and asthma would make him susceptible to tuberculosis; "all around me," as the poet wrote in an autobiographical memoir, "Between Sea and Moor" (in *Towards the Human: Selected Essays,* 1986) "the village was palpitant with the symptoms of tuberculosis which the young and the middle-aged . . . were dying from" (p. 76). Tuberculosis was common on Lewis; because of the islanders' lack of immunity to the bacterial infection, they risked contracting it during visits to the Scottish mainland.

From the age of five, Smith attended Bayble school and began instruction in what was to him a foreign language—English. His memory of first encountering the language was indistinct, though another contemporary, a writer from nearby Harris, Finlay J. Macdonald, instructed by his teacher with the one alien English word, "Sit," described it sardonically as being treated like a dog being trained for Crufts, a famous English dog-breeders' show. At home Smith spoke Gaelic; at school, and at the Nicolson Institute in Stornoway, which Smith attended on a scholarship from the age of eleven, he spoke English. To some degree—which he was to regret later—Smith identified Gaelic with the oppression of his religious upbringing, while English was the language he associated with education, emancipation, and things outside his home village. In this respect he considered himself something of a split personality. At Nicolson, however, he was taught by a fine classics teacher, Mr. Traill, who instilled in him a love of Latin. The classics—and especially the Dido and Aeneas episode in Virgil's *Aeneid,* emblematic of the conflict between duty and passion—frequently underpin his later writing.

Added to this mix—poverty, Calvinism, a divided linguistic heritage—was the legacy of World War I and the sinking of the *Iolaire*; as a result of a navigational error, this ship ran aground, and two hundred Lewis men returning home from the war drowned on New Year's morning 1919, in sight of the island's shores. Reverberations of this tragedy were certainly being felt when Smith was growing up. Furthermore, World War II broke out when Smith was eleven. The war sent out, as he wrote in "Between Sea and Moor," "long searching tentacles from vast unimaginable distances to pick off one by one a number of the older boys of the village who drowned in oceans which they had never seen except on a dusty globe in the village schoolroom" (p. 77).

At age seventeen, in September 1945, Smith left Lewis for the first time to attend Aberdeen University, where he studied English. Once on the mainland he took a train—something he had never seen before—to Aberdeen, where, on the station platform upon his arrival, he encountered a blind beggar, holding out a cap for pennies. This experience made a deep impression on Smith: on Lewis, the community would have cared for the man.

Despite this introduction to life off the island, Smith's time at university seems to have been a happy one. He was an avid learner, and graduated with honors in English in 1949. He later attributed his positive feelings about his university years to the fact that no one known to him had died during that time—an expression of the pervasiveness of death in his background.

By 1952, following a year's teacher training at Jordanhill College, Glasgow, and two years' compulsory National Service—he was a sergeant in the Education Corps—Smith began a twenty-five-year career as a high school English teacher, initially in Clydebank, Glasgow, from 1952 to 1955, then in the west coast Highland town of Oban from 1955 to 1977. During this period he kept up a remarkable level of productivity, typing his work on a battered old typewriter—his tatty typescripts (Conn, 2001, p. 92) were objects to marvel at—and living with his mother on Combie Street in Oban. Christina Smith died in 1969. In 1977 Smith married Donalda Logan, an event which brought him great happiness. Smith's marriage and the experience of being a stepfather to Donalda's sons, Alisdair and Peter, helped humanize him; his wife was extroverted and cheerful, and much liked by Smith's friends and acquaintances. Furthermore, she could drive—Smith himself was a lifelong pedestrian—and she often acted as a supportive companion at his readings. As the Scottish poet and dramatist Stewart Conn has pointed out, photographs of Smith after his marriage show a relaxed and youthful presence rather different from the somewhat edgy personality revealed in earlier images. As he aged, Smith seemed to grow younger.

Smith's marriage coincided with his decision to take early retirement from teaching. For the last twenty-one years of his life he worked as a freelance writer, and was a popular performer at readings, where his own particular brand of humor, and the prose accounts of Murdo Macrae, Smith's personification of the absurdities of life as refracted through an island sensibility, acted as a foil to the barer realities of the more serious poems. Murdo is the Scottish Don Quixote, and those close to the poet recognized something of Smith in the character's quirky take on existence.

Though marriage brought him happiness, it did not entirely protect him from his own psychological vulnerabilities. In 1982 Smith had a nervous breakdown—the experience of which he later used as material for his novel *In the Middle of the Wood* (1987). An intellectual man, whose single collection of essays was titled *Towards the Human,* as if he felt that humanity was a condition he aspired to rather than possessed, Smith later credited the breakdown with restoring to him a sense of connection with the human race. As he said in a 1998 interview with Gerry Cambridge, "I think for a long period I was very introverted, but after [my breakdown] I seemed to become more relaxed as far as people were concerned" (p. 50). A note of lightness and gaiety began to enter the poetry thereafter, as Smith demonstrated his ability to celebrate the moment.

Literary honors and awards were a frequent part of Smith's later life; elected as a Fellow of the Royal Society of Literature in 1971, he received an Order of the British Empire (OBE) in 1980, was writer-in-residence for the University of Aberdeen from 1985 to 1987, receiving an honorary D.Litt. from that institution the following year; his *Collected Poems* of 1992 received a Saltire Prize, one of Scotland's premier literary awards, as well as a special commendation from the Poetry Book Society.

In 1998, when Smith was diagnosed with cancer of the esophagus, he showed no sign of lessening his remarkable output; the disease, however, progressed rapidly. Treated in Glasgow's Southern General Hospital, and looked after in his last days by his wife, Smith died at home in Taynuilt, Argyll, Scotland, on 15 October 1998, about a week before the release of his book *The Leaf and the Marble* (1998), a long love poem dedicated to his wife. His funeral was in Taynuilt; at a crowded memorial service held for him in Helensburgh the week after his death, several mourners entered, sat at the back, and after listening to the proceedings for a few minutes, embarrassedly got up and left—they had come to the wrong service. It was a misalignment that the poet, with his characteristic pleasure in the unpredicted, might well have chuckled over.

THE NOVELS AND SHORT STORIES

The critical consensus seems to be that Smith's novels generally lack the distinction of his poetry. Among the more interesting novels are *In the Middle of the Wood,* a semiautobiographical account of a writer's descent into paranoia and nervous breakdown, and *The Last Summer* (1969), again with a strong autobiographical tone, which recounts the final island summer of Malcolm, a student studying for university. It is notable for its local color and early elucidation of what would become Smith's major themes.

The primary exception among the novels in terms of its literary merit is Smith's first, *Consider the Lilies* (1968), written in around ten days. It tells the story of an old Highland woman, Mrs. Scott, threatened with eviction during the period of the Highland Clearances, sometime between 1792 and the 1850s, when landlords cleared the land of crofters, people who worked smallholdings, or small farms, to make way for pastureland for the grazing of sheep. While the novel has a historical basis, Smith wrote that he didn't intend it to be read for historical accuracy—it has been criticized for its faulty chronology—but as a study of the psychology of its central character.

At the novel's opening Mrs. Scott is portrayed as a standard fundamentalist. Threatened with eviction, she seeks out the local church minister, who refers to the evictions as something brought on by the crofters' godlessness—a heavily ironic assertion with respect to the straitened old woman. Returning home after this encounter, she falls in a burn, or creek, and ends up recuperating in the house of Donald Macleod, a local freethinker and atheist more fundamentally charitable than the minister and whom Mrs. Scott had previously regarded with great mistrust. Over the course of the novel Mrs. Scott experiences a softening of attitude toward Macleod; she sees the minister for what he is, and resolves never again to attend his church. The novel ends with the threat of imminent eviction, but also the sense that Mrs. Scott has undergone a necessary shift in perspective. *Consider the Lilies,* like the poetry, delineates the conflict between dogma and free expression, an openness to joy. Mrs. Scott can be seen as a counterpoint to the persona addressed in Smith's poem "Old Woman," from his 1965 poetry collection *The Law and the Grace.* Unlike the woman in the poem, Mrs. Scott, however, is, redeemingly, still open to change.

Smith's short stories also explore many of the same themes as the poetry, and like the novels they are frequently semiautobiographical. The title story of his 1973 collection *The Black and the Red*—the black symbolic of dogma, the red of all that is life-affirming, if dangerous—takes the form of a series of letters from a young island man, newly attending university, to his fundamentalist mother. The letters increase in rebelliousness and a sense of liberation as the son frees himself from the strictures of his mother and background. "The Professor and the Comics," meanwhile, is a defense of high art as against mediocre postmodernist works which patronize readers. In "The Play," a teacher, Mark, attempts to engage an underachieving class by having the students write and perform their own play; banal as the production turns out, it is rooted in the dilemmas of their lives and has the stamp of veracity (*Mr. Trill in Hades, and Other Stories,* 1984).

Perhaps the peak of Smith's achievement as a short story writer is "Murdo," the title character of which Smith celebrated in a series of prose vignettes, later collected in *Thoughts of Murdo..* "Murdo" tells the story of Murdo Macrae, who has given up his job in a bank to try and be a writer. He is obsessed with the white mountain he can see through the window, a complex symbol of death and artistic aspiration. He is a true outsider who baffles his conventional wife, a man plagued by abstruse philosophical questions and hypersensitively alive to the anomalies, absurdities, and contradictions of living. The story is recounted in a rapid, almost manic and yet strangely deadpan prose in a series of sketches with only a tenuous narrative line. On its surface, the story is richly comic. But on closer reading, the knockabout absurdities take on a darker cast. Here the story's narrator recalls an incident in Murdo's primary school experience. The quote is from the story as it appears in *Listen to the Voice: Selected Stories* (1993).

> One day [his teacher] asked him to write an essay with the title, "My Home." Murdo wrote twenty pages about a place where there were large green forests, men with wings, aeroplanes made of diamond, and rainbow-coloured stairs.
>
> She said to him, "What does all this stuff mean? Are you laughing at me or what?" She gave him two strokes of the belt.
>
> After that Murdo grew very good at counting, and he could compute in his head in seconds 1,005 x 19. This pleased the schoolmistress and when the inspector visited the school she showed him Murdo with great pride. "This boy will make a perfect clerk," said the inspector, and he gave him a hard white sweet.
>
> (p. 225)

To the figures of authority in young Murdo's life, imagination is suspect, and creativity is dealt with harshly, through corporal punishment—the belt, or "tawse," was a regular feature of Scottish classrooms as recently as the 1970s. "Murdo" paints a blackly comic picture of fundamentalist island life.

THE EARLY POEMS: THE LONG RIVER AND "THE WHITE NOON"

Of the nineteen poems in Smith's first collection, *The Long River* (1955), only four made it into his 1992 *Collected Poems*. These were the Audenesque "The Dedicated Spirits"; two poems about his childhood environment, "Poem of Lewis," which conjures the harshness of life on the island, where "they have no time for the fine graces / of poetry," and "Some Days Were Running Legs," an energetic evocation of boyhood energy and foreboding; and, lastly, "Anchored Yachts on a Stormy Day," an impressively fluent sonnet.

These first poems showed Smith to be a notable craftsman, an impression confirmed by "The White Noon," the title of a selection of poems included in *New Poets 1959: Iain Crichton Smith, Karen Gershon, Christopher Levenson* (1959), edited by Edwin Muir. The ready fluency of the poems in "The White Noon," however, serve often to obscure the poet's subjects; the poems seem to favor technique over the development of voice. An exception is the dramatic monologue "The Widow"; the speaker is a resentful woman whose overly literary teacher husband has died from a stroke. It begins by informing an unknown listener, "That's his harem on the shelves." As it continues, the speaker begins to address the shade of her husband, haranguing him for a childless marriage. The straightforward voice of the speaker is unencumbered by the rhetorical intrusions that characterize many of the weaker poems in the selection. In some ways a companion piece, "School Teacher" is a portrait of a woman teacher who, teaching for forty years, has lost the meaning of the work. She confiscates a red apple from a pupil, and locks it in her "loved desk," where it lies, "soon to decay." Her desk, while "loved," is also what permits her to hide the apple, an act symbolic in microcosm of her own wasted life.

THISTLES AND ROSES

Smith's first important volume of poems was *Thistles and Roses* (1961); its title shows the poet's awareness of what can be seen in his mature work as the poles of his sensibility— "thistles" being emblematic of the toughness of his upbringing and background, and "roses" of the achieved world of art to which he aspired. It is in this book that some of Smith's major poetic themes are introduced: the suffering of the old, sensuality and spontaneity versus religious dogma, the examination of the fact of death. The frequently anthologized "Old Woman"—poems under this title appear frequently throughout Smith's work—written in nimble and efficient quatrains, with a deft, fluent movement from stanza to stanza, recounts the death of an old woman in the presence of her husband and the poem's narrator. The latter is outraged:

> There I sat
> imprisoned in my pity and my shame
> that men and women having suffered time
> should sit in such a place, in such a state
>
> and wished to be away, yes, to be far away
> with athletes, heroes, Greek or Roman men
> who pushed their bitter spears into a vein
> and would not spend an hour with such decay.

Smith invokes a classical reference here as a way, perhaps, of distancing himself from the full glare of the present, the way fundamentalists of his experience used dogma as a way of protecting themselves from their own suffering humanity. Where his mother had the Bible, he had the classics. The authority of voice and plainness of diction that distinguishes this incarnation of the "Old Woman" poem appears in other poems in this volume, as in this piece, which begins:

> Dying is not setting out
> in a full flower of sails.
> More complex ropes are taut
> across the blue pulse.
>
> ("Dying Is Not Setting Out")

The sonnet "John Knox" pits the grim founder of Scottish Calvinism against the "harlot"

Catholic Mary, queen of Scots. The pair met four times, most significantly at Holyrood Palace, Edinburgh, on 4 September 1561. In Smith's sonnet Knox is "the scything wind," and Mary is "the rich corn" which it reaps. Fundamentalism is regarded as a kind of absolute as compared with the flamboyance of the Scottish queen, who was fond of ceremony, pomp, and literature. "The shearing naked absolute blade has torn / Through false French roses to her foreign cry." Smith uses adjectives as cogently as Auden, who was an early influence on his poetry. Here, despite Smith's reaction against Calvinism, the narrator grants it "absolute" power, piling up the adjectives in its favor relentlessly: they give the phrase a manic urgency. Mary's "cry" is "foreign," both literally and to the spirit of unemotional Calvinism, in which crying would be considered unseemly.

Calvinism versus sensuality was a theme Smith would return to in the four-part "Love Songs of a Puritan." Section two opens: "My eyes are heresies to the clear / and grave theology yours speak to me." Here, in an ironic twist, the Puritan speaker is the heretic; the loved one's gaze conveys its own theology, that of the physical body and the moment. The sequence closes:

All things that speak of surety and grace
proclaim us heretic from our proper place
though venomous devils preach against the light
which opens heavens at her precious feet.
Yet even these by sneers and laughs make known
the dear theology they now disown.

The "theology" is that, presumably, of erotic love posited as a good. Though the "venomous devils" preach against it, the very ferocity of their reaction is proof that the theology is a real one, and serves to advertise it. Whereas Presbyterianism sees itself as a chosen religion, Smith ironically reverses its position to a reactionary one. The loved one here becomes the truly religious, and love the true religion.

The graceful vignette "By Ferry to the Island" confirms Smith's increasing skill. Through six delicately modulated five-line stanzas the narrator describes visiting "the bare island" on a day trip among other visitors; he notices a dead

seagull, white breasted and "so pure . . . that it made more dear / the lesser white around us." A woman is present in a white dress, and "The fool sparkled his wit that she might hear / new diamonds turning on her naked finger." The woman is unmarried; "the fool" courts her. At the day's end, as the visitors go home, the narrator sees the moon rising and finds

in the heart
the image of the gull and of that dress,
both being white and out of the darkness rising
the moon ahead of us with its rusty ring.

The moon is ringed, presumably by haze, which is "rusty" as the moon is red, being not yet fully clear of the horizon. The "ring" connects in the reader's mind with the potential "new diamonds" on the unmarried woman's finger. The purity of the gull's white breast, the white of the unmarried woman's dress, and the soon-to-be-white moon, its tarnished nimbus here implying both venerability and shabbiness, all gleam in complex consort together in the reader's mind. The poem resists paraphrase.

THE LAW AND THE GRACE

Following *Deer on the High Hills* (1962), a philosophical meditation somewhat in the manner of Wallace Stevens—with a glance at the Gaelic bard Duncan Ben MacIntyre's famous "Ban Dorain," which Smith also translated into English—*The Law and the Grace* appeared in 1965. It shared like its major predecessor a title marked by antithesis: the "Law" representing both Smith's inherited but dismissed Presbyterianism and, he pointed out, the strictness of the verse forms he often wrote in; the "Grace" being both the energy and gifted happenstance of a true poem, and everything unpredictably fortuitous in life. Numerous pieces in the book elucidate Smith's new awareness of these antipathies. His poem "Lenin" takes an interestingly different approach from that of Hugh MacDiarmid whose 1957 work *Three Hymns to Lenin*, venerates the Russian Communist leader; Smith's poem may be seen as a poetic response to this text. While for MacDiarmid, Lenin's willfulness and single-mindedness were admirable, for Smith these qualities recall the dour, life-denying character traits of religious fundamentalists. He asserts that admirers of Lenin's qualities, in an ironic double take, "purge [their] envy of unadult iron," when the true dialectic is to turn

in the infinitely complex, like a chain
we steadily burn through, steadily forge and burn
not to be dismissed in any poem
by admiration for the ruthless man
nor for the saint but for the moving on
into the endlessly various, real, human,
world which is no new era, shining dawn.

The poem's last eight and a half lines unwind as a single sentence, the longest in the poem, helping to embody the process they describe. Smith in this poem and others is opening himself, or attempting to, to "the endlessly various"; he dismisses the utopian ideal, and seems willing to settle for the diminished ordinary, despite its limitations.

Several poems in this volume return to Smith's obsession with the old woman figure. *The Law and the Grace*'s "Old Woman" portrays a Presbyterian widow, bitter and alone. Her mouth is "set," her eyes "cold"; she

never learned,
not even aging, to forgive
our poor journey and our common grave
while the free daffodils
wave in the valleys and on the hills
the deer look down with their instinctive skills,
and the huge sea
in which your brothers drowned sings slow
over the headland and the peevish crow.

The poem's first six stanzas, describing the obdurate old woman, are each end-stopped. Only in the final three stanzas as quoted above does the poem break, as "Lenin" did, from its gritted stance; the rhythmic bounce of the last two stanzas buttresses the relative vigor of those—perhaps ironically—"waving" daffodils, and the instinctive deer. The gaiety of nature, the "grace," with the exception of that "peevish crow," which, traditionally associated with death, seems linked in its peevishness to the old woman, is set against the doctrine held by the central character. Time

and again Smith returns to such characters; in the twelve-line poem "Face of an Old Highland Woman" he scrutinizes with a sort of awed fascination her features, which are "not the Mona Lisa's / staring from a submarine / greenness of water." The art of Europe is elsewhere. Instead, the woman's eyes are "like lochs staring up / from heather gnarled by a bare wind"; she is the personification of "the God of fist and bone."

Against such characters he sets "Two Girls Singing." The poet is traveling on a bus in winter; as it gets dark, two girls begin to sing, and continue their singing for miles. It's not the song's words or tune that interests him, but the simple fact of "the human sweetness in that yellow, / the unpredicted voices of our kind." It is the girls' action he praises, not the quality of the performance. The "yellow" may be both the sodium street lamps, emblematic of a certain bureaucratic order and, perhaps, the glary yellow light of the bus itself.

Four years were to pass before Smith's next main collection, *From Bourgeois Land* (1969); in the interim he appeared in *Three Regional Voices: Iain Crichton Smith, Barry Tebb, Michael Longley* (1968). One of Smith's poems in this collection, "Money-Man Only," showed the poet developing a theme which he would continue in the 1969 volume. The speaker of this poem condemns a figure he perceives—somewhat presumptuously, it may seem to the reader—as materialistic. While the urgency of Smith's tone and his verbal fluency are impressive, the subject of the poem is oversimplified and dehumanized in a way which Smith would later castigate. With considerable irony, Smith's speaker "excommunicate[s]" the materialist from his "undesigned / church of the crooked spire," with its "minister wearing his clown's cloak." Perhaps the most interesting thing to note about the poem is that the speaker, in portraying his own humanistic values and sensibilities, persists in taking his images from organized religion.

FROM BOURGEOIS LAND

The moralistic tone of "Money-Man Only" reappears in Smith's next collection, an attempted indictment of bland contemporary society, in which Smith contrasts the artist with the "bourgeois"—a catchall term which, though not completely explained, Smith seems to associate with a comfortable mediocrity and an over-regard for money and respectability—generally in the artist's favor. A dozen of its thirty-nine untitled poems are included in the *Collected Poems*. Smith is unable to embrace the Calvinism of his childhood, and equally uncomfortable with the banalities of contemporary living; the most powerful poems in this volume tend to be either those in which Smith's attention is ironically focused on himself, or in which the sheer energy of his anger propels the verse. Among the former is "In Youth," which contrasts the easy scorn of callow inexperience with what growing older demonstrates; the mocking youth becomes the one who walks "in self-protection from the gangs who prowl / . . . foes of those burdened by 'the true and real.'" Among the latter pieces is "What's Your Success?" addressed to an unnamed person, but one with "chains," "baubles," and "rings." The poem sets earthly and temporal success against the scrutiny of "the great dead" poets whose "marble faces" the narrator is constantly observed by. The poem, four spry couplets which employ half-rhymes, closes:

> Over terraced houses
> these satellites rotate and in deep spaces
>
> the hammered poetry of Dante turns
> light as a wristwatch, bright as a thousand suns.

As often with Smith at a poem's closure, he achieves liftoff by sheer force of utterance and nimble technique. Dante's poetry is "hammered": it is the product of passionate, even violent, craftsmanship. The verse ends in a dazzle of comparison: the wristwatch is at once homely, small, intricate, and man-made; the suns are natural massive forces. The penultimate line's iambic pentameter with a weak third stress leads into the awestruck and resonant final line, in which the two phrases each begin with a strong stress on a rhyming word, followed by a rhythmic leap to the next strong stress in each phrase—on "wrist," and the first syllable of "thousand"—

which in its energy helps to reinforce the poem's meaning.

The collection closes with "'Children, Follow the Dwarfs,'" an invocation to children not to settle for ordinariness and bourgeois living. Jauntily written in couplets with an anapestic bounce, it advises against alignment with "the Man with the Smiling Face, / . . . the Lady with the Flowery Dress," and, in a phrase that could be described as pure Auden, "the Rinsoed Boy who is forever clean." The poem's closing lines encourage the children addressed to

> Follow your love, the butterfly, where it spins
> over the wall, the hedge, the road, the fence,
> and love the Disordered Man who sings like a river
> whose form is Love, whose country is Forever.

The poem reacts against set patterns, predictability, respectability. The commas in the second line quoted allow the sentence to mimic the flitting movement of the butterfly. The poem values difference and the unexpected, exhorts its readers not to settle for the conventional but to cherish "disorder," as a way toward creativity and joy.

LINES REVIEW *POEMS AND* HAMLET IN AUTUMN

Smith's next few collections, at least in the verse in English, show him moving away from his obsession with his Lewis upbringing—which may have been many things, but "bourgeois" was not among them—and confronting contemporary urban society in poems that were included in a special issue (June 1969) of the Scottish poetry magazine *Lines Review* devoted to his work, some of which are included in his *Collected Poems*. These pieces include "The House We Lived In" and "Return to the Council House." Both are written in trim four-line stanzas, and in their references to "green" and "blue" point up the sectarian aggression still prevalent in society in the west of Scotland: green stands for Celtic, a Catholic football team; blue for Rangers, a Protestant one. Smith's experience as a teacher also begins to show in his work. In "In the Classics Room," an attractive female student is transformed by the narrator into Dido, lover of Aeneas, whom Aeneas left to found Rome; the student's teacher, dazed by her attractiveness, becomes "this Roman whose glasses reflect [her] fire"; his legs "twitch uncontrollably like an infant's"; the book he is holding "shakes like a leaf." The classics help, paradoxically, to both set in perspective and intensify the present in Smith's poems. The dutiful teacher continues his lesson, though, when faced by this Dido of the classroom, the book in his hand, a symbol of civilization, is converted to a mere leaf, an organic friable object subject to decay. Hers, it may be implied, is the greater power.

Smith's "Homage to George Orwell" is a five-part piece examining the role, at times somewhat surreally, of art in society. Is art created at the expense of the common man? Section 2 comprises this classic brief poem:

In my little house
on a distant island
I used to scribble poems
on an oil-skinned table.
But I didn't know
what I've learnt to know—
what inhuman pressures
keep a line of verse
on its own course.
How a cult of slaves
kept in their fixed place
the elaborated lines
of a Greek vase.

However true its central assertion that art is built finally upon societal brutality and subjugation, the poem's simplicity carries conviction. Plain diction and conversational speech—"I used to scribble poems" —contrast sharply with the Latinate "inhuman pressures," "the elaborated lines"; the diction tends to increase in complexity as the poet explicates what he has "learnt to know."

Despite the plainspokenness here, increasingly in the 1972 collection *Hamlet in Autumn,* Smith makes sudden free-associational leaps in his poems. Sometimes these are stunningly effective, at other times confusing, though his gift as a phrase-maker often results in his lines being lodged in the reader's mind. The second stanza of "On a Summer's Day," for example, begins:

"I have studied your face across the draughtsboard. / It is freckled and young." Then follows the wholly unexpected third line: "Death and summer have such fine breasts." In "Party," the volume of Francis Bacon's nudes the narrator looks through is "a butcher's shop of graduated screams," while in "The Letter," in which the narrator writes a questioning letter to God—in a tone of manic urgency which prefigures that of Smith's tragicomic antihero, Murdo Macrae—he asks:

Why did you put the rabbit in the belly of the fox?
Why did you put man in the box of his days?
Why did you build us of frail bones?
Why did you give us hearts
to suffer hubbub and sorrow,
why aren't they like watches,
small, circular, golden?

Such forthright questions are rare in contemporary British poetry, which tends in tone toward an ironic knowingness. Smith's work of this period is genuinely exploratory, even to the point of being obsessive, which gives it both its power and its sense of monotony.

His Lewis upbringing is replaced as the subject of these poems with a focus on Smith's new urban experience; in "Gaelic Songs" the narrator hears the songs from "a city studio" on radio. Gaelic being a tongue which seems very much organic to its landscape—the Hebrides and Northern Scotland, where it is still spoken—the narrator elucidates the maritime and cultural associations the songs have for him. The songs are bounded on either side by other radio programs, presumably in English. The narrator concludes, of the songs, that

Now they are made of crystal
taking just a moment
between two programmes
elbowing them fiercely
between two darknesses.

"Gaelic Songs" takes its strength as a poem from its tone of calm factuality. The description of the songs as "crystal" gives them an artificial brilliance; they have ossified, they are no longer alive; the language in which they are written has

IAIN CRICHTON SMITH

become an object, something precious. The "two [English] programmes" aggressively "elbow" the more passive older tongue, and the two darknesses recall both the silence prior to the development of the language and the threat of its extinction.

LOVE POEMS AND ELEGIES

Smith's mother died in 1969, and Smith's preoccupation with her life, death, and his own relationship to her shapes the opening of Smith's 1972 collection, *Love Poems and Elegies.* In poems such as "You Lived in Glasgow," "You Told Me Once" "My Sailor Father," "That Island Formed You," "Contrasts," "The Space-ship," and "Of the Uncomplicated Dairy Girl," Smith both praises, investigates, and argues with the meaning of his mother's life. In "Contrasts," five three-line stanzas, each beginning with the word "Against," Smith uses the repetition with dogmatic irony to offer alternatives to his mother's beliefs. It opens:

Against your black I set the dainty deer
stepping in mosses and in water where
there are miles of moorland under miles of air.

The spry randomness and otherness of the deer in their seemingly boundless environment is given nineteen words of description, compared with the bleak binary "your black." The rhythmically lively verse echoes the "stepping" of the animals themselves. Luxuriousness, variety, opulence, is celebrated in the face of narrowed simplicities. Elsewhere, however, in "Of the Uncomplicated Dairy Girl," the mother is remembered less combatively in a delicate lyric which imagines her, still unmarried, before "the beat of metal wings," presumably the outbreak of World War I. The poet asks that

Of the uncomplicated dairy girl
in gown that's striped in blue and red
feeding the hens in a windy spring
by the green wooden shed
where shade after quick shade
endlessly shuttles let me speak
and speak unsorrowing.

Here the woman is vibrantly dressed; even the shed is green. She is feeding the hens, which will lay eggs—an image of fruitfulness—and everything is in motion in the windy spring day, season of hope; only the hens make "quick" shadows as they chase after food. The poem offers a lyric snapshot of Smith's mother at a period when her life was still all potential and could have developed differently. With "let me speak" the poet seems to invoke, or empower, his own objectivity and separateness.

Though it was just three years before Smith's next major collection, *The Notebooks of Robinson Crusoe* (1975), in the interim he published smaller groups of poems, including three notable long sequences, "By the Sea" and "The White Air of March," in a selection in *Penguin Modern Poets 21* (1974), and "Orpheus" in *Orpheus and Other Poems* (1974). "The White Air of March," somewhat Eliotesque in tone, is a sixteen-part sequence, part satire, part aspiration for a nobler Scotland, in which the Isle of Skye's stunning Cuillin mountain range forms a symbol of the loftiness of the imagination and of art. The sequence shares something of the disenchantment of *From Bourgeois Land.* Like "By the Sea," it cannot be considered wholly successful, though it has its moments. It begins:

This is the land God gave to Andy Stewart—
We have our inheritance.
There shall be no ardour, there shall be indifference.
There shall not be excellence, there shall be the
 average.
We shall be the intrepid hunters of golf balls.

Andy Stewart, at one time a popular singer of faux-traditional Scottish songs, a kilted Scottish entertainer, and this vision of a mediocre Scotland which owes something to Hugh MacDiarmid's scorn, as professed in his poetry, for ordinary contemporary life, is set against the Cuillins, which "stand and will forever stand," and the truth tellers, worthy of praise: "Dostoevsky, Nietzsche, Kierkegaard, / Kafka." The poem contrasts interestingly with the desire for ordinary life expressed in "Lenin"; it shows the poet still attracted to obsessive single-mindedness, though here an artistic one. The piece exists primarily on the level of opinionated assertion, finishing, somewhat unconvincingly, with a vision of, "In the white air of March / A new mind." In the less formal pieces, which lack the resonance of rhyme to bolster content, Smith's poetry works best not at the level of rhetorical argument but during serendipitous passages when the poem's verbal leaps reveal new connections. His attempts to convey a personal belief or truth can lead him into the type of religious sermonizing he consistently aligned himself against.

Smith's tendency to preach in his poems lessened considerably after meeting Donalda Logan. In "Helplessly," a brief lyric published in *Poems for Donalda* (1974), Smith described the effect that his future wife's presence had on him. He is "a grey street" which, on her appearance, becomes full of "a noise of cars / the cries of flower sellers / the shaking out of antique pictured rugs." His wife's gaiety of spirit and boisterousness overcomes his tendency to brood. It was to be a relationship and marriage which would sustain the poet to the end of his life.

THE NOTEBOOKS OF ROBINSON CRUSOE

Aspects of his relationship with Donalda seem to be revealed in his new book, *The Notebooks of Robinson Crusoe, and Other Poems* (1975). Only five of its poems, and a considerably shortened version of the book's title sequence—twenty parts, now unnumbered, of the original forty-one—appear in the *Collected Poems*. Among them is a blank verse piece, "Incident," told from the point of view of a woman wondering whether her new partner will accept her children from a previous relationship. She observes them interacting, and her initial doubt of his ability to integrate turns into pleasure as she realizes that her new partner has turned his eyes away from the clouds to "her and the common earth." Attentiveness to "the common earth" made Smith's later work less rarefied, more accepting. The poet in these poems is becoming humanized.

In this new volume, however, Smith's narrator is still struggling with questions of identity, isolation, and exile. The sequence, much of it prose, is somewhat heavy going: Crusoe wishes to be "a man without memory"; remembering is too

painful. He prays, and compares his more fortunate lot with that of "spastics, idiots, physically ruined men," and asks, at the end of a litany of harsh fates that he has escaped, "Why then am I not happy?" The figure of Crusoe functions as an ideal correlative for the alienated artist, brooding in his solitude, who says that, as "my own god worshipping my own images, I would not wish to enter, unshaven and hairy, the monotonous climate of the mediocre, but would prefer my extreme pain to their temperate ordinariness." The narrator here is simply another incarnation of that of "The White Air of March." The sequence closes with Crusoe/Smith leaving his island and thirty years of solitude to reenter the world of mankind: he emerges from his dwelling place of "sparse iron into the vast cinema of sensation," like the child of Presbyterianism entering the modern world. The sequence lacks the saving comedy of "Chomei at Toyama," a monologue of another solitary outsider, written by the British poet Basil Bunting; "The Notebooks of Robinson Crusoe" will most likely be read mainly out of duty by literary scholars.

IN THE MIDDLE

The follow-up collection to *The Notebooks of Robinson Crusoe* partakes of a similar harshness; the poems of *In the Middle* (1977) delineate an often strictured world, where "Everyone illuminates his acre / with a hugged torch" ("The Torches"). "Tears are Salt," however, a twenty-four-line lyric in terse quatrains, shows Smith's facility for the surprising image. The poem points out how "reality breaks in on us / while we are acting so well / on our tiny stages":

Suddenly reality is there
with its large crude torch
shining it into our eyes
and into our guts.
The sunbeam just passing
is carrying a coffin
as a bee will carry pollen
home to its hive.

While the reader may well object that humanity acting on its tiny stages is equally reality, Smith implies that it is when at its most brutal that reality is most fundamental and "truest"; gentrified living is an affectation: a perception the bleak realities of Lewis must have helped confirm. (Smith later seemed to favor such affectation, simply because it was possible for him to do so.) The noun "guts" reinforces the starkness. The second stanza quoted is a gem of concision; the sunbeam carries the coffin not literally but because it is emblematic of time, which may mean death for someone, by the moment the sunbeam arrives at its destination; by comparing it to a bee carrying pollen with which to make honey, the poem's narrator implies that death, in one sense, is creative, "the mother of beauty," as Wallace Stevens called it.

When Smith asserts through images, as in the example above, his assertions can work well. When he makes generalizations about, for example, differences between the sexes in "Women," however, he seems on shakier ground. "The sap of women" is "bewildered and angry," he tells us, while "Man often strolls down an avenue of ideas, / his hands in his pocket, cool and lenient." The problem with such generalizations is that they are almost meaningless. The reader knows that there are equable women, as certainly as there are bitter, angry, and confused men.

THE EXILES

The Exiles (1984) shows Smith grappling not just with what Lewis had meant for him personally, but with its history of emigration, largely caused by poverty, war, and the search for a better life. For Smith, emigration was an accustomed fact: he had relatives in Canada, South Africa, and Australia. Exile, including mental exile from one's own self, is a frequent theme. It gives the book a rather gloomy air. In "There Is No Sorrow," Smith writes:

There is no sorrow worse than this sorrow
the dumb grief of the exile
among villages that have strange names
among the new rocks.

Many readers, of course, may imagine considerably worse sorrows and feel that Smith's case is too black and white; given the grim topography and culture of Lewis he delineated, it's equally possible to imagine people glad to leave it. He projects a personal grief as if it were universal, though in "No Return" realizes that, for him, a return to Lewis is not an option: the narrator, like the island, has changed too much. Many of the volume's weaker poems worry at this central theme of exile; the best of them approach it obliquely. These include the fine miniature, "Owl and Mouse," and the fiercely elegiac "At the Funeral of Robert Garioch." "Owl and Mouse," eight lines set out as four unrhyming couplets, depicts an owl which has caught a mouse and is "waft[ing] home" under a brilliant moon. The poem concludes:

All seems immortal but for the dangling mouse,
an old hurt string among the harmony
of the masterful and jewelled orchestra
which shows no waste soundlessly playing on.

Of course, the owl is mortal too; what is truly immortal is the principle—this is the "harmony," and the "jewelled orchestra." This little gemlike poem, with its image of the self-conducting orchestra, conveys very well something of the eeriness of the natural world. Present is the poet's sympathy for the damaged in the shape of the mouse, the "exile" here: while the rest of the scene runs with a clockwork efficiency and precision, the imperfect mortal mouse is, nonetheless, vital to the perfection of the performance. It is the equivalent of "the cult of slaves" which helped produce the "elaborated lines of a Greek vase" in Smith's earlier poem "Homage to George Orwell."

This unexpectedness of description is a quality also shared by "At the Funeral of Robert Garioch." Garioch, a skilled satirical poet who wrote in contemporary Scots, died at the age of eighty-two in 1981. The poem's setting is "halfway April"; the flowers are out, the first birds are singing, and the minister blesses the cremation, "his voice fat and voluptuous / his enunciation pure," as Smith writes, with some distaste. The coffin slides into the incinerator, and the poem closes:

IAIN CRICHTON SMITH

Poet, the flowers are open
even when we are dead
even when the power has gone
from our right arms.
The flowers open in flame.
The coffin slides home.
Fugitive April becomes
A tremendous summer.

Nature goes inexorably on, despite our personal tragedies. The blossoming of the flowers is linked with the cremating fire—destruction and creation are conjoined. It is death that permits "fugitive April" to become "a tremendous summer."

A more ambitious poem is "Iolaire," which is prefaced by a note describing the 1919 tragedy when a ship bound for Lewis went aground, resulting in the loss of two hundred men returning home after World War I. The speaker in Smith's poem is an elder of the Presbyterian church on the island. The piece has a strange, hallucinogenic quality, opening with the repeated construction "It seemed," as if the speaker is unable or unwilling to validate his own account:

It seemed that I
touched my fixed hat which seemed to float and then
the sun illumined fish with naval caps,
names of the vanished ships. In sloppy waves,
in the fat of water, they came floating home
bruising against their island.

The "fish," in a surreal image, may be drowned sailors still wearing their naval caps braided with the names of the ships they had served on. "Bruising" is a painful, ironic verb in this context. The speaker uses brief staccato sentences, especially as the poem closes, and he himself floats in the water, conveying his own frantic grasping for reason. The poem ends:

I kneel from you.
This water soaks me. I am running with
its tart sharp joy. I am floating here
in my black uniform. I am embraced
by these green ignorant waters. I am calm.

It is uncertain here—the speaker has just touched the blond head of a drowned sailor—whether the "you" he is kneeling "from" is the sailor or God. (Smith doesn't capitalize references to God in the poem.) There is a sense of fear in the kneeling "from"; not kneeling "to," which would be more expected. The speaker is "embraced" by the water; he undergoes a new—and perhaps ambiguous—baptism in the same seawater that has been witness to such tragedy.

A LIFE

Both of Smith's next collections show the poet turning away to some extent from the existential gloom of previous work. As it appears in Smith's *Collected Poems,* the six-part autobiographical sequence *A Life* is subtitled: "Lewis, 1928–1945"; "Aberdeen University, 1945–1949"; "National Service, 1950–1952"; "Clydebank and Dumbarton, 1952–1955"; "Oban, 1955–1982"; and "Taynuilt, 1982–." One notable characteristic is how the sequence picks up once the poet leaves Lewis at the age of seventeen. In the first part of the sequence, Smith states that "The island is the anvil where was made / the puritanical heart"; life on Lewis is "Life without Art, the minimum"; its "meagre furniture" appalls the narrator. Lewis is dealt with in a series of twelve verse vignettes, which, however, have their livelier moments, describing in the poet's adolescence, with a straightforwardness reminiscent of Philip Larkin, "the bum / divine and rounded" of a pupil who "sits / behind a desk that's scored beneath her tits." In church the narrator notices "the fifty-year-old girl" he used to know, her face now "curdled and gaunt"; retrospection and a sense of sadness govern the section. However, things heat up in the, by comparison, bustling social and cultural milieu of Aberdeen: the stimuli of a university education and the attractions of girls press in on the young poet: "We are such fiery fleshy tenements." Teaching the alphabet to the illiterate as part of his National Service, in four sections he captures something of the squalid messiness of army life, while "Clydebank and Dumbarton" charts some of the young poet's early high-school-teaching experiences. Facing rambunctious urban pupils, he realizes, "The chalk's a ghostly dust for such as these." Looking back on Glasgow from "green Argyll," he finds it "a yellow labyrinth"—yellow, emblematic of streetlights, is often a negative color in Smith's poetry—a place of "tubercular bloom"—while the fourteen-part "Oban" closes with several pieces examining the changing relationship between pupils and teachers. There has been a switch of power, in the pupils' favor: "long ago" the teachers "played on their pupils like violins"; whereas

Now there is hubbub.
They are the chancy
scouts of the frontiers
and the chiming pentameters
have forsaken them.

By "Taynuilt, 1982–" (Taynuilt being the village that Smith and his wife eventually settled in) he is a freelance writer, retired from teaching and aspiring "to make literature." He occupies the "cold marble cell which will forgive / only the best and truest." He is to be a student of "the vases and the stone"—or art—"though not forgetting human voices too." This closing part has an anecdotal feel—"What have I done today?"—section 2 begins, and then duly records the poet's activities. Here Smith writes in a more impressionistic free verse, and the poems gain in gaiety what they have lost in verbal resonance. The word "joy" begins to make frequent appearances; the poet begins purely to celebrate the moment. The section at times has a sparkling vivacity, like a spring day when sunlight reflects off many brilliant surfaces. In section 5, Smith writes, addressing God, the "supreme author":

Such joy, such joy! Do not recall us to You.
Let us go on our way rejoicing
down all the possible avenues we can take.

The poet praises manifold possibilities; he is a world away from the strict religion of his upbringing, and also from the need to respond to it defensively. Instead he simply praises what he sees as its opposite, a world full of "possible avenues."

THE VILLAGE AND OTHER POEMS

Smith's next collection, *The Village and Other Poems* (1989), largely showed him following his own avenue. The book's title poem, vignettes of the village in which the narrator lives, is a fifty-part sequence of meditations, impressions, and imaginings, written in a mix of metered and free verse, sporadically rhymed. Smith's imaginative faculties are strongly at work. Here is section 10:

The little red van
buzzes about the village.
Letters from England, Canada, New Zealand.
We communicate with each other
because of a driver
with a small black moustache.
Little red van
at the edge of the ocean
dodging among the trees
with no salt on it.

This vignette, haiku-like in its seeming artlessness, conveys something of the childlike aspect of Smith's vision. The post van—red in Britain—"buzzes" around the village, like a bee or, more ominously, like a wasp. There is a bizarre note of comedy in lines 4–6; the observation has a curious, vivid simplicity. The correspondents are able to be in contact with one another, in this time before e-mail, because of the actions of the postman, whose "small black moustache" initially conjures, absurdly, Hitler or Charlie Chaplin. In the closing stanza, the little red van, which is "at the edge" of an ocean, often indicative of exile, grief, and sadness in Smith—because of its "dodging," is too rapid for the salt—another frequently bitter or astringent motif in Smith's work—to settle on it. This strange little poem is utterly simple verbally. It could have been written by a ten year old. Yet—a characteristic of a good deal of his work—it does not easily yield to paraphrase.

Many of the sections in "The Village" have a similar jauntiness. While the narrator of "At the Sale" in *From Bourgeois Land* lets out a howl of existential anguish at being among the cast-off bric-a-brac of humankind, in section 33 of the new poem, "on a breezy morning" the poet visits the local market with his wife. He recalls Socrates, bald like himself, strolling on another morning through a Greek market and observing, cynically, how little one really needed in the world, to which Smith rejoins that he loves all the color, and "the sly / cries of the salesmen." This is so different, in its attitude of acceptance, from the poetic stance of *From Bourgeois Land,* that it almost reads like the work of another writer. Both technically and in terms of their sensibility, the poems are looser. Smith's experiences had taught him that to judge others "bourgeois" may say as much about oneself as about the judged. "The Village" is finally a paean to transience, attempts to catch the living present, as D. H. Lawrence wished to in his poems. Smith's answer to dogma is hymns to "the wind of everyday."

Of course, the poet hasn't wholly left previous themes. Poems in the book's second section include a piece on his complex emotions on looking at a photograph ("Photograph of Emigrants"), while poems such as "TV" and "Christmas" grimly delineate aspects of contemporary life, though in the latter, at least, not without some saving black humor. Christmas is the time when "the children gather round the tree in simple greed"; enmity is sardonically evoked:

Who did not send us a Christmas card this year?
We shall have our revenge on them. And who sent
a cheaper card than the dear one we sent them?
See how on the father patiently slicing the turkey
the son's eyes are fixed. Soon I will be your master.
I already feel the power refreshing my arm.

Plain as this language is, the poet hasn't lost his sensitivity to the powerful verb: that "refreshing" is finely judged.

As if in recognition of the aesthetic journey that the poet has made, the volume's closing poem, titled "Listen"—half a request, half an imperative—tracks his development. It begins with the triumphant line, "Listen, I have flown through darkness towards joy. . . ." It closes:

I had not believed that the stony heads
would change to actors and actresses,
and that the grooved armour of statues
would rise and walk away
into a resurrection of villages,
townspeople, citizens, dead exiles,
who sing with the salt in their mouths,
winged nightingales of brine.

Deathliness, the dogma of childhood, has become life; the armorial statues, which could be emblematic of that dogma, have become the living, and despite the sadness of those "dead exiles" they still "sing" to the poet; they are "brine" but, nonetheless, "nightingales," and not only nightingales but "winged" ones, as he feels compelled to tell us; they can fly as well as sing. The closing stanzas enact, in their enjambment from penultimate to final stanza, the resurrection they describe.

ENDS AND BEGINNINGS

Ends and Beginnings appeared some five years later, in 1994—the nearly four-hundred-page *Collected Poems* had appeared in the interim, in 1992—and showed a poet of impressive facility who was, perhaps, overproducing. The book's six sections and 152 pages contained much of interest but little that was singularly outstanding—an observation which could be made of Smith's later poetry in general.

Ends and Beginnings displays most of Smith's major themes: Lewis is revisited in memory, there are poems castigating dogma—two of which end in the same five lines—and the habitual "Old Lady" returns, as does the rampant materialist in the new poem "Come, Fool." There is a strange little poem about the death of a pet cat, Champers, which just avoids bathos, and a long poem on the Israeli-Palestinian conflict, "Conversion," which looks forward in tone to Smith's next work, *The Human Face* (1996). The collection has a somewhat arbitrary feel; it shows Smith open to impressions and willing to write about almost anything. "Early Spring" begins in inconsequential commonplaces—"The crocuses are out in January / in their green and purple / and I have seen the gorse as well"; tagged on at the end is an anecdote about an old man finding coffin wood among graves which he used to make violins. The poem ends where, the reader feels, it should have started. But while the poems often don't work as a whole, because of Smith's facility as a phrase maker and the quirky unexpectedness of some of his images, which shine like surprising flowers in a winter wood, few poems are entirely without interest.

IAIN CRICHTON SMITH

The best of them exemplify Smith's own observation in "No Muses," that poetic inspiration is more likely to come from commonplaces such as "a flash from a piece of glass or from an old mirror" than from lofty musings. The book's most successful poems tend to be the shortest; they include "The Revenant," a mysterious little piece in which, apparently, the narrator's mother returns to him in a vision, and "Nurses," which praises the fresh youth of nurses "among these coughing, wheezing, shouting old men." Smith is strongly on the side of life here; the empathy he showed earlier for the old and infirm now shifts to their caretakers. In "The Gaelic Proverb" he subverts the purported wisdom of a proverb which has it that "sad is the state of the house / without a child or cat," by ascribing to the house a Presbyterian narrowness that constricts its inhabitants. "A Story," meanwhile, is a curious, almost surreal account of a fight between a Glasgow taxi driver and a "madman" over an unpaid fare, while "Shakespeare," despite a certain confusion of images, vividly depicts Shakespeare as an ominously soaring buzzard—a large British hawk—whose shadow "flies across the grass"; the poem ends, "My pen is a small beak, nibbling, nervous. / Acres are swallowed by that confident shade."

THE HUMAN FACE

By the mid-1990s, Smith obviously felt ready for a long, ambitious poem; *The Human Face*—its title perhaps derived from William Blake's poem "A Divine Image," in which the "human face is a furnace seal'd," and also recalling Edwin Muir's fine sonnet "The Face"—was published in 1996. Described by Smith's English publisher, Carcanet, as "an impassioned poem-essay" with "the humane scope and sweep of the major poems of [Hugh] MacDiarmid and [Sorley] Maclean," it is a three-hundred-stanza, 1,798-line polemic in a version of "standard Habbie," one of the favored stanzas of Robert Burns and other eighteenth-century Scottish poets. It is a difficult form: its six-line stanzas have the rhyme scheme *aaabab*; every line has four beats, except the fourth and the last, which have two. Smith gets over the

technical difficulty by considerably loosening the form, not wholly successfully; at times he enjambs from one stanza to the next, and the result is to break up the integrity of the stanza, which traditionally expressed one complete thought.

In *The Human Face,* Smith attempts that almost impossible task, to write a didactic poem which is also interesting. The theme of the poem is world violence, for which Smith largely blames religious dogma, which, in positing the existence of a soul and an afterlife, he asserts, devalues earthly existence. The poem at times comes across as the versified concerns of a philosopher, though it lacks a philosopher's intellectual rigor. Smith, in his essay on MacDiarmid, "The Golden Lyric," observed that the latter would not make the claim of offering original thought in his work. Similarly, Smith, in not addressing a particular reality, theorizes along well-worn lines, and the poem, perhaps consequently, takes on a hectoring tone. Societal concern is laudable, but it often translates thinly into poetry, especially when not rooted in concrete particulars. MacDiarmid or MacLean at their best *The Human Face* certainly is not. Instead, the vocative "O" is overused, often in introducing an ironic phrase; the rhyming is inexact, and the register relatively abstract. Elsewhere in the poem there is a note of, it appears, unintended bathos, as if Murdo Macrae had suddenly taken hold of Smith's pen:

The way he speaks, the way he walks,
the shape and glamour of his socks . . .
these all show him as the fox
the hound must kill

The sudden transformation into a fox of a man wearing "glamorous" socks has a distinctly cartoonish element, and it is difficult to see what that "shape" is doing there: socks are, relatively speaking, always the same shape. Smith may be lampooning the "hound" here, the bigoted individual, but this is by no means clear.

At times, too, the poet addresses the reader as if he or she were the enemy, the terrorist, though it is unlikely that a person with terrorist inclinations would be reading a book such as this: "that twisted face / contorted by your ethics is / your human brother, not a prize / for your revolver," he advises. Inflated phrases—"Perfidious dogma," "Superficial anthologies of ills"—vie with ill-judged banality and clichéd wisdom: "We need our yesterdays, it's true"; "that life is dicey, we can grant."

In *The Human Face* we see the transformation of a wholly individual poet into a purveyor of worthy concerns. When Smith expounds instead of focusing on documentary detail, he proves to be as confused and muddleheaded on the world's ills as everyone else. His gift is not for such large-scale speculation but for the jeweled miniatures, the queer, quirky leaps of perception, and the singularities of phrasing that are his trademark. *The Human Face* reads like the work of a writer who feels he should write a poem; beyond its worthy sentiments, it lacks a feeling of true compulsion.

THE LEAF AND THE MARBLE

Published just a few days after Smith's death, *The Leaf and the Marble* in its title again hints at the polarity found throughout Smith's poetry. Written when the poet was emerging from a depression, it is an extended love poem to his wife, Donalda, with an "Epilogue" in the form of an exquisite brief poem in five sections based on a painting from the Eighteenth Dynasty of Egypt (which illustrates the cover of the Carcanet edition) titled *Back of Tutankhamun's Throne,* showing King Tutankhamen and his wife Akhesenamun; he sits lightly on his throne; she stands, and has her right hand on his shoulder; they gaze at each other. The book was begun on a holiday in Rome when Smith saw a Judas tree flowering among ruins. The "leaf" of the book's title represents the eternal renewal of nature, the indomitable spirit of his wife, immortality in transience, openness to experience; the marble, meanwhile, is associated with the imperialism of Rome, unwielding will, and the obdurate Presbyterian religion of the poet's mother and of his youth. Written in two parts primarily in a delicate short-lined free verse, it opens resoundingly with "The Green Leaf":

My doughty one,
when I think of you
I think of light leaves in Rome
above the marble—
green leaves, green leaves!

. . .

Not the statues,
no, not the statues,
those imperial riders—
no, but the green leaves
of early April.

The entire poem circles around the leaf/marble, spontaneity/willfulness dualism; the leaf in its "untheatricality," the "gift of life," is dwelt upon somewhat obsessively by the poet; rising from a deeper emotional center, however, the book carries more emotional weight than its predecessor. A frequent motif is the poet rising from Avernus, the entrance to the underworld, into the spring light. He celebrates radiance, flowers, light; the verb "sparkle" does overtime.

Section 2 finds the poet back in Scotland, celebrating the local in his Highland vicinity. He acknowledges, for him, the difficulty of living without the succor of dogma:

More terrible
even than Rome is this
encounter with the leaf, at which
we do not worship. More terrible
this lack of dogma, this light, this
unstructured library. More
innocent this unjudged fire, this
scent of the arbitrary. At night
there are millions of jewels, a shop
burning in space.

The image of the starry night as a shop, perhaps a jeweler's, is typically unexpected and fresh. It is a practical image, perhaps suggestive of commerce and transaction, of the vibrantly human from which Smith had formerly shied away, and might well still have done. The poem finishes with his invocation that he "tremble"; "let my sail tremble, / a diaphanous poppy," he asks. The islander from Lewis imagines his life, naturally enough, as a voyage; though the cost of the voyaging is fear, he still wishes to pay the price.

IAIN CRICHTON SMITH

A COUNTRY FOR OLD MEN; *AND* MY CANADIAN UNCLE

This substantial volume, over one hundred pages of poetry which Smith sent to his English publisher Carcanet not long before he died, shows that the poet was attempting to develop in his craft. Published posthumously in 2000, it is divided into two sections, the ironically titled "A Country for Old Men"—derived from W. B. Yeats's poem "Byzantium," in which the world of the sensual young is "No country for old men"—which is a gathering of shorter poems, few longer than a half page; and the closing anecdotal sequence of twenty-one vignettes in blank verse, often spoken by the poet's uncle, Torquil, who immigrated to Canada.

New in the first section are eight sequences of "Shorts," attempts at epigrams, often strictly formal, which, mainly unsuccessful, illustrate the difficulty of this compact form; they do, however, show the poet trying out new voices, even humor, and his four-line "Pheasant in a Cemetery," which is "brilliant red / among the annotated dead," provides a ready-made image for his affirmation of life. Among the other poems, "The Wedding" is a fine example of Smith's delicate lyric voice. It is two rhyming quatrains which form a clear-eyed epithalamium for "the netted bride" and her husband. The adjective "netted" shows Smith's gift for the apt yet unforeseen qualifier: the implication is that the woman is netted like a fish, though she may also still be wearing her bridal veil, its fine mesh resembling a sort of net. The qualifier may be both conceptual and literal. Also included here is an eerie poem about the *Titanic,* which switches inexplicably from third to first person near the poem's close. The houses of the great ship's privileged passengers "fall through the waves"; one of the passengers asks, "How did our handbags fill with water?" The brutality of ocean and the homeliness of personal artifacts such as handbags are shockingly conjoined. Smith also writes a praise poem for his contemporary, the Scottish poet Edwin Morgan, for whom it is "mandatory" "to swim out / into the impassioned light / and glint of the new." Morgan manages as second nature what Smith must strive toward.

"My Canadian Uncle," for such a lengthy sequence, lacks a strong narrative drive, but it is full of vivid particulars which engage the reader's attention. The poet is on a visit to Canada, staying with his eighty-five-year-old uncle. Through the poem the uncle recounts his emigration by boat in 1912 and his own packed biography. This is interspersed with sections by the narrator about the new experiences of being in Canada, along with reminiscences, by both the narrator and his uncle, of their native Lewis; these often employ Smith's typical contrasting imagery. So, in section 9, the poet watches "a green snail feeding on a black," glad to see "the black snail die / in the fresh green innocence of Canada."

By the closing section, the Canadian trip is over; the uncle dies later in the year. Rather than think of him dead, Smith prefers, in the narrative's last lines,

to think of him telling stories in his house,
huge, craggy, confident, while that velvet rose
glowed in the garden below squawking crows.

In these closing lines of his last published volume, Smith opts for life over the life denying, a movement that almost all his work traced. The "velvet rose," image of life, cultivation, and perhaps art, which, earlier in the poem, the uncle had carefully watered, is set against "the squawking crows," probably symbolic of the religious dogma which Smith fought against all his life. It is a complex image, however; the crows, though trivialized in the description of them as "squawking," are still capable of flight, and situated above the rose.

Smith develops throughout his oeuvre a humane liberality and generous sensibility, although, paradoxically, it may well be that the most lasting work, certainly among the poetry, is that in which he wrestles with the imposed mind-set of his upbringing, when the "law" and the "grace" are held in a thrumming tension. The later work, often looser in structure, has moments of astonishing imagery, and at their best the earlier poems form an impressive charting of a personal, yet distinctly Scottish, predicament, in a poetry of that "hammered" craftsmanship which Smith so praised in Dante.

IAIN CRICHTON SMITH

SELECTED BIBLIOGRAPHY

I. COLLECTED WORKS. *Collected Poems* (Manchester, U.K., 1992; 2d ed. 1995); *The Red Door: The Complete English Stories 1949–76*, ed. by Kevin MacNeil (Edinburgh, 2001); *The Black Halo: The Complete English Stories 1977–98*, ed. by Kevin MacNeil (Edinburgh, 2001).

II. POETRY. *The Long River* (Edinburgh, 1955); "The White Noon," in Edwin Muir, ed., *New Poets 1959: Iain Crichton Smith, Karen Gershon, Christopher Levenson* (London, 1959); *Burn is Aran* [Bread and Water] (Glasgow, 1960); *Thistles and Roses* (London, 1961); *Deer on the High Hills* (Edinburgh, 1962); *Biobuill is Sanasan Reice* [Bibles and Advertisements] (Glasgow, 1965); *The Law and the Grace* (London, 1965); *Three Regional Voices: Iain Crichton Smith, Barry Tebb, Michael Longley* (London, 1968); *At Helensburgh* (Belfast, 1968); *Lines Review 29* (June 1969; special issue devoted exclusively to Smith's poetry); *From Bourgeois Land* (London, 1969); *Selected Poems* (London and Chester Spring, Pa., 1970); *Hamlet in Autumn* (Edinburgh, 1972); *Love Poems and Elegies* (London, 1972); *Eadar Fealla-Dha is Glaschu* [Between Comedy and Glasgow] (Glasgow, 1974); *Orpheus and Other Poems* (Preston, U.K., 1974); *Poems for Donalda* (Belfast, 1974); *The Notebooks of Robinson Crusoe, and Other Poems* (London, 1975); *The Permanent Island: Gaelic Poems*, translations of poems from *Biobuill is Sanasan Reice* and *Eadar Fealla-Dha is Glaschu* (Edinburgh, 1975); *In the Middle* (London, 1977); *River, River: Poems for Children* (Edinburgh, 1978); *Selected Poems 1955–1980*, ed. by Robin Fulton (Edinburgh 1981); *Na h-Eilthirich* [The Exiles] (Glasgow, 1983); *The Exiles* (Manchester and Dublin, 1984); *Selected Poems* (Manchester, U.K., 1985); *A Life* (Manchester, U.K., 1986); *An t-Eilean Agus an Cana* [The Island and the Language] (Glasgow, 1987); *The Village and Other Poems* (Manchester, U.K., 1989); *Ends and Beginnings* (Manchester, U.K., 1994); *The Human Face* (Manchester, U.K., 1996); *The Leaf and the Marble* (Manchester, U.K., 1998); *A Country for Old Men; and My Canadian Uncle* (Manchester, U.K., 2000).

III. NOVELS. *Consider the Lilies* (London, 1968, republished under the title *The Alien Light*, Boston, 1969); *The Last Summer* (London, 1969); *My Last Duchess* (London, 1971); *Goodbye, Mr. Dixon* (London, 1974); *An t-Aonoran* [The Loner] (Glasgow, 1976); *An End to Autumn* (London, 1978); *On the Island* (London, 1979); *A Field Full of Folk* (London, 1982); *The Search* (London, 1983); *The Tenement* (London, 1985); *In the Middle of the Wood* (London, 1987); *Na Speuclairean Dubha* [The Dark Glasses] (Glasgow, 1989); *The Dream* (London, 1990).

IV. SHORT STORIES. *An Dubh is an Gorm* [The Black and the Blue] (Aberdeen, U.K., 1963); *Maighstirean is Ministearan* [Masters and Ministers] (Inverness, U.K., 1970); *Survival Without Error, and Other Stories* (London, 1970); *The Black and the Red, and Other Stories* (London, 1973); *An T-Adhair Ameireaganach* [American Sky] (Inverness, U.K., 1973); *The Village* (Inverness, U.K., 1976); *The Hermit, and Other Stories* (London, 1977); *Am Bruadaraiche* [The Dreamer] (Stornoway, U.K., 1980); *Murdo and Other Stories* (London, 1981); *Mr. Trill in Hades, and Other Stories* (London, 1984); *Selected Stories* (Manchester, U.K., 1990); *Listen to the Voice: Selected Stories* (Edinburgh, 1993); *Thoughts of Murdo* (Edinburgh, 1993).

V. OTHER WORKS. *The Golden Lyric: An Essay on the Poetry of Hugh MacDiarmid* (Preston, U.K., 1967); *Towards the Human: Collected Essays* (Edinburgh, 1986).

VI. INTERVIEWS. Lorn McIntyre, "Poet in Bourgeois Land," in *Scottish International* (September 1971);); Aonghas Macneacail, "Iain Crichton Smith," in *Stand Magazine* 30, no. 1 (winter 1988–89); Bill Duncan, "Iain Crichton Smith in Conversation," in *Chapman* 73 (summer 1993); Gerry Cambridge, "Iain Crichton Smith at Seventy: The Poet in Conversation in Brownsbank Cottage," in *The Dark Horse* 6 (spring 1998).

VII. BIOGRAPHICAL AND CRITICAL WORKS. Robin Fulton, "Iain Crichton Smith," in his *Contemporary Scottish Poetry: Individuals and Contexts* (Edinburgh, 1974); Alan Taylor, "Hell and Back Again," in *Scotland on Sunday* (29 March 1992); Carole Gow, *Mirror and Marble: The Poetry of Iain Crichton Smith* (Edinburgh, 1992); Colin Nicholson, ed., *Iain Crichton Smith: Critical Essays* (Edinburgh, 1992); John Blackburn, *The Poetry of Iain Crichton Smith* (Aberdeen, U.K., 1993); Alan Riach, "Iain Crichton Smith: An Appreciation," in *PN Review* 25, no. 4, 1998; Aonghas Macneacail, "A Rare and Precious Miracle," in *West Highland Free Press* (23 October 1998); Catherine Deveney, "Survival of the Wittiest," in *Scotland on Sunday* (5 July 1998); Alasdair Macrae, "Remembering Iain Crichton Smith," in *Dark Horse* 8 (autumn 1999); Edwin Morgan, "The Contribution of Iain Crichton Smith," in *Scotlit* 23 (winter 2000); Stewart Conn, "A Human Trembling: Iain Crichton Smith," in his *Distances: A Personal Evocation of People and Places* (Dalkeith, U.K., 2001).

EMMA TENNANT

(1937–)

Jennifer E. Dunn

EMMA TENNANT IS firmly a figure of the British literary establishment, yet her precise identity as a writer is difficult to define. She is nothing if not rebellious, questioning the literary canon by rewriting its classics, satirizing feminism, and mocking the eccentricities of the aristocracy into which she was born. Tennant's fiction defies labels, although she is often called a feminist writer for her consistent focus on female experience and identity. In her treatment of the supernatural and the improbable, the allure and mystery of the past, and the terror that these provoke in both her characters and her audience, Tennant is fundamentally an artist of the neogothic, although she draws on a wide range of genres and literary traditions. Plucking techniques from science fiction and magic realism as well as the gothic novel, and concentrating on themes as widely varied as the occult, psychoanalysis, and myth, her novels are puzzling and often structurally fractured. Tennant is not always an easy read: her best novels refuse closure and suspend meaning, as if purposefully designed to frustrate the reader. The best way to approach Tennant is to remember that in her work she experiments with the convergence of different forms and forces, and with the unclear boundary between real and unreal that results from this play.

LIFE

Emma Christina Tennant was the first child of Christopher Tennant, the second baron Glenconner, and his second wife, Elizabeth Powell. With its glamorous connections, wealth, and eccentricity, the history of the Tennant family is as fantastic as one of Tennant's novels. Emma Tennant's great-grandfather, Charles Tennant, was the grandson of an earlier Tennant who invented the bleaching process; he expanded the family enterprise into one of the first multinational corporations, with properties as far as Spain and Trinidad. He also established the family seat at Peebles in the Scottish Borders, a gothic-styled castle named Glen. After being made a peer, he married his two children into aristocratic families. His daughter Margot became the wife of Herbert Asquith, England's prime minister from 1908 to 1916. His son Edward, the first baron Glenconner and Emma Tennant's grandfather, married Pamela Wyndham and had five children. Their eldest son, Edward, was killed at the battle of the Somme during World War I, and the entail established by Charles passed to the second son, Christopher. Christopher Tennant married twice: first to Pamela Paget and then to Elizabeth Powell. From his first marriage came two sons: Colin, the second baron Glenconner, and James. The family estate and wealth passed through this branch of the family. From Christopher's second marriage came Emma Tennant and two siblings, Tobias and Catherine. The Tennant reputation for high connections and eccentricity was augmented by Christopher's generation. His sister Clare, a divorcée several times over, included among her husbands Alfred, Lord Tennyson's, grandson Lionel. His brother David was a notorious socialite who founded the Gargoyle Club in London in 1925. The youngest brother, Emma's uncle Stephen, was known as the outrageous and beautiful eccentric who seduced the poet Siegfried Sassoon. In the 1950s the friendship between Colin Tennant and Princess Margaret, the sister of Queen Elizabeth II, fueled tabloid rumors of an engagement. The rumors proved false; the two never married, although Colin gave the princess a villa on the Caribbean island of Mustique as a wedding gift. Colin himself married the daughter of the earl of Leicester and had three sons, all of whom suffered tragedies that fueled more tabloid headlines, this time about "the Tennant curse."

Although she was born in London, on 20 October 1937, Emma spent her early childhood at Glen. She writes in her memoirs about discovering long-forgotten letters and notebooks detailing the lives of these earlier Tennants; as if determined to live up to, or perhaps outdo, her predecessors, Tennant went on to lead a remarkably unconventional adulthood. She was educated at St. Paul's Girls' School in London until the age of fifteen, and then spent a year at a finishing school in Oxford. After this, she stayed in Paris, informally studying art history, before returning to her parents' home in Regent's Park to be presented as a debutante. Princess Margaret attended her coming-out ball in 1955. In the years between this and her marriage, the teenage Emma had an affair with an older man, which resulted in an abortion. In 1957 she was married in a gold dress to Sebastian Yorke, son of the writer Henry Green. Although they had a son, Matthew, the marriage didn't last. Tennant left their home in Chelsea to travel, establishing friendships with writers, including Gore Vidal and Bruce Chatwin, along the way. She also wrote for *Queen* magazine in London, spent time in New York working for *Vogue,* and wrote her first novel, *The Colour of Rain.* In 1962 she formally divorced Yorke, and in 1963 *The Colour of Rain* was published. In the same year, she married Christopher Booker, editor of the satiric journal *Private Eye.* She was remarried in 1968, this time to the journalist Alexander Cockburn, with whom she had a daughter, Daisy, in 1969. This marriage ended in divorce in 1973, when Tennant gave birth to a second daughter, Rose, by Michael Dempsey, a writer. In 1975 Tennant founded the literary magazine *Bananas,* which she ran until 1978. During these years, Tennant cultivated friendships with many of the writers published in the magazine. She also began an affair with the poet Ted Hughes in 1977, after his marriage to the American poet Sylvia Plath and Plath's suicide in 1963. Tennant calls the time between 1977 and 1984 "the years of evil fortune": the

deaths of family and friends were accompanied by her own bout with cancer (*Burnt Diaries,* p. 214). During this time and as of 2003, she lived with Tim Owens, a writer, and proved herself a prolific writer by publishing novels on an almost yearly basis.

BANANAS *AND THE NOTTING HILL SCENE*

The table of contents of the first *Bananas* reveals an impressive list of contributors, including Heathcote Williams, Ted Hughes, Claud Cockburn, J. G. Ballard, and Elaine Feinstein. Later issues of the magazine include work by Peter Redgrove, Sylvia Plath, and Angela Carter. Most of these writers were personal friends of Tennant during the mid-to-late 1970s, and her Notting Hill home was the site of regular *Bananas* parties and informal gatherings. The magazine itself was a showcase for new and established talent, a "literary newspaper" that promoted experimental short fiction but also printed poetry, essays, and artwork in every issue.

Tennant edited *Bananas* from 1975 until 1978, when, for financial reasons, she handed editorship over to Abigail Mozley (who ran it under the same name until 1981). During Tennant's tenure as editor, the magazine was critically acclaimed and received Arts Council funding. One sign of the magazine's success was the steady support it received from a sizable group of talented contributors. Tennant was offered several of Ted Hughes's poems and his neogothic story "The Head" for publication. Angela Carter's story "In the Company of Wolves," later included in her well-known work *The Bloody Chamber* (1979), was first published in the magazine. *Bananas* also featured Sara Maitland's early work and previously unpublished pieces by Sylvia Plath. Tennant even included her own work: her gothic short story "Rigor Beach" appeared in the first issue in 1975.

In 1976 Elaine Feinstein introduced Tennant to Ted Hughes. The meeting was uneventful, although Tennant confesses that she was already fascinated by the future poet laureate of Britain, the man at the center of a legend in which "Sylvia [Plath] stands for the martyred female and

EMMA TENNANT

Hughes for the murderous male." In a 1999 memoir, Tennant recalls her attraction to Hughes:

> A sizeable part of me wishes to abandon allegiance to the martyr and saint and throw myself at Ted Hughes. I am embarrassedly aware that I'm not the only one to suffer from this suppressed desire. I've laughed about it with friends: we refer to it as the Bluebeard or Mr. Rochester syndrome . . . a need on the part of certain women to become involved with a man known for his terrifying and unacceptable treatment of members of their sex.
>
> (*Burnt Diaries,* pp. 48–49)

Although she resolves to resist Hughes's allure, she nonetheless "throws herself" at the poet when they meet a second time. An affair soon follows, although the two see each other infrequently: Tennant was running *Bananas* and raising two small children; Hughes had remarried and was involved in affairs with other women as well. Their relationship was over by 1979, but Tennant's writing—her autobiographies as well as her fiction—reflect a lingering fascination with this period of her life, with the dark, magical prose she published in *Bananas,* and with the gothic mystery of bluebeards and their muses.

THE EARLY NOVELS

One may tentatively suggest a split between Tennant's pre- and post-*Bananas* writing. Before the publication of her seminal work, *The Bad Sister,* in 1978, Tennant's concerns were those of the modernists: the limitations of realism and representing perception. The pre-*Bananas* novels show some of the aesthetic qualities of postmodernism, like mixed genres, parody, and experimentalism. But they lack the extreme self-consciousness, or metafictional aspect, of full-blown postmodernist writing. Tennant's early novels are less concerned with the context of their own creation than with the fictional reality they create—its plots, characters, and their processes of perception. Tennant's early agenda is to represent that reality as contextual, fluid, and subjective. This is essentially a project developed by earlier modernists such as James Joyce and Virginia Woolf.

Tennant's first novel, however, *The Colour of Rain,* falls somewhat outside this characterization. A realist social satire, it portrays the tensions between several young couples living in London. Adopting the style of Henry Green, Tennant's then father-in-law, it is written almost entirely in dialogue. Affairs and gossip form the novel's brief plot, exposing the futility and emptiness of married life within the upper middle class. *The Colour of Rain* caused a minor uproar. Tennant's publisher submitted it for the Formentor Prize in 1964, and one of the judges denounced it as an example of "the decadence of English writing." Tennant did not publish for another ten years.

When she wrote again, she turned to nonrealist approaches. *The Time of the Crack* (1973; republished under the title *The Crack*) is a tale of apocalypse. An immense and unexplained crack forms along the Thames River in London, fostering chaos and a sense of the surreal. The novel traces the movements of a Playboy bunny named Baba as she meets characters who find different meanings in the crack: a fortune-teller predicting matriarchy, businessmen seeking profit, scholars uselessly debating the event's significance. Like so many of Tennant's novels, *The Time of the Crack* destabilizes the meanings behind political, economic, and intellectual discourses by rendering their agendas ridiculous. The novel adopts the framework of science fiction (a fantastic event, a futuristic-apocalyptic setting), but unlike sci-fi, its tone is tongue-in-cheek: this fantasy is self-conscious of its absurdity. *The Time of the Crack*'s value lies in its vivid, strange imagery and its wry twisting of the generic conventions it adopts. When the "apocalypse" reverses itself and the crack disappears, Tennant's characters are still wandering; they have learned nothing from their encounter with chaos. And although the novel becomes increasingly like a fable, with less-than-subtle preaching about the dangers of commerce and modern "knowledge," the novel ends without example or closure. The final scene depicts a minor character floating in a hot-air balloon above a world that has been transformed, unpredictably, into a meaningless feminist utopia. We can only assume that Baba and the rest of the characters have been lost in the new social order that seems as meaningless as its sudden, chaotic creation.

The Last of the Country House Murders (1974) centers on the eccentric Jules Tanner and Mr. Haines, respectively the "victim" and "detective" in a staged murder to take place at Tanner's estate, Woodiscombe Manor. By the end of the story, Tanner is haunted by the ghost of his father and an old lover, and pestered by a former fiancée; tourists line up outside the manor to try to "solve" the murder case; and an army advances out of nowhere. As these different plots and agendas overlap, the question of who murders whom, and why, is completely confused. As in *The Time of the Crack,* a sense of the surreal gradually turns into absurdity, although *The Last of the Country House Murders* is a less disturbing—and therefore, a less accomplished—novel: the story's outcome returns the reader to a recognizable world, where a rational explanation of the events transforms the surreal narrative into a facile murder mystery that recalls the board game Clue.

In some respects, *Hotel de Dream* (1976) is a transitional text. Like the novels before it, there is no first-person protagonist: characters from widely different backgrounds are again brought together, this time in a dingy boardinghouse where their dream lives overlap. The events that unfold reveal the desires and pretensions of a timid closet feminist (Mrs. Scranton), an overbearing novelist (Cecilia Houghton), and her class-conscious admirer (Mr. Poynter). The surrealist aspects and dream portions of the narrative offer disturbing scenarios. Cecilia Houghton's characters come to life and try to murder their creator, but are finally trapped within her depressing plotlines. The Amazonian collective of Mrs. Scranton's dreams clashes with Mr. Poynter's highly ordered dream city, and the free sexuality of her subconscious is juxtaposed with the sexual exploitations of his. *Hotel de Dream* is darker than its predecessors: it is the first time Tennant mingles social satire with such explicit explorations of identity and unconscious desire in the context of a destabilized external world. The novel hints at what is to come in *The Bad Sister* and *Wild Nights* (1979), with their more intense focus on the forces that shape the experience of subjectivity and reality. While these early texts reflect the 1960s milieu of rebellion and experimentation, their parody of realism belies a certain dependency on and perpetuation of earlier literary concerns, particularly modernism's antirealism and preoccupation with representing human consciousness. Tennant's use of absurdity, ironic imagery, and surrealism indicate her postmodernist tendencies, but only on a technical level. *The Time of the Crack* and *Hotel de Dream,* for instance, show only traces of textual self-consciousness and self–interrogation, important postmodernist approaches that expand upon the simpler problems of form and representation. Whereas *The Bad Sister* dramatizes the problems of discourse and narrative, these earlier texts remain preoccupied with formal innovation, the rejection of realism, and the relationship between consciousness and reality. Stylistically and thematically, they are less interesting and less accomplished than her later work. Aside from sometimes muddled plots, they offer little challenge to the reader. Irony is transparently gained by the simple juxtaposition of contradictory images: Playboy bunnies cavorting with feminists, an Amazonian collective submitting to rape by soldiers, a detective entangled in the disputes of wealthy eccentrics. Their style wavers hesitantly and sometimes distractingly between social realism and fantasy. And, perhaps because there is no first-person narrator, we gain only a fleeting sense of the characters. At times, they feel like props used merely to enhance the novels' absurd landscapes. With the exception of *Hotel de Dream,* these novels only partially explore the relationship between subjectivity, discourse, and reality.

In many ways, these three early texts are awkward prototypes, for in the later work this meshing of different genres, traditions, and techniques develops into a more complex style that not only frustrates categorization, but also problematizes the categories, assumptions, and expectations that accompany the experience of reading. As if trying to find what mode most suits her talents, Tennant experiments with different projects before settling on the wider thematic range and dark literary pastiche that characterize her strongest and most appealing writing.

DEVELOPMENT OF THE LATER FICTION

Pastiche—bringing together aspects of different sources—is characteristic of postmodernist writing. One example would be the use of fairy-tale characters in a modern setting, or mythological imagery in a detective story. Such unconventional pairings have the same function as surrealism: they create a sense of the bizarre. Pastiche calls attention to the creation of a text, or its context. The reader is forced to notice how a text works, and how it draws on or plays with previous literary models. This self-awareness of the text, and the awareness it provokes in the reader, is central to postmodernism. Postmodernism works on the idea that reality is structured like a narrative: what we think is real or true is contextual, and like a story, created. Ideas, discourses, reality—all of which are kinds of texts—can therefore be re-created.

For Tennant, the possibilities of re-creation apply to all kinds of "narratives," from specific literary texts, genres, and traditions to constructions of reality, subjectivity, and gender. Tennant's post-*Bananas* novels can be labeled postmodernist because of the implications of this revisionist agenda. Many of the novels, including *The Bad Sister, Queen of Stones* (1982), *Faustine* (1992), and *Tess* (1993) are explicit reworkings of earlier novels. Often, Tennant is rewriting more than one text. *The Bad Sister,* for instance, takes its plot from a nineteenth-century novel, but its conventions, style, and imagery from fairy tales, magic realist fiction, and the classic gothic novel. Thematically, *The Bad Sister* destabilizes ideas about feminism, identity, and reality—suggesting that these discourses are simply stories that can be retold in any number of ways. The problems of stories and storytelling are central to Tennant's later fiction. So too are the themes of magic and fantasy. What is real or unreal, what one should believe or discard, is often the problem Tennant's protagonists face. More specifically, her characters are faced with the confusing forces of feminism and patriarchy and the inherited narratives of literature, myth, psychology, and class. If Tennant participates in the postmodernist projects of destabilizing discourses and playing with narrative, she also has her own agenda: to turn stories inside out and reveal the dark, forceful power they hold over us.

THE NEOGOTHIC NOVELS

While all of the post-*Bananas* novels are revisionist in some respect, some are less realist than others. *The Bad Sister, Wild Nights, Queen of Stones,* and *Woman Beware Woman* (1983; published in the United States under the title *The Half-Mother*) are all based on earlier texts, but predominantly rework gothic conventions and themes.

The Bad Sister is based on the Scottish poet James Hogg's *Confessions of a Justified Sinner* (1824). Hogg's novel, set in eighteenth-century Scotland, is the story of Robert Wringhim, the disowned son of the laird of Dalcastle, who is raised by an extremist Calvinist preacher. Under his adoptive father's influence, he comes to believe that he is "saved." (Calvinism holds that fate in the afterlife is determined before birth.) When Wringhim falls under the spell of a mysterious companion known as Gil-martin, he uses the doctrine of predestination to justify murdering his elder brother, George Colwan, and gaining his father's estate. Gil-martin then tricks Wringhim into further depravity. The structure of the novel is twofold: the central narrative is Wringhim's story, conveyed in his personal memoirs. These have been collected by an editor, who offers "evidence" and his own commentary to lend the story an aura of truth. A gothic mystery posing as a "historical account," *Confessions of a Justified Sinner* explores fanaticism and moral vulnerability. Yet while the novel can be read as a tale of temptation—Gil-martin is possibly Satan—it is fundamentally a story about the unknown. Gil-martin may be the devil, but he could also be a hallucination, the result of Wringhim's warped moral perspective and hatred for his family. The editor's account, which feigns objective analysis, never resolves the events. The novel offers a disturbing picture of the possibility of the supernatural, and how this possibility so easily alters reality and identity.

The Bad Sister, set in the late twentieth century, parallels Hogg's plot. The story centers on the murders of Michael and Ishbel Dalzell, members of a prominent Scottish family. The suspect is Dalzell's illegitimate daughter, known as Jane Wild. As in Hogg's *Confessions,* an editor has gathered and presented evidence on the case. The book is a collection of news articles, interviews, specialist reports, and the editor's own commentary. This material surrounds Jane Wild's diary, which details the events of her life prior to the murders and her own disappearance. Like Wringhim, Jane Wild has been cast off by her biological father. She spends her childhood in a cottage on his estate bordering the Ettrick Forest. Although Jane is raised there by her mother, she falls under the influence of her mother's companion, Meg. Meg is possibly one of Dalzell's former mistresses, which might explain her intense hatred of him. During Jane's childhood, Meg heads a feminist commune that terrorizes the Dalzell family. Later, at the time of Jane's journal, she founds a similar cult in London. All of her followers take the surname Wild. Meg's extremist feminism parallels the warped Calvinism in Hogg's text. She uses this ideology to justify violence. After Dalzell's murder, she makes the following statement to Jane's friend Stephen: "It was a ritual killing. The left hand performs the act figuratively, the right hand performs it literally. There is no difference between the two. He was the incarnation of capitalism. We have incarnated our disapproval of him" (p. 40). She uses similar rhetoric to encourage Jane's hatred of her half sister Ishbel.

At the point where the journal begins, Jane is working as a film critic in London and living with her boyfriend, Tony Marten. The relationship is emotionally empty, and Jane is burdened by the intrusions of Tony's malicious mother. Her own mother seems to have disappeared, but Meg is still a strong presence in her unhappy life. The journal describes dreamlike journeys that Meg "sends" to Jane. These sometimes involve flashbacks to Jane's childhood; at other times, Jane turns into an androgynous being and flies to mysterious landscapes. It is during these journeys that she sees her "bad sister," Ishbel, who takes the form of Tony's ex-girlfriend Miranda. In these visions, Jane also encounters a vampiric Meg and a strange male figure named Gil-martin. Gradually, these journeys blend into Jane's everyday life: she leaves Stephen's house only to find herself in a mysterious forest; in bed with Tony, she floats out of her body and sees herself talking to Meg. Finally, a plan emerges from the visions: Meg asks Jane to kill her bad sister, Ishbel-Miranda, in exchange for Gil-martin. Jane is obsessed with carrying out the plan. She never questions Meg's—or her own—sanity, but does become intensely paranoid. She convinces herself that Mrs. Marten is plotting to kill her, and is conspiring with Ishbel-Miranda. The journal ends with a surreal account of a costume party, where Jane finds and kills a woman she believes is her sister. This moment is confusing: once the murder has happened, the setting changes. Jane is suddenly in Meg's house, giving her "the girl," then she is in a dream-journey again, changing shape and joining Gil-martin in the hills of Scotland. At no point does Jane tell us who or what Gil-martin is, except to say he is her "other half."

If Jane's account is unclear, the editor's investigations only confuse things more. Michael Dalzell is killed at home by one or two unknown women, suspected to be Jane and Meg. But there is no mention of her father's death in the journal, and Jane never plots his murder; she only wants to kill her sister. Ishbel, on the other hand, is found dead on a street while Jane is seen at a party; yet other witnesses claim to have seen Jane at the murder site that night. Finally, after reading the journal, the editor goes to Scotland, where there have been recent disturbances in the Ettrick Forest. There, in a clearing reputed to be haunted, he finds a body. It is a "hermaphroditic" woman who looks like Jane, pierced through the heart with a wooden stake. The editor concludes that the remains are Jane's, but the murders remain unsolved. The editor briefly wonders how Meg and Gil-martin were involved, but concludes that "these were of course the over-tired and agitated

EMMA TENNANT

wanderings of my mind" (p. 222). His final explanation is that a shepherd randomly thrust the stake into the mound.

The Bad Sister offers several narrative authorities and undermines them all. The events outlined in the journal make no sense, and yet we cannot read them as a fantastic account because they are mired in a real murder case. Yet the editor's "objective" narrative contradicts itself: the "facts" of the case—witness reports, a psychoanalytic evaluation, local lore, and interviews with Jane's acquaintances—are not fully consistent with each other or with the journal. The editor's credibility is further undermined by the novel's final moment, when he/she compares Mrs. Marten to Meg. This similarity corresponds with descriptions in the journal, where Meg and Mrs. Marten are both represented as supernatural persecutors. Jane visits Meg's innocent-looking house, "a nest for an old woman with fleecy hair," where Meg becomes a vampire and drinks her blood (p. 128). A few pages later, Jane encounters Mrs. Marten and observes: "Her hair was like the wool on the distaff of the wicked old woman who puts a castle to sleep for a hundred years—her whole person was the spindle, which pricks you through and through" (p. 137). Many of the characters are confused by subtle pairings like this one. Meg and Mrs. Marten, Ishbel and Miranda, Jane and Gil-martin—we cannot be sure that any of these characters are entirely distinct from one another. The self-destabilizing quality of the journal breaks through into the external narrative(s). We cannot believe the editor's fragile insistence on logic: "rational" explanations are always contradicted by "supernatural" ones that refer us back to the journal whose authority is already suspect. A psychoanalyst's conclusion that Jane is schizophrenic seems to explain everything—but then there is the undeniable situation of "Jane's" corpse—which ultimately goes unexplained. In the end, even this "scientific" analysis makes no sense. Fiction and fact, psychosis and reality—the boundaries are endlessly confused.

This confusion, though it makes for a frustrating reading experience, is the point of Tennant's fiction. She is not only deconstructing conventional binaries—reality and fantasy, reason and madness—but also complicating inherited narratives. In the case of *The Bad Sister,* she explicitly rewrites and feminizes Hogg's *Confessions.* Hogg's male-centered story becomes one about sisterhood and feminist politics, patriarchy and the roles it assigns women. If Robert Wringhim is trapped between religion and sin, then Jane Wild is caught between versions of herself: the vampiric feminist, the abandoned and resentful daughter, the unhappy girlfriend, the murderer. Yet all of these identities blend into one, just as Jane and her "bad sister" are two aspects of one identity. The issue of good and evil and the question of temptation are not as clear in Tennant's novel as they are in Hogg's. Nor is the usefulness of feminism. Meg's "Wild" women, who exist outside society's moral system, are a parody of the feminist "wild zone," the theoretical space women occupy outside patriarchal language.

Some critics have objected to Tennant's wry commentary on feminism. Pauline Palmer, for instance, admits she is offended by *The Bad Sister'*s "prejudiced" portrayal of feminism as a "terrorist subculture" (p. 143). Yet, this criticism overlooks the real significance of such representations. By associating extremist feminism with spells and vampires, Tennant is both poking fun at the fear of feminism that leads to such caricatures, and pointing out the potentially dangerous side of identity politics. In *The Bad Sister,* the feminist is evil because she is blinded by man-hating fanaticism and the dysfunctional tenets of a purely theoretical discourse. Instead of promoting sisterhood and more equal relations between genders, Meg's feminism insists on violence and hatred and accomplishes nothing. For all that, however, *The Bad Sister* is a feminist text. Feminism seeks new perspectives on the status quo. Feminist literature is often concerned, therefore, with rewriting gender roles and subjectivity. *The Bad Sister* does both, as well as offering a different perspective on feminism. This is merely part of Tennant's overall agenda, which is to reveal and question the discourses that shape women's identities. In *The Bad Sister,* as well as *Wild Nights, Queen of Stones,* and *Woman Beware Woman,* the most prominent discourse being rewritten is the tradition—often thought of as a "women's tradition"—of the gothic novel. All of these texts use gothic tropes: a vulnerable heroine "pursued" by a hero-villain, forbidding domestic spaces, haunted landscapes, the sense of the past impending on the present, and most importantly, the presence or possibility of supernatural forces. A typical gothic plot concerns a mystery involving one or all of these aspects. The action and atmosphere of the novel are enhanced by a sense of tension, usually provoked by old scandals and/or a subplot of escape and pursuit. *The Bad Sister* alters gothic conventions, just as it alters Hogg's text; but the primary pattern is still there. In some cases, the basic gothic structure overlaps with other genres, including fairy tales and magic realism. This pastiche is a postmodernist twist, a means of drawing on previous narratives and models while simultaneously deconstructing and rewriting them.

Tennant's 1979 novel, *Wild Nights,* wavers back and forth between a gothic family drama and a child's fairy tale. A memoir of a childhood spent in the mysterious hills of the north, it centers on the perceptions of a first-person unnamed narrator and her witch-like aunt, Zita. There is no conventional plot; the circumstances of the narrative are even less clear than those in *The Bad Sister.* The narrator tells us about Zita's yearly visits to the family home, which bring the end of summer and also transform the gloomy family estate:

> When my aunt Zita came, there were changes everywhere. The days outside, which were long and white at that time of year, closed and turned like a shutter, a sharp blue night coming on sudden and unexpected as a finger caught in a hinge. The house shrank; the walls seemed to lean inwards.
>
> (p. 9)

When Zita visits, the world reverts to an older, more supernatural era. The electricity goes out; ghosts appear in the halls; the narrator and Zita ride on the back of the north wind to attend midnight parties in exotic locations. While the narrator's mother is uncomfortable with these changes, and dislikes Zita for provoking them, the narrator finds herself drawn to the magic that

surrounds her aunt. She creeps through the transformed house, discovering rooms filled with old belongings, portraits of deceased relatives, and, one day, Zita entwined in the arms of her own brother's ghost. She also develops a friendship with a boy from the village, observes the clashes between Zita and the other women in the family, and witnesses the villagers burn Zita on a pyre as winter finally settles over the landscape.

It is a strange story, filled with vivid descriptions of magical events. In the narrator's eyes, the world becomes a fairy tale in which she attends fantastical balls, the morning frost is "brittle as icing sugar," women are burned to death, and mysterious aunts bear the seasons of the year in their wake. Like *The Bad Sister,* the irrational movements of the narrative convey a different reality, one that straddles the border between fantasy and fact. The magic, however playful and intriguing, is associated with darker truths—the narrator's isolation in the north and her obsessive curiosity about her family, her mother's bitterness, the possibility of incest in earlier generations, and Zita's strange death. Precisely because this darkness frames the story, and fails to provoke surprise in the narrator, *Wild Nights* persistently raises the question of narrative authority. Who is telling this story, and why? What is really happening? Is Zita a real person, a metaphor for autumn, or a child's fantasy? The narrator reveals nothing about herself but her strange perspective of her insular world. We have no idea if these events are imagined or real, if she is mad, or if her family is. At the center of this mystery is the family house, a looming structure with endless rooms and ancient furnishings, where ghosts hide and the walls seem alive. At times, the house merges with the landscape around it, is invaded by autumn leaves or by the dead atmosphere of winter. It is the gothic castle of earlier novels, a dark, secretive place that houses and perhaps compels the strange events that occur within it. Zita is its gothic heroine, trapped by the allure of the house and pursued by her own past, the obsessive eyes of her niece, and the fatal darkness of her own magic.

Queen of Stones continues to develop the themes of *The Bad Sister* and *Wild Nights*; though it is a more coherent novel, it does frustrate interpretation. A group of girls goes missing for a few days, and one of them never returns. Her headless body washes up on shore soon after the other girls are found. There is again an editor, who supplies different reports, which are interspersed with his/her own "recreation" of the events. Unlike Jane Wild's journal, which purports to be a firsthand account, we know from the start that the editor's re-creation is a fiction. He/she even offers a "bibliography" at the end of the text, which includes a well-known study of fairy tales, Sigmund Freud's case study on hysteria ("Dora"), and other psychoanalytical texts. All of these sources have an obvious influence on the editor's account.

The events, according to the editor, are as follows. On a walk through the countryside, a group of schoolgirls is separated from their chaperone by a sudden fog. The girls become lost in a maze of walking paths, make their way to the shore, and then to a rocky peninsula cut off from the mainland by the fog, where they wait until the weather clears. The group's leader is thirteen-year-old Bess Plantain, the eldest daughter of a wealthy family. Accompanying her are her younger sister Jane (eleven) and some of her classmates; the daughter of the Plantains' maid, Laurie Strang (thirteen); and several six-year-old schoolchildren. According to the editor's reconstruction, the group descends quickly into a savage state, and new rivalries lead to violence. Portraying Bess as Queen Elizabeth and Laurie Strang as Mary, queen of Scots, the editor explores the group dynamics that lead to the ritualized beheading of a socially awkward eleven-year-old named Melanie.

The narrative is a feminized version of William Golding's *Lord of the Flies* (1954), a similar account of schoolboys stranded on an empty island. *Queen of Stones* takes on the mythic quality of that earlier narrative by suggesting that underneath a girl's civilized exterior are "primitive" desires and fears, and a tendency to regress to violence. The events are explained by classic psychoanalytic theory: Bess is hysterical, torn by memories of past abuse, desire for her father's attention, sexual attraction to Laurie, and fear of

menarche. It is telling that Bess finally menstruates after the ordeal is over. Her persistent cough, thought to be a symptom of hysteria, disappears at the same time. The whole experience is presented as "cathartic," the manifestation and resolution of Bess's unconscious worries and guilt. This is a parody of the Dora case. The psychoanalytic explanation leaves many issues unexplored, such as class tension between the girls and the supernatural elements that surface in the re-creation. Psychoanalysis is revealed as a self-undermining discourse: it is blind to its own (often sexist) assumptions.

The narrative rewrites the discourses that problematically "explain" the female psyche (like psychoanalysis) or exclude females altogether (like *Lord of the Flies*). Like the novels discussed above, it draws on more than one genre. Fairy-tale themes recur in the narrative, as well as gothic conventions. The Plantain house looms in the background of the story, as well as the dark figures of Bess's father and her abusive uncle. Yet the hero-villain is also Bess herself: the vulnerable girl becomes an evil queen with the power to torment and kill. The landscape, especially the island, is the haunted terrain of the gothic novel, where supernatural events are possible, and nature is at times a terrifyingly sentient force.

Other of Tennant's novels written in the neogothic vein include *Alice Fell* (1980), *Woman Beware Woman,* and *Sisters and Strangers: A Moral Tale* (1990). These novels set out to do what *The Bad Sister* does, but their use and revision of gothic tropes is typically less effective. Whereas the three novels discussed above use the gothic to examine and rewrite various discourses, these others tend to use it merely for setting or plot enhancement. In *Woman Beware Woman,* there are a few magical events that lead the reader to question the reliability of the narrator. This hint of uncertainty calls the plot and background of the story into question. The novel puts pressure on the act of storytelling, suggesting that perspective, memory, and desire are all contextual and changing forces affecting narration. But it does not do this consistently or forcefully enough to sustain its point. Ambiguity, so effective in *The Bad Sister,* fails to work in the same way here.

There are similar weaknesses in the other novels. *Alice Fell* depends on imagery rather than the play of discourse to convey a sense of the bizarre, which sometimes overpowers the weak plot to the point of confusion. *Sisters and Strangers,* which rewrites the story of Eve, offers an interesting juxtaposition of modern-day society and that timeless story of gender roles, yet is straightforward in its plot and feminist agenda. It does not question its own narrative authority or its politics. Considered alone, these novels are interesting examples of experimental writing, and reveal how influential feminist and psychoanalytic theories were at the time they were written. Yet in comparison to Tennant's more complex neogothic novels, they appear unpolished and one-dimensional—not truly representative of Tennant's considerable talents, but pointing the way to some of her later, less accomplished writing.

THE CONVENTIONAL REVISIONIST NOVELS

Novels like *Woman Beware Woman* show two different strands in Tennant's work: one that uses gothic tropes to complicate many discourses at once, and another that rewrites specific texts and stays within the confines of realism. Sometimes the more conventional novels are successful in the same way that the neogothic novels are. The 1993 work *Tess,* for example, uses standard realist narration, yet manages to explore writing and rewriting, and how this shapes history and social change. Some of the other conventional novels written around the same time, however, fail to work on a more complex level. Tennant's sequels to Jane Austen novels offer little if any challenge to the original texts; they read like predictable romances meant for the sole purpose of entertainment. They are almost a mockery of Tennant's other mode of writing. These are the two extremes of her later fiction—disturbing and complicated books that are haunted by the texts they rewrite, and potboilers that cater to generic expectations without questioning them.

Tess draws on Thomas Hardy's *Tess of the d'Urbervilles* (1891). Hardy's novel, considered one of his greatest works, is about the trials of the milkmaid Tess Durbeyfield, the descendent of a fallen noble family. Tess's beauty and innocence invite exploitation at the hands of Alec d'Urberville (a nouveau aristocrat whose family has bought the d'Urberville name). Alec rapes and thereby dishonors Tess, but she later falls in love with and marries a man named Angel Clare. Angel, however, is repelled by Tess as soon as he learns her history, and he abandons her. After returning to farm work, Tess finds herself once again in the hands of Alec. By this time, Tess is a changed woman. She murders Alec, and this act of vengeance is Tess's undoing. She is executed for her crime, and the final scene of the novel depicts Angel joining hands with Tess's younger sister, Liza-Lu. The novel works on a large scope: it is a story about class and gender relations as well as individual suffering.

Tennant's *Tess* is a combination of different narratives. The primary narrative, the story of Tess and Liza-Lu Hewitt, sisters growing up in the 1950s and 1960s, is intertwined with the story of Hardy himself. Told in retrospect by the aged Liza-Lu, the narrative moves across time. She recounts Hardy's life at the turn of the century, his appalling treatment of his wives, and his rumored affairs. She speculates on his obsession with various incarnations of the "Ruined Maid": Tess, the protagonist of his most famous novel; the young actress who takes the role of Tess in his play; and that actress's daughter, who plays Tess many years later. This view of Hardy allows Liza-Lu to reread the fate of his legendary heroine. Liza-Lu says:

> For all Hardy's apparent compassion for Tess . . . he was as guilty as the next man. His compassion was an exquisite cruelty. Hardy used the execution of Tess for the crime of murdering her first and hateful lover as a final, tender way of killing the woman he loves. . . . For her prime disobedience to man, her ruler, her father, her seducer, Tess must swing.
>
> (p. 82)

The sisters' father, John Hewitt, takes on Hardy's role as domineering father-seducer almost a century later. He is a cold man who loves the swans he raises more than his wife and daughters. Liza-Lu says: "Our father, you see, was born in the last great age of punishment for women—he was a Victorian. . . . Like the swans he tended at Abbotsbury, our father liked to think of women as silent, mute" (p. 84). His cruelest actions are reserved for his "favourite swan," his eldest daughter, Tess. From childhood, her misbehavior is punished with physical and sexual abuse. When John Hewitt finds young Tess sexually experimenting with a neighborhood boy, he beats and rapes her in front of Liza-Lu. A few years later, he discovers her in the same act and locks her in his barn for several days.

Yet, even while Tess is subjected to such horrific treatment, she is exposed to new ideas about "free love" and women's liberation. She estranges her father by dating the musician Gabriel Bell, starting a singing career, and becoming pregnant out of wedlock. Liza-Lu is her constant companion during this rebellion. But their father casts Tess off, unable to reconcile these developments with his outdated ideal of femininity and his sadistic desire to control the women around him. By embracing a new discourse that promises equality between the sexes, the sisters seem to escape their father. But Liza-Lu's story quickly reveals that the rhetoric of the 1960s, and of women's liberation in particular, is not what it seems. Gabriel Bell, "the new man," is not the enlightened companion he pretends to be. Following in the steps of Angel Clare, Gabriel abandons Tess Hewitt once she becomes pregnant. He also has affairs with other women, including Liza-Lu. In retrospect, Liza-Lu sees that the ideals of sexual liberation were hardly useful for a young pregnant woman seeking a dependable partner. She notes that even new birth control methods failed to provide the freedom they promised: "[the] sudden 'choice' [offered by the Pill] only succeeded in removing any possible moral reasons for men to take the consequences for their actions" (p. 30).

And it turns out that the sisters fail to escape their father after all. Tess's infant daughter, Mary, is the product of her father's continued rapes, although Tess lets everyone believe that the baby belongs to Gabriel. In a terrible cycle of incest, John Hewitt then abuses Mary, his daughter/granddaughter. Liza-Lu discovers him in the act, and Mary is sent away to Gabriel, who eagerly claims "his" daughter while still renouncing Tess. Like Hardy's heroine, Tess Hewitt and her daughter are fated to suffer at the hands of the man who created them. The aged Liza-Lu, who tells this story to Mary's daughter, Baby Tess, laments the inevitability of the pattern. She is painfully aware of her own role in the story, how she fell asleep one afternoon and allowed Mary to wander into John Hewitt's hands: "My part was written for me long ago and I sleep through the consequences" (pp. 206–207). She mourns that "little Mary, whose father is her grandfather, will have to go the same way as her mother and all the Tesses before her" (p. 207).

Tess is a realist novel, and more conventional than Tennant's neogothic novels. It does, however, have Tennant's signature lack of closure. Tess finally murders her father, but it is an empty victory: her father's death cannot undo what has happened to her and her daughter. Liza-Lu acknowledges her own participation in this ongoing history, how she must observe and narrate the cycle of victimization without being able to defy it. Yet at the same time, she tells the story to Baby Tess in the hope that, this time, the pattern can be escaped. The novel is inconclusive because it presents so many conflicting emotions: hope clashes with a sense of futility, and murderous anger overlaps with meek submission. The reader is left wondering if Liza-Lu's story is cautionary or visionary, how much Tess Hewitt—or Tess Durbeyfield—is to blame for her own fate, and if women can ever liberate themselves from the roles exemplified by literature's "greatest" suffering heroines.

Tennant's Austen novels, which include *Pemberly: The Sequel to Pride and Prejudice* (1993; published in the United States as *Pemberly; or, Pride and Prejudice Continued*), *An Unequal Marriage: Pride and Prejudice Continued* (1994; published in the United States as *An Unequal Marriage; or, Pride and Prejudice Twenty Years Later*), *Elinor and Marianne: A Sequel to Jane*

Austen's Sense and Sensibility (1996), and *Emma in Love: Jane Austen's Emma Continued* (1996), are very different from *Tess.* Like *Tess,* they are clearly based on a specific text. In the case of *Tess,* however, the tone and style of Tennant's writing are different from Hardy's, and the text is an explicit challenge to the voice and implications of the original novel. The novel is also self-conscious of its relation to the earlier work: in fact, Liza-Lu's awareness of storytelling and revision is what structures the story. The Austen novels, on the other hand, adopt Jane Austen's diction, ironic tone, and descriptive style. Instead of revising Austen's novels, they begin where her narratives left off. There are virtually no new characters or developments. Both of the sequels to *Pride and Prejudice* center on Elizabeth and Darcy's married life and the trials that arise from their tendency to be "proud" or "prejudiced." Both sequels have happy endings that resolve these small conflicts; they follow the trajectory set by Austen's novel exactly. *Emma in Love,* however, is more deviant. In Tennant's sequel, Emma becomes dissatisfied with her marriage and has an affair with a woman. This may seem like either an outrageous sales ploy or a risky take on Austen's proper heroines (and *Emma in Love* did stir controversy among Austen fans). Yet it can also be read as an ironic commentary on the original text. In Austen's novel, Emma is obsessed with matchmaking and yearns for marriage. Emma's brief and highly "inappropriate" affair with a sensual woman in Tennant's sequel is perhaps a parody of Austen's preoccupation with conventional romance. The affair also points to problems with Austen's representations of love. In the sequel, it is the lack of passion in Emma's marriage that leads to her affair. The original *Emma* glosses over the possibility that marriage can fail or be unhappy; it also focuses on social institutions of love instead of passion or sexual desire. Despite Austen's famed irony, her novels tend to idealize heroines and relationships that comply with social norms. Tennant is generally faithful to Austen, but she sometimes uses the sequel format to highlight what has been ignored or omitted in the original text.

Tennant's gothic tropes, which work to destabilize discourse, are replaced in *Tess* and the Austen sequels with references to narration and textuality. Liza-Lu calls attention to her role as narrator, and emphasizes that the stories she tells are always involved with other stories. The reader is plunged into a world of interlaced narratives where fact and fiction are not always distinct. The neogothic novels raise the possibility of the supernatural to accomplish this; when it succeeds, doing this without gothic tropes is perhaps a more sophisticated and subtle technique. In the case of *Tess,* the reader is forced to question the act of narration, and to see that discourses taken as truths are no more than stories that can be critiqued, rewritten, or even discarded. Thus, Tennant makes Hardy's story of Tess's victimization into a story about sadistic men and the women who defy them. *Tess* is particularly interesting and successful because it takes on so many different discourses simultaneously. In addition to the Hardy legend, Liza-Lu questions constructions of history and fate, environmental change, the subjection of women, the myths of Victorian and 1960s culture, and feminist rhetoric. Like *The Bad Sister, Tess* is a critique of solutions as well as problems: in both novels, the uncertainties of making change—through feminism or through revisionist literature—are revealed.

Tennant's other realist novels are also revisionist, and focus on the question of narratives and female identity. *Faustine* (1992) is the story of a woman tempted, like Faust, by the devil. She is granted eternal youth and movie-star fame, but loses her sense of self in the process. *Two Women of London: The Strange Case of Ms. Jekyll and Mrs. Hyde* (1989) is based on Robert Louis Stevenson's *The Strange Case of Dr. Jekyll and Mr. Hyde* (1886). As with earlier novels, the reader must access the main narrative of *Two Women of London* through conflicting pieces of evidence: newspaper articles and investigative reports document the double personality of Eliza Jekyll, who cannot reconcile her desire for beauty and independence with her identity as a single mother. The story centers on the murder of an important politician and a serial rapist prowling Eliza Jekyll's neighborhood. One of Eliza's acquaintances, an artist, depicts the rapist's victims in a huge collage. Her piece concentrates the main issues of the narrative—split identity, victimization, and art's power—in one image:

> The unknown woman is . . . spread over multipanels so that a portion of her brooding, bruised face looks out with sudden ferocity from a corner of the gallery—or, again, a curtain of gold-silk hair with a gash of red torn flesh for a mouth looms from a suspended raft. There is too much pain to allow for an easy judgement—but two art critics (male) are staring up at the pictures with something very like fear and scorn.
>
> (p. 15)

It is interesting that the collage disturbs in such different ways. Tennant's realist novels have a similar effect. At times her revisions of cherished texts provoke disdain in critics, who see her work as a facile and/or transgressive act of appropriation. Other critics recognize the potential usefulness in doing exactly that. Yet most often, whether her writing appeals or disgusts, it shocks. Both her neogothic and realist revisions create unease because they reveal that truth and representation are never solid, stable, or trustworthy: her texts undermine the discourses—the stories—that shape who we are.

OTHER WRITING

Tennant's other fiction includes *The Adventures of Robina* (1986), a "memoir" of a twentieth-century debutante written in the style of Daniel Defoe's *Moll Flanders* (1722). *Adèle: Jane Eyre's Hidden Story* (2002), is a "sequel" to the Charlotte Brontë novel *Jane Eyre* (1847). Tennant has also written *Black Marina* (1985), *The House of Hospitalities* (1987) and *A Wedding of Cousins* (1988), *The Magic Drum* (1989), and *Felony: The Private History of the Aspern Papers* (2002). All of these novels have gothic and/or revisionist characteristics. Many are mysteries, or are set in mysterious or bizarre settings. Tennant has also written several children's books. *The Ghost Child* (1984) and *Princess Cinderella and Her Wicked Sisters* (1996) are particularly interesting for their respective gothic and revisionist qualities.

Tennant's autobiographical writing has received some attention, perhaps because her family has appeared in tabloids for decades. *Strangers: A Family Romance* (1998) is a speculative account of her notorious ancestors and their life at Glen before her birth. The book draws on the personal notebooks of Tennant's grandmother and Tennant's own early memories of Scotland. Her later autobiographies are more personal memoirs. *Girlitude: A Memoir of the 50s and 60s* (1999) details Tennant's debutante years, her marriages, and her entrance into the literary establishment. *Burnt Diaries* (1999) covers her life in Notting Hill in the 1960s, as well as her affair with Ted Hughes. The latter book received mixed reviews: some critics were intrigued by Tennant's perspective on the enigmatic Hughes, who died in 1998, while others felt that its publication was an insensitive gesture to Hughes's recently widowed wife. *The Ballad of Sylvia and Ted* (2001; published in the United States as *Sylvia and Ted: A Novel*), a fictionalized account of Hughes and Sylvia Plath's notorious marriage, caused similar controversy. More recently, Tennant has written about her family's Greek home in *A House in Corfu: A Family's Sojourn in Greece* (2001). Her articles are regularly published in British newspapers such as the *Guardian,* and she has written introductions to editions of Kate Chopin's *The Awakening* (1992) and Hardy's *Fellow Townsmen* (2003).

RECEPTION AND CRITICISM

Tennant's writing has received regular attention from high-circulation periodicals in Britain, such as the *Guardian* and the *London Review of Books.* Almost all of her novels, including *The Colour of Rain,* have been praised for their accomplished technique. The neogothic novels, especially *The Bad Sister,* are consistently admired for their vivid descriptions and shifting perspectives. Karl Miller, in his 1978 review of *The Bad Sister,* noted its "romantic wildness." Tennant's more conventional novels have provoked different reactions. The Austen sequels tend to either delight or enrage readers. In a 1993 review of

Pemberly, Kathryn Hughes reveals the reasoning behind both sentiments:

> The reproduction of tone and character is faultless. True, Tennant allows herself to peer into Elizabeth and Darcy's bedroom in a manner which would have been impossible for Jane Austen, but she does it with such grace that her gentle voyeurism seems to extend rather than intrude upon our understanding of the original.
>
> (p. 44)

Hughes also questions why such a talented writer would bother with "literary ventriloquism," adding, "For despite all the fancy arguments about intertextuality and knowing pastiche, the fact is that writing sequels to fabulous best-sellers represents a commercial and artistic safe bet."

The same suspicion pervades reviews of the better (and more "literary") revisionist texts. Ruth Pavey (1993) praises aspects of Tess, but finally suggests that the novel is nothing more than a fad: "Thomas Hardy's *Tess,* as an example of the real thing in literature, shines through this fashionable trammelling" (p. 37) Tennant's memoirs and *The Ballad of Sylvia and Ted* have been similarly branded. Some reviewers find them fascinating while others think them a tasteless attempt to cash in on old scandals.

For all her popularity in the literary limelight, there has been little scholarly commentary on Tennant's work. Though her fiction deserves one, there is no authoritative study. The critical debate has been confined to a small number of journal articles and brief analyses in women's writing studies. She is most often described as a magic realist or fantasy writer akin to Angela Carter. Both use fairy tales, gothic tropes, and magic realism in their fiction, but Tennant is more of a revisionist. The common comparison between the two is somewhat unfair because it overlooks the scope of Tennant's writing. Whereas Carter's fiction clearly falls under the genre of magic realism and dark comedy, Tennant draws on many genres and sources at once, and problematizes them all. "Magic realism" is therefore too simplistic a label. The "neogothic" tag is insufficient for the same reason, although it is the most prominent quality of her work. Many critics read Tennant as a gothic feminist. Some, such as

Paulina Palmer and Amy Levin, have studied Tennant's dark representations of female institutions, such as feminism and sisterhood. Palmer, as noted above, objects to Tennant's portrayal of feminists as vampires. Levin, in her book *The Suppressed Sister: A Relationship in Novels by Nineteenth- and Twentieth-Century British Women* (1992), offers an insightful psychoanalytic reading of *The Bad Sister,* but overlooks the fact that Tennant's fiction consistently anticipates and parodies psychoanalytic interpretations. Other critics look at Tennant's more specific gothic tropes. In *Myth and Fairy Tale in Contemporary Women's Fiction* (2001), Susan Sellers writes about Tennant's vampires (comparing her to the popular novelist Anne Rice). Palmer, in her book *Lesbian Gothic: Transgressive Fictions* (1999), studies Tennant's undertones of homoeroticism as a form of gothic transgression. In "Emma Tennant: The Secret Lives of Girls," Marilyn C. Wesley constructs Tennant's novels as "ghost stories" representing the long-neglected inner lives of adolescent girls.

Other critics focus on the metafictional aesthetic of Tennant's work rather than her gothicism. In his 1995 article "Newstories: Fiction, History and the Modern World," Peter Widdowson writes about Tennant's layered narratives in *Two Women of London.* He notes that her use of textual self-consciousness as a mode of commentary on literature, politics, and other themes makes her a typical postmodernist. Steven Connor offers a similar argument. In his 1994 piece, "Rewriting Wrong: On the Ethics of Literary Revision," he writes: "In contemporary fiction, telling has become compulsorily belated, inextricably bound up with retelling, in all its idioms: reworking, translation, adaptation, displacement, imitation, forgery, plagiarism, parody, pastiche" (p. 79).

These two latter positions are typical interpretations of Tennant's revisionist agenda. More generally, Tennant criticism locates her work within the field of feminist postmodernism. The interesting possibility that her novels problematize this aesthetic/agenda just as they question so many other discourses has been largely overlooked.

CONCLUSION

Because Emma Tennant's fiction incorporates a wide range of genres, it is no surprise that she has been labeled in different ways. Her novels function on many levels, calling attention to assumptions about canon and genre. Her fiction occupies more than one niche: she is adept in her use of magic realist, fantastic, gothic, and postmodernist aesthetic conventions. Yet she refuses to submit to the confines of any one of these modes of writing. Rather, she questions the traditions she draws on in order to accomplish her more important project: destabilizing the acts of the telling and reading of narratives. As a postmodernist writer, she is important because she both practices and questions the aesthetics of postmodernism. As a feminist, she offers a different view of feminism as well as new considerations of old texts from a female perspective. To offer a revision of any one text or genre is to call attention to our literary heritage and the way we read. If this is literature's project during the latter half of the twentieth century and into the twenty-first century, Tennant is a writer who has both exploited and explored it in many different ways.

SELECTED BIBLIOGRAPHY

I. NOVELS. *The Colour of Rain* (London, 1963; Boston, 1988); *The Time of the Crack* (London and New York, 1973), republished under title *The Crack*; *The Last of the Country House Murders* (London, 1974; Boston, 1985); *Hotel de Dream* (London, 1976; Boston, 1986); *The Bad Sister* (New York, 1978); *Wild Nights* (London, 1979; New York, 1980); *Alice Fell* (London, 1980); *Queen of Stones* (London, 1982); *Woman Beware Woman* (London, 1983), published in the United States as *The Half-Mother* (Boston, 1983); *Black Marina* (London, 1985); *The Adventures of Robina: By Herself: Being the Memoirs of a Débutante at the Court of Queen Elizabeth II* (London and Boston, 1986); *The House of Hospitalities* (London and New York, 1987); *A Wedding of Cousins* (London and New York, 1988); *Two Women of London: The Strange Case of Ms. Jekyll and Mrs. Hyde* (London and Boston, 1989); *The Magic Drum* (London and New York, 1989); *Sisters and Strangers: A Moral Tale* (London, 1990); *Faustine* (London and Boston, 1992); *Pemberly: The Sequel to Pride and Prejudice* (London, 1993), published in the United States as *Pemberly; or, Pride and Prejudice Continued* (New York, 1993); *Tess* (London, 1993); *An Unequal Marriage: Pride and Prejudice Continued* (London, 1994), published in the United States as *An Unequal Marriage; or, Pride and Prejudice Twenty Years Later* (New York, 1994); *Elinor and Marianne: A Sequel to Jane Austen's Sense and Sensibility* (London and New York, 1996); *Emma in Love: Jane Austen's Emma Continued* (London, 1996); *The Ballad of Sylvia and Ted* (Edinburgh, 2001), published in the United States as *Sylvia and Ted: A Novel* (New York, 2001); *Felony: The Private History of the Aspern Papers* (London, 2002); *Adèle: Jane Eyre's Hidden Story* (New York, 2002; London, 2003).

II. CHILDREN'S FICTION. *The Boggart* (London, 1980); *The Search for Treasure Island* (London, 1981); *The Ghost Child* (London, 1984); *Dare's Secret Pony* (London, 1991); *Princess Cinderella and Her Wicked Sisters* (London, 1996).

III. AUTOBIOGRAPHICAL WORKS. *Strangers: A Family Romance* (London, 1998; New York, 1999); *Burnt Diaries* (Edinburgh, 1999); *Girlitude: A Memoir of the 50s and 60s* (London, 1999); *A House in Corfu: A Family's Sojourn in Greece* (London, 2001; New York, 2002).

IV. WORKS EDITED AND INTRODUCED. *Bananas* 1–11 (London, 1975–1978); *The Saturday Night Reader* (London, 1979); Introduction to Kate Chopin, *The Awakening* (New York, 1992); Introduction to Thomas Hardy, *Fellow Townsmen* (London, 2003).

V. INTERVIEWS. John Haffenden, ed., "Emma Tennant," in his *Novelists in Interview* (London and New York, 1985); Emma Crichton-Miller, "Wednesday Women: Stevenson's Rocket—Interview with Novelist Emma Tennant," in *Guardian* (31 May 1989).

VI. CRITICAL STUDIES AND REVIEWS. Karl Miller, Review of *The Bad Sister*, in *New York Review of Books* 9 (November 1978); Moira Monteith, ed., *Women's Writing: A Challenge to Theory* (Brighton, U.K., and New York, 1986); Paulina Palmer, *Contemporary Women's Fiction: Narrative Practice and Feminist Theory* (Jackson, Miss., 1989); Gary Indiana, "Novel 2: Emma Tennant's Higher Powers," in *Village Voice Literary Supplement* 95 (May 1991); Amy K. Levin, *The Suppressed Sister: A Relationship in Novels by Nineteenth- and Twentieth-Century British Women* (Lewisburg, Pa., 1992); Ruth Pavey, Review of *Tess*, in *New Statesman and Society* (16 April 1993); Kathryn Hughes, Review of *Pemberly*, in *New Statesman and Society* (26 November 1993); Steven Connor, "Rewriting Wrong: On the Ethics of Literary Revision," in Theo D'Haen and Hans Bertens, eds, *Liminal Postmodernisms: The Postmodern, the (Post-)Colonial, and the (Post-)Feminist* (Amsterdam, 1994); Peter Widdowson, "Newstories: Fiction, History, and the Modern World," in *Critical Survey* 7, no. 1 (1995); Patricia Juliana Smith, *Lesbian Panic: Homoeroticism in Modern British Women's Fiction* (New York, 1997); Paulina Palmer, *Lesbian Gothic: Transgressive Fictions* (New York, 1999); Carol Anderson, "Emma Tennant, Elspeth Barker, Alice Thompson: Gothic Revisited," in Aileen Christianson and Alison Lumsden, eds., *Contemporary Scottish Women Writers* (Edinburgh, 2000); C. Marilyn Wesley, "Emma Tennant: The Secret Lives of Girls," in Abby H. P. Werlock, ed., *British Women Writing Fiction* (Tuscaloosa, Ala., 2000); Susanne Schmid, "Fantasy and Realism in Emma Tennant's *Wild Nights* and *Queen of Stones*," in Beate Neumeier, ed., *Engendering Realism and Postmodernism* (Amsterdam, Netherlands, 2001); Susan Sellers, *Myth and Fairy Tale in Contemporary Women's Fiction.* (Houndmills, U.K., and New York, 2001).

JOHN TREVISA

(ca. 1342–1402)

Jane Beal

JOHN TREVISA, A medieval Christian translator, inherited an understanding of the world's linguistic diversity from histories, commentaries, sermons, popular folklore, and the remarks of other translators about the Tower of Babel. Ultimately traceable to Genesis 11, these sources describe a world that once shared a language known to all, but which fell into confusion after God's divine intervention. According to the biblical version of the story, the descendents of the survivors of the Flood began to construct a tower of brick and tar on the plain of Shinar. Their goal was to build it high enough to reach the heavens. God came down to observe the construction of this tower and the city around it and concluded that for one people speaking one language, who had begun such an ambitiously high tower, nothing would be impossible. Genesis records that God decided to confuse the language the people were speaking so that they would not understand one another. As a result, the people were scattered far and wide, away from the city and the tower they were building and over the whole earth. The tower came to be known as the Tower of Babel because "babel" sounds like the Hebrew word for "confusion."

This Bible story provided the explanation for the variety of languages in the world. At the same time, it necessitated what John Trevisa called a "double remedy" for the problem of linguistic confusion. The double remedy consisted of the reestablishment of one language in the West—the Latin spoken, written, and read in the churches, royal courts, and law courts of the Middle Ages—and the institution of translation as a means of fostering mutual understanding among those who did not know Latin. These remedies were especially significant in times of linguistic change, when the vernacular languages were competing directly with Latin for prominence in everyday

life. In fourteenth-century England, for example, a trilingual situation emerged wherein English, French, and Latin were spoken in different contexts with varying degrees of comprehension on the part of both speakers and listeners, writers and readers. It was in this situation that John Trevisa would come to play such a significant role as a translator.

John Trevisa translated several written works from Latin into English during his lifetime as part of his scholarly endeavors at Oxford and his priestly duties for the Berkeley family in Gloucestershire. His translations apparently enjoyed a modest circulation in manuscript form, but they gained a larger audience through the fifteenth-century printed editions of the English *Polychronicon* produced by William Caxton and Wynkyn de Worde and through the sixteenth-century editions of *De Proprietatibus Rerum (On the Properties of Things)*. Trevisa himself acquired a reputation as a Bible translator (which he may or may not have deserved, as we shall see) and was so designated in an address to the reader that prefaced the King James Bible (1611). The historical, scientific, and biblical translations Trevisa performed make his life, works, and worldview worthy of closer examination.

CHILD OF CORNWALL

The exact date of John Trevisa's birth is unknown. However, because he entered Exeter College, Oxford (1362), and because David Fowler argues that he did so at about age twenty, we can approximate Trevisa's birth date as being somewhere around 1342. Trevisa may have begun studies at Exeter before or after age twenty, however, and therefore a birth date of 1342 is conjectural.

JOHN TREVISA

The exact place of Trevisa's birth is similarly unknown, but several factors contribute to the likelihood that Trevisa was born in Cornwall: his Cornish last name; his admittance to Exeter College, Oxford, which had been specifically established for students from the diocese of Exeter (Devon and Cornwall); Trevisa's original notes on Cornwall or matters pertaining to it in his translation of the universal history book, the *Polychronicon;* remnants of Cornish vocabulary in Trevisa's English translations; and the testimony of sixteenth-century writers like John Bale and Raphael Holinshed who believed that the translator was born in Cornwall. Through an accident in seventeenth-century scholarship, wherein the birthplace of John Trevisa was confused with that of one Peter Trevisa, later critics came to believe that Trevisa was born in Crocadon in St. Mellion near Saltash, Cornwall. Now, however, most scholars suppose that Trevisa was born in one of the three Cornish towns that bear his last name (and from which it is ostensibly derived), most probably Trevessa in St. Enoder, since some extant legal records point to the existence of members of a Trevisa family living in the environs of Trevessa in St. Enoder beginning before 1328. This is particularly significant because Trevessa is part of the manor of Tygembreth (or Degembris) which was owned by the Berkeley family of Gloucestershire, England, and Lord Thomas IV of Berkeley was John Trevisa's employer and patron later in life.

As with many medieval men and women of note, no surviving documents exist from which to derive crucial information about John Trevisa's childhood. His parents, their professions (and hence socioeconomic class), his siblings (if any), their baptisms, marriages, and deaths all remain obscure. However, the rhythm of Trevisa's life before Oxford can be reconstructed from what is known about the sociopolitical situation of Cornwall and the influence of the church on daily life in the mid-fourteenth century.

During Trevisa's youth, Cornwall was a duchy technically governed by the oldest son of England's king, the Black Prince. However, the prince was not often in Cornwall to rule it. Instead, he was frequently in France, campaigning in the ongoing war to claim French territory for the English throne. Cornwall, like the rest of England, was embroiled in the conflict, and Cornwall served by providing coastal ports for English ships as well as Cornish men to attack or defend against French aggressors arriving by sea. The Hundred Years' War (1337–1453), as it came to be known, brought about many tensions, disruptions, and deaths in Cornwall, but not nearly as many as the Black Death did. Between 1348 and 1350, perhaps twenty thousand persons in Cornwall died from the plague. This tremendous loss of life effected the Cornish economy, which was fueled primarily by agriculture and the tin trade, and the production of crops and tin fell as a result. The loss of life also effected the church in Cornwall, which decreased numerically as priests administering the sacraments to the sick and dying contracted the plague themselves.

Despite the loss of its ministers, the church continued to influence daily life considerably in Cornwall (as elsewhere in England and Europe) during this period. The seven sacraments of the church defined the stages of a medieval person's life, and the annual liturgy determined its rhythm. The sacraments included baptism, confirmation, the Eucharist, matrimony, penance, holy orders, and extreme unction, and these provided structure for medieval human lives from the cradle to the grave. In a similar manner, the church's liturgy provided structure and comfort each year. As a young man, Trevisa would have participated in church feasts and holy days along with the rest of his community. On such occasions, he listened to priests preaching their sermons, telling Bible stories and exhorting their parishioners to live holy lives, love God, and treat their neighbors as they would like to be treated.

Preaching figured significantly in Trevisa's early and later life. As a young man, Trevisa became familiar with different types of preachers and different scenes of preaching. According to canon law, priests, deacons, and subdeacons who had preferment and the care of souls entrusted to them (that is, bishops and curates) could legally preach, but preaching was also accomplished by others who were specially licensed to do so, including monks, mendicants, friars, university

244

graduates in theology, vicars, chaplains, pardoners, and recluses. Trevisa would have had the opportunity to see bishops and curates in their pulpits, typically on Sunday during the mass or after it, and those who were specially licensed in various places: streets, markets, ecclesiastical and extra-ecclesiastical grounds. Trevisa knew the two major types of sermons derived from the church's two calendars (the Temporale and the Sanctorale): *sermones ad tempore* and *sermones de sanctis.*

The Temporale first focused on five major Christian holidays—Christmas, Epiphany, Easter, Ascension, and Whitsunday (that is, Pentecost)—while the Sanctorale focused on saints' lives and miracles. Another genre of sermons consisted of the *sermones ad status,* words addressed to the various estates of medieval society and geared toward exhortation of particular audiences. The effect of these preachers, preaching scenes, and sermons combined to make an impression on Trevisa as a youth, an effect apparently so considerable that it would motivate him to become a priest and preacher himself. As an adult priest and translator, he would both preach sermons and translate them; Trevisa's translation of Richard FitzRalph's Latin sermon into English is a notable example.

Before becoming ordained as a priest, however, Trevisa first obtained his initial education, probably at a grammar school and possibly at Glasney Collegiate church in Cornwall, and then attended Exeter and Queen's College, Oxford.

SCHOLAR AT OXFORD

John Trevisa was almost continuously in residence at Exeter, then known as Stapledon Hall, from 1362 until he transferred to Queen's in 1369. At Exeter he earned his master's of theology, and at Queen's he continued his studies, though he did not apparently receive his doctorate. In 1370 he was ordained a priest, and by 1387 he could dedicate his first major translation, the *Polychronicon,* to Sir Thomas, lord of Berkeley. Despite periodic gaps in the college records, it appears that Trevisa was a scholar at Oxford between 1362 and 1387, fully twenty-five

years of his life. In order to understand this period of Trevisa's personal growth and development, it will be useful to consider the course and content of his education, his conflicts with authority while at Queen's, his travels, and his transition into the service of the Berkeley family.

Trevisa's university training followed a predetermined pattern. Within the colleges at Oxford, students undertook a seven-year course in the arts to prepare themselves to study theology, law, or medicine. The arts curriculum consisted of the trivium (grammar, rhetoric, dialectic) and the quadrivium (arithmetic, geometry, astronomy, music); students learned and demonstrated their learning through a structured series of disputations. A student would stand to respond to an initial examination with a master of grammar or logic, and later, as a "questionist," he answered to four regent masters in another oral examination. After this, he could enter debates as a bachelor with students of lower status and lecture to them as well. After a few years, the bachelor would dispute on a subject of his own choosing (a "quodlibet"), and if he did well, he was given official permission to begin the process necessary to become a master of arts within the next year.

Trevisa completed this seven-year course in the arts at Exeter by 1369 and entered Queen's as a magister. He commenced his residency with the probable intention of pursuing a doctorate. How far he got in his studies, however, is difficult to determine because the records for the college during Trevisa's time there are incomplete. The condition of the records may be the result of a disagreement between northern and southern fellows of the college over who ought to have been the new provost. Trevisa was closely involved in this disagreement, and it may have disrupted his doctoral studies in theology or prevented their completion. The disagreement, which broke out in 1376, resulted from the objection of several fellows, including Trevisa, to the election of one Thomas Carlisle (a northern man) over William Frank (a southern man). The disagreement necessitated both ecclesiastical and royal intervention for resolution. With evidence collected under the direction of Alexander Neville, archbishop of York, as support, King Richard II eventually ruled in favor of Thomas Carlisle; Trevisa and other dissenters were expelled. They did not go peacefully, but in 1378 (or before), took the college seal, several books, and other college properties and apparently continued to act as a college despite the royal decision. The disagreement was resolved in favor of the northern faction, but matters were apparently settled between disputants so that Trevisa could rent rooms peaceably enough at Queen's from 1383 to 1387 and from 1394 to 1396.

Trevisa's adventures were not limited to political and legal maneuvering with his college, however. As we know from notes he inserted in his translation of the *Polychronicon,* sometime before 1385 he traveled on the European continent, visiting Aachen in Germany, Aix-les-Bains in Savoy, and Breisach. Trevisa's reasons for undertaking this journey (or journeys) are unknown, but Trevisa himself mentions bathing in the fair, clear baths at Aix-les-Bains, which were reputed to have a healthful effect on ailing persons.

If Trevisa pursued his doctoral studies assiduously while at Queen's, his pursuit would have followed a typical pattern, just as his arts course had. In the first four years, Trevisa and other doctoral students heard lectures and disputations on the Bible and the *Sentences* of Peter Lombard. The *Sentences* contained a synthesis of church doctrine and functioned as the theology textbook of the period. After four years, students could oppose in a disputation and later respond to opposition. After seven years, students applied to become bachelors and lecture on the *Sentences* themselves; they would dispute others at their same level. Bachelors would lecture on the *Sentences* for a year and the Bible for a year. After completing the necessary lectures, bachelors could begin the disputations that would lead to the receipt of the doctorate.

The disputations in the "inception process" lasted many days. The candidate would preach at St. Mary's and then participate in preliminary disputes on the evening before inception. On the day of the inception, he disputed with the next candidate in line for inception, then argued the opposite viewpoint with a regent or senior master, and finally concluded by restating his own solution to the problem or question he had posed. The candidate then received the doctorate, which was a general permission to teach, a duty he would undertake immediately, lecturing on the Bible and instructing students for at least a year thereafter. Although we do not know if Trevisa reached this stage at Queen's, the influence of disputation in the educational process at Oxford clearly influenced one of his original compositions, the *Dialogue between a Lord and a Clerk.*

It is possible that Trevisa stopped short of inception because he was preoccupied with other matters, including the aforementioned trouble which arose within Queen's College itself. In any case, by 1387, when he dedicated the *Polychronicon* to Sir Thomas Berkeley, Trevisa was serving the Berkeley family of Gloucestershire. Although the exact date of Trevisa's appointment is not known, scholars think Trevisa joined the family in 1374 and became its chaplain in 1379. Since Trevisa rented rooms at Oxford after this date, it is clear that his association with the university continued during (and perhaps as a part of) his employment with the Berkeley family.

PRIEST OF GLOUCESTERSHIRE

Trevisa was ordained a priest in 1370 while still at the college of Queen's Hall, Oxford, but he later replaced Master David of Melksham as vicar of Berkeley (Fowler, p. 94). In an extant record of 1374, Master David is referred to as the *former* tenant of Stinchcombe, his home, which implies that he had either moved or died by 1374. Because no later records mention David, scholars conclude that he had died, thus leaving the vicarage of Berkeley open to Trevisa. Unfortunately no known record testifies to the exact date on which Trevisa was instituted vicar, but one "Johannes vicarius de Berkeleye" paid taxes levied by Parliament in 1379, so most likely John Trevisa was vicar of Berkeley by that date.

In his new position Trevisa had three key roles: secular priest, vicar of Berkeley, and personal chaplain to the Berkeley family. As a secular priest, Trevisa was committed to working in the world (saeculum), which meant he was explicitly not a member of the regular orders, those ecclesiastical institutions for monks and other brothers living in community according to a certain rule (regula), such as the Benedictine rule or the Augustinian rule, for example. Trevisa could administer the sacraments of the church to the people of his parish, and he could thereby be involved in their daily lives, particularly by baptizing infants, confirming young people in the church, saying mass and administering the Eucharist, conducting marriage ceremonies, hearing confession and assigning penance, preaching regularly, and giving the last rites to the dying.

When he took Master David's place in the church at Berkeley, Trevisa became a vicar as well as a priest. A vicar is a priest of a parish acting in place of the rector or he is a representative of a religious community to which tithes belong. In Trevisa's case, the majority of the tithes of the Berkeley church went to the canons of St. Augustine's Abbey, Bristol, and he received a smaller salary out of those same tithes. With this salary, Trevisa was supposed to appoint and pay for a chaplain at the chapel of Stone, but a case brought to Bishop Wakefield by the parishioners of Stone states that Trevisa failed to do this, perhaps because his income was limited. How this case was resolved is unclear. However, Trevisa received additional income when Sir Thomas Berkeley made him a canon of the Collegiate Church of Westbury-on-Trym and awarded him the prebend of Woodford. A canon is a clergyman associated with a collegiate church; a collegiate church is a church endowed to support a chapter, or group, of canons; and a prebend is a portion of the revenues from the collegiate church given to support individual canons. Woodford was the location associated with the Collegiate Church of Westbury-on-Trym from which Trevisa's stipend derived, so the location as well as the revenue it generated is known as a prebend.

It is worth noting that Trevisa's right to the prebend was disputed by Robert Wattes, the dean of Westbury-on-Trym, who wanted it given to one Thomas Cone. Three legal documents associated with the case indicate that rival supporters of Trevisa and Wattes actually came to blows over the matter within the church itself. Trevisa's supporters decided to physically occupy Woodford, and the dean's supporters were briefly imprisoned at Berkeley Castle. Watts and Cone protested through legal channels, but in 1390, a year after the dispute, Watts gave up his deanery at Westbury and Trevisa retained his Westford prebend thereafter. It seems that King Richard II saw no reason to support Watts or Cone, who made an appeal to him, when Trevisa's patron, Sir Thomas Berkeley, was loyal and supportive of the king's rights and policies. Clearly Trevisa's role as Lord Berkeley's chaplain did not harm his rights to the prebend associated with Westbury-on-Trym.

As chaplain to the Berkeley family, Trevisa was attached to the chapel in Berkeley Castle and said prayers on behalf of the Berkeley family. In an epistle to Lord Berkeley which prefaces the *Polychronicon* in several manuscripts, Trevisa specifically calls himself Lord Berkeley's "priest and beadsman," where the latter term refers to prayers said by following beads (a type of rosary). Some of Trevisa's work as a priest and man of prayer would have been carried out in the Chapel of St. John the Baptist in Berkeley Castle, which is now the Morning Room, and it is worth imagining Trevisa in that setting. The chapel ceiling was engraved with a transcription of an Anglo-Norman translation of passages from the Apocalypse, and they describe, among others things, the darkening of the heavenly lights and a flying eagle warning of the angelic trumpets whose sounding will bring woe to the earth at the end of time. Under these revelatory words, Trevisa would have heard confession and conducted mass and preached sermons, probably in Latin and English, specifically for the edification of the Berkeley family.

The patronage of the Berkeley family clearly provided for Trevisa's material needs, and it may have also inspired (or required) him to undertake the two major translations in which he mentions Sir Thomas Berkeley: the *Polychronicon,* which Trevisa finished translating into English in 1387, and *De Proprietatibus Rerum,* which he completed in 1398. Trevisa also translated four minor works, but he does not indicate when he translated any of them, so one or more of the works may have preceded his association with the Berkeley family. He has had additional works attributed to him, but not definitively. In modern times Trevisa has become best known for his role as a medieval translator, and so his conception of translation and the task of the translator deserve consideration.

For Trevisa, translation meant bringing knowledge across from one language to another, as the etymology of the Latin noun *translatio* suggests, or changing and exchanging it between languages, as the meaning of the Middle English *tornyng* ("turning" or "translation") implies. As a translator, Trevisa aimed to be intelligent, idiomatic, and accurate, and he states specifically in the *Epistle* that he is committed to translating word for word except when in so doing he would corrupt or endanger the sense of a given passage. His theory is sometimes at odds with his practice, but whether he was aware of this or not remains an open question. Still, in comparison with other self-styled translators, like Chaucer, Trevisa was a fairly close translator of his original Latin texts. He greatly admired the history of Bible translation and believed that the Holy Spirit had inspired it. To the extent that he placed himself in that tradition, he sought to acquire authority for his vernacular translations of various Latin works.

A closer examination of Trevisa's original works and major translations, minor translations, and the works attributed to him will reveal a fuller picture of Trevisa's translation praxis.

ORIGINAL WORKS AND MAJOR TRANSLATIONS

Trevisa's three original works are closely associated with his first major translation, the *Polychronicon.* Trevisa composed an original dialogue, known as the *Dialogue between a Lord and a Clerk on Translation,* and a dedicatory epistle to Lord Berkeley to accompany his English translation. In addition, he composed over 120 notes which he inserted into the text of the *Polychronicon.* These notes, which can be considered together with notes Trevisa interpolated in other translations, constitute a third original "work" in Trevisa's canon.

The genre of Trevisa's *Dialogue* reveals much about its purpose. It is an "unequal" dialogue modeled on academic debates between a master teacher and a student. Trevisa sets it up as a conversation between a Lord and a Clerk, a contest wherein the Lord clearly has the upper hand, both socially and argumentatively. The Lord argues in favor of vernacular translation while the Clerk opposes it with questions and challenges. At the conclusion of the dialogue, the Clerk agrees to translate the *Polychronicon,* and in a brilliant reversal, asks for God's inspiration (and hence authority) to perform the task of translation.

Clearly there are some parallels between the fictional Lord and Clerk of the dialogue and historical Sir Thomas Berkeley and John Trevisa. Both the real and constructed lords are patrons interested in translation; both the real and imagined clerks are translators turning the Latin *Polychronicon* into English. However, it should be remembered that Trevisa is constructing a generic dialogue, within specific generic constraints, in order to make points in favor of vernacular translation. That he does not hesitate to represent the Clerk in an occasionally negative or self-deprecating light suggests the translator's own humor. It does not mean, as some critics have supposed, that the actual lord of Berkeley articulated the strongest arguments for translation and that the real Trevisa was a reluctant translator at best. Trevisa set up the unequal dialogue so that the Lord, who has the greater authority, would be able to endorse the practice of vernacular translation. Such endorsement was a necessary response to the suspicion translation and translators faced before, during, and after the fourteenth century.

Through the interaction of the Lord and the Clerk, Trevisa reveals several aspects of his theory, practice, and understanding of translation. On a theoretical level, he sees Babel as the explanation for the diversity and difficulty of languages; at the same time, he acknowledges that God has a "double remedy" for this problematic situation: Latin for a few and translators for the rest. He admits to a distinction between what is necessary and what is profitable but uses the idea of profitability to extend the idea of necessity. He acknowledges the role of the Holy Spirit on both the theoretical and practical levels of translation. Trevisa pays considerable attention to the practical side of translation, noting the complex degrees of Latin literacy, the barriers to obtaining proficiency, and the variations among clerical, noble, and lower-class lay audiences. By reiterating the history of Bible translation, he recalls not only the Holy Spirit—inspired paraphrases like Caedmon's but also the revision translation entails, as when he references Origen's two translations of the Bible and Jerome's thrice-translated Psalter. In addition, Trevisa very insightfully observes that preaching in English also constitutes English translation at the most fundamental and practical level. Finally, he clearly evinces concern for the way in which audiences perceive and receive translations when the Clerk articulates his fear that he will be reproached for errors in the translation of the *Polychronicon*. Trevisa is then able to focus on his goal: a skillful rather than perfect translation.

Trevisa's dedicatory epistle to Sir Thomas Berkeley, is both briefer than the dialogue and generically distinct from it. Trevisa frames the *Dialogue* as a fictional debate, the *Epistle* as a dedication to a patron. The first is outside of, even though it may comment upon, Trevisa's historical circumstances; the second is directly concerned with them. As a separate genre, the *Epistle* has different conventions and implications. In this case, it develops key ideas from the *Dialogue* about translation theory and practice, clarifies the role of Trevisa the translator, and probably indicates something of the realistic rather than constructed role of Sir Thomas Berkeley. In the first part, Trevisa greets his patron, identifies himself, and restates his task: to translate the *Polychronicon*. In the second part, Trevisa resolves to work hard and responds in advance to any detractors, whom he calls "backbiters" and "evil speakers," who might deride his effort. The third part, and the longest, gives some interesting details about Trevisa's translation practices. The final part is a benedic-

tion which asks for God's blessing on the life of Sir Thomas Berkeley.

The third part of Trevisa's *Epistle* deserves attention because in it Trevisa makes no fewer than seven points about his translation of the *Polychronicon*. First, he clearly states that his goal is a "clear and plain" translation which can be "known and understood." He then explains that in order to accomplish this, he will, in general, translate word for word. Active verbs in Latin will be active in English, and passive verbs in Latin will be passive in English, and the order of the words will not be changed. However, the translator admits, occasionally he will change verbal forms and word order. Furthermore, he will also add a reason or explanation for a word to tell what it means (the interpolated notes). "But," he insists, "for all such changing, the meaning shall stand and not be changed." He explains that though some things will be changed for the sake of a comprehensible translation, some words will not be translated, including the names of some places and persons. He lists eighteen such words, among them Mount Sinai, Bethlehem, and Jerusalem. He concludes this section by saying that if any man can make a better and more profitable translation of the books of the chronicle, he hopes that God will reward him. This remark implies that making another, better translation would be difficult, but it also leaves open the possibility for revision, which is yet another vital part of the process of translation.

Trevisa's *Epistle* thus indicates much of what his readers will see in his English *Polychronicon*, including the interpolated notes, which he implies are simple explanations of unknown words. In fact, they are much more than that; they aim both to instruct and to persuade. The notes fall into roughly five categories (with exceptions and some overlap): definitions, explanations, amplifications, cross-references, and arguments. Often the notes, especially longer ones, perform more than one of these functions. Definitions of terms, including etymologies, are by far the most numerous, while explanations of concepts and geographical place-names run a close second. Amplifications are typically explanations with additional evidence. Amplificatory notes relate to the text which precedes them and contain supplementary material or evidence which occasionally refers to Trevisa's personal experience. Most of Trevisa's cross-references are intratextual, referring to other places in the *Polychronicon* itself.

Trevisa's notes are not marginal or interlinear in the sense that a Latin Bible glossed with an Anglo-Saxon translation might be. Rather, they appear composed in blocks, inserted between translated passages of the *Polychronicon,* and are included in each extant English manuscript of the chronicle as part of the text itself. The notes vary in length, consisting of as few as four words and as many as four hundred. They are usually, although not always, signed with Trevisa's name to indicate his authorship and distinguish the text of the notes from other blocks of text in the chronicle. The notes frequently precede or follow the notes of the compiler of the Latin *Polychronicon,* Ranulf Higden, and are apparently modeled on them, though they also appear separately from these. Ranulf Higden authored more than twice as many interpolations as Trevisa did, and many of the texts attributed to other authorities can be attributed to the compiler who paraphrased, revised, and rewrote them.

Trevisa's notes address a plethora of subjects, both directly and indirectly, including the definition of "hyperbole," the uniqueness of the Phoenix, the greatness of Rome, the complexity of the Labyrinth, the inefficacy of St. Patrick's Purgatory, Cornwall's place among the shires of England, the use of English in grammar schools, the nature of the crocodile, lunar and solar and Olympic calendars, the life and second death of Lazarus, the adoption of children, the historicity of King Arthur, the objectionable actions of various monks, and so forth. Trevisa's last note, the colophon, thanks God for the completion of the English *Polychronicon* on 18 April 1387 in the tenth year of King Richard and the thirty-fifth year of the life of Sir Thomas, lord of Berkeley. These notes reveal many of Trevisa's thoughts and opinions, and they constitute an original work in their own right. The notes exist in direct relationship to Trevisa's English translation of the Latin *Polychronicon.* Trevisa's third original work and first major translation were thus

initially made possible by the efforts of the compiler of the chronicle, Ranulf Higden.

Ranulf Higden was a Benedictine monk at St. Werburgh's Abbey in Chester for most of his life. In addition to the *Polychronicon,* he also compiled or composed several minor works, including a mirror (advice book) for curates, a book of Latin grammar (no longer extant), a treatise on the calendar, a manual on the art of preaching, and a collection of sermons. Two collections of *Distinctiones,* commentaries on the Bible, have also been attributed to him. His Latin *Polychronicon* enjoyed a tremendous reputation in the compiler's lifetime, being used on the European continent and in the English king's court on at least one known occasion. It survives in over one hundred manuscripts and, in addition to being translated by Trevisa, was translated by another unknown translator in the fifteenth century. As a universal history of the world, the *Polychronicon* provided a vast amount of historical information to both the learned and the curious.

Ranulf was interested in all of world history, but he was particularly interested in glorifying England's place in that history. So it is not surprising that he chose to write a universal chronicle with a national bias. The genre of the *Polychronicon* defines the inclusive scope of its contents as well as its emphasis on the English nation. Eusebius of Caesarea (ca. A.D. 260–340) provided the chronology for this type of universal history, drawing up in table form a list of dates from Assyrian, Hebrew, Egyptian, Greek, and Roman histories. Augustine (A.D. 354–430) famously provided the concept of two cities, an earthly one and a heavenly one, and he situated it in a Christian narrative of history made up of six ages. Following Augustine, medieval historians believed the six ages to have the same beginning and ending points, more or less, so that the first age consisted of the time from Adam to Noah; the second, from Noah to Abraham; the third, from Abraham to David; the fourth, from David to the Babylonian captivity; the fifth, from the captivity to the birth of Jesus Christ. Everyone living since the birth of Christ lives in the sixth age which will culminate in the Last Judgment.

Like some of his predecessors, Ranulf combined a Christian historical view with a secular one, interweaving the narrative of the six ages with a Hellenistic one based upon a sequence of four great empires. He differed from other universal chroniclers in that he began the *Polychronicon* with a geographical survey of the known world which ends with a detailed description of England. In so doing, he may have been imitating a national chronicler, Bede, who begins the *Ecclesiastical History of the English People* (A.D. 731) with a geographical description of England, albeit one on a smaller scale than Ranulf's. After his geographical survey, Ranulf goes on to relate the history of the world from Creation to the fourteenth century.

In producing the *Polychronicon,* Ranulf wrote a chronicle in *compilatio* form for a learned, Latinate English audience and, as the manuscript circulation history shows, a Continental audience as well. Through the English translation of John Trevisa, the *Polychronicon* reached a much wider vernacular audience. The fourteenth-century manuscript circulation of the English *Polychronicon* may have been somewhat limited, but William Caxton's new edition of it in 1482—together with a new "Prohemye" and updated *Liber Ultimus,* an eighth and last book which Caxton wrote for this edition—guaranteed the Chronicle's survival and influence. In a similar manner, the 1535 and 1592 printed editions of Trevisa's second major translation, his English version of Bartolomaeus Anglicus's *De Proprietatibus Rerum* (*On the Properties of Things*), ensured and secured a wider audience for Trevisa's work.

The life of Bartolomaeus Anglicus is known only in part. He was born in England, most probably before 1200, and he may have been educated at Oxford and later Paris. At Paris, he may have lectured on the whole Bible and written sermons. He joined the Order of Friars Minor, that is, the Franciscans, and he was sent from France to Saxonia, the eastern part of Germany, as a reader and lecturer on the Bible in 1231. About 1245, he completed his famous encyclopedia, *De Proprietatibus Rerum.* He may also have been that Bartholomaeus who was the minister provincial of Bohemia from 1255 to 1256. Bartolomaeus Anglicus died in 1272.

Generically speaking, Bartolomaeus's *De Proprietatibus Rerum* is an encyclopedia of medieval knowledge, both scientific and theological. It consists of nineteen books, possibly because the number nineteen combined the twelve signs of the zodiac and the seven planets in order to signify universality. The books are arranged to discuss "The Great Chain of Being," beginning with God and descending to consider the angels, the soul, the human body, and the properties of humanity—such as mortality, motherhood, and dreams—as well as illness and poisons. Beginning with book 8, the encyclopedia considers aspects of the physical world, including the macrocosm (the world and heavenly bodies), seasons and times, elements like fire and air, birds, water, earth, geography, precious stones and metals, herbs and plants, animals, and finally accidents, those qualities, events, or entities that medieval philosophy considered contingent upon the existence of something else, such as colors, odors, tastes, liquids, eggs, numbers, measures, weights, and music. The encyclopedia contains an obviously rich and diverse amount of knowledge about the world from a medieval perspective.

Trevisa completed his translation of this fascinating textbook in 1398. He may have originally encountered it during his studies at Oxford and later recognized it as part of the *Polychronicon.* Although Ranulf Higden did not acknowledge it (and may not have realized it), his citations from Priscian's *Cosmographia* in the *Polychronicon* are actually citations from Bartolomaeus's *De Proprietatibus Rerum.* Wherever Trevisa found it, by translating it he provided his later medieval and early modern readers with an English encyclopedia which combined Augustinian interpretations of the Bible with an Aristotelian understanding of the natural sciences.

Trevisa's translation of Bartolomaeus's *De Proprietatibus Rerum* may at first seem to be a radically different undertaking than his translation of the *Polychronicon.* However, the works share a common bond: both explain and contextualize Scripture, one in a historical sense and the other in a scientific sense. As such, these works would have been particularly useful for priests and other churchmen serving under or alongside John Trevisa in Gloucestershire. While the works were clearly supported by Sir Thomas Berkeley, they were intended for a larger audience, one of clerics who could then use them to compose sermons to edify the laity. This raison d'être justifies the minor translations of John Trevisa as well.

MINOR TRANSLATIONS

Although Trevisa's four shorter translations cannot be dated precisely by either internal or external evidence, they can be put in a logical chronological order based on their relationship to Trevisa's major translations, interests, and historical circumstances. Trevisa probably encountered FitzRalph's *Defensio Curatorum* (*Defense of Curates*) while he was a student at Oxford and translated it sometime between 1362 and 1385. His translation of the *Dialogus inter Militem et Clericum* (*Dialogue between a Soldier and a Clerk*) would likewise fall into this period, as it probably served as a model for the original dialogue which Trevisa composed to accompany the completed *Polychronicon* around 1387 or later. Because the *Dialogus* always appears before the *Defensio* in the manuscripts where both appear, it is possible that, of the two, the *Dialogus* was written first.

Trevisa's translation of the *Evangelium Nicodemi* (*Gospel of Nicodemus*) may have come before or after his translation of the *Polychronicon*. If before, it would have appeared around the same time as the Wycliffite Bible translations; the Early Version of the Wycliffite Bible was completed in the 1370s/1380 and the Later Version was completed in 1384 or later. If after, Trevisa's gospel translation would fall conveniently into the gap of time left between 1387, when Trevisa completed the *Polychronicon*, and 1398, when he completed the English *De Proprietatibus Rerum*.

In that same gap, Trevisa may have translated the *De Regimine Principum* (*Concerning the Rule of Princes*), a mirror for princes, which could have been intended as a vernacular advice manual for the beleaguered King Richard II or a justificatory (if indirect) piece of rhetoric for his deposition. (As noted in the *Historia Vitae et Regni Ricardi II* by the Monk of Evesham, Lord Berkeley held a meeting of the nobility in Berkeley Church which increased the momentum toward the deposition of the king, a deposition which finally occurred in the summer of 1399.) Alternatively, Trevisa may have translated *De Regimine Principum* when King Henry V assumed the throne in order to advise the new monarch and steer him away from the mistakes of his predecessor.

Given this provisional chronology, it is possible to consider each of Trevisa's four minor translations, beginning with the *Dialogue between a Soldier and a Clerk*. The Latin *Dialogus*, sometimes also known as the *Disputatio inter Militem et Clericum*, has been attributed to William of Ockham, Marsilius of Padua, and Pierre DuBois. William of Ockham has been the most popular choice of the three, being acknowledged repeatedly in later printed editions. Marsilius of Padua is suggested along with William in Vatican MS Borghese 29, and Pierre DuBois was proposed by a modern critic. Whoever the author, the content of the work—a debate over the exercise of power by church and state—suggests origins in a late thirteenth-century controversy between the French King Philip IV and Pope Boniface VIII.

Around 1297, king and pope were particularly at odds over the king's right to tax the clergy for "the defense of the realm." The pope was interested in funding another crusade while the king wanted to pay for the continuing war with England. As the disagreement intensified, people chose sides. The king's own tutor Aegidius Romanus, for example, wrote an eloquent apology for papal authority. The author of the *Dialogus inter Militem et Clericum* wrote an equally impassioned defense of regal power. The king is not mentioned directly in the dialogue, but Pope Boniface is, specifically in a speech by the Soldier expressing astonishment over the pope's "new statute" declaring that he has lordship over all secular lords, princes, kings, and emperors.

In Trevisa's translation, the dialogue begins with the Clerk and ends with the Soldier, a shift which reveals where the argumentative power finally lies. Like Trevisa's original dialogue, this one is an "unequal" debate in which one man—in this case, the Soldier—dominates. The Clerk asks provocative questions and makes brief objections, but the bulk of the conversation is in the Soldier's voice. The Soldier argues that kings and princes have the right to tax the lands of the church "for defense of the common profit." The Clerk, in response, argues that kings and princes are subject to the spiritual lordship of the church. This debate between *temporalité* (temporal power) and *spiritualité* (spiritual or ecclesiastical power) reveals the ways in which the boundaries of church and state were being negotiated in the later Middle Ages. The disputants both use quotations and examples from "Holy Writ," translated or paraphrased from the Latin Vulgate, to supply evidence in support of their arguments. Ironically, it is the Soldier, rather than the ecclesiastically trained Clerk, who uses biblical evidence the most extensively and persuasively.

Trevisa's English translation stays fairly close to the substance of the Latin original, but he does include one extensive note correcting a misleading theological point made by the Soldier. The Soldier makes a distinction between the power that Christ had during his manhood on earth and the power he had once he returned to God the Father. He uses this distinction to argue that the power given to Peter and his successors, the popes, is limited to the power Christ exercised while on earth when, in humility, he did not exercise power over temporal rulers. However, Trevisa denies this distinction in a long and significant note wherein he states: "For all the time of Christ's manhood, that was before his Passion, was the time of his might, power, and majesty." Trevisa then lists evidence in support of this point, including the fact that Christ turned water into wine, healed the sick, commanded the sea, fed the five thousand, and gave his disciples power over all devils and fiends. Although it seems that Trevisa agrees with the basic argument of the Soldier in the *Dialogue,* namely that temporal lords have the right to tax church lands

to defend the realm, he does not allow any part of that argument to impinge on the power and majesty of Christ Jesus.

Trevisa's English *Defense of Curates* approaches the right of kings to appropriate the wealth of the church from another direction. It was written by a bishop as an appeal to the pope to reform or dissolve the fraternal orders. If that were done, then the unclaimed wealth which would result would be available to temporal powers.

Trevisa's *Defense of Curates* is a sermon which defends secular priests (curates) by virulently attacking the monastic and fraternal orders. Its author, Richard FitzRalph, wrote it in an emotional and intellectual passion inspired by a conflict he found himself embroiled in while in Ireland. As an English bishop in the Irish see of Armagh, FitzRalph was trying to reconcile hostilities between Irish and English parishioners, a process which was being undermined by friars offering confession and giving absolution without the bishop's license to disputants on either side, disputants who justified everything from theft to arson and murder by invoking "frontier law." Whereas the bishop wanted to hold parishioners accountable and compel them to pay restitution where appropriate, the friars apparently did not want to do so, and the civil war in the see continued unabated. By 1356, when he returned to England, FitzRalph had completed *De Pauperie Salvatoris,* in which he argued for the dissolution of the fraternal orders, and in 1357 he presented his case against the fraternal orders to the papal court at Avignon, from whence comes the *Defensio Curatorum.*

FitzRalph's sermon is a thematic one, returning more than once to John 8 and the phrase, in Trevisa's translation, "Demeth nought by the face but rigtful doom ye deem" (Judge not by the surface but give righteous judgment). Since FitzRalph is addressing the pope and arguing the preeminence of parish priests (curates) over friars, he urges the pope to judge rightfully between him and the friars, though he (ironically) insists that he is not arguing for the destruction of the fraternal orders. He sets out nine points in support of his position. These points notably invoke the authority of Christ (points 1–4), attack church legislation taken as supportive of fraternal begging (points 5–7), and insist on the proper relationship between the people of a parish and their parson (points 8–9).

FitzRalph's opinions created quite a stir at Oxford in the ongoing tensions between secular and regular churchmen, and Trevisa certainly became familiar with the terms of the debate when he arrived at the university. He also chose sides, in effect, by being ordained a priest and seeking a secular benefice. His translation of FitzRalph's sermon reflects his own strongly held opinions in the matter, opinions which he rearticulates quite boldly in several anti-fraternal notes included in the *Polychronicon*. Trevisa's position, it is worth noting, was shared by Wycliffe and many members of the English nobility. If the monasteries were dissolved, these men reasoned, monastic wealth should go to the lords and king of England. In fact, as we have seen, this is precisely the argument made in the *Dialogus inter Militem et Clericum.*

The *Dialogus* and the *Defensio,* when taken together, demonstrate Trevisa's support of temporal power and interest in church reform. Trevisa could clearly see the need for the imposition of limitations on ecclesiastical power. However, his advocacy of ecclesiastical reforms in no way implied a disbelief in God's power as manifested in Christ. His translation of the *Gospel of Nicodemus* reveals a particular interest in the lordship Christ demonstrated through the Harrowing of Hell after the Crucifixion.

The *Gospel of Nicodemus* has an older and more complicated history of transmission and translation than any of the other works Trevisa is known to have translated. Its narrative developed in stages between the second and fifth centuries, and titles adopted by Zbigniew Izydorczyk (1997) effectively name those stages: *Acta Pilati* (Acts of Pilate) indicates the earliest forms as well as the Greek and Eastern versions (second to fourth centuries); *Evangelium Nicodemi* indicates the Latin texts (fifth century and later); *Gesta Pilati* (Deeds of Pilate) indicates the first two sections of the Latin version, comprising Christ's Passion and Joseph of Arimathea's story, while *Descen-*

sus Christi ad inferos (Descent of Christ into the Inferno) indicates the third section about the Harrowing of Hell; and the *Gospel of Nicodemus* refers to the gospel generally, to European vernacular translations, and specifically in this case, to John Trevisa's fourteenth-century Middle English translation.

The *Gospel of Nicodemus* is an apocryphal gospel. As an apocryphon, it stands outside the established canon of Scripture found in the Bible. It was sometimes included as the fifth gospel after John in *evangelaria* (books containing collections of the gospels apart from other Old and New Testament writings), and it attained an amazing level of popularity in western Europe. It is demonstrably dependent on the older canonical gospels (Matthew, Mark, Luke, and John) and was never included in the church's official canon of scripture. As a generic gospel, however, it is narrative of Christ's Passion, Resurrection, and Ascension, extending the canonical gospel story beyond this point by telling the stories of Joseph of Arimathea and the Harrowing of Hell.

The *Gospel of Nicodemus* begins when Jewish leaders approach Pilate accusing Jesus of calling himself king, breaking the Sabbath, and attempting to subvert Jewish law. When Jesus arrives to face his accusers, the messenger who had been sent for him spreads his *fasciale* (kerchief or napkin) for Jesus to walk over, and the imperial standards bow down before him. Pilate's wife, Procula, sends her husband a message to let Jesus go on account of a dream she has had, but the drama of accusation continues until Jesus is charged with blasphemy, a crime punishable by death. Several persons, including Nicodemus and Veronica, defend Jesus and tell of the signs and wonders he performed, but in the end, following the account of Luke 23, Jesus is condemned, crucified, and buried. Joseph of Arimathea places the body in his own tomb.

Jewish leaders imprison Joseph for his actions, but when they return to deal with him more severely after the Sabbath, they find his prison cell empty. At this point, the high priests and scribes learn from the guards that angels have announced Christ's Resurrection to some women, and they quickly pay for the guards' silence. Then they receive reports that three Galilean rabbis have seen Jesus, who first instructed his followers and then ascended into heaven. Again the Jewish leaders pay for silence, sending messengers meanwhile to find Joseph in Arimathea. Joseph comes to Jerusalem and reports that Jesus set him free from his prison cell. According to Joseph, the resurrected Jesus raised many others to life with him, including Simeon's sons Leucius and Carinus. Summoning the two brothers, the high priests order them to tell their story. Leucius and Carinus ask for pen and paper and write down the account of the Harrowing of Hell.

The account is highly allegorical, with Death and Hell having speaking parts along with Satan against Jesus, Isaiah, David, Enoch, Elijah, and the Good Thief. Essentially it is a drama in which Jesus enters Hell, conquers Satan, and translates the waiting souls to the care of the Archangel Michael in the terrestrial paradise. Once it is finished in written form, Leucius gives his account to the Jewish leaders Annas, Caiaphas, and Gamaliel while Carinus gives his to Nicodemus and Joseph. The brothers are transfigured forthwith, then disappear. In comparing the two written narratives, the Jews see that they are absolutely identical. Nicodemus and Joseph bring the story to Pilate, who writes it down and places it in his records.

In translating the *Gospel of Nicodemus,* Trevisa included two notes, one explaining the date of Christ's Passion and the other defining the words "amen" (as "so must it be") and "alleluia" (as "praise ye and hear God all at once, and also, Lord save thou me"). He may also have added an unsigned interpolation near the beginning of the second chapter summarizing further information from the canonical gospels about Judas's betrayal and the accusations made before Pilate by the scribes and high priests. On the whole, the translation is a good one, and it reveals Trevisa's theological, pastoral, and probably personal interest in Christ's Harrowing of Hell. It is easiest to relate the translation thematically to the information about Christ's life in the *Polychronicon* and to Trevisa's interpolated notes about life after death, but it can also be related to Trevisa's entire corpus of translations through a consideration of

audience. Trevisa's translations were composed for a very broad audience that included clerics, and through their preaching, the laity as well as the most socially elevated members of medieval English life, the kings and princes and rulers for whom he may have translated the *Gospel of Nicodemus* and for whom he certainly composed *De Regimine Principum (Concerning the Rule of Princes)* years later.

Aegidius Romanus originally composed *De Regimine Principum* about 1270–1285 for the son of the king of France, who would himself be crowned King Philip IV the Fair in 1285. Aegidius Romanus was a member of the order of the Hermits of Saint Augustine; he studied theology at Paris and later became Philip IV's tutor. In his treatise, the author acts as a proponent of strongly exercised kingship, limited primarily by the king's own dedication to morality and law. Generically the treatise is a mirror for princes (an advice book for rulers).

Trevisa's translation, following the structure of the Latin original, consists of three books: book 1 on the king's rule of himself; Book 2 on the king's rule of his household; and book 3 on the king's rule of the realm. The first book contains an introduction setting out the order of the work and the profit to be obtained from the content. There follows a section on the virtues, another on the passions, and a final one on manners. The second book describes how a king ought to approach his marriage, his children, and his household. The final book sets forth how the king ought to rule a city and his entire kingdom, whether in peace or in war.

Trevisa's translation contains no interpolated notes and survives in only one manuscript, Bodleian Library MS Digby 233.

TRANSLATIONS ATTRIBUTED TO TREVISA

David Fowler has argued that John Trevisa may have composed the B-text of *The Vision of Piers Plowman* originally. This assertion has been met with critical skepticism. Most scholars consider William Langland the author and reviser of the various texts of *Piers Plowman.* More persuasive has been Fowler's argument that Trevisa may have been one of the Wycliffite Bible translators, an argument which Fowler first set forth in his article "John Trevisa and the English Bible." Ronald Waldron (1988) challenged Fowler's position in his own article "John Trevisa and the Use of English," but the possibility that Trevisa was a Wycliffite Bible translator nevertheless remains outstanding. Certainly Trevisa was preeminently qualified to undertake Bible translation, and he attended Queen's College, Oxford, with one of the known translators, Nicholas Hereford. Trevisa furthermore translated many biblical passages within in his own known works of translation.

Another scholar attributed *De Re Militari,* a military treatise, to Trevisa's corpus of translations. However, in 1925, after Trevisa's date of death was established as being no later than 1402, William Perry observed the treatise could not be Trevisa's because it had been composed (according to a manuscript colophon) in 1408. Perry also argued against including *On the Bygynnyng of the World and the Ende of Worldes* in Trevisa's canon of translations, though this time on linguistic grounds (for example, the absence of doublets for translation of single terms; the occurrence of compound subjects, rare elsewhere in Trevisa's works; the position of objects, adjectives, and adverbs, and so on). Furthermore, the translation contains no signed interpolations by Trevisa.

Some scholars have also thought that Trevisa might be responsible for the Anglo-Norman inscriptions on the walls and ceiling of the Berkeley Castle Chapel, but as D. A. Trotter (1990) has shown, they probably date to the thirteenth century.

WORLDVIEW OF JOHN TREVISA

Trevisa's belief in Christ and his position in the Catholic Church in fourteenth-century England fundamentally shaped his view of the world. His ideas about his identity, other people, relationships, faith, the nature of the world, space, time, and language were all inherently contingent upon Christian interpretations of biblical texts and ideas. Trevisa inherited his worldview from his predecessors in the church, and that view was shaped and changed by his contemporaries at Oxford University and employment in the Berkeley household. As we have seen, Trevisa's life and canon of translations reveal many aspects of his ideology, but I would argue that the *Polychronicon* exemplifies it. As a history of the world known to the medieval West, the *Polychronicon* sets forth a medieval Christian worldview. It does so nowhere more vividly than in the maps which accompany its Latin versions and in its first book, called a *mappamundi* (map of the world) by Ranulf Higden and Trevisa's translation, which is a survey of world geography in prose. By examining these two parts of the *Polychronicon,* the graphic map and the prose one, it will be possible to gain a fuller, more precise understanding of Trevisa's worldview.

Medieval maps of the world can reveal medieval worldviews just as they once helped to shape them. These maps relate historical, theological, and symbolic information in a geographical framework. Matters of scale, proportion, and the depiction of spatial relationships typically serve the narrative and rhetorical purposes of the maps. In a sense, the maps are pictorial chronicles, graphic representations of theological interpretations of history. This is obvious to modern people, who can recognize medieval maps' striking difference from our own, but it was also clear to the medieval mapmakers and their viewers. Ranulf Higden seems to have been particularly aware of the relationship between cartography and history when he produced the graphic *mappamundi* which accompanies the Latin *Polychronicon.* Nineteen copies of differing versions of Ranulf's map survive, mostly in Latin manuscripts of the *Polychronicon,* and these give insight into the medieval worldview which recipients of the *Polychronicon* inherited from the past.

Ranulf's autograph of the chronicle, Huntington MS 132, contains a circular or oval *mappamundi* quite possibly in the chronicler's own hand. Despite this model, Ranulf's *mappamundi* survives in different forms. Specifically, extant copies are in the shapes of circles, ovals, and mandorlas, also known as *vesicae piscis* (fish bladders). They probably developed in that order, that is, from circle to oval to mandorla. Hugh of St. Victor suggests that maps of the world were drawn in an oval shape because that was supposedly the shape of Noah's ark. The idea that the world ought to conform to the shape of Noah's ark speaks to the biblical ideas that informed the making of medieval maps, including Ranulf's.

Indeed, Ranulf's map did not appear in a vacuum. It draws on earlier medieval maps of the world and represents the transitional stage of world mapping before the "discoveries" of the fifteenth and sixteenth centuries. At their most basic, earlier medieval maps, exemplified in the sixth-century *mappamundi* of Isidore of Seville, have a T-O structure. In a T-O map, the "O" is the *mare oceanum,* the ocean sea or the ocean river, which surrounds everything. The "T" consists of two water bodies: the vertical stem is the Mediterranean Sea, separating Europe and Africa, and the crossbar is typically identified with the Danube (also known as the Don or the Tanais), separating Asia (on top) from Europe and Africa (below). The crossbar could include additional waterways and bodies as well. Pictorially speaking, water framed medieval maps, but ideologically, biblical history gave them their shape and content.

For instance, in medieval *mappaemundi* the world is divided in thirds and assigned to the sons of Noah who survived the Flood. Asia is identified with Shem, Europe with Japhet, and Africa with Cham. This division ultimately traces its roots to Genesis 9:18–19 (translated from the Vulgate): "These are the sons of Noah who came out of the ark, Shem, Cham and Japhet, and furthermore, Cham is the father of Canaan. These three are the sons of Noah and from these all humankind was scattered over the whole earth." The story which follows this passage explains how Noah became drunk from the wine of the vineyard that he planted after the Flood and, lying uncovered in his tent, was spied by his son, Cham. Cham reveals his father's situation to his brothers, who cover their father's nakedness; when Noah wakes and learns what has transpired, he curses Cham to enslavement to his brothers, Shem and Japhet. Thus Cham's association with

Canaan in the Jewish Tanakh and with Africa in medieval maps became a form of justification for later conflict, conquest, and imperialism. As Ranulf's *Polychronicon* records in book 1, chapter 7, drawing on Pliny and Priscian, and which Trevisa translates (here given in a modernized translation of John Trevisa):

> Asia is the most in quantity, Europe is less, and equal in number of people, *but Africa is least of all* the three parties both in place and in number of people, and therefore some men, that know men and lands, record but two parts of the earth only, Asia and Europe, and *they recorded that Africa belongs to Europe,* for Africa is narrow in breadth, and evil doers, corrupt air, wild beasts and venomous move in it (emphases added).

Formulations such as this lay the intellectual groundwork for the rape of Africa in succeeding centuries. Indeed, the circulation of the printed editions of the *Polychronicon* in the fifteenth and sixteenth centuries ensured that many eyes read this specific passage. However, neither medieval maps in general nor Ranulf's map in particular pictorially represent European possession of Africa; rivers, in the shape of a "T" sometimes symbolically identified with Christ's cross, maintain divisions between them.

Biblical influence gives shape in yet another way to medieval world maps: their orientation. Unlike most modern Western maps, the true north for most medieval maps and their viewers was the east, which was designated *Oriens* in Latin, the direction of the rising sun. The east is located at the top of many medieval maps (though not all) and occasionally, as in copies of Ranulf's map, identified with the terrestrial paradise. Thus at the top of the map in Huntington MS 132, the figures of a man and a woman, Adam and Eve with a leafy tree (obviously corresponding to the Tree of the Knowledge of Good and Evil) represent Paradise and, more relevantly, the Fall. By placing Paradise in the east and Adam and Eve at the top of the world map, Ranulf and other mapmakers demonstrate pictorially that the world exists under the shadow of the Fall. In some other maps, such as one thirteenth-century Psalter map in British Library Additional MS 28681, Christ is enthroned over the symbolic representation of

Adam, Eve, and the Tree, indicating his lordship over the world and the consequences of the Fall.

In addition, Jerusalem is often given a prominent place, sometimes at or near the center of medieval maps, and in the famous Hereford map, Christ's cross is placed above it. At least one scholar has been at pains to dispel the idea that Jerusalem is *always* placed at the center of medieval world maps, including Ranulf's, but in Ranulf's case, his objection does not quite hold. In British Library Royal MS 14.C.XII, a mandorla-type *mappamundi,* Jerusalem and Rome hold equidistant positions from one another in the center of the map with Jerusalem in the superior position. In British Library Royal MS 14.C.IX, Jerusalem is represented as a church or temple with a steeple in a red circle just above the center of the map and plainly marked with its name. In Huntington MS 132, the map again appears to depict Jerusalem as a building, thus differentiating it from the landscape around it. It is possible to quibble about whether or not Jerusalem is in the *exact* center of these maps, but it is clearly not on the sidelines or in the margins.

It is worth noting that Ranulf clearly describes Jerusalem's centrality in book 1, chapter 14 of the *Polychronicon:* "Haec itaque terra Judaea opulenta est, frugifera. . . . quae in medio sui velut in umbilico terrae urbem habet Jerusalem," or in a modernized version of Trevisa's translation, "This land of Judea is rich and fruitful . . . and has in the middle, as if it were the navel of the earth, the city of Jerusalem." Jerusalem's place in the center of medieval world maps and its metaphoric designation as the "navel of the world" stems, in part, from Ezekiel. Ezekiel 5:5 suggests that all other nations and lands surround Jerusalem (translated from the Vulgate): "This the Lord God says: This is Jerusalem, in the middle of the nations I have placed her, and in the circle of her lands." The Vulgate translation of the Hebrew *tabûr* (center) in a later passage, Ezekiel 38:12, is "umbilicus terrae," that is, the navel of the world. Hence there is a biblical and linguistic explanation for Jerusalem's place, but there is also, of course, a theological one. Paul's famous analogy in Galatians imagines a relationship between an earthly and a heavenly Jerusa-

lem; Augustine picks this up in *The City of God against the Pagans,* and the Middle Ages runs with it. Pictorial representations of Jerusalem in medieval world maps thus constitute symbolic allusions to Pauline and Augustinian thought.

It should be pointed out that Ranulf's graphic map does not appear with all or even most of the Latin *Polychronicon* manuscripts, nor does it accompany John Trevisa's English translation of the *Polychronicon.* Ronald Waldron has speculated that empty front pages in some English *Polychronicon* maps may have been left blank to accommodate a graphic *mappamundi* which ultimately remained uncopied. Of course, an argument from absence is difficult to prove. However, the Latin and English versions of the *Polychronicon* itself contain an entire book, book 1, called therein a *mappamundi,* and it provides an even more detailed account of a medieval worldview than a graphic map would have in any case.

The prose *mappamundi* is divided into sixty chapters which concern about twenty-three countries and several islands, including some in Asia (India, Parthia, Assyria, Judea, Canaan, Egypt, Scythia, Capadocia), Africa (which receives a scant two chapters, one on Ethiopia, Libya, and Getula and the other on Numidia, Mauritania, and Phoenicia), and Europe (Greece, Rome, Germany, Gaul or France, Spain, Ireland, Scotland, Wales, and England). The *mappamundi* claims to use a variety of authorities, including Priscian, Augustine, Isidore of Seville, Pliny, Bede, Paul the Deacon, Solinus, Basilius, Josephus, Peter Comestor, Tully, Trogus, Giraldus Cambrensis, the Bible, Orosius, Jerome, William of Malmesbury, Hugguccio, Pseudo-Methodius, Martin, John of Salisbury, Valerian, Pseudo-Turpin, Herodotus, Alfred of Beverly, Geoffrey of Monmouth, and Marianus Scotus. Certain authors are used more heavily in some sections than in others. For example, Giraldus contributes a great deal to the descriptions of Ireland and Wales. Isidore of Seville, however, is used pretty much throughout. The book begins with "Inde," a pun on "India" and "end" in Middle English, and concludes with England. England's hindmost position indicates its foremost importance in the scheme here, as the compiler and translator make abundantly clear in their prefaces. Yet compiler and translator also take time to describe the wonders and marvels of the wider world in a variety of instances. Its order and proportions indicate their priorities, and the assembly of authorities indicates just how many influential medieval writers shared (or shaped) some aspect of Ranulf Higden and John Trevisa's worldview.

Just as John Trevisa's predecessors shaped his worldview, so too did Trevisa help to shape the worldview of later generations of English people. Trevisa's translation of the *Polychronicon* became accessible to fifteenth-century audiences when Caxton printed it, first in part and then as a whole, in two different books: in *The Description of Britain,* which contained chapters on England from book 1 and the first woodcut of an English landscape, and in a complete edition of Trevisa's English *Polychronicon.* Caxton's decision to print the first book, with a focus on England, reflects the commitment demonstrated by both Ranulf Higden and John Trevisa to celebrating English nationality. In his prefaces, Ranulf declared that he compiled the *Polychronicon* for "the cause of Britain," and in his interpolated notes, Trevisa insisted on Cornwall's integral place in the English nation. It is no surprise, then, that Caxton's printed editions of the *Polychronicon* also perpetuated the celebration of such nationalism.

Trevisa's English nationalism was part of his outlook, as was his intense loyalty to Cornwall, but his faith in Christ defined his worldview. His profession as a priest, his canon of original works and translations, and his English version of book 1 of the *Polychronicon,* the *mappamundi,* all provide clear evidence of this. For Trevisa, life's ultimate goal, as suggested by his conclusion to the *Dialogue between a Lord and a Clerk,* was to see God's "blissful face in joy without any end." We may hope that he attained it.

SELECTED BIBLIOGRAPHY

I. MANUSCRIPTS. A list of manuscripts containing the works of John Trevisa may be found in David Fowler, *The Life and Times of John Trevisa, Medieval Scholar* (Seattle, Wash., 1995).

II. ORIGINAL WORKS. "Trevisa's Original Prefaces on Translation: A Critical Edition," ed. by Ronald Waldron, in Edward Donald Kennedy, Ronald Waldron, and Joseph S. Wittig, eds., *Medieval English Studies Presented to George Kane* (Woodbridge, Suffolk, U.K., and Wolfeboro, N.H., 1988).

III. MAJOR TRANSLATIONS. *Polychronicon,* 9 vols., ed. by Joseph Rawson Lumby, Rolls Series (London, 1865–1886); *On the Properties of Things: John Trevisa's Translation of Bartholomaeus Anglicus, De Proprietatibus Rerum,* 3 vols., ed. by M. C. Seymour et al. (Oxford, 1975–1988).

IV. MINOR TRANSLATIONS. *Dialogus inter Militem et Clericum, Richard FitzRalph's Sermon "Defensio Curatorum," and Methodius, "The Bygynnyng of the World and the Ende of Worldes" by John Trevisa,* ed. by William Perry, EETS 167 (London, 1925); *The Gospel of Nicodemus, translated by John Trevisa,* ed. by H. C. Kim, Ph.D. dissertation (University of Washington, 1963).

V. CRITICAL STUDIES. For a partial survey of Trevisa criticism to 1984, see A. S. G. Edwards, "John Trevisa," in *Middle English Prose: A Critical Guide to Major Authors and Genres* (New Brunswick, N.J., 1984). Three critical pieces of importance published prior to 1984 and consulted for this essay include Gerald Robert Owst, *Preaching in Medieval England: An Introduction to Sermon Manuscripts of the Period, c. 1350–1450* (Cambridge, 1926); V. H. Galbraith, "An Autograph MS of Ranulph Higden's *Polychronicon,*" *Huntington Library Quarterly* 23 (1959); and John Taylor, *The Universal History of Ranulf Higden* (Oxford, 1966).

Since 1984, scholars have published the following studies or editions of Trevisa and his work: David Woodward, "Medieval *Mappaemundi,*" in *The History of Cartography,* Vol. 1: *Cartography in Prehistoric, Ancient, and Medieval Europe and the Mediterranean,* ed. by J. B. Harley and David Woodward (Chicago, 1987); Anne Hudson, *The Premature Reformation: Wycliffite Texts and Lollard History* (Oxford and New York, 1988); Ronald Waldron, "John Trevisa and the Use of English," *Proceedings of the British Academy* 74 (1988); Ralph Hanna 3d, "Sir Thomas Berkeley and His Patronage," *Speculum* 64 (1989); Ronald Waldron, "Trevisa's Celtic Complex Revisited," *N&Q* 234 (1989).

D. A. Trotter, "The Anglo-Norman Inscriptions at Berkeley Castle," *Medium Aevum* 59, no. 1 (1990); Ronald Waldron, "The Manuscripts of Trevisa's Translation of the *Polychronicon,*" *Modern Language Quarterly* 51 (1990); Ronald Waldron, "Dialect Aspects of Manuscripts of Trevisa's Translation of the *Polychronicon,*" in Felicity Riddy, ed., *Regionalism in Late Medieval Manuscripts and Texts* (Cambridge and Rochester, N.Y., 1991); Ronald Waldron and Henry Hargreaves, "The Aberdeen Manuscript of Trevisa's Translation of the *Polychronicon* (AUL MS 21): A Workshop Crisis and Its Resolution," *Scriptorium* 46 (1992); David Fowler, *John Trevisa,* English Writers of the Late Middle Ages Series (Newcastle upon Tyne, U.K., 1993); H. Leith Spencer, *English Preaching in the Late Middle Ages* (Oxford and New York, 1993); David Fowler, *The Life and Times of John Trevisa, Medieval Scholar* (Seattle, Wash., 1995); J. A. Burrow and Thorlac Turville-Petre, eds., "Dialogue between a Lord and a Clerk," in *A Book of Middle English,* 2d ed. (Oxford, 1997); Evelyn Edson, *Mapping*

JOHN TREVISA

Time and Space: How Medieval Mapmakers Viewed Their World, British Library Studies in Map History, vol. 1 (London, 1997); Zbigniew Izydorczyk, *The Medieval Gospel of Nicodemus: Texts, Intertexts, and Contexts in Western Europe* (Tempe, Ariz., 1997); Fiona Somerset, *Clerical Discourse and Lay Audience in Late Medieval England* (Cambridge and New York, 1998); Stephen Shepherd, "Dialogue between a Lord and a Clerk on Translation (Extract)" and "Epistle to Thomas, Lord Berkeley, on the Translation of Higden's *Polychronicon,*" in Joycelyn Wogan-Browne et. al., eds., *The Idea of the Vernacular: An Anthology of Middle English Literary Theory, 1280–1520* (University Park, Pa., 1999).

Ronald Waldron, "Doublets in the Translation Techniques of John Trevisa," in C. J. Kay and L. M. Sylvester, eds., *Lexis and Texts in Early English: Studies Presented to Jane Roberts,* Costerius New Series 133 (Rodopi, 2000); Ronald Waldron, "The Mind of John Trevisa," *Journal of the Royal Institute of Cornwall* (2001); Jane Beal, *John Trevisa and the English* Polychronicon: *Authority and Vernacular Translation in Late-Medieval England,* Ph.D dissertation (University of California, Davis, 2002); William Mark Ormond, ed., "Mapping Identity in John's Trevisa's English *Polychronicon*: Chester, Cornwall, and the Translation of English National History," in *Fourteenth-Century England,* vol. 3 (London: 2003).

260

DENTON WELCH

1915–1948

David Breithaupt

THE BRIEF LIFE of Maurice Denton Welch reeks of romance and the exotic. Welch was born in Shanghai on 29 March 1915 into a financially comfortable family that included three older brothers; his father, Joseph Welch, ran a trading business, shipping tea to England from Shanghai, where he based his company. As a young man, Welch experienced both the English countryside and the mysteries of China's most cosmopolitan city.

Joseph Welch's trading business had been handed down from his father, John Knox. It had roots reaching back to 1842, when the British invaded Shanghai, ending the Opium War of 1839 and resulting in the Treaty of Nanking, which opened Shanghai's gates to the West. Welch's mother, Rosalind Bassett, was an American descended from a branch of the Russell family that founded New Bedford, Massachusetts. Her strong faith in Christian Science would serve Welch to the end of his short life. According to Michael De-la-Noy in his book *Denton Welch: The Making of a Writer* (1984), Welch's faith in Christian Science was informal but "perhaps because it was so strongly associated with his mother, never entirely left him" (p. 31). A shared love of Shanghai's small antique and junk shops helped her and her youngest son stave off the loneliness of shuttling between continents. Welch's older brothers, William, Paul, and Tom, were in school in England when he was born, and he stayed with his mother in Shanghai until he was old enough to follow them. The time alone with his mother forged a close bond, since his father was often away, absorbed in his tea company and frequently emotionally distant when he was home.

Despite such periods of separation from his father and brothers, Welch enjoyed some idyllic moments during his childhood. He particularly remembered the summer of 1922, in Wei-hai-Wei on Half-Moon Bay, spent in a cliff house. His brother Paul was with him, and the two of them spent hours searching for shells along the coastline. Although not as athletic as his brother, Welch spent many hours hiking, biking, and swimming. He and Paul had a secret spot for picnicking alone.

The same year saw the awakening and precocious development—Welch was seven—of his love of designing costumes, drawing, and painting. He drew whatever caught his eye, including dress designs for his mother. He also started writing music, and the beauty of his compositions helped ease his mother through a prolonged period of illness. Her death in 1926 of kidney disease dealt a catastrophic blow to the eleven-year-old boy.

Welch returned to England after his mother died and began his matriculation at St. Michaels, in Sussex. Evelyn Sparks, a family friend, offered to keep house for him. Welch wrote next to nothing in his journals about his time at St. Michaels, apart from a description or two of predictably unhappy Christmases. Most clues to his feelings while he was at prep school are to be found in two later novels, *Maiden Voyage* (1943) and *In Youth Is Pleasure* (1945).

In 1929, Welch relocated to Repton Preparatory School, where his older brother Paul was still a student. It was no improvement over St. Michaels. Later, Welch wrote the poet Alex Comfort: "Early adolescence was, to me, what I can only describe as a *sordid* and fearful time. I was frightened of everything and everything seemed sullied and 'slimed-over' with this fear. It is only just lately (I am now 26) that I have come to realize what an unpleasant time it was" (Phillips, p. 25).

DENTON WELCH

Though Welch grew up with a strong appreciation of literature, it wasn't until he was enrolled at Repton that he discovered his strong attraction to books and writing. Nonetheless, Repton became so distasteful to him that he ran away, with no plans at all except to view the cathedrals of northern England. When he ran out of money and was finally captured by local police, he returned to Repton with hero status. He was no longer the sickly wimp but a brave escapee whose bars could no longer contain him. More important than this schoolboy escapade was his decision to change his academic focus from art to literature. He continued to paint as he developed his writing style, however, and in 1933, at the age of eighteen, Welch enrolled at the Goldsmith College in New Cross at London.

CATASTROPHE

It was at Goldsmith that Welch would spend his last two years as a walking man, able to move about without the aid of a helper or wheelchair. For it was near the end of Welch's second year that he suffered a tragic accident that almost ended his life.

In 1935, as spring break neared, Denton decided to bicycle to visit his Aunt Edith and her husband, the Reverend Thomas Kane, who lived by Leigh Vicarage near Reigate for the Whitsun weekend. It was a good day's bike ride to the north of England, perfect for a weekend trip and catching up on family sagas.

He was peddling along the road when a car traveling too fast struck him. He awoke to the sound of a police officer asking him how he felt; he had almost no memory of the accident. Welch, it seems, had suffered injuries so severe that he almost died. Investigators deduced that the car wheels actually went over his body, causing a broken ankle, rampant bruising, and a fracture of the spine. He was only twenty years old.

The accident caused temporary paralysis from the chest downward. Welch struggled between life and death for weeks, his condition worsening when he contracted tuberculosis of the spine. According to his own accounts, at one point he weighed less than seventy pounds. He eventually regained use of his arms and after many months of treatment was able to walk again with a form of spastic paralysis. Because of the fracture, he suffered ongoing paralysis of his bladder and kidneys, which caused periodic infections of those organs, resulting in random bouts of fever. Blinding headaches and high blood pressure were yet more problems.

As sometimes happens amid tragedy, a twist of fate changed the direction of Welch's life. A doctor named Easton (renamed "Dr. Farley" in Welch's novel *A Voice Through a Cloud* [1950]) took charge of Welch when he transferred to a private hospital. The friendship that developed between the two was believed by many to have saved Welch's life. Easton, with his amazing bedside manner, was able to heal Welch's spirit as well as his body, and the doctor proved to be an outlet for Welch's emotional needs as his father should have been. When Dr. Easton announced he was taking a new position and leaving the hospital, Welch attempted to follow him and continue their relationship, but this did not work out. Instead Welch rented a flat outside London, on Hadlow Road. Here he met his landlady, Evelyn (Evie) Sinclair, the model for Miss Hellier in *A Voice Through a Cloud* and in time one of Welch's closest friends. Fortunately Welch had become wealthy enough not to have to work, after inheriting a trust fund from his mother on his twenty-first birthday, with additional money paid out by insurance and the court as a result of the accident.

He worked hard at regaining his interest in art and building his strength and was eventually able to take short walks with a cane. When he achieved moments that were relatively pain-free, he wasted no time filling up volumes of his journals. He also started working on several short stories. Such progress came simultaneously with the grim knowledge that he would never fully recover and that his life would be cut short.

Welch was of course exempt from the war. In 1940 he and Evie Sinclair moved to a flat at the Hopgarden at Platt in London. Not long after, an air raid over London bombed their new home, destroying enough to force them to seek new quarters. It was their first real brush with the war,

262

which previously had been only an ongoing story in the papers. A series of disrupting moves continued until the two finally settled near Tonbridge, Kent, at Pitt's Folly Cottage, a large room with a big kitchen and bath housed over a garage. Though frequently confined to bed, Welch painted and sketched when his health permitted. An exhibition of his paintings at the Leicester Gallery in 1941 led to the sale of one of the works to Dame Rose Macauley, a writer Welch admired, and other commissions followed. In 1942 his father died. Welch's journals indicate he felt little or no direct sense of loss of this admittedly remote figure in his life; rather, his most immediate concern was the continuance of his stipend. The same year Welch published his first story in *Horizon* magazine. "A Visit with Sickert" was based on a meeting he had had with the well-known English painter Walter Sickert; the story was later republished in a posthumous collection, *A Last Sheaf* (1951).

Welch received a postcard the following year from Eric Oliver, a young man working for the Kent War Agricultural Executive Committee, who admired his paintings and the published story. The two became friends and eventually lovers despite differences in temperament and background; Oliver was also to serve as Welch's unofficial agent. They seemed an unlikely pair, but after a few weeks, that mysterious chemistry that so often unites people bound them in friendship. Books, writing, and Oliver's knowledge of the outdoors so impressed Welch that they became roommates eight months after they met. Oliver helped Welch with the physical chores he still could not perform. Correspondingly, Evie Sinclair's role as Welch's caretaker diminished, and she developed a life of her own.

Welch's final years were a frenzy of creative activity. In 1943 he published his first novel, *Maiden Voyage*, a resounding critical success. He continued various writing projects, working on short stories, journals, and his next novel, *In Youth Is Pleasure*, published in 1945.

His health continued to worsen, however, and on 30 December 1948 Denton Welch died in his sleep, leaving an unfinished novel, *A Voice Through a Cloud*. The cause of death was high blood pressure and pyelitis, inflammation of the pelvis and kidneys. He was only thirty-three years old. Despite great pain, he had never stopped writing. As his early supporter Dame Edith Sitwell said of him, "He was born to write."

MAIDEN VOYAGE

Denton Welch could have easily spent the last decade of his life in a haze of medication, absorbed only in his pain and recovery. Fortunately he was more productive than many healthy writers, producing three novels, dozens of short stories, a very large collection of journals, and even a slim volume of poetry.

Maiden Voyage, probably begun in late 1940 or early 1941, drew heavily on Welch's early life and was inspired at least in part by a reading of J. R. Ackerley's *Hindoo Holiday* (1932), which directed the format of this autobiographical novel. Welch completed the book in a few concentrated months of writing. It made the rounds of publishers and was widely rejected until Herbert Read asked to interview Welch. The two men met at Read's club, The Reform, in Pall Mall, and Welch was honored to sit in Henry James's old chair. Read offered Welch a £50 advance and suggested that Welch design the jacket and title page. The book, published on 7 May 1943, was listed as "autobiography" in some libraries and reviews, and Welch was criticized in certain quarters for calling his book a novel when its contents followed the events of his life so closely. Writers such as D. H. Lawrence (in *Sons and Lovers*) and Somerset Maugham (in *Of Human Bondage*) had taken similar liberties, but Welch went further, writing in the first person and calling his protagonist "Denton Welch." The novel's title recalls the author's escape from Repton Preparatory School. In the retelling, Welch's youthful enthusiasm for getting away from Repton and visiting his favorite sights of northern England is replaced by exhaustion and anxiety as his funds diminish. He seeks shelter with relatives, who eventually lead him back to Repton. Welch is surprised to find himself enjoying the status of an outlaw, which he vastly prefers over his former status as a sissy. In addition to this unexpected promotion, Welch receives an invitation from his father to come to Shanghai when the school term is over. Ecstatic, he is able to carry on through the rest of the school term. Welch is about to embark on another "maiden voyage" and prepares his bags for the trip.

Of course Welch is familiar with Shanghai and its environs from his childhood and continued visits to the city to see his father, but this time he has the opportunity for a journey he did not expect: his father suggests he explore the interior of China. The older man appreciates his son's love of collectibles and presents a like-minded friend, Mr. Butler, as companion. The trip to the interior will be yet another maiden voyage.

The journey proves to be somewhat risky, with China unstable in the years before World War II. The travelers endure shakedowns by soldiers who evict them from their train in the middle of the night, leaving them stranded, and later escape gunfire. With nerves worn thin from stress, Welch quickly tires of Mr. Butler and his fussy ways.

The two return safely to Shanghai, and Welch prepares to return to England. Here Welch highlights the tension in his relationship with his father, describing his father's apathy as the time nears for him to go, this time to attend art school. A final conflict with his father ensues when he takes, without asking, several of his mother's belongings. It is not the taking without asking that upsets his father so much, nor even the loss of the objects, so much as his intuition that his son favored his mother over him.

Maiden Voyage contains a number of themes Welch was to explore further in later writings: journeys that end in self-revelation, generally concerning relationships or sexuality; alienation from the world and from the family. Isolation and rejection were themes that haunted the author to his dying days.

Beyond this is Welch's ability to create deep and powerful personal myth out of even the seemingly mundane events of modern life. (Indeed. William S. Burroughs, in an introduction to a recent edition of *In Youth Is Pleasure*, gave students looking for writing ideas the following advice: Read anything by Denton Welch.) As the Welch biographer Robert Phillips has

pointed out, this aspect of Welch's work may best be described through the words of Joseph Campbell, who, in *The Hero with a Thousand Faces* helped define the use of myth in contemporary life:

> The mythological hero, setting forth from his commonday hut or castle, is lured, carried away, or else voluntarily proceeds to the threshold of advantage. There he encounters a shadow presence that guards the passage. The hero may defeat or conciliate this power or go alive into the kingdom of the dark.
>
> (pp. 245–246)

Campbell, outlining what could happen to the hero in his quest, finally concludes:

> if the powers have blessed the hero, he now sets forth under their protection (emissary); if not, he flees and is pursued (transformation flight, obstacle flight). At the return threshold the transcendental powers must remain behind; the hero re-emerges from the kingdom of dread (return, resurrection). The boon that he brings restores the world (elixir).
>
> (pp. 245–246)

Campbell's description well describes Welch's first novel: Welch awakens one day to the dreariness of his "commonday hut" and leaves. Despite its exotic setting, *Maiden Voyage* is a series of personal departures, not high adventure or the stuff of thrillers, yet Welch's writing carries the reader forward as surely as the most riveting bestseller.

IN YOUTH IS PLEASURE

With *Maiden Voyage,* Welch entered into a circle of writers that included Edith Sitwell, E. M. Forster, and Evelyn Waugh. Although the thrill of inclusion was mitigated by the overwhelming distractions of fame, Welch nevertheless began work on *In Youth Is Pleasure* (1945), whose hero is Orville Pym, another thinly disguised version of Welch. The action is much more limited in this second book and more reliant on the poetic and descriptive form. The difference in tone is best indicated by the book's title, which denotes a certain amount of sarcasm. Though Welch does not come near to depicting a childhood as wretched as say, Oliver Twist's, he does portray the frustrations and anxieties of adolescence.

In Youth Is Pleasure is the story of Pym's vacation at a grand hotel on the Thames with his father and two older brothers. The time span is condensed, and the writing is finely tuned and crafted, as demonstrated in his rendering of this commonplace event:

> He walked slowly into the dark water and lay down flat. His exultation passed into a more sober delight. Water always soothed him. He felt calm and peaceful.
>
> As he floated he felt the sun hot on his face, and on the parts of his chest and arms which were still above the water. The rest of his body was tingling with cold.
>
> "I'm like one of those Baked Alaskas," he thought, "one of those lovely puddings of ice-cream and hot sponge."
>
> (p. 33)

Pym is self-absorbed, his mother is dead, and his father is a distant parent, fond of drink and the occasional use of opium. Pym's loneliness is increased by his father's insistence that no one speak his wife's name, as if not saying her name could somehow stop the grieving process. Pym feels further alienated by his older brothers, who find their young sibling too insignificant to bother with.

Feeling exiled from his family sets the stage for Pym's wanderings and daydreams. He fears growing up and facing his sexuality, about which he is confused. He even hopes his voice will not change and dreads the ritual of daily shaving.

Pym's struggle with his sexuality is a major theme of the book. His sleep is often troubled by erotic dreams, one of which has him "lying full length in an enormous open wound" (p. 9). He also takes advantage of his isolation for several episodes of masturbation, a subject that wasn't written about in novels for at least the next twenty-five years.

Homoerotic images appear throughout the book. When Pym orders peach Melba for dessert, he remarks on the "buttock-like shape of the fruit" (p. 7). Elsewhere, he spies on two young men and an older man canoeing and camping by a lake. The young boys are tanned, healthy, and idealized while the older man represents manhood at its peak. The older man acts sadistically, abusing the young men physically and verbally. Though the sexuality and rough treatment of the boys appears to appeal to Pym, he seems aware only of the natural outdoor life the three are living. Pym declares, "'If only . . . I could live by myself in a tent by the river! If I could hunt for my food, and get brown and fierce and hard all over! I could search in the fields for mushrooms, berries and roots, I might even try eating grass.'"

After Pym's encounter with the trio, he begins to sink deeper into himself. He seems to want to disappear from the world and performs strange rituals, including shutting himself in a closet and the bottom drawer of a large dresser. He begins to recall the tales heard in his youth of Chinese torture boxes kept in dark dungeons. Pym, with his increasing fear of growing old, decides to stunt his growth by confining himself to a small cabinet drawer, not able to leave for even a brief break to eat or bathe. Once these fantasies are dispensed with, Pym plays the role of Peeping Tom and is caught, after a quick chase, by a London headmaster whose mission is to bring young campers to a site for outings. Pym, who has often dreamed of being a slave, is delighted with the idea and confesses to the headmaster: "I don't understand how to live, what to do." The old man tells Pym that he has not allowed himself to grow since the death of his mother, and explains to the boy that: "you can't stop still at your mother's death."

The episode with the headmaster ends with Pym playfully tying him up. The headmaster is not amused and cuffs Pym on the head as he escapes from his ties. Deep down, Pym feels that this latest attempt to escape from himself has failed once more. Though he has come closer to having some of the answers he needs, such as those pertaining to his deceased mother, he still has failed to confront and question the nature of his true homoerotic identity.

Finally Pym meets an older married woman named Aphra, who prefers his sexual innocence

DENTON WELCH

to the more heavily charged sexuality of his older brothers. Pym readily attaches himself to Aphra as a replacement for his long-gone mother. He decides to attend a dance being held at the Grand Hotel with the idea of dressing as a girl. In the quiet of his room he begins to paint himself, starting with his cheeks and lips, with lipstick stolen from Aphra. He works on his hair by fluffing it up and, finally, undresses and paints his nipples with rouge until they look like flattened strawberries. He continues by adding rouge to his fingertips, toes, and earlobes. Pym completes his costume by painting gashes and spots all over his body.

Not surprisingly, Pym's plan for becoming a big hit at the dance comes to exactly the opposite. A group of older teenagers quickly ejects him from the gym, dashing his hopes of impressing Aphra and his older brothers. As he wanders the night, he accidentally comes across his rival brother Charles, making love to Aphra in the woods. As Aphra had recently begun to breast-feed her baby, warm jets of milk shoot into the air as Charles kisses and touches her breasts. Pym's reaction to the scene is simply that of one's mother giving milk to another instead of him. Aphra's unfaithfulness to her husband and her own deceitfulness with Pym serve only to reinforce the young boy's disillusionment with women. As the novel draws to a close, Pym's self-absorption is disturbed by the vacation's end and the preparation for a new school year. On the train back, he meets up with an older boy also returning to school. The older boy senses that Pym is different from other boys and begins to attack him. The older boy takes out a pair of nail clippers, and holding Pym down, trims his eyelashes. Pym's long lashes, of which he had been so proud, will never grow back. He begins to scream: "he knew he could not stop, that he had been working to this scream all his life" (p. 152).

Pym is saved by his older brother Ben, who kicks the attacker in his groin. But it is too late— Pym has been symbolically emasculated. What had been a quick summer of introspection concludes for him as disaster. He is sure of only one thing now: that he will never find his proper place in the world.

Welch's subject matter in this novel, homosexuality and masturbation, was radical for the mid-1940s. Though readers today can hardly be shocked by the ideas in *In Youth Is Pleasure,* his poetic prose style and intimate rendering of adolescent turmoil make the book a classic.

A VOICE THROUGH A CLOUD

Whereas *In Youth Is Pleasure* focused on its protagonist's mental anguish, *A Voice Through a Cloud* (1950) is about the world of physical pain. Welch called the book "a work of art spun like a delicately lovely spider's web out of his own entrails" (Phillips, p. 116). It begins with the book's hero, Maurice, taking a spontaneous bike ride to his uncle's house while on break from art school. Maurice was not used to riding along busy roadsides, traveling mostly on quiet country lanes during school holidays. After a few brief stops for refreshments, he continues his trip, riding carefully and close to the curb. He does not recall the actual accident—being struck by a woman driver approaching him from behind. Later, he recalls the aftermath:

> I heard a voice through a great cloud of agony and sickness. The voice was asking questions. It seemed to be opening and closing like a concertina. The words were loud as the swelling notes of an organ, then they finally melted to the tiniest wiry tinkle of water in a glass.
>
> (p. 13)

A Voice Through a Cloud has been compared to other novels of physical and mental suffering, such as Thomas Mann's *The Magic Mountain,* Dostoyevsky's *The Idiot,* and Sylvia Plath's *The Bell Jar.* John Updike described Welch's book as a novel in which "agony precedes psychology; introspection takes place only as pain's monopoly loosens" (Phillips, p. 109).

As Maurice begins the slow process of recovery, he reflects on the immediate aftermath of the accident: "There was a confusion in my mind between being brought to life—forceps, navel

266

DENTON WELCH

cords, midwives—and being put to death—ropes, axes and black masks" (p. 13). A fraction of his former self, he has a new life to adjust to, that of an invalid, dependent on many others. The new people in his life will be nurses and orderlies, who are distant and hardly capable of sympathy. An absence of spirituality extends throughout the hospital where Maurice is taken. This spiritual void extends to the doctors, creating indifference as painful to Maurice as the injuries caused by his accident. He begins to reflect on how the staff fails to realize that they are the main connections to reality for the patient. "Nobody seemed to realize that this was the only thing on earth. People didn't know that it was waiting for them quietly, patiently."

Maurice is determined to fight for his recovery and takes the first step by writing his brother to help him transfer to a private hospital, where he is later to meet Dr. Farley, modeled on Welch's own physician, Dr. Easton. It is only when this transaction occurs that Maurice takes his first physical steps, marking a turning point in his recovery.

While finishing *A Voice Through a Cloud,* Welch put down his pen in mid-sentence and died, leaving his third novel unfinished at the young age of thirty-three. The novel stops as Maurice makes a surprise visit to Dr. Farley with his companion, Miss Hellier, during which they are treated with cool politeness. The doctor is about to make a call to a patient who lives near the address of a rental apartment that Maurice and Miss Hellier are interested in viewing. The story ends as Dr. Farley drives his two guests to their destination. It is frustrating to the reader not to witness the end of Maurice's much anticipated visit to his doctor. The novel is published as Welch left it, forever leaving its readers to imagine how it might have ended.

SHORT STORIES

Even when Welch was in the middle of a longer work, he would often pause to work on a shorter piece of fiction. These pieces were not diversions from his novels but serious, well-crafted works whose inspiration could strike him at any time.

Brave and Cruel (1948) and *A Last Sheaf* (1951) were published posthumously, the latter edited by Welch's friend and lover, Eric Oliver. The stories in *Brave and Cruel* exhibit a wide range of writing techniques. Sketches such as "Narcissus Bay" and "Leaves from a Young Person's Notebook" were perhaps influenced by the impressionistic paintings of the time. These pieces provide an interesting contrast to other, more polished works in the collection, such as "The Trout Stream" and "The Fire in the Wood," which are far more structured and approach novella length ("Brave and Cruel," the longest, consumes the entire second half of the book). The collection begins with "The Coffin on the Hill," which features a family's Easter trip up-river on a houseboat. The narrator, now an adult, recalls himself as a youngster fraught with anxiety and fear. He talks to dolls for company and is terrified of the boat's cook, who tells him superstitious tales such as why the river current runs so rapidly: it's the spirits of drowned people, he says, who will pull the boy down if he falls overboard.

A journey within a journey begins when the boat pulls up to shore. The young boy climbs a nearby hill and discovers a graveyard, where the family decides (of all places) to have a picnic. After eating, the boy explores on his own and finds a wide-open grave with a cheap wooden coffin at the bottom. He can even see a small piece of cloth sticking out from beneath the coffin lid.

It is at this young age that the boy discovers the ultimate fate of humankind. Jolted, he runs back to his family, only to discover that they have left. He panics until he finds his mother in the tomb garden. Desperate to tell his mother the realization he has just reached, he knows his mother will not care to discuss such matters. Still, he thinks, "she seemed the very opposite of all the coffin held, but this only made my confusion worse, for I knew she would come to it at last; and that knowledge was unbearable" (p. 17).

As the family returns home, the boy ponders his discovery of mortality. He decides to throw his doll Lymph Est, his closest companion, into the river as a symbolic sacrifice. He notices that

DENTON WELCH

the drowned spirits do not drag his doll down yet senses that it is doomed as it floats away, perhaps representing his lost innocence, for now he knows the destiny of all humans. Thus another of Welch's journeys ends in a soul-shattering and life-altering manner.

"The Barn," next in the volume, is not quite as complex as its predecessor. The narrator, named Denton, is being teased by his older brother as he tries to skid his bicycle correctly. The older brother continues his teasing, accusing Denton of preferring the company of old ladies to that of boys. Denton's father asks him to take a note to Mrs. Singleton, their landlady. Denton does so reluctantly, only to find the landlady half-dressed. Mrs. Singleton, who had come to the door thinking Denton was one of her daughters, is shocked and runs to her bedroom to dress. She returns fully clothed and completely made up, "making me feel that it was I who appeared before her in a semi-naked and disgusting condition" (p. 22).

Denton flees to the barn and distracts himself from the situation by pretending to be a monkey, then a slave, and, finally, a prisoner. He is interrupted by a tramp asking for a night's shelter in the barn. As the boy tries to tell the tramp he would like to rough it too and join him, the tramp politely tells him he is too young and soft. The boy again feels mocked and inadequate. Nonetheless, he finally joins the tramp in the hay during the night and sleeps next to him. But when morning comes, the tramp takes to the road, and Denton is rejected once again. In a projection of homosexual desire, the boy compares Mrs. Singleton to the tramp, finding the latter's skin hard and desirable and his landlady's fleshy and repulsive. We find the narrator on the brink of discovery as he examines himself and his desires.

"Narcissus" is the story of four men and one woman returning from a mountaintop, with two of the men shackled, their hands behind their backs. The woman is bloodied and injured. The third man seems to have saved her from an even bloodier fate. The scene is witnessed by a boy (the narrator) and his friends, and the rest of the day is tainted by the violence he witnessed. The playmates are peaceful until the boy tells them what he has witnessed, and they now turn to play-

ing cruel tricks upon each other. One girl suggests hanging her governess and the boy begins to turn on his best friend. What influence could witnessing this violence have had upon the children? Welch leaves the conclusion up to the reader.

"Leaves from a Young Person's Notebook" anticipates *A Voice Through a Cloud* as it follows the story of a young boy condemned to view life from his sickbed. The young boy can only record what he sees from the window of his sickroom, and he eventually becomes confused over what is reality and fantasy. The effect is not unlike a Kafka novel, in which the reader weighs the sanity of the narrator against the reality of the day-to-day world.

The much anthologized "When I Was Thirteen" concerns adolescent awakening, including the struggle for sexual identity. Written in the first person, it recalls a trip Welch took to Switzerland. The trip is a Christmas holiday, and the unnamed narrator decides to improve his skills at skiing. During practice runs he meets a boy from his own school named Archer, who is about the same age and has comparable skills at skiing. But Archer is more knowledgeable about sexual matters. The narrator asks Archer what "illegitimate" means, and Archer informs him that the term refers to a child born out of wedlock. The narrator does not believe such a thing is possible and that marriage, and not just sex alone is needed to have intimate relations. "I had a vague idea that some particular reckless people attempted, without being married, to have children in places called 'nightclubs,' but they were always unsuccessful and this made them drink, and plunged them into the most hectic gaiety" (p. 60).

In many ways, Archer is an exact opposite of the narrator. The latter reads classics while the former reads comics and cheap novels filled with sex. Archer is bold and knowing, whereas the narrator is hesitant and inexperienced in worldly matters. These are the differences that make the narrator look up to Archer. However, the narrator's older brother warns him that Archer has a bad reputation at school—about what he does not say.

It isn't until the narrator's older brother leaves on a two-day guided tour, leaving him alone at the hotel, that the narrator really begins to spend time with Archer. The attractions are strong; Archer is the forbidden fruit, a slightly older boy who knows how to smoke and drink and all about the dark secrets of sex. The two decide to go skiing and have a picnic. Archer proves to be an excellent companion, providing the narrator with one of the best days he has ever had. Upon returning to the lodge to have dinner, the narrator has a bit too much to drink, which eventually leads him into Archer's extra bunk. First, though, the two take turns bathing, during which Archer asks to have his back scrubbed, then scratched, followed by a foot rub. Perhaps this is what the narrator's older brother was hinting at when warning his brother about Archer.

In the end, Archer makes no overt passes, but takes the narrator's shoes off, loosens his tie, and tucks him carefully into bed. Archer even has tea ready for him in the morning when he awakens. The good times end when the older brother returns earlier than expected and assumes the worst between Archer and his brother, imagining a tryst. The older brother chases the narrator around the room, trying his best to give him a good whipping. If the reader's mind had not been prejudiced by the older brother's suspicions, the story would have been a clean and simple episode.

Motivation for friendship is more obvious in "The Judas Tree." The action revolves around an art student and a retired schoolteacher, described as a dandy. The schoolmaster wants to acquire a painting that depicts the hanging of Judas. He has many paintings of Judas, most of which are Last Supper scenes, and we can only guess why the teacher identifies with this figure. Perhaps he is guilty about his homosexuality and feels that in some way he is betraying his companions or mankind in general because of his sexuality. A picture of Judas as he is hanged would allow the teacher to work out his guilt in transference.

The schoolmaster asks the student to paint the picture he desires so much. After relentless pressure the student agrees, at which point he begins to avoid his eccentric patron. He later regrets his actions, sensing the man's loneliness and pain, and tries to make up for his neglect of the project. The student is rejected in his attempts to make amends and ends by feeling Judaslike.

"Brave and Cruel" is narrated by a successful writer and painter named Dave, who proceeds to tell the story of a certain Micki Beaumont. Micki is proud of the many women he has duped and of his finesse as a liar. When Dave paints an oil portrait of Micki, he is thrust into his subject's reality and is shocked by the confrontation.

Dave is a firm believer that certain social classes should not try to rise above their appointed station in life. Welch subtly transforms the two men's roles as the story continues, remaking Micki as the nobler of the two. It becomes apparent that Welch prefers the honesty of those who are down and out and forced to lie and steal to the artificial stuffiness of London's upper class. Though both Dave and Micki have their unsavory aspects, both see themselves in ways they never would have had they not met, with Dave's revealing oil portrait of Micki and Micki's realization that for all his faults he had not succumbed to the class snobbishness of Dave. The final question posed by "Brave and Cruel" is about defining who the real criminals in the world might be.

FRAGMENTS, POEMS, AND JOURNALS

The only medium with which Welch struggled unsuccessfully was poetry. Critics generally panned this work, which at best was weakly derivative of A. E. Housman. Welch himself was never satisfied with it, and that is perhaps why so little survives (Only sixty-seven of his poems are collected in book form.). The following work, simply called "Poem," published in the posthumous book *Dumb Instrument* (1976), contains many of Welch's (and Housman's) familiar touches and phrases:

A few years back
with drink and love
the rowdy boys were gay;
But I sat still
to wonder at
and watch their play.

Now I am sad
And long to catch
that bright, uprushing flame;
But all the drinks
Are drunk now
And the feet are lame.

Even as a footnote to readers seeking insight into Welch's method, the poetry falls short.

Welch's journals, on the other hand, which have drawn favorable comparisons to Ned Rorem's *Paris Diary* (1966) and W. N. P. Barbellion's *The Journal of a Disappointed Man* (1919), have been mined for insights into Welch's craftsmanlike approach to writing. Welch wrote about how slowly he worked, often writing as little as four paragraphs a day; frequently he was slowed by blinding headaches. He frequently wrote entries about his conscious use of symbol in his work, which sheds some light on ongoing debates among scholars who argue that too much symbolism has been read into Welch's work.

Many entries convey the excitement of arriving at an important thought, idea, or discovery. Oftentimes Welch sketched an outline for a book, leaving behind fragments of serious work he lost interest in or simply failed to complete. The current published edition of his journals is, unfortunately, a selection (spanning 1942–1948), comprising only half of his work in this form. Some parts were cut to avoid embarrassment to those still living. We can only hope that one day soon a complete edition will be published.

Welch's life leaves readers with a list full of "what ifs." What if Welch had not had his accident? Would he have been so introspective? Would he have followed his painting career? What if he had lived another twenty years? What would have interested him if he had?

Since his death Welch's reputation has risen, sunk, gone into dormancy, rebloomed. Perhaps if he were alive today to see how his literary reputation has grown, he would no longer need to utter his primal scream.

SELECTED BIBLIOGRAPHY

I. NOVELS. *Maiden Voyage* (London, 1943); *In Youth Is Pleasure* (London, 1945); *A Voice Through a Cloud* (London, 1950).

II. SHORT STORY COLLECTIONS. *Brave and Cruel* (London, 1948); *A Last Sheaf* (London, 1951).

III. OTHER WORKS. "A Visit with Sickert," short story published in *Horizon Magazine* (November 1942); *The Denton Welch Journals,* ed. by Jocelyn Brooke (London, 1952); *I Left My Grandfather's House* (London, 1958); *Denton Welch: A Selection from His Published Works,* ed. by Jocelyn Brooke (London, 1963). *Dumb Instrument* (poems) ed. by Jean-Louis Chevalier (London, 1976).

IV. BIOGRAPHY AND CRITICISM. Robert Phillips, *Denton Welch* (New York, 1974); Michael De-la-Noy, *Denton Welch: The Making of a Writer* (New York, 1984); Brendan Lemon, "A Model Short Form," *Christopher Street* 8 (1984); Caleb Crain, "It's Pretty, But Is It Broken?" *New York Times Book Review* 148 (1999); P. N. Furbank, "Like Steam Escaping," *London Review of Books* 24 (2002); Selina Hastings, "A Fragile, Precocious Talent," *Spectator* 288 (2002); Frances Spalding, "A Talent for Tidiness," *Times Literary Supplement* (2002).

CHARLES WALTER STANSBY WILLIAMS

1886–1945

Charles Robert Baker

THE FEW PUBLISHED photographs of Charles Williams present a man who appears to be much older than he actually is, a long-faced, tight-lipped, bespectacled man with a broad brow. Nowhere in Williams's visage is there to be found the childlike merriment evident in photographs of his friend C. S. Lewis or the elfin mischievousness of another friend, J. R. R. Tolkien. A photograph included in Alice Mary Hadfield's *Charles Williams: An Exploration of His Life and Work* (1983) shows Williams and fellow poet William Butler Yeats in an informal pose; Yeats, with arms folded across his stomach, wears an amused grin, Williams looks as grave as an undertaker. Nothing in Williams's outward appearance betrays the fact that he was a man filled with romantic passions and supernatural imaginings.

CHILDHOOD, EDUCATION, AND OXFORD UNIVERSITY PRESS

Charles Williams was born on 20 September 1886 in the northern London community of Holloway. All biographical accounts report that Williams enjoyed a secure and peaceful childhood in a loving household. His father, Walter Williams, on the other hand, had grown up in a troubled environment. Walter's birth had cost his mother her life, and he was raised by his grandmother. His father's next marriage was to a troublesome woman who caused a great deal of unpleasantness before abandoning Walter and his father permanently. Walter may have harjbored some feelings of responsibility for his father's chronic unhappiness, since he delayed his own marriage in order to provide the man financial assistance.

For several years, Walter was engaged to Mary Wall, the daughter of a cabinet maker, James Wall. Mary's brother Charles and sister Alice were lively and intelligent companions for the betrothed, all sharing a love of literature and history. Indeed, Charles Wall wrote several books on English antiquities that he published himself. Walter, not to be outdone by his future brother-in-law, had adopted an uncle's name, Stansby, as a pseudonym and wrote stories, plays, and poems. Some of these had been published in Charles Dickens's magazine, *Household Words*. Finally, in 1884 the Anglican Church solemnized Walter and Mary's exchange of vows. Walter accepted the sacraments of baptism and confirmation just prior to his marriage and began a long and faithful membership in the Church of England.

Williams began attending services at St. Anne's Church with his family at the age of three. Walter and Mary Williams, whose family had grown to include a daughter, Edith (1889), were devout and joyous Anglicans who often attended both Sunday services and Williams was far from reluctant to be taken with them. Indeed, in her unpublished manuscript, "Memories of Early Days at Home," Edith Williams recalls her mother saying that young Charles "marched into church as if he owned the place." Williams became as familiar with St. Anne's as he was with his own home. A relatively new church, St. Anne's was built in 1871 and incorporated all the lofty splendors of late Victorian architecture. The Anglican service and the vast scope of the edifice combined to inspire awe in Williams and his family. Alice Mary Hadfield wrote in her biography, *Charles Williams: An Exploration of His Life and Work*, "The lofty building expanded their familiar home life into another, while the music and singing, the regular yet changing marvel of the psalms and collects, filled their minds with strength, wonder and refreshment" (p. 5).

Another essential bonding element of the family was its devotion to the world of letters. Walter Williams shared his love of literature with his young children, reciting poems and instilling the basics of writing and recognizing letters. By the age of five Williams was an avid reader and, although it stretched the family's finances, he was enrolled in a private school, St. Mary Magdalene. Shortly thereafter, however, a crisis occurred that briefly disrupted this idyllic life.

Walter Williams worked as a clerk for a firm of importers. It was his job to correspond with French and German clients. The firm had suffered two serious setbacks and it stood on precarious financial ground. Additionally, Walter's vision began to deteriorate, making it difficult for him to perform his duties. In 1894 the firm dissolved and Walter found himself jobless and nearly blind. A specialist advised him to leave the coal-smoke that clouded London and move away from the city if he wished to retain what sight he had left. Into this dilemma stepped Walter's brother-in-law, Charles Wall. Wall made it possible for the Williams family to move to the village of St. Albans, twenty miles northwest of the polluted city air. There he provided additional assistance by making arrangements for Walter and Mary to purchase an empty shop "The Art Depot," that was located between a tobacconist and a tailor. Wall also stocked the shop with the necessary merchandise, stationery and art supplies. The property included a large house and garden. Indeed, the house was so large that the Williamses were able to rent out two of its rooms and thereby augment their income from the shop.

Williams was enrolled in the St. Albans Abbey School where he proved to be an indifferent student who nonetheless managed to win annual prizes for his classwork. His father's library provided him a vast array of subjects to explore but Williams found that literature and history gave him the most satisfaction: the historical romances of Dumas, the scientific fantasies of Verne, the gothic tales of Hawthorne, and the heart breaking novels of Dickens. The large house in St. Albans was also the site of many family poetry recitations and amateur theatricals. A particular pleasure Williams enjoyed while growing up in St. Albans was long walks with his father. Together they discussed poetry and Williams's first attempts at creating it. Williams always remembered his father as his first and best teacher and paid one of many poetic tributes to him in these lines from the title poem of his 1920 collection, *Divorce,*

Each to his teachers,—nor of mine,
Though long and lofty be the line,
    Shall any, sir, be set
More high in this poor heart than you
Who taught me all the good I knew
    Ere Love and I were met:

The family business suffered all the financial uncertainties inherent in such ventures. It became evident that Walter was not the man to run things and Mary took over. Fortunately it was during a period of solvency that Williams won a small scholarship to University College in London. The scholarship was enough to pay for tuition; Mary paid for the remaining fees, books, supplies, and commuter fares. Seventeen-year-old Williams immersed himself in the study of mathematics, literature, languages, and history. The poet A. E. Housman instructed him in Latin. Housman's *A Shropshire Lad* was still wildly popular when Williams entered his classroom in 1903, but the elegiac, somewhat sentimental poetry, with its combination of classical tradition and modernist economy, does not seem to have made an impression on the poet Williams became. Housman did, however, provide Williams with a fine example of a professional poet and lecturer.

The strain that supplementing Williams's scholarship caused the family finances reached a breaking point after two years and he was forced to withdraw from University College. Nineteen years old and without any marketable skills, Williams had little choice but to take a civil service examination and hope that he qualified for some sort of government employment. His test scores, however, were too low. It is remarkable that he did not simply help in the family business but for some unexplained reason that solution was not viable. As he had before, Charles Wall provided a solution to the Williams'ss family dilemma. He found work for the restless young man at the Methodist Bookroom in London. The job, which consisted of packing books in boxes, must have proved exceedingly boring to the inquisitive young man. He kept his mind active and fed by teaching at the Abbey Sunday School, attending night classes at the Working Man's College, and participating in the meetings of two debating societies.

Through the college and the debating societies, Williams met others who shared his passion for the written word. He enjoyed the good-humored camaraderie of a wide circle of friends who critiqued each other's poetry and discussed the burning issues of their times, but it was one man in particular who opened a door for Williams that would make all the difference in his life. Fred Page was an editor at Oxford University Press with the arduous task of proofreading seventeen volumes of William Makepeace Thackeray for publication. Page was allowed an assistant and he suggested to the publisher that Charles Williams would be an ideal choice. Williams was hired by Oxford University Press on 9 June 1908 to work for Page in the Paper, Printing and Proofreading Department, and he remained with the publishing house until his death thirty-seven years later.

MARRIAGE AND EARLY POETRY

The year 1908 was momentous for Williams in another way. In addition to finding a suitable place for himself among London's community of working men and women, he found the missing ingredient that he later proclaimed was absolutely essential for a complete life: Love. It was while he was helping decorate for a Christmas party at St. Alban's that he met and fell in love with Florence Conway. We know from the preface to Anne Ridler's *The Image of the City and Other Essays* (1958) that the tall, twenty-three-year-old Williams was quite shy about approaching Miss Conway. Florence remembered during the first

five minutes of their meeting that she thought she had never met a man who said so little, and for the rest of the evening that she had never met a man who said so much. For his part, Williams was completely enthralled. Soon he composed eighty-four sonnets that he presented to Florence in January for her approval. He called the sequence *The Silver Stair* (1912), and in it we find the first stirrings of Williams's imagination in regard to love's source and its ultimate cost. Even in the most exuberant exultations of feeling Williams reminds himself of love's ultimate end.

I love her. O! what other word could keep
   In many tongues one clear immutable sound,
   Having so many meanings? It is bound,
First, to religion, signifying: "The steep
Whence I see God," translated into sleep
   It is: "Glad waking," into thought: "Fixed ground;
   A measuring-rod," and for the body: "Found."
These know I, with one more, which is: "To weep."
            (Sonnet 38, lines 1–8)

Williams at first may have meant the poems to be nothing more than aids in his courtship of Florence, but he showed them to Page, who in turn sent them to Alice Meynell. Meynell was at that time gaining a considerable reputation as a Roman Catholic poet whose most successful poems dealt with religious mysteries. She met with Williams and was so impressed with the young man and his work that she offered, along with her husband, Wilfrid Meynell, to have *The Silver Stair* published at their expense by the London firm of Herbert & Daniel. In November 1912, Williams's poetry made its first appearance to the reading public. It raised little interest, however, outside his circle of friends and his colleagues at Oxford University Press. Williams was not discouraged; the favorable recognition he received from Meynell in addition to that from Humphrey Milford, who was soon to be named Publisher at Oxford University Press, and Sir Walter Raleigh, Professor of Poetry at Oxford, was enough to spur Williams on to produce more poems.

Williams's courtship with Florence continued despite the fact that her family found the young man unsuitable. The couple also had to deal with the ever-increasing demands on Williams's salary by his family's failing business. Marriage, even an official announcement of engagement had to be delayed. When the Great War broke out in August 1914, Williams was spared the horrors of the bloody battlefields by being declared medically unfit. He was not spared the horrors of losing two of his best friends, however. While Williams did civilian war duty in London and St. Albans, his close comrades, Harold Eyers and Ernest Nottingham, died in France. Poetry ceased for a while.

Williams buried himself in his work at the press, which at that time was located in Amen Corner near St. Paul's Cathedral. In addition to two ambitious works the press was preparing for the tercentenary of Shakespeare's death, Williams had a part in the publication of *The Oxford Book of Mystical Verse* (1917). One contributor in particular caught Williams's attention, A. E. Waite. Waite, a poet with a strong interest in the occult, was the leader of a secret, ritualistic society, the Order of the Golden Dawn. Williams knew of Waite's scholarship in Grail (or Graal, as Williams preferred to spell it) literature, a subject that fascinated Williams. Waite and his order were to play a significant role in Williams's development as a poet and theologian but most particularly as a novelist.

In 1917, feeling himself firmly established at Oxford University Press, Williams married Florence on 17 April. They both moved from their families' homes into a small apartment in north London. In that same year Williams's second book of poetry, *Poems of Conformity,* was published. Like *The Golden Stair,* it caused little stir among reviewers and readers. The title is somewhat misleading, coming as soon as it did after Williams's marriage. The "conformity" he writes of, however, is not that of a newlywed adjusting to married life; instead it is human love conforming itself to the holy love it shares with God in Christ. These are love poems of a different sort; instead of extolling love's impact upon the human recipient, Williams marvels at his personal discovery that love, particularly in its physical expression, unites the couple with the divine and is as sacramental as any rite of the church. Although Williams confesses in one poem that more wisdom is to be found at a lover's breast than on one's knees at prayer, he docs not abandon the church. He instead adds a sexual dimension to Jesus' commandment "to love one another."

Another volume of poetry published three years later bears a misleading title, *Divorce* (1920). Although Williams experienced the stressful anxieties and disappointments inherent in marriage, these poems do not reflect a desire to bring an end to it. Rather they explore the forces that divorce us from one another: schism, illness, death, and, indeed, our own lack of dedication. *Divorce* is the antithesis of *Poems of Conformity* in much the same way Blake's *Songs of Innocence* is shadowed by *Songs of Experience.*

A fourth volume of poetry, *Windows of Night,* was published in 1925. Although the collection includes many poems of intimacy and affection, the overall tone is one of unrelenting pessimism. It is clear that Williams's joy in his discovery that we are joined to Christ through our expressions of love has matured to acceptance of the fact that in our union with Christ we are subject to the same betrayal and death as He.

DOMESTIC DIFFICULTIES
AND THE OTHER WOMAN

There are a few outer occurrences that can account for Williams's inner turmoil, his pessimism, indeed his self-loathing, at this time. In 1922 his friend, mentor, confidante, and benefactor Alice Meynell died. That same year his only child, Michael Stansby Williams, was born. It appears that Williams was temperamentally unsuited for fatherhood; in letters to friends he often complains that the baby, like Christ, came not to bring peace but a sword. Additionally, he found himself resenting the redirection of his wife's affection and attention caused by Michael's arrival. His exploration of the divine through physical intimacy with Florence was often interrupted or made impossible by her motherly devotion to her child.

Domesticity was in conflict with his development as a writer and he gained reprieve from its demands, as well as some additional income, by accepting an invitation for the London County Council to give a series of lectures at the Holloway Literary Institute. Williams's evening classes, which began in 1924 and continued until 1939, gave him a much-needed opportunity to express and exchange ideas with a broad range of people. Young and old, office workers and day laborers crowded into his classroom and enthusiastically took part in the discussions. This was far different from the reception his ideas received at home. Indeed, he had renamed his wife "Michal" after the biblical daughter of King Saul. In 2 Samuel 6:16 Michal sees King David leaping for joy and dancing naked before the ark of the Covenant as it enters his city, "and she despised him in her heart." She rebukes him for acting like a fool and exposing himself to "the handmaids of his servants." King David replies, "And I will yet be more vile than thus, and will be base in mine own sight: and of the maidservants which thou hast spoken of, of them shall I be had in honour." Florence not only accepted that her husband used this name for her publicly, privately, and in his poems, she fully adopted it as her own and identified herself as "Michal" for the rest of her life. In doing so she made it clear to Williams that the differences of temperament that existed between them would have to coexist with the affection they enjoyed.

Another element of disruption was added when in 1924 Oxford University Press moved from the rather cramped quarters at Amen Corner to a much larger building, Amen House. The extra square footage allowed for the creation of a much-needed reference library. The woman hired to be the librarian was pretty, twenty-three-year old Phyllis Jones. Williams found himself struck by her beauty and intelligence; he also found himself confused by the passion she stirred in him. He believed wholeheartedly, along with the quintessential Victorian poet of holy matrimony, Coventry Patmore, in the sanctity of married love, yet now, in his late thirties, Williams felt that belief challenged as never before. It was time to collect his thoughts on the matter, and he did so in his first book of prose, *Outlines of Romantic Theology.*

Williams is quick to declare what he does not mean by the word "Romantic."

> This term does not imply, as will inevitably at first be thought, a theology based merely on fantasy and dream, and concerning itself only with illogical sentimentalities. It is a theology as exact as any other kind, but having for cause and subject those experiences of man which, anyhow in discussions of art, are generally termed "Romantic". The chief of these is romantic love; that is, sexual love between a man and a woman, freely given, freely accepted, and appearing to its partakers one of the most important experiences in life—a love which demands the attention of the intellect and the spirit for its understanding and its service.
>
> (p. 7)

Williams is also quick to clarify that although his observations are based on orthodox Christian theology, specifically the rites and dogmas of the Church of England as set forth in the *Book of Common Prayer,* he does not intend to correct or deny other religions. Indeed, it is his own church that is taken to task for neglecting to address the issue of marriage as a sacrament. He finds that the church exhorts the newly married couple to observe their moral duties and avoid divorce but says nothing about how to ensure that their initial love, that which led them to be joined in Christ through the matrimonial sacrament, will survive the weaknesses and temptations to which flesh is heir. To fill this void, Williams offers his own suggestions in chapters entitled "The New Testament in Romantic Theology," "The Mass in Romantic Theology," and "Dangers and Safeguards." chapter Six, "Doctors and Document," is of interest to Williams scholars since it contains the first explorations of two subjects that dominate Williams's later works: Dante's *Vita Nuova* and Malory's *Morte D'Arthur.* The manuscript of *Outlines of Romantic Theology* (1990) was refused by two publishers and remained unpublished until 1990.

Whatever insight he may have gained from his ruminations proved to be not enough to substantially change his domestic circumstances. The marriage endured the challenge posed not only by Phyllis but by other women through the years

CHARLES WALTER STANSBY WILLIAMS

who were mesmerized by Williams's teachings. Glen Cavaliero sums up the importance of Phyllis in the introduction to his book *Charles Williams: Poet of Theology* (1983):

> But this second love, perhaps for the very reason that it was never fulfilled and was only for a while returned, seems to have caused a self-questioning that was to result in the release of his full creative powers. It forced upon him the tragic awareness of a division within the good. Williams'ss innate pessimism and his thwarted romanticism made him peculiarly susceptible to this contradictory situation, which was to be a leading theme in his writings of the 1930s.
>
> (p. 5)

His fascination with Phyllis prompted him to write letters and poetry to her and embark on other, more ambitious, literary projects as well. In April 1927, an invited audience beheld a production of Williams's *The Masque of the Manuscript* in the library at Amen House with Phyllis in the starring role of Phillida. Other masques (with Phyllis always in a central role as either Phillida or Celia) and poems followed. While she was flattered by this intelligent older man's attentions to her, she did not love him. After ten years, Phyllis left the publishing house and married, but she never left Williams's thoughts and prayers; her essence appears as various characters in his later works, and they remained friends for the rest of their lives.

AN OXFORD (UNIVERSITY PRESS) EDUCATION

For an intelligent man who, for whatever reason, could not earn a university degree, there could not have been a better substitute than employment at Oxford University Press. And if that intelligent man also wished to be a published author, employment at the press opened doors of opportunity for him that otherwise would probably have been shut tight. Williams's keen intellect and natural instincts as a poet encouraged publisher Humphrey Milford to entrust him with ever-increasing editorial responsibilities. The selections for and the introduction to Oxford's *A Book of Victorian Narrative Verse* (1927) were

solely Williams's, and he collaborated with Milford and Page on *The Oxford Book of Regency Verse* (1928). Williams contributed to such standard reference works as *The Oxford Companion to English Literature* and *The Oxford Dictionary of Quotations*. An autodidact, he was certainly qualified to take on these scholarly tasks. A great deal of the work Williams did at the press involved editing and proofreading texts for Oxford's World's Classics and Standard Authors series. Thus, relatively quickly, Williams acquired an immense working knowledge of the world's greatest literature. Additionally, Williams read the manuscripts of many of the best-known writers of his day and passed his opinions on to Milford. New works by Eliot, Auden, Housman and others came under Williams's scrutiny, and through his correspondence with them these luminaries of modern English poetry became aware of him and his work.

Milford continued to take risks with Williams's own work. By 1929 Oxford had published three of Williams's books of poetry that were remarkable for their unsalability. According to Hadfield, Oxford's traveling salesmen were given these instructions when presenting a work by Williams, "Do *please* impress on your customers that it is *not* a book of minor poems but a collection that shall rank high in the scale of contemporary literature. . . . There is no doubt that Williams will one day be recognized as a very fine poet, and *then* those who possess early editions will be lucky!" (Hadfield, p. 52). In spite of the lack of interest in Williams, Milford decided to publish his verse play *A Myth of Shakespeare* in 1929. This highly imaginative play proved popular enough to warrant a second printing, and that was encouragement enough for Milford to publish Williams's *Three Plays* in 1931. The plays, all of them in verse, were *The Witch, The Rite of the Passion,* and *The Chaste Wanton.* All three have the death of love as their subject. Love dies at the hands of pure evil in *The Witch,* Love dies on the cross as part of God's redemptive plan for mankind in *The Rite of the Passion,* and, in the thinly veiled story of his crisis of conscience regarding Williams's love for Phyllis, Love dies through the sublimation of forbidden sexual desires in *The Chaste Wanton*. All three are somewhat weighted down by ornate language, but the curious reader will find in them the seeds of Williams's later pronouncements on the mysterious duality of human experience.

Williams's growing reputation as a literary critic was enhanced by the 1930 publication of his *Poetry at Present*. The sixteen essays are directed to Williams's particular audience, those who, like his students at his evening lectures, are not academics in the usual sense of the word but rather ordinary men and women who, after a day of work, enjoy a bit of culture. This is not to imply that Williams did not take this work seriously; indeed, part of Williams's success among his audience was the fact that he constantly challenged his readers to think beyond the limits of their areas of intellectual comfort. As he says in the preface, "This book is meant as an introduction to the works of certain contemporary poets, for those readers who do not know them, while not being, it is hoped, entirely without interest for those who do." The poets included are: Thomas Hardy, Robert Bridges, A. E. Housman, Rudyard Kipling, W. B. Yeats, W. H. Davies, Walter de la Mare, G. K. Chesterton, John Masefield, Ralph Hodgson, Wilfrid Gibson, Lascelles Abercrombie, T. S. Eliot, Edith, Osbert, and Sacheverell Sitwell, Robert Graves, and Edmund Blunden.

Each essay is introduced by a brief biographical statement and bibliography, then follows a keen analysis of the poet's work, work he clearly admires. These are not, however, essays written by minor poet who seeks to curry favor with those of established greatness; indeed, Williams is not reluctant to display outrage when he finds fault with a poem. For instance, when presenting these lines from Hardy's "Without Ceremony" (The example as printed in *Poetry at Present* contains a mistake: "To vanish . . . " should read "To be gone . . . "),

It was your way, my dear,
To vanish without a word
When callers, friends, or kin,
Had left, and I hastened in
To rejoin you, as I inferred.

Williams is quick to shout, "'As I inferred'! 'Inferred'! the circumlocution! the word bullied into its place for the sake of the rhyme!" (*Poetry at Present,* p.10). But neither is Williams reluctant to promote his own work and perhaps gain something by association. Each essay concludes with a laudatory poem written by Williams in the fashion of the poet concerned. The Hardy essay contains this end piece:

He knew the Comic Muse, and made her free
    of seedtime and of harvest, barn and mill;
      and—sole since Shakespeare—with a happy skill
restored her to her wise rusticity:
he knew the large debate of Destiny,
    disputing with itself of its own will,
shape and close moth of loveliest Tragedy.
All the vast movement of the worlds he saw,
proceeding and returning through the void
    of metaphysic to each dire event:
      Imagination with a deep content
beholds each crisis fashioned and destroyed
by that unswerving and unresting law.

                    (*Poetry at Present,* p.17)

The book did not make much of an impression on critics, but the public responded favorably enough to merit a second printing. Indeed, a few of the poets included in the volume wrote letters of admiration and appreciation. Gibson wrote: "I have now read all the articles with deep interest and much appreciation. I need hardly say how proud and pleased I was to find myself among the 'significant' poets" (Hadfield, p. 80). Blunden wrote that Williams's book "is by far the best thing of its kind I know" (Hadfield, p. 80). As satisfying as his reception as a literary critic must have been for Williams, he did not sit on those laurels long; he was soon surprised to find himself recognized for his achievements in a far different form of writing.

HUMAN AND HOLY RELATIONSHIPS

Before beginning a study of the novels of Williams, it is helpful to have an understanding of his views of human interaction and responsibility. Williams's views were formed by his idea of the city. Except for one brief trip to Paris in January

CHARLES WALTER STANSBY WILLIAMS

1938 to deliver a lecture, "On Byron and Byronism," at the Sorbonne, Williams spent his entire life in and around London. Unlike many of his contemporaries who regarded the city as a place of corruption and decay and who sought the meaning of life on earth through Nature, Williams saw the city as the model of God's kingdom on earth and viewed the relevance of pastoral beauty with a city-dweller's skepticism. Through his daily interactions with his fellow citizens and his unswerving belief in the teaching of the Anglican Church, Williams developed a theory of human relationships based on three principles: exchange, substitution, and co-inherence.

Williams believed that all humanity exists in fellowship with not only the living but also the dead as well. We all share common needs that are met through a process of exchange. One simple example of exchange would be the creation of a birthday cake. Taken to its earliest state and followed to completion a birthday cake has many creators: the farmer who raises the wheat, the miller who grinds it into flour, the poultry man who sells the eggs, the dairyman who provides the milk, people in other parts of the world who harvest sugarcane, and many others. Without each of these providers working in a harmonious process of exchange of goods and services and money, neither the cake nor the providers of the ingredients could exist. When done properly the principle of exchange creates a society in which everyone benefits. Trouble arises when an individual or group or entire nation denies the principle and acts in a manner that is completely self-serving. A petty thief is a good example of someone who acts outside the principle, someone who simply takes what he wants without exchanging something else of value. If the thief is caught, his punishment often includes not only the return of the goods but payment of a fine as well. If the crime is particularly heinous, the offender is removed from society for a while. The principle also applies to mankind's relationship with God. Williams found the supreme embodiment of the principle of exchange in the Holy Eucharist wherein the gifts of the people to God, the elements of bread and wine, are accepted by God who in turn converts them into

his gift to the people, the body and blood of his Son, Jesus Christ. As with the thief, however, those who refuse to act their part in relation to God are separated from God for a time but ultimately pardoned and released to begin anew. Continued refusal results in the ultimate separation from God, eternal damnation in Hell.

Closely associated with the principle of exchange is the principle of substitution. Williams took the admonition by St. Paul in Galatians 6:2, "Bear ye one another's burdens, and so fulfill the law of Christ," quite literally. Using the example of Christ on the cross, Williams developed the idea that we, being one in the body of Christ, not only could but also are required to take on one another's burdens as he carried our sins. A taunt from the bystanders at the Crucifixion offers the best definition of substitution: in Mark 15:31 someone among the chief priests and scribes says, "He saved others; himself he cannot save." In other words, Jesus who was capable of healing others, indeed, to the point of raising his friend Lazarus from the grave, is incapable of doing the same for himself as he hangs helplessly upon the cross. Williams does not see Jesus' plight as a defeat, however; he sees it as proof that we do not achieve salvation by our own solitary efforts but through our dedicated devotion to the principles of substitution and exchange with others.

That idea leads to Williams's third principle, co-inherence. That principle is not unique to Williams; indeed it is as old as the Gospels and the concept of the Holy Trinity. In John 15:4 Jesus says, "Abide in me, and I in you. As the branch cannot bear fruit of itself, except it abide in the vine; no more can ye, except ye abide in me." The key word is "in." Co-inherence is not the same thing as coexistence. Coexistence means to exist together, whereas co-inherence means that we exist or abide in one another and are inseparable from all creation, past, present and future. We help each other "bear fruit" through the processes of exchange and substitution.

Another concept helpful in understanding Williams and his work is that of the Way of Affirmation of Images and the Way of Rejection of Images. Simply put, both Ways are pathways to God. Those who choose the Way of Affirmation, and this included Williams, seek God in all of creation; from the most mundane and ordinary and even unpleasant areas of human art and activity, to the most glorious. They see a reflection of God in everything. Those who choose the Way of Rejection do not deny that God is reflected in images; rather they choose to rid themselves of all mere representations in hopes of reaching the genuine article. Both are valid paths, and they co-inhere. Their co-inherence is best defined by one of Williams's trademark sayings, "This also is Thou, neither is this Thou." To the follower of Affirmation, the image points the way to God; to the follower of Rejection the image is a distraction. Williams warns throughout his works that there is a danger in following either way exclusively; too much Affirmation can lead to subservient idolatry and too much Rejection can lead to heretical denial. And neither way is easier than the other. As Williams writes in *The Figure of Beatrice* (1943),

> It is not to be rashly assumed that the Way of Affirmation is much easier than the Way of Rejection. To affirm the validity of an image one does not at the moment happen to like or want—such as that of one's next door neighbor—is as harsh as to reject an image—such as oneself as successful—which one does happen to like and want.
>
> (p. 13)

For Williams anything can be an image: poetry, music, fine art, religious services, acts of charity graciously and unself-consciously done, a beautiful woman. All contain the seed of transcendence, a glimpse of the heavenly kingdom. It is helpful to keep these concepts—co-inherence, substitution, exchange, the Way of Affirmation and the Way of Rejection—in mind as one reads any of Williams's work, but they are especially helpful in making one's way through the difficulties of his novels.

THE "ENTERTAINMENTS"

It was quite by accident that the first of Williams's seven novels, or "entertainments" as he preferred to call them, was published. In 1925 he had written a sensationalistic novel, *The Black Bastard* (later retitled *The Adepts of Africa*); it was followed in 1926 by *The Corpse*. He presented both manuscripts, parts one and two of an intended trilogy, to Faber and Faber and to Knopf. Both publishing houses rejected the works, and they were consigned to a wooden box in Williams's office, presumably never to be seen again. During an office clean-up in 1929, however, Williams's typist, Jocelyn Harris, came across the manuscript of *The Corpse*. Although Williams instructed her to throw it away, she instead sent it to Victor Gollancz. Gollancz, who had only recently started his publishing house, Victor Gollancz, Ltd., read the manuscript in one night and offered Williams a contract. The title, Gollancz insisted, must be changed, and Williams, who was at that time editing Milton's *Paradise Lost,* chose *War in Heaven.*

War in Heaven (1930) was the first of Williams's novels to be published, but it was not the first to be written. *Shadows of Ecstasy,* a revision of *The Black Bastard,* was written earlier but not published until 1933. The reader who chooses to study the novels of Williams in the order in which he wrote them is met with some challenges in *Shadows of Ecstasy.* Indeed it is, despite its exciting though thoroughly implausible plot, the least satisfying of the seven. There is a sense that Williams did not stand with one side or the other in the central conflict and thus leaving the reader wondering what message the author is attempting to convey. Perhaps that is why this novel was held back and not published until four other, more accessible novels had met with some popular success.

The central character of *Shadows of Ecstasy* is Nigel Considine. Considine has come to the University of London to lecture on his findings in South America and Africa. He claims that Western civilization has become stagnant due to its dependence on logic and science and its reluctance to look beneath the surface of experience to find the mysteries that lie there. What Considine has learned through his contact with the native cultures along the Amazon and Zambesi Rivers is that Western man is content with mere shadows or external embodiments, whereas the so-called primitive peoples of the world are much more in tune with the true meaning of life. He claims that by redirecting the energy spent on grasping at the shadows of those things that give ecstasy one can achieve immortality. This seems harmless enough, and some of the novel's characters see merit in Considine's call to reject the shadows and follow his example. It soon becomes clear that Considine's goal is not the winning of a few converts; indeed he desires nothing less than complete world domination. To achieve this end he has rallied the African nations in armed rebellion against Europe. African troops invade London and add to the terror inflicted by bombs dropped from African aircraft.

> I have let the English feel panic, panic such as they have not felt since the Vikings raided their coasts and burned their towns a thousand years ago. They have been afraid of their feelings, of ecstasy and riot and savage glee; they have frozen love and hated death. And I have shown them these things wild and possibly triumphant; and what fear of a thousand armies will not do, fear of their own passions will.
>
> (p.152)

Ultimately, Considine, whose strict adherence to his principles has allowed him to live for more than two hundred years, is felled by one of his followers. Without their leader, the rebellions cease, and some normalcy returns to the lives of the novel's characters. In the final chapter, however, a submarine appears at Considine's seaside estate and spirits his body away, leaving the reader with many questions. Is Considine dead or merely wounded? Will he revive, either through the effects of some mystical rite performed by his followers or through natural healing, and return to complete his work?

War in Heaven opens with a scene that is in the finest traditions of detective fiction. That is not surprising, since at the time of its writing Williams was reviewing mystery novels for a London newspaper, the *News-Chronicle*. "The telephone bell was ringing wildly, but without result, since there was no-one in the room but the corpse" (*War in Heaven*, p. 7). The investigation of the murder of the unfortunate man leads to Gregory Persimmons, a retired publisher and devotee of the occult, in whose former office the body had been found. The reader learns that Persimmons and his cohort Sir Giles Tumulty have discovered that the cup used by Jesus at the Last Supper, the Holy Graal, has somehow found its way to the parish church in Fardles, England. They want the cup, believing it can help them in their dark arts. A war ensues between those who would use the cup for evil, Persimmons and Tumulty, and those who are the cup's protectors and servants, Julian Davenant, the Anglican archdeacon of Fardles, first among them. The archdeacon is a splendid portrait of the true man of God, a man who has subdued his own will in order to become an agent for the will of God. He is also the embodiment of the balance between the Way of Affirmation of Images and the Way of Rejection of Images, regarding the Graal as a reflection of God's love but in actuality nothing more than a silver cup. He tells one of the Graal's defenders, "In one sense, of course, the Graal is unimportant—it is a symbol less near Reality now than any chalice of consecrated wine" (p. 37).

The Graal is stolen, recovered, and stolen again in a series of almost Wodehousian misadventures, but the humor ceases and the deadly seriousness of Persimmons's evil intentions sets the tone for the novel's final chapters. Persimmons, who has acquired the Graal for a third time, concocts a scheme whereby to lure the archdeacon to a pharmacy in London where two of the Graal's champions and the Graal itself are being held. Persimmons's trickery is matched by Williams who cleverly inserts an intervening chapter, "The Search for the House." The action in that chapter revolves around the continuing police investigation of the murder that occurred in chapter 1 and involves a disappearing building and the surrender of Persimmons. What led the arch-villain to turn himself in to the police is revealed in the two concluding chapters.

The archdeacon, secure in the knowledge that he is doing God's will arrives at the chemist's shop and is seized and bound by Persimmons and his fellow practitioners of black magic. He suffers the despair of feeling the power of God leaving him as he faces his enemies. Yet even in his overwhelming desolation he is able to say to himself, "This also is Thou." The archdeacon and the Graal are to be used in a bizarre occult rite wherein Persimmons attempts to recall the soul of the murdered man, a man, it turns out, Persimmons killed, and place it in the archdeacon's body. The obscenity is interrupted by the arrival of a man who has made appearances throughout the story, dispensing advice, comfort, and warnings. He is now revealed in his entire archangelic glory as Prester John, the mythical Eastern king-priest who is also the Keeper of the Grail in some of the Arthurian legends. He puts a stop to the evil being committed, sends Persimmons out to pay for his crimes, and restores the Graal to the archdeacon. The next day the king-priest celebrates a mass at Fardles. Through a clever exchange of lower case "h" for upper case, Williams transforms the celebrant into the true High Priest, Christ himself. During the service the archdeacon hears his name called from the altar three times; he begins to ascend the chancel steps but falls softly to the ground, dead. At that "the Graal and its Lord were gone" (p. 255).

Williams's next three novels follow the same storyline as *War in Heaven*; a supernatural object or force turns up and creates an unbalance in the lives of those who encounter it. In *Many Dimensions* (1931) the object of power is a stone that once rested in the crown of Solomon. In *The Place of the Lion* (1931) all the elemental, invisible forces that rule the world are unleashed. Finally, the original pack of Tarot cards brings havoc and horror to those who fall within its power in *The Greater Trumps* (1932). There are two later novels that break from this pattern and focus more on Williams's principles of substitution and exchange: *Descent into Hell* (1937) and *All Hallows' Eve* (1945).

Descent into Hell is unique in Williams's fiction in that there is no clearly identifiable villain; there are only common, everyday sorts of people who live common, everyday sorts of lives. Pauline Anstruther is a young woman who, after the death of her parents, has come to live with her grandmother, Margaret Anstruther in the fashionable London suburb, Battle Hill. Other inhabitants of this community include a well-known playwright, Peter Stanhope, and a military historian, Lawrence Wentworth. The action of the novel centers on the rehearsal of a play that Stanhope has offered to the locals for an amateur production. He becomes aware that something is troubling Pauline, and she confesses to him that from an early age she has been followed by an apparition that is her exact double. She is terrified that if the doppelganger ever catches up with her she will lose her sanity. Stanhope instructs her in the possibility of a goodness that is so good as to be terrifying; he also explains the principle of substitution and exchange. It is up to Pauline to come face-to-face with her double, but Stanhope will take her fear of the encounter onto himself. Initially Pauline thinks Stanhope's offer is silly and impossible but she soon finds that her terror has vanished, that she can fully enjoy those simple pleasures life has to offer, and that she too is capable of providing the same help to others. By admitting her need for help and, more importantly, accepting it, Pauline has entered the joy of the co-inherence and starts her journey toward a full and courageous life.

A parallel story reveals how denial of the co-inherence and refusal to participate in substitution and exchange leads to ultimate damnation. Wentworth is plagued by fears, as was Pauline; he, however, keeps them to himself. He has a recurring nightmare, a vision of himself holding onto a seemingly endless rope suspended in space. Above there is light; below there is darkness. Although the rope is knotted and he could climb toward the light, Wentworth chooses the easy descent. In his waking hours he makes the same easy, selfish choices that further isolate him from the co-inherence. Every occasion for joy that is possible for him he rejects or perverts: he prefers to envy rather than celebrate a fellow historian's success, he creates an imaginary double, a succubus, of a woman he is attracted to rather than pursue the more difficult course of human interaction, and, when asked to provide his expert advice on the military costumes to be used in Stanhope's play, he lies about their authenticity in order to return quickly to his solitary fantasy life. Finally, he reaches the end of the rope; he no longer has the option of ascending and he falls into a state of idiotic madness.

In *Descent into Hell,* Williams argues that it is the seemingly innocuous choices we make in our lives that propel us toward salvation or damnation. He also proposes that we live in eternity, that all that ever happened exists simultaneously with the present. Pauline, for example, is able to perform charitable acts of kindness to two deceased men; one a relatively recent suicide who is trying to find his way back to the salvation of the city, and a distant Anstruther relative whose fear of fire Pauline takes onto herself thereby freeing him to face his Marian martyrdom rejoicing in God's goodness as he is burned at the stake. The ability of the dead to aid the living is explored in Williams's last novel, published a month before his death, *All Hallows' Eve* (1945).

THE ARTHURIAN POEMS

It would perhaps be helpful to the first-time reader of Williams's two volumes of poems that concern "The Matter of Britain," that is, the stories of King Arthur, to understand what the poems are not. They are not a retelling of the familiar tales written by Geoffrey of Monmouth, Thomas Malory, and Lord Tennyson. Indeed, the poems do not tell a story at all, and Williams presupposes, and indeed the poems demand, a thorough understanding of those early works. The poems may be considered as meditations on certain aspects of the ancient stories or as a once familiar landscape seen from a different vantage point.

Taliessin Through Logres (1938) begins with a three-stanza prelude that is enticing in its obscurity. In the first stanza, the emperor, whose glory extends to the ends of the earth, establishes a kingdom in Britain. Misrule of this new kingdom is the subject of the second stanza, and finally invading Muslims disrupt the unity of the empire. Williams's vision of the Empire is represented by a drawing that served as endpapers in the first edition of *Taliessin Through Logres;* it shows that part of the world that stretches from Britain to the Far East as a reclining nude woman. Each part of the woman's body represents a specific area and its corresponding function. For instance, the woman's reproductive organs are placed over Jerusalem, the birthplace of Christianity; her breasts lie across Gaul, the place of universities that provide the nourishing milk of learning. The hands are placed upon Rome where the hands of the pope perform the Holy Eucharist; the buttocks are over Caucasia, a place of innocent sensual pleasures. The head of this organic body is Logres, the realm of Arthur and Merlin. Logres, which rhymes with "progress," is an ancient name for that area of Britain that was inhabited by the Celts during the time of Arthur's kingdom. The name comes from the Welsh "Lloegyr." The figure's calves and feet dangle just below Arabia and are threatened by tentacles that arise from a hellish region Williams calls P'o-lu.

Anyone looking for a chronological story is immediately corrected by the next poem, "Taliessin Returns to Logres." We are not told where he has been or very much about who he is, other than that he is a bard who was raised by Druids. He has sailed across the Channel in search of Arthur's camp and rides horseback for three days through a forbidding wood inhabited by fearsome specters before he finds it. But he rides unafraid with his harp slung across his back, for he is obviously a Christian who believes that "the Mercy," one of many names Williams uses to identify God, will protect him. His arrival is suitably dramatic:

I saw a Druid light
burn through the Druid hills,
as the hooves of King Arthur's horse
rounded me in the night.
I heard the running of flame
faster than fast through Logres
into the camp by the hazels
I Taliessin came.

There follows a lengthy poem, "The Vision of the Empire," that describes in detail the organic whole of creation. Young Arthur meets Merlin who calls upon him to rid the nation of the evil King Cradlemas and build Camelot in "The Calling of Arthur." "Mount Badon" is a stirring battle poem wherein Taliessin is not only the king's poet but a captain in the king's cavalry as well. Williams uses his notion that all of history is happening simultaneously in eternity to great effect in this poem. At one point in the battle, Taliessin, who is holding his troops in back until the right moment, has a vision of Virgil composing *The Aeneid.* He sees the Roman poet searching for just the right word and when his stylus begins to write, Taliessin knows it is time for his troops to enter the fray.

Civilised centuries away, the Roman moved.
Taliessin saw the flash of his style
dash at the wax; he saw the hexameter spring
and the king's sword swing; he saw, in the long field,
the point where the pirate chaos might suddenly yield,
the place for the law of grace to strike.
He stood in his stirrups; he stretched his hand;
hc fetched the pen of his spear from its bearer;
his staff behind signed to their men.

The battle is won, Arthur is crowned, and the next several poems reflect life in Logres. There are love poems, poems of exchange and substitution, particularly "Taliessin on the Death of Virgil" and poems relating the fall of Logres. A second book of Arthurian poems was published six years later, *The Region of the Summer Stars* (1944). The first poem in this collection, "The Calling of Taliessin," is a long narrative that answers many of the questions about Taliessin that readers of the first book may have had. We learn of Taliessin's birth and upbringing among the Druids, his decision to travel to Byzantium to learn more about a new myth that had begun to circulate, that of a man who was crucified and rose from the dead. On his way he has a vision of Merlin and Brisen, Merlin's sister. Merlin gives Taliessin a glimpse of the future and the role he, Taliessin, has to play. The wizard is aware, however, that all may not go as planned, and he instructs Taliessin to gather a household about him during his travels so that the king's poet, as he will become, and his followers may carry on the principles of substitution and exchange if Arthur's kingdom falls. Such a gathering of souls is accomplished, and "The Founding of the Company" declares,

The Company throve by love, by increase of peace,
by the shyness of saving and being saved by others
the Christ-taunting and Christ-planting maxim
which throughout Logres the excellent absurdity held.

Poems of life within the Company follow. The penultimate poem, "The Meditation of Mordred," is a vivid reminder of the perils faced by those who scorn the co-inherence. Finally there is the masterful poem that presents virtually all of Williams's ideas and beliefs, "The Prayers of the Pope."

The poems in these two volumes have carried the onus of being regarded as "difficult" since they first appeared, and indeed they do require much of the reader. Perhaps the best way to approach them is by reading them out loud, discovering thereby the internal rhyme schemes, the unevenness of the lines, and the pounding consonants and alliteration reminiscent of early Anglo-Saxon poetry. As a reader makes him- or herself familiar with some of the more obscure places and personages of Arthurian mythology, Williams's poems will reveal multilayered depths of meaning. The effort expended in understanding Williams's Arthurian poetry, or any "difficult" poetry whether it is that of the Beowulf poet or Seamus Heaney, is immensely rewarded.

OXFORD AND THE INKLINGS

In 1939, England declared war on Nazi Germany, and many enterprises housed in London found it prudent to move their offices and essential staff away from the city that was soon to become the primary target of Hitler's bombers. The London offices of the Oxford University Press were relocated to Southfield House, Oxford, and it was there Williams remained for the duration of the war. Williams's disappointment in being forced to leave his familiar and beloved city was heightened by his wife's decision to remain behind with their son. Oxford did, however, offer a convivial company of like-minded writers and poets. Foremost among them was C. S. Lewis.

Lewis and Williams had exchanged letters of mutual admiration in 1936, Williams praising Lewis' *The Allegory of Love,* and Lewis returning the compliment on Williams's *The Place of the Lion.* Now that Williams was in Oxford, Lewis, a longtime fellow and lecturer in English literature at Magdalen College, was determined to make use of him. Despite Williams's lack of a degree, Lewis secured a lectureship for him at the university. Throughout the war, Williams lectured regularly on Milton, Shakespeare, Wordsworth and others. His lectures were very popular and always well attended. T. S. Eliot, who had met Williams in the 1920s and who became a close friend when Williams's play, *Thomas Cranmer of Canterbury* (1936), was being produced for the Canterbury Festival, describes Williams's style as a lecturer:

> As a platform speaker, he was certainly unusual, and had, to an exaggerated degree, some of those mannerisms which uninspired speakers should most sedulously avoid. He was never still: he writhed and swayed; he jingled coins in his pocket; he sat on the edge of the table swinging his leg; in a torrent of speech he appeared to be saying whatever came into his head from one moment to the next. But what would have been the ruin of another lecturer contributed to Williams's success; he held his audience in rapt attention, and left with them the contagion of his own enthusiastic curiosity.
>
> (Preface to *All Hallows' Eve,* p. xii)

Away from the gothic halls and classrooms, Williams enjoyed the company of a mixed group of writers known as The Inklings. Lewis was the recognized leader of this fellowship and meetings were held in his rooms at Magdalen and occasionally at local pubs, either The White Horse or The Eagle and Child. Members, such as Owen Barfield and J. R. R. Tolkien, would read from their works-in-progress and open the floor to discussion. Williams was a regular attendee and exerted a powerful influence on atheist turned pantheist Lewis's decision to embrace Christianity.

Oxford was a relatively peaceful place during the war years. Although concerned about the horrors being faced by his wife and son in London, Williams found it possible, in addition to his duties at the press and his lecture schedule at the university, to produce much work. Poetry, plays and fiction were put aside for a while and he concentrated on nonfiction. Most of the work from 1938 through 1945 focused on an objective study of what can be called the theology of romantic love, a subject he had first addressed in an earlier work, *Outlines of Romantic Theology.* Throughout his adult life Williams believed that physical, romantic love revealed a greater dimension of God than one found while on one's knees in church. Although he recognized the shortcomings of the Anglican Church, he attended services regularly.

The first of these studies, *He Came Down from Heaven* (1938), is dedicated to his wife and suggests that it was through her that he found the conjoining of human love and Christianity: "To Michal by whom I began to study the doctrine of glory." The work is divided into two parts: the first part exploring God's relationship with humanity and the second our relationship with one another. *The Descent of the Dove* (1939) follows the emergence of the Holy Spirit in the Christian church from the Ascension of Christ to the outbreak of World War II.

For Williams, God and Heaven are nonnegotiable facts that we are free to affirm or reject. His next two books present the consequences of rejection and the means by which those who have strayed may be reunited with the co-inherence. *Witchcraft* (1941) addresses the misuse or perversion of images, the reality of evil, and the church's historical use of the devil as a necessary adversary. *The Forgiveness of Sins* (1942), which was dedicated to The Inklings, examines how the Spirit of Love prevails against the darkness of sin and rejection. Williams begins with a survey of how forgiveness is enacted in the plays of Shakespeare, follows with a history of forgiveness as expressed by the church, and concludes with his theories on how forgiveness should operate among mankind.

Perhaps the most successful attempt to explain his theories and principles of substitution, exchange, co-inherence, affirmation of images, rejection of images, and romantic theology can be found in Williams's *The Figure of Beatrice* (1943). For Williams, the story of Dante Alighieri (1265–1321) and Beatrice Portinari (1266—1290) represents the ultimate expression of his philosophy. Dante first saw Beatrice in their native city of Florence when he was nine years old and she was eight. His Beatrician moment came nearly ten years later when she first spoke to him. The curious stirrings of love enjoyed by Dante at that moment caused the poet to embark on a lifelong search for the source of such bliss. In Beatrice, Dante saw not only a beautiful woman but also the very essence of God's love for mankind, thereby recognizing the act of falling in love as a religious as well as a romantic experience. Williams investigates thoroughly Dante's poetic expression of his experience as recorded in *La Vita Nuova* (1292) and *Divina Commedia* (1310–1314). The Dante that emerges from Williams's work is far from being a long-dead, medieval Italian poet; indeed, he is presented as a vital voice that speaks to a universal and contemporary search for meaning.

A LATE RECOGNITION AND AN UNEXPECTED DEATH

In 1943, Williams, at the age of fifty-seven, received that which he had sought some forty years earlier: a university degree. In recognition of his tireless devotion to the school, Oxford University awarded Williams an honorary Master of Arts degree. Although much appreciated, the degree made very little difference to Williams's persistent economic anxieties. He continued in his usual pattern of working for the press in the morning, lecturing in the evenings, and finding what time he could for his writing.

The exhausting pace of his life may have been a contributing factor in the overall decline of his health during his last two years. On 10 May 1945, one day after the official end of World War II in Europe, Williams was admitted to Radcliffe Hospital in Oxford suffering from extreme digestive pain. It was a recurrence of a gastrointestinal problem for which he had undergone surgery eleven years earlier. Corrective surgery was performed on 14 May. Although the surgery was routine, Williams never regained consciousness and died the following day.

It is difficult to assess the impact of Williams's work on the general public. He never achieved the literary status of Lewis or Tolkien, and most of his works have long been out of print, although a surge of interest in Tolkien's *The Hobbit* (1937) and *The Lord of the Rings* (1954–1955) during the 1960s prompted Eerdmanns to reissue Williams's novels. His impact on his fellow writers, members of The Inklings, is evident in the publication of *Essays Presented to Charles Williams* (1947). This posthumous tribute to Williams gives the reader a glimpse of what a meeting of The Inklings must have been like. Lewis, Tolkien, Barfield, and Dorothy L. Sayers (who credits Williams with encouraging her to read Dante) made contributions that reveal their admiration for the man and his writings.

The question "Who is Charles Williams?" is difficult to answer. The sheer volume of his work in a variety of genres presents a problem to those who try to categorize him; his originality and depth of thought as well as his unique and sometimes difficult mode of verbal expression makes even the best attempt to summarize one of his novels or poems seem fatuous. Eliot wrote in the preface to *All Hallows' Eve:*

> To have known the man would have been enough; to know his books is enough; but no one who has known both the man and his works would have willingly foregone either experience. I can think of no writer who was more wholly the same man in his life and in his writings. What he had to say was beyond his resources, and probably beyond the resources of language, to say once for all through any one medium of expression. Hence, probably, the variety of forms in which he wrote: the play, the poem, the literary or philosophical essay, and the novel. Conversation for him was one more channel of communication. And just as his books attract and hold the reader's interest from the start, but have a great deal in them which only reveals itself on re-reading, so the man himself and an immediate charm and likeability, a radiation of benevolence and amiability which, while it concealed nothing, yet left the best of him to disclose itself gradually on better acquaintance.
>
> (p. xi)

It may be that the best answer to the question "Who is Charles Williams?" is found in the churchyard of St. Cross, Holywell, Oxford. There at his gravesite is a simple marker that reads: "Charles Williams. Poet. Under the Mercy."

SELECTED BIBLIOGRAPHY

I. POETRY AND VERSE PLAYS. *The Silver Stair* (London, 1912); *Poems of Conformity* (London, 1917); *Divorce* (London, 1920); *Windows of Night* (London, 1925); *An Urbanity* (London, 1925); *The Carol of Amen House* (London, 1927); *The Masque of the Manuscript* (London, 1927); *A Myth of Shakespeare* (London, 1929); *The Masque of Perusal* (London, 1929); *Heroes and Kings* (London, 1930); *The Masque of the Termination of Copyright* (London, 1930); *Three Plays: The Witch, The Rite of Passion, The Chaste Wanton* (London, 1931); *A Myth of Francis Bacon* (London, 1932); *Thomas Cranmer of Canterbury* (London, 1936); *Taliessin Through Logres* (London, 1938); *Judgment at Chelmsford* (London, 1939); *The Region of the Summer Stars* (London, 1944); *The House of the Octopus* (London, 1945).

II. NOVELS. *War in Heaven* (London, 1930; Grand Rapids, Mich., 1965); *The Place of the Lion* (London, 1931; Grand Rapids, Mich., 1965); *Many Dimensions* (London, 1931; Grand Rapids, Mich., 1965); *The Greater Trumps* (London, 1932; Grand Rapids, Mich., 1976); *Shadows of Ecstasy* (London, 1933; Grand Rapids, Mich., 1965); *Descent Into Hell* (London, 1937; Grand Rapids, Mich., 1965); *All Hallows' Eve* (London, 1945; Grand Rapids, Mich., 1969).

III. BIOGRAPHIES. *Bacon* (London, 1933); *James I* (London, 1934); *Rochester* (London, 1935); *Queen Elizabeth* (London, 1936); *Henry VII* (London, 1937); *Flecker of Dean Close* (London, 1946).

IV. LITERARY CRITICISM. *Poetry at Present* (London, 1930); *The English Poetic Mind* (London, 1932); *Reason and Beauty in the Poetic Mind* (London, 1933); *The Figure of Beatrice: A Study of Dante* (London, 1943; Rochester, N.Y., 1994); "The Figure of Arthur" in *Arthurian Torso* (London, 1948).

V. THEOLOGY. *He Came Down from Heaven* (London, 1938; Grand Rapids, Mich., 1984); *The Descent of the Dove: A History of the Holy Spirit in the Church* (London, 1939; Grand Rapids, Mich., 1965); *Witchcraft: A History of Black Magic in Christian Times* (London, 1941); *The Forgiveness of Sins* (London, 1942; New York, 1959).

VI. LETTERS. *Letters to Lalage: The Letters of Charles Williams to Lois Lang-Sims,* ed. and with a commentary by Lois Lang-Sims; introduction by Glen Cavaliero (Kent, Ohio, 1989); *To Michal from Serge: Letters from Charles Williams to His Wife, Florence, 1939–1945,* ed. by Roma A. King Jr. (Kent, Ohio, 2002).

VII. COLLECTED WORKS. *Arthurian Torso: Containing the Posthumous Fragment of "The Figure of Arthur" by Charles Williams and a Commentary on the Arthurian Poems of Charles Williams by C. S. Lewis* (London, 1948); *The Image of the City and Other Essays,* ed. by Anne Ridler (London, 1958); *Collected Plays by Charles Williams,* ed. by John Heath-Stubbs (London, 1963); *Outlines of Romantic Theology: With Which Is Reprinted Religion and Love in Dante: The Theology of Romantic Love,* ed. and introduced by Alice Mary Hadfield (Grand Rapids, Mich., 1990); *Charles Williams* (Includes *Taliessin Through Logres, The Region of the Summer Stars* and uncollected and unpublished Arthurian poems), ed. and introduced by David Llewellyn Dodds (Cambridge, 1991); *Charles Williams: Essential Writings in Spirituality and Theology,* ed. by Charles Hefling (Boston, 1993); *Masques of Amen House,* ed. by David Bratman, introduced by Hubert J. Foss (Minnetonka, Minn., 2000).

VIII. BIBLIOGRAPHY. Lois Glenn, *Charles W. S. Williams: A Checklist* (Kent, Ohio, 1975).

IX. BIOGRAPHICAL AND CRITICAL STUDIES. Alice Mary Hadfield, *An Introduction to Charles Williams* (London, 1959); Mary McDermott Shideler, *The Theology of Romantic Love: A Study in the Writings of Charles Williams* (Grand Rapids, Mich., 1962); Robert J. Reilly, *Romantic Religion: A Study of Barfield, Lewis, Williams and Tolkien* (Athens, Ga., 1971); Humphrey Carpenter, *The Inklings* (London, 1978); Agnes Sibley, *Charles Williams* (Boston, 1982); Glen Cavaliero, *Charles Williams: Poet of Theology* (London and Grand Rapids, Mich., 1983); Alice Mary Hadfield, *Charles Williams: An Exploration of His Life and Work* (London, 1983); Thomas T. Howard, *The Novels of Charles Williams* (New York, 1983); Roma A. King Jr., *The Pattern in the Web: The Mythical Poetry of Charles Williams* (Kent, Ohio, 1990); *The Rhetoric of Vision: Essays on Charles Williams,* ed. by Charles A. Hutter and Peter J. Schakel (Lewisburg, Pa., 1996); Colin Duriez and David Porter, *The Inklings Handbook: A Comprehensive Guide to the Lives, Thought and Writings of C. S. Lewis, J. R. R. Tolkien, Charles Williams, Owen Barfield and Their Friends* (London, 2001).

MASTER INDEX

The following index covers the entire British Writers series through Supplement IX. All references include volume numbers in boldface Roman numerals followed by page numbers within that volume. Subjects of articles are indicated by boldface type.

"All Things Ill Done" (Cameron), **Supp. IX:** 23–24

All Trivia (Connolly), **Supp. III:** 98

All What Jazz: A Record Diary, 1961–1968 (Larkin), **Supp. I:** 286, 287–288

Allan Quatermain (Haggard), **Supp. III:** 213, 218

"Allegiance, An" (Wallace-Crabbe), **VIII:** 315

Allegory of Love: A Study in Medieval Tradition (Lewis), **Supp. III:** 248, 249–250, 265

Allen, John, **IV:** 341, 349–350, 352

Allen, Walter Ernest, **V:** 219; **VI:** 257; **VII:** xvii, xxxvii, 71, 343

Allestree, Richard, **III:** 82

Allott, Kenneth, **IV:** 236; **VI:** xi, xxvii, 218

Allott, Miriam, **IV:** x, xxiv, 223n, 224, 234, 236; **V:** x, 218

All's Well That Ends Well (Shakespeare), **I:** 313, 318

"Allusion to the Tenth Satire of the Second Book of Horace" (Rochester), **II:** 259

Almayer's Folly (Conrad), **VI:** 135–136, 148; **Retro. Supp. II:** 70–71

Almeria (Edgeworth), **Supp. III:** 158

"Aloe, The" (Mansfield), **VII:** 173–174

Alone (Douglas), **VI:** 293, 294, 297, 304, 305

Alpers, Antony, **VII:** 176

"Alphabetical Catalogue of Names . . . and Other Material Things Mentioned in These Pastorals, An" (Gay), **III:** 56

Alphabetical Order (Frayn), **Supp. VII:** 60

"Alphabets" (Heaney), **Retro. Supp. I:** 131

Alphonsus, King of Aragon (Greene), **VIII:** 139–140

Alps and Sanctuaries (Butler), **Supp. II:** 114

"Alps in Winter, The" (Stephen), **V:** 282

Alroy (Disraeli), **IV:** 296, 297, 308

"Altar, The" (Herbert), **II:** 128

"Altar of the Dead, The" (James), **VI:** 69

"Altarwise by owl–light" (Thomas), **Supp. I:** 174–176

Alteration, The (Amis), **Supp. II:** 12–13

"Alternative to Despair, An" (Koestler), **Supp. I:** 39

Althusser, Louis, **Supp. IV:** 90

Alton, R. E., **I:** 285

Alton Locke (Kingsley), **V:** vii, xxi, 2, 4; **VI:** 240

"Altruistic Tenderness of LenWing the Poet, The" (Cameron), **Supp. IX:** 19

Altus Prosator (tr. Morgan, E.), **Supp. IX:** 169

Alvarez, A., **II:** 125n

Alvíssmál, **VIII:** 231

Amadeus (Shaffer), **Supp. I:** 326–327

Amadis of Gaul (tr. Southey), **IV:** 71

Amado, Jorge, **Supp. IV:** 440

Amalgamemnon (Brooke-Rose), **Supp. IV:** 99, 110–111, 112

Amateur Emigrant, The (Stevenson), **V:** 389, 396

"Amateur Film–Making" (Fuller), **Supp. VII:** 73

Amazing Marriage, The (Meredith), **V:** 227, 232, 233, 234

Ambarvalia: Poems by T. Burbidge and A. H. Clough, **V:** 159–160, 161, 170

Ambassadors, The (James), **VI:** 55, 57–59; **Supp. IV:** 371

"Amber Bead, The" (Herrick), **II:** 106

Amberley, Lady, **V:** 129

"Ambiguities" (Fuller), **Supp. VII:** 73

Ambler, Eric, **Supp. IV:** 1–24

Amboyna (Dryden), **II:** 305

Amelia (Fielding), **III:** 102–103, 105; **Retro. Supp. I:** 81, 89–90

"Amen" (Rossetti), **V:** 256

Amendments of Mr. Collier's False and Imperfect Citations (Congreve), **II:** 339, 340, 350

America. A Prophecy (Blake), **III:** 300, 302, 307; **Retro. Supp. I:** 39, 40–41

America I Presume (Lewis), **VII:** 77

American, The (James), **VI:** 24, 28–29, 39, 67

American Ghosts and Other World Wonders (Carter), **Supp. III:** 91

American Notes (Dickens), **V:** 42, 54, 55, 71

American Scene, The (James), **VI: 54, 62–64,** 67

American Senator, The (Trollope), **V:** 100, 102

American Visitor, An (Cary), **VII:** 186

"Americans in My Mind, The" (Pritchett), **Supp. III:** 316

"Ametas and Thestylis Making Hay–Ropes" (Marvell), **II:** 211

Aminta (Tasso), **II:** 49

"Amir's Homily, The" (Kipling), **VI:** 201

Amis, Kingsley, **Supp. II: 1–19; Supp. IV:** 25, 26, 27, 29, 377; **Supp. V:** 206

Amis, Martin, **Supp. IV: 25–44,** 65, 75, 437, 445

"Among All Lovely Things My Love Had Been" (Wordsworth), **IV:** 21

"Among School Children" (Yeats), **VI:** 211, 217

Among the Believers: An Islamic Journey (Naipaul), **Supp. I:** 399, 400–401, 402

Amores (tr. Marlowe), **I:** 276, 290

Amoretti and Epithalamion (Spenser), **I:** 124, 128–131

Amorous Cannibal, The (Wallace-Crabbe), **VIII:** 319, 320–321

"Amorous Cannibal, The" (Wallace-Crabbe), **VIII:** 319

Amorous Prince, The; or, The Curious Husband (Behn), **Supp. III:** 26

"Amos Barton" (Eliot), **V:** 190

Amours de Voyage (Clough), **V:** xxii, 155, 156, 158, 159, 161–163, 165, 166–168, 170

Amphytrion; or, The Two Sosias (Dryden), **II:** 296, 305

"Ample Garden, The" (Graves), **VII:** 269

Amrita (Jhabvala), **Supp. V:** 224–226

"Amsterdam" (Murphy), **Supp. V:** 326

Amusements Serious and Comical (Brown), **III:** 41

"Amy Foster" (Conrad), **VI:** 134, 148

An Duanaire: An Irish Anthology, Poems of the Dispossessed, 1600–1900 (Kinsella), **Supp. V:** 266

An Giall (Behan), **Supp. II:** 71–73

Anacreontiques (Johnson), **II:** 198

"Anactoria" (Swinburne), **V:** 319–320, 321

"Anahorish" (Heaney), **Retro. Supp. I:** 125, 128

Anand, Mulk Raj, **Supp. IV:** 440

"Anarchist, An" (Conrad), **VI:** 148

Anathemata, The (Jones), **Supp. VII:** 167, 168, 169, 170, 175–178

Anatomy of Exchange–Alley, The (Defoe), **III:** 13

Anatomy of Frustration, The (Wells), **VI:** 228

Anatomy of Melancholy (Burton), **II:** 88, 106, 108; **IV:** 219

Anatomy of Oxford (eds. Day Lewis and Fenby), **Supp. III:** 118

Anatomy of Restlessness: Selected Writings, 1969–1989 (Chatwin), **Supp. IV:** 157, 160; **Supp. IX:** 52, 53, 61

"Ancestor" (Kinsella), **Supp. V:** 274

"Ancestors" (Cornford), **VIII:** 106

"Anchored Yachts on a Stormy Day" (Smith, I. C.), **Supp. IX:** 211

Ancient Allan, The (Haggard), **Supp. III:** 222

Ancient and English Versions of the Bible (Isaacs), **I:** 385

"Ancient Ballet, An" (Kinsella), **Supp. V:** 261

"Ancient Historian" (Wallace-Crabbe), **VIII:** 311

Ancient Lights (Ford), **VI:** 319, 320

"Ancient Mariner, The" (Coleridge), **III:** 330, 338; **IV:** viii, ix, 42, 44–48, 54, 55; **Retro. Supp. II:** 53–56

"Ancient Sage, The" (Tennyson), **IV:** 329

"Ancient to Ancients, An" (Hardy), **VI:** 13

"And country life I praise" (Bridges), **VI:** 75

"And death shall have no dominion" (Thomas), **Supp. I:** 174

And Our Faces, My Heart, Brief as Photos (Berger), **Supp. IV:** 94, 95

And Then There Were None (Christie), *see Ten Little Niggers*

And What if the Pretender Should Come? (Defoe), **III:** 13

Anderson, Lindsay, **Supp. IV:** 78

Anderson, Sherwood, **VII:** 75

Anderton, Basil, **II:** 154, 157

"Andrea del Sarto" (Browning), **IV:** 357, 361, 366; **Retro. Supp. II:** 27–28

Andrea of Hungary, and Giovanna of Naples (Landor), **IV:** 100

Andreas, **Retro. Supp. II:** 301

"Andrey Satchel and the Parson and Clerk" (Hardy), **VI:** 22

Androcles and the Lion (Shaw), **VI:** 116, 124, 129; **Retro. Supp. II:** 322

"Andromeda" (Hopkins), **V:** 370, 376

Andromeda Liberata (Chapman), **I:** 235, 254

Ane Prayer for the Pest (Henryson), **Supp. VII:** 146, 148

Boswell, James, **III:** 54, 107, 110–115, 117, 119–122, **234–251; IV:** xv, xvi, 27, 88n, 280; **Retro. Supp. I:** 145–149

"Boswell and Rousseau" (Leigh), **III:** 246n

Boswell for the Defence 1769–1774 (ed. Pottle and Wimsatt), **III:** 249

Boswell in Extremis 1776–1778 (ed. Pottle and Weis), **III:** 249

Boswell in Holland 1763–1764 (ed. Pottle), **III:** 249

Boswell in Search of a Wife 1766–1769 (ed. Brady and Pottle), **III:** 249

Boswell: Lord of Auchinleck 1778–1782 (ed. Pottle and Reed), **III:** 249

Boswell on the Grand Tour: Germany and Switzerland 1764 (ed. Pottle), **III:** 249

Boswell on the Grand Tour: Italy . . . 1765–1766 (ed. Brady and Pottle), **III:** 249

Boswell: The Ominous Years 1774–1776 (ed. Pottle and Ryskamp), **III:** 249

Boswelliana . . . Memoir and Annotations by the Rev. Charles Rogers (Rogers), **III:** 249

Boswell's Book of Bad Verse (ed. Werner), **III:** 249

Boswell's London Journal 1762–1763 (ed. Pottle), **III:** 249

Boswell's Notebook, 1776–1777 (Boswell), **III:** 244, 249

"Botany Bay Eclogues" (Southey), **IV:** 60

Bothie of Tober–na–Vuolich, The (Clough), **V:** 155, 156, 158, 159, 161–164, 166, 167, 169, 170

Bothie of Toper–na–Fuosich, The (Clough), **V:** 170

Bothwell (Swinburne), **V:** 314, 330, 331, 332

Botticelli, Sandro, **V:** 345

Bottle Factory Outing, The (Bainbridge), **Supp. VI:** 18–20, 24, 27

"Bottle Imp, The" (Stevenson), **V:** 396

Bottle in the Smoke, A (Wilson), **Supp. VI:** 304, 307

Bottle's Path and Other Stories (Powys), **VIII:** 249, 255

Boucicault, Dion, **V:** 415; **VII:** 2

Bouge of Court, The (Skelton), **I:** 83, 84–85

Boughner, D. C., **I:** 186

"Bourgeois Psychology" (Caudwell), **Supp. IX:** 45

Boursault, Edme, **II:** 324, 332

Bow Down (Harrison), **Supp. V:** 164

"Bow in the Cloud, The" (Nicholson), **Supp. VI:** 215

Bowen, Elizabeth, **Supp. II: 77–95; Supp. IV:** 151, 500, 514

Bowen, Stella, **VI:** 324

Bowen's Court (Bowen), **Supp. II:** 78, 84, 91

Bowers, Fredson, **II:** 44

Bowles, Caroline, **IV:** 62, 63

"Bowling Alley and the Sun, or, How I Learned to Stop Worrying and Love America, The" (Lodge), **Supp. IV:** 373

Bowra, C. M., **VI:** 153

Bowra, Maurice, **V:** 252–256, 260

Boy and the Magic, The (tr. Fry), **Supp. III:** 195

Boy Comes Home, The (Milne), **Supp. V:** 299

Boy Hairdresser, The (Orton), **Supp. V:** 363, 364, 367

Boy in the Bush, The (Lawrence), **VII:** 114; **Retro. Supp. II:** 230–231

Boy: Tales of Childhood (Dahl), **Supp. IV:** 204, 205, 206, 208, 225

Boy Who Followed Ripley, The (Highsmith), **Supp. V:** 171

"Boy Who Talked with Animals, The" (Dahl), **Supp. IV:** 223, 224

Boy with a Cart, The; Cuthman, Saint of Sussex (Fry), **Supp. III:** 191, 194, 195, 196

Boyd, H. S., **IV:** 312

Boyer, Abel, **II:** 352

Boyhood: Scenes from Provincial Life (Coetzee), **Supp. VI:** 77–78

Boyle, Robert, **II:** 23, 95

Boys Who Stole the Funeral, The: A Novel Sequence (Murray), **Supp. VII:** 270, 284–286

"Boys' Weeklies" (Orwell), **Supp. III:** 107

Bradbrook, M. C., **I:** xi, 292, 329; **II:** 42, 78; **VII:** xiii–xiv, xxxvii, 234

Bradbury, Ray, **III:** 341

Bradbury, Malcolm, **Supp. IV:** 303, 365

Braddon, Mary Elizabeth, **V:** 327; **VIII: 35–52**

Bradley, A. C., **IV:** 106, 123, 216, 235, 236

Bradley, F. H., **V:** xxi, 212, 217

Bradley, Henry, **VI:** 76

Brady, F., **III:** 249

Braine, John, **Supp. IV:** 238

Brand (Hill), **Supp. V:** 199, 200–201

Brander, Laurence, **IV:** xxiv; **VII:** xxii

Brantley, Ben, **Supp. IV:** 197–198

Branwell Brontë (Gerin), **V:** 153

Branwell's Blackwood's (periodical), **V:** 109, 123

Branwell's Young Men's (periodical), *see Branwell's Blackwood's*

Brass Butterfly, The (Golding), **Supp. I:** 65, 75

"Brassneck" (Armitage), **VIII:** 5

Brassneck (Hare and Brenton), **Supp. IV:** 281, 282, 283, 284–285, 289

Brave and Cruel (Welch), **Supp. IX:** 267–269

"Brave and Cruel" (Welch), **Supp. IX:** 267, 269

Brave New World (Huxley), **III:** 341; **VII:** xviii, 200, 204

Brave New World Revisited (Huxley), **VII:** 207

"Bravest Boat, The" (Lowry), **Supp. III:** 281

Brawne, Fanny, **IV:** 211, 216–220, 222, 226, 234

Bray, Charles, **V:** 188

Bray, William, **II:** 275, 276, 286

Brazil (Gilliam), **Supp. IV:** 442, 455

"Breach, The" (Murray), **Supp. VII:** 276

"Bréagh San Réilg, La" (Behan), **Supp. II:** 73

"Break My Heart" (Golding), **Supp. I:** 79

"Break of Day in the Trenches" (Rosenberg), **VI:** 433, 434

"Breake of day" (Donne), **Retro. Supp. II:** 88

Breakfast on Pluto (McCabe), **Supp. IX:** 127, 135–136, 138

"Breaking Ground" (Gunn), **Supp. IV:** 271

"Breaking the Blue" (McGuckian), **Supp. V:** 287

Breath (Beckett), **Supp. I:** 60; **Retro. Supp. I:** 26

Brecht, Bertolt, **II:** 359; **IV:** 183; **VI:** 109, 123; **Supp. II:** 23, 25, 28; **Supp. IV:** 82, 87, 180, 194, 198, 281, 298

"Bredon Hill" (Housman), **VI:** 158

Brendan (O'Connor), **Supp. II:** 63, 76

Brendan Behan's Island (Behan), **Supp. II:** 64, 66, 71, 73, 75

Brendan Behan's New York (Behan), **Supp. II:** 75

Brennoralt (Suckling), *see Discontented Colonel, The*

Brenton, Howard, **Supp. IV:** 281, 283, 284, 285

Brethren, The (Haggard), **Supp. III:** 214

"Breton Walks" (Mahon), **Supp. VI:** 168, 172

Brett, Raymond Laurence, **IV:** x, xi, xxiv, 57

Brickfield, The (Hartley), **Supp. VII:** 131–132

Bricks to Babel (Koestler), **Supp. I:** 37

Bridal of Triermain, The (Scott), **IV:** 38

"Bride and Groom" (Hughes), **Supp. I:** 356

"Bride in the 30's, A" (Auden), **Retro. Supp. I:** 8

Bride of Abydos, The (Byron), **IV:** xvii, 172, 174–175, 192

Bride of Frankenstein (film), **III:** 342

Bride of Lammermoor, The (Scott), **IV:** xviii, 30, 36, 39

Brides of Reason (Davie), **Supp. VI:** 106–107

"Brides, The" (Hope), **Supp. VII:** 154

"Bride's Prelude, The" (Rossetti), **V:** 239, 240

Brideshead Revisited (Waugh), **VII:** xx–xxi, 290, 299–300; **Supp. IV:** 285

"Bridge, The" (Thomas), **Supp. III:** 401

"Bridge for the Living" (Larkin), **Supp. I:** 284

"Bridge of Sighs, The" (Hood), **IV:** 252, 261, 264–265

Bridges, Robert, **II:** 160; **V:** xx, 205, 362–368, 370–372, 374, 376–381; **VI:** xv, **71–83**, 203

Brief History of Moscovia . . . , A (Milton), **II:** 176

Brief Lives (Aubrey), **I:** 260

Brief Lives (Brookner), **Supp. IV:** 131–133

Brief Notes upon a Late Sermon . . . (Milton), **II:** 176

Children's Encyclopedia (Mee), **Supp. IV:** 256

"Child's Christmas in Wales, A" (Thomas), **Supp. I:** 183

"Child's Calendar, A" (Brown), **Supp. VI:** 71

Child's Garden of Verses, A (Stevenson), **V:** 385, 387, 395; **Retro. Supp. I:** 264

Child's History of England, A (Dickens), **V:** 71

Child's Play: A Tragi–comedy in Three Acts of Violence With a Prologue and an Epilogue (Hill, R.), **Supp. IX:** 115–116

Chimeras, The (Mahon), **Supp. VI:** 173

Chimes, The (Dickens), **V:** 42, 64, 71

"Chimney Sweeper" (Blake), **III:** 297; **Retro. Supp. I:** 36, 42

China. A Revised Reprint of Articles from Titan . . . (DeQuincey), **IV:** 155

China Diary (Spender), **Supp. II:** 493

Chinamen (Frayn), **Supp. VII:** 57–58

"Chinese Button, The" (Brooke-Rose), **Supp. IV:** 103

"Chinese Letters" (Goldsmith), *see Citizen of the World, The*

"Chinese Lobster, The" (Byatt), **Supp. IV:** 155

Chinese Love Pavilion, The (Scott), **Supp. I:** 259, 263

"Chinoiserie" (Reading), **VIII:** 273

"Chip of Glass Ruby, A" (Gordimer), **Supp. II:** 232

Chit–chat (periodical), **III:** 50

Chitty Chitty Bang Bang (film, Dahl), **Supp. IV:** 213

Chitty Chitty Bang Bang (Fleming), **Supp. IV:** 212–213

Chivers, Thomas Holley, **V:** 313

Chloe (Meredith), **V:** 231n, 234

Chloe Marr (Milne), **Supp. V:** 310

Choice of Kipling's Prose, A (Maugham), **VI:** 200, 204

"Choir School" (Murphy), **Supp. V:** 328

Chomei at Toyama (Bunting), **Supp. VII:** 4, 6–7

Chomsky, Noam, **Supp. IV:** 113–114

"Chorale" (Hope), **Supp. VII:** 158

Chorus of Disapproval, A (Ayckbourn), **Supp. V:** 3, 9–10, 14

Christ a Compleat Saviour in His Intercession (Bunyan), **II:** 253

Christ and Satan, **Retro. Supp. II:** 301

Christ in the Cupboard (Powys), **VIII:** 255

Christ Stopped at Eboli (Levi), **VI:** 299

"Christ Surprised" (Jennings), **Supp. V:** 217

"Christ upon the Waters" (Newman), **Supp. VII:** 298

Christabel (Coleridge), **II:** 179; **III:** 338; **IV:** ix, xvii, 29, 44, 48–49, 56, 218, 313; **Retro. Supp. II:** 58–59

Christe's Bloody Sweat (Ford), **II:** 88, 100

"Christening" (Murphy), **Supp. V:** 322

Christian Behaviour (Lewis), **Supp. III:** 248

Christian Behaviour . . . (Bunyan), **II:** 253

Christian Captives, The (Bridges), **VI:** 83

Christian Dialogue, A (Bunyan), **II:** 253

Christian Ethicks (Traherne), **II:** 190, 191, 201

Christian Hero, The (Steele), **III: 43, 44,** 53

Christian Morals (Browne), **II:** 149, 153, 154, 156; **III:** 40

Christie, Agatha, **III:** 341; **Supp. II: 123–135; Supp. III:** 334; **Supp. IV:** 500

Christina Alberta's Father (Wells), **VI:** 227

Christina Rossetti (Packer), **V:** 251, 252–253, 260

Christina Rossetti: A Divided Life (Battiscombe), **V:** 260

Christina Stead (Brydon), **Supp. IV:** 463

Christina Stead: A Biography (Rowley), **Supp. IV:** 459

"Christine's Letter" (Coppard), **VIII:** 96

"Christmas" (Smith, I. C.), **Supp. IX:** 221

"Christmas Antiphones" (Swinburne), **V:** 325

"Christmas at Sea" (Stevenson), **V:** 396

Christmas at Thompson Hall (Trollope), **V:** 102

Christmas Books (Dickens), **V:** 71

Christmas Carol, A (Dickens), **V:** xx, 42, 56–57, 71

"Christmas Carol, A" (Swinburne), **V:** 315

"Christmas Childhood, A" (Kavanagh), **Supp. VII:** 194

Christmas Comes But Once a Year (Chettle, Dekker, Heywood, Webster), **II:** 68, 85

"Christmas Day in the Workhouse" (Wilson), **Supp. I:** 153, 157

Christmas Eve and Easter Day (Browning), **Retro. Supp. II:** 25–26

"Christmas Garland Woven by Max Beerbohm, A" (Beerbohm), **Supp. II:** 45

Christmas Garland, A (Beerbohm), **Supp. II:** 45, 49

Christmas His Masque (Jonson), **Retro. Supp. I:** 165

Christmas Holiday (Maugham), **VI:** 377

"Christmas Life, The" (Cope), **VIII:** 80

"Christmas Oratorio, A" (Auden), **Retro. Supp. I:** 10–11

"Christmas Storms and Sunshine" (Gaskell), **V:** 15

Christmas–Eve and Easter–Day (Browning), **IV:** 357, 363, 370, 372, 374

Christopher, John, **Supp. V:** 22

Christopher and His Kind (Isherwood), **VII:** 318

"Christopher At Birth" (Longley), **VIII:** 167

Christopher Columbus (MacNeice), **VII:** 406

"Christopher Columbus and Queen Isabella of Spain Consummate Their Relationship" (Rushdie), **Supp. IV:** 452

"Christopher Marlowe" (Swinburne), **V:** 332

Christopher Marlowe in Relation to Greene, Peele and Lodge (Swinburne), **V:** 333

Christ's Hospital, A Retrospect (Blunden), **IV:** 86

"Christ's Hospital Five–and–Thirty Years Ago"(Lamb), **IV:** 42, 76

"Chronicle, The" (Cowley), **II:** 198

Chronicle Historie of Perkin Warbeck, The (Ford), *see Perkin Warbeck*

chronicle history, **I:** 73

Chronicle of Carlingford series (ed. Fitzgerald), **Supp. V:** 98

Chronicle of Friendships, A, 1873–1900 (Low), **V:** 393, 397

Chronicle of Queen Fredegond, The (Swinburne), **V:** 333

Chronicle of the Cid (tr. Southey), **IV:** 71

"Chronicle of the Drum, The" (Thackeray), **V:** 17, 38

Chronicles (Hall), **II:** 43

Chronicles of Barset (Trollope), **Supp. IV:** 231

Chronicles of Clovis, The (Saki), **Supp. VI:** 240–243, 245, 249

Chronicles of Narnia, The (Lewis), **Supp. III:** 247, 248, **259–261**

Chronicles of the Canongate (Scott), **IV:** 39

Chroniques (Froissart), **I:** 21

"Chronopolis" (Ballard), **Supp. V:** 22

"Chrysalides" (Kinsella), **Supp. V:** 262

Chrysaor (Landor), **IV:** 96

Church, Dean R. W., **I:** 186

Church and Queen. Five Speeches, 1860–1864 (Disraeli), **IV:** 308

"Church–floore, The" (Herbert), **Retro. Supp. II:** 178–179

"Church Going" (Larkin), **Supp. I:** 277, 279, 280, 285

"Church Service" (Vaughan), **II:** 187

"Church Windows, The" (Herbert), **II:** 127

"Churche-Floore, The" (Herbert), **II:** 126

Church in Crisis, The (Wilson), **Supp. VI:** 305

"Churches of Northern France, The" (Morris), **V:** 293, 306

Churchill, Caryl, **Supp. IV: 179–200**

Churchill, Lady Randolph, **VI:** 349

Churchill, Winston, **III:** 27; **VI:** xv, 261, 274, **347–362,** 369, 385, 392; **Supp. III:** 58–59; speeches, **VI:** 361

Churchill by His Contemporaries (ed. Eade), **VI:** 351n, 361

"Church–monuments" (Herbert), **II:** 127

"Church–warden and the Curate, The" (Tennyson), **IV:** 327

"Churl and the Bird, The" (Lydgate), **I:** 57

Chymist's Key, The (tr. Vaughan), **II:** 185, 201

Cibber, Colley, **I:** 327; **II:** 314, 324–326, 331, 334, 337

Cicadas, The (Huxley), **VII:** 199

"Cicero and His Brother" (Landor), **IV:** 90, 91

Ciceronianus (Harvey), **I:** 122

Ciceronis Amor: Tullies Love (Greene), **VIII:** 135, 143

"George and the Seraph" (Brooke-Rose), **Supp. IV:** 103

George Bernard Shaw (Chesterton), **VI:** 344

George Crabbe and His Times (Huchon), **III:** 273*n*

George Eliot (Stephen), **V:** 289

George Eliot: Her Life and Books (Bullet), **V:** 196, 200–201

George Eliot, Selected Essays, Poems and Other Writings (Byatt), **Supp. IV:** 151

George Eliot's Life as Related in Her Letters and Journals (ed. Cross), **V:** 13, 200

George Gissing: Grave Comedian (Donnelly), **V:** 427*n*, 438

"George Herbert: The Art of Plainness" (Stein), **Retro. Supp. II:** 181

George Moore: L'homme et l'oeuvre (Noel), **VI:** 98, 99

George Orwell (Fyvel), **VII:** 287

George Passant (Snow), **VII:** 324, 325–326

George Silverman's Explanation (Dickens), **V:** 72

George's Ghosts (Maddox), **Retro. Supp. I:** 327, 328

George's Marvellous Medicine (Dahl), **Supp. IV:** 204–205

"Georgian Boyhood, A" (Connolly), **Supp. III:** 1–2

Georgian Poetry 1911–1912 (ed. Marsh), **VI:** 416, 419, 420, 453; **VII:** xvi; **Supp. III:** 45, 53–54, 397

Georgics of Virgil, The (tr. Day Lewis), **Supp. III:** 118

"Georgina's Reasons" (James), **VI:** 69

Gerard; or, The World, the Flesh, and the Devil (Braddon), **VIII:** 49

Gerald: A Portrait (du Maurier), **Supp. III:** 134–135, 138–139

Gerard Manley Hopkins: A Critical Symposium (Kenyon Critics), **V:** 382

Gerard Manley Hopkins: The Classical Background . . . (Bender), **V:** 364–365, 382

Géricault, Théodore, **Supp. IV:** 71–72, 73

Gérin, Winifred, **V:** x, xxvii, 111, 151, 152, 153

Germ (periodical), **V:** xxi, 235–236, 249

"German Chronicle" (Hulme), **Supp. VI:** 139

"Germinal" (Russell), **VIII:** 290

"Gerontion" (Eliot), **VII:** 144, 146, 147, 152; **Retro. Supp. II:** 123–124

Gerugte van Reen (Brink), **Supp. VI:** 49

Gesta Romanorum, **I:** 52 53

"Gethsemane" (Nicholson), **Supp. VI:** 214

Get Ready for Battle (Jhabvala), **Supp. V:** 228–229

"Getting at Stars" (Armitage), **VIII:** 4

Getting Married (Shaw), **VI:** 115, 117–118

"Getting Off the Altitude" (Lessing), **Supp. I:** 240

Getting On (Bennett), **VIII:** 20, 21, 25–26

"Getting Poisoned" (Ishiguro), **Supp. IV:** 303

"Getting there" (Kelman), **Supp. V:** 249

Getting to Know the General (Greene), **Supp. I:** 1, 13, 14, 17

Geulincx, Arnold, **Supp. I: 44**

"Geve place ye lovers" (Surrey), **I:** 120

"Geysers, The" (Gunn), **Supp. IV:** 268, 269, 276

Ghastly Good Taste (Betjeman), **VII:** 357, 361

Ghost Child, The (Tennant), **Supp. IX:** 239

Ghost in the Machine, The (Koestler), **Supp. I:** 37, 38

Ghost of Lucrece, The (Middleton), **II:** 3

Ghost Orchid, The (Longley), **VIII:** 175–177

"Ghost Orchid, The" (Longley), **VIII:** 175–176

Ghost Road, The (Barker), **Supp. IV:** 45, 46, 57, 61–63

Ghost Trio (Beckett), **Retro. Supp. I:** 29

"Ghost–Crabs" (Hughes), **Supp. I:** 349, 350; **Retro. Supp. II:** 206

"Ghostkeeper" (Lowry), **Supp. III:** 285

"Ghostly Father, The" (Redgrove), **Supp. VI:** 228

"Ghosts" (Redgrove), **Supp. VI:** 228, 236

"Ghosts" (Reid), **Supp. VII:** 327

Giants' Bread (Christie), **Supp. II:** 133

Giaour, The (Byron), **III:** 338; **IV:** xvii, 172, 173–174, 180, 192

Gibbon, Edward, **III:** 109, 221–233; **IV:** xiv, xvi, 93, 284; **V:** 425; **VI:** 347, 353, 383, 390*n*

Gibbons, Brian, **II:** 281

Gibson, W. W., **VI:** 416

Gide, André, **V:** xxiii, 402

Gidez, Richard B., **Supp. IV:** 326, 339–340

Gifford, William, **II:** 96; **IV:** 133

"Gift of Boxes, A" (Longley), **VIII:** 176

"Gigolo and Gigolette" (Maugham), **VI:** 370

Gil Blas (tr. Smollett), **III:** 150

Gil Perez, The Gallician (tr. FitzGerald), **IV:** 344

Gilbert, Elliott, **VI:** 194

"Gilbert" (Brontë), **V:** 131–132

Gilbert, Peter, **Supp. IV:** 354

Gilbert, Sandra, **Retro. Supp. I:** 59–60

"Gilbert's Mother" (Trevor), **Supp. IV:** 505

Gilchrist, Andrew, **Retro. Supp. I:** 46

Gilfillan, George, **I:** 98

"Gilles de Retz" (Keyes), **VII:** 437

Gilliam, Terry, **Supp. IV:** 455

Gillman, James, **IV:** 48–49, 50, 56

Gilman, Charlotte Perkins, **Supp. III:** 147

Gilpin, William, **IV:** 36, 37

Gilson, Étienne, **VI:** 341

"Gin and Goldenrod" (Lowry), **Supp. III:** 282

"Ginger Hero" (Friel), **Supp. V:** 113

Ginger, You're Barmy (Lodge), **Supp. IV:** 364–365, 368–369, 371

Giorgione da Castelfranco, **V:** 345, 348

"Giorgione" (Pater), **V:** 345, 348, 353

"Gipsy Vans" (Kipling), **VI:** 193, 196

"Giraffes, The" (Fuller), **VII:** 430, **Supp. VII:** 70

"Girl" (Kincaid), **Supp. VII:** 220, 221, 223

"Girl at the Seaside" (Murphy), **Supp. V:** 313, 318

Girl in Winter, A (Larkin), **Supp. I:** 286, 287

Girl, 20 (Amis), **Supp. II:** 15–16; **Supp. IV:** 29

Girl Weeping for the Death of Her Canary (Greuze), **Supp. IV:** 122

"Girl Who Loved Graveyards, The" (James), **Supp. IV:** 340

Girlhood of Mary Virgin, The (Rossetti), **V:** 236, 248, 249

Girlitude: A Memoir of the 50s and 60s (Tennant), **Supp. IX:** 239

Girls in Their Married Bliss (O'Brien), **Supp. V:** 334, 337–338

"Girls in Their Season" (Mahon), **Supp. VI:** 167

Girls of Slender Means, The (Spark), **Supp. I:** 200, 204, 206

"Girls on a Bridge" (Mahon), **Supp. VI:** 174

Gisborne, John, **IV:** 206

Gísla saga Súrssonar, **VIII:** 241

Gismond of Salerne (Wilmot), **I:** 216

Gissing, George, **V:** xiii, xxii, xxv–xxvi, 69, **423–438; VI:** 365; **Supp. IV:** 7–8

Gittings, Robert, **Supp. III:** 194

"Give Her A Pattern" (Lawrence), **II:** 330*n*

Give Me Your Answer, Do! (Friel), **Supp. V:** 127–128

"Given Heart, The" (Cowley), **II:** 197

Giving Alms No Charity . . . (Defoe), **III:** 13

Gladiators, The (Koestler), **Supp. I:** 27, 28, 29*n*

"Glanmore Revisited" (Heaney), **Retro. Supp. I:** 132

"Glanmore Sonnets" (Heaney), **Supp. II:** 276

Glanvill, Joseph, **II:** 275

"Glasgow 5 March 1971" (Morgan, E.), **Supp. IX:** 162

"Glasgow Green" (Morgan, E.), **Supp. IX:** 158

"Glasgow October 1971" (Morgan, E.), **Supp. IX:** 162

Glass–Blowers, The (du Maurier), **Supp. III:** 136, 138

Glass Cell, The (Highsmith), **Supp. V:** 174

Glass Cottage, A Nautical Romance, The (Redgrove), **Supp. VI:** 230–231

Glass of Blessings, A (Pym), **Supp. II:** **377–378**

Glass Town chronicles (Brontës), **V:** 110–111

Gleanings from the Menagerie and Aviary at Knowsley Hall (Lear), **V:** 76, 87

Gleckner, R. F., **IV:** 173, 194

Glen, Heather, **III:** 297

Glendinning, Victoria, **Supp. II:** 78, 80, 90, 95

"Green Hills of Africa" (Fuller), **VII:** 429, 432

"Green Leaf, The" (Smith, I. C.), **Supp. IX:** 223

Green Man, The (Amis), **Supp. II:** 13–14

"Green Mountain, Black Mountain" (Stevenson), **Supp. VI:** 256–257, 261–262, 266

Green Shore, The (Nicholson), **Supp. VI: 219–220**

Green Song (Sitwell), **VII:** 132, 135, 136

"Green Tea" (Le Fanu), **III:** 340, 345

Greene, Graham, **VI:** 329, 370; **VII:** xii; **Supp. I: 1–20; Supp. II:** 311, 324; **Supp. IV:** 4, 10, 13, 17, 21, 157, 365, 369, 373–374, 505; **Supp. V:** 26; **Retro. Supp. II: 151–167**

Greene, Robert, **I:** 165, 220, 275, 286, 296, 322; **II:** 3; **VIII: 131–146**

Greene's Arcadia (Greene). *See Menaphon*

Greenlees, Ian Gordon, **VI:** xxxiii

"Greenshank" (MacCaig), **Supp. VI:** 192

Greenvoe (Brown), **Supp. VI:** 64, **65–66**

"Greenwich—Whitebait" (Thackeray), **V:** 38

Greenwood, Edward Baker, **VII:** xix, xxxvii

Greenwood, Frederick, **V:** 1

Greer, Germaine, **Supp. IV:** 436

Greg, W. R., **V:** 5, 7, 15

Greg, W. W., **I:** 279

Gregory, Lady Augusta, **VI:** 210, 218, **307–312, 314–316,** 317–318; **VII:** 1, 3, 42

Gregory, Sir Richard, **VI:** 233

Greiffenhagen, Maurice, **VI:** 91

Gremlins, The (Dahl), **Supp. IV:** 202, 211–212

"Grenadier" (Housman), **VI:** 160

Grenfell, Julian, **VI:** xvi, 417–418, 420

"Gretchen" (Gissing), **V:** 437

"Gretna Green" (Behan), **Supp. II:** 64

Grettis saga, **VIII:** 234–235, 238, 241

Greuze, Jean–Baptiste, **Supp. IV:** 122

Greuze: The Rise and Fall of an Eighteenth Century Phenomenon (Brookner), **Supp. IV:** 122

Greville, Fulke, **I:** 160, 164; **Supp. IV:** 256

Grey Area (Self), **Supp. V:** 402–404

Grey Eminence (Huxley), **VII:** 205

Grey of Fallodon (Trevelyan), **VI:** 383, 391

"Grey Woman, The" (Gaskell), **V:** 15

Greybeards at Play (Chesterton), **VI:** 336

Greyhound for Breakfast (Kelman), **Supp. V:** 242, 249–250

"Greyhound for Breakfast" (Kelman), **Supp. V:** 250

"Grief" (Browning), **IV:** 313, 318

Grief Observed, A (Lewis), **Supp. III:** 249

"Grief on the Death of Prince Henry, A" (Tourneur), **II:** 37, 41

Grierson, Herbert J. C., **II:** 121, 130, 196, 200, 202, 258; **Retro. Supp. II:** 173

Grigson, Geoffrey, **IV:** 47; **VII:** xvi

Grim Smile of the Five Towns, The (Bennett), **VI:** 250, 253–254

Grímnismál, **VIII:** 230

Grimus (Rushdie), **Supp. IV:** 435, 438–439, 443, 450

Gris, Juan, **Supp. IV:** 81

"Grisly Folk, The" (Wells), **Retro. Supp. I:** 96

Groatsworth of Wit, A (Greene), **I:** 275, 276; **VIII:** 131, 132

Grænlendinga saga, **VIII:** 240

Grosskurth, Phyllis, **V:** xxvii

Grote, George, **IV:** 289

Group of Noble Dames, A (Hardy), **VI:** 20, 22

"Grove, The" (Muir), **Supp. VI:** 206

"Growing, Flying, Happening" (Reid), **Supp. VII:** 328

"Growing Old" (Arnold), **V:** 203

Growing Pains: The Shaping of a Writer (du Maurier), **Supp. III:** 135, 142, 144

Growing Points (Jennings), **Supp. V:** 217

Growing Rich (Weldon), **Supp. IV:** 531, 533

Growth of Love, The (Bridges), **VI:** 81, 83

Growth of Plato's Ideal Theory, The (Frazer), **Supp. III:** 170–171

"Grub First, Then Ethics" (Auden), **Retro. Supp. I:** 7, 13

Grünewald, Mathias, **Supp. IV:** 85

Gryffydh, Jane, **IV:** 159

Gryll Grange (Peacock), **IV:** xxii, 166–167, 170

Grylls, R. Glynn, **V:** 247, 260; **VII:** xvii, xxxviii

Guardian (periodical), **III:** 46, 49, 50

Guardian, The (Cowley), **II:** 194, 202

Guarini, Guarino, **II:** 49–50

Gubar, Susan, **Retro. Supp. I:** 59–60

Guerrillas (Naipaul), **Supp. I:** 396–397

Guest of Honour, A (Gordimer), **Supp. II:** 229–230, 231

Guide Through the District of the Lakes in the North of England, A (Wordsworth), **IV:** 25

Guide to Kulchur (Pound), **VI:** 333

Guido della Colonna, **I:** 57

Guild of St. George, The, **V:** 182

Guillaume de Deguilleville, **I:** 57

Guillaume de Lorris, **I:** 71

"Guilt and Sorrow" (Wordsworth), **IV:** 5, 45

"Guinevere" (Tennyson), **IV:** 336–337, 338

Guise, The (Marlowe), *see Massacre at Paris, The*

Guise, The (Webster), **II:** 68, 85

"Guitarist Tunes Up, The" (Cornford), **VIII:** 114

Gulliver's Travels (Swift), **II:** 261; **III:** 11, 20, **23–26,** 28, 35; **VI:** 121–122; **Supp. IV:** 502; **Retro. Supp. I:** 274, 275, 276–277, 279–282

Gun for Sale, A (Greene; U.S. title, *This Gun for Hire*), **Supp. I:** 3, 6–7, 10; **Retro. Supp. II:** 153

Gunn, Ander, **Supp. IV:** 265

Gunn, Thom, **Supp. IV: 255–279**

Gunnlaugs saga ormstunga, **VIII:** 239

Guns of Navarone, The (film, Ambler), **Supp. IV:** 3

Gurdjieff, Georges I., **Supp. IV:** 1, 5

Gurney, Ivor, **VI:** 416, **425–427**

Gussow, Mel, **Retro. Supp. I:** 217–218

Gutch, J. M., **IV:** 78, 81

Guthlac, **Retro. Supp. II:** 303

Gutteridge, Bernard, **VII:** 422, 432–433

Guy Domville (James), **VI:** 39

Guy Mannering (Scott), **IV:** xvii, 31–32, 38

Guy of Warwick (Lydgate), **I:** 58

Guy Renton (Waugh), **Supp. VI:** 274–275

Guyana Quartet (Harris), **Supp. V:** 132, 133, 135

Guzman Go Home and Other Stories (Sillitoe), **Supp. V:** 410

Gyðinga saga, **VIII:** 237

Gylfaginning, **VIII:** 243

"Gym"(Murphy), **Supp. V:** 328

Gypsies Metamorphos'd (Jonson), **II:** 111*n*

"Gyrtt in my giltetesse gowne" (Surrey), **I:** 115

"Healthy Landscape with Dormouse" (Warner), **Supp. VII:** 380

"Hee–Haw" (Warner), **Supp. VII:** 380

"House Grown Silent, The" (Warner), **Supp. VII:** 371

H. G. Wells and His Critics (Raknem), **VI:** 228, 245, 246

H. G. Wells: His Turbulent Life and Times (Dickson), **VI:** 246

H. G. Wells: The Critical Heritage (ed. Parrinder), **VI:** 246

Ha! Ha! Among the Trumpets (Lewis), **VII:** 447, 448

Habeas Corpus (Bennett), **VIII:** 25

Habermas, Jürgen, **Supp. IV:** 112

Habington, William, **II:** 222, 237, 238

Habit of Loving, The (Lessing), **Supp. I:** 244

"Habit of Perfection, The" (Hopkins), **V:** 362, 381

Hadjinicolaou, Nicos, **Supp. IV:** 90

"Hag, The" (Herrick), **II:** 111

Haggard, H. Rider, **Supp. III: 211–228; Supp. IV:** 201, 484

Haight, Gordon, **V:** 199, 200, 201

Hail and Farewell (Moore), **VI:** xii, 85, 88, 97, 99

"Hailstones" (Heaney), **Supp. II:** 280

"Hair, The" (Caudwell), **Supp. IX:** 37

Hakluyt, Richard, **I:** 150, 267; **III:** 7

Hale, Kathleen, **Supp. IV:** 231

"Hale, sterne superne" (Dunbar), **VIII:** 128–129

"Half–a–Crown's Worth of Cheap Knowledge" (Thackeray), **V:** 22, 37

Half–Mother, The (Tennant), *see Woman Beware Woman*

Halidon Hill (Scott), **IV:** 39

Halifax, marquess of, **III:** 38, 39, 40, 46

Hall, Donald, **Supp. IV:** 256

Hall, Edward, **II:** 43

Hall, Joseph, **II:** 25–26, 81; **IV:** 286

Hall, Radclyffe, **VI:** 411; **Supp. VI: 119–132**

Hall, Samuel (pseud., O'Nolan), **Supp. II:** 322

"In Deep and Solemn Dreams" (Tennyson), **IV:** 329
"In Defence of Milton" (Leavis), **VII:** 246
"In Defense of Astigmatism" (Wodehouse), **Supp. III:** 454
"In Defense of the Novel, Yet Again" (Rushdie), **Supp. IV:** 455
"In dungeons dark I cannot sing"(Brontë), **V:** 115–116
In Excited Reverie: A Centenary Tribute to William Butler Yeats, 1865–1939 (ed. Jeffares and Cross), **VI:** 224
"In Flanders Fields" (McCrae), **VI:** 434
"In from Spain" (Powys), **VIII:** 251
"In God We Trust" (Rushdie), **Supp. IV:** 434, 456
"In Good Faith" (Rushdie), **Supp. IV:** 437, 450
In Good King Charles's Golden Days (Shaw), **VI:** 125, 127, 129
In Her Own Image (Boland), **Supp. V:** 48
"In Her Own Image" (Boland), **Supp. V:** 48, 49
"In His Own Image" (Boland), **Supp. V:** 48–49
"In Lambeth Palace Road" (Fuller), **Supp. VII:** 76
In Light and Darkness (Wallace-Crabbe), **VIII:** 311
"In Love for Long" (Muir), **Supp. VI:** 206–207
"In Me Two Worlds" (Day Lewis), **Supp. III:** 126
"In Memoriam" (Longley), **VIII:** 169
In Memoriam (Tennyson), **IV:** xxi, 234, 248, 292, 310, 313, 323, 325–328, 330, 333–338, 371; **V:** 285, 455
"In Memoriam, Amada" (Reid), **Supp. VII:** 333
"In Memoriam (Easter, 1915)" (Thomas), **VI:** 424–425; **Supp. III:** 403, 404
"In Memory of Ernst Toller" (Auden), **Retro. Supp. I:** 9
"In Memory of Eva Gore–Booth and Con Markiewicz" (Yeats), **VI:** 217
"In Memory of Major Robert Gregory" (Yeats), **Retro. Supp. I:** 331
"In Memory of my Cat, Domino" (Fuller), **Supp. VII:** 77
"In Memory of My Mother" (Kavanagh), **Supp. VII:** 198
"In Memory of Sigmund Freud" (Auden), **VII:** 379; **Retro. Supp. I:** 1
"In Memory of W. B. Yeats" (Auden), **VI:** 208; **Retro. Supp. I:** 1, 9
"In Memory of Zoe Yalland" (Motion), **Supp. VII:** 264
"In my craft or sullen art" (Thomas), **Supp. I:** 178
"In My Dreams" (Smith), **Supp. II:** 466
In My Good Books (Pritchett), **Supp. III:** 313
"In My Own Album" (Lamb), **IV:** 83
In Our Infancy (Corke), **VII:** 93
In Our Time (Hemingway), **Supp. IV:** 163

In Parenthesis (Jones), **VI:** xvi, 437–438, **Supp. VII:** 167, 168, 169, 170, 171–175, 177
In Patagonia (Chatwin), **Supp. IV:** 157, 159, 161, 163–165, 173; **Supp. IX:** 53–55, 56, 59
"In Praise of Lessius His Rule of Health" (Crashaw), **II:** 181n
"In Praise of Limestone"(Auden), **VII:** 390, 391; **Retro. Supp. I:** 12
In Praise of Love (Rattigan), **Supp. VII:** 320–321
"In Procession" (Graves), **VII:** 264
In Pursuit of the English (Lessing), **Supp. I:** 237–238
"In Santa Maria del Popolo" (Gunn), **Supp. IV:** 262
In Search of Love and Beauty (Jhabvala), **Supp. V:** 223, 233
"In Sickness and in Health" (Auden), **Retro. Supp. I:** 10
In Single Strictness (Moore), **VI:** 87, 95, 99
"In Sobieski's Shield" (Morgan, E.), **Supp. IX:** 158, 164
"In Such a Poise Is Love" (Reid), **Supp. VII:** 328–329
"In Summer" (Wallace-Crabbe), **VIII:** 311
"In Tenebris II" (Hardy), **VI:** 14
In the Middle (Smith, I. C.), **Supp. IX:** 217–218
In the Middle of the Wood (Smith, I. C.), **Supp. IX:** 209
In the Beginning (Douglas), **VI:** 303, 304, 305
In the Cage (James), **VI:** 67, 69
"In the City of Red Dust" (Okri), **Supp. V:** 352
"In the Classics Room" (Smith, I. C.), **Supp. IX:** 214–215
In the Country of the Skin (Redgrove), **Supp. VI:** 230
In the Days of the Comet (Wells), **VI:** 227, 237, 244
"In the Garden at Swainston" (Tennyson), **IV:** 336
"In the Great Metropolis" (Clough), **V:** 164
In the Green Tree (Lewis), **VII:** 447
In the Heart of the Country (Coetzee), **Supp. VI:** 76, **80–81**
"In the House of Suddhoo" (Kipling), **VI:** 170
In the Labyrinth (Robbe–Grillet), **Supp. IV:** 116
In the Meantime (Jennings), **Supp. V:** 219
In the Night (Kelman), **Supp. V:** 256
"In the Night" (Jennings), **Supp. V:** 211–212
"In the Night" (Kincaid), **Supp. VII:** 220
"In the Nursery" (Stevenson), **Supp. VI:** 264
In the Pink (Blackwood), **Supp. IX:** 14–15
"In the Ringwood" (Kinsella), **Supp. V:** 260
"In the rude age when science was not so rife" (Surrey), **I:** 115–116
"In the Same Boat" (Kipling), **VI:** 193

In the Scales of Fate (Pietrkiewicz), **Supp. IV:** 98
In the Seven Woods (Yeats), **VI:** 213, 222
In the Shadow of the Glen (Synge), **Retro. Supp. I:** 295–296
"In the Snack–bar" (Morgan, E.), **Supp. IX:**158
In the South Seas (Stevenson), **V:** 396
In the Stopping Train (Davie), **Supp. VI:** 112
"In the Stopping Train" (Davie), **Supp. VI:** 112
In the Twilight (Swinburne), **V:** 333
"In the Vermilion Cathedral" (Redgrove), **Supp. VI:** 234
In the Year of Jubilee (Gissing), **V:** 437
"In This Time" (Jennings), **Supp. V:** 214
"In Time of Absence" (Graves), **VII:** 270
"In Time of 'The Breaking of Nations'" (Hardy), **Retro. Supp. I:** 120
"In Time of War" (Auden), **Retro. Supp. I:** 9
"In to thir dirk and drublie days" (Dunbar), **VIII:** 121
In Touch with the Infinite (Betjeman), **VII:** 365
In Which We Serve (Coward), **Supp. II:** 154
In Wicklow, West Kerry, and Connemara (Synge), **VI:** 309, 317
"In Youth" (Smith, I. C.), **Supp. IX:** 214
In Youth is Pleasure (Welch), **Supp. IX:** 261, 263, 264–266
Inadmissible Evidence (Osborne), **Supp. I:** 330, 333, 336–337
"Inarticulates" (MacCaig), **Supp. VI:** 191
Inca of Perusalem, The (Shaw), **VI:** 120
"Incarnate One, The" (Muir), **Supp. VI:** 208
"Incantata" (Muldoon), **Supp. IV:** 428–429, 430, 431–432
"Incendiary Method, The" (Murray), **Supp. VII:** 273
"Inchcape Rock, The" (Southey), **IV:** 58
"Incident" (Smith, I. C.), **Supp. IX:** 217
"Incident in the Life of Mr. George Crookhill" (Hardy), **VI:** 22
"Incident on a Journey" (Gunn), **Supp. IV:** 256, 258–259
Incidents at the Shrine (Okri), **Supp. V:** 347, 348, 352, 355–356
"Incidents at the Shrine" (Okri), **Supp. V:** 356–357
Incidents in the Rue Laugier (Brookner), **Supp. IV:** 135–136
Inclinations (Firbank), **Supp. II:** 201, 202, 209–211
Inclinations (Sackville–West), **VII:** 70
Incline Our Hearts (Wilson), **Supp. VI:** 307
Incognita; or, Love and Duty Reconcil'd (Congreve), **II:** 338, 346
Inconstant, The; or, The Way to Win Him (Farquhar), **II:** 352–353, 357, 362, 364
Incredulity of Father Brown, The (Chesterton), **VI:** 338
"Incubus, or the Impossibility of Self–Determination as to Desire (Self), **Supp. V:** 402

Jake's Thing (Amis), **Supp. II:** 16–17; **Supp. IV:** 29

Jakobson, Roman, **Supp. IV:** 115

"Jam Tart" (Auden), **Retro. Supp. I:** 6

Jamaica Inn (du Maurier), **Supp. III:** 139, 144, 145, 147

James, Henry, **II:** 42; **III:** 334, 340, 345; **IV:** 35, 107, 319, 323, 369, 371, 372; **V:** x, xx, xiv–xxvi, 2, 48, 51, 70, 95, 97, 98, 102, 191, 199, 205, 210, 295, 384, 390–392; **VI:** x–xi, 5, 23–69, 227, 236, 239, 266, 320, 322; list of short stories and novellas, **VI:** 69; **Supp. II:** 80–81, 89, 487–488, 492; **Supp. III:** 47–48, 60, 217, 437; **Supp. IV:** 97, 116, 133, 153, 233, 243, 371, 503, 511

James, M. R., **III:** 340

James, P. D., **Supp. II:** 127; **Supp. IV:** **319–341**

James, Richard, **II:** 102

James, William, **V:** xxv, 272; **VI:** 24

James IV (Greene), **VIII:** 142

James and the Giant Peach (Dahl), **Supp. IV:** 202, 213, 222

James and the Giant Peach (film), **Supp. IV:** 203

"James Honeyman" (Auden), **Retro. Supp. I:** 8

James Joyce and the Making of AUlysses" (Budgen) **VII:** 56

"James Lee's Wife" (Browning), **IV:** 367, 369

Jamie on a Flying Visit (Frayn), **Supp. VII:** 56–57

Jane and Prudence (Pym), **Supp. II:** **370–372**

Jane Austen: The Critical Heritage (ed. Southam), **IV:** 122, 124

Jane Austen's Literary Manuscripts (ed. Southam), **IV:** 124

Jane Eyre (Brontë), **III:** 338, 344, 345; **V:** xx, 106, 108, 112, 124, 135, **137–140**, 145, 147, 148, 152; **VII:** 101; **Supp. III:** 146; **Supp. IV:** 236, 452, 471; **Retro. Supp. I:** 50, 52, 53–55, 56, 58–60

"Janeites, The" (Kipling), **IV:** 106

"Jane's Marriage" (Kipling), **IV:** 106, 109

"Janet's Repentance" (Eliot), **V:** 190–191; **Retro. Supp. II:** 104

Janowitz, Haas, **III:** 342

"January 12, 1996" (Longley), **VIII:** 177

Janus: A Summing Up (Koestler), **Supp. I:** 35, 37, 38–39

Japp, A. H., **IV:** 144*n*, 155

Jarrell, Randall, **VI:** 165, 194, 200; **Supp. IV:** 460

"Jars, The" (Brown), **Supp. VI:** 71–72

"Jasmine" (Naipaul), **Supp. I:** 383

"Jason and Medea" (Gower), **I:** 54, 56

"Je est un autre" (Durrell), **Supp. I:** 126

"Je ne parle pas Français" (Mansfield), **VII:** 174, 177

"Je ne regretted rien" (Morgan, E.), **Supp. IX:** 165

"Je t'adore" (Kinsella), **Supp. V:** 263

"Jealousy" (Brooke), **Supp. III:** 52

Jeames's Diary; or, Sudden Wealth (Thackeray), **V:** 38

Jean de Meung, **I:** 49

Jeeves (Ayckbourn and Webber), **Supp. V:** 3

"Jeeves and the Hard–Boiled Egg" (Wodehouse), **Supp. III:** 455, 458

Jeeves and the Tie That Binds (Wodehouse), *see Much Obliged*

"Jeeves Takes Charge" (Wodehouse), **Supp. III:** 456, 457–458

Jeffares, Alexander Norman, **VI:** xxxiii–xxxiv, 98, 221

Jefferson, D. W., **III:** 182, 183

Jeffrey, Francis, **III:** 276, 285; **IV:** 31, 39, 60, 72, 129, 269

Jeffrey, Sara, **IV:** 225

Jenkin, Fleeming, **V:** 386

Jenkyn, D., **Supp. IV:** 346

Jennings, Elizabeth, **Supp. IV:** 256; **Supp. V:** **205–221**

"Jenny" (Rossetti), **V:** 240

Jenyns, Soame, **Retro. Supp. I:** 148

Jerrold, Douglas, **V:** 19

Jerrold, W. C., **IV:** 252, 254, 267

"Jersey Villas" (James), **III:** 69

Jerusalem (Blake), **III:** 303, 304–305, 307; **V:** xvi, 330; **Retro. Supp. I:** 45–46

Jerusalem Sinner Saved (Bunyan), *see Good News for the Vilest of Men*

Jerusalem the Golden (Drabble), **Supp. IV:** 230, 231, 238–239, 241, 243, 248, 251

Jesus (Wilson), **Supp. VI:** 306

Jess (Haggard), **Supp. III:** 213

Jesting Pilate (Huxley), **VII:** 201

Jew of Malta, The (Marlowe), **I:** 212, 280, **282–285, 310**; **Retro. Supp. I:** 208–209

Jew Süss (Feuchtwanger), **VI:** 265

Jewel in the Crown, The (Scott), **Supp. I:** 266–267, 269–270

Jeweller of Amsterdam, The (Field, Fletcher, Massinger), **II:** 67

"Jews, The" (Vaughan), **II:** 189

Jhabvala, Ruth Prawer, **Supp. V:** **223–239**

Jill (Larkin), **Supp. I:** 276, 286–287

Jill Somerset (Waugh), **Supp. VI:** 273

Jimmy Governor (Clune), **Supp. IV:** 350

Jitta's Atonement (Shaw), **VI:** 129

"Joachim du Bellay" (Pater), **V:** 344

Joan and Peter (Wells), **VI:** 240

Joan of Arc (Southey), **IV:** 59, 60, 63–64, 71

Joannis Miltonii Pro se defensio . . . (Milton), **II:** 176

Job (biblical book), **III:** 307

Jocasta (Gascoigne), **I:** 215–216

Jocelyn (Galsworthy), **VI:** 277

"Jochanan Hakkadosh" (Browning), **IV:** 365

Jocoseria (Browning), **IV:** 359, 374

"Joe Soap" (Motion), **Supp. VII:** 260–261, 262

"Johann Joachim Quantz's Five Lessons" (Graham), **Supp. VII:** 116

"Johannes Agricola in Meditation" (Browning), **IV:** 360

Johannes Secundus, **II:** 108

"John Betjeman's Brighton" (Ewart), **Supp. VII:** 37

John Bull's Other Island (Shaw), **VI:** 112, **113–115**; **Retro. Supp. II:** 320–321

John Caldigate (Trollope), **V:** 102

"John Clare" (Cope), **VIII:** 82

"John Fletcher" (Swinburne), **V:** 332

John Gabriel Borkman (Ibsen), **VI:** 110

"John Galsworthy" (Lawrence), **VI:** 275–276, 290

John Galsworthy (Mottram), **VI:** 271, 275, 290

"John Galsworthy, An Appreciation" (Conrad), **VI:** 290

"John Gilpin" (Cowper), **III:** 212, 220

John Keats: A Reassessment (ed. Muir), **IV:** 219, 227, 236

John Keats: His Like and Writings (Bush), **IV:** 224, 236

John Knox (Muir), **Supp. VI:** 198

"John Knox" (Smith, I. C.), **Supp. IX:** 211–212

John M. Synge (Masefield), **VI:** 317

John Marchmont's Legacy (Braddon), **VIII:** 44, 46

"John Norton" (Moore), **VI:** 98

"John of the Cross" (Jennings), **Supp. V:** 207

"John Ruskin" (Proust), **V:** 183

John Ruskin: The Portrait of a Prophet (Quennell), **V:** 185

John Sherman and Dhoya (Yeats), **VI:** 221

John Thomas and Lady Jane (Lawrence), **VII:** 111–112

John Woodvil (Lamb), **IV:** 78–79, 85

Johnnie Sahib (Scott), **Supp. I:** 259, 261

Johnny I Hardly Knew You (O'Brien), **Supp. V:** 338, 339

Johnny in the Clouds (Rattigan), see*Way to the Stars, The*

Johnson, Edgar, **IV:** 27, 40; **V:** 60, 72

Johnson, James, **III:** 320, 322

Johnson, Joseph, **Retro. Supp. I:** 37

Johnson, Lionel, **VI:** 3, 210, 211

Johnson, Samuel, **III:** 54, 96, **107–123,** 127, 151, 275; **IV:** xiv, xv, 27, 31, 34, 88n, 101, 138, 268, 299; **V:** 9, 281, 287; **VI:** 363; **Retro. Supp. I:** **137–150**; and Boswell, **III:** 234, 235, 238, 239, 243–249; and Collins, **III:** 160, 163, 164, 171, 173; and Crabbe, **III:** 280–282; and Goldsmith, **III:** 177, 180, 181, 189; dictionary, **III:** 113–116; **V:** 281, 434; literary criticism, **I:** 326; **II:** 123, 173, 197, 200, 259, 263, 293, 301, 347; **III:** 11, 88, 94, 139, 257, 275; **IV:** 101; on Addison and Steele, **III:** 39, 42, 44, 49, 51; **Supp. IV:** 271

Johnson, W. E., **Supp. II:** 406

Johnson over Jordan (Priestley), **VII:** 226–227

"Joker, The" (Wallace-Crabbe), **VIII:** 315–316

"Joker as Told" (Murray), **Supp. VII:** 279

Joking Apart (Ayckbourn), **Supp. V:** 3, 9, 13, 14

Jolly Beggars, The (Burns), **III:** 319–320

Junius Manuscript, **Retro. Supp. II:** 298–299, 301

Junk Mail (Self), **Supp. V:** 406–407

"Junkie" (Morgan, E.), **Supp. IX:** 164

Juno and the Paycock (O'Casey), **VII:** xviii, 4–5, 6, 11

Jure Divino (Defoe), **III:** 4, 13

Jusserand, Jean, **I:** 98

Just Between Ourselves (Ayckbourn), **Supp. V:** 3, 13

Just So Stories for Little Children (Kipling), **VI:** 188, 204

Just Vengeance, The (Sayers), **Supp. III:** 336, 350

Justice (Galsworthy), **VI:** xiii, 269, 273–274, 286–287

Justine (Durrell), **Supp. I:** 104, 105, 106

Juvenal, **II:** 30, 292, 347, 348; **III:** 42; **IV:** 188

Kafka, Franz, **III:** 340, 345; **Supp. IV:** 1, 199, 407, 439

Kafka's Dick (Bennett), **VIII:** 29–30

Kain, Saul, pseud. of Siegfried Sassoon

Kaisers of Carnuntum, The (Harrison), **Supp. V:** 164

Kakutani, Michiko, **Supp. IV:** 304

Kalendarium Hortense (Evelyn), **II:** 287

Kallman, Chester, **Supp. IV:** 422, 424; **Retro. Supp. I:** 9–10, 13

Kama Sutra, **Supp. IV:** 493

Kane, Sarah, **VIII:** 147–161

Kangaroo (Lawrence), **VII:** 90, 107–109, 119

Kant, Immanuel, **IV:** xiv, 50, 52, 145

Kanthapura (Rao), **Supp. V:** 56

"Karain: A Memory" (Conrad), **VI:** 148

Karl, Frederick R., **VI:** 135, 149

Karl–Ludwig's Window, (Saki), **Supp. VI:** 250

"Karshish" (Browning), **IV:** 357, 360, 363

Katchen's Caprices (Trollope), **V:** 101

"Kathe Kollwitz" (Rukeyser), **Supp. V:** 261

Katherine Mansfield (Alpers), **VII:** 183

Kathleen and Frank (Isherwood), **VII:** 316–317

Kathleen Listens In (O'Casey), **VII:** 12

"Katina" (Dahl), **Supp. IV:** 210

Kavan, Anna, **Supp. VII:** 201–215

Kavanagh, Julia, **IV:** 108, 122

Kavanagh, Dan, pseud. of Julian Barnes

Kavanagh, Patrick, **Supp. IV:** 409, 410, 412, 428, 542; **Supp. VII:** 183–199; **Retro. Supp. I:** 126

Kazin, Alfred, **Supp. IV:** 460

Keats, John, **II:** 102, 122, 192, 200; **III:** 174, 337, 338; **IV:** viii–xii, 81, 95, 129, 178, 196, 198, 204–205, 211–237, 255, 284, 316, 323, 332, 349, 355; **V:** 173, 361, 401, 403; **Supp. I:** 218; **Supp. V:** 38; **Retro. Supp. I:** 183–197

Keats and the Mirror of Art (Jack), **IV:** 236

Keats Circle, The: Letters and Papers . . . (Rollins), **IV:** 231, 232, 235

Keats: The Critical Heritage (ed. Matthews), **IV:** 237

Keats's Publisher: A Memoir of John Taylor (Blunden), **IV:** 236

Keble, John, **V:** xix, 252

"Keel, Ram, Stauros" (Jones), **Supp. VII:** 177

"Keen, Fitful Gusts" (Keats), **IV:** 215

Keep the Aspidistra Flying (Orwell), **VII:** 275, 278–279

"Keep the Home Fires Burning" (Novello), **VI:** 435

Keeton, G. W., **IV:** 286

Kell, Joseph, *see* Burgess, Anthony

Kellys and the O'Kellys, The (Trollope), **V:** 101

Kelman, James, **Supp. V:** 241–258

Keneally, Thomas, **Supp. IV:** 343–362

Kenilworth (Scott), **IV:** xviii, 39

Kennis van die aand (Brink), **Supp. VI:** 47–48, 49

Kept (Waugh), **Supp. VI:** 270

Kept in the Dark (Trollope), **V:** 102

Kermode, Frank, **I:** 237; **V:** 344, 355, 359, 412, 420; **VI:** 147, 208

Key of the Field, The (Powys), **VIII:** 255

Key to Modern Poetry, A (Durrell), **Supp. I:** 100, 121–123, 125, 126, 127

Key to My Heart, The (Pritchett), **Supp. III:** 324–325

"Key to My Heart, The" (Pritchett), **Supp. III:** 324

Key to the Door (Sillitoe), **Supp. V:** 410, 415

Keyes, Sidney, **VII:** xxii, 422, 433–440

Keynes, G. L., **II:** 134; **III:** 289n, 307, 308, 309

Kickleburys on the Rhine, The (Thackeray), **V:** 38

Kid (Armitage), **VIII:** 1, 4–6

"Kid" (Armitage), **VIII:** 5

Kidnapped (Stevenson), **V:** 383, 384, 387, 395; **Retro. Supp. I:** 266–267

"Kill, A" (Hughes), **Supp. I:** 352

"Killary Hostel" (Murphy), **Supp. V:** 328

Killham, John, **IV:** 323n, 338, 339; **VII:** 248–249

Killing Bottle, The (Hartley), **Supp. VII:** 123

Killing Kindness, A (Hill, R.), **Supp. IX:** 114–115, 117, 122

Killing the Lawyers (Hill, R.), **Supp. IX:** 123

Killing Time (Armitage), **VIII:** 1, 15–16

"Killing Time" (Harrison), **Supp. V:** 156

Kiltartan History Book, The (Gregory), **VI:** 318

Kiltartan Molière, The (Gregory), **VI:** 316, 318

Kiltartan Poetry Book, The (Gregory), **VI:** 318

Kilvert, Francis, **V:** 269; **Supp. IV:** 169

Kim (Kipling), **VI:** 166, 168, 169, 185–189; **Supp. IV:** 443

Kincaid, Jamaica, **Supp. VII:** 217–232

Kind Are Her Answers (Renault), **Supp. IX:** 173–174

"Kind Ghosts, The" (Owen), **VI:** 447, 455, 457

Kind Keeper, The; or, Mr Limberham (Dryden), **II:** 294305

Kind of Alaska, A (Pinter), **Supp. I:** 378

Kind of Anger, A (Ambler), **Supp. IV:** 16, 18–20

"Kind of Business: The Academic Critic in America, A" (Lodge), **Supp. IV:** 374

Kind of Scar, A (Boland), **Supp. V:** 35

"Kindertotenlieder" (Longley), **VIII:** 169–170

Kindness in a Corner (Powys), **VIII:** 248, 249, 256

Kindness of Women, The (Ballard), **Supp. V:** 24, 28, 31, 33

Kindly Light (Wilson), **Supp. VI:** 299, 308

Kindly Ones, The (Powell), **VII:** 344, 347, 348, 349, 350

King, Francis Henry, **VII:** xx, xxxviii; **Supp. IV:** 302

King, Bishop Henry, **II:** 121, 221; **Supp. VI:** 149–163

King, Kimball, **Supp. IV:** 194–195

King, S., **III:** 345

King, T., **II:** 336

King and No King, A (Beaumont and Fletcher), **II:** 43, 45, 52, 54, 57–58, 65

King Arthur; or, The British Worthy (Dryden), **II:** 294, 296, 305

"King Arthur's Tomb" (Morris), **V:** 293

"King Billy" (Morgan, E.), **Supp. IX:** 158

"King Duffus" (Warner), **Supp. VII:** 373

"King James I and Isaac Casaubon" (Landor), **IV:** 92

King James Version of the Bible, **I:** 370, 377–380

King John (Shakespeare), **I:** 286, 301

"King John's Castle" (Kinsella), **Supp. V:** 260

King Lear (Shakespeare), **I:** 316–317; **II:** 69; **III:** 116, 295; **IV:** 232; **Supp. II:** 194; **Supp. IV:** 149, 171, 282, 283, 294, 335; **Retro. Supp. I:** 34–35

King Log (Hill), **Supp. V:** 186–189

King Must Die, The (Renault), **Supp. IX:** 178–180, 187

"King of Beasts" (MacCaig), **Supp. VI:** 189

King of Hearts, The (Golding), **Supp. I:** 82

King of Pirates, The . . . (Defoe), **III:** 13

King of the Golden River, The; or, The Black Brothers (Ruskin), **V:** 184

"King of the World, The" (Coppard), **VIII:** 92

"King Pim" (Powys), **VIII:** 248, 249

King Solomon's Mines (Haggard), **Supp. III:** 211, 213, 215–217, 218–219, 227; **Supp. IV:** 484

King Stephen (Keats), **IV:** 231

King Victor and King Charles (Browning), **IV:** 373

"Kingdom of God, The" (Thompson), **V:** 449–450

"Kingdom of Heaven, The" (Powys), **VIII:** 256

Kingdom of the Wicked, The (Burgess), **Supp. I:** 186, 193

Kingdoms of Elfin (Warner), **Supp. VII:** 369, 371, 381

Macdonald, George, **V:** 266; **Supp. IV:** 201

Macdonald, Mary, **V:** 266, 272

McElroy, Joseph, **Supp. IV:** 116

McEwan, Ian, **Supp. IV:** 65, 75, **389–408; Supp. V: xxx**

McGann, Jerome J., **V:** 314, 335

McGrotty and Ludmilla (Gray, A.), **Supp. IX:** 80, 89

McGuckian, Medbh, **Supp. V: 277–293**

McHale, Brian, **Supp. IV:** 112

Machiavelli, Niccolò, **II:** 71, 72; **IV:** 279; **Retro. Supp. I:** 204

"Machine Stops, The" (Forster), **VI:** 399

McInherny, Frances, **Supp. IV:** 347, 353

Mack, Maynard, **Retro. Supp. I:** 229

Mackail, J. W., **V:** 294, 296, 297, 306

McKane, Richard, **Supp. IV:** 494–495

Mackay, M. E., **V:** 223, 234

Mackenzie, Compton, **VII:** 278

Mackenzie, Henry, **III:** 87; **IV:** 79

MacKenzie, Jean, **VI:** 227, 243

MacKenzie, Norman, **V:** 374n, 375n, 381, 382; **VI:** 227, 243

McKenney, Ruth, **Supp. IV:** 476

Mackenzie, Sir George, **III:** 95

"Mackery End, in Hertfordshire" (Lamb), **IV:** 83

MacLaren, Moray, **V:** 393, 398

McLeehan, Marshall, **IV:** 323n, 338, 339

Maclure, Millar, **I:** 291

Macmillan's (periodical), **VI:** 351

MacNeice, Louis, **VII:** 153, 382, 385, **401–418; Supp. III:** 119; **Supp. IV:** 423, 424

Macpherson, James, **III:** 336; **VIII: 179–195; Supp. II:** 523

Macready, William Charles, **I:** 327

McTaggart, J. M. E., **Supp. II:** 406

Mad Forest: A Play from Romania (Churchill), **Supp. IV:** 179, 188, 195–196, 198, 199

Mad Islands, The (MacNeice), **VII:** 405, 407

Mad Lover, The (Fletcher), **II:** 45, 55, 65

"Mad Maids Song, The" (Herrick), **II:** 112

"Mad Mullinix and Timothy" (Swift), **III:** 31

Mad Soldier's Song (Hardy), **VI:** 11

Mad World, My Masters, A (Middleton), **II:** 3, 4, 21

Madagascar; or, Robert Drury's Journal (Defoe), **III:** 14

Madame Bovary (Flaubert), **V:** xxii, 429; **Supp. IV:** 68, 69

"Madame de Mauves" (James), **VI:** 69; **Supp. IV:** 133

"Madame Rosette" (Dahl), **Supp. IV:** 209–210

Madan, Falconer, **V:** 264, 274

Maddox, Brenda, **Retro. Supp. I:** 327, 328

"Mademoiselle" (Stevenson), **Supp. VI:** 255

Mademoiselle de Maupin (Gautier), **V:** 320n

Madge, Charles, **VII:** xix

"Madman and the Child, The" (Cornford), **VIII:** 107

Madness of George III, The (Bennett), **VIII:** 31–33

Madoc (Muldoon), **Supp. IV:** 420, 424–427, 428

"Madoc" (Muldoon), **Supp. IV:** 422, 425–427, 430

Madoc (Southey), **IV:** 63, 64–65, 71

"Madoc" (Southey), **Supp. IV:** 425

"Madonna" (Kinsella), **Supp. V:** 273

Madonna and Other Poems (Kinsella), **Supp. V:** 272–273

Madonna of the Future and Other Tales, The (James), **VI:** 67, 69

"Madonna of the Trenches, A" (Kipling), **VI:** 193, **194–196**

Madras House, The (Shaw), **VI:** 118

Madwoman in the Attic, The (Gilbert/Gubar), **Retro. Supp. I:** 59–60

Maggot, A (Fowles), **Supp. I:** 309–310

"Magi" (Brown), **Supp. VI:** 71

Magic (Chesterton), **VI:** 340

Magic Box, The (Ambler), **Supp. IV:** 3

Magic Drum, The (Tennant), **Supp. IX:** 239

Magic Finger, The (Dahl), **Supp. IV:** 201

"Magic Finger, The" (Dahl), **Supp. IV:** 223–224

Magic Toyshop, The (Carter), **III:** 345; **Supp. III:** 80, 81, 82

Magic Wheel, The (eds. Swift and Profumo), **Supp. V:** 427

Magician, The (Maugham), **VI:** 374

Magician's Nephew, The (Lewis), **Supp. III:** 248

Magician's Wife, The (Moore, B.), **Supp. IX:** 141, 145–146

Maginn, William, **V:** 19

"Magna Est Veritas" (Smith), **Supp. II:** 471, 472

"Magnanimity" (Kinsella), **Supp. V:** 263

Magnetic Mountain, The (Day Lewis), **Supp. III:** 117, 122, 124–126

Magnetick Lady, The (Jonson), **Retro. Supp. I:** 165

Magnificence (Skelton), **I:** 90

"Magnolia" (Fuller), **Supp. VII:** 78

Magnus (Brown), **Supp. VI: 66–67**

"Magnus" (Macpherson), **VIII:** 186

Magnusson, Erika, **V:** 299, 300, 306

Magus, The (Fowles), **Supp. I:** 291, 292, 293, **295–299**, 310

Mahafty, John Pentland, **V:** 400, 401

Mahon, Derek, **Supp. IV:** 412; **Supp. VI: 165–180**

"Mahratta Ghats, The" (Lewis), **VII:** 446–447

Maid in the Mill, The (Fletcher and Rowley), **II:** 66

Maid in Waiting (Galsworthy), **VI:** 275

Maid Marian (Peacock), **IV:** xviii, 167–168, 170

Maid of Bath, The (Foote), **III:** 253

"Maid of Craca, The" (Macpherson), **VIII:** 186, 187

"Maiden Name" (Larkin), **Supp. I:** 277

Maiden Voyage (Welch), **Supp. IX:** 261, 263–264

Maiden's Dream, A (Greene), **VIII:** 142

Maid's Tragedy, The (Beaumont and Fletcher), **II:** 44, 45, **54–57,** 58, 60, 65

Maid's Tragedy, Alter'd, The (Waller), **II:** 238

Mailer, Norman, **Supp. IV:** 17–18

"Maim'd Debauchee, The" (Rochester), **II:** 259–260

"Main Road" (Pritchett), **Supp. III:** 316–317

Mainly on the Air (Beerbohm), **Supp. II:** 52

Maitland, F. W., **V:** 277, 290; **VI:** 385

Maitland, Thomas, pseud. of Algernon Charles Swinburne

Maitū njugīra (Ngũgĩ wa Thiong'o/Ngũgĩ wa Mīriī), **VIII:** 216, 224, 225

Maiwa's Revenge (Haggard), **Supp. III:** 213

Majeske, Penelope, **Supp. IV:** 330

Major, John, **Supp. IV:** 437–438

Major Barbara (Shaw), **VII:** xv, 102, 108, **113–115,** 124; **Retro. Supp. II:** 321

Major Political Essays (Shaw), **VI:** 129

Major Victorian Poets, The: Reconsiderations (Armstrong), **IV:** 339

Make Death Love Me (Rendell), **Supp. IX:** 192–194

Make Thyself Many (Powys), **VIII:** 255

"Maker on High, The" (tr. Morgan, E.), see *Altus Prosator*

Makin, Bathsua, **Supp. III:** 21

Making Cocoa for Kingsley Amis (Cope), **VIII:** 67, 69, 70–74, 81

Making History (Friel), **Supp. V:** 125

Making of a Poem, The (Spender), **Supp. II:** 481, 492

Making of an Immortal, The (Moore), **VI:** 96, 99

"Making of an Irish Goddess, The" (Boland), **Supp. V:** 44–45

Making of the English Working Class, The (Thompson), **Supp. IV:** 473

Making of the Representative for Planet 8, The (Lessing), **Supp. I:** 252, 254

"Making Poetry" (Stevenson), **Supp. VI:** 262

Mal vu, mal dit (Beckett), **Supp. I:** 62

Malayan trilogy (Burgess), **Supp. I:** 187

Malcolm Lowry: Psalms and Songs (Lowry), **Supp. III:** 285

Malcolm Mooney's Land (Graham), **Supp. VII:** 104, 106, 109, 113–115, 116

Malcontent, The (Marston), **II:** 27, 30, **31–33,** 36, 40, 68

Malcontents, The (Snow), **VII:** 336–337

Male Child, A (Scott), **Supp. I:** 263

Malign Fiesta (Lewis), **VII:** 72, 80

Malinowski, Bronislaw, **Supp. III:** 186

Mallet, David, **Supp. III:** 412, 424–425

Malone, Edmond, **I:** 326

Malone Dies (Beckett), **Supp. I:** 50, 51, 52–53, 63; **Supp. IV:** 106; **Retro. Supp. I:** 18, 22–23

Malory, Sir Thomas, **I: 67–80; IV:** 336, 337; **Retro. Supp. II: 237–252**

Malraux, André, **VI:** 240

"Maltese Cat, The" (Kipling), **VI:** 200

Malthus, Thomas, **IV:** xvi, 127, 133

Mamillia: A Mirror, or Looking-Glasse for the Ladies of England (Greene), **VIII:** 135, 140

"Man"(Herbert), **Retro. Supp. II:** 176–177

"Man"(Vaughan), **II:** 186, 188

Man, The (Stoker), **Supp. III:** 381

Man Above Men (Hare), **Supp. IV:** 282, 289

"Man and Bird" (Mahon), **Supp. VI:** 168

"Man and Boy" (Heaney), **Retro. Supp. I:** 132

Man and Boy (Rattigan), **Supp. VII:** 318, 320

"Man and Dog" (Thomas), **Supp. III:** 394, 403, 405

Man and Literature (Nicholson), **Supp. VI:** 213, 223

Man and Superman: A Comedy and a Philosophy (Shaw), **IV:** 161; **VI: 112–113,** 114, 127, 129; **Retro. Supp. II:** 309, 317–320

Man and Time (Priestley), **VII:** 213

Man and Two Women, A (Lessing), **Supp. I:** 244, 248

Man and Wife (Collins), **Supp. VI:** 102

Man Born to Be King, The (Sayers), **Supp. III:** 336, 349–350

"Man Called East, The" (Redgrove), **Supp. VI:** 236

Man Could Stand Up, A (Ford), **VI:** 319, 329

Man Does, Woman Is (Graves), **VII:** 268

"Man Friday" (Hope), **Supp. VII:** 164–165

"Man From the Caravan, The" (Coppard), **VIII:** 96

Man from the North, A (Bennett), **VI:** 248, 253

"Man from the South" (Dahl), **Supp. IV:** 215, 217–218

"Man I Killed, The" (Hardy), **Retro. Supp. I:** 120

"Man in Assynt, A" (MacCaig), **Supp. VI:** 191

Man in My Position, A (MacCaig), **Supp. VI: 191–192**

Man Lying On A Wall (Longley), **VIII:** 166, 172–173

"Man Lying On A Wall" (Longley), **VIII:** 172

Man Named East, The (Redgrove), **Supp. VI:** 235–236

Man of Destiny, The (Shaw), **VI:** 112

Man of Devon, A (Galsworthy), **VI:** 277

Man of Honour, A (Maugham), **VI:** 367, 368

Man of Law's Tale, The (Chaucer), **I:** 24, 34, 43, 51, 57

Man of Mode, The; or, Sir Fopling Flutter (Etherege), **II:** 256, 266, 271, 305

Man of Nazareth, The (Burgess), **Supp. I:** 193

Man of Property, A (Galsworthy), **VI:** 271, 272, 273, 274, 275, 276, 278, 282–283

Man of Quality, A (Lee), **II:** 336

Man of the Moment (Ayckbourn), **Supp. V:** 3, 7–8, 10

"Man Was Made to Mourn, a Dirge" (Burns), **III:** 315

"Man Who Changes His Mind, The" (Ambler), **Supp. IV:** 5

"Man Who Could Work Miracles, The" (Wells), **VI:** 235

"Man Who Died, The" (Lawrence), **VII:** 115; **Retro. Supp. II:** 233

Man Who Loved Children, The (Stead), **Supp. IV:** 460, 467–470, 473

"Man Who Loved Islands, The" (Lawrence), **VII:** 115

"Man Who Walked on the Moon, The" (Ballard), **Supp. V:** 33

Man Who Was Thursday, The (Chesterton), **VI:** 338

Man Who Wasn't There, The (Barker), **Supp. IV:** 45, 46, 56–57

"Man with a Past, The" (Hardy), **VI:** 17

"Man with Night Sweats, The" (Gunn), **Supp. IV:** 276–277

Man with Night Sweats, The (Gunn), **Supp. IV:** 255, 257, 274–278

"Man with the Dog, The" (Jhabvala), **Supp. V:** 236

"Man with the Twisted Lip, The" (Doyle), **Supp. II:** 171

Man Within, The (Greene), **Supp. I:** 2; **Retro. Supp. II:** 152

"Man Without a Temperament, The" (Mansfield), **VII:** 174, 177

"Mana Aboda" (Hulme), **Supp. VI:** 136

Manalive (Chesterton), **VI:** 340

Mañanas de abril y mayo (Calderón), **II:** 312*n*

Manchester Enthusiasts, The (Arden and D'Arcy), **Supp. II:** 39

"Manchester Marriage, The" (Gaskell), **V:** 6*n*, 14, 15

Manciple's Prologue, The (Chaucer), **I:** 24

Manciple's Tale, The (Chaucer), **I:** 55

"Mandela" (Motion), **Supp. VII:** 266

Mandelbaum Gate, The (Spark), **Supp. I: 206–208,** 213

Mandelstam, Osip, **Supp. IV:** 163, 493

Manet, Edouard, **Supp. IV:** 480

Manfred (Byron), **III:** 338; **IV:** xvii, 172, 173, 177, **178–182,** 192

Mangan Inheritance, The (Moore), **Supp. IX:** 144, 148, 150–151, 153

"Manhole 69" (Ballard), **Supp. V:** 21

"Manifesto" (Morgan, E.), **Supp. IX:** 163

Manifold, John, **VII:** 422, 426–427

Manin and the Venetian Revolution of 1848 (Trevelyan), **VI:** 389

Mankind in the Making (Wells), **VI:** 227, 236

Manly, J. M., **I:** 1

"Man–Man" (Naipaul), **Supp. I:** 385

Mann, Thomas, **II:** 97; **III:** 344; **Supp. IV:** 397

Manner of the World Nowadays, The (Skelton), **I:** 89

Mannerly Margery Milk and Ale (Skelton), **I:** 83

Manners, Mrs. Horace, pseud. of Algernon Charles Swinburne

"Manners, The" (Collins), **III:** 161, 162, 166, 171

Manning, Cardinal, **V:** 181

Manoeuvring (Edgeworth), **Supp. III:** 158

"Manor Farm, The" (Thomas), **Supp. III:** 399, 405

"Mans medley" (Herbert), **Retro. Supp. II:** 181–182

Manservant and Maidservant (Compton-Burnett), **VII:** 62, 63, 67

Mansfield, Katherine, **IV:** 106; **VI:** 375; **VII:** xv, xvii, **171–184,** 314; list of short stories, **VII:** 183–184

Mansfield Park (Austen), **IV:** xvii, 102–103, 108, 109, 111, 112, 115–119, 122; **Retro. Supp. II:** 9–11

Mantissa (Fowles), **Supp. I:** 308–309, 310

Manto, Saadat Hasan, **Supp. IV:** 440

Mantz, Ruth, **VII:** 176

Manuel (Maturin), **VIII:** 207, 208

"Manus Animam Pinxit" (Thompson), **V:** 442

Many Dimensions (Williams, C. W. S.), **Supp. IX:** 281

Manzoni, Alessandro, **III:** 334

Map, Walter, **I:** 35

Map of Love, The (Thomas), **Supp. I:** 176–177, 180

"Map of the City, A" (Gunn), **Supp. IV:** 262, 274

Map of the World, A (Hare), **Supp. IV:** 282, 288–289, 293

Map of Verona, A (Reed), **VII:** 423

Mapp Showing . . . Salvation and Damnation, A (Bunyan), **II:** 253

Mapplethorpe, Robert, **Supp. IV:** 170, 273

Mara, Bernard, *see* Moore, Brian

Marble Faun, The (Hawthorne), **VI:** 27

March of Literature, The (Ford), **VI:** 321, 322, 324

"Marchese Pallavicini and Walter Landor" (Landor), **IV:** 90

Marching Soldier (Cary), **VII:** 186

"Marching to Zion" (Coppard), **VIII:** 91–92

"Marchioness of Stonehenge, The" (Hardy), **VI:** 22

Marconi's Cottage (McGuckian), **Supp. V:** 284, 286–287

Marcus, Jane, **Retro. Supp. I:** 306

Marcus, S., **V:** 46, 73

Marfan (Reading), **VIII:** 262, 274–275

Margaret Drabble: Puritanism and Permissiveness (Myer), **Supp. IV:** 233

Margaret Ogilvy (Barrie), **Supp. III:** 3

Margin Released (Priestley), **VII:** 209, 210, 211

Margoliouth, H. M., **II:** 214*n*, 219

Mari Magno (Clough), **V:** 159, 168

Maria; or, The Wrongs of Woman (Wollstonecraft), **Supp. III:** 466, **476–480**

"Mariana" (Tennyson), **IV:** 329, 331

"Mariana in the South" (Tennyson), **IV:** 329, 331

Mariani, Paul L., **V:** 373*n*, 378, 382

Marianne Thornton (Forster), **VI:** 397, 411

Marie (Haggard), **Supp. III:** 214

Perimeter: Caroline Blackwood at Greenham Common, On the (Blackwood), **Supp. IX:** 14–15

Peripatetic, The (Thelwall), **IV:** 103

Perkin Warbeck (Ford), **II:** 89, 92, 96, 97, 100

Perkin Warbeck (Shelley), **Supp. III:** 371

Perkins, Richard, **II:** 68

Permanent Red: Essays in Seeing (Berger), **Supp. IV:** 79, 81

Pernicious Consequences of the New Heresie of the Jesuites . . . , The (tr. Evelyn), **II:** 287

Peronnik the Fool (Moore), **VI:** 99

Perry, Thomas Sergeant, **VI:** 24

Persian Boy, The (Renault), **Supp. IX:** 185–186

"Persian Eclogues" (Collins), **III:** 160, 164–165, 175

"Persian Passion Play, A" (Arnold), **V:** 216

Personae (Pound), **Supp. III:** 398

Personal and Possessive (Thomas), **Supp. IV:** 490

Personal Heresy, The: A Controversy (Lewis), **Supp. III:** 249

Personal History, Adventures, Experience, and Observation of David Copperfield, The (Dickens), *see David Copperfield*

Personal Landscape (periodical), **VII:** 425, 443

Personal Places (Kinsella), **Supp. V:** 272

"Personal Problem" (Kavanagh), **Supp. VII:** 198

Personal Record, A (Conrad), **VI:** 134, 148; **Retro. Supp. II:** 69

Personal Reminiscences of Henry Irving (Stoker), **Supp. III:** 381

Persons from Porlock (MacNeice), **VII:** 408

Persse, Jocelyn, **VI:** 55

Persuasion (Austen), **IV:** xvii, 106–109, 111, 113, 115–120, 122; **Retro. Supp. II:** 12–13

"Perturbations of Uranus, The" (Fuller), **Supp. VII:** 73

"Pervasion of Rouge, The" (Beerbohm), **Supp. II:** 45

"Pessimism in Literature" (Forster), **VI:** 410

Petals of Blood (Ngũgĩ), **VIII:** 212, 215, 220–221

Peter Bell (Wordsworth), **IV:** xviii 2

Peter Bell the Third (Shelley), **IV:** 203, 207

"Peter Grimes" (Crabbe), **III:** 283, 284–285

Peter Ibbetson (du Maurier), **Supp. III:** 134, 135, 136, 137, 138, 139

Peter Pan; or, The Boy Who Would Not Grow Up (Barrie), **Supp. III:** 2, **6–8**

Petrarch's Seven Penitential Psalms (Chapman), **I:** 241–242

Peveril of the Peak (Scott), **IV:** xviii, 36, 37, 39

Pfeil, Fred, **Supp. IV:** 94

Phaedra (tr. Morgan), **Supp. IX:** 157

Phaedra (Seneca), **II:** 97

Phaedra's Love (Kane), **VIII:** 148, 149, 156

"Phaèthôn" (Meredith), **V:** 224

"Phallus in Wonderland" (Ewart), **Supp. VII:** 36

Phantasmagoria (Carroll), **V:** 270, 273

Pharos, pseud. of E. M. Forster

Pharos and Pharillon (Forster), **VI:** 408

Pharsalia (tr. Marlowe), **I:** 276, 291

Phases of Faith (Newman), **V:** 208n

"Pheasant in a Cemetery" (Smith, I. C.), **Supp. IX:** 224

"Phebus and Cornide" (Gower), **I:** 55

Philadelphia, Here I Come! (Friel), **Supp. V:** 111, 116–118

Philanderer, The (Shaw), **VI:** 107, 109; **Retro. Supp. II:** 312

Philaster (Beaumont and Fletcher), **II:** 45, 46, **52–54**, 55, 65

Philby Conspiracy, The (Page, Leitch, and Knightley), **Supp. II:** 302, 303, 311–312

Philip (Thackeray), *see Adventures of Philip on His Way Through the World, The*

Philip Larkin (Motion), **Supp. VII:** 253

Philip Sparrow (Skelton), **I:** 84, 86–88

Philip Webb and His Work (Lethaby), **V:** 291, 292, 296, 306

Philips, Ambrose, **III:** 56

Philips, Katherine, **II:** 185

Phillips, Caryl, **Supp. V:** **379–394**

Phillipps, Sir Thomas, **II:** 103

Phillips, Edward, **II:** 347

"Phillis is my only Joy" (Sedley), **II:** 265

"Phillis, let's shun the common Fate" (Sedley), **II:** 263

Phillpotts, Eden, **VI:** 266

"Philosopher, The" (Brontë), **V:** 134

"Philosopher and the Birds, The" (Murphy), **Supp. V:** 318

Philosopher's Pupil, The (Murdoch), **Supp. I:** 231, 232–233

Philosophical Discourse of Earth, An, Relating to . . . Plants, &c. (Evelyn), **II:** 287

Philosophical Enquiry into the Origin of Our Ideas of the Sublime and Beautiful, A (Burke), *see On the Sublime and Beautiful*

Philosophical Essays Concerning Human Understanding (Hume), **Supp. III:** 238

Philosophical Lectures of S. T. Coleridge, The (ed. Cobum), **IV:** 52, 56

"Philosophical View of Reform, A" (Shelley), **IV:** 199, 209; **Retro. Supp. I:** 254

"Philosophy of Herodotus" (De Quincey), **IV:** 147–148

Philosophy of Melancholy, The (Peacock), **IV:** 158, 169

Philosophy of Nesessity, The (Bray), **V:** 188

Philosophy of Rhetoric (Richards), **Supp. II:** 416, 423

Philosophy of the Unconscious (Hartmann), **Supp. II:** 108

Phineas Finn (Trollope), **V:** 96, 98, 101, 102

Phineas Redux (Trollope), **V:** 96, 98, 101, 102

Phoenix (Storey), **Supp. I:** 408, 420

Phoenix, The, **Retro. Supp. II:** 303

Phoenix, The (Middleton), **II:** 21, 30

Phoenix and the Turtle, The (Shakespeare), **I:** 34, 313

"Phoenix Park" (Kinsella), **Supp. V:** 264

"Phoenix Rose Again, The" (Golding), **Supp. I:** 66

Phoenix Too Frequent, A (Fry), **Supp. III:** 194–195, 201–202

Photographs and Notebooks (Chatwin, B.), **Supp. IX:** 61–62

"Photograph of Emigrants" (Smith, I. C.), **Supp. IX:** 221

Physicists, The (Snow), **VII:** 339–340

Physico'Theology (Derham), **III:** 49

"Pibroch" (Hughes), **Supp. I:** 350

Picasso, Pablo, **Supp. IV:** 81, 87, 88

Piccolomini; or, The First Part of Wallenstein, The (Coleridge), **IV:** 55–56

Pickering, John, **I:** 213, 216–218

Pickwick Papers (Dickens), **V:** xix, 9, 42, 46–47, 48, 52, 59, 62, 71

Pico della Mirandola, **II:** 146; **V:** 344

"Pictor Ignotus, Florence 15" A (Browning), **IV:** 356, 361; **Retro. Supp. II:** 27

"Pictorial Rhapsody, A" (Thackeray), **V:** 37

Picture and Text (James), **VI:** 46, 67

"Picture of a Nativity" (Hill), **Supp. V:** 186

Picture of Dorian Gray, The (Wilde), **III:** 334, 345; **V:** xxv, 339, 399, 410–411, 417, 419; **Retro. Supp. II:** 368

"Picture of Little T. C. in a Prospect of Flowers, The" (Marvell), **II:** 211, 215

"Picture This" (Motion), **Supp. VII:** 266

Picturegoers, The (Lodge), **Supp. IV:** 364, 367–368, 369, 371, 372, 381, 382

"Pictures" (Kelman), **Supp. V:** 250

Pictures at an Exhibition (Thomas), **Supp. IV:** 487–488

"Pictures from a Japanese Printmaker" (Redgrove), **Supp. VI:** 234

"Pictures from an Ecclesiastical Furnisher's" (Redgrove), **Supp. VI:** 234

Pictures from Italy (Dickens), **V:** 71

Pictures in the Hallway (O'Casey), **VII:** 9, 12

Pictures of Perfection (Hill, R.), **Supp. IX:** 121, 122–123

Picturesque Landscape and English Romantic Poetry (Watson), **IV:** 26

"Piece of Cake, A" (Dahl), **Supp. IV:** 208, 209

"Pied Beauty" (Hopkins), **V:** 367; **Retro. Supp. II:** 196

"Pied Piper of Hamelin, The" (Browning), **IV:** 356, 367

Pied Piper of Lovers (Durrell), **Supp. I:** 95

"Pier Bar" (Murphy), **Supp. V:** 328

Pier'Glass, The (Graves), **VII:** 263–264

Pierrot mon ami (Queneau), **Supp. I:** 220

Piers Plowman (Langland), **I:** **1–18**

Pietrkiewicz, Jerzy, **Supp. IV:** 98

Pygmalion (Shaw), **VI:** xv, 108, 115, 116–117, 120; **Retro. Supp. II:** 322
"Pylons, The" (Spender), **Supp. II:** 48
Pym, Barbara, **Supp. II: 363–384**
Pynchon, Thomas, **Supp. IV:** 116, 163
Pynson, Richard, **I:** 99
Pyramid, The (Golding), **Supp. I:** 81–82; **Retro. Supp. I:** 100–101
"Pyramis or The House of Ascent" (Hope), **Supp. VII:** 154
"Pyramus and Thisbe" (Gower), **I:** 53–54, 55
"Qua cursum ventus" (Clough), **V:** 160
Quadrille (Coward), **Supp. II:** 155
"Quaint Mazes" (Hill), **Supp. V:** 191
"Quality of Sprawl, The" (Murray), **Supp. VII:** 278–279
Quality Street (Barrie), **Supp. III:** 6, 8
"Quantity Theory of Insanity, The" (Self), **Supp. V:** 402
Quantity Theory of Insanity, The: Together with Five Supporting Propositions (Self), **Supp. V:** 395, 400–402
Quare Fellow, The (Behan), **Supp. II:** 65, **68–70,** 73
Quaritch, Bernard, **IV:** 343, 346, 348, 349
Quarles, Francis, **II:** 139, 246
"Quarrel, The" (Cornford), **VIII:** 113
Quarterly Review (periodical), **IV:** xvi, 60–61, 69, 133, 204–205, 269–270; **V:** 140
Quartermaine, Peter, **Supp. IV:** 348
Quartet (Rhys), **Supp. II:** 388, **390–392,** 403
Quartet in Autumn (Pym), **Supp. II: 380–382**
Queen, The; or, The Excellency of Her Sex (Ford), **II:** 88, 89, 91, 96, 100
"Queen Annelida and False Arcite" (Browning), **IV:** 321
Queen Is Crowned, A (Fry), **Supp. III:** 195
Queen Mab (Shelley), **IV:** xvii, 197, 201, 207, 208; **Retro. Supp. I:** 245–246
Queen Mary (Tennyson), **IV:** 328, 338
Queen of Corinth, The (Field, Fletcher, Massinger), **II:** 66
Queen of Hearts, The (Collins), **Supp. VI:** 95
"Queen of Spades, The" (Pushkin), **III:** 339–340, 345
Queen of Stones (Tennant), **Supp. IX:** 231, 233–235
Queen of the Air, The (Ruskin), **V:** 174, 180, 181, 184
Queen of the Dawn (Haggard), **Supp. III:** 222
Queen Sheba's Ring (Haggard), **Supp. III:** 214
Queen Victoria (Strachey), **Supp. II: 512–514**
Queen Was in the Parlor, The (Coward), **Supp. II:** 141, 146
Queen Yseult (Swinburne), **V:** 333
Queenhoo' Hall (Strutt), **IV:** 31
"Queenie Fat and Thin" (Brooke' Rose), **Supp. IV:** 103
Queen' Mother, The (Swinburne), **V:** 312, 313, 314, 330, 331, 332

Queen's Tragedy, The (Swinburne), **V:** 333
Queery Leary Nonsense (Lear), **V:** 87
Quennell, Peter, **V:** xii, xviii, 192, 193, 194; **VI:** 237; **Supp. III:** 107
Quentin Durward (Scott), **IV:** xviii, 37, 39
"Quest, The" (Saki), **Supp. VI:** 249
Quest sonnets (Auden), **VII:** 380–381; **Retro. Supp. I:** 2, 10
"Question, A" (Synge), **VI:** 314
"Question, The" (Shelley), **IV:** 203
"Question for Walter, A" (Longley), **VIII:** 163–164
"Question in the Cobweb, The" (Reid), **Supp. VII:** 326
Question of Attribution, A (Bennett), **VIII:** 30, 31
"Question of Place, A" (Berger), **Supp. IV:** 92
Question of Proof, A (Day Lewis), **Supp. III:** 117, 131
Question of Upbringing, A (Powell), **VII:** 343, 347, 350, 351
Questions about the . . . Seventh' Day Sabbath (Bunyan), **II:** 253
"Questions in a Wood" (Graves), **VII:** 268
"Qui laborat orat" (Clough), **V:** 160
"Quidditie, The" (Herbert), **Retro. Supp. II:** 179
Quiet American, The (Greene), **Supp. I:** 7, 13, 14; **Supp. IV:** 369; **Retro. Supp. II:** 160–161
Quiet Life, A (Bainbridge), **Supp. VI:** 17, 21–22, 26–27
Quiet Memorandum, The (Pinter), **Supp. I:** 374
"Quiet Neighbours" (Warner), **Supp. VII:** 371
Quiet Wedding (Rattigan), **Supp. VII:** 311
"Quiet Woman, The" (Coppard), **VIII:** 93
"Quiet Woman of Chancery Lane, The" (Redgrove), **Supp. VI:** 235, 237
Quigley, Austin E., **Retro. Supp. I:** 227
Quiller' Couch, Sir Arthur, **II:** 121, 191; **V:** 384
Quillinan, Edward, **IV:** 143n
Quinlan, M. J., **III:** 220
Quinn Manuscript, **VII:** 148
Quintessence of Ibsenism, The (Shaw), **VI:** 104, 106, 129
"Quintets for Robert Morley" (Murray), **Supp. VII:** 278, 283
Quinx (Durrell), **Supp. I:** 119, 120
"Quip, The" (Herbert), **II:** 126
"Quis Optimus Reipvb. Status (What Is The Best Form of the Commonwealth?)" (More), **Supp. VII:** 238
"Quite Early One Morning" (Thomas), **Supp. I:** 183
"Quitting Bulleen" (Wallace-Crabbe), **VIII:** 316
Quoof (Muldoon), **Supp. IV:** 418–421, 422, 423, 425
"R. I. P." (Gissing), **V:** 43

R.L.S. and His Sine Qua Non (Boodle), **V:** 391, 393, 397
"Rabbit Catcher, The" (Hughes), **Retro. Supp. II:** 217–218
Rabelais, François, **III:** 24; **Supp. IV:** 464
Rachel Papers, The (Amis), **Supp. IV:** 26, 27, 28–29, 30
Rachel Ray (Trollope), **V:** 101
Racine, Jean Baptiste, **II:** 98; **V:** 22
Racing Demon (Hare), **Supp. IV:** 282, 294–296, 298
Radcliffe (Storey), **Supp. I:** 408, 410, 414, 415–416, 418–419
Radcliffe, Ann, **III:** 327, 331–332, 333, 335–338, 345; **IV:** xvi, 30, 35, 36, 111, 173, 218; **Supp. III:** 384
Radiant Way, The (Drabble), **Supp. IV:** 231, 234, 247–249, 250
Radical Imagination, The (Harris), **Supp. V:** 140, 145
Rafferty, Terrence, **Supp. IV:** 357, 360
Raffety, F. W., **III:** 199n
Raft of the Medusa, The (Géricault), **Supp. IV:** 71–72
"Rage for Order" (Mahon), **Supp. VI:** 170
Rage of the Vulture, The (Unsworth), **Supp. VII:** 356, 357, 359–360
Raiders' Dawn (Lewis), **VII:** 445, 448
Rain (Maugham), **VI:** 369
"Rain" (Thomas), **VI:** 424; **Supp. III:** 400, 401
"Rain Charm for the Duchy" (Hughes), **Supp. I:** 365; **Retro. Supp. II:** 214
"Rain Horse, The" (Hughes), **Supp. I:** 348
"Rain in Spain, The" (Reid), **Supp. VII:** 328
"Rain Stick, The" (Heaney), **Retro. Supp. I:** 132–133
Rain upon Godshill (Priestley), **VII:** 209, 210
Rainbow, The (Lawrence), **VI:** 232, 276, 283; **VII:** 88, 90, 93, **98–101; Retro. Supp. II:** 227–228
Raine, Kathleen, **III:** 297, 308
"Rainy Night, A" (Lowry), **Supp. III:** 270
Raj Quartet (Scott), **Supp. I:** 259, 260, 261–262, **266–272**
"Rajah's Diamond, The" (Stevenson), **V:** 395
Rajan, B., **VI:** 219
Rake's Progress, The (Auden/Kallman), **Retro. Supp. I:** 10
Raknem, Ingwald, **VI:** 228
Ralegh, Sir Walter, **I: 145–159,** 277, 278, 291; **II:** 138; **III:** 120, 122, 245; **VI:** 76, 157; **Retro. Supp. I:** 203–204
Raleigh, Sir Walter, *see* Ralegh, Sir Walter
Ralph the Heir (Trollope), **V:** 100, 102
"Ram, The" (Armitage), **VIII:** 12
Rambler (Newman), **Supp. VII:** 299
Rambler (periodical), **II:** 142; **III:** 94, 110–111, 112, 119, 121; **Retro. Supp. I:** 137, 140–141, 149
Rambles Among the Oases of Tunisia (Douglas), **VI:** 305

Resurrection at Sorrow Hill (Harris), **Supp. V:** 144

Resurrection of the Dead, The, . . . (Bunyan), **II:** 253

"Retaliation" (Goldsmith), **III:** 181, 185, 191

"Reticence of Lady Anne, The" (Saki), **Supp. VI:** 245

"Retired Cat, The" (Cowper), **III:** 217

"Retirement" (Vaughan), **II:** 187, 188, 189

"Retreat, The" (King), **Supp. VI:** 153

"Retreate, The" (Vaughan), **II:** 186, 188–189

"Retrospect" (Brooke), **Supp. III:** 56

"Retrospect: From a Street in Chelsea" (Day Lewis), **Supp. III:** 121

"Retrospective Review" (Hood), **IV:** 255

"Return, The" (Conrad), **VI:** 148

"Return, The" (Muir), **Supp. VI:** 207

"Return, A" (Russell), **VIII:** 284

"Return from the Freudian Islands, The" (Hope), **Supp. VII:** 155–156, 157

"Return from the Islands" (Redgrove), **Supp. VI:** 235

Return of Eva Peron, The (Naipaul), **Supp. I:** 396, 397, 398, 399

Return of the Druses, The (Browning), **IV:** 374

"Return of the Iron Man, The" (Hughes), **Supp. I:** 346

Return of the King, The (Tolkien), **Supp. II:** 519

Return of the Native, The (Hardy), **V:** xxiv, 279; **VI:** 1–2, 5, 6, 7, 8; **Retro. Supp. I:** 114

Return of the Soldier, The (West), **Supp. III:** 440, 441

Return of Ulysses, The (Bridges), **VI:** 83

Return to Abyssinia (White), **Supp. I:** 131

Return to My Native Land (tr. Berger), **Supp. IV:** 77

Return to Night (Renault), **Supp. IX:** 175

Return to Oasis (Durrell), **VII:** 425

"Return to the Council House" (Smith, I. C.), **Supp. IX:** 214

Return to Yesterday (Ford), **VI:** 149

Returning (O'Brien), **Supp. V:** 339

"Returning, We Hear the Larks" (Rosenberg), **VI:** 434–435

Revaluation (Leavis), **III:** 68; **VII:** 234, 236, 244–245

"Reveille" (Hughes), **Supp. I:** 350

Revelations of Divine Love (Juliana of Norwich), **I:** 20–21

Revenge for Love, The (Lewis), **VII:** 72, 74, 81

Revenge Is Sweet: Two Short Stories (Hardy), **VI:** 20

Revenge of Bussy D'Ambois, The (Chapman), **I:** 251–252, 253; **II:** 37

Revenger's Tragedy, The, **II:** 1–2, 21, 29, **33–36,** 37, 39, 40, 41, 70, 97

Revengers' Comedies, The (Ayckbourn), **Supp. V:** 3, 10

Reverberator, The (James), **VI:** 67

"Reverie" (Browning), **IV:** 365

Reveries over Childhood and Youth (Yeats), **VI:** 222

Reversals (Stevenson), **Supp. VI:** 255–256

"Reversals" (Stevenson), **Supp. VI:** 256

Review of some poems by Alexander Smith and Matthew Arnold (Clough), **V:** 158

Review of the Affairs of France, A . . . (Defoe), **III:** 13; **Retro. Supp. I:** 65

Review of the State of the British Nation, A (Defoe), **Retro. Supp. I:** 65

"Reviewer's ABC, A" (Aiken), **VII:** 149

Revised Version of the Bible, **I:** 381–382

Revolt in the Desert (Lawrence), **Supp. II:** 288, 289–290, 293

Revolt of Aphrodite, The (Durrell), *see Tunc; Nunquam*

Revolt of Islam, The (Shelley), **IV:** xvii, 198, 203, 208; **VI:** 455; **Retro. Supp. I:** 249–250

"Revolt of the Tartars" (De Quincey), **IV:** 149

"Revolution" (Housman), **VI:** 160

Revolution in Tanner's Lane, The (Rutherford), **VI:** 240

Revolution Script, The (Moore, B.), **Supp. IX:** 141, 143

Revolutionary Epick, The (Disraeli), **IV:** 306, 308

Revolving Lights (Richardson), **Retro. Supp. I:** 313–314

Revue des Deux Mondes (Montégut), **V:** 102

"Revulsion" (Davie), **Supp. VI:** 110, 112

"Rex Imperator" (Wilson), **Supp. I:** 155, 156

"Reynard the Fox" (Masefield), **VI:** 338

Reynolds, G. W. M., **III:** 335

Reynolds, Henry, **Supp. IV:** 350

Reynolds, John, **II:** 14

Reynolds, John Hamilton, **IV:** 215, 221, 226, 228, 229, 232, 233, 253, 257, 259, 281

Reynolds, Sir Joshua, **II:** 336; **III:** 305

"Rhapsody of Life's Progress, A" (Browning), **IV:** 313

"Rhapsody on a Windy Night" (Eliot), **Retro. Supp. II:** 121–122

Rhetor (Harvey), **I:** 122

"Rhetoric" (De Quincey), **IV:** 147

"Rhetoric" (Jennings), **Supp. V:** 218

"Rhetoric and Poetic Drama" (Eliot), **VII:** 157

"Rhetoric of a Journey" (Fuller), **Supp. VII:** 72

Rhetoric of the Unreal: Studies in Narrative and Structure, Especially of the Fantastic, A (Brooke-Rose), **Supp. IV:** 97, 99, 115, 116

"Rhineland Journal" (Spender), **Supp. II:** 489

Rhoda Fleming (Meredith), **V:** xxiii, 227n, 234

"Rhodian Captain" (Durrell), **Supp. I:** 124

Rhododaphne (Peacock), **IV:** 158, 170

Rhyme? and Reason? (Carroll), **V:** 270, 273

Rhyme Stew (Dahl), **Supp. IV:** 226

Rhys, Jean, **Supp. II: 387–403; Supp. V:** 40; **Retro. Supp. I:** 60

"Rhythm and Imagery in British Poetry" (Empson), **Supp. II:** 195

"Ribblesdale" (Hopkins), **V:** 367, 372; **Retro. Supp. II:** 191

Riceyman Steps (Bennett), **VI:** 250, 252, 260–261

Rich, Barnaby, **I:** 312

Rich Get Rich (Kavan), **Supp. VII:** 208–209

Richard II (Shakespeare), **I:** 286, 308

Richard III (Shakespeare), **I:** 285, 299–301

"Richard Martin" (Hood), **IV:** 267

Richard Rolle of Hampole, **I:** 20

Richards, I. A., **III:** 324; **V:** 367, 381; **VI:** 207, 208; **VII:** xiii, 233, 239; **Supp. II:** 185, 193, **405–431**

Richard's Cork Leg (Behan), **Supp. II:** 65, 74

Richards, Grant, **VI:** 158

Richardson, Betty, **Supp. IV:** 330

Richardson, Dorothy, **VI:** 372; **VII:** 20; **Supp. IV:** 233; **Retro. Supp. I:** 313–314

Richardson, Elaine Cynthia Potter, *see* Kincaid, Jamaica

Richardson, Joanna, **IV:** xxv, 236; **V:** xi, xviii

Richardson, Samuel, **III: 80–93,** 94, 98, 333; **VI:** 266 **Supp. II:** 10; **Supp. III:** 26, 30–31; **Supp. IV:** 150; **Retro. Supp. I:** 80

"Richt Respeck for Cuddies, A" (tr. Morgan, E.), **Supp. IX:** 168

Ricks, Christopher, **Supp. IV:** 394, 398

Riddarasögur, **VIII:** 236

"Riddle of Houdini, The" (Doyle), **Supp. II:** 163–164

Riddle of Midnight, The (film, Rushdie), **Supp. IV:** 436, 441

"Ride from Milan, The" (Swinburne), **V:** 325, 333

Riders in the Chariot (White), **Supp. I:** 131, 132, 133, 136, **141–143,** 152

Riders to the Sea (Synge), **VI:** xvi, 308, 309, 310–311; **Retro. Supp. I:** 296

Riding, Laura, **VI:** 207; **VII:** 258, 260, 261, 263, 269; **Supp. II:** 185; **Supp. III:** 120

Riding Lights (MacCaig), **Supp. VI:** 181, **185–186,** 190, 194

Riffaterre, Michael, **Supp. IV:** 115

Rigby, Elizabeth, **V:** 138

Right at Last and Other Tales (Gaskell), **V:** 15

Right Ho, Jeeves (Wodehouse), **Supp. III:** 458, 461

Right to an Answer, The (Burgess), **Supp. I:** 187, 188–189, 190, 195, 196

Righter, Anne, **I:** 224, 269, 329

Rights of Great Britain asserted against the Claims of America (Macpherson), **VIII:** 193

Rígsþula, **VIII:** 231

Rilke, Rainer Maria, **VI:** 215; **Supp. IV:** 480

Rimbaud, Jean Nicolas, **Supp. IV:** 163

"Rime of the Ancient Mariner, The" (Coleridge), *see* "Ancient Mariner, The"

"There Is Nothing" (Gurney), **VI:** 426–427

"There was a Saviour" (Thomas), **Supp. I:** 177, 178

"There was a time" (Thomas), **Supp. III:** 404

"There was an old Derry down Derry" (Lear), **V:** 82

"There Was an Old Man in a Barge" (Lear), **V:** 83

"There Was an Old Man of Blackheath" (Lear), **V:** 86

"There Was an Old Man of Three Bridges" (Lear), **V:** 86

"There was never nothing more me pained" (Wyatt), **I:** 103

"There Will Be No Peace" (Auden), **Retro. Supp. I:** 13

"There's Nothing Here" (Muir), **Supp. VI:** 208

"Thermal Stair, The" (Graham), **Supp. VII:** 114

"These Summer–Birds did with thy Master stay" (Herrick), **II:** 103

These the Companions (Davie), **Supp. VI:** 105, 109, 111, 113, 117

These Twain (Bennett), **VI:** 258

"Theses on the Philosophy of History" (Benjamin), **Supp. IV:** 87

Thespian Magazine (periodical), **III:** 263

"Thespians at Thermopylae, The" (Cameron), **Supp. IX:** 19

"They" (Kipling), **VI:** 199

"They" (Sassoon), **VI:** 430

"They" (Wallace-Crabbe), **VIII:** 322

"They All Go to the Mountains Now" (Brooke-Rose), **Supp. IV:** 103

"They Are All Gone into the World of Light!" (Vaughan), **II:** 188

They Came to a City (Priestley), **VII:** 210, 227

"They flee from me" (Wyatt), **I:** 102

"They Shall Not Grow Old" (Dahl), **Supp. IV:** 210, 224

They Walk in the City (Priestley), **VII:** 217

They Went (Douglas), **VI:** 303, 304, 305

"Thief" (Graves), **VII:** 267

Thierry and Theodoret (Beaumont, Fletcher, Massinger), **II:** 66

Thieves in the Night (Koestler), **Supp. I:** 27–28, 32–33

"Thin Air" (Armitage), **VIII:** 11

"Thing Itself, The" (Wallace-Crabbe), **VIII:** 321

Things That Have Interested Me (Bennett), **VI:** 267

Things That Interested Me (Bennett), **VI:** 267

Things We Do for Love (Ayckbourn), **Supp. V:** 3–4, 12–13

Things Which Have Interested Me (Bennett), **VI:** 267

"Thinking as a Hobby" (Golding), **Supp. I:** 75

"Thinking of Mr. D." (Kinsella), **Supp. V:** 260

Thinking Reed, The (West), **Supp. III:** 442

"Thir Lady is Fair" (Dunbar), **VIII:** 122

"Third Journey, The" (Graham), **Supp. VII:** 109

Third Man, The (Greene), **Supp. I:** 11; **Retro. Supp. II:** 159

"Third Person, The" (James), **VI:** 69

Third Policeman, The (O'Nolan), **Supp. II:** 322, **326–329,** 337, 338

"Third Prize, The" (Coppard), **VIII:** 96

Third Satire (Wyatt), **I:** 111

Thirteen Such Years (Waugh), **Supp. VI:** 272–273

Thirteenth Tribe, The (Koestler), **Supp. I:** 33

"30 December" (Cope), **VIII:** 80

"38 Phoenix Street" (Kinsella), **Supp. V:** 268

Thirty–Nine Steps, The (Buchan), **Supp. II:** 299, 306; **Supp. IV:** 7

36 Hours (film), **Supp. IV:** 209

"Thirty–Three Triads" (Kinsella), **Supp. V:** 264

"This Be the Verse" (Larkin), **Supp. I:** 284

"This bread I break" (Thomas), **Supp. I:** 174

"This England" (Thomas), **Supp. III:** 404

This England: An Anthology from Her Writers (ed. Thomas), **Supp. III: 404–405**

This Gun for Hire (Greene), *see Gun for Sale, A*

This Happy Breed (Coward), **Supp. II:** 151, 154

"This Hinder Nicht in Dunfermeling" (Dunbar), **VIII:** 122

"This Is No Case of Petty Right or Wrong" (Thomas), **VI:** 424; **Supp. III:** 395

"This Is Thyself" (Powys), **VIII:** 247

This Is Where I Came In (Ayckbourn), **Supp. V:** 3, 11, 13

"This Is Your Subject Speaking" (Motion), **Supp. VII:** 257

"This Last Pain" (Empson), **Supp. II:** 184–185

This Life I've Loved (Field), **V:** 393, 397

"This Lime Tree Bower My Prison" (Coleridge), **IV:** 41, 44; **Retro. Supp. II:** 52

This Misery of Boots (Wells), **VI:** 244

This My Hand (Caudwell), **Supp. IX:** 33, 35, 37, 39–40, 46

This Real Night (West), **Supp. III:** 443

This Sporting Life (Storey), **Supp. I:** 407, **408–410,** 414, 415, 416

This Sweet Sickness (Highsmith), **Supp. V:** 172–173

This Time Tomorrow (Ngũgĩ), **VIII:** 213, 222

This Was a Man (Coward), **Supp. II:** 146

"This was for youth, Strength, Mirth and wit that Time" (Walton), **II:** 141

This Was the Old Chief's Country (Lessing), **Supp. I:** 239

This Year of Grace! (Coward), **Supp. II:** 146

"Thistles" (Hughes), **Retro. Supp. II:** 205–206

Thistles and Roses (Smith, I. C.), **Supp. IX:** 211–212

Thom Gunn and Ted Hughes (Bold), **Supp. IV:** 256, 257

"Thom Gunn at 60" (Hall), **Supp. IV:** 256

Thomas, D. M., **Supp. IV: 479–497**

Thomas, Dylan, **II:** 156; **Supp. I: 169–184; Supp. III:** 107; **Supp. IV:** 252, 263

Thomas, Edward, **IV:** 218; **V:** 313, 334, 355, 358; **VI:** 420–421, **423–425; VII:** xvi, 382; **Supp. III: 393–408**

"Thomas Bewick" (Gunn), **Supp. IV:** 269

"Thomas Campey and the Copernican System" (Harrison), **Supp. V:** 151

Thomas Carlyle (Campbell), **IV:** 250

Thomas Carlyle (Froude), **IV:** 238–239, 250

Thomas Cranmer of Canterbury (Williams, C. W. S.), **Supp. IX:** 284

Thomas De Quincey: A Biography (Eaton), **IV:** 142, 156

Thomas De Quincey: His Life and Writings (Page), **IV:** 152, 155

"Thomas Gray" (Arnold), **III:** 277

Thomas Hardy: A Bibliographical Study (Purdy), **VI:** 19

Thomas Hardy and British Poetry (Davie), **Supp. VI:** 115

Thomas Hobbes (Stephen), **V:** 289

Thomas Hood (Reid), **IV:** 267

Thomas Hood and Charles Lamb (ed. Jerrold), **IV:** 252, 253, 267

Thomas Hood: His Life and Times (Jerrold), **IV:** 267

Thomas Love Peacock (Priestley), **IV:** 159–160, 170

Thomas Nabbes (Swinburne), **V:** 333

Thomas Stevenson, Civil Engineer (Stevenson), **V:** 395

Thomas the Rhymer, **IV:** 29, 219

Thompson, E. P., **Supp. IV:** 95, 473

Thompson, Francis, **III:** 338; **V:** xxii, xxvi, 439–452

Thompson, R., **II:** 288

Thomson, George, **III:** 322

Thomson, James, **III:** 162, 171, 312; **Supp. III:** 409–429; **Retro. Supp. I:** 241

Thor, with Angels (Fry), **Supp. III:** 195, 197–198

"Thorn, The" (Wordsworth), **IV:** 6, 7

Thornton, R. K. R., **V:** 377, 382

Thornton, Robert, **III:** 307

Thorsler, Jr., P. L., **IV:** 173, 194

Those Barren Leaves (Huxley), **VII:** 79, 199, 202

Those Were the Days (Milne), **Supp. V:** 298

Those Were the Days: The Holocaust through the Eyes of the Perpetrators and Bystanders, **Supp. IV:** 488

Those Who Walk Away (Highsmith), **Supp. V:** 175

"Thou art an Atheist, *Quintus,* and a Wit" (Sedley), **II:** 265–266

"Thou art fair and few are fairer" (Shelley), **IV:** 203

"Thou art indeed just, Lord" (Hopkins), **V:** 376, 378

Time of Hope (Snow), **VII:** xxi, 321, 324–325
Time of the Crack, The (Tennant), **Supp. IX:** 229–230
Time of My Life (Ayckbourn), **Supp. V:** 3, 8, 10, 11, 13, 14
"Time of Plague, The" (Gunn), **Supp. IV:** 277
Time of the Angels, The (Murdoch), **III:** 341, 345; **Supp. I:** 225–226, 227, 228
"Time of Waiting, A" (Graves), **VII:** 269
Time Present (Osborne), **Supp. I:** 338
"Time the Tiger" (Lewis), **VII:** 74
Time to Dance, A (Day Lewis), **Supp. III:** 118, 126
Time to Go, A (O'Casey), **VII:** 12
Time to Keep, A (Brown), **Supp. VI:** 64, 70
Time Traveller, The: The Life of H. G. Wells (MacKenzie and MacKenzie), **VI:** 228, 246
"Timekeeping" (Cope), **VIII:** 81
"Timer" (Harrison), **Supp. V:** 150
Time's Arrow; or The Nature of the Offence (Amis), **Supp. IV:** 40–42
Time's Laughingstocks and other Verses (Hardy), **VI:** 20
Times (periodical), **IV:** xv, 272, 278; **V:** 93, 279
Times Literary Supplement, **Supp. IV:** 25, 66, 121
"Time–Tombs, The" (Ballard), **Supp. V:** 21
Timon of Athens (Shakespeare), **I:** 318–319, 321; **II:** 70
Tin Drum, The (Grass), **Supp. IV:** 440
Tin Men, The (Frayn), **Supp. VII:** 51–52, 64
Tinker, C. B., **III:** 234n, 249, 250
"Tinker, The" (Wordsworth), **IV:** 21
Tinker, Tailor, Soldier, Spy (le Carré), **Supp. II:** 306, **311–313,** 314
Tinker's Wedding, The (Synge), **VI:** 311, 313–314; **Retro. Supp. I:** 296–297
"Tintern Abbey" (Wordsworth), *see* "Lines Composed a Few Miles Above Tintern Abbey"
Tiny Tears (Fuller), **Supp. VII:** 78
"Tipperary" (Thomas), **Supp. III:** 404
"Tirade for the Mimic Muse" (Boland), **Supp. V:** 49
Tireless Traveller, The (Trollope), **V:** 102
"Tiresias" (Tennyson), **IV:** 328, 332–334, 338
"Tiriel" (Blake), **III:** 298, 302; **Retro. Supp. I:** 34–35
"Tirocinium; or, A Review of Schools" (Cowper), **III:** 208
'Tis Pity She's a Whore (Ford), **II:** 57, 88, 89, 90, 92–93, 99, 100
Tit–Bits (periodical), **VI:** 135, 248
"Tithe Barn, The" (Powys), **VIII:** 248, 249
Tithe Barn, The and The Dove and the Eage (Powys), **VIII:** 248
"Tithon" (Tennyson), **IV:** 332–334; *see also* "Tithonus"
"Tithonus" (Tennyson), **IV:** 328, 333
Title, The (Bennett), **VI:** 250, 264

Title and Pedigree of Henry VI (Lydgate), **I:** 58
Titmarsh, Michael Angelo, pseud. of William Makepeace Thackeray
Titus Andronicus (Shakespeare), **I:** 279, 305; **II:** 69
"Titus Hoyt, 1 A" (Naipaul), **Supp. I:** 385
"To a Black Greyhound" (Grenfell), **VI:** 418
"To a Brother in the Mystery" (Davie), **Supp. VI:** 113–114
"To a Butterfly" (Wordsworth), **IV:** 21
"To a Cretan Monk in Thanks for a Flask of Wine" (Murphy), **Supp. V:** 318
"To a Cold Beauty" (Hood), **IV:** 255
"To a Comrade in Flanders" (Owen), **VI:** 452
"To a Devout Young Gentlewoman" (Sedley), **II:** 264
"To a Fat Lady Seen from the Train" (Cornford), **VIII:** 102
"To a *Fine Singer,* who had gotten a *Cold; . . .*" (Wycherley), **II:** 320
"To a Fine Young *Woman . . .*" (Wycherley), **II:** 320
"To a Friend in Time of Trouble" (Gunn), **Supp. IV:** 274, 275
"To a Friend mourning the Death of Miss—" (Macpherson), **VIII:** 181
"To A. L." (Carew), **II:** 224–225
"To a Lady in a Letter" (Rochester), **II:** 258
To a Lady More Cruel Than Fair (Vanbrugh), **II:** 336
"To a Lady on Her Passion for Old China" (Gay), **III:** 58, 67
"To a Lady on the Death of Colonel Ross . . ." (Collins), **III:** 166, 169
"To a Louse" (Burns), **III:** 315, 317–318
"To a Mountain Daisy" (Burns), **III:** 313, 315, 317, 318
"To a Mouse" (Burns), **III:** 315, 317, 318
"To a Nightingale" (Coleridge), **IV:** 222
"To a Skylark" (Shelley), **III:** 337
"To a Snail" (Moore), **Supp. IV:** 262–263
"To a Very Young Lady" (Etherege), **II:** 267
"To Althea from Prison" (Lovelace), **II:** 231, 232
"To Amarantha, That She Would Dishevell Her Haire" (Lovelace), **II:** 230
"To Amoret Gone from Him" (Vaughan), **II:** 185
"To Amoret, of the Difference 'twixt Him, . . ." (Vaughan), **II:** 185
"To an English Friend in Africa" (Okri), **Supp. V:** 359
"To an Old Lady" (Empson), **Supp. II:** 182–183
"To an Unborn Pauper Child" (Hardy), **Retro. Supp. I:** 121
"To an Unknown Reader" (Fuller), **Supp. VII:** 78
"To and Fro" (McEwan), **Supp. IV:** 395
"To Anthea" (Herrick), **II:** 105–106, 108
"To Any Dead Officer" (Sassoon), **VI:** 431
To Asmara (Keneally), **Supp. IV:** 346

"To Augustus" (Pope), **Retro. Supp. I:** 230–231
"To Autumn" (Keats), **IV:** 221, 226–227, 228, 232
To Be a Pilgrim (Cary), **VII:** 186, 187, 191, 192–194
"To Be a Poet" (Stevenson), **Supp. VI:** 260
"To Be Less Philosophical" (Graves), **VII:** 266
"To Blossoms" (Herrick), **II:** 112
"To Call Paula Paul" (McGuckian), **Supp. V:** 286
To Catch a Spy (Ambler), **Supp. IV:** 4, 17
"To cause accord or to agree" (Wyatt), **I:** 109
"To Celia" (Johnson), **IV:** 327
"To Charles Cowden Clarke" (Keats), **IV:** 214, 215
"To Certain English Poets" (Davie), **Supp. VI:** 110
"To Charles Cowden Clarke" (Keats), **Retro. Supp. I:** 188
"To Constantia Singing" (Shelley), **IV:** 209
"To Daffodills" (Herrick), **II:** 112
"To Deanbourn" (Herrick), **II:** 103
"To Dianeme" (Herrick), **II:** 107, 112
"To E. Fitzgerald" (Tennyson), **IV:** 336
"To Edward Thomas" (Lewis), **VII:** 445
"To E. L., on his Travels in Greece" (Tennyson), **V:** 79
"To Electra" (Herrick), **II:** 105
"To Everlasting Oblivion" (Marston), **II:** 25
"To Fanny" (Keats), **IV:** 220–221
"To George Felton Mathew" (Keats), **IV:** 214
"To Germany" (Sorley), **VI:** 421
"To God" (Gurney), **VI:** 426
"To Helen" (Thomas), **Supp. III:** 401
"To His Coy Mistress" (Marvell), **II:** 197, 198, 208–209, 211, 214–215; **Retro. Supp. II:** 259–261
"To his inconstant Friend" (King), **Supp. VI:** 151
"To His Lost Lover" (Armitage), **VIII:** 8
"To His Love" (Gurney), **VI:** 426
"To His Lovely Mistresses" (Herrick), **II:** 113
To His Sacred Majesty, a Panegyrick on His Coronation (Dryden), **II:** 304
"To His Sweet Savior" (Herrick), **II:** 114
"To His Wife" (Hill), **Supp. V:** 189
"To Hope" (Keats), **Retro. Supp. I:** 188
"To Ireland in the Coming Times" (Yeats), **Retro. Supp. I:** 330
"To J. F. H. (1897–1934)" (Muir), **Supp. VI:** 206
"To Joan Eardley" (Morgan, E.), **Supp. IX:** 165
"To Julia, The Flaminica Dialis, or Queen–
To Keep the Ball Rolling (Powell), **VII:** 351
"To King Henry IV, in Praise of Peace" (Gower), **I:** 56
"To Leonard Clark" (Graham), **Supp. VII:** 116

Tomlin, Eric Walter Frederick, **VII:** xv, xxxviii

"Tomlinson" (Kipling), **VI:** 202

"Tomorrow" (Conrad), **VI:** 148

"Tomorrow" (Harris), **Supp. V:** 131

"Tomorrow Is a Million Years" (Ballard), **Supp. V:** 26

Tomorrow Morning, Faustus! (Richards), **Supp. II:** 427–428

"Tom's Garland" (Hopkins), **V:** 376

"Tone of Time, The" (James), **VI:** 69

"Tongues of Fire" (Wallace-Crabbe), **VIII:** 325

Tonight at 8:30 (Coward), **Supp. II:** 152–153

Tono–Bungay (Wells), **VI:** xii, 237–238, 244

Tonson, Jacob, **II:** 323; **III:** 69

"Tony Kytes, The Arch–Deceiver" (Hardy), **VI:** 22

"Tony White's Cottage" (Murphy), **Supp. V:** 328

"Too Dearly Bought" (Gissing), **V:** 437

Too Good to Be True (Shaw), **VI:** 125, 127, 129

"Too Late" (Browning), **V:** 366, 369

Too Late the Phalarope (Paton), **Supp. II:** 341, **351–353**

Too Many Husbands (Maugham), **VI:** 368–369

"Too Much" (Muir), **Supp. VI:** 207

"Toot Baldon" (Motion), **Supp. VII:** 253

Top Girls (Churchill), **Supp. IV:** 179, 183, 189–191, 198

Topkapi (film), **Supp. IV:** 4

"Torridge" (Trevor), **Supp. IV:** 501

"Tortoise and the Hare, The" (Dahl), **Supp. IV:** 226

Tortoises (Lawrence), **VII:** 118

Tortoises, Terrapins and Turtles (Sowerby and Lear), **V:** 76, 87

"Torturer's Apprenticeship, The" (Murray), **Supp. VII:** 280

"Tory Prime Minister, Maggie May . . . , A" (Rushdie), **Supp. IV:** 456

Totemism (Frazer), **Supp. III:** 171

"Totentanz" (Wilson), **Supp. I:** 155, 156, 157

Tottel's Miscellany, **I:** 97–98, 114

Touch (Gunn), **Supp. IV:** 257, 264, 265–266

"Touch" (Gunn), **Supp. IV:** 265–266

Touch and Go (Lawrence), **VII:** 120, 121

Touch of Love, A (screenplay, Drabble), **Supp. IV:** 230

Touch of Mistletoe, A (Comyns), **VIII:** 54–55, 56, 58–59, 65

Tour Thro' the Whole Island of Great Britain (Defoe), **III:** 5, 13; **Retro. Supp. I:** 75–76

Tour to the Hebrides, A (Boswell), *see Journal of a Tour to the Hebrides*

Tourneur, Cyril, **II:** 24, 33, **36–41,** 70, 72, 85, 97

Toward Reality (Berger), *see Permanent Red: Essays in Seeing*

"Toward the Imminent Days" (Murray), **Supp. VII:** 274

"Towards an Artless Society" (Lewis), **VII:** 76

Towards the End of Morning (Frayn), **Supp. VII:** 53–54, 65

Towards the Human (Smith, I. C.), **Supp. IX:** 209

Towards the Mountain (Paton), **Supp. II:** 346, 347, 351, 359

Towards Zero (Christie), **Supp. II:** 132, 134

Tower, The (Fry), **Supp. III:** 194, 195

Tower, The (Yeats), **VI:** 207, 216, 220; **Retro. Supp. I:** 333–335

Towers of Silence, The (Scott), **Supp. I:** 267–268

Town (periodical), **V:** 22

"Town and Country" (Brooke), **VI:** 420

"Town Betrayed, The" (Muir), **Supp. VI:** 206

Townley plays, **I:** 20

Townsend, Aurelian, **II:** 222, 237

Townsend Warner, George, **VI:** 485

Town–Talk (periodical), **III:** 50, 53

"Trace Elements" (Wallace-Crabbe), **VIII:** 323

"Track 12" (Ballard), **Supp. V:** 21

Trackers of Oxyrhyncus, The (Harrison), **Supp. V:** 163, 164

Tract 90 (Newman), *see Remarks on Certain Passages of the 39 Articles*

"Tractor" (Hughes), **Retro. Supp. II:** 211

Tracts for the Times (Newman), **Supp. VII:** 291, 293

"Traction–Engine, The" (Auden), **Retro. Supp. I:** 3

"Tradition and the Individual Talent" (Eliot), **VII:** 155, 156, 163, 164

"Tradition of Eighteen Hundred and Four, A" (Hardy), **VI:** 22

Tradition of Women's Fiction, The (Drabble), **Supp. IV:** 231

Tradition, the Writer and Society (Harris), **Supp. V:** 145, 146

"Traditional Prize Country Pigs" (Cope), **VIII:** 82–83

"Traditions, Voyages" (Wallace-Crabbe), **VIII:** 318

Traffics and Discoveries (Kipling), **VI:** 204

"Tragedy and the Essay, The" (Brontë), **V:** 135

Tragedy of Brennoralt, The (Suckling), **II:** 226

Tragedy of Byron, The (Chapman), **I:** 233, 234, 241n, 251

Tragedy of Count Alarcos, The (Disraeli), **IV:** 306, 308

Tragedy of Doctor Faustus, The (Marlowe), **Retro. Supp. I:** 200, 207–208

"Tragedy of Error, A" (James), **VI:** 25

Tragedy of Sir John Van Olden Barnavelt, The (Fletcher and Massinger), **II:** 66

Tragedy of Sophonisba, The (Thomson), **Supp. III:** 411, 422, 423, 424

Tragedy of the Duchess of Malfi, The (Webster), *see Duchess of Malfi, The*

Tragedy of Tragedies; or, The Life . . . of Tom Thumb, The (Fielding), *see Tom Thumb*

"Tragedy of Two Ambitions, A" (Hardy), **VI:** 22

Tragic Comedians, The (Meredith), **V:** 228, 234

Tragic History of Romeus and Juliet, The (Brooke), **I:** 305–306

Tragic Muse, The (James), **VI:** 39, **43–55, 67**

"Tragic Theatre, The" (Yeats), **VI:** 218

Tragical History of Doctor Faustus, The (Hope), **Supp. VII:** 160–161

Tragical History of Dr. Faustus, The (Marlowe), **III:** 344

Traherne, Thomas, **II:** 123, **189–194, 201–203**

Trail of the Dinosaur, The (Koestler), **Supp. I:** 32, 33, 36, 37

Traill, H. D., **III:** 80

Train of Powder, A (West), **Supp. III:** 439–440

Trained for Genius (Goldring), **VI:** 333

Traité du poeme épique (Le Bossu), **III:** 103

Traitor's Blood (Hill, R.), **Supp. IX:** 117

"Trampwoman's Tragedy, The" (Hardy), **VI:** 15; **Retro. Supp. I:** 120

transatlantic review (periodical), **VI:** 324

Transatlantic Sketches (James), **VI:** 67

"Transfiguration, The" (Muir), **Supp. VI:** 207

Transformed Metamorphosis, The (Tourneur), **II:** 37, 41

"Transients and Residents" (Gunn), **Supp. IV:** 271, 273

transition (quarterly periodical), **Supp. I:** 43n

Transitional Poem (Day Lewis), **Supp. III:** 117, 121–123

"Translation of Poetry, The" (Morgan, E.), **Supp. IX:** 168–169

Translations (Friel), **Supp. V:** 123–124

Translations and Tomfooleries (Shaw), **VI:** 129

"Translations from the Early Irish" (Kinsella), **Supp. V:** 264

Translations of the Natural World (Murray), **Supp. VII:** 281–282

"Transparencies" (Stevenson), **Supp. VI:** 262

Traps (Churchill), **Supp. IV:** 179, 180, 183–184, 188, 198

Traulus (Swift), **III:** 36

Travelers (Jhabvala), **Supp. V:** 230

"Traveller" (Kinsella), **Supp. V:** 263

Traveller, The (Goldsmith), **III:** 177, 179, 180, 185–186, 191; **Retro. Supp. I:** 149

"Traveller, The" (Stevenson), **Supp. VI:** 254, 265

"Travelling" (Healy), **Supp. IX:** 106

Travelling Behind Glass (Stevenson), **Supp. VI:** 256–257

"Travelling Behind Glass" (Stevenson), **Supp. VI:** 257, 261

"Travelling Companion, The" (Kinsella), **Supp. V:** 261

"Travelling Companions" (James), **VI:** 25, 69

Travelling Grave, The (Hartley), *see Killing Bottle, The*

Viper and Her Brood, The (Middleton), **II:** 3, 33

Virchow, Rudolf, **V:** 348

Virgidemiarum (Hall), **II:** 25

Virgil, *see* Vergil

Virgin and the Gipsy, The (Lawrence), **VII:** 91, 115

Virgin in the Garden, The (Byatt), **Supp. IV:** 139, 145–147, 149

"Virgin Mary to the Child Jesus, The" (Browning), **IV:** 313

"Virgin Russia" (Cameron), **Supp. IX:** 19

Virginia (O'Brien), **Supp. V:** 334

Virginia Woolf: A Biography (Bell), **VII:** 38; **Retro. Supp. I:** 305

Virginia Woolf Icon (Silver), **Retro. Supp. I:** 305

Virginians, The (Thackeray), **V:** 29, **31–33,** 38

Virginibus Puerisque and Other Papers (Stevenson), **V:** 395; **Retro. Supp. I:** 262

Vision, A (Yeats), **VI:** 209, 213, 214, 222

"Vision, The" (Burns), **III:** 315

"Vision and Prayer" (Thomas), **Supp. I:** 178

Vision of Bags, A (Swinburne), **V:** 333

Vision of Battlements, A (Burgess), **Supp. I:** 185, 187, 195–196

Vision of Cathkin Braes, The (Morgan, E.), **Supp. IX:** 160–163

"Vision of Cathkin Braes, The" (Morgan, E.), **Supp. IX:** 163

Vision of Delight, The (Jonson), **Retro. Supp. I:** 165

Vision of Don Roderick, The (Scott), **IV:** 38

Vision of Gombold Proval, The (Orton), **Supp. V:** 365–366, 370

Vision of Judgement, A (Southey), **IV:** 61, 71, 184–187

Vision of Judgment, The (Byron), **IV:** xviii, 58, 61–62, 132, 172, 178, **184–187,** 193

"Vision of Poets, A" (Browning), **IV:** 316

"Vision of the Empire, The" (Williams, C. W. S.), **Supp. IX:** 282

"Vision of the Last Judgment, A" (Blake), **III:** 299

"Vision of the Mermaids, A" (Hopkins), **V:** 361, 381

Vision of the Three T's, The (Carroll), **V:** 274

"Vision of that Ancient Man, The" (Motion), **Supp. VII:** 260, 261

Vision of William Concerning Piers the Plowman . . . , The (ed. Skeat), **I:** 17

Visions of the Daughters of Albion (Blake), **III:** 307; **Retro. Supp. I:** 39–40

"Visit in Bad Taste, A" (Wilson), **Supp. I:** 157

"Visit to Grandpa's, A" (Thomas), **Supp. I:** 181

"Visit to Morin, A" (Greene), **Supp. I:** 15, 18

"Visit to the Dead, A" (Cameron), **Supp. IX:** 27

"Visitation, The" (Jennings), **Supp. V:** 212

Visitations (MacNeice), **VII:** 416

"Visiting Hour" (Kinsella), **Supp. V:** 273

"Visiting Hour" (Murphy), **Supp. V:** 326

Visiting Mrs. Nabokov and Other Excursions (Amis), **Supp. IV:** 42, 43

"Visiting Rainer Maria" (McGuckian), **Supp. V:** 286

"Visitor, The" (Bowen), **Supp. II:** 81

"Visitor, The" (Dahl), **Supp. IV:** 219–220

Visitor, The (Orton), **Supp. V:** 363, 367

"Visitors, The" (Fuller), **Supp. VII:** 77

"Visits, The" (James), **VI:** 49, 69

"Visits to the Cemetery of the Long Alive" (Stevenson), **Supp. VI:** 264

Vita Nuova (tr. Rossetti), **V:** 238

"Vitai Lampada" (Newbolt), **VI:** 417

Vittoria (Meredith), **V:** 227–228, 234

Vivian (Edgeworth), **Supp. III:** 158

Vivian Grey (Disraeli), **IV:** xvii, 293–294, 297, 299, 308

Vivisector, The (White), **Supp. I:** 132, 145–146

Vizetelly (publisher), **VI:** 86

"Voice, The" (Brooke), **Supp. III:** 52

"Voice, The" (Hardy), **VI:** 18

"Voice from the Dead, A" (Connolly), **Supp. III:** 111

"Voice of Nature, The" (Bridges), **VI:** 79

"Voice of the Ancient Bard, The" (Blake), **Retro. Supp. I:** 37

"Voice of Things, The" (Hardy), **Retro. Supp. I:** 121

Voice Over (MacCaig), **Supp. VI:** 194

Voice Through a Cloud, A (Welch), **Supp. IX:** 262–263; 266–267, 268

Voices in the City (Desai), **Supp. V:** 54, 59–60, 72

Voices of the Stones (Russell), **VIII:** 290

"Voices of Time, The" (Ballard), **Supp. V:** 22, 24, 29, 34

Volpone (Jonson), **I:** 339, 343–344, 348; **II:** 4, 45, 70, 79; **V:** 56; **Retro. Supp. I:** 163, 164

Vǫlsunga saga, **VIII:** 231

Voltaire, **II:** 261, 348; **III:** 149, 235, 236, 327; **IV:** xiv, 290, 295, 346; **Supp. IV:** 136, 221

"Voltaire at Ferney" (Auden), **Retro. Supp. I:** 8

Vǫlundarkviða, **VIII:** 230

"Volunteer, The" (Asquith), **VI:** 417

Volunteers (Friel), **Supp. V:** 111, 112, 121–122

Vǫluspá, **VIII:** 230, 231, 235, 243

Vonnegut, Kurt, Jr., **III:** 341; **Supp. IV:** 116

Vortex, The (Coward), **Supp. II:** 139, 141–143, 144, 149

Voss (White), **VII:** 31; **Supp. I:** 130, 131, **138–141,** 142

Votive Tablets (Blunden), **IV:** 86

Vox clamantis (Gower), **I:** 48, 49–50

"Vox Humana" (Gunn), **Supp. IV:** 261–262

Voyage, The (Muir), **Supp. VI:** 204, **206–207**

Voyage In the Dark (Rhys), **Supp. II:** **394–396**

Voyage of Captain Popanilla, The (Disraeli), **IV:** 294–295, 308

"Voyage of Mael Duin," **Supp. IV:** 415–416

Voyage of the Dawn Treader, The (Lewis), **Supp. III:** 248, 260

Voyage Out, The (Woolf), **VII:** 20, 27, 37; **Retro. Supp. I:** 307, 315–316

Voyage That Never Ends, The (Lowry), **Supp. III:** 276, 280

Voyage to Abyssinia, A (tr. Johnson), **III:** 107, 112, 121; **Retro. Supp. I:** 139

Voyage to New Holland, A (Dampier), **III:** 24

Voyage to the Island of Love, A (Behn), **Supp. III:** 37

Voyage to Venus (Lewis), **Supp. III:** 249

Voyages (Hakluyt), **I:** 150, 267; **III:** 7

"Voyages of Alfred Wallis, The" (Graham), **Supp. VII:** 110

Vulgar Errors (Browne), *see Pseudodoxia Epidemica*

Vulgar Streak, The (Lewis), **VII:** 72, 77

"Vulgarity in Literature" (Huxley), **V:** 53; **VII:** 198

"Vulture, The" (Beckett), **Supp. I:** 44

W. B. Yeats, Man and Poet (Jeffares), **VI:** 223

W. B. Yeats: The Critical Heritage (Jeffares), **VI:** 224

"W. Kitchener" (Hood), **IV:** 267

W. Somerset Maugham and the Quest for Freedom (Calder), **VI:** 376n

Waagen, Gustav Friedrich, **III:** 328

Wager, William, **I:** 213

Waggoner, The (Wordsworth), **IV:** 24, 73

"Wagner" (Brooke), **Supp. III:** 53

Wagner the Werewolf (Reynolds), **III:** 335

Wagstaff, Simon, pseud. of Jonathan Swift

Waif Woman, The (Stevenson), **V:** 396

Wain, John, **VI:** 209

Wainewright, Thomas, **V:** 405

Waingrow, W., **III:** 249

Waith, Eugene, **II:** 51, 64

"Waiting" (Self), **Supp. V:** 402

"Waiting at the Station" (Thackeray), **V:** 25

"Waiting for Breakfast" (Larkin), **Supp. I:** 277

"Waiting for Columbus" (Reid), **Supp. VII:** 334

Waiting for Godot (Beckett), **I:** 16–17; **Supp. I:** 51, 55–56, 57, 59; **Supp. IV:** 281, 429; **Retro. Supp. I:** 17–18, 20–21, 23–24; **Retro. Supp. II:** 344

"Waiting for J." (Ishiguro), **Supp. IV:** 303

Waiting for the Barbarians (Coetzee), **Supp. VI:** 75–76, **81–82**

Waiting for the Telegram (Bennett), **VIII:** 28

"Waiting Grounds, The" (Ballard), **Supp. V:** 21, 22

"Waiting in Hospital" (Cornford), **VIII:** 113

White–Eagles over Serbia (Durrell), **Supp. I:** 100
Whitehall, Harold, **V:** 365, 382
Whitelock, Derek, **Supp. IV:** 348
"Whitewashed Wall, The" (Hardy), **Retro. Supp. I:** 120
Whitman, Walt, **IV:** 332; **V:** 418; **VI:** 55, 63; **Supp. IV:** 163, 487
Whitsun Weddings, The (Larkin), **Supp. I:** 276, **279–281,** 285
"Whitsun Weddings, The" (Larkin), **Supp. I:** 285
"Whitsunday" (Herbert), **II:** 125
"Whitsunday in Kirchstetten" (Auden), **VII:** 396, 397
"Who Are These Coming to the Sacrifice?" (Hill), **Supp. V:** 191
Who Are You? (Kavan), **Supp. VII:** 214
"Who Goes Home?" (Day Lewis), **Supp. III:** 130
Who Guards a Prince? (Hill, R.), **Supp. IX:** 117
Who Is Sylvia? (Rattigan), **Supp. VII:** 317
"Who Needs It?" (Blackwood), **Supp. IX:** 9
Who was Changed and Who was Dead (Comyns), **VIII:** 53, 60–61
Who Was Oswald Fish? (Wilson), **Supp. VI: 300–301**
Whole Armour, The (Harris), **Supp. V:** 132, 134, 135
Whole Duty of Man, The (Allestree), **III:** 82
"Whole of the Sky, The" (Armitage), **VIII:** 11
"Whole Truth, The" (Motion), **Supp. VII:** 256
Whole Works of Homer, The (Chapman), **I:** 235
Whoroscope (Beckett), **Supp. I:** 43; **Retro. Supp. I:** 19
"Who's Who" (Auden), **Retro. Supp. I:** 2
Whose Body? (Sayers), **Supp. III:** 334, 336–338, 340, 350
"Whose Endless Jar" (Richards), **Supp. II:** 426, 429
Whose Is the Kingdom? (Arden and D'Arcy), **Supp. II:** 39, 40–41
"Whoso list to hunt" (Wyatt), **I:** 101, 109
"Why Brownlee Left" (Muldoon), **Supp. IV:** 409, 410, 415, 418, 426
Why Come Ye Not to Court? (Skelton), **I:** 92–93
Why Do I Write? (Bowen), **Supp. II:** 80, 81, 91
Why Frau Frohmann Raised Her Prices and Other stories (Trollope), **V:** 102
"Why Has Narrative Poetry Failed" (Murphy), **Supp. V:** 320–321
"Why I Have Embraced Islam" (Rushdie), **Supp. IV:** 437
"Why I Ought Not to Have Become a Dramatic Critic" (Beerbohm), **Supp. II:** 54
"Why Not Take Pater Seriously?" (Fletcher), **V:** 359
Why Scots Should Rule Scotland (Gray, A.), **Supp. IX:** 80, 85

"Why She Would Not" (Shaw), **VI:** 130
"Why Should Not Old Men Be Mad?" (Yeats), **Retro. Supp. I:** 337
Why So, Socrates? (Richards), **Supp. II:** 425
"Why the Novel Matters" (Lawrence), **VII:** 122
"Why We Are in Favour of This War" (Hulme), **Supp. VI:** 140
"Why Write of the Sun" (Armitage), **VIII:** 3
Wi the Haill Voice (tr. Morgan, E.), **Supp. IX:** 168
"Wicked Tunge Wille Sey Amys, A" (Lydgate), **I:** 57
Wide Sargasso Sea (Rhys), **Supp. II:** 387, 389, **398–401,** 441; **Retro. Supp. I:** 60
Widow, The (Middleton), **II:** 3, 21
"Widow, The" (Smith, I. C.), **Supp. IX:** 211
Widow Ranter, The (Behn), **Supp. III:** 34
Widow Ranter, The (Belin), **II:** 305
"Widower in the Country, The" (Murray), **Supp. VII:** 271
Widower's Son, The (Sillitoe), **Supp. V:** 410, 414, 415, 425
Widowers' Houses (Shaw), **VI:** 104, 107, 108, 129; **Retro. Supp. II:** 310–312
"Widowhood System, The" (Friel), **Supp. V:** 113
Widowing of Mrs. Holroyd, The (Lawrence), **VII:** 120, 121
Widow's Tears, The (Chapman), **I:** 243–244, 245–246
Widsith, **Retro. Supp. II:** 304
Wiene, Robert, **III:** 342
Wife for a Month (Fletcher), **II:** 65
Wife of Bath, The (Gay), **III:** 60, 67
Wife of Bath's Prologue, The (Chaucer), **I:** 24, 34, 39, 40
Wife of Bath's Tale, The (Chaucer), **I:** 27, 35–36
"Wife of Ted Wickham, The" (Coppard), **VIII:** 95
"Wife Speaks, The" (Day Lewis), **Supp. III:** 125
Wife's Lament, The, **Retro. Supp. II:** 305
Wilberforce, William, **IV:** 133, 268; **V:** 277
Wild Ass's Skin, The (Balzac), **III:** 339, 345
"Wild Boar and the Ram, The" (Gay), **III:** 59
Wild Body, The (Lewis), **VII:** 72, 77, 78, 79
"Wild Colonial Puzzler, The" (Wallace-Crabbe), **VIII:** 318
Wild Duck, The (Ibsen), **VI:** ix
"Wild Flowers" (Howard), **V:** 48
Wild Gallant, The (Dryden), **II:** 305
Wild Garden, The; or, Speaking of Writing (Wilson), **Supp. I:** 153, 154–155, 156, 158, 160
Wild Goose Chase, The (Fletcher), **II:** 45, 61–62, 65, 352, 357
Wild Honey (Frayn), **Supp. VII:** 61
Wild Irish Boy, The (Maturin), **VIII:** 207, 209
Wild Knight, The (Chesterton), **VI:** 336

Wild Nights (Tennant), **Supp. IX:** 230, 233–234
Wild Swans at Coole, The (Yeats), **VI:** 207, 213, 214, 217; **Retro. Supp. I:** 331
"Wild with All Regrets" (Owen), **VI:** 446, 452, 453
Wilde, Oscar, **III:** 334, 345; **V:** xiii, xxi, xxv, xxvi, 53, 339, **399–422; VI:** ix, 365; **VII:** 83; **Supp. II:** 43, 45–46, 48, 50, 51, 53, 54, 141, 143, 148, 155; **Supp. IV:** 288; **Retro. Supp. II:** 314–315, **359–374**
Wilder Hope, The: Essays on Future Punishment . . . (De Quincey), **IV:** 155
"Wilderness, The" (Keyes), **VII:** 439
Wilderness of Zin (Woolley and Lawrence), **Supp. II:** 284
Wildest Dreams (Ayckbourn), **Supp. V:** 3, 10, 12, 14
"Wildgoose Chase, A" (Coppard), **VIII:** 95
"Wilfred Owen and the Georgians" (Hibberd), **VI:** 460
Wilfred Owen: War Poems and Others (Hibberd), **VI:** 446, 459
"Wilfred Owen's Letters" (Hibberd), **VI:** 460
Wilhelm Meister (Goethe), **IV:** 241; **V:** 214
Wilhelm Meister's Apprenticeship (tr. Carlyle), **IV:** 241, 250
Wilkes, John, **IV:** 61, 185
Wilkes, Thomas, **II:** 351, 363
Wilkie, David, **IV:** 37
Wilkins, George, **I:** 321
Wilkinson, Martin, **Supp. IV:** 168
"Will, The" (Donne), **Retro. Supp. II:** 91
Will Drew and Phil Crewe and Frank Fane . . . (Swinburne), **V:** 333
"Will o' the Mill" (Stevenson), **V:** 395
Will Warburton (Gissing), **V:** 435, 437
"Will Ye No' Come Back Again?" (Wallace-Crabbe), **VIII:** 323
Willey, Basil, **II:** 145, 157; **Supp. II:** 103, 107, 108
"William and Mary" (Dahl), **Supp. IV:** 218, 219
William B. Yeats: The Poet in Contemporary Ireland (Hone), **VI:** 223
William Blake (Chesterton), **VI:** 344
William Blake (Swinburne), **V:** 313, 314, 317, 329–330, 332
William Cobbett (Chesterton), **VI:** 341, 345
"William Cobbett: In Absentia" (Hill), **Supp. V:** 183
"William Congreve" (Swinburne), **V:** 332
William Dunbar, Selected Poems (Dunbar), **VIII:** 119
William Morris (Bloomfield), **V:** 306
William Morris, Artist, Writer, Socialist (Morris), **V:** 301, 305
"William Morris as I Knew Him" (Shaw), **VI:** 129
William Pitt . . . an Excellent New Ballad . . . (Boswell), **III:** 248
William Posters trilogy (Sillitoe), **Supp. V:** 410, 413, 421–424